Welfare Law

**The International Library of Essays in Law and Legal Theory**
*Series Editor: Tom D. Campbell*

*Schools*

**Natural Law, Vols I & II** *John Finnis*
**Justice** *Thomas Morawetz*
**Law and Economics, Vols I & II** *Jules Coleman and Jeffrey Lange*
**Critical Legal Studies** *James Boyle*
**Marxian Legal Theory** *Csaba Varga*
**Legal Reasoning, Vols I & II** *Aulis Aarnio and Neil MacCormick*
**Legal Positivism** *Mario Jori*
**American Legal Theory** *Robert Summers*
**Law and Language** *Fred Schauer*
**Sociological Theories of Law** *Kahei Rokumoto*
**Rights** *Carlos Nino*
**Law and Psychology** *Martin Levine*
**Feminist Legal Theory** *Frances Olsen*
**Law and Society** *Werner Krawietz*

*Areas*

**Criminal Law** *Thomas Morawetz*
**Tort Law** *Ernest Weinrib*
**Contract Law, Vols I & II** *Larry Alexander*
**Anti-Discrimination Law** *Christopher McCrudden*
**Consumer Law** *Iain Ramsay*
**International Law** *Martti Koskenniemi*
**Property Law, Vols I & II** *Elizabeth Mensch and Alan Freeman*
**Constitutional Law** *Mark Tushnet*
**Procedure** *Denis Galligan*
**Evidence and Proof** *William Twining and Alex Stein*
**Administrative Law** *Denis Galligan*
**Child Law** *Harry Krause*
**Family Law, Vols I & II** *Harry Krause*
**Welfare Law** *Peter Robson*
**Medicine and the Law** *Bernard Dickens*
**Commercial Law** *Ross Cranston*
**Communications Law** *David Goldberg*
**Environmental Law** *Michael Blumm*
**Conflict of Laws** *Richard Fentiman*
**Law and Religion** *Wojciech Sadurski*
**Human Rights Law** *Philip Alston*
**European Community Law, Vols I & II** *Francis Snyder*

*Legal Cultures*

**Comparative Legal Cultures** *Csaba Varga*
**Law and Anthropology** *Peter Sack*
**Hindu Law and Legal Theory** *Ved Nanda*
**Islamic Law and Legal Theory** *Ian Edge*
**Chinese Law and Legal Theory** *Michael Palmer*
**Socialist Law and Legal Theory** *W. Butler*
**Japanese Law and Legal Theory** *Koichiro Fujikura*
**Law and Development** *Anthony Carty*
**Jewish Law and Legal Theory** *Martin Golding*
**Legal Education** *Martin Levine*

*Future Volumes*

Labour Law, Common Law and Legal Theory, Civil Law and Legal Theory, African Law and Legal Theory, Legal Ethics and Cumulative index.

# Welfare Law

*Edited by*

Peter Robson

*Reader in Law*
*University of Strathclyde*

NEW YORK UNIVERSITY PRESS
REFERENCE COLLECTION

Manufactured in Great Britain

First published in the U.S.A. in 1992 by
NEW YORK UNIVERSITY PRESS
Washington Square
New York NY 10003

**Library of Congress Cataloging-in-Publication Data**
Welfare law / edited, Peter Robson.
p. cm. – (The International library of essays in law and legal theory. Areas)
Includes bibliographical references and index.
ISBN 0-8147-7426-1
1. Public welfare–Law and legislation. I. Robson, Peter, 1947- II. Series.
K1960.Z9W45 1992
344'.03–dc 20
[342.43] 92-956
CIP

# Contents

# Acknowledgements

The editor and publishers wish to thank the following for permission to use copyright material.

Acta Sociologica for essays: Birte Siim (1987), 'The Scandinavian Welfare States – Towards Sexual Equality or a New Kind of Male Domination?', *Acta Sociologica*, **30**, pp. 255–70, and Göran Therborn (1987), 'Welfare States and Capitalist Markets', *Acta Sociologica*, **30**, pp. 237–54.

The American Academy of Political and Social Science for the essay: S.M. Miller, Martin Rein, Pamela Roby and Bertram M. Gross (1967), 'Poverty, Inequality and Conflict', *Annals of the American Academy of Political Science*, **373**, pp. 16–52. Copyright © The American Academy of Political Science.

The American Political Science Association for the essay: Robert E. Goodin (1985), 'Vulnerabilities and Responsibilities: An Ethical Defense of the Welfare State', *The American Political Science Review*, **79**, pp. 775–87.

Blackwell Publishers for essays: Ian Loveland (1987), 'Welfare Benefits, Administrative Discretion, and the Politics of the "New Urban Left"', *Journal of Law and Society*, **14**, No. 4, pp. 474–94, Rudolf Klein (1980), 'The Welfare State: A Self-inflicted Crisis?', *The Political Quarterly*, **51**, pp. 24–34, and Richard M. Titmuss (1971), 'Welfare "Rights", Law and Discretion', *The Political Quarterly*, **42**, pp. 113–32.

Cambridge University Press for essays: Hilary Land (1978), 'Who Cares for the Family?', *Journal of Social Policy*, **7**, pp. 257–84, T.H. Marshall (1972), 'Value Problems of Welfare Capitalism', *Journal of Social Policy*, **1**, pp. 15–32, Adrian Sinfield (1978), 'Analyses in the Social Division of Welfare', *Journal of Social Policy*, **7**, pp. 129–56, and Desmond S. King and Jeremy Waldron (1988), 'Citizenship, Social Citizenship and the Defence of Welfare Provision', *British Journal of Political Science*, **18**, pp. 415–43. Copyright © The Cambridge University Press.

Canadian Journal of Political Science for the essay: Caroline Andrew (1984), 'Women and the Welfare State', *Canadian Journal of Political Science*, **XVII**, pp. 667–83.

Critical Social Policy and Mary McIntosh (1981), 'Feminism and Social Policy', *Critical Social Policy*, **1**, pp. 32–42. Copyright © Critical Social Policy and Mary McIntosh.

Government and Opposition for the essay: Geraint Parry (1985), 'Welfare State and Welfare Society', *Government and Opposition*, **20**, pp. 287–96. Copyright © Government and Opposition.

Harold Ober Associates Incorporated for the essay: Oscar Lewis (1966), 'The Culture of Poverty', *Scientific American*, **215**, pp. 19–25.

Harvard Law Review for the essay: Frank I. Michelman (1969), 'On Protecting the Poor Through the Fourteenth Amendment', *Harvard Law Review*, **83**, pp. 7–59. Copyright © (1969) by the Harvard Law Review Association.

Robert S. Lynd for the essay: Herbert J. Gans (1972), 'The Positive Functions of Poverty', *American Journal of Sociology*, **78**, No. 2, pp. 275–89. Copyright © Robert S. Lynd.

New Left Review for the essay: Ian Gough (1975), 'State Expenditure in Advanced Capitalism', *New Left Review*, **92**, pp. 53–92.

Routledge Chapman & Hall for the essay: Peter Townsend (1954), 'Measuring Poverty', *British Journal of Sociology*, **5**, pp. 130–7.

U.S. Department of Labor for the essay: Mollie Orshansky (1969), 'How Poverty is Measured', *Monthly Labor Review*, pp. 37–41.

The Yale Law Journal and Fred B. Rothman & Co. for essays: Joel F. Handler (1983), 'Discretion in Social Welfare: The Uneasy Position in the Rule of Law', *The Yale Law Journal*, **92**, pp. 1270–86. Reprinted by permission of The Yale Law Journal Company and Fred B. Rothman & Co. for The Yale Law Journal, Vol. **92**, pp. 1270–86, William H. Simon (1983), 'Legality, Bureaucracy, and Class in the Welfare System', *The Yale Law Journal*, **92**, pp. 1198–269. Reprinted by permission of The Yale Law Journal Company and Fred B. Rothman & Co. from The Yale Law Journal, Vol. **92**, pp. 1198–269, and Charles A. Reich (1965), 'Individual Rights and Social Welfare: The Emerging Legal Issues', *The Yale Law Journal*, **74**, pp. 1245–57. Reprinted by permission of The Yale Law Journal Company and Fred B. Rothman & Co. from The Yale Law Journal, Vol. **74**, pp. 1245–57.

Every effort has been made to trace all the copyright holders but if any have been inadvertently overlooked the publishers will be pleased to make the necessary arrangement at the first opportunity.

# Series Preface

The International Library of Law and Legal Theory is designed to provide important research materials in an accessible form. Each volume contains essays of central theoretical importance in its subject area. The series as a whole makes available an extensive range of valuable material which will be of considerable interest to those involved in the research, teaching and study of law.

The series has been divided into three sections. The Schools section is intended to represent the main distinctive approaches and topics of special concern to groups of scholars. The Areas section takes in the main branches of law with an emphasis on essays which present analytical and theoretical insights of broad application. The section on Legal Cultures makes available the distinctive legal theories of different legal traditions and takes up topics of general comparative and developmental concern.

I have been delighted and impressed by the way in which the editors of the individual volumes have set about the difficult task of selecting, ordering and presenting essays from the immense quantity of academic legal writing published in journals throughout the world. Editors were asked to pick out those essays from law, philosophy and social science journals which they consider to be fundamental for the understanding of law, as seen from the perspective of a particular approach or sphere of legal interest. This is not an easy task and many difficult decisions have had to be made in order to ensure that a representative sample of the best journal essays available takes account of the scope of each topic or school.

I should like to express my thanks to all the volume editors for their willing participation and scholarly judgement. The interest and enthusiasm which the project has generated is well illustrated by the fact that an original projection of 12 volumes drawn up in 1989 has now become a list of some 60 volumes. I must also acknowledge the vision, persistence and constant cheerfulness of John Irwin and the marvellous work done by Mrs Margaret O'Reilly and Mrs Sonia Bridgman.

TOM D. CAMPBELL
Series Editor
*The Faculty of Law*
*The Australian National University*

# Introduction

## The Background to Welfare

Welfare provision is the modern 'civilized' response to the problem of poor people in society. Poor people have not always been seen as a threat to social stability.[1] However, the views of the early Christian Fathers and the Thomist version of the virtues of mendicancy were largely displaced in public policy with fear and distrust from the 14th century.[2] The treatment of poor people ranged from criminalization to degradation over the next five centuries. The workhouse symbolizes this approach to poverty, with its strong overtones of punishment. With the rise of Darwinian notions of social progress, policy towards the poor was extended to allow for improvement through regimented disciplined work. The underlying concept was the division of the poor into deserving and undeserving. The latter merited encouragement and could be assisted and taught to make a worthwhile contribution to society.[3]

The rise of a powerful alternative explanation of the causes of poverty and the solution to the problem in socialism produced a variety of policy responses. These welfare mechanisms I have characterized as the 'civilized' way of treating poverty. They are located in a hybrid view of the causes of social inequality; these are partly perceived as structural as well as also stemming from personal inadequacies. Some merit the attention of the community, whilst others are best left to the market. There is no obvious rationale for the distinctions that have been made historically. As we shall see, welfare mechanisims have been conceived in a limited way, constructed with the world of the able-bodied male industrial worker in mind. The concentration on this dominant client group stemmed, of course, from the power of the organized working class in industrial society. Yet even for this dominant client group, the system has revealed a variety of inadequacies in its provision for the shared risks covered by welfare mechanisms. Thus the nature of unemployment has been unsuited to short-term unemployment insurance schemes which have been a prevalent form of combatting this major traditional cause of poverty. In addition, the relationship between inadequate wages and low benefit levels has been chronic within the welfare schemes operated this century. For those groups whose needs are not covered by the dominant thrust of welfare policies, the limitations have been even more severe. The sexual division of labour in relation to childbearing and family nurturing means that women have been disadvantaged and restricted by the concentration of welfare policies on full-time waged workers. The basis of systems in insurance and waged work means that those with long-term illness and disability have also benefited significantly less well than the dominant client group.

The legal structures within which these policies operate have provided an expanding (though low-status) area of work for legal practitioners in the past 25 years. The range and nature of the problems confronting lawyers have mirrored the political debates which have raged about the extent and limitations of welfare. However, the contribution of lawyers to this broader debate has been limited.[4]

## The Academic and Professional Context

This selection attempts to highlight the major theoretical issues which have preoccupied practitioners and academics involved in the welfare field in the recent past. Two general riders need to be added at this juncture since they have a bearing on the selection process. First, there has been extensive book writing in this area, sometimes to the detriment of journal articles. This tendency has been exacerbated by the delays in journal publication and the improvements in the technology of book production so that more extended up-to-date monographs have been feasible. Thus debates have not always been fully represented in journals. In addition, like other new areas where there is an extensive range of clients with immediate problems and a limited range of experts available, there has been a tendency for many journals to concentrate on technical rather than theoretical questions. Thus journals which have been in existence in Britain for over a decade (like the *Journal of Social Welfare Law and Legal Action*) yield minimal major theoretical perspectives which might be of interest to those outside Britain. Other journals are even more specifically practical in their contents, concentrating on keeping welfare practitioners up to date with recent case law and tribunal decisions[5] or addressing narrow policy options in particular areas.[6] The thrust of one major recent contribution[7] is to concentrate on the specifics of recent British developments in the detailed policies covering such areas as housing, income support and child care. The basic framework of analysis centres on the rule of law. Substantive changes which have been introduced to reduce the extent of community provision for the unprivileged are discussed in terms of whether the review and appeal mechanisms are adequate to the task of defending 'social welfare principles'. The contributors to this volume are not explicit about what such social welfare principles involve. Nor are the authors happy with the impact of the past decade of right-wing politics on the poor and unprivileged. However their discussions concentrate on concrete details rather than involve any elaboration of social welfare principles. Engagement with this debate is nonetheless to be welcomed from the legal community and augurs well for the future.

Another problem in this area is the strong tendency towards ethnocentricity in much work in Britain and the United States. Given the complexity of the law relating to welfare arrangements, this is perhaps unsurprising but it does mean that much interesting work is written for consumption within a particular legal and political culture and its possible wider implications are not always made clear.[8] Sometimes the claims made for research work may be ambitious and difficult to assess. For instance, one essay about social control through welfare legislation concerns the 'suitable home' requirement for Aid to Dependent Children in Florida in the mid 1960s.[9] In another discussion of the crisis of political legitimacy being experienced by the welfare state, the author concludes that the choice offered is between the end of the welfare state and violent revolution. This is based on a survey of 240 people living in Kent in the winter of 1980.[10]

The parameters of welfare law are not easily drawn. In practice the teaching of welfare law as a subject in British universities and colleges ranges beyond income support into housing, health, discrimination and child law.[11] It is taught both as a separate entity and together with taxation.[12] Academic treatments have thus attempted to give a view of how the various interventions of the local and national state have an impact on the life chances of poor people. In its broadest conception this involves a consideration of the issues of health, education and discrimination. Of course the boundaries which are drawn for the purpose of instruction bear only a limited resemblance to the overall politico/social analysis of the situation of poor people.

Why lawyers are interested in the problems of the poor is itself a matter of major debate within both Britain and the United States. This has been ascribed variously to altruism,[13] lawyers' self-interest,[14] a reaction to the unacceptable reality of Stalinism,[15] the inability of municipal Left politics to deal effectively with poverty,[16] as well as an attempt by careerist law teachers to create new empires[17] or simply to engage in the problems of poor people rather than work for rich or corporate clients.[18] The specialist journals recognize a range of issues likely to be dealt with by lawyers working in the welfare field. For a fully rounded view of welfare, it would be ideal to include these broader issues of social policy such as health, housing and education. However the literature in these areas is sufficiently self-contained and so extensive as to make such a broad project both problematic and unfeasible. In similar vein the dimension of racial disadvantage is dealt with elsewhere in this series.

In addition, a separate but related debate and literature have sprung up about the delivery of the advice and assistance services available to the poor.[19] Central to this work is a conception of what it is that lawyers and other advice agencies are trying to do on behalf of the poor; there is considerable overlap in the background assumptions informing these kinds of practical lawyers' and advisers' strategies.[20] For the purposes of this collection it is proposed to limit the coverage to those areas of social and legal policy where the local or national state seeks to supplement the market mechanism by providing income support.

## Issues in Welfare Law

Debates about state income support – welfare – and the role of law are relatively recent. They initially concentrated upon the removal from the supervision of the courts of determinations by expert welfare tribunals which was a feature of post-war Britain.[21] In Britain and the United States welfare issues as an area of legal practice and teaching have been largely a feature of the past 20 years. Over this period the major theme which has dominated debates about welfare law has been the function of welfare mechanisms. There has been concern on the political Left that welfare has provided a version of what (the Conservative) Prime Minister Balfour described as an 'antidote to socialism'.[22] Welfare has been perceived as a way of softening the edges of the market allocation of goods and services. More than that, welfare services have been functional to the operation of capitalism without altering the fundamental way of making decisions about production.[23] On the Right there has been concern about the cost of welfare. This has been expressed both about money paid unnecessarily as well as the negative impact of welfare on initiative or incentives.[24] Related themes are the fiscal crisis and the crisis of confidence in the welfare state.[25] What differentiates much of this discussion is the presentation of the political debate in terms of the desirability of welfare mechanisms rather than as apolitical technical questions.

This debate has not always been conducted using the typology indicated here. There have also been reassessments of the nature of poverty and its relationship to structural features of the political economy. In place of a simple choice between the Left/Right dichotomy, some writers have suggested that industrial change has rendered the language of class irrelevant or meaningless in the post-industrial economy. According to them, the problem is no longer how to secure adequate protection for wage labourers in and out of work, but how to treat a whole category of individuals who lack economically viable skills and whose children are likely to remain in the same position.[26]

Related to this cataclysmic view of the future of work for whole sectors of society is a reappraisal of the basis and function of welfare. Just as arguments about the creation of an underclass suggest that a group is emerging who will not be able to participate effectively in society, it is claimed that such groups already exist.[27] This argument has been applied to the work of women and their hidden and largely unrecognized role in servicing the economy.[28] Literatures have developed which have important theoretical implications for the whole question of what welfare can achieve in relation to its impact on women.[29] Directly related to the notion of welfare being an aspect of the world of waged work is the treatment of disabled people.[30] The political implications for these two groups have particularly called into question the British approach to welfare where the theoretical importance of the insurance principle is based on contributions in work.[31]

## Selection of this Collection of Essays

The themes which these essays highlight have dominated debates over the role of law and welfare. They are grouped into five separate but related topics. These divisions are necessarily heuristic and readers will observe overlap as writers range beyond the major issue in which they are engaged. Part I of the collection documents the central debate about the measurement of poverty. It starts with an early essay by Peter Townsend in which he sets out human needs and hence what amounts to poverty as largely determined by the accepted modes of behaviour of the communities in which people live. Hence inability to match such a yardstick would be a feature of a relative view of poverty. Peter Townsend used the work of Mollie Orshansky as a counterpoint in his later writings and an example of this alternative position is included. It was a reaction to this kind of approach which was a feature of Townsend's major developed work, *Poverty in the United Kingdom*, published at the end of the 1970s.[32] This theme is developed in work by Miller, Rein, Roby and Gross where the notion of inequality is broadened from income inequality to cover not just capital assets but other factors affecting life chances. Thus the importance of health education and other services and their distribution becomes a crucial feature in the evaluation of the extent of poverty in society. Poverty and inequality in this view are interrelated, and the solution of one becomes entwined with the eradication of the other.

A rather different way of seeing poverty is found in Oscar Lewis' essay on the culture of poverty. The author of the celebrated *The Children of Sanchez*[33] provides a concise account of the centrality of culture in approaching poverty. In different arenas the notion that the problems of poor people are cultural is one which has from time to time struck a chord with politicians and social scientists alike. It conveniently absolves the rest of society from any direct responsibility for the lot of the oppressed. Space restraints necessitate the omission of John Veit-Wilson's assessment at the end of the 1980s[34] of the practical implications of adopting a relativist approach to poverty which do not provide a privileged position to the expert. Similarly of interest is the challenging essay by Stein Ringen[35] to the effect that poverty has been wildly overestimated. He is highly critical of poverty studies in the late 1970s and 1980s and suggests that their findings are largely invalid – no more, he claims, than statements of opinion. This bold assertion met with a spirited response from David Donnison.[36]

The related theme of appropriate responses to poverty comprises Part II of this collection. Debates about the nature of poverty and responses to it tend to assume that the 'problem' of poverty demands a response. Adrian Sinfield draws on the framework of Richard Titmuss to examine the way in which welfare ranges into the economic, political and social spheres. The fact that the benefits of welfare (conceived in this wider way) continue and still today are enjoyed by a wide range of the managerial and professional sectors of society has had a profound impact for both the supporters and detractors of the principle of universal welfare. The success of the middle class on expanding the range of welfare goods provided and dominating their distribution connects with a theme developed by Kirk Mann which space did not allow to be included.[37] Mann points to the fact that in the representation of welfare as a product of the struggles of the working class, the divided nature of the working class has not been fully appreciated. Looking across Western Europe, Göran Therborn suggests that the historical circumstances in which individuals and groups find themselves determine their response to the goods at stake under welfare capitalism.

These views contrast with a strand of writing which characterizes welfare issues less in terms of political struggles than in terms of the language and spirit of social values. In the essays by Goodin and King and Waldron, the nature of the responsibilities and rights involved in community provision for the weak and vulnerable is discussed in the context of the United States and Britain. A related theme (which space did not allow to be included) is developed by Pekka Kosonen[38] – namely the tensions between collectivity and individualism in modern Scandinavian states.

At a more general level, Part III documents the relationship between political and economic systems and the functions of poverty and its various treatments. The work of T.H. Marshall overlaps the two different kinds of concerns identified in Parts II and III. In the essay selected here he provides a classic account of the post-ideology view of welfare: it is the civilizer of capitalism. As Herbert Gans points out, however, the existence of poverty may also be functional for capital, but alternatives are posited. This view of why poverty persists provides a link into the writings from the political left. Ian Gough provides a Marxist explanation of how the expansion of state expenditure in relation to welfare involves contradictions which imply restructuring. Rudolf Klein suggests that it is necessary to overhaul thinking on what it is that welfare policies should provide in order to withstand the onslaught from advocates of the market and other opponents of welfare. This is a theme which Ramesh Mishra has developed in his work.[39] The full realization in the Reagan years that some restructuring was inevitable was analysed tellingly elsewhere by Vicente Navarro.[40] This 'crisis of the welfare state' was the subject of extensive writings in the 1980s. Geraint Parry provides a summary of the themes which emerged from this discussion, partly revolving around the notion that a new situation had been reached in the nature of welfare provision. This was a product not so much of political ideology but of structural factors such as the decline of the welfare state's economic base. Recently Peter Taylor-Gooby has provided a valuable overview of the range of options which appear to present themselves to policymakers as a result of these developments; the accuracy of his prediction will prove of interest.[41]

The theoretical concerns of legal writers provide the theme for Part IV. These concerns have concentrated on how any given welfare provision should be distributed. This has centred on the chronic question of the role of rights and discretion within welfare distribution systems. The struggle between universal benefits available to all and selective ones available on an income or means test has been debated in different contexts. At the level of practical politics, the competing efficiency of means testing as a mechanism of targeting need has been claimed,[42] as opposed to the cheaper administration and more satisfactory take-up amongst the needy of universal rights.[43] These debates have traditionally derived from a political commitment either to the notion of discretion on the one hand or to citizenship rights on the other. There is also a more crucial role perceived for those operating within systems of broad constitutional rights of citizenship. The call for action from lawyers to engage in welfare work by Charles Reich provides a coherent account from a major writer in this American rights-based perspective. How to put such a project into effect is examined at length in Frank Michelman's essay. He discusses the protection of the poor through invoking broad constitutional principles. How these issues fared in practice in the ensuing decade and the implications for the rule of law are the subject of the essays by Simon and Handler. Reich's theme is taken up by Richard Titmuss in the context of Britain together with the expanded role of discretion in the British post-War welfare system. The relationship between rights and discretion is the theme Robert Goodin explores. This part concludes with Ian Loveland's discussion of the relationship between this question of discretion in welfare and practical politics.

Finally, Part V covers the significance of gender in determining the ways in which welfare law and policy have been constructed. Hilary Land's essay makes the basic point in its title – 'Who cares for the family?' That primary responsibility for family care is allocated to women is a cultural construct with significant repercussions for the role of women and the operation of power in society. The significance of the role of women's demands in discussions of future social policy is stressed by Mary McIntosh who urges the crucial need to reconceptualize welfare. Hilary Rose takes up the same notion elsewhere.[44] While class implications must not be lost sight of, it is central to her thesis that welfare is perceived as based on the paid and unpaid labour of women. This theme of male domination and its specific form in relation to welfare systems are explored in the final essays by Caroline Andrew, Virginia Sapiro and Birte Siim in the context of Canada, the United States and Scandinavia.

## Debates for the Future

The rationale behind the selection of these 25 essays has been to give a flavour of both the debates which have preoccupied the academic community and welfare practitioners, as well as to highlight some areas where there is likely to be conflict in the future. The issue of defining poverty has been the subject of much controversy; it rests at the core of questions about how societies understand the causes of poverty. Insofar as defining the problem determines an appropriate response, then this is an area where writing has been extensive. Rejecting a view of poverty as a matter of an absolute standard was commonplace in the writings of the late 1960s.[45] The implication of such relative approaches to poverty was a move towards redistribution of wealth and income.[46] Accordingly the preference for thinkers from the political Right has been to argue that an absolute standard of poverty is viable. The advantages of such an approach are twofold; in addition to setting an identifiable limit on public expenditure, there are psychological advantages to be gained from the minimalist state.[47] Thus we find Joseph and Sumption urging the acceptance of an absolute standard in the late 1970s[48] and in the early 1980s Hermione Parker suggesting that the morale of the poor had been sapped by welfare benefits.[49] This debate appeared to shift significantly during the 1980s when political questions were presented as apparently largely technical: what measurement of poverty would likely command a significant degree of consensual support? With politicians reticent about committing themselves[50] to any firm position on welfare policy goals, this is perhaps understandable.

A major thrust of the early work on post-Second World War poverty was to assess the implications of interpreting poverty as a socially constructed phenomenon. If poverty had its basis in the economic and political relations operative in a society, how could such a problem be untangled? The various analyses of this issue were distinct. Whilst poverty was a societal construct, its actual nature was variously seen as a matter of changing people's values and beliefs, of transferring goods, of making effective power accessible or of offering equal opportunities. Poverty was seen in various ways as an issue of citizenship. What distinguishes this set of debates is the absence of an overtly political analysis. The economic structure is assumed to be given.

In the essays on the political and economic context of welfare, the debate is largely about the relationship between capitalism as an economic system and welfare structures that have been developed within capitalism in the 20th century. The economic structure here is not taken as given: it is assumed to be the problem by writers of the political Left. As indicated above, this is an area where debate has been particularly extensive.

Less fundamentally in conflict, at first blush, have been the differences of emphasis over rights and discretion. Those concerned with welfare as a matter of rights based in citizenship are nonetheless committed to a very different conception of the relationship between the individual and the community from those prepared to rely on official and unofficial charity as the bulwark against deprivation of social resources. Whether or not the debate is constructed in terms of entrenched rights or outside such a framework has an impact on the centrality of the debate to the political programmes underpinning action for the deprived. Only where that group is denied an authentic political voice does the legalist preoccupation enjoy a primacy in anti-poverty strategy.

A developing concern of writing on welfare in the 1980s has been the position of women under welfare. Starting with Elizabeth Wilson's *Women and the Welfare State*,[51] the relationship between women's oppression and welfare systems has been extensively documented both in journals and books. The extent to which social provision – for sickness, retirement, unemployment and, surprisingly, childbearing and rearing – bears the stamp of male-orientated policies is remarkable in the field of welfare provision.[52]

In this volume there is an attempt both to characterize the major themes which have preoccupied writers, as well as to impose a coherence on the developments which may be tangential. That is to say, the development of welfare structures is not solely dependent on the interplay of academic arguments, but on concrete struggles and the fate of political programmes. Which of these is likely to triumph depends on the external economic factors within which political struggles operate and debates are conducted. In popular culture there are pessimistic as well as optimistic views of the future for the poor in society.[53] Whether welfare mechanisms can steer a course between such apocalyptic views of the lot of the poor is not easy to gauge. Confidence in the civilized response is low at the time of writing. Despite indications in the 1990s of confidence from Eastern Europe, what is clear is that the market is manifestly incapable of providing solutions for the poor and the community that are acceptable to any of its participants.

## Notes

1 R. Schlatter (1951), *Private Property*, London: Allen and Unwin.
2 Statutes punishing begging and vagrancy were enacted throughout Britain in the 14th century; see F.F. Piven and R. Cloward (1972), *Regulating the Poor*, London: Tavistock.
3 See the work of the C.O.S. discussed in K. Woodroofe (1962), *From Charity to Social Work in England and the United States*, London: Tavistock, and the farm colony movement in the early 20th century. In addition this took an official form in the 1920s; see D. Colledge (1989), *Labour Camps*, Sheffield: Sheffield Popular Publishing.
4 *Thatcher's Law* (the special issue of the *Journal of Law and Society* **16** (1989)) and specifically Pete Alcock's essay at p. 97 are cited by Michael Freeman in his introduction to *Critical Issues in Welfare Law*, London: Stevens, 1990. To this one might reasonably add P. Alcock and P. Harris (1982), *Welfare Law and Order*, London: Macmillan.
5 The publications *Adviser* (NCAB/Shelter) and *Welfare Rights Bulletin* (CPAG) are excellent examples of this kind of work in Britain.
6 The monthly journal of the Child Poverty Action Group *Poverty* is an example, as is *SCOLAG* (the journal of the Scottish Legal Action Group).
7 M. Freeman (ed.) (1990), *Critical Issues in Welfare Law*, London: Stevens.
8 W. Birdsall and J. Hankins (1985), 'The Future of Social Security' in *Annals of the American Academy of Political and Social Science*, **479**, 82.
9 R. Chilton (1970), 'Social Control through Welfare Legislation', *Law and Society Review*, **5** (2), 205.
10 P. Taylor-Gooby (1980), 'Legitimation Deficit, Public Opinion and the Welfare State', *Sociology*, **17**, 165.
11 Amongst such diverse institutions as the Universities of Leicester, Queen's Belfast, Strathclyde and Dundee.
12 Edinburgh and Warwick Universities provided early examples of the 'taxation' approach.
13 In their first issues, the founders of *LAG* and *SCOLAG* indicated the prominence of altruism in their thinking; these issues exhibited this to a high degree.
14 Z. Bankowski and G. Mungham (1976), *Images of Law*, London: Routledge and Kegan Paul.
15 Cyril Glasser saw the Congress of the CPSU when Khruschev denounced Stalin as the crucial turning point for the Left in Great Britain, leading to a shift from party politics to single issues; unpublished paper at Ford Foundation Workshop on welfare law, July 1977.
16 On the structural issues involved, see B. Hindess (1971), *The Decline of Working Class Politics*, London: MacGibbon & Kee.
17 Z. Bankowski and G. Mungham (1976), 'Warwick University Ltd (Continued)', *British Journal of Law and Society*, **1**, 179.
18 This also took the form of a debate about whether the subject should be called poverty law; see C. Smith and D. Hoath (1975), *Law and the Underprivileged*, London: Routledge & Kegan Paul.
19 T. Prosser (1983), *Test Cases for the Poor*, London: Child Poverty Action Group; also the Roach and Roach/Piven and Cloward (1978–79) debate in *Social Problems*, **26**, 160–71, 172–78 and 267–70.
20 Contrast, first, F. Pivan and R. Cloward (1972), *Regulating the Poor*, London: Tavistock, and, second, the work of the Community Development Projects in Britain (such as *Gilding the Ghetto*, 1978) with the Legal Action Group's rights-based strategy.
21 A.T. Denning (1949), *Freedom under the Law*, London: Stevens.
22 It is perhaps a measure of the impact of the political Right in the 1980s that welfare systems in New Zealand and Scandinavia are under serious threat in the 1990s. Welfare has also been

characterized as 'an island of socialism in a sea of capitalism': T. Novak (1988), *Poverty and the State*, Milton Keynes: Open University Press.

23 I. Gough (1979), *The Political Economy of the Welfare State*, London: Macmillan; N. Ginsburg (1979), *Class, Capital and Social Policy*, London: Macmillan; P. Alcock and P. Harris (1982), *Welfare, Law and Order*, London: Macmillan.

24 R. Boyson (ed.) (1971), *Down with the Poor*, London: Churchill; H. Parker (1982), *The Moral Hazards of Social Benefits*, London: Institute of Economic Affairs.

25 J. O'Connor (1973), *The Fiscal Crisis of the State*, New York: St Martin's Press; R. Mishra (1984), *The Welfare State in Crisis*, Brighton: Wheatsheaf.

26 R. Dahrendorf (1985), *Law and Order*, London: Stevens.

27 M. Harrington (1984), *The New American Poverty*, New York: Holt, Rinehart and Winston. This work connects these two themes.

28 C. Cockburn (1977), *The Local State*, London: Pluto.

29 C. Glendinning and J. Millar (eds) (1987), *Women and Poverty in Britain*, Brighton: Wheatsheaf; G. Pascall (1986), *Social Policy*, London: Tavistock; C.V. Baldock and B. Cross (eds) (1983), *Women, Social Welfare and the State*, Sydney: George Allen and Unwin.

30 D. Stone (1985), *The Disabled State*, Basingstoke: Macmillan; D. Guthrie (ed.) (1981), *Disability*, London: Macmillan; E. Topliss and B. Gould (1981), *A Charter for the Disabled*, Oxford: Basil Blackwell and Martin Robertson.

31 A. Ogus and E. Barendt (1989), *Law of Social Security*, London: Butterworths, Chapters 4 and 7.

32 London: Harmondsworth, 1979.

33 London: Secker and Warburg, 1962.

34 John Veit-Wilson (1987), 'Consensual approaches to poverty lines and social security', *Journal of Social Policy*, **16**, 184–211.

35 Stein Ringen (1988), 'Direct and indirect measures of poverty', *Journal of Social Policy*, **17**, 351–65.

36 David Donnison (1988), 'Defining and measuring poverty: a reply to Stein Ringen', *Journal of Social Policy*, **17**, 367–74.

37 Kirk Mann (1986), 'The making of the claiming class: the neglect of agency in analyses of the welfare state', *Critical Social Policy*, **15**, 62–74.

38 Pekka Kosonen (1987), 'From Collectivity to Individualism in the Welfare State', *Acta Sociologica*, **30**, 281–93.

39 Ramesh Mishra (1986), 'The Left and the Welfare State: a critical analysis', *Critical Social Policy*, **15**, Spring, 4–19.

40 Vicente Navarro (1982), 'The Crisis of the International Capitalist Order and its Implications for the Welfare State', *Critical Social Policy*, **2** (1), 43–62.

41 Peter Taylor-Gooby (1989), 'Current developments in the sociology of welfare', *British Journal of Sociology*, **4**, 637–56.

42 A.W. Dilnot, J.A. Kay and C.N. Morris (1984), *The Reform of Social Security*, Oxford: Clarendon Press.

43 J. Bradshaw (1985), 'Tried and found wanting: the take-up of means tested benefits' in S. Ward (ed.) (1985), *DHSS in Crisis*, London: Child Poverty Action Group.

44 Hilary Rose (1981), 'Rereading Titmuss: The Sexual Division of Welfare', *Journal of Social Policy*, **10** (4), 477–501.

45 P. Townsend (ed.) (1970), *The Concept of Poverty*, London: Heinemann; K. Coates and R. Silburn (1970), *Poverty: the forgotten Englishmen*, Harmondsworth: Penguin.

46 J. Kincaid (1973) (2nd edition, 1975), *Poverty and Equality in Britain*, Harmondsworth: Penguin.

47 R. Boyson (1971), *Down with the Poor*, London: Churchill.

48 K. Joseph and J. Sumption (1979), *Equality*, London: J. Murray.

49 H. Parker (1982), *The Moral Hazards of Social Benefits*, London: Institute of Economic Affairs. The point is also made in H. Parker (1989), *Instead of the Dole*, London: Routledge in the context of the emergence of an underclass stemming from structural changes in work, as well as the nature of the benefits system and its failure to offer adequate flexibility to meet such changes.

50 The language of the 1980s has shifted to talk in terms of expenditure targets. Hence in Britain

Conservatives like ex-Prime Minister Margaret Thatcher and Social Security Minister Nicholas Scott have consistently stressed that there was no official poverty line.

51 Red Rag Collective, 1974 and the extended 1977 version under the same title, London: Tavistock; see also E. Wilson (1980), *Only Halfway to Paradise*, London: Tavistock.

52 It was originally planned to incorporate a section on another group oppressed by the way in which welfare has been constructed around the interests of a dominant group – the able–bodied. However, for reasons of space this section could not be included. Again it also seemed to be an area where much of the writing on the construction of the welfare world in terms of the able-bodied had taken place in books rather than journal articles.

53 Lou Reed (1988): 'Give me your tired, your poor, I'll piss on 'em, That's what the Statue of Bigotry says, Your poor huddled masses, let's club 'em to death and get it over with', *Dirty Blvd*, New York: Sire Records. Tracy Chapman (1988): 'Poor people gonna rise up, And get their share, Poor people gonna rise up, And take what's theirs, *Talkin' Bout a Revolution*, Elektra/Asylum Records.

# Part I
# The Definition of Poverty

# [1]

# Measuring Poverty

PETER TOWNSEND

ONE OF the basic aims of social policy in the years immediately following the war was the elimination of poverty. In order to find how far this aim has been realized there must be adequate inquiries from time to time in the form of social surveys which adopt certain definite standards of measurement. In the ten years preceding the war at least ten surveys of the extent and causes of poverty in particular areas were carried out. In the nine years since the war only one study of this type has been published. This in itself may be an indication that the problem of poverty is less pressing than it was, but, on the evidence of a single study, we cannot claim much detailed knowledge about the living conditions of poorer people, or about the effects of the new social security services. The aim of this article is to consider on what basis this knowledge may be acquired in the future. I will discuss briefly the standards used in measuring poverty in the past, and in the course of this will argue for an entirely different approach.

The standard selected is important not only to the research worker intent on measuring the extent of poverty or general living conditions in any locality. A standard of a similar kind has been used in framing social policy. Social security benefit payments are intended to be related to a rough standard of subsistence, and this relation will have to be considered when the quinquennial review of the social security scheme is presented to Parliament in the near future. It is therefore appropriate to examine what is meant by a subsistence or poverty standard.

The sociological study and measurement of poverty in this country dates from the pioneering work of Charles Booth and B. Seebohm Rowntree at the end of the last century. [1, 2] In introducing his study Rowntree said,

> The families living in poverty may be divided into two sections:
>
> (1) Families whose total earnings are insufficient to obtain the minimum necessaries for the maintenance of merely physical efficiency. Poverty falling under this head may be described as "primary" poverty.
>
> (2) Families whose total earnings would be sufficient for the maintenance of merely physical efficiency were it not that some portion of it is absorbed by other expenditure, either useful or wasteful. Poverty falling under this head may be described as "secondary" poverty.

The " minimum necessaries for the maintenance of merely physical efficiency " were calculated by estimating the nutritional needs of adults and children and by translating such needs into quantities of different foods and hence into money terms, and by adding on to these figures certain minimum sums for clothing, fuel and household sundries, according to the size of family. The poverty line for a family of five was, food 12*s*. 9*d*., clothing 2*s*. 3*d*., fuel 1*s*. 10*d*., household sundries 10*d*., totalling 17*s*. 8*d*. per week. Rent was treated as unavoidable outlay and was added to this sum. A family was considered to be in poverty if its total income fell short of the poverty line plus rent. The studies that followed in the next forty years adopted the same approach and although there were some minor alterations, the standards used for measuring poverty were broadly the same, adjusted according to change in prices, as that used by Rowntree in 1899. [3, 13] In the 1930s a standard applicable to 1899 and converted by means of a price index based on articles purchased in 1904 was taken to be the best method of measuring poverty. [4, 14] By and large the changes in the conditions of life brought about in the intervening years were ignored.

In 1936 Rowntree made a second survey of York, in the course of which he used a more generous standard of poverty. This differed in degree, but not in kind, from the standard used at the end of the last century. The list of necessaries was lengthened to include compulsory insurance contributions, trade union subscriptions, travelling to and from work, and personal sundries such as a daily newspaper, a little stationery, and a few other odds and ends. A similar list was adopted in his and G. R. Lavers' Third Survey of York, *Poverty and the Welfare State*, 1951. A discussion of these standards and of those used in earlier surveys will be found in " Poverty : Ten Years after Beveridge ". [15]

In considering all these poverty standards in detail, one cannot help feeling that they are too arbitrary. If clothing, money for travel to work and newspapers are considered to be " necessaries " in the conventional sense, why not tea, handkerchiefs, laundry, contraceptives, cosmetics, hairdressing and shaving, and life insurance payments ? Are we indeed so sure that a list of necessaries must exclude cigarettes, beer, toys for children, Christmas gifts and cinema entertainment ? The question of what were regarded or what ought to have been regarded as necessaries was very rarely raised in any of the surveys.

In attempts to reduce the arbitrariness of the standards some investigators had tried to find out the actual spending of families on certain items. In 1899 and 1936 Rowntree based his allowances for clothing and fuel and light on information and opinions passed on to him by " a large number of working people ", though in 1936 he admitted that in arriving at an allowance for personal sundries " I was forced to rely largely on my own judgment ", and in both years his findings on the food consumption and expenditure of 18 and 28 families respectively did not affect his formulation of the poverty line. In the third survey of York in 1950 Rowntree found out the spending of

29 women on clothing and household sundries, and of 32 men on clothing and fuel and light. In the last case, for example, the amounts to be included in the poverty standard for women's and children's clothing and for household sundries were based on the average expenditure of three women whose expenditure on these items was the smallest of those from whom information was obtained. Finding out the expenditure of the poorest families on clothing, fuel and light and household sundries is perhaps a less arbitrary method of compiling a standard, but why should these items be selected from budgets for consideration and not others as well? And secondly, does the average expenditure of those who spend least on clothing or fuel provide a standard of what people *need to spend* on such items to be out of poverty?

The most defensible constituent of the poverty line has always been the amount allocated to food. Experts on nutrition have worked out the average nutritive needs of broad classes of the population, in terms of calories, proteins, vitamins, iron, calcium and so on. These needs, as stated earlier, can be translated into quantities of different foods and from foods into money terms. The diet, as derived, gives adequate nutrition at the lowest possible cost, and demands considerable knowledge of the most nutritious and cheapest foods on the market. It may well be argued that few families have the knowledge or opportunity to attain such a standard. In a study of the diets of 28 families in different income groups in his 1936 survey of York Rowntree said:

> It is true that, at 1936 prices, a family of five could be adequately fed for this sum (20*s.* 6*d.*), but . . . the housewife must possess an unusual amount of knowledge of the nutritive value of different foodstuffs. Among the 28 families, some of which were very poor, not one succeeded in selecting a dietary anything like as economical as that used in our minimum standard of living (p. 173).[1]

The same point applies to the half-yearly papers on the cost of a "human needs" diet, which stem from the standard used by Rowntree in 1936, written by Miss T. Schulz of the Oxford University Institute of Statistics.[2] If indeed few working-class families attain this standard, then it may not be a practicable one to use in measuring poverty.

The main fault in the standards used has been their lack of relation to the budgets and customs of life of working people. Many who are considered to be above the poverty line because their income exceeds the total cost of meeting basic needs do, in fact, spend less on the individual items included in the standard—food, clothing, fuel and light and household sundries—

[1] In the *New Survey of London Life and Labour*, Vol. VI, p. 320, discussing working-class culinary and dietetic standards, Miss F. A. Livingstone argued that full weight must be given "to all the handicaps and difficulties, such as cramped space, absence of storage, defective water supply or cooking apparatus, and the severe limitation of time arising from other pressing duties", besides working-class "habits and prejudices".

[2] In a summary of her studies Miss Schulz said: "It needed, indeed, exceptional knowledge of food values as well as considerable skill in cooking for the adequate nutrition of a family to be attained at the figures of cost computed by us since 1941."—*Human Needs Diets from 1936 to 1949*, Bulletin of the Oxford University Institute of Statistics, October, 1949.

simply because they spend money on other things. This can be illustrated by comparing the poverty standards used immediately before the war (and the subsistence standard outlined in the Beveridge Report) with the budgets of poorer families in 1938, details of which were collected by the Ministry of Labour. [16] Lord Beveridge, for example, arguing for a subsistence standard similar in kind to the poverty lines used in the surveys before the war, allowed a man, wife and three small children 53*s.* 3*d.* a week at 1938 prices, including 31*s.* for food (58 per cent of the total). But in 1938 families of the same size with roughly the same total income were spending less than 22*s.* on food (41 per cent of the total income).[1] How those on the borderline of poverty ought to spend their money is a very different thing from how they do spend their money. It would be unrealistic to expect them, as in effect many social investigators have expected them, to be skilled dieticians with marked tendencies towards puritanism.

In all the definitions of poverty in the social surveys there is the implication that many poor people ought to limit their spending to a short list of "necessaries" laid down by those in charge of the surveys and that if they did not do this they were in poverty only through their own fault. "Our definition is such that a family is deemed to be in poverty if the joint income of the members, ***supposing it were all available and wisely spent***, would not suffice to purchase for them the necessaries of life . . ." (p. 148, *Social Survey of Merseyside* [my italics]). Many critics fastened on to the large numbers in what Rowntree called "secondary" poverty as evidence of the need for moral regeneration, and said that these people lacked merely strength of will to pull themselves out of poverty. It was not appreciated that many in this class would have needed virtues of self-denial, skill and knowledge not possessed by any other class of society, if they were to spend their money as it was thought they should spend it.

Judgments of one social class on another are notoriously untrustworthy and things which are treated as necessaries by one group may not be so regarded by another. A few drinks in a pub on a Saturday night after watching the local football match may be as necessary, in the conventional sense, to membership of the poorest stratum of society as a Savile Row suit and business meetings over lunch at the Savoy to membership of a wealthier stratum of society. Recent experience of the effects of unemployment in the cotton towns in Lancashire showed that when incomes were reduced from a full wage to an unemployment insurance allowance many families were apt to cut down on things such as meat and fruit in order not to forgo an occasional visit to a cinema or football match. [17] In considering the spending habits of poorer people, it seems that due regard must be paid to the conventions sanctioning membership of their community, to the influence of economic and social measures currently adopted by society as a whole, such as rationing welfare foods services, food subsidies and indirect taxes,

[1] Based on data in "The Cost of a Family", A. M. Henderson, *The Review of Economic Studies 1949–50*, Vol. XVII (2).

and to the standards encouraged by advertisers,[1] the press, the B.B.C. and the Church.

### A New Standard

The pattern of spending among poor people is largely determined by the accepted modes of behaviour in the communities in which they live, and these, in turn, are determined to some extent by the practices adopted by the society as a whole through central and local government. A yardstick for measuring poverty can only be devised in the light of knowledge about family budgets. How can this be done with the least arbitrariness?

One improvement was suggested in a study of a Birmingham community, carried out in 1939 and published in 1942. [13] In this study poverty was measured in two ways: (i) by comparing *net income* (i.e. total income less rent, compulsory insurances, and fares to and from work) with an assumed minimum standard of expenditure on food, fuel, light, clothing and cleaning materials; and (ii) by comparing with a minimum standard of expenditure on food the *balance out of housekeeping money theoretically available for food*, after paying the assumed minimum on non-food items in (i) plus voluntary insurances and regular hire-purchase instalments. The first, the usual type of measurement adopted in social surveys, was said to take "less account of actualities" and the second was "a more realistic measure of the standard of sufficiency of the family". But it was acknowledged that both these methods could be criticized, though the second to a lesser extent, for "ignoring certain types of necessary expenditure, such as that on household utensils, medical treatment, and holidays, as well as expenditure on tobacco, beer, newspapers, and recreation, which are, to say the least of it, customary" (p. 47).

The second method, although open to many of the criticisms expressed above, gives prominence to expenditure on food as a criterion of poverty. In future, it would seem reasonable to accept such a criterion, with certain qualifications, simply because nutritional needs are more susceptible of measurement than clothing, fuel and other needs.

The following procedure might be justifiable in future surveys: (i) The collection of data relating to the food consumption and expenditure as well as the income of working-class households; (ii) The comparison of this data, assembled according to constitution of household and income group, with a scale of nutritive needs, such as that in the Report of the Committee on Nutrition of the British Medical Association, 1950; (iii) The isolation, from all those securing minimum nutrition, of, say, the 25 per cent in the various household groups who achieve it on the smallest incomes, or rather, the

[1] "To (the advertiser) a bride is not a young woman on the edge of a great adventure; she is a conditioned consumer who, by buying the right cosmetics and rignt brassiere has captured her man, and who, when she returns from her honeymoon, will go into the grocer's and automatically recite those branded names which have been the most loudly dinned into her ears for the last twenty-one years."—*The Shocking History of Advertising*, E. S. Turner, 1952, p. 12.

smallest incomes less one or two fixed involuntary overheads, such as rent and compulsory insurances. The average total expenditure of these households, less the overheads, according to their different sizes, can be taken as the poverty line.

Such a standard may be justified on the ground that it is, in fact, attained by a fair proportion of working-class people, and is therefore realistic. It would obviate the need for subjective decisions about the sums of money required for clothing, fuel and light and so on. Inevitably, a subjective element remains, and this is involved in the choice of the proportion of working-class households whose members have an adequate diet and whose spending is to be considered in fixing the standard. But this element need not be obtrusive, particularly if the choice is made with full knowledge of the budgetary patterns of different families, and with full knowledge of the dispersion, and the reasons for the dispersion, around the budgetary mean of each income and household group.

Part of the information essential to the application of this method is already obtained in the course of the National Food Survey. The latest Report on this, for 1951 [18], analyses the adequacy of diet by social class, but the classes are rather broadly defined,[1] and the diet and expenditure of those in the lowest income group is not set out in any detail. A great deal of information about family budgets will issue from the new survey of household expenditure being made at present by the Ministry of Labour. It is to be hoped that this will be tabulated by household size and constitution, for each income group.

It is true that the method suggested is basically a method of measuring the extent of malnutrition not attributable to wasteful spending, but I think it would give the fairest index of poverty, particularly if the results gained by its use were correlated with other findings based on standards of overcrowding, household amenities, education and so on.

## The Level of Benefit Payments

The different approach which has been urged has an important bearing on the standards adopted in social policy for benefit payments. Lord Beveridge, in his *Report on Social Insurance and Allied Services*, formulated a subsistence standard very similar to the poverty lines used in the social surveys before the war, as a reasonable way of fixing benefit rates. This was generally regarded as the " central idea " of the Beveridge Plan. [19, 20] Lord Beveridge has himself reaffirmed this point in recent months. The National Assistance scales are determined by means of a similar standard, and although the National Insurance scales fall short of the Beveridge standard, they are still

[1] The sample was divided into the following income groups: £20 and over per week (1 per cent of the population), £13–£20 (2 per cent), £8–£13 (13 per cent), £4 10*s.*–£8 (64 per cent), and under £4 10*s.* per week (20 per cent).

in principle related to it. Neither the Labour nor the Conservative Party has explicitly abandoned this principle.

Whether, in fact, the subsistence basis for benefit payments should be accepted by the nation in the future is one of the fundamental questions that will have to be faced by Parliament next year when the quinquennial review of social security is considered. The adoption of a true subsistence minimum would add greatly to the costs of the scheme. It is true that in recent years an increasing number of people have received wages during sickness and have entered superannuation schemes, and income from the social security services in times of adversity may therefore be less important now than it was. For short periods of unemployment or sickness people seem to manage quite well, because, apart from insurance payments, they frequently get deferred wages, trade union allowances and P.A.Y.E. refunds, and need to purchase few items of clothing or household materials. (Large families should not be included in this category.) There would appear to be a case for two scales, one for a short and one for a long period of need. It may be true, too, that payments to the old should be lower than those to other people in continuing need, but this is a matter for further inquiry. In any event, the acceptance of a standard such as the pre-war poverty line or the Beveridge subsistence minimum implies that poor working-class people should and could live as social scientists and administrators think they should live. There has been little attempt to discuss the distinction between "luxuries" and "necessities" in terms of economic and social sanctions for spending behaviour, nor in terms of individual and class differences. And there has been no attempt to distinguish between the humanly attainable and the desirable in the pattern of family budgets.

I have tried to set out the difficulties of arriving at a satisfactory standard for measuring poverty, which can be used in social surveys, and the difficulties of eliminating class judgments from that standard. The conclusion seems to be that the problem of whether or not a family is in poverty is best decided by finding whether its expenditure, save for one or two involuntary overheads, such as rent and compulsory insurances, is less than that which actually secures minimum nutrition for a large number of working-class families.

## REFERENCES

1. London: *Life and Labour of the People in London*, Charles Booth.
2. York: *Poverty: A Study of Town Life*, B. S. Rowntree.
3. A Survey of Five Towns: *Livelihood and Poverty*, A. L. Bowley and A. R. Burnett-Hurst, 1915, and *Has Poverty Diminished?* A. L. Bowley and Margaret H. Hogg, 1925.
4. London: *New Survey of London Life and Labour*, 1930–5.
5. Merseyside: *Social Survey of Merseyside*, ed. D. Caradog-Jones, 1934.
6. Southampton: *Work and Wealth in a Modern Port*, P. Ford, 1934.
7. Sheffield: *A Survey of the Standard of Living in Sheffield*, A. D. K. Owen, 1934.

8. Miles Platting (Manchester): *Poverty and Housing Conditions in a Manchester Ward*, John Inman, 1934.
9. Plymouth: *A Social Survey of Plymouth*, 1935.
10. York: *Poverty and Progress*, B. S. Rowntree, 1941.
11. Bristol: *The Standard of Living in Bristol*, H. Tout, 1938.
12. Six Towns: *Men Without Work*, A report made to the Pilgrim Trust, 1938.
13. Kingstanding (Birmingham): *Nutrition and Size of Family*, M. S. Soutar, E. H. Wilkins and P. Sargant Florence, 1942.
14. "A New Calculation of the Poverty Line", R. F. George, *Journal of the Royal Statistical Society*, 1937.
15. "Poverty: Ten Years After Beveridge", *Planning*, No. 344, August 4, 1952.
16. *Weekly Expenditure of Working Class Households in the United Kingdom in 1937–38*, Detailed Tables, July, 1949.
17. "Social Security and Unemployment in Lancashire", *Planning*, No. 349, December 1, 1952.
18. "Domestic Food Consumption and Expenditure, 1951", *Report of the National Food Survey Committee*, 1953.
19. *England's Road to Social Security*, Karl de Schweinitz, 1943.
20. "After the Beveridge Report", *Planning*, No. 205, April 20, 1943.

# [2]

Established 1845 SCIENTIFIC AMERICAN October 1966 Volume 215 Number 4

# The Culture of Poverty

*Does membership in a group that has been poor for generations constitute belonging to a separate culture? A study of Puerto Ricans in both Puerto Rico and New York indicates that it does*

by Oscar Lewis

Poverty and the so-called war against it provide a principal theme for the domestic program of the present Administration. In the midst of a population that enjoys unexampled material well-being—with the average annual family income exceeding $7,000—it is officially acknowledged that some 18 million families, numbering more than 50 million individuals, live below the $3,000 "poverty line." Toward the improvement of the lot of these people some $1,600 million of Federal funds are directly allocated through the Office of Economic Opportunity, and many hundreds of millions of additional dollars flow indirectly through expanded Federal expenditures in the fields of health, education, welfare and urban affairs.

Along with the increase in activity on behalf of the poor indicated by these figures there has come a parallel expansion of publication in the social sciences on the subject of poverty. The new writings advance the same two opposed evaluations of the poor that are to be found in literature, in proverbs and in popular sayings throughout recorded history. Just as the poor have been pronounced blessed, virtuous, upright, serene, independent, honest, kind and happy, so contemporary students stress their great and neglected capacity for self-help, leadership and community organization. Conversely, as the poor have been characterized as shiftless, mean, sordid, violent, evil and criminal, so other students point to the irreversibly destructive effects of poverty on individual character and emphasize the corresponding need to keep guidance and control of poverty projects in the hands of duly constituted authorities. This clash of viewpoints reflects in part the infighting for political control of the program between Federal and local officials. The confusion results also from the tendency to focus study and attention on the personality of the individual victim of poverty rather than on the slum community and family and from the consequent failure to distinguish between poverty and what I have called the culture of poverty.

The phrase is a catchy one and is used and misused with some frequency in the current literature. In my writings it is the label for a specific conceptual model that describes in positive terms a subculture of Western society with its own structure and rationale, a way of life handed on from generation to generation along family lines. The culture of poverty is not just a matter of deprivation or disorganization, a term signifying the absence of something. It is a culture in the traditional anthropological sense in that it provides human beings with a design for living, with a ready-made set of solutions for human problems, and so serves a significant adaptive function. This style of life transcends national boundaries and regional and rural-urban differences within nations. Wherever it occurs, its practitioners exhibit remarkable similarity in the structure of their families, in interpersonal relations, in spending habits, in their value systems and in their orientation in time.

Not nearly enough is known about this important complex of human behavior. My own concept of it has evolved as my work has progressed and remains subject to amendment by my own further work and that of others. The scarcity of literature on the culture of poverty is a measure of the gap in communication that exists between the very poor and the middle-class personnel—social scientists, social workers, teachers, physicians, priests and others—who bear the major responsibility for carrying out the antipoverty programs. Much of the behavior accepted in the culture of poverty goes counter to cherished ideals of the larger society. In writing about "multiproblem" families social scientists thus often stress their instability, their lack of order, direction and organization. Yet, as I have observed them, their behavior seems clearly patterned and reasonably predictable. I am more often struck by the inexorable repetitiousness and the iron entrenchment of their lifeways.

The concept of the culture of poverty may help to correct misapprehensions that have ascribed some behavior patterns of ethnic, national or regional groups as distinctive characteristics. For example, a high incidence of common-law marriage and of households headed by women has been thought to be distinctive of Negro family life in this country and has been attributed to the Negro's historical experience of slavery. In actuality it turns out that such households express essential traits of the culture of poverty and are found among diverse peoples in many parts of the world and among peoples that have had no history of slavery. Although it is now possible to assert such generalizations, there is still much to be learned about this difficult and affecting subject. The absence of intensive anthropological studies of poor families in a wide variety of national contexts—particularly the lack of such studies in socialist countries—remains a serious handicap to the formulation of dependable cross-cultural constants of the culture of poverty.

My studies of poverty and family life have centered largely in Mexico. On occasion some of my Mexican friends have suggested delicately that I turn to a study of poverty in my own country. As a first step in this direction I am currently engaged in a study of Puerto Rican families. Over the past three years my staff and I have been assembling data on 100 representative families in four slums of Greater San Juan and some 50 families of their relatives in New York City.

Our methods combine the traditional techniques of sociology, anthropology and psychology. This includes a battery of 19 questionnaires, the administration of which requires 12 hours per informant. They cover the residence and employment history of each adult; family relations; income and expenditure; complete inventory of household and personal possessions; friendship patterns, particularly the *compadrazgo*, or godparent, relationship that serves as a kind of informal social security for the children of these families and establishes special obligations among the adults; recreational patterns; health and medical history; politics; religion; world view and "cosmopolitanism." Open-end interviews and psychological tests (such as the thematic apperception test, the Rorschach test and the sentence-completion test) are administered to a sampling of this population.

All this work serves to establish the context for close-range study of a selected few families. Because the family is a small social system, it lends itself to

**WATERFRONT SHACKS of a Puerto Rican slum provide a sharp contrast to the modern construction that characterizes the prosperous parts of San Juan's Santurce district (*rear*). The author has found that residents in clearly delineated slum neighborhoods such as this one often have a community sense similar to that characteristic of villagers in rural areas. Such *esprit de corps* is**

the holistic approach of anthropology. Whole-family studies bridge the gap between the conceptual extremes of the culture at one pole and of the individual at the other, making possible observation of both culture and personality as they are interrelated in real life. In a large metropolis such as San Juan or New York the family is the natural unit of study.

Ideally our objective is the naturalistic observation of the life of "our" families, with a minimum of intervention. Such intensive study, however, necessarily involves the establishment of deep personal ties. My assistants include two Mexicans whose families I had studied; their "Mexican's-eye view" of the Puerto Rican slum has helped to point up the similarities and differences between the Mexican and Puerto Rican subcultures. We have spent many hours attending family parties, wakes and baptisms, responding to emergency calls, taking people to the hospital, getting them out of jail, filling out applications for them, hunting apartments with them, helping them to get jobs or to get on relief. With each member of these families we conduct tape-recorded interviews, taking down their life stories and their answers to questions on a wide variety of topics. For the ordering of our material we undertake to reconstruct, by close interrogation, the history of a week or more of consecutive days in the lives of each family, and we observe and record complete days as they unfold. The first volume to issue from this study is to be published next month under the title of *La Vida, a Puerto Rican Family in the Culture of Poverty—San Juan and New York* (Random House).

uncommon among participants in the culture of poverty; although gregarious, they seldom manage to become well organized.

There are many poor people in the world. Indeed, the poverty of the two-thirds of the world's population who live in the underdeveloped countries has been rightly called "the problem of problems." But not all of them by any means live in the culture of poverty. For this way of life to come into being and flourish it seems clear that certain preconditions must be met.

The setting is a cash economy, with wage labor and production for profit and with a persistently high rate of unemployment and underemployment, at low wages, for unskilled labor. The society fails to provide social, political and economic organization, on either a voluntary basis or by government imposition, for the low-income population. There is a bilateral kinship system centered on the nuclear progenitive family, as distinguished from the unilateral extended kinship system of lineage and clan. The dominant class asserts a set of values that prizes thrift and the accumulation of wealth and property, stresses the possibility of upward mobility and explains low economic status as the result of individual personal inadequacy and inferiority.

Where these conditions prevail the way of life that develops among some of the poor is the culture of poverty. That is why I have described it as a subculture of the Western social order. It is both an adaptation and a reaction of the poor to their marginal position in a class-stratified, highly individuated, capitalistic society. It represents an effort to cope with feelings of hopelessness and despair that arise from the realization by the members of the marginal communities in these societies of the improbability of their achieving success in terms of the prevailing values and goals. Many of the traits of the culture of poverty can be viewed as local, spontaneous attempts to meet needs not served in the case of the poor by the institutions and agencies of the larger society because the poor are not eligible for such service, cannot afford it or are ignorant and suspicious.

Once the culture of poverty has come into existence it tends to perpetuate itself. By the time slum children are six or seven they have usually absorbed the basic attitudes and values of their subculture. Thereafter they are psychologically unready to take full advantage of changing conditions or improving opportunities that may develop in their lifetime.

My studies have identified some 70 traits that characterize the culture of poverty. The principal ones may be described in four dimensions of the system: the relationship between the subculture and the larger society; the nature of the slum community; the nature of the family, and the attitudes, values and character structure of the individual.

The disengagement, the nonintegration, of the poor with respect to the major institutions of society is a crucial element in the culture of poverty. It reflects the combined effect of a variety of factors including poverty, to begin with, but also segregation and discrimination, fear, suspicion and apathy and the development of alternative institutions and procedures in the slum community. The people do not belong to labor unions or political parties and make little use of banks, hospitals, department stores or museums. Such involvement as there is in the institutions of the larger society—in the jails, the army and the public welfare system—does little to suppress the traits of the culture of poverty. A relief system that barely keeps people alive perpetuates rather than eliminates poverty and the pervading sense of hopelessness.

People in a culture of poverty produce little wealth and receive little in return. Chronic unemployment and underemployment, low wages, lack of property, lack of savings, absence of food reserves in the home and chronic shortage of cash imprison the family and the individual in a vicious circle. Thus for lack of cash the slum householder makes frequent purchases of

SAN JUAN SLUM AREA in the Santurce district sprawls along the edge of the tidal inlet (*top*) that connects the city's harbor with San José Lake. Rickety buildings have been erected on stilts beyond the high-water line and narrow alleyways crisscross the district. Compared to this area, many of New York's worst slum areas, such as the ones that appear below, are nearly middle-class.

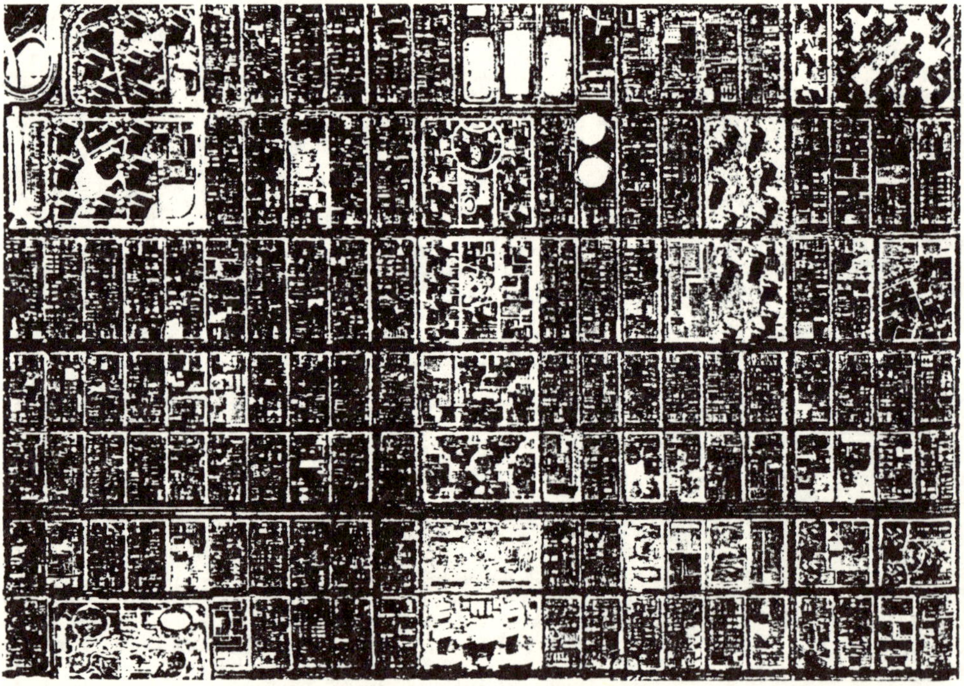

EL BARRIO, the original nuclear Latin-American slum area of Manhattan, occupies the greater part of this aerial photograph. Lying roughly between Central Park and the East River north of 99th Street and south of 125th Street in Manhattan, this is the area that received the pioneer Puerto Rican immigrants to New York in the early years of this century. Photograph was made in 1961.

small quantities of food at higher prices. The slum economy turns inward; it shows a high incidence of pawning of personal goods, borrowing at usurious rates of interest, informal credit arrangements among neighbors, use of secondhand clothing and furniture.

There is awareness of middle-class values. People talk about them and even claim some of them as their own. On the whole, however, they do not live by them. They will declare that marriage by law, by the church or by both is the ideal form of marriage, but few will marry. For men who have no steady jobs, no property and no prospect of wealth to pass on to their children, who live in the present without expectations of the future, who want to avoid the expense and legal difficulties involved in marriage and divorce, a free union or consensual marriage makes good sense. The women, for their part, will turn down offers of marriage from men who are likely to be immature, punishing and generally unreliable. They feel that a consensual union gives them some of the freedom and flexibility men have. By not giving the fathers of their children legal status as husbands, the women have a stronger claim on the children. They also maintain exclusive rights to their own property.

Along with disengagement from the larger society, there is a hostility to the basic institutions of what are regarded as the dominant classes. There is hatred of the police, mistrust of government and of those in high positions and a cynicism that extends to the church. The culture of poverty thus holds a certain potential for protest and for entrainment in political movements aimed against the existing order.

With its poor housing and overcrowding, the community of the culture of poverty is high in gregariousness, but it has a minimum of organization beyond the nuclear and extended family. Occasionally slum dwellers come together in temporary informal groupings; neighborhood gangs that cut across slum settlements represent a considerable advance beyond the zero point of the continuum I have in mind. It is the low level of organization that gives the culture of poverty its marginal and anomalous quality in our highly organized society. Most primitive peoples have achieved a higher degree of sociocultural organization than contemporary urban slum dwellers. This is not to say that there may not be a sense of community and *esprit de corps* in a slum neighborhood. In fact, where slums are isolated from their surroundings by enclosing walls or other physical barriers, where rents are low and residence is stable and where the population constitutes a distinct ethnic, racial or language group, the sense of community may approach that of a village. In Mexico City and San Juan such territoriality is engendered by the scarcity of low-cost housing outside of established slum areas. In South Africa it is actively enforced by the *apartheid* that confines rural migrants to prescribed locations.

The family in the culture of poverty does not cherish childhood as a specially prolonged and protected stage in the life cycle. Initiation into sex comes early. With the instability of consensual marriage the family tends to be mother-centered and tied more closely to the mother's extended family. The female head of the house is given to authoritarian rule. In spite of much verbal emphasis on family solidarity, sibling rivalry for the limited supply of goods and maternal affection is intense. There is little privacy.

The individual who grows up in this culture has a strong feeling of fatalism, helplessness, dependence and inferiority. These traits, so often remarked in the current literature as characteristic of the American Negro, I found equally strong in slum dwellers of Mexico City and San Juan, who are not segregated or discriminated against as a distinct ethnic or racial group. Other traits include a high incidence of weak ego structure, orality and confusion of sexual identification, all reflecting maternal deprivation; a strong present-time orientation with relatively little disposition to defer gratification and plan for the future, and a high tolerance for psychological pathology of all kinds. There is widespread belief in male superiority and among the men a strong preoccupation with *machismo*, their masculinity.

Provincial and local in outlook, with little sense of history, these people know only their own neighborhood and their own way of life. Usually they do not have the knowledge, the vision or the ideology to see the similarities between their troubles and those of their counterparts elsewhere in the world. They are not class-conscious, although they are sensitive indeed to symbols of status.

The distinction between poverty and the culture of poverty is basic to the model described here. There are numerous examples of poor people whose way of life I would not characterize as belonging to this subculture. Many primitive and preliterate peoples that have been studied by anthropologists suffer dire poverty attributable to low technology or thin resources or both. Yet even the simplest of these peoples have a high degree of social organization and a relatively integrated, satisfying and self-sufficient culture.

In India the destitute lower-caste peoples—such as the Chamars, the leatherworkers, and the Bhangis, the sweepers—remain integrated in the larger society and have their own panchayat institutions of self-government. Their panchayats and their extended unilateral kinship systems, or clans, cut across village lines, giving them a strong sense of identity and continuity. In my studies of these peoples I found no culture of poverty to go with their poverty.

The Jews of eastern Europe were a poor urban people, often confined to ghettos. Yet they did not have many traits of the culture of poverty. They had a tradition of literacy that placed great value on learning; they formed many voluntary associations and adhered with devotion to the central community organization around the rabbi, and they had a religion that taught them they were the chosen people.

I would cite also a fourth, somewhat speculative example of poverty dissociated from the culture of poverty. On the basis of limited direct observation in one country—Cuba—and from indirect evidence, I am inclined to believe the culture of poverty does not exist in socialist countries. In 1947 I undertook a study of a slum in Havana. Recently I had an opportunity to revisit the same slum and some of the same families. The physical aspect of the place had changed little, except for a beautiful new nursery school. The people were as poor as before, but I was impressed to find much less of the feelings of despair and apathy, so symptomatic of the culture of poverty in the urban slums of the U.S. The slum was now highly organized, with block committees, educational committees, party committees. The people had found a new sense of power and importance in a doctrine that glorified the lower class as the hope of humanity, and they were armed. I was told by one Cuban official that the Castro government had practically eliminated delinquency by giving arms to the delinquents!

Evidently the Castro regime—revising Marx and Engels—did not write off the so-called *lumpenproletariat* as an inherently reactionary and antirevolutionary

**PUERTO RICAN BOYS in a Manhattan upper East Side neighborhood use the fenced-off yard of a deserted school as an impromptu playground. The culture of poverty does not cherish childhood as a protected and especially prolonged part of the life cycle. Sexual maturity is early, the male is accepted as a superior and men are strongly preoccupied with *machismo*, or masculinity.**

force but rather found in them a revolutionary potential and utilized it. Frantz Fanon, in his book *The Wretched of the Earth,* makes a similar evaluation of their role in the Algerian revolution: "It is within this mass of humanity, this people of the shantytowns, at the core of the *lumpenproletariat,* that the rebellion will find its urban spearhead. For the *lumpenproletariat,* that horde of starving men, uprooted from their tribe and from their clan, constitutes one of the most spontaneous and most radically revolutionary forces of a colonized people."

It is true that I have found little revolutionary spirit or radical ideology among low-income Puerto Ricans. Most of the families I studied were politically conservative, about half of them favoring the Statehood Republican Party, which provides opposition on the right to the Popular Democratic Party that dominates the politics of the commonwealth. It seems to me, therefore, that disposition for protest among people living in the culture of poverty will vary considerably according to the national context and historical circumstances. In contrast to Algeria, the independence movement in Puerto Rico has found little popular support. In Mexico, where the cause of independence carried long ago, there is no longer any such movement to stir the dwellers in the new and old slums of the capital city.

Yet it would seem that any movement—be it religious, pacifist or revolutionary—that organizes and gives hope to the poor and effectively promotes a sense of solidarity with larger groups must effectively destroy the psychological and social core of the culture of poverty. In this connection, I suspect that the civil rights movement among American Negroes has of itself done more to improve their self-image and self-respect than such economic gains as it has won although, without doubt, the two kinds of progress are mutually reinforcing. In the culture of poverty of the American Negro the additional disadvantage of racial discrimination has generated a potential for revolutionary protest and organization that is absent in the slums of San Juan and Mexico City and, for that matter, among the poor whites in the South.

If it is true, as I suspect, that the culture of poverty flourishes and is endemic to the free-enterprise, pre-welfare-state stage of capitalism, then it is also endemic in colonial societies. The most likely candidates for the culture of poverty would be the people who come from the lower strata of a rapidly changing society and who are already partially alienated from it. Accordingly the subculture is likely to be found where imperial conquest has smashed the native social and economic structure and held the natives, perhaps for generations, in servile status, or where feudalism is yielding to capitalism in the later evolution of a colonial economy. Landless rural workers who migrate to the cities, as in Latin America, can be expected to fall into this way of life more readily than migrants from stable peasant villages with a well-organized traditional culture, as in India. It remains to be seen, however, whether the culture of poverty has not already begun to develop in the slums of Bombay and Calcutta. Compared with Latin America also, the strong corporate nature of many African tribal societies may tend to inhibit or delay the formation of a full-blown culture of poverty in the new towns and cities of that continent. In South Africa the institutionalization of repression and discrimination under *apartheid* may also have begun to promote an immunizing sense of identity and group consciousness among the African Negroes.

One must therefore keep the dynamic aspects of human institutions forward in observing and assessing the evidence for the presence, the waxing or the waning of this subculture. Measured on the dimension of relationship to the larger society, some slum dwellers may have a warmer identification with their national tradition even though they suffer deeper poverty than members of a similar community in another country. In Mexico City a high percentage of our respondents, including those with little or no formal schooling, knew of Cuauhtémoc,

**MOTHER AND DAUGHTER stand together by the door of a run-down apartment building on upper Park Avenue. Because common-law marriage offers the female participant in the culture of poverty more protection of her property rights and surer custody of her children than formal marriage does, the mother is usually the head of the household and family ties are to her kin and not the father's.**

Hidalgo, Father Morelos, Juárez, Díaz, Zapata, Carranza and Cárdenas. In San Juan the names of Rámon Power, José de Diego, Baldorioty de Castro, Rámon Betances, Nemesio Canales, Lloréns Torres rang no bell; a few could tell about the late Albizu Campos. For the lower-income Puerto Rican, however, history begins with Muñoz Rivera and ends with his son Muñoz Marín.

The national context can make a big difference in the play of the crucial traits of fatalism and hopelessness. Given the advanced technology, the high level of literacy, the all-pervasive reach of the media of mass communications and the relatively high aspirations of all sectors of the population, even the poorest and most marginal communities of the U.S. must aspire to a larger future than the slum dwellers of Ecuador and Peru, where the actual possibilities are more limited and where an authoritarian social order persists in city and country. Among the 50 million U.S. citizens now more or less officially certified as poor, I would guess that about 20 percent live in a culture of poverty. The largest numbers in this group are made up of Negroes, Puerto Ricans, Mexicans, American Indians and Southern poor whites. In these figures there is some reassurance for those concerned, because it is much more difficult to undo the culture of poverty than to cure poverty itself.

Middle-class people—this would certainly include most social scientists—tend to concentrate on the negative aspects of the culture of poverty. They attach a minus sign to such traits as present-time orientation and readiness to indulge impulses. I do not intend to idealize or romanticize the culture of poverty—"it is easier to praise poverty than to live in it." Yet the positive aspects of these traits must not be overlooked. Living in the present may develop a capacity for spontaneity, for the enjoyment of the sensual, which is often blunted in the middle-class, future-oriented man. Indeed, I am often struck by the analogies that can be drawn between the mores of the very rich—of the "jet set" and "café society"—and the culture of the very poor. Yet it is, on the whole, a comparatively superficial culture. There is in it much pathos, suffering and emptiness. It does not provide much support or satisfaction; its pervading mistrust magnifies individual helplessness and isolation. Indeed, poverty of culture is one of the crucial traits of the culture of poverty.

The concept of the culture of poverty provides a generalization that may help to unify and explain a number of phenomena hitherto viewed as peculiar to certain racial, national or regional groups. Problems we think of as being distinctively our own or distinctively Negro (or as typifying any other ethnic group) prove to be endemic in countries where there are no segregated ethnic minority groups. If it follows that the elimination of physical poverty may not by itself eliminate the culture of poverty, then an understanding of the subculture may contribute to the design of measures specific to that purpose.

What is the future of the culture of poverty? In considering this question one must distinguish between those countries in which it represents a relatively small segment of the population and those in which it constitutes a large one. In the U.S. the major solution proposed by social workers dealing with the "hard core" poor has been slowly to raise their level of living and incorporate them in the middle class. Wherever possible psychiatric treatment is prescribed.

In underdeveloped countries where great masses of people live in the culture of poverty, such a social-work solution does not seem feasible. The local psychiatrists have all they can do to care for their own growing middle class. In those countries the people with a culture of poverty may seek a more revolutionary solution. By creating basic structural changes in society, by redistributing wealth, by organizing the poor and giving them a sense of belonging, of power and of leadership, revolutions frequently succeed in abolishing some of the basic characteristics of the culture of poverty even when they do not succeed in curing poverty itself.

# [3]

## Poverty, Inequality, and Conflict

By S. M. Miller, Martin Rein, Pamela Roby, and Bertram M. Gross

Abstract: Groping concern with poverty has ushered in the much more controversial issue of inequalities within the affluent society. In America, relative deprivation is a more important aspect of "poverty" than poor physical conditions. Income alone is an inadequate indicator of level of living. This paper proposes six dimensions for the measurement of well-being: income, assets, basic services, social mobility and education, political position, and status and satisfaction. Questions of "who does and should get what" within each of these dimensions are issues arousing acrimonious debate. Social indicators are suggested which would create greater awareness of the extent of inequalities and make discussions of inequalities more useful. These indicators will not tell us what choices to make in inequality-reduction, but they can prevent us from complacently ignoring the fact that choices *are* being made.

*S. M. Miller, Ph.D., New York City, is Professor of Education and Sociology, New York University, and Program Advisor in Social Development, Ford Foundation. His publications include Social Class and Social Policy (forthcoming), Comparative Social Mobility (1960), and The Dynamics of the American Economy (1956).*

*Martin Rein, Ph.D., Bryn Mawr, Pennsylvania, is Associate Professor of Social Work and Social Research, Bryn Mawr College.*

*Pamela Roby, New York City, is Research Assistant to S. M. Miller, Instructor of Educational Sociology, New York University, and Research Assistant, Russell Sage Foundation.*

*Bertram M. Gross, see page 208.*

THE acceptable term "poverty" has become the way of discussing the more disturbing issue of inequality. "Poverty" has not been fully recognized as the shorthand for a much broader idea because the historic subsistence connotations of the term "poverty" still survive. The result is that we have furious debates which fail to clarify issues. For some, it will come as a shock to learn that their words are the prose of inequality; for others, their statements will surprise them when parsed into nineteenth-century sensibilities about pauperism.

The "discovery" of poverty in the United States did not take place because part of the population lived in worse circumstances than before. Some of those characterized as poor do live in as difficult conditions as the poor of previous generations, but, by and large, that is not the situation of "poverty" today. Some of our contemporary "poor" live on diets or in shelter inadequate for physical survival, but that is far from typical. Nor are most of those characterized as "in poverty," paupers or dependents whose only financial support comes from government.

Nonetheless, worsened conditions, threatened physical survival, and pauperism, singly or together, characterize the historic concern with poverty. In low-income societies, physical survival is often threatened; in nineteenth-century England, pauperism was the focus; in the desperate depression of the 1930's in the United States, a decline in living standards was the issue.

Today, these are not the main issues within the high-income industrial societies. The growing and groping concern with poverty in these societies is a consequence of revelations about inequality. The euphoria of economic growth following World War II overwhelmed doubts about the emphasis on materialism. Economic justice was not an issue, as there was confidence that all in society, especially those at the bottom, were benefiting from expansion. The bigger economic pie was being cut so that the bottommost groups received larger slices.

Gradually, a disturbing recognition upset affluent complacency. The problems of those at the bottom had not been eradicated. The proportion of national income going to the bottommost group has probably not increased in the United States or in most other economies. New forms of division and stratification may be emerging. A man's having a car or a washing machine does not assure that he is a full citizen of society, nor that his children have equal access to decent jobs or education, nor that he lives in decent housing.

Obviously, this kind of "poverty" is different. It is relative deprivation, a comparative position of losing out, that characterizes those who are termed "poor" in the affluent society. The historic term of "poverty," once applied to low-income families in industrializing societies, is found wanting when stretched to the highly industrialized society.

"Poverty," then, has ushered in the issue of inequalities in the affluent society. The ancient term, with its imagery of eliminating starvation and rags, cloaks the new agenda of reducing disparities and inequities. The discussants of poverty are divided on the important questions of which kinds of issues are important and how wide the gap between groups must be before it can be deemed significant.

*To be deeply and frontally concerned about relativities is to address oneself to the nature of the divisions and stratifications in society: How large should the divisions be among various groups in society? What are the bases of monetary and status rewards? In what ways can the mechanisms that disburse rewards be changed? In attempting to obtain these changes, how much controversy and agitation to get these changes is desirable or acceptable?*

But not all agree on this new agenda; some argue for the desirability of placing the income poverty line at a low level in order to discourage dependency or governmental activity which interferes with market forces. Nonetheless, even proponents of these latter approaches have some concern with relativities. They adjust the income poverty line to changes in the general standard of living, though at a slower rate than those who would more frankly embrace a relative approach.

The social welfare term "poverty" does not incur the disturbance aroused by the political term "inequality." But the ambiguity of our use of "poverty" is preventing the full-scale examination of the issues of inequality: Who gets what? Who does and should benefit from government subsidization? What shape do we wish the income and social profiles of this country to have?

These are difficult questions producing acrimonious debate. Obviously, adherence to the historic view of poverty will lead to a set of indicators which is inadequate for the depiction of the course of inequalities. Furthermore, it is much easier to show progress in social achievement when a fixed income line is employed as a poverty standard; if standards were based upon relativities, we could have the politically embarrassing situation of nonexistent progress. The lack of progress measured by these indicators of inequality would lead many policy officials to argue for a different concept of poverty. Policy critics, however, would advocate the use of these indicators and the augmentation of resources which go to the underclass. *Thus, the conceptualizations of problems can mold policy objectives and constraints.*

This conclusion argues for the importance of having multiple conceptualizations and producers of social indicators. In our view, not all users of indicators have the same needs: indicators can be used for spotting problems and unmet needs, detecting trends and their changes, or assessing policies. Much of the contemporary discussion of indicators is in terms of the policy operators, not the outsiders—the independent, external, critical groups. The needs of official agencies for social indicators of poverty may be different, for example, from those of civil rights groups. Our concern in this essay is to look at the poverty and inequality issues more from the perspectives of nongovernmental groups than from those of official agencies.[1]

In studying social indicators, two perspectives are possible: one moves from the problem to needed indicators; the other, the assessment of current policies, moves from programs to indicators. Because of space limitations, we are viewing poverty in terms of the problems rather than the programs. Both perspectives are needed.

## POVERTY—AN INCOME OR SOCIAL CONDITION?

Much of the current discussion of poverty is posed in terms of an income line: How many families and individuals are living below this line, adjusted for family size and other conditions? At what rate is this number being reduced? The availability of these figures and the historic view of poverty in

[1] We will not discuss the inequalities which affect other than low-income groups, for example, youth, women, and minority groups.

terms of pauperism lead to the emphasis on the income figures. But income is only *one* of the dimensions of poverty and inequality today.

In the last third of this century, we need new approaches to the quality of life in every country. We suggest that *a minimum approach by government in any society with significant inequalities must provide for rising minimum levels not only of incomes, assets, and basic services, but also of self-respect and opportunities for social mobility and participation in many forms of decision-making.*

The approach which we suggest broadens the economic perspective from a narrow concern with "income." The starting point is Titmuss' conceptualization of income as the "command over resources over time." [2] This moves us to a growing concern with assets as disguised income and as the source of future income (pensions) and with services as an increasingly important ingredient of a standard of life. But even this expanded perspective fails to measure all the concerns that we have today in dealing with poverty and inequality. The concern is also with the individual's political role, the opportunities for his children, and his self-respect. This broadened view of "the command over resources" requires us to range beyond the economic. Many of the hesitations about "the war on poverty" in the United States have occurred because it has been viewed through an exceedingly narrow income lens. Poverty is not only a condition of economic insufficiency; it is also social and political exclusion.[3]

The general position which we espouse in this paper is that income alone is an inadequate indicator of level of living. Movement along the varied dimensions of well-being is not always synchronized—advance or loss along one dimension does not necessarily mean that similar movement occurs on the other dimensions. For example, although the current income of two families may be the same, the level of living of one may be vastly below that of the other because of the families' different housing conditions.

We frequently refer in the following analysis to the poorest of the poor, for we suspect that their conditions are more difficult than that of the rest of the poor and that their interests, by and large, are neglected in current discussions of poverty programs.

We shall discuss, then, six dimensions of well-being—income, assets, basic services, education and social mobility, political position, and status and self-respect. The longest discussion concerns income because there is a complicated literature of immediate policy significance in this area. But we do not mean to minimize thereby the other neglected dimensions of well-being.

## INCOMES

Most discussions of poverty center about the income line or level which differentiates the poor from the nonpoor. How to define that line is obviously important, but two other aspects are also important. These are the stability and the source of income. Be-

[2] Richard M. Titmuss, *Income Distribution and Social Change* (London: G. Allen and Unwin, 1962) and *Essays on the Welfare State* (New Haven, Conn.: Yale University Press, 1958). See also Bertram Gross (ed.), *Action under Planning* (New York: McGraw-Hill, 1966), chap. vii. This approach has been expanded by Bertram Gross and S. M. Miller in an unpublished paper.

[3] See S. M. Miller and Frank Riessman, "The New Income," *Social Class and Social Policy* (New York: Basic Books, forthcoming). Also, S. M. Miller and Pamela Roby, "Class, Status, and Power Revisited," a paper presented to the American Sociological Association, San Francisco, August 1967.

cause the source of individuals' incomes affects their social honor, it will be discussed under the section on status.

*Level*

There are three basic approaches to defining an adequate level of income. The first defines poverty thresholds in relation to a cost-of-living budget estimate. This is the "poverty line" approach which marks current policy. The second defines the adequacy level in relation to mean or median family income for the United States. The third views poverty in terms of the share of total national income going to the bottom 10, 20, or 30 per cent of the population.

*Budget-oriented approaches*

Obviously, the line which separates the poor from the nonpoor or the poorer from the poor is not clear-cut. A fundamental issue in delineating the cutoff point between the poor and the others is whether poverty is to be considered as barest survival or as inadequacy in terms of prevailing standards. A second issue that veers into the technical is how many gradations and modifications should be made for varying conditions (family size and composition, regional cost differences, and the like) which affect the assessment of need.

Within the budget-oriented approaches, wide variations exist in the placement of the poverty line. Obviously, the aim is to provide an "adequate" level of income; immediately, the issue then becomes "adequate for what?" An income level that permits a family to "survive" is one thing; an income level that brings families closer to prevailing standards is quite another; and an income level that provides a stimulus for social mobility, a great concern of the war on poverty, is probably still another. Where the line is drawn will deeply affect the number and characteristics of those who are defined as "poor." And it will as deeply affect the assessment of failure or success in poverty-reduction efforts.

We believe that poverty lines based upon budget-oriented approaches will continue to be inadequate because of the deep political implications which each upward adjustment involves. Although a budget-based poverty line may be rapidly falling farther behind the rising standard of living enjoyed by the rest of the population, it will not be adjusted upward until that change appears politically feasible. For this reason, we believe that, in the United States, it is more appropriate to use the comparative approach to poverty (for instance, to define families as suffering from income poverty if they are below one-half of the nation's median income) or to view poverty in terms of the income share going to units in the lower end of the income distribution.[4] In this way, the criteria delineating the poor would automatically be shifted upward with the general society's rising level of living and would be more independent of political issues.

*Comparative income*

What is the scope and character of poverty when we move from budget-oriented approaches to a comparative approach? In this procedure, median or mean family income for the United States is taken as the standard; the poverty line is 50 per cent of the standard, and the line for the poorest of the poor could be 33 or 25 per cent of the standard.[5] This approach openly

[4] Of course, the comparative or income share approaches would be inadequate in countries in which a large proportion of the population is living at or beneath a minimum subsistence level.

[5] The median is the point which breaks a distribution in half: 50 per cent of the popu-

TABLE 1—PERCENTAGE OF U. S. FAMILIES CLASSIFIED AS POOR BY RELATIVE AND ABSOLUTE STANDARDS, 1947–1960

| YEAR | MEDIAN INCOME (1959 DOLLARS) | PERCENTAGE OF FAMILIES WITH INCOME | | |
|---|---|---|---|---|
| | | Less than one-half the median† | Less than $3,000 (1959 prices) | Less than $2,000 (1959 prices) |
| 1947 | 3,957 | 19.0 | 33.9 | 19.1 |
| 1948 | 3,868 | 19.4 | 34.7 | 19.8 |
| 1949 | 3,807 | 20.1 | 35.9 | 21.3 |
| 1950 | 4,036 | 20.0 | 33.0 | 19.8 |
| 1951 | 4,164 | 19.0 | 30.9 | 17.9 |
| 1952 | 4,277 | 19.0 | 29.3 | 17.8 |
| 1953 | 4,627 | 19.9 | 27.1 | 16.8 |
| 1954 | 4,530 | 20.7 | 28.7 | 18.1 |
| 1955 | 4,817 | 19.9 | 25.9 | 16.0 |
| 1956 | 5,129 | 19.5 | 23.6 | 14.2 |
| 1957 | 5,148 | 20.0 | 23.5 | 14.2 |
| 1958 | 5,143 | 19.9 | 23.8 | 14.1 |
| 1959 | 5,417 | 19.9 | 22.7 | 13.4 |
| 1960 | 5,547 | 20.2 | 22.1 | 13.2 |

† Estimated by interpolation.

Source: Victor R. Fuchs, "Toward a Theory of Poverty," in Task Force on Economic Growth and Opportunity, *The Concept of Poverty* (Washington, D. C.: Chamber of Commerce of the United States, 1965).

embraces the notion that a poverty condition is a relative phenomenon—the poor are those who have fallen behind the grades and standards of the society as a whole, as Galbraith stated.[6]

Using the standard of 50 per cent of median family income, the poverty line was $2,774 in 1960.[7] Twenty per cent of the nation's families in 1960 were living below this level, that is, they were "in poverty." This contrasts with Orshansky's figure, which showed 24 per cent of 1960 households in poverty, and converges with the Council of Economic Advisors' approach, which found that 20 per cent of the country's families had incomes below $3,000 (1962 prices) in 1960.[8]

The trend data are particularly striking: *the median income standard shows that the percentage of poor has not declined since 1947.* Between 1947 and 1960, as shown in Table 1, although families with incomes less than $3,000 (1959 prices) declined from 33.9 per cent to 20.2 per cent, families with incomes less than one-half the median increased from 19 per cent to 20.2 per cent.

*Poverty as income share*

A third way of looking at the income component of poverty is in terms of the share of total national income that goes to the bottom 10, 20, or 30 per cent. In this approach, poverty is simply regarded as inequality. It is the income fate of a specific group at the bottom of society that is the issue. Obviously, from this perspective, we cannot have trends in the numbers and percentages of poor. The question instead will be: How well is the bottom group doing? (Some critics of poverty efforts have not always understood that talking about poverty as income share prevents talking about trends in the extent of poverty.)

Data on the size distribution of income are available, but not in great detail. The discouraging report, as shown

lation is above the point, 50 per cent below. The mean is the conventional average; all incomes are totaled and then divided by the number of incomes. The mean 1962 family income was $8,151; the median family income was $5,747.

[6] John K. Galbraith, *The Affluent Society* (Boston: Houghton Mifflin, 1958).

[7] Victor R. Fuchs, "Toward a Theory of Poverty," in Task Force on Economic Growth and Opportunity, *The Concept of Poverty* (Washington, D.C.: Chamber of Commerce of the United States, 1965), p. 75.

[8] In 1965, 19 per cent of all households (families and unrelated individuals) were poor, according to the Social Security Administration's poverty-income standard. See *The Annual Report of the Council of Economic Advisors* (Washington, D.C.: U.S. Government Printing Office, 1967), p. 40.

TABLE 2—DISTRIBUTION OF TOTAL MONEY INCOME RECEIVED BY EACH FIFTH AND THE TOP 5 PER CENT OF FAMILIES AND UNRELATED INDIVIDUALS, 1947 TO 1962

| YEAR | TOTAL | CENSUS (TOTAL MONEY INCOME) | | | | | |
|---|---|---|---|---|---|---|---|
| | | Lowest fifth | Second fifth | Middle fifth | Fourth fifth | Highest fifth | Top 5 per cent |
| 1962 | 100.0 | 3.3 | 10.5 | 17.3 | 24.6 | 44.2 | 17.3 |
| 1961 | 100.0 | 3.3 | 10.0 | 17.0 | 24.5 | 45.2 | 18.2 |
| 1960 | 100.0 | 3.4 | 10.3 | 17.4 | 24.4 | 44.5 | 17.9 |
| 1959 | 100.0 | 3.4 | 10.4 | 17.6 | 24.3 | 44.3 | 17.6 |
| 1958 | 100.0 | 3.5 | 10.7 | 17.8 | 24.6 | 43.4 | 16.9 |
| 1957 | 100.0 | 3.5 | 10.8 | 18.0 | 24.7 | 43.1 | 16.8 |
| 1956 | 100.0 | 3.4 | 10.6 | 17.5 | 24.5 | 44.0 | 17.5 |
| 1955 | 100.0 | 3.3 | 10.6 | 17.4 | 24.6 | 44.2 | 18.0 |
| 1954 | 100.0 | 3.1 | 10.2 | 17.5 | 24.7 | 44.5 | 17.7 |
| 1953 | 100.0 | 3.2 | 10.8 | 17.5 | 24.6 | 43.9 | 17.6 |
| 1952 | 100.0 | 3.5 | 10.7 | 17.2 | 24.0 | 44.6 | 18.9 |
| 1951 | 100.0 | 3.5 | 11.2 | 17.5 | 24.3 | 43.6 | 17.6 |
| 1950 | 100.0 | 3.2 | 10.4 | 17.2 | 24.1 | 45.1 | 18.2 |
| 1949 | 100.0 | 3.3 | 10.5 | 17.1 | 24.1 | 45.0 | 17.9 |
| 1948 | 100.0 | 3.6 | 10.7 | 17.1 | 23.9 | 44.8 | 18.1 |
| 1947 | 100.0 | 3.6 | 10.6 | 16.7 | 23.5 | 45.6 | 18.8 |

Source: Herman P. Miller, *Income Distribution in the United States* (A 1960 Census Monograph; Washington, D. C.: U. S. Government Printing Office, for the United States Bureau of the Census, 1966), p. 21.

in Table 2, is that the percentage of total money income going to the bottom 20 per cent of families and unrelated individuals has hovered between 3 and 4 per cent since 1947. Total money income going to the lowest quintile declined from 3.6 per cent in 1947 and 1948 to 3.3 per cent in 1961 and 1962. Over the years from 1950 to 1960, the share fluctuated from 3.1 per cent to 3.5 per cent, but never attained the 3.6 per cent of 1947 and 1948.[9] Great progress has not been made in increasing the share of the bottom 20 per cent, despite the decline in the share of the top 5 per cent. Indeed, the earlier focusing on the decline of the top 5 per cent led to the facile conclusion of an income revolution in which all Americans were partaking of economic expansion.[10]

[9] The slight decline in the percentage of income held by the bottom quintile may be accounted for by the changing composition of households. A much greater percentage of aged poor live alone now than ten years ago. This change increases the percentage of low-income households. The shares received by the middle and fourth quintiles rose between 1947 and 1962 while the percentage of total money income held by the highest quintile declined—Herman P. Miller, *Income Distribution in the United States* (A 1960 Census Monograph; Washington, D.C.: U.S. Government Printing Office, for the United States Bureau of the Census, 1966), p. 21.

[10] A technical aside: Economic statisticians, despite their inventiveness, have failed to innovate new measures of income inequality. The Gini coefficient, the most popular tool for estimating inequality in income distribution, is not sensitive to the question of which points in the distribution suffer most from inequality. New measures of inequality are needed for the more complicated concerns of today. One example is top-bottom ratios which compare the share of the top income group—for instance, the upper tenth—with

Which families are most likely to be in the bottom levels of the nation's income distribution? The University of Michigan Survey Research Center's Reports on Consumer Finances show that, in 1964, 42 per cent of the South, as compared with 24 or 25 per cent of other regions, had aggregate family incomes falling within the nation's bottom three income deciles. Of the aged (persons aged 65 and over), 28 per cent fell within the lowest deciles and two-thirds within the lowest three deciles of the nation's income distribution. Twenty-four per cent of nonwhite as compared with 9 per cent of white families had incomes falling within the bottom decile, and 58 per cent of nonwhite families in contrast to 27 per cent of white families fell within the bottom 30 per cent of the nation's income distribution.[11]

The data on income shares should be much more detailed so that it would be possible to compare what is happening to various groups (aged, employed, minority groups, and the like) of the poor within cities of varying size, in regions, and in urban-rural areas. We especially need information on the income shares of Negroes by place of residence, age, and employment status, for it is clear that the problem of Negroes is not only achieving a better level of living but also reducing the gap between them and the rest of society. As American society turns more squarely to the issues of inequality, better and more detailed information on income shares will be needed.

*Perspectives on income lines*

Is there one best way of measuring the extent of and trends in poverty? Can these various approaches be reduced to one? We doubt it. In part, this is because different interest groups prefer various ways of thinking about poverty. Those concerned with economic growth in the context of price stability would move toward definitions of poverty along a compressed budget approach; civil rights groups would focus on the income share going to Negroes. Behind these different orientations and stresses is the uncertainty about what poverty means in the affluent society.

In our view, budget-oriented approaches are inadequate. The better ones, like Orshansky's, sneak in relative issues under the guise of absolute standards. Since our outlook is to avoid ambiguity, and since we believe that, over the long run, forthright discussion of issues best meets the needs of the underclass, we advocate clear-cut presentation of poverty data in terms of inequality.[12]

The inequality emphasis leads to concern with the bottom 20 per cent generally and the bottom 10 per cent particularly. It may be difficult to be concerned about the plight of persons within the bottom 20 per cent of the United States when their incomes would make them well off in many other societies. While we should not blind ourselves to the magnitude and severity of poverty in other nations, we should not thereby minimize the extent of the poverty problem in our midst.

the share of the bottom group. For a useful approach, see Harry T. Oshima, "The International Comparison of Size Distribution of Family Incomes, with Special Reference to Asia," *Review of Economics and Statistics*, 44 (1962). Bruce Russett has done some interesting work in probing different approaches to inequality measurement.

[11] Survey Research Center, University of Michigan, *1965 Survey of Consumer Finances* (Ann Arbor: University of Michigan Press, 1966), Tables 1-5, p. 19.

[12] Note that a political theory is involved in the choice of ambiguity or clarity in depicting the extent of a problem. Our orientation, it should be noted, goes against the stance of most "successful" politicians.

*Stability of income*

Variations in income can be viewed in two ways: variation within a year and variations between years. The assured and stable income within a year of white-collar persons is becoming the principal income-differentiating dimension between them and blue-collar workers, who frequently earn higher incomes. The confidence that income is assured for all of the year is an important amenity apart from the level of income. White-collar workers' obtaining of income in predictable weekly or monthly amounts helps them to make decisions governing their activity.

To what extent the poor's income is stable over the year is unclear. Louis Ferman's notion of an "irregular economy" of the poor would suggest that even within the low level of income of the poor there are sizable gyrations in income levels. While some of the poor, like those on welfare, have a somewhat assured but low income, many have an uncertain and unpredictable income, dependent on economic circumstances and their wits. Data on the within-a-year income stream of various groups of the poor would be useful.

The variation of income over the years is obviously more important than the within-year changes.[13] Are the poor, no matter what income approach is used, the same group from year to year except for a relative few who escape? Or is the composition of poverty constantly changing with some falling and some more climbing out? Or do many of those who escape one year move up only as far as the near-poor level and then fall back into poverty? Is there a pull-out–fallback syndrome with families moving back and forth across the poverty line, never much above or below?

Data gathered by the Survey Research Center (see Table 3) reveal considerable mobility between the bottom third and the other two-thirds. Of the spending unit heads aged fifty-five to sixty-four who had incomes in the bottom third in 1928, 51 per cent were in the bottom, 30 per cent in the middle, and 18 per cent in the top third in 1960. Obviously, there is much more income mobility than is implicit in most discussions of the poverty population. The question remains, however: "Who moved?" Did families at the bottom of the lowest third experience the same amount of mobility as those at the top of the third? Is there a low-income group who do not experience much improvement, while the rest of the poor in any year is made up of families who are temporarily in poverty?

There is great need for a longitudinal study of family income employing a cohort (the same group) that is studied over time with an oversampling of the poor and near-poor. An important item in the study would be delineation of the factors in shifts in income. For example, to what extent has a family moved across the poverty line because of a demographic shift (for instance, a child marrying at the age of eighteen and leaving the family) which may not reflect great changes in family well-being? Or is movement out of poverty due to additional wage-earners, to income gains of the main wage-earner, or to improved transfer payments? Cohort analysis is probably the most important instrument for measuring family income and the other dimensions of well-being discussed below.

The policy implications of income mobility are very important. Should

[13] Otis Dudley Duncan has redirected our attention to this problem. It is possible to conceptualize income poverty in terms of a lifetime rather than a year. In this perspective, the poor would be those families whose lifetime income is below a lifetime poverty-income line.

TABLE 3—POSITIONS OF SPENDING UNIT HEADS IN INCOME DISTRIBUTIONS OF EARLIER YEARS: 1928–1960 (EXPRESSED AS PERCENTAGES)

**1955 Position**

| | Group Aged 55 to 64 in Early 1961 | | | | Group Aged 45 to 54 in Early 1961 | | | | Group Aged 35 to 44 in Early 1961 | | | |
|---|---|---|---|---|---|---|---|---|---|---|---|---|
| 1960 Position | Bottom Third | Middle Third | Top Third | Total | Bottom Third | Middle Third | Top Third | Total | Bottom Third | Middle Third | Top Third | Total |
| Bottom Third | 69 | 27 | 6 | 100 | 69 | 24 | 9 | 100 | 63 | 27 | 12 | 100 |
| Middle Third | 30 | 51 | 18 | 100 | 27 | 51 | 21 | 100 | 27 | 48 | 24 | 100 |
| Top Third | 0 | 24 | 75 | 100 | 3 | 27 | 69 | 100 | 12 | 24 | 63 | 100 |
| Total | 100 | 100 | 100 | | 100 | 100 | 100 | | 100 | 100 | 100 | |

**1947 Position**

| | Group Aged 55 to 64 in Early 1961 | | | | Group Aged 45 to 54 in Early 1961 | | | | Group Aged 35 to 44 in Early 1961 | | | |
|---|---|---|---|---|---|---|---|---|---|---|---|---|
| 1960 Position | Bottom Third | Middle Third | Top Third | Total | Bottom Third | Middle Third | Top Third | Total | Bottom Third | Middle Third | Top Third | Total |
| Bottom Third | 57 | 30 | 15 | 100 | 60 | 21 | 20 | 100 | 45 | 30 | 24 | 100 |
| Middle Third | 33 | 42 | 24 | 100 | 30 | 48 | 24 | 100 | 27 | 39 | 33 | 100 |
| Top Third | 9 | 27 | 63 | 100 | 9 | 30 | 57 | 100 | 27 | 30 | 45 | 100 |
| Total | 100 | 100 | 100 | | 100 | 100 | 100 | | 100 | 100 | 100 | |

**1940 Position**

| | Group Aged 55 to 64 in Early 1961 | | | | Group Aged 45 to 54 in Early 1961 | | | |
|---|---|---|---|---|---|---|---|---|
| 1960 Position | Bottom Third | Middle Third | Top Third | Total | Bottom Third | Middle Third | Top Third | Total |
| Bottom Third | 54 | 30 | 18 | 100 | 51 | 27 | 21 | 100 |
| Middle Third | 33 | 39 | 24 | 100 | 30 | 42 | 27 | 100 |
| Top Third | 12 | 33 | 62 | 100 | 15 | 33 | 54 | 100 |
| Total | 100 | 100 | 100 | | 100 | 100 | 100 | |

**1928 Position**

| | Group Aged 55 to 64 in Early 1961 | | | |
|---|---|---|---|---|
| 1960 Position | Bottom Third | Middle Third | Top Third | Total |
| Bottom Third | 51 | 27 | 21 | 100 |
| Middle Third | 30 | 39 | 30 | 100 |
| Top Third | 18 | 33 | 51 | 100 |
| Total | 100 | 100 | 100 | |

Source: Calculated from 1961 *Survey of Consumer Finances, op. cit.*, p. 76, Table 5–3.

attention be concentrated on the potentially mobile to give them a secure hold on the nonpoor rungs of the income ladder or on those immobile at the bottom of the ladder? If the poor are not a stable group, are those present policies concerned with breaking "the culture of poverty" well-aimed?

Our own discussions below inadequately mirror the issue of shifting and permanent groups in poverty. The problem of minimum levels in various areas of well-being is enormously complicated by the existence of large numbers who are temporarily below the poverty level.

## ASSETS

Current income in an inadequate indicator of the economic position of a family. First, it does not provide an adequate basis for comparing poor and nonpoor groups, since some of the income of the nonpoor is received in ways (for example, capital gains) purposely designated to appear as nonincome in order to reduce taxation. Second, current income inadequately reflects the future command over resources. Savings and pension accumulations are important in the future picture. Further, they affect present satisfactions by providing confidence about the future. Third, past expenditures affect present well-being, as in the case of household furnishings. Fourth, income does not always adequately reflect the character of housing. Fifth, the aged with low incomes (and others temporarily with low income) may have nonpoverty levels of living because of the use of their accumulated assets.

Consequently, we have included a variety of items under the loose appellation of assets. (We do not discuss capital gains since they are included in discussions of income level.) For symmetry as much as for substance, we have included housing under assets, thereby treating rental units as though they, too, were owner-occupied. Other assets are consumers' durables, savings, and insurance.

### *Housing*

There are two ways of thinking about housing goals. One is in terms of relativities. How close to "average" levels should the existence of the poor be? For example, should the housing space available to the poor have a minimum level of half of the dwelling space per unit of the nonpoor? A second approach is in terms of presumably scientifically derivable standards of need and subsistence. Clearly, this is what is implied in the budget analyses of food needs. In housing, there is a minimal public health standard of density per room. This standard is regarded as scientific rather than cultural or political.[14] The Bureau of the Census in 1960 used certain visible defects to classify housing as "deteriorating" or "dilapidated."[15] It also gathered data on water supply, toilet and bathing facilities, sources of water, and sewage disposal.

By Census criteria, 16 per cent of all housing units were classified as either deteriorating or dilapidated in 1960. Units with incomes under $2,000 are nearly two and a half times as likely to be living in such substandard dwelling places as persons in the total population.[16]

Unfortunately, any assessment of changes over time must be very rough because of the change in the Census definition of substandard housing.[17] Oscar Ornati, comparing trends in the percentage of income groups living in any type of substandard housing, esti-

[14] In general, we support the use of relativities rather than absolute standards. Fixed standards have the political value of being "beyond politics," thus producing feasibility, but we doubt that, over a term of years, standards can move up rapidly to keep pace with an economy that is swiftly expanding. In general, our aim is to have forthright discussions of inequalities rather than improvements through subterfuge. We do not have confidence in subterfuge as an enduring political device.

[15] See *U.S. Census of Housing, 1960,* Vol. A: *Metropolitan Housing,* Final Report, HC (2)-1, p. lxii.

"Deteriorating housing needs more repair than would be provided in the course of regular maintenance. Such housing has one or more defects of an intermediate nature that must be corrected if the unit is to continue to provide safe and adequate shelter.

"Dilapidated housing does not provide safe and adequate shelter and in its present condition endangers the health, safety, or well-being of the occupants. Such housing has one or more critical defects; or has a combination of intermediate defects in sufficient number or extent to require considerable repair or rebuilding; or is of inadequate original construction. The defects are either so critical or so widespread that the structure should be extensively repaired, rebuilt, or torn down." It is doubtful if these concepts are adequate for the post-World War II period.

[16] Thirty-nine per cent of those with incomes under $2,000, as compared with 20 per cent of the $3,000–$3,999 income category, lived in substandard units.

[17] Deteriorated housing with plumbing was classified as substandard in 1960 but not in 1950.

mates that the lowest income group had the least proportionate improvement in housing between 1950 and 1960.[18] On the other hand, it should be noted that 74 per cent of homeowners with incomes under $3,000 lived in sound housing in 1959,[19] and 4 per cent had houses valued at $25,000 or more in 1964.[20]

When we move beyond standards of sheer adequacy to broader criteria of space, facilities, and housing style, the differences between the poor and nonpoor become more marked. On the financial side, 30 per cent of the houses owned by nonfarm families with under $3,000 incomes were valued at under $5,000, as compared with only 9 per cent of those owned by all nonfarm homeowning families in 1963.[21] Fifty-four per cent of the families in the lowest, as compared with only 14 per cent of families in the highest, income quintile did not own their own home.[22]

The poor put a higher percentage of their income into housing.[23] More importantly, do the poor get less for their housing dollar? The data are lacking here. The unavailability of insurance in poor housing areas indicates that low-income families attain little security for their housing dollar. The poor are also less able to maintain or enhance their housing investment.[24] The unavailability of loan funds for low-income persons as well as the low income itself make financing of expensive repairs or additions very difficult.

The subsidy system is believed to even out the differences between the poor and nonpoor. But a full view of subsidies which includes foregone taxes as well as direct transfers, reveals that the nonpoor benefit more from federal housing activity than the poor! If the loss in taxes resulting from the deductibility of interest payments on mortgages is compared with direct housing subsidies to the poor, the former is two and a half times the latter: the nonpoor have federal housing benefits of $2.9 billion, the poor, of $820 million.[25] (The indirect benefits to the nonpoor of Federal Housing Administration (FHA) government insurance, which lowers interest charges, are not included in these calculations.)

The poorest benefit very little from federal housing expenditures. They are usually ineligible for public housing because they have very low incomes, present housekeeping problems, or live in areas where public housing is very scarce.[26] In an analysis of four New York City housing projects, Ornati found that, on the average, the median educational attainment of household heads was higher in housing projects

[18] Oscar Ornati, *Poverty Amid Affluence* (New York: Twentieth Century Fund, 1966), p. 179.

[19] Sixty-one per cent of families and individuals with under $3,000 incomes living in rented units had "sound" housing in 1959, *U.S. Census of Housing, op. cit.,* pp. 1–6, Table A-4.

[20] University of Michigan, Survey Research Center, *1964 Survey of Consumer Finances* (Ann Arbor: University of Michigan Press, 1965), p. 88.

[21] University of Michigan, Survey Research Center, *1963 Survey of Consumer Finances* (Ann Arbor: University of Michigan Press, 1964), p. 88.

[22] University of Michigan, Survey Research Center, *1965 Survey of Consumer Finances* (Ann Arbor: University of Michigan Press, 1966), p. 117.

[23] *1964 Survey of Consumer Finances, op. cit.,* p. 31. In 1964, nonfarm rent-paying families with less than $3,000 incomes paid a median monthly rent of $45 as compared with $65 paid by those with $3,000–$4,900 incomes.

[24] *Ibid.,* p. 35. Only 18 per cent of nonfarm families with under $3,000 incomes, as compared with 34 per cent of the total nonfarm population, had housing addition and repair expenditures of over $49 in 1964.

[25] Alvin L. Schorr, "National Community and Housing Policy," *Social Service Review,* (1965), p. 434.

[26] Alvin L. Schorr, "Housing" (Manuscript, August 1965), p. 6. Almost 60 per cent of substandard housing is in rural areas.

than in adjoining tracts. Nearly half of the families occupying public housing in 1963 were not poor.[27] The rent subsidy program provided for in 1965 legislation, as Schorr has pointed out, is also directed primarily toward those at the high end of the low-income scale.

*Consumers' durables*

Consumers' durables are today an important component of the level of living. Current income inadequately indicates the command over resources of this kind. We believe that enormous variations exist in the possession of durables among low-income families, but information is very spotty. Interpretations of the meaning of possessions have added to the confusion.[28]

One of the problems in ascertaining whether working-class families were becoming "middle class" was the assumption that to own certain things indicated a zeal for the middle-class value system. Aside from the imputation of a peculiar status concern in purchases, this reasoning suffered from the inadequate realization that better-off families were moving much beyond working-class families in consumers' purchases—when workers' families were buying toasters, middle-class families were moving on to bun-warmers and the like.

Similarly, one is easily surprised at the variety and cost of household appliances available to the poor. For example, in New York City, 95 per cent of low-income families have television sets. By contrast, the nonpoor have had significant gains. They use planes to visit distant relatives, while video-tape machines automatically record the television programs missed when away from home.

Comparisons should take into consideration the lower quality of furnishings of the poor. For example, many of the washing machines of low-income families are old, hand-operated washers in need of major repairs, as is obvious on the porches of homes in the hollows of Appalachia. Also, the poor pay more, so that expenditure is an inadequate indicator of value.

What standard of consumers' durables should be used for the poverty line? One is in terms of minimal needs which home economists and other specialists could define: What is the supply of durables that every family should have? In essence, many durables are no longer in the luxury class. For example, a refrigerator might be considered as part of a basic durables minimum. In some areas of the country, a car might be. Home furnishings of beds, chairs, tables, and some pictures might be another. Constructing a minimum durables standard would require attention to the average durable levels of nonpoor families and some estimate of what is a reasonable gap in terms of service and esthetics. Presumably, the policy that flows from this approach is to insure that each family has the ingredients of the minimum durables standards. Welfare departments have constructed such budgets, though at very low levels. Families have no choice in what kind of items they would like to have.

A different approach would maximize choice among the low-income. The dollar value of the durables of the nonpoor would be the basis of a standard of durables for the poor. The latter would have funds available to them up to perhaps one-half of the value of the nonpoor's durables and could spend the available amounts on whatever durables they pleased.

*These two approaches illustrate that the nature of indicators—in this case*

[27] David Caplovitz, *The Poor Pay More* (New York: Free Press, 1963).

[28] S. M. Miller and Frank Riessman, "Are Workers Middle Class?", *Dissent* (1962).

*physical or monetary quantities—may affect the character of policy.*

*Savings*

Liquid assets are not only an important protector against emergencies; they also can break the fall into poverty. For want of savings, any emergency drains a low-income family. Debt ensues; the family may have to move and change employment. Savings not only provide some psychological security; they are an important instrument in maintaining or improving economic conditions.

Savings are obviously concentrated: 25 per cent of spending units in the highest income quintile (top fifth), as compared with less than 9 per cent in the bottom three quintiles, had liquid assets totaling over $5,000 in 1960.[29] The form of asset-holding is important, for it affects the possibility of assets increasing in value or yielding income: 62 per cent of families with incomes of $15,000 and over had stockholdings valued at $1,000 or more; 3 per cent of families with under 3,000 income held stock above this level. (Most of these families were over 65.)[30]

From the point of view of inequality, it is important to pay attention to savings and other forms of assets. If income alone is considered, then the differences between the poor and nonpoor appear narrower than they are. For example, the asset level of the nonpoor aged not only puts them in a higher income bracket than the aged poor, but provides a stream of income over the future. (Many assets are forms of deferred income.)

What should be the goal in the area of liquid assets? The minimum level of liquid assets should be twice the weekly income. Achievement of this goal is difficult, since the poor might well utilize savings for current needs, so that a long-run asset-building program would become a current income program.

*Insurance*

The average American who lives to the age of 65 can expect to live for another fifteen years. A tenth or more of the current income of many individuals is devoted to providing security for their later years. Thus, the command over future resources is a major concern of Americans today. It affects not only the calculation of current income but the satisfactions and security derived from earnings. Because of space limitations, we address ourselves only to the issue of insuring against income losses because of age, ignoring unemployment and other insurances.

The present methods of protecting against old age serve to worsen inequalities: the concentration of income among the aged is greater than it is among younger age groups or for the nation as a whole. In 1960 the upper 20 per cent of families headed by a person over 64 received 52 per cent of that group's aggregate income, as compared with 42 per cent received by the upper fifth of the nation as a whole and 37 per cent of the age group 25 to 34.[31] Less than 0.5 per cent of families with incomes under $3,000 in 1964, as compared with 2 per cent of all families, had savings in the form of retirement funds or old-age pensions.[32]

[29] *1960 Survey of Consumer Finances, op. cit.*, p. 79.

[30] *1964 Survey of Consumer Finances, op. cit.*, p. 96.

[31] Herman Miller, *op. cit.*, p. 75.

[32] *1964 Survey of Consumer Finances, op. cit.*, p. 114. At each income level, persons who contribute to private pension funds save more in a given year than those who do not contribute, and tend to devote the same fraction of their income to life insurance—Margaret S. Gordon, *The Economics of Welfare Policies* (New York: Columbia University Press, 1963), p. 50.

As Margaret Gordon has pointed out, although Congress in recent years has tended to adjust upward Old Age Survivors, Disability and Health Insurance benefits proportionately with increases in the consumer price index, the question may be raised whether a special cost-of-living index for the aged should be constructed. This procedure might make a marked difference because of pronounced increases in the cost of certain items, such as medical care, which figure prominently in the budgets of elderly people.[33]

The system of transfer through public assistance only partially reduces the inequalities of private savings and returns and the distribution of social security and private pension benefits.[34] With the extension of life and the concern about the future, deferred income in the form of pensions should be an important consideration in today's assessment of economic well-being.

In regarding pension accumulations as an important aspect of one's standard of living before 65, a difficult question emerges. The public welfare system will provide aid to the aged with low incomes; in 1965, 2.1 million aged persons (over 64) received public assistance in the form of Old Age Assistance.[35] Can we consider different levels of pension accumulations today as important when welfare will be available for those who are poor in their old age? One response to this is that welfare is stigmatizing. Another is that welfare payments are low, so that while an income "floor" is available, it does not provide much security and confidence about the future. Depending on public authorities to provide a small amount of money to keep one going is quite different from having a guaranteed future. In reality, even this low welfare floor is only a grating: 22 per cent of the aged still fall beneath the poverty line.[36]

## BASIC SERVICES

Income and assets are important components of the command over resources, but they do not include the increasingly important area of services. These services include education and training, health, neighborhood amenities, protection, social services, and transportation. In the high-income society, services compose a high and increasing proportion of expenditures and furnish important segments of total satisfaction and well-being.

The connection between family income and basic services is close but incomplete. A fairly well-to-do rural family can have inadequate immediate health care because no health center is nearby, while an urban low-income family may have access to an excellent medical teaching center. Or, two families with the same low level of income can be in very different environments—one in an overcrowded area with few recreational facilities, poor sanitation and garbage control, inadequate police protection, and little transportation; the other, in a high-density area which has outstanding services. This example illustrates the contention that in Sweden the poor are less worse off than in the United States because their low incomes are *not* associated with poor basic services.

[33] Margaret S. Gordon, *op. cit.*, p. 55.

[34] No one who lives out the fifteen years of past-65 expectancy has paid into social security as much as he receives from it. The payment from social security is based more on the symbolism of contribution than on actual contribution. Musgrave found that, in 1954, effective social insurance tax rates were regressive over the income distribution as a whole and fairly uniform for tax brackets under $5,000—Gordon, *op. cit.*, p. 25.

[35] *Social Security Bulletin* (February 1967), pp. 1, 44.

[36] Mollie Orshansky, "More about the Poor in 1964," *Social Security Bulletin*, (May 1966), p. 5.

Below, we discuss five issues in conceptualizing and measuring basic services. First, basic services are usually associated with the public sector, but this is not inevitable. The growth of fringe benefits in private employment means that many basic services are provided through employment. In the United States, many hospital insurance plans and health services are provided by private employers; over-all, fringe benefits comprise about 20 per cent of the wage bill, a smaller share than in many other countries. While the history of the growth of basic services for the poor has, to a large extent, meant the enlargement of the public sector, this may not be intrinsic to the development of the services. Indeed, in England, conservative groups like the Institute of Economic Affairs are strongly insisting that more and better basic services can be provided through increased reliance on the market.[37] The sharp distinction between public and private sectors may be increasingly unuseful.

Second, are basic services to be considered as amenities or investments? As amenities, services directly increase the consumption of individuals. They are not means to the attainment of other resources; they are themselves important components of the level of living. As investments, however, they are ways of improving the capacity of individuals to gain access to resources through the private market: for example, better health services and better transportation to jobs increase the individual's or the family's capacity to earn.

The trend of liberal thought is to transmute goals into means. What is desirable as a goal is not defended on that basis but on the contention that it is instrumental to the achievement of other goals. Rationality—the effectiveness of a program to achieve another program—supplants desirability—a program is desired of itself. We strongly doubt that many of the things we characterize as investments in human resources, for example, health programs, are really effective methods to increase earning capacity.[38] Consequently, we prefer to look at basic services as amenities rather than as investments in human resources development.

A third problem discussed earlier in connection with income is the question of what the goals are in the area of basic services. Is the objective a minimum or adequate level? Or is the objective a question of relative distribution between those at the bottom and other groups in society? In the second case, it is a question of distribution of resources; in the first, it is a question of standards. Adequacy is the major criterion in an essential thing like health services, but as general conditions improve in a society, questions of relative distribution assume greater importance.

Fourth, a particularly sensitive problem is the connection between services and well-being. Do services actually contribute to improved circumstances of life or is their usefulness overstated? For example, some evidence suggests that personal health services (as contrasted with public health measures) do not have a high impact upon physical well-being. Similar questions have been raised about the effectiveness of case-work services and psychotherapy.

Since we measure most services by their costs and quantities, we do not

[37] On the other hand, the recommendations of the Institute of Economic Affairs and similar groups largely ignore the issue of reductions in inequalities.

[38] Martin Rein and S. M. Miller, "Poverty, Policy, and Choice," in Leonard Goodman (ed.), *Economic Progress and Social Welfare* (New York: Columbia University Press, 1996). A version of this article appears in *Trans-Action* (October 1967).

have an estimate of their yield, especcially to people of different income levels, as the services may yield more to one group than to another. This differential yield could be a product of differences in quality. What purports to be the same basic service, for example, school education, can be widely varying in quality.

Fifth is the issue of the availability versus the utilization of services. To some analysts, the issue is services available to a particular population. If the group does not use it, for whatever reason, that is their own prerogative; we cannot then condemn the service organization for the resultant inequitable distribution of its resources to the nonpoor. The contrasting notion is that the issue is actual delivery of the services. Availability of service is not sufficient: direct efforts are needed to cope with the obstacles which result in low utilization by the poor. The problem of utilization is especially acute with the isolated groups and the poorest of the poor.

We deal below with these basic services: health, neighborhood amenities, transportation, and legal and social services. The field of education will be discussed in the following section with our analysis of social mobility.

### *Health*

The poor of all ages consult doctors, dentists, and medical specialists less frequently than do the nonpoor.[39] The rate of visits to physicians' offices, as compared with telephone or hospital clinic visits, also declines with income. Short-stay hospital utilization, in terms of rates of discharges, age for age, is somewhat less for low-income than high-income persons.[40] Utilization of immunization and pediatric services has also been found to be inversely related to income.[41]

Do the poor use health services less because they are healthier? The answer is probably no. Charlotte Muller succinctly summarizes the findings: "Identifying the low-income group is tantamount to identifying a high probability of medical need as shown by various indexes of prevalence and severity of disabling illness." [42]

While low-income persons (under $2,000 family income) made less than a third as many dental visits per year as high-income persons (family incomes over $7,000), nearly four times as many low-income as high-income persons required extractions when they made dental visits.[43] Although persons with low family incomes had lower rates of hospitalization, they required more days of care when they were hospitalized.[44] Restricted activity days as well as bed-disability days are over twice as frequent in the lowest as in the highest income group.[45] The lowest income

39 4.6 physician consultations were made per year by persons with family income under $2,000 as compared with 5.7 by those with family income over $7,000; youth under fifteen in families with under $2,000 made 3.0 visits as compared with 5.7 made per year by youth in families with income over $7,000. *Over three times as many dental visits* were made per year by persons with incomes over $7,000 as by those with family income under $2,000—U.S., Department of Health, Education, and Welfare, "Health Status and Family Income: United States," *Vital and Health Statistics: Data from the National Health Survey,* Series 10, No. 9 (May 1964); and Charlotte Muller, "Income and the Receipt of Medical Care," *American Journal of Public Health,* 55 (April 1965), p. 514.

40 U.S., Department of Health, Education, and Welfare, *op. cit.*

41 Oscar Ornati, *op. cit.*, p. 75.

42 Muller, *op. cit.*, p. 517.

43 Muller, *ibid.*, p. 514.

44 U.S., Department of Health, Education, and Welfare, *op. cit.*, p. 15.

45 These contrasts are found even after the higher proportion of aged among the lowest income group are allowed for—U.S., National Health Survey, *Health Statistics,* Series B-7, B-8, B-10, Washington, D.C., 1960.

class also has the highest rates of heart diseases, diabetes mellitus, arthritis, and diseases of female genital organs.[46]

The pattern of mortality rates is similar to that of illnesses. In major United States cities, higher infant mortality rates generally prevail in nonwhite areas. Nationally, the gap between death rates for white and nonwhite infants is increasing.[47] Fetal loss varies with instability of income, measured by husband's unemployment history.[48]

The relationship between infrequent health care, poor health, and low income is more intricate than an analysis based solely upon these data would indicate.[49] Income is only one aspect of poverty. The complexity of the interrelationships among the dimensions of poverty and health is demonstrated by Hauser and Kitagawa's recent analysis of mortality in the United States. Both education and income vary inversely with mortality; but, although education differentials in mortality are larger than income differentials for women, the opposite is true for men.[50]

Education is more highly correlated with the frequency of visits to physicians than is income.[51] Persons who lack health education are frequently unable to identify and care for minor symptoms in time to prevent major medical problems. Lack of experience with professionals also causes the poor to hesitate to seek their help before an ailment is severe. Others who have experienced difficulty in communicating their needs or have felt stigmatized and out-of-place within professional surroundings will delay their return as long as possible. In some areas of the country, great strides appear to have been made in health services for the poor, but most regions need enormous improvements.[52]

[46] Ornati, *op. cit.*, p. 75.

[47] In 1964, the nonwhite infant death rate was 41.1 per 100,000, a level not recorded for white infants since 1941—*Trans-Action*, Vol. 4, No. 5 (April 1967), p. 4. The maternal mortality rate among Mississippi Negroes is 15.3 per 10,000 live births, more than six times the national average for whites of 2.5—Elinor Langer, "Who Makes Our Health Policy?", *Physicians' Forum* (June 1967).

[48] Ronald Freedman, Lolagene C. Coombs, and Judith Friedman, "Social Correlates of Fetal Mortality," *The Milbank Memorial Fund Quarterly*, Vol. 44 (1966), p. 337. The data are from intensive interviews obtained by the Detroit Area Study of the University of Michigan.

[49] Charles Kadushin takes exception with the findings summarized above. He concludes: "The fact is that the lower classes are not more likely than the middle class to have a disease or condition but they do react more violently to it and are more concerned about it. Nonetheless, neither sociologists nor public health researchers have for the most part taken proper note of the split between getting sick and reacting to it," "Social Class and the Experience of Ill Health," *Sociological Inquiry*, 34 (Winter 1964) and in "Health and Social Class," *New Society*, December 24, 1964, p. 10. Aaron Antonovsky challenges Kadushin's analysis in a soon-to-be-published paper.

[50] Evelyn M. Kitagawa and Philip M. Hauser, "Education and Income Differentials in Mortality: United States, 1960," University of Chicago Population Center (Manuscript, 1967). The mortality index for men, age 25 to 64, with less than five years of schooling was 49 per cent higher than for men with some college; it was 86 per cent higher for men with less than $2,000 family income than for men with over $10,000 income. For women the rate was 98 per cent higher for those with less than five years of education than for college alumnae, and 41 per cent higher for those with less than $2,000 family income than for those with over $10,000. Because the Census definition of income, which was used in the analysis, does not take into account savings and oher forms of capital or the income decline which generally occurs prior to death, the authors judge education to be a better indicator of Social-Economic State (SES) than income for the purposes of their study.

[51] Ornati, *op. cit.*, p. 74.

[52] Gouverneur Ambulatory Care Unit of Beth Israel Hospital in New York's Lower East Side and other agencies in the largest

What criteria are to be used to judge the quality of services?[53] Patient-satisfaction? Recovery rates? Professional evaluations? Each has its pitfalls. The difficulties involved in developing these indicators are amplified by questions of professional authority. Nonetheless, a few assessments have been made of professional care. A study of expectant mothers in metropolitan Boston showed that the percentage judged to have received satisfactory medical care rose steadily with income.[54]

But poor treatment is not confined to the poor, nor excellent care to the well-to-do. Sliding scales mean that higher dollar figures for medical expenditures do not necessarily reflect better care. Good health care is frequently distributed on the basis of neither medical nor financial need, but on the basis of the medical interest of the patient's case or the patient's ability to manipulate the system.

Obviously, income affects the ability of a family to obtain medical services for which it must pay, and to purchase hospital and surgical insurance which will cover a portion of potential medical expenses.[55] Muller reports, however, that for every dollar spent by consumers or financed by their premiums and the payments of employers, or by insurance carriers on their behalf, or by philanthropies, another 25 cents is spent out of the public treasury.[56] Much of this public spending is channeled to the poor, but, as Alvin Schorr has pointed out, the neediest do not necessarily receive their share of the benefits of public programs.

What are the goals in health? The goals can be specified in terms of services—the distribution and utilization of services—and in terms of mortality and

United States cities now employ professionals as well as nonprofessionals who speak many dialects of Chinese as well as Spanish.

[53] A formal test of the major criteria is developed in Bertram Gross, "What Are Your Organization's Objectives?", *Human Relations* (August 1965).

[54] Muller, *op. cit.*, p. 517. See also J. Ehrlich, M. A. Morehead, and R. E. Trussell, *The Quantity, Quality, and Costs of Medical and Hospital Care Secured by a Sample of Teamster Families in the New York Area* (New York: School of Public Health and Administrative Medicine, Columbia University, 1962) and M. A. Morehead, *et al.*, *A Study of the Quality of Hospital Care Secured by a Sample of Teamster Family Members in New York City* (New York: School of Public Health and Administrative Medicine, Columbia University, 1964). These studies document how frequently the care received by members of a union through traditional sources proved inadequate. The relationships between quality of care and hospital and physician characteristics are analyzed. The proportion of consumption and income going to medical care is relatively high in the lowest income group (9.3 per cent), declining to 6.3 per cent at $4,000, staying close to this proportion as income continues to rise. High proportionate expenditure in low-income groups is only partly due to age (67 was the average age of heads of families with under $1,000 incomes). The average per capita family medical expenditure is $100 for families with below $3,000 income and $248 for families with income over $15,000—Muller, *op. cit.*, p. 519. Between 1953 and 1958 the mean gross family expenditure for personal health services increased considerably more among low-income rather than high-income families. Families with under $2,000 income experienced a 27 per cent increase; those with $2,000-$3,499, a 49 per cent increase; and those with $7,500 and over, a 16 per cent increase—Olin Anderson, Patricia Collette, and J. J. Feldman, *Changes in Family Medical Care Expenditures and Voluntary Health Service: A Five Year Resurvey* (London: Oxford University Press, 1963), p. 17.

[55] While many doctors donate outstanding services to low-income patients or use sliding scales, the share of industrial and philanthropic services in private spending is small—4½ per cent out of $23.8 billion private expenditures for medical service (Muller, *op. cit.*, p. 512).

[56] Alvin Schorr, *Children*, 11, 4: 129, (July–August, 1964). This point is made by Brian Abel-Smith in his seminal essay, "Whose Welfare State?," in Norman MacKenzie (ed.), *Conviction* (London: MacGibbon & Kee, 1959).

morbidity. Are health and longevity areas in which our society no longer finds class differences acceptable? We have the odd feeling that American society implicitly argues for equality of outcome in health and longevity—and for inequality in the distribution of services!

To reduce the disparities among the rich and poor may require more than rectifying the distribution of services. In mental retardation, where there are pronounced differences in incidence, the mother's conditions of life during the prenatal period are undoubtedly more important than medical services. Health is not only a reflection of health services.

The adequacy of health services is a general problem in our society. Despite enormous expenditures, the United States has fallen behind many other nations in crucial indicators of health. The plight of the poor is directing attention to the general medical situation, with the possibility of improved health services for all.

*Neighborhood amenities*

Neighborhood amenities refer to such important influences on the character of a habitat as sanitation control; police and fire protection; recreational facilities; libraries, parks, and playgrounds; and the condition of streets and roads. What we are attempting to convey by neighborhood amenities are conditions which are usually collectively provided for a neighborhood through public expenditures of one kind or another.

A common observation in many large cities is to note the differences in the sanitation pick-up for low-income and better-off neighborhoods. In low-income neighborhoods, especially those which are not politically important or are opposed to the party in power, sanitation pickup is sporadic, infrequent, and very inadequate. The areas that complain the most and are strongly organized are most likely to get satisfactory garbage control. As a result, the poorest are likely to have inadequate sanitation and garbage control.

A common complaint in many low-income areas is inadequate police protection. This complaint is coupled with grievances about police brutality. Arguments about excessive police force do not mean that police *aid* is not desired.[57]

The Senate Ribicoff Hearing's data show that the citizens of Harlem and Watts are concerned about the inadequate availability of police as well as the excessive use of force by police. Data across the country on the degree of police availability and activity in low-income areas are hard to obtain. Due to the high incidence of crime in these areas, there is a general impression that there is inadequate police protection in these areas. Of course, the underlying issue is the extent to which having more police would drastically reduce this rate. The kinds and quality of police services are the important issues.[58] The objectives of police services are still being debated, and important new programs have been recommended.

Similarly, the data on the availability of fire protection in low-income areas are very spotty. We know that in-

[57] *New York Times*, September 4, 1967, Section 1, p. 1. Data from a survey conducted by the J. F. Kraft public opinion organization in Harlem and released by Senator Ribicoff suggest that residents are more concerned about police protection than police brutality. The persons interviewed wanted more instead of fewer police in neighborhoods.

[58] In a random sample of 10,000 householders during the summer of 1965, the National Opinion Research Center found that almost 14 per cent of the Negroes interviewed, as compared with only 3 per cent of the whites, responded that police respectfulness "toward people like yourself was not so good"—Philip H. Ennis, "Crime Victims and the Police," *Trans-Action*, 4, 7 (June 1967), p. 42.

surance companies are reluctant to insure in these areas. It would be useful to try to develop some index of police and fire protection which would mirror changes over time in the degree of availability of such facilities.

An adequate measure of recreational facilities is difficult to construct. This is partly because transportation to distant recreational facilities is differentially distributed. Patricia Sexton found:

> There are more parks and recreation areas in the upper-income areas of Detroit than in the lower-income areas. The smallest amount of park space per 10,000 people is found in the oldest part of the city . . . where the lowest-income groups live. In one large section of this area (130,000 population), there are only 2.6 acres of recreation area per 10,000 people—as compared with 30 acres in the highest-income area.

Children in these areas also tend to be much less mobile than children in upper-income areas. Poorer children (because their parents usually do not have cars or the money for travel or summer camps or even for local bus transportation) are virtually imprisoned in the crowded areas where they live. When recreation facilities in these areas are not adequate, it is very difficult for lower-income children to go elsewhere to find them.[59] Limited evidence on use of national parks seems to suggest that the national parks are more likely to be used by middle-income rather than lowest-income people. On the other hand, some ethnic groups which have a history of outdoor use, like the Puerto Ricans, are probably more likely than other groups to use park facilities.

Museums and libraries seem to be disproportionately used by the nonpoor, although trend data are exceedingly sparse. These facilities, which are expensive, tend to be concentrated in their uses among a limited segment of a population. This, it could be argued, is the result of low-income ideas about museums rather than of questions of effective delivery. However, efforts to try to decentralize such facilities and make them interesting and attractive to the poor might be effective, at least some believe. Thomas Hoving, Metropolitan Museum director, argues otherwise—art museums lose what they have to offer in the way of relief from the routine world when they are set up in store fronts. Therefore, his efforts are oriented toward bringing the poor to the central museum.

It would be useful to develop cultural indices which would reveal the use of facilities such as museums and libraries. These indices could indicate the degree of success of concerted policies to deepen the use of these facilities by poor and low-educated groups. The use of museums and libraries by socialist-oriented workers in Poland and other European nations suggests that some gains could be made.[60]

### *Public transportation*

Public transportation is of more importance to the poor than the nonpoor. Today, job opportunities are multiplying in the suburbs, out of reach of the poor in the center-city. Low-income persons cannot afford costly long-distance commuting by car and generally lack other transportation alternatives.[61]

[59] Patricia Sexton, *Education and Income* (New York: Viking Press, 1961), pp. 143–144.

[60] See Feleks Gross, *The Polish Worker: A Study of a Social Stratum* (New York: Roy, 1945). César Grâna notes that when the school children of polyglot New York do visit a museum, they find themselves "the guests of a mansion conceived, not only as a monument to 'values,' but as a re-enactment of the patrician past"—César Grâna, "The Private Lives of Public Museums," *Trans-Action*, 4, 5, (1965), pp. 23–24.

[61] Dorothy K. Newman, "The Decentralization of Jobs," *Monthly Labor Review* (May 1967). It would cost a worker in Harlem $40 a month to commute by public transpor-

On the other hand, they cannot afford, or are not permitted because of racial discrimination, to live near the new factories, hospitals, commercial buildings, schools, and stores in the periphery of the city. A minimum level of access to transportation is important.

*Legal services*

Our society prides itself that all are equal before the law. In practice, the bright-minded and better-educated are better treated by judicial officials and have easier access to better legal services than do the poor. In the case of the law, the goal obviously is that the low-income citizen should be as well treated as the better-off. But this would mean an equal distribution of legal services—a far cry from our present situation.[62]

Jerome Carlin, after studying lawyer's ethics in New York City, described the present state of legal services for the poor:

> The best trained, most technically skilled, and ethically most responsible lawyers are reserved to the upper reaches of business and society. This leaves the least competent, least well-trained, and least ethical lawyers to the smaller business concerns and lower-income individuals. As a result, the most helpless clients who most need protection are least likely to get it.
>
> The uneven character of legal services, moreover, leads to a highly selective development of the law itself. Those areas that reflect the interest of large corporations and wealthy individuals are most likely to be elaborated; law dealing with the poor and other disadvantaged groups, particularly in the consumer, landlord-tenant, welfare, and domestic relations areas, remains largely neglected and underdeveloped.
>
> Whatever efforts have been made by leaders of the profession to cope with these problems have been largely ineffective. Lack of leadership is particularly evident in the failure of the organized bar to seek and to support new forms of legal representation that might help in extending legal services to a larger segment of the population.[63]

A series of decisions like the cases of *Gideon* v. *Wainwright* and *Brotherhood of Railroad Trainmen* v. *Virginia* and the surprising success of the Office of Economic Opportunity (OEO) in promoting legal services to the poor have reduced the disparities between the legal conditions facing the poor, and the services available to them, and the situations of the nonpoor.[64] But a gap continues; how wide it is, is uncertain, and it would be useful—and not impossible—to construct and maintain indices of legal treatment and services.[65]

## SOCIAL MOBILITY AND EDUCATION

The poverty programs of the Economic Opportunity Act of 1964 were largely youth programs; the intent was to break the connection between the situation of low-income parents and the prospects of their children. These were

tation to work in an aircraft plant in Farmingdale, Long Island; in a parts plant in Yonkers, Westchester; or in a basic chemical plant on Staten Island.

[62] In New York City, fewer than 5 per cent of the lawyers report that the median income of their clients is under $5,000 a year, although half of the total families and unrelated individuals in New York City have incomes under this amount. Conversely, 70 per cent of the lawyers in New York City report that the median income of their clients is in excess of $10,000, though fewer than 10 per cent of New York's families and unrelated individuals receive incomes that high—U.S., Department of Health, Education, and Welfare, *Extension of Legal Services to the Poor.*

[63] Jerome E. Carlin, *Lawyers' Ethics: A Survey of the New York City Bar* (New York: Russell Sage Foundation, 1966), p. 177.

[64] See Jerome E. Carlin and Jan Howard, "Legal Representation and Class Justice," *UCLA Law Review,* 12 (January 1965), p. 432.

[65] 372 U.S. 335 (1963) and 377 U.S. 1 (1964).

programs aimed at increasing the rate of intergenerational social mobility of low-income youth.[66] More generally, questions of equality and social justice involve issues of social mobility. Life chances are defined largely as questions of opportunity for an individual to rise occupationally in his lifetime or for his children to move into the better situations of the society, thus surpassing the economic level of his parents.

Education is increasingly the route to social mobility in our credential-oriented society. For this reason, we discuss it in this section rather than in the preceding section on basic services. While education has many dimensions other than its contribution to occupational advance, this dimension is the major attraction of education at this point. Educational sophistication is also protection against bureacratic manipulation. It is an aid in learning how to get services. And, for Negroes in particular, it is a barrier to offhand humiliating treatment, especially by police.

Why treat social mobility independently? Does not improvement in family income *automatically* result in improvement in social mobility chances? The data as shown in Figure 1 do not support this conclusion: the education of a family, in most situations, is more important than the income of the family in affecting how far the youth goes in school. Furthermore, two families of the same income obviously fare quite differently in other respects if the offspring of one have a much better chance of higher education and resulting better job prospects than the other. To some extent, then, social mobility is a dimension of well-being deserving of separate attention. It is one of most crucial indicators of a socially democratic society.

*Education*

We deal first with data on education, then with the social mobility data. In education, we can look at various types of indicators. One level of indicators is the expenditures data—how much is spent on children of different income levels? The Syracuse University study of school expenditures, by Alan Campbell, Jesse Burkhead, Seymour Sachs, and associates, shows that in 1962, in thirty-five of the largest metropolitan areas, expenditures in central cities—where there are many children of low-income families—was $145 per pupil less than in their contiguous suburbs—where there are few children of low-income families.[67] One of the most disturbing findings in the investigation is that state funds go relatively more to the suburbs than to the cities; in state aid, suburban schools receive forty dollars more per pupil than city schools. Even more disconcerting, the gap between cities and suburbs is growing: the 1962 difference did not exist in 1958, for then the two areas were spending the same amount.

The importance of school expenditures is indicated by the finding that the proportion of National Merit finalists is related to a locality's support for education.[68]

When differences in the quality of the product—the return per dollar of expenditures—are considered, the gap

[66] A contrasting approach toward improving social conditions tends to be family-oriented, more concerned with the aged than youth. These two approaches are discussed in S. M. Miller, "Poverty," in *Proceedings*, Sixth World Congress of Sociology, 1967.

[67] The report is summarized in the *Carnegie Quarterly*, 14 (Fall 1966). The Coleman Report on education has some contradictory evidence, but it is highly debatable. The data reported in Morgan *et al.*, *Income and Welfare in the United States*, *op. cit.*, tends to support the general notion of differences in per capita educational expenditures between high- and low-income communities.

[68] Robert C. Nichols, "The Financial Status of National Merit Finalists," *Science*, 149 (September 1965), p. 1071.

FIGURE 1—PERCENTAGE OF YOUTH, AGE 16–20, WHO ARE ENROLLED IN OR ATTENDED COLLEGE, BY FATHER'S EDUCATION AND FAMILY INCOME, 1960

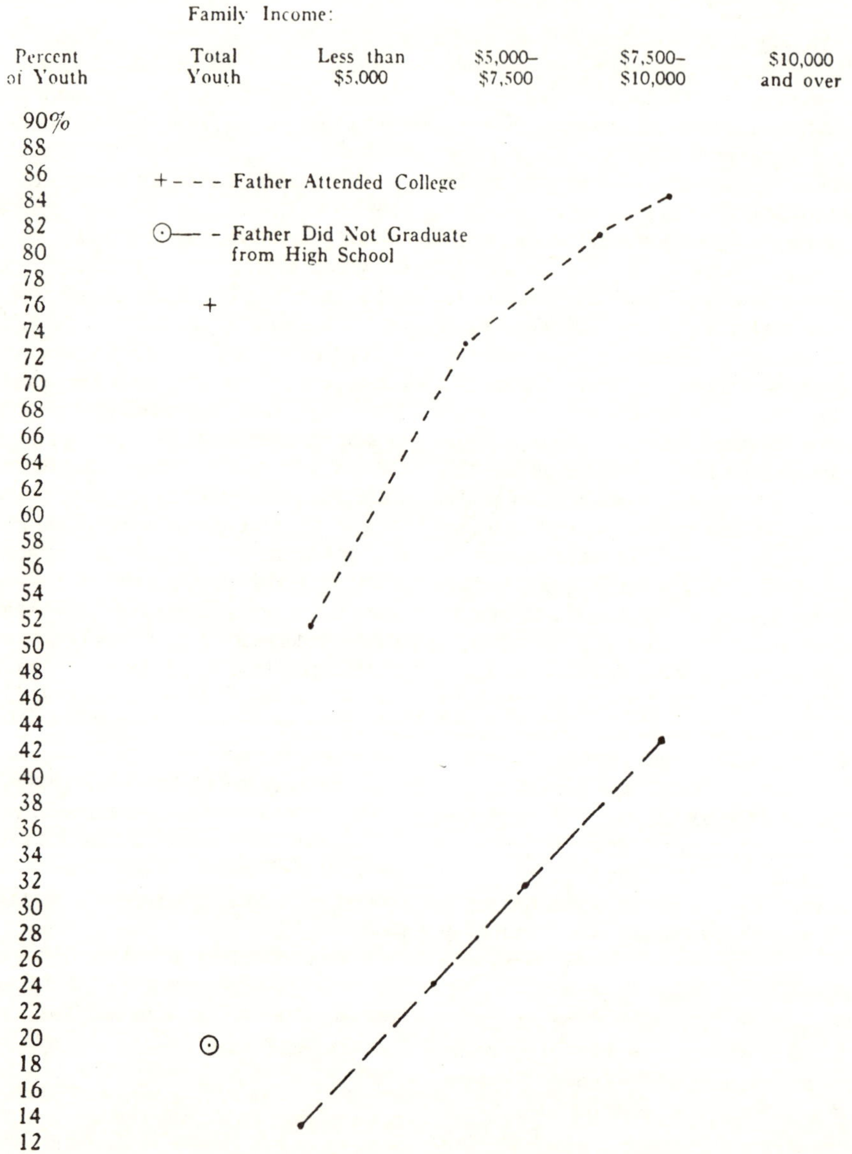


Source: Pamela Roby, "The Economic Prospects of High School Dropouts, Graduates, and College Graduates," Youth Development Center, Syracuse University, 1965 (mimeographed). Adapted from U.S., Bureau of the Census, *Current Population Reports,* P-20, No. 110 (July 24, 1961), Table 10, p. 15.

TABLE 4—PERCENTAGE OF MALE HIGH SCHOOL GRADUATES WHO ENTERED COLLEGE WITHIN ONE YEAR AFTER COMPLETING HIGH SCHOOL, BY APTITUDE PERCENTILE AND FAMILY INCOME.[a]

| FAMILY INCOME | APTITUDE LEVEL, PERCENTILE | | | | |
|---|---|---|---|---|---|
| | 0–49.9 | 50–74.9 | 75–89.9 | 90–97.9 | 98–100 |
| Less than $3,000 | 19.6 | 48.2 | 75.4 | 87.9 | 100.0 |
| $3,000–$5,999 | 27.3 | 52.5 | 73.3 | 86.7 | 96.1 |
| $6,000 $8,999 | 31.9 | 59.7 | 80.6 | 88.6 | 95.2 |
| $9,000–$11,999 | 40.2 | 66.8 | 83.9 | 92.5 | 95.9 |
| $12,000 plus | 49.7 | 79.7 | 90.1 | 96.7 | 98.5 |

[a] Calculated from Hearings before Subcommittee on Education, Committee on Education and Labor, House of Representatives, 88th Congress, 1st and 2nd Sessions.

is probably even larger than the gross education figures indicate. It is likely that there are fewer and poorer services rendered per dollar in low-income schools than in higher-income schools.

Data for the city of Detroit in the late 1950's show that for children in families in the below $7,000 income category, 18 per cent of the total teaching time is by "Emergency Substitutes in Regular Positions," as compared with 5.5 per cent for the children in families with above $7,000 family incomes.[69] According to Project Talent findings, teacher experience is highly correlated with student achievement.

Table 4 indicates that adequate college financial aid is probably available—to the top 2 per cent of the nation's youth. For even those who fall within two to ten percentage points from the top in ability, family income is an important determinant of who shall go to college.

Median educational attainment levels of the low-income and Negroes are growing. But here, particularly, the absolute level is probably not as important as the relative level. For if the low-income children increase their median levels while the children of the higher-income change theirs even more, the former may not be much advantaged in terms of job prospects. In interpreting median data, it is important to recognize that more years of high school have much less importance than the jump to a high school diploma. Although the over-all difference in educational attainment is narrowing, *the difference between the percentage of whites and nonwhites with high school diplomas or college educations has remained the same over the past decade.*

Goals of education for the low-income are much more significantly stated in terms of what percentage should be high school or college *graduates* than in terms of median years of education.

Despite the staggering amount of educational statistics, gaps still exist. Needed are statistics for localities on the distribution and quality of educational statistics. Units smaller than a city are needed. On the product side, data are needed on the achievement of students. It is important to link expenditures to attainments for specific localities—a need not met in the important national testing program which Ralph Tyler has been urging and the organizations of school officials have been resisting. Studies of charts of students from their entrance into school through maturity would be particularly useful; the objective would be to discern the influences of school characteristics on their achievements.

[69] Patricia C. Sexton, *op. cit.*, p. 120.

### *Mobility*

The social mobility rates that we are concerned about are intergenerational. We ignore in this discussion intragenerational mobility—the changes in occupations of an individual over his lifetime—or stratum mobility—the changes in income and other benefits of an occupation compared to other occupations. These are both important processes, to which not enough attention has been paid in current discussions of mobility. Nor do we discuss geographic mobility, which is frequently, though not necessarily, involved in the patterning of social mobility. And we ignore all the difficulties intrinsic to mobility studies.[70]

Surprisingly, the United States has lagged behind many other nations in conducting a national study which was mainly addressed to issues of social mobility. In 1962, this lack was remedied in the very useful investigation by the Bureau of the Census which was stimulated by, and conducted in close co-operation with, the sociologists Otis Dudley Duncan and Peter Blau. We will use this study. It would be rewarding to conduct such a study every five years to see changes in the rates and patterns of social mobility in the United States.

Children of families at the bottom of the occupational hierarchy had much less chance of moving into upper-level jobs than children born in families at these levels. A son of a Negro manual worker has less than a quarter of the chance of a white-collar non-Negro son to get into a white-collar job. The chance of the white manual worker's son is slightly more than half that of the latter.[71]

The degree of stability of upper-level families is an indication of the openness of society (as well as of economic change and growth). Here, we find downward mobility from the nonmanual into the manual classes to be 22 per cent in the United States, 42 per cent in Great Britain, 37 per cent in Denmark, and 44 per cent in Canada.[72]

The Negro data are disturbing. The Negro mobility rate from lower manual occupations is about half (51 per cent) that of the white from these same occupations. More disturbing is the finding that among Negro sons of white-collar fathers, 72.4 per cent went into manual occupations, as compared with 23.4 per cent of non-Negro sons. This rate of downward mobility is spectacular, even when we allow for the likelihood that, for some, the movement may be into manual occupations that pay as well or better than marginal middle-class occupations.[73]

The Negro data indicate the inadequacies of utilizing national figures. Data for regions of the country would probably show that the South has a much lower rate of social mobility than other parts of the country.

What is the target in social mobility? Obviously, income, the occupational and social contacts of families, the know-how, and the educational support all combine to make it difficult to reduce sharply competitive advantages. But substantial reduction of differences is possible. Specific targets over a ten- and twenty-year period are probably desirable to reduce social mobility differen-

[70] S. M. Miller, "Comparative Social Mobility," *Current Sociology*, IX-1 (1960), chap. i.

[71] Otis Dudley Duncan, Survey Research Center, University of Michigan, unpublished tabulations.

[72] The foreign data are from S. M. Miller, "Comparative Social Mobility," *op. cit.*: they are for earlier years than the U.S.A. figures. But the earlier U.S.A. data suggest that there is a significant gap in downward fluidity between the U.S.A. and a number of other nations.

[73] The statements in this paragraph are based on special, unpublished tabulations by Otis Dudley Duncan. We are grateful to him for his willingness to let us publish them before his own material appears.

tials. The improvement of the education of those at the bottom, the reduction of the emphasis on educational credentials as intrinsic to occupational entrance, and the more effective reliance on upgrading and training on the job are among the ways that social mobility patterns can become political questions.

Cutting the link between parent's position and child's is one of the core goals of a fluid society. (One can argue the position that the goal is only to break the link for those at the bottom, not those in already more advantaged positions.) Careful collection and analysis of data of this kind are essential to keeping the issue under public scrutiny.

## POLITICAL POSITION

The improvement of economic position does not always bring with it advances in political position. Indeed, many analysts argue that it is the inconsistency between rising economic power and stunted political power that is most likely to make a group revolutionary or militant. A major part of Max Weber's implicit critique of Marx's theory of class is to stress the possible disjunctures between economic and social and political positions.

Historically, the movement towards political advance of the bottommost groups has been a striving for citizenship rights of suffrage. The nineteenth century in Europe can be seen as a long-drawn-out struggle for the extension of voting rights to the disenfranchised. The fight was largely won by World War I in most countries that employ the term "democratic." The formal, legal right to vote is no longer an issue in most countries. The actual use and importance of that right is the more important question today, with the disturbing exception of Negroes in the American South, who still suffer from concerted efforts to limit their voting.

As Scammon's data show,[74] the frequency of voting decreases the lower the income. Some would argue, as one may infer from Berelson,[75] that it is desirable to have a low voting rate among the low-income and low-educated because they are likely to be ill-informed, antidemocratic voters. But the general sentiment would be that democracy is defined, in part, as the integration of the low-income into the political process.

What should be the target for the voting of the low-income? No group has 100 per cent voting rates. To move to the level of the higher-income group ($10,000 and over), the rate is 84.9 per cent, in contrast to the 49.6 per cent rate in families below $2,000 and the 57.6 per cent rate in the $2,000–$2,999 range. The largest jump in rates is between the $3,000–$4,999 and the $5,000–$7,999 rate, where the change is from the 62.7 to the 72.4 per cent level.[76] This latter figure might well serve as the goal for voting rights among the low-income.[77]

To achieve this level would require not only eliminating the *de facto* resistances to Negro voting, but also reducing the varied requirements that limit voting—for example, residence requirements, English-language literacy, and loss of voting rights because of imprisonment.[78] Increasing the ease of

[74] Richard M. Scammon, "Electoral Participation," *Social Goals and Indicators for American Society*, Vol. I, THE ANNALS, Vol. 371 (May 1967), Table 4, p. 63.

[75] Bernard Berelson, Paul F. Lazarsfeld, and W. N. McPhee, *Voting* (Chicago: University of Chicago Press, 1954).

[76] Scammon, *op. cit.*, p. 63.

[77] Here, as elsewhere in this paper, we are not discussing the inequalities which affect other than the low-income. In the case of youth, the obvious point is the issue of the lowering of the voting age to eighteen.

[78] David Caplovitz and other students of Harlem voting patterns contend that when adjustments are made for noneligibles, the

voting may also be necessary—more polling places, longer polling hours, and elimination of registration, so that only one visit is needed in order to vote. A third barrier to voting is, of course, a lack of interest in voting and the political process—whether due to apathy or to a feeling that the issues and candidates are not important or do not involve a significant choice.

The implicit notion here is that low voting rates among the low-income should not be regarded as only a defect of the nonvoters but as a criticism of the political process.

Voting is but one level of the issue of political rights. Another is that of the importance of the vote. This leads to the question which underlies the agitation about reapportionment: Are voters in different areas securing equal representation in a legislative body, whether it be Congress, a state assembly, or a city council? At another, more subtle level, the question is: Do the representatives of the low-income groups have as much sensitivity to their constituents' interests and wishes as do the representatives of higher-income groups? Indicators of this type are difficult, but not impossible, and are best developed and maintained by nongovernmental groups. The simplest form is the American Federation of Labor–Congress of Industrial Organizations (AFL–CIO) report on the voting records on key labor issues of congressmen and senators. The main issues (and positions) for low-income individuals could be delineated,[79] and representatives from low-income districts could be rated on how they stood on these issues; this could be done by civil rights and poverty groups. If similar measures were maintained for higher-income groups, it would be possible to see if there are large differences in the sensitivity of representatives of different socioeconomic groups.[80] It would seem a "natural" for civil rights groups and poverty groups like the Citizens' Crusade against Poverty to maintain such indices.

"Sensitivity of representatives" perhaps begs the issue because the question frequently is: Are the legislative decisions of deep significance to low-income voters? If the issues are marginal in importance, then the sensitivity of the representatives is not central. The radical critics raise the question whether the overlap of the two main parties buries crucial issues of redistribution, since the effort is to appeal to a mythical voter of the center. From the point of view of the low-income, to what extent are the issues that come before legislative bodies of central importance? Are their glaring needs untouched? This analysis could be done both absolutely and relatively (the total number of issues relevant to the low-income and the ratio

voting rate in this locality is as high as in high-income neighborhoods. If this is so, increasing the ease of voting is not important. On the other hand, some data show that a lower proportion of registered low-income than high-income persons actually do vote.

[79] What the needed response is on a particular issue from the point of view of a particular income or socioeconomic grouping is not undebatable. But there would be a high degree of agreement on most issues, whether by a panel of experts thinking in terms of a particular group or by a sample of the group itself. At least, this is a testable proposition.

[80] Since most voting districts are not homogeneous (and the larger, the greater the heterogeneity), a representative would have to be rated in terms of his sensitivity to a particular group, rather than to the district as a whole. A less direct way of measuring sensitivity is the MacRae method of seeing to what extent a district is a potential swing district. The higher the potential, the greater the sensitivity of the representatives. Are low-income districts more likely than high-income districts to favor one candidate or party so overwhelmingly that a representative feels little pressure for responding to his constituents' needs and feelings?

of these issues to the number relevant to the nonpoor). Obviously, a mode of analysis along these lines is exceedingly difficult and could best be pursued outside the government.

Indeed, except for voting rates, it is likely that most appraisals of performance in the political realm can only be carried through by independent groups. This is the result not only of the strong repercussions of these views and the likelihood of manipulation of results for partisan purposes, but, more importantly, of the fact that competing indicators and interpretations are inevitable and desirable. Different groups and interests would want quite different sets of information and would interpret them in very contrasting ways.

Our analysis so far has been at the level of voting and representation. But a good deal of what is important in terms of political position and process is not in the development of policy but in its administration. The militant attacks on "the welfare state" are, in part, sparked by concerns about administrative injustices and inhumanity. A modern view of political process and power must analyze the relationships of individuals to bureaucracies. The proliferation of governmental agencies means that a good deal of what affects the life of the poor emanates from bureaucracies and bureaucrats. Important decisions are made administratively as well as legislatively. The way in which agency officials treat the low-income may be more important than the law which the officials purport to administer.

First, the *quality of treatment* is one important aspect of bureaucratic functioning. The issue of decency in behavior of officials towards citizen-clients has been raised most sharply recently in the realm of public welfare, where there have been charges of invasion of privacy (checking of homes in "midnight raids," to see if there is evasion of the "no man in the home rule"), the utilization of welfare as a means of social control, and generally humiliating treatment of clients by welfare officials.[31] How to set up indicators of quality of treatment is not clear; perhaps it is easiest to do this if treatment is governed by rights and rules.

Where aid (money and services) is provided to the poor, the latter's claim to this aid is frequently ambiguous. Do they have rights as citizens to these services or are they dependents who lose the privilege of rights because of their dependent status? Increasingly, the issue is raised (see, for example, the report of the 1966 Advisory Committee on Public Welfare) that the provisioning of cash and services becomes a right for individuals. If an individual is refused aid, he should be able to appeal—if necessary, to an adjudicating body that is independent of the agency. If he is poorly treated, he could protest and demand to have the official punished. The example of police review boards leaps to mind.

Second, it would be possible to work up indicators of *rights* and *grievances*. To what extent do programs in aid of the poor have statements of rights that are meaningful and effective? Does an agency have a grievance procedure which meets the criteria of effectiveness (the history of union experiences with grievance procedures would probably offer many ways of evaluating procedures): Who uses it, on what issues, with what results? Indicators of rights and grievances could be developed by governmental agencies, but would undoubtedly be limited; outside groups would be more effective in formulating more comprehensive indicators.

Third, in a "pluralistic society," the interests of individuals are represented

[31] Charles A. Reich, "Individual Rights and Social Welfare: The Emerging Legal Issues," *The Yale Law Journal*, 74 (1965).

by organizations and associations. To what extent is the pluralism of American society democratic? Do the low-income have effective representative organizations? Do other groups? How involved are the low-income in the discussions of their groups? What changes are taking place?

Several studies show that membership in voluntary associations increases with status and that membership in associations increases interest in presidential elections.[82] Gradations within the low-income strata are important. In a study of New York City poor, David Caplovitz found that "for the sample as a whole, and within each racial group, the more solvent families more often belong to the voluntary associations." This suggests that the relationship between voluntary-association membership, voting, and social class found in the general population "occurs within the lower class as well; the less the financial stability of the low income family, the less its participation in the life of the broader community." [83]

Quality of treatment, rights and grievance, and representation are important and inadequately supplied today by bureaucracies. But a new demand has emerged which is insufficiently represented in indicators of these types. This fourth issue has been dramatically phrased in that ambiguous phrase of "maximum feasible participation," the right to share in the decision-making of administrative agencies. Since so many important decisions are made outside the realm of the legislature, administrative law-making and allocations become increasingly important. While the demand for participation has had many different sides to it —many initially supported it because it would reduce the psychological feeling of powerlessness—in this context, participation is clearly a political act of involvement in important decisions which are nonlegislative. OEO is experimenting with indicators of grass-roots involvement in local community action programs, and, hopefully, these indicators may be adaptable to broader use, as participation issues are much wider than poverty programs.

The new politics will increasingly involve the relationships of citizens to the welfare state's apparatus. While the participation issue has just begun to be raised in terms of the poor, it will increasingly be raised for other groups in society. The issues of the welfare state are most acute for the poor, but affect other citizens as well. It may be that the call for political participation in decision-making on a wider scale is not a call for reduction of inequalities, as better-off citizens also have limited participation. But their losses from inadequate sharing in decision-making may be less important to them than to the poor, who are so deeply affected by bureaucratic practices. Refinements of measures of "participation" are needed.

A fifth issue is that of the psychological feeling of powerlessness.[84] The poor feel less able to control their des-

[82] Charles R. Wright and Herbert H. Hyman, "Voluntary Association Memberships of American Adults: Evidence from National Sample Surveys," *American Sociological Review*, 23 (1958).

[83] David Caplovitz, *op. cit.*, pp. 133–134.

[84] Melvin Seeman, "On the Meaning of Alienation," *American Sociological Review*, 24 (1959), pp. 783–791. Seeman identifies five alternative meanings of alienation: powerlessness, meaninglessness, normlessness, isolation, and self-estrangement. Blauner demonstrates that because the conditions of work and existence in various industrial environments are quite different, the industry in which the man works is fateful in furthering or abating each of the five dimensions of alienation examined by Seeman—Robert Blauner, *Alienation and Freedom: The Factory Worker and His Industry* (Chicago: University of Chicago Press, 1964).

tinies than do other groups in society. "The government," "they," and "city hall" loom large, threatening and immovable to many of the poor. Changes in the feeling of powerlessness would not only affect willingness to try to vote, to make changes and share in decision-making, but they may also have importance in their own right as constituting an important state of well-being. Indicators of changes in feelings of powerlessness could be constructed on the basis of the studies of alienation and anomie (indeed, they have been involved in some evaluations of poverty programs). Public opinion surveys could provide relevant data on the indicators. It may turn out that feelings of "powerlessness" are segmented politically. Some institutions may appear to be more permeable than others, and indicators of particular institutions may be necessary.

As with all subjective indicators, the danger of manipulation is important: policies may successfully aim at making people feel more politically powerful even though their political potency has not grown. Here again, it would be important for nongovernmental groups to gauge independently the realistic significance of changed feelings of powerlessness. (And the converse may occur: increased political control without decreased feelings of powerlessness.)

We have talked about power in the political realm, whether at the federal state, local, or bureaucratic-organizational level. As Dahrendorf has asserted, "class is about power."[85] The conflict about authority is the universal issue of which the Marxist concern with property is a special though important case.[86] We have not addressed power and authority relationships in the workplace, a sixth dimension of power.

The jobs of the poor are less frequently rationalized than the jobs of the better-off;[87] they are less frequently organized into unions; low-skilled workers are more easily replaceable than high-skilled workers, so that employers can be more forceful with the former. Or so it would seem. Indicators of workplace independence and participation would be useful to develop, for the nature of job authority is an important part of well-being, even if we do not fully recognize it as such today.[88]

We suspect that the discussions of democracy in the political process will be supplemented in the next years by the reopening of questions about authority at work, although not necessarily in the old forms of socialist ownership or of shibboleths of worker participation.

### STATUS AND SATISFACTION

Why is status important? As we have pointed out earlier, a gain in income that is stigmatized diminishes the satisfactions of the income-recipients. Further, it may be that a major issue of the poor today is their social exclusion, rather than their income level. Being included in society—which means being accorded respect and accepted in social and political relations with others—is increasingly an important part of the issue of inequality.[89]

[85] Ralf Dahrendorf, "Recent Changes in the Class Structure of European Societies," *Daedalus*, 93 (Winter 1964).

[86] Ralf Dahrendorf, *Class and Class Conflict in Industrial Society* (Stanford, Calif.: Stanford University Press, 1959).

[87] Blauner has reported the wide variations of responsibility and freedom among blue-collar jobs. He has reopened a number of important issues—Robert Blauner, *op. cit.*

[88] S. M. Miller and Ira Harrison, "Types of Dropouts—The Unemployables," in Arthur Hartak and William Gomberg (eds.), *Blue Collar World* (Englewood Cliffs, N.J.: Prentice-Hall, 1964).

[89] We do not discuss mass and other styles of culture in this paper. But issues of culture will probably re-emerge as important; they have done so very forcefully with regard to Negro culture and history.

Status refers to the views that others hold of an individual. This view affects the way in which individuals are treated —with approval or with disapprobation, with respect or dishonor. The "two nations" of Disraeli and Harrington, the have's and the have-not's, are divided not only by income and hope, but by respect as well. The immediate view is that the gulf between the have's and have-not's has been reduced, but a more accurate view is probably that more individuals are now have's and are acceptable. What about those left behind in the general advance of society? Are they less likely now to be viewed as subhuman, undeserving of attention? There probably has been a growth of humanity, but there still is a sizable difference in the ways in which the low-income and others are regarded.

The United States no longer has a legal basis for dishonor in the form of laws requiring discrimination against minority groups. But the practices of discrimination frequently exist—on the job, in housing, in public facilities, and in education. Data for overt discrimination are difficult to collect. Crucial activities and localities could be studied, however, to see changes in discrimination patterns and frequency. National cross-sections of minority-group members could be studied over time (preferably as a panel) to see whether they have had changing experiences with discrimination. In the case of discrimination, the goal is clear-cut: the total elimination of discrimination on the basis of race, religion, ethnic extraction, and income.

Discrimination is the most striking case of status barriers. But it is not the main dimension today. The more important dimensions surround the prestige of various groupings in society and the nature of the interactions among groups. Data are lacking on the ways in which low-income groups are rated by others. The most common data available are those on occupational prestige; they uniformly show that the occupations held by the low-income are at the bottom. In 1947 and 1963, janitors, bartenders, sharecroppers, garbage-collectors, street-sweepers, and shoeshiners were ranked among the bottom ten in prestige of ninety occupations in nationwide samples.

But what is the goal in reduction of prestige differences? We do not anticipate complete equality here, but some reduction in the range of differences. Unfortunately, we have not been able to find data dealing with compression or expansion of the occupational-prestige range within a nation. Setting specific goals would require more knowledge of trends. The greater difficulty is that the policies to follow are not clear.[90]

Studies of communities have revealed the stratification and exclusions which occur.[91] These studies report the fact of different ratings, but not the span of the differences in ratings. It would seem not too difficult to develop measures of the differences among groups, whether stratified by income, occupation, or more complex sets of measurements. The use of these measures over time would inform our guesses as to whether the gulfs among strata are increasing or decreasing.

[90] Robert W. Hodge, Paul M. Siegel, and Peter H. Rossi, "Occupational Prestige in the United States: 1925–1963," in Reinhard Bendix and S. M. Lipset (eds.), *Class Status and Power* (New York: Free Press, 1966), Table 1, p. 325.

[91] Cf. Robert S. Lynd and Helen M. Lynd, *Middletown: A Study in Contemporary American Culture* (New York: Harcourt, Brace, 1929); W. Lloyd Warner, "The Yankee City Series," and *American Life: Dream and Reality* (Chicago: University of Chicago Press, 1953); and Arthur Vidich and Joseph Bensman, *Small Town in Mass Society* (Princeton, N.J.: Princeton University Press, 1958).

One simple measure does already exist, but its interpretation is subject to considerable controversy. This indicator is the degree and kind of interaction which exists among individuals and families of different economic standing. (In many community studies, especially those influenced by Warner, position in the community is defined by reputation, an assessment which is influenced by the patterns of interaction among families of a community. The measure that we seek would require arraying individuals on an indicator such as income and then studying the differences in interaction patterns.) The evidence is unmistakable—low rates of cross-class, nonjob interaction.

The target here is unclear. Should the goal be random sorting of interaction so that individuals of high income (or education) are as likely to associate with individuals of low income as with their income peers? Should the goal be that ethnic-group members associate no more frequently with fellow ethnics than with nonethnics? Many would argue for ethnic solidarity—at least for political purposes—among deprived groups like Negroes. While we lack clarity about goals for a society that, in rhetoric at least, is pictured as socially democratic, information over time on these patterns would still be useful in depicting the extent to which gulfs among groups are being narrowed.

Interestingly, it is in this area of contact, social distance, and social honor that we have the greatest difficulty in specifying targets. For in this sensitive area, the cloudy, ambiguous slogans of American values and goals provide little direction. A more systematic collection of the kinds of information suggested here may force re-examination of broad tenets and specific behaviors which are poorly articulated or understood.

The basis for and the way in which one receives income affect the satisfactions derived from income. In American society, income that is not obtained directly or indirectly from work or education (for example, scholarships) is likely to be demeaned. Some 15 per cent of adult units with under $1,000 income received payments in the form of public welfare, accompanied by demeaning means tests.

Transfer payments to upper, unlike lower, income groups generally have the seal of social acceptance. Social security, government payments to farmers, and indirect subsidies in the form of tax deductions, allowances, and exemptions are generally accepted forms of government transfers. Fifty-five per cent of total 1963 government payments to farmers went to the top 11 per cent of all farmers, those with farm sales of $20,000 and over.[92]

Many of the discussions of the reform of the welfare system are concerned with the importance of removing the stigma associated with receiving income in this way. The concern is largely, though not exclusively, with the degradation of the means-test ceremonials. In effect, then, we are in the midst of a *politicalization of status* where the distribution of stigma through the distribution of income and services is being challenged. Stigma is now a political issue; the demand is for mechanisms, like the negative income tax, welfare rights, or family allowances, which reduce the possibilities of families' having low status because of the way that they procure income. (In part, too, as we shall discuss shortly, the effort is to change the recipients' views of themselves by removing the stigmatizing procedures.) While it would be difficult to construct, an index of income stigma

[92] Theodore Schultz, "Public Approaches to Minimize Poverty," in Leo Fishman (ed.), *Poverty Amid Affluence* (New Haven, Conn.: Yale University Press, 1966).

would be a useful indicator in measuring poverty movement.[93]

Our discussion of status has been of external views of the poor. But a very important area is the way that the poor look upon themselves. A significant aspect of satisfactory life is the degree of acceptance of self, the agreeability of self-image, the satisfactions with life. In addition to statistical data of actual inequalities, indicators are needed of individuals' perceptions of inequalities in each dimension of well-being: incomes, assets, basic services, social mobility and education, political position, and status. In England, Runciman has demonstrated the extent to which attitudes toward social inequalities have failed to correspond with the facts of inequality, whether economic, social, or political.[94] These are difficult issues to discuss in the context of policies without being reminded of *1984*; but the dangers of their manipulation should not prevent us from first exploring some issues, even if, on civil libertarian, democratic grounds, we later decide that we do not wish to pursue study and action along these lines.

In contrast to the "good savage, healthy and free" view of the poor, most measures show that they enjoy life less than do other groups. As one would expect in an industrial, instrumentally oriented society, the available data are largely about job satisfaction and morale. Here, the results are almost all in the same direction: the higher the job level, the greater the degree of job satisfaction: for example, only 16 per cent of unskilled auto workers as compared with over 90 per cent of mathematicians and urban university professors reported that they would try to get into a similar type of work if they could start over again.[95]

According to the findings of Bradburn and Caplovitz' study on happiness, job dissatisfaction is an instance of relative deprivation. Men in a low socioeconomic position in prosperous communities were found more dissatisfied with their jobs than similar men in depressed communities.[96]

Studies of mental health show the highest rate of severe illness among the lowest socioeconomic groups. For example, in the most famous survey,[97] class V, the bottom group, had a schizophrenic rate of 895 per 100,000 while class I-II had a rate of 111. Unfortunately, as in most studies, this investigation is marred by the possibility of underenumerating of illness in the upper-income groups. More complex assessments of mental health show that the bottommost class is characterized by more emotional instability than higher-placed groups.[98]

[93] This measure may run the danger of perpetuating stigmatizing practices.

[94] W. G. Runciman, *Relative Deprivation and Social Justice: A Study of Attitudes to Social Inequality in Twentieth-Century England* (Berkeley and Los Angeles: University of California Press, 1966).

[95] Harold Wilensky, "Varieties of Work Experience," in Henry Borow (ed.), *Man in a World of Work* (Boston: Houghton Mifflin, 1964), p. 137.

[96] Norman M. Bradburn and David Caplovitz, *Reports on Happiness: A Pilot Study of Behavior Related to Mental Health* (Chicago: Aldine, 1965).

[97] August B. Hollingshead and Frederic Redlich, *Social Class and Mental Illness* (New York: John Wiley and Sons, 1958), p. 232.

[98] Srole and his associates surveyed midtown Manhattan by interviewing a cross-section of residents of their homes. Persons classified as "well" rose steadily from 9.7 per cent in the lowest socioeconomic category (F) to 24.4 per cent in the highest (A): those classified as "impaired" declined from 33.7 to 16.4 per cent in the second highest category and then rose slightly to 17.5 per cent in the highest SES. The term "incapacitated" was applied to category F, 3.3 per cent of category B, and 1.9 per cent of category A. Studies of this kind are subject to the criticism that similar symptoms may not have the same implications and intensity in groups differentially placed in society. See

As a goal, the reduction of mental illness, especially severe mental illness, among lower socioeconomic groups would be important, as well as reducing the rates as rapidly as they are reduced among the higher groups.

The importance of dignity, satisfaction, self-respect, and self-image is evidenced in Negroes' calling for institutional settings, especially in schools, which foster the development of positive self-images. While, in part, this demand is clearly political in terms of power, at another level it is a psychologically based demand, insisting that the development among Negroes of positive attitudes toward themselves is a responsibility of society. While one can argue about the best way to do this—whether "black power" and separate institutions are the only instruments—the intent of the goal—positive self-image—is one which many would accept as a societal obligation. *The differential distribution of positive feelings about one's self is perhaps the essence of inequality.*

Recently, studies have been aimed at studying the elusive issue of happiness.[99] These studies, which provide a base for the development of time-series investigations of the nation's psychological well-being, indicate that positive and negative feelings vary independently of each other. Again, the interrelationships among education and income are complex. Education and happiness are positively related for those who earn less than $7,000 a year, but negatively related among wealthier people.[100]

The Bradburn-Caplovitz study of happiness in four medium-size communities demonstrates the importance of many items which are not included in the definition of an "adequate level of income." Going for a ride in a car as well as eating in a restaurant several times a week and participating in or watching games or sports activities are related to positive feelings. The degree of a community's economic depression is reflected in the happiness of lower, but not higher, socioeconomic groups. Economic privation through loss of job, low income, or increased vulnerability to economic stress with increasing age were found to affect the feelings of individuals most greatly.[101]

In dealing with status and self-respect, we are in the most troublesome realms, where manipulation and invasion of privacy are grave threats. But the ultimate tests of inequality are not only in income alone; societies with fairly similar income profiles can have enormous differences in the distribution of other values. The dangers should not obscure the recognition of what the ultimate objectives are, nor should the seeming neutrality of the material elements of well-being lead us into taking easy measurements which eliminate study of the new demands that are being made of the affluent society. For example, in the kibbutz, it has been reported that the differential of greatest importance in affecting people's treatment by others and view of themselves is length of stay in the kibbutz.[102] "Stratification" was pronounced, despite the equality in the distribution of income.

L. Srole, T. S. Langner, S. T. Michael, M. K. Opler, and T. A. C. Rennie, *Mental Health in the Metropolis* (New York: McGraw-Hill, 1962).

[99] Cf. Norman M. Bradburn and David Caplovitz, *op. cit.;* G. Gurin, J. Veroff, and S. Feld, *Americans View Their Mental Health* (New York: Basic Books, 1960); L. Srole, T. S. Langner, S. T. Michael, M. K. Opler, and T. A. C. Rennie, *op. cit.;* Derek L. Phillips, "Social Participation and Happiness," *American Journal of Sociology,* 72, 5 (March 1967).

[100] Bradburn and Caplovitz, *op. cit.,* p. 11.

[101] *Ibid.,* pp. 46, 63.

[102] Eva Rosenfeld, "Social Stratification in a Classless Society," *American Sociological Review,* 16 (December 1951).

## CONCLUSION

A specific timetable of inequality-reduction is needed. Without clear-cut targets we cannot assess our progress. In income, we would urge that we set as a goal the reduction of the number of families below a family poverty line to 5 per cent by 1975. (The line should move in relation to prices and general economic advance.) We could seek to expand the share of income going to the bottom 20 per cent by 2 per cent to 3 per cent in the next ten years. In other discussions, specific targets should be set up. The absence of concrete targets hinders the building up of interest groups and the intense counterplay of competing strategies.

In emphasizing the importance of inequality and of its varied forms, we are not implicitly arguing the case that there should not be any important distinctions among individuals. Rather, we believe that a number of inequalities are much greater than many realize and that they are hard to defend on the basis even of an economically rational allocation of benefits. We are also critical of them on the basis of our view of what is a desirable society.[103]

We believe that greater awareness of the extent of inequalities, an awareness which would be deepened by the presentation of the kinds of indicators suggested here, would make possible more useful discussions of inequality: How many differences and what kind are we really willing to live with?

It could be argued that unconscious inequality is preferable to conscious inequality, that if society is unaware of the degree of inequality and of the processes leading to it, society is less damaging to disadvantaged individuals than if there were a sorting out of the disadvantaged. This is a danger, eloquently expressed by Michael Young in *The Rise of the Meritocracy.*

But we do find it hard to accept the notion that *at this time* unawareness of inequalities is more kind to the disadvantaged than public discussion of these inequalities.

> Considered only in terms of opportunity and power, class [that is, inequality] appears as a unilateral possession of privileges, a greater accumulation of benefits and powers in one sector of society than another. But class is clearly more than this. It is a universal loss. There is one human need it violates in all members of society, oppressors and oppressed alike; the need of men for each other. It is in its aspects as a pure human *division,* rather than an economic or political disparity, which is most often ignored and yet which wholly describes class.[104]

One does not have to embrace the idea of complete equality to feel that reductions in inequality are desirable.[105]

The fact that many of the poor in the United States would be well off in low-income societies suggests that more is involved in "poverty" than just low levels of the physical conditions of life. The issues of relative deprivation appear to be more important. In that perspective, we must increasingly turn to the indicators of inequality as well as of "poverty," which implies a scientific standard of subsistence. The second half of the twentieth century requires

[103] For interesting discussions of inequality, see W. G. Runciman, *op. cit.;* Bertram de Jouvenel, *The Ethics of Redistribution* (Cambridge, England: Cambridge University Press, 1952); Lee Rainwater, "Towards A Society of Average Men," unpublished; and Robin Blackburn, "Inequality and Exploitation," *New Left Review,* No. 42 (March–April 1967).

[104] Perry Anderson, "Sweden: A Study in Social Democracy," *New Left Review* (May 1961).

[105] See S. M. Miller and Martin Rein, "Poverty, Inequality, and Policy," in Howard Becker (ed.), *Social Problems* (New York: John Wiley & Sons, 1966).

more sensitive instruments than the nineteenth century.

Poverty is "income-insufficiency," but it is more than that in the affluent society. To be able to discuss poverty and inequality requires an understanding of the changing dynamics and desirable products of the society. As in many other cases—for example, the indictment of education because of its inadequate development of low-income youngsters has probably improved education for all—the situation of the poor is forcing social scientists and actionists to understand better the society in which the disturbing questions of humanity still haunt the economic cornucopia. *The issues of distribution—who should get what—inevitably lead to questioning the character of the "what."*

Social indicators will not tell us what choices to make between growth and inequality-reduction, between spending money on health services or education, between price increases or expansion, and the like. But they can prevent us from ignoring the fact that we are making choices. Effective measurements will improve our ability to comprehend which kinds of programs are likely to be useful for a particular purpose. But we believe that the hopes for compelling evaluations and knowledge are at least premature. Rather, we look to new knowledge brought out by social indicators to direct us, freshly and more acutely, to the issues of choice that are frequently ignored in a political rhetoric and a social science which lag behind the subtleties of late twentieth-century life. Social indicators can arouse groups, outside the government as well as within, to delineate what "progress" is and how well it is being achieved and distributed. In these assessments, low consensus will emerge. The ensuing debates would be around the central issues of a just society. Social indicators would then contribute to useful conflict rather than to evasive complacency.

# [4]

# Perspectives on poverty 2 How poverty is measured

MOLLIE ORSHANSKY

COUNTING THE POOR is an exercise in the art of the possible. For deciding who is poor, prayers are more relevant than calculation because poverty, like beauty, lies in the eye of the beholder. Poverty is a value judgment; it is not something one can verify or demonstrate, except by inference and suggestion, even with a measure of error. To say who is poor is to use all sorts of value judgments. The concept has to be limited by the purpose which is to be served by the definition. There is no particular reason to count the poor unless you are going to do something about them. Whatever the possibilities for socioeconomic research in general, when it comes to defining poverty, you can only be more subjective or less so. You cannot be nonsubjective.

## Defining the issue

In the Social Security Administration, poverty was first defined in terms of the public or policy issue: To how many people, and to which ones, did we wish to direct policy concern. Even when we bore this aim in mind, the level of living we used to separate the "haves" from the "have nots" could be as generous or as rigorous as we pleased. The level could be understated so that everyone who was counted in the "have not" group really did not have enough. If we did the reverse, we ran the risk of counting some who should not be there. There is, in short, no one perfect scheme and no value-free scheme.

Since we were attempting to illustrate the level of public concern, we wanted to be sure that every family or consumer unit had its fair chance to be numbered among those who would be considered as needing attention. Indeed, it was precisely to insure consideration of the needs of large families as well as small, and of young people as well as old, that we refined the initial standard developed by the Council of Economic Advisers. Their standard said that any family of two or more with less than $3,000 annual income, and any single person living alone with less than $1,500, would be considered poor for purposes of antipoverty program planning—but not for program eligibility. This original standard led to the odd result that an elderly couple with $2,900 income for the year would be considered poor, but a family with a husband, wife, and four little children with $3,100 income would not be.

Moreover, when we looked at the poor distributed demographically, by comparison with the total population, we made some unusual discoveries. For example, the percentage of the families classified as poor who had no children was higher than that for the population as a whole; and to make it even more unrealistic, the percentage of the poor families with four children or more was actually less than the representation of such families in the population. We did not think this was correct, so we tried to vary the poverty line—the necessary minimum of resources—with the size and composition of the family. The reason this had not been done by the Council is that no such data were available to them then.

## Setting the benchmark

A concept which can help influence public thinking must be socially and politically credible. We need benchmarks to distinguish the population group that we want to worry about. A benchmark should neither select a group so small, in relation to all the population, that it hardly seems to deserve a general program, nor so large that a solution to the problem appears impossible. For example, in the 1930's, President Roosevelt said, "I see before me one-third of a Nation ill-clothed,

Mollie Orshansky is a social insurance research analyst in the Office of Research and Statistics, Social Security Administration.

ill-housed, and ill-fed." This fraction is now part of our history. No matter how we get our number today, if more than a third of the population is called poor, it will lose value as a public reference point.

At the Social Security Administration, we decided that we would develop two measures of need, and state, on the basis of the income sample of the Current Population Survey, how many and what kinds of families these measures delineated. It was not the Social Security Administration that labeled the poverty line. It remained for the Office of Economic Opportunity and the Council of Economic Advisers to select the lower of the two measures and decide they would use it as the working tool. The best you can say for the measure is that at a time when it seemed useful, it was there. It is interesting that few outside the Social Security Administration ever wanted to talk about the higher measure. Everybody wanted only to talk about the lower one, labeled the "poverty line," which yielded roughly the same number of people in poverty as the original $3,000 measure did, except that fewer families with more children were substituted for a larger number of older families without children.

### Thresholds of poverty

We have developed two poverty thresholds, corresponding to what we call the "poor" and the "near-poor." These thresholds are set separately for 124 different kinds of families, based on the sex of the head, the number of children under 18, the number of adults, and whether or not the household lives on a farm. The threshold is defined as an attempt to "specify the minimum money income that could support an average family of given composition at the lowest level consistent with the standards of living prevailing in this country. It is based on the amount needed by families of different size and type to purchase a nutritionally adequate diet on the assumption that no more than a third of the family income is used for food."[1] The two thresholds were developed from food consumption surveys conducted by the Department of Agriculture in 1948 and 1955. These revealed that the average expenditure for food by all families was about one-third of income.[2]

An assumption was made that the poor would have the same flexibility in allocating income as the rest of the population but that, obviously, their margin for choice would be less. The amount allocated to food from the average expenditure was cut to the minimum that the Agriculture Department said could still provide American families with an adequate diet. We used the low cost plan to characterize the near poor and for the poor an even lower one, the economy food plan, which postulated 70 cents a person for food each day, assuming that all foods would be prepared at home. The Agriculture Department estimates that only about 10 percent of persons spending that amount or less actually were able to get a nutritionally adequate diet.

Our research revealed that in 1966, on the average, a nonfarm family of four would require an income of about $65 a week to meet the poverty threshold; for the near-poor level, it would take about $20 more. It is important to remember that these income criteria are derived solely from the estimated cost of the minimum diet and its presumed relationship to other daily necessities. We made only two decisions—how much we would allow for food in the low cost plan and the economy plan, and what would be the relationship of food to other income. The index is arbitrary in that it relies only on income as the criterion of poverty, but income statistics happen to be the only ones currently available on a regular basis. If we want to be able to apply our standard to see how many and what kinds of families fall below it, we have no choice but to base it on whatever statistics are available.

### Criticisms of the index

A lot has been said about the limitations of the Social Security Administration's poverty index. Critics point out that the concept refers only to current income and ignores assets and other money income. It specifies no list of goods and services

[1] Mollie Orshansky, "Measuring Poverty," *The Social Welfare Forum, 1965* (New York, Columbia University Press, 1965).

[2] See U.S. Department of Agriculture publications: *Food Consumption of Urban Households, With an Appraisal of Method,* Agriculture Information Bulletin 132, October 1954; *Food Consumption in Households in the United States,* Household Food Consumption Survey, 1955, Report 1, December 1956; and *Family Food Plans and Food Costs,* Home Economics Research Report 20, November 1962.

other than food, yet we know that for many families, particularly Negro families and those with several children, the cost of housing may be even more critical. Our index assumes that if the food expenditure is cut to a minimum below the level that the average family with more money spends, everything else would be cut in proportion; yet it is obvious this is not always possible, at least not for housing. Some people argue that the index makes no adjustment and no allowance for income in kind, except for farmers. Some people find that the index is weak because it ignores year-to-year changes in income. Others do not like it because it ignores life's nonmonetary satisfactions.

All of these criticisms have merit, but let us start from bottom to top. If money alone will not solve poverty, without it nothing else will work either! It is still a necessary if not a sufficient condition. It should also be remembered that in a money economy, housing, food, and medical care received free are not substitutes for things for which people must have cash.

To ignore assets is one of the more serious defects, but the income data that are available regularly from the Current Population Survey provide no asset data. In any case, studies by Dorothy Projector and Gertrude Weiss show that except among the aged, there are few low income households with lots of assets.[3]

New studies, from which we are awaiting the results, will tell us the asset holdings of poor families. We did prorate assets when we were surveying the aged in 1962; it made little difference in the income position of most aged families.[4] The survey was a very nice statistical artifact, but it was based on several assumptions which were not applicable to families other than the aged, and one of them would not even work for the aged. We assumed all assets could be converted into an annuity at 4 percent. We then worked out average length of life by age and sex, and joint survivorship rates for husbands and wives, to estimate how much more money a person would have if he used up the annuity in the remaining years of life. We had to assume that family size would never increase, and that there would be either two, or one, or no persons, as the mates died. We had to assume that whatever assets a person had at the beginning of the study would not be replenished once they were used up. This, too, would be an unreasonable assumption for younger families. Even for the aged, it was somewhat unrealistic. Because if assets are going to be prorated, why should one person have to start prorating at age 65 and another, because he was 83 when he came under study, not have to do it until now? In addition, some forms of assets, despite what economists think, are not regarded as negotiable by people who own them.

[3] Dorothy S. Projector and Gertrude S. Weiss, *Survey of Financial Characteristics of Consumers* (Washington, Federal Reserve System, 1966).

[4] See Mollie Orshansky, "Who's Who Among the Poor," *Social Security Bulletin*, July 1965.

### Income flow and consumption

With respect to the temporary income thesis, we really do not know much about income flow of families and how it affects consumption. Farmer and business families, perhaps more than others, are subject to the hazards of planned and unplanned poverty, because they can use their income in 1 year for their business and improve their prospects for the future. As for the argument that nonmoney income should be included in determining who is poor, one can say with confidence that inclusion of all the free medical care and the food stamps received by the poor and of all the benefits that go to the middle class, including health insurance benefits, expense accounts, vacations, free tuition, and commodity discounts, would hardly change the result; nonmoney income, like income tax benefits, would go mainly to the nonpoor. Thus, the full effect of incorporating these benefits into the income distribution, if we were honest, might be to skew it even more than now; and since poverty is relative, the poverty line would have to be moved up.

It is very difficult to know from the mere figures representing family expenditure and consumption patterns which actions are taken consciously, as a matter of free choice, and which reflect the long-term constraint of insufficient funds not only within a family but in a community. Some have questioned why we do not make regional or organizational differentials in the poverty line except for farm versus nonfarm families. One reason is the lack of evidence that, at the poverty line or near it, with a very small discretionary spending allowance, there is much difference from one area to another in the cost of living.

The value of consumption appears to be superior to income as a measure of poverty status. Of course, income standards are chosen only because they are to be used as a proxy for consumption potential. Shifting to consumption as a reference unit does not eliminate problems of measurement and definition. It merely exchanges old problems for new ones. For example, the consumer expenditure studies, on which we depend so much, tell us about total purchase commitments rather than cash outlay. "Buy now, pay later" may be on every television and radio program, but government expenditure schedules still do not acknowledge them. Also we do not have, in most of our surveys, the total consumer potential in terms of inventory of stocks on hand at home, as well as current purchasing. In addition, we still face the question of how to value goods received without direct outlay. A retail value—if it is known—might be a good measure, although often (as in the case of food) the items do not replace what the family actually buys.

Also, if you are thinking of counting the value of an owned home in the income-consumption matrix, should it be set at a fair return for investment, as economists often do? Or, at the saving, if any, over what a neighbor in similar circumstances pays for rent? Space standards for owned housing are usually set much higher than for rented housing—a six-room owned house may be compared with a three-room rental unit. There remain a host of problems of arbitrary selection: If, for instance, one category is used as a proxy for all others, as we use food, the question is which category should it be? In the Social Security Administration's case, which food pattern should be used?

## Alternative poverty measures

There is another method of defining poverty, which is now often discussed. In place of complicated methods of deciding on a budget of one form or another, it substitutes the statement that families are called poor if their incomes fall below a stated proportion of median income at a given time. This "formula" has the virture of simplicity and uniformity; it also has a serious deficiency in that it sets one relative measure of need for all kinds of families. Thus, it becomes very difficult to devise a measure which has this kind of simplicity and yet to provide for rapid progress and attention to the groups that we worry about. Under such a scheme, they need receive no special attention as long as they maintain their current relative position.

The break-even point was used some time ago. This would select as the critical income point the amount at which, on the average, expenditures by families matched income, so that there would be no deficit and no savings. Now, however, with the use of credit and installment buying and the never-ending list of wants, deficit is found among a good many families of relatively high incomes. At low income points, some families cannot spend more than their income would permit because they cannot get credit.

In any case, there is no one method that does not suffer from some difficulty that renders it less usable for some purposes than for others.

## Uses of the present index

One of the difficulties encountered in the use of the poverty index is that the data used are not adequate for the applications. However, we feel that the directional differences among population groups with poverty risk, and the relative orders of magnitude of these differences, are meaningful even if the absolute numbers are weak. They can tell us about special problems in disadvantaged areas such as the South, or slums versus suburbs, and the difficulties of minority groups. They can help us heal the sores economic growth alone cannot heal. The index we now have has pointed out little that people might not have otherwise suspected, but it has served to give us some broad gages of the severity of the problem.

Despite what Social Security and other programs have done, one finds, upon ranking persons by age and poverty, that the aged did not improve in terms of poverty status as much as the young did over the last 7 years. Although we knew that there must be some people who worked and yet were poor, many of us tended to equate poverty among young families with either having too many children (whatever too many means) or with unemployment. As it turns out, a substantial number of families are in poverty even when the man works all year. Though most large families that are poor would obviously be somewhat better off if they had fewer children, many of them have so little income that they would be poor even then. Present surveys of poverty and low income are based on the Current Population Survey sample and thus exclude persons in institutions, many of whom are among the poorest. They also measure poverty on the basis of the total income of all related persons living together. Thus, in the families where people have to double up because an old woman has no money of her own, or a mother and child do not have money of their own, we mask the fact that this is a group of persons who do not have the essentials for independent living.

Wherever the poverty line is, there are two things that ought to be done to it—and we really do not know how to do them. First, how to adjust a poverty line to conform to changes in productivity. Second, even if the poverty line is adjusted for the rise of productivity, how to measure the impact of price change on consumers' living at or below the margin.

### Income maintenance programs

The Economic Opportunity Act has authorized several new mechanisms which we continually think of as the antipoverty program. But the aggregate poverty gap, which in 1967 was about $9.7 billion, is the deficiency in income relative to need for the whole group of poor people. Taking into account all of the people's sources of income, including the income they receive from public support programs, such as public assistance, veterans programs, and unemployment insurance, one must say that most of the antipoverty effort, in terms of putting money into the hands of people, is still made under programs other than those of the Office of Economic Opportunity.

We have, for the first time, information on income collected by the Census Bureau for 1965, showing separately, in addition to earnings, the amount of the family's income received from social security, public assistance, and various other programs. Obviously, the data are not entirely correct. We suspect, for example, that the numbers we get on public assistance are an understatement, rather than overstatement, for a variety of reasons. We also know that we do not have enough information about the timing and the overlap of the programs. Even if the family identifies the program of aid and can give the appropriate information at the time of the census interview, all that is published is a net figure for the year. With the data we have, we cannot take into account the fact that a person may be getting public assistance for 2 months waiting for a social security claim to be processed, or may be getting money from unemployment insurance before appealing for public assistance.

It is a revelation to find that despite the remarks we hear on how we do not want to give handouts to the poor, getting money from the government in the form of a regular monthly check is really not unusual. It is becoming almost a universal experience. Almost 19.5 million households reported in 1965 that they had received some government payments. For the aged, it was mostly social security; for younger families, particularly for the women and children, it was mostly public assistance. Even with all their limitations, these programs have changed the poverty profile a good deal.

In 1966, there were 10.9 million households in poverty (counting one-person units as well as families as a household). Using the 1965 relationships, one may assume that the number of poor households would have been 16 million had there not been programs of income maintenance. In other words, instead of 1 in every 5 households being poor, 1 in every 4 would have been poor.

Only two-thirds of all households that would be poor with no public payments receive any help. Of those poor as we now count them—after all payments—fully half have received no help at all from a public income program. Of those who do receive public assistance, 5 out of 6 remain poor after they get assistance. By contrast, social security, less restrictive in other income that beneficiaries may have, lifts more than half the household poor without their payments into the nonpoor ranks. Thus, though existing public welfare programs do much to lessen the number of poor they could do much more. It is clear that for many already receiving help from public programs it is the degree of that help that must be increased if they are to escape poverty, but new programs or extensions of existing ones are required for those now in poverty and receiving no help at all.

# Part II
# The Nature of Poverty and Responses to It

# [5]

*Jnl Soc. Pol.* 7, 2, 129–56 

# Analyses in the Social Division of Welfare*

ADRIAN SINFIELD†

ABSTRACT

Richard Titmuss's 'The Social Division of Welfare' has been neglected as a framework for assessing changes in social policy and society. The analytical, as opposed to the descriptive, value of the original essay becomes more evident, and more significant, when the relations between the social divisions of labour and welfare are examined in terms of the distribution of benefits and services through the public, fiscal and occupational systems; the growth and differential recognition of needs and 'man-made' states of dependency; the variations in the primary objectives of welfare including control; the interrelationship of the different systems and the ways in which they legitimate the existing social structure. This paper seeks to show that, combined with a consideration of power and the state, time and security and the institutions of capitalism, the ideas of the original essay encourage a more dynamic analysis of the impact of the three systems of welfare on society than has so far been attempted.

---

'The Social Division of Welfare: Some Reflections on the Search for Equity' was delivered by Richard Titmuss as the sixth Eleanor Rathbone Memorial Lecture on 1 December 1955, at the University of Birmingham. Subsequently republished as the second chapter of *Essays on 'The Welfare State'*,[1] it has probably become the most cited paper in the British literature of social policy and planning, and possibly in the United States as well. Indeed many new students, who find references to it scattered throughout reading lists and studies, may come to see it as one of the most established parts of

* This article is based on discussions over the last three years, and in particular on a paper given to a British Sociological Association study group seminar in February 1975. My attempts to develop these themes have been helped by comments from colleagues and students, and I particularly wish to acknowledge my debt to A. B. Atkinson, Malcolm Cross, Joan Higgins, Dennis Marsden, S. M. Miller, R. A. Pinker, Garth Plowman, Giovanni Sgritta, Dorothy Sinfield, Peter Townsend and Alan Walker. I hope that this revised text shows the benefit of their always thoughtful and often trenchant criticisms.

† Senior Lecurer in Sociology, University of Essex.

1 R. M. Titmuss, 'The Social Division of Welfare: Some Reflections on the Search for Equity', Liverpool University Press, Liverpool, 1956; republished in R. M. Titmuss, *Essays on 'The Welfare State'*, Allen and Unwin, London, 1958, pp. 34–55.

the conventional wisdom of social policy and gain little sense of its original impact and the intellectual excitement it generated.

The essay discussed the growth of 'essentially three different systems of "social services": Social Welfare, Fiscal Welfare and Occupational Welfare'.[2] The first is the traditional area of social administration, the five services of 'the welfare state' which 'are treated as "social service" expenditure since they represent flows of payment through the central government account'.[3] I have described these as the 'public system of welfare' or 'public welfare' because 'social welfare' does not seem to denote public provision sufficiently clearly.

Fiscal welfare was described by Titmuss in 1955 as 'allowances and reliefs from income tax, though providing similar benefits and expressing a similar purpose in the recognition of dependent needs [as social or public welfare which] are not however treated as social service expenditure'.[4] The tax saving must be treated as a transfer payment in any analysis of the distribution and redistribution of resources. By 1973 Titmuss had extended this 'in total, to reliefs, allowances and deductions under direct systems of taxation, central and local, and such "taxes" as National Insurance (or social security) so-called contributions'.[5] Occupational welfare covers benefits received by an employee through or as a result of his employment over and beyond the public benefits such as national insurance. It includes the range of services and resources somewhat dismissively known as 'fringe benefits' as well as much industrial welfare provision.

Although these three distinct systems have become a part of social policy vocabulary for classification or description, I have gained the impression from some teachers and students that, whatever its original merits, the ideas behind this particular essay are now somewhat tired and out of date. By contrast I have found myself forced back time and time again to this particular paper for a framework with which to analyse the full extent of changes in policy over the last decade. This essay in particular has always seemed to me to justify Richard Titmuss's reputation as a seminal thinker in social policy.[6] At the same time, to continue the metaphor, the seed has not been sufficiently systematically and thoroughly cultivated, and in the two decades following its original planting we have done very little to develop and improve the strain.

[2] R. M. Titmuss, *Social Policy: An Introduction*, Allen and Unwin, London, 1974, p. 137.
[3] Titmuss, *Essays on 'The Welfare State'*, p. 44. [4] *Ibid.*
[5] Titmuss, *Social Policy*, pp. 136–7.
[6] For a wider discussion of Titmuss's work see Paul Wilding, 'Richard Titmuss and Social Welfare', *Social and Economic Administration*, 10:3 (1976); D. A. Reisman, *Richard Titmuss: Welfare and Society*, Heinemann, London, 1977; Robert Pinker, 'Social Policy and Social Justice', *Journal of Social Policy*, 3:1 (1974); and Margaret Gowing, 'Richard Morris Titmuss', *Proceedings of the British Academy*, Vol. LXI, 1975.

In this article I aim to outline the core elements of the 1955 paper and, in developing them, to indicate why the concept of the social division of welfare must be included in any sociological analysis of social policy as 'the underlying as well as the professed rationale by which social institutions and groups' are developed or created 'to ensure social preservation or development'.[7] In the final sections I will attempt to show that the interaction of the different themes in Titmuss's original paper deserves much closer examination and sustained analysis, especially when combined with certain other key sociological concepts that have received insufficient attention from most of us who are engaged in the study of social policy.

## THE SOCIAL DIVISIONS OF WELFARE AND LABOUR

The very concept of a social division of welfare underlines the link with the stratification system of a society and the need to relate analyses of the two. The division of welfare, observed Titmuss, derives not from any difference in intended function or aim but 'from an organisational division of method, which, in the main, is related to the division of labour in complex, individuated societies'.[8] With some exceptions in *Income Distribution and Social Change* and his introduction to Tawney's *Equality*,[9] Titmuss himself never systematically explored or developed the point which he made in the original essay. The developments in policy in recent years, much more than research, have made the significance of the link much clearer. Others who have employed the concept have generally confined themselves to illustrating the division of welfare and have shown little concern for exploring it further and in particular investigating its causes and its relation to the division of labour. Both the initial causes and any subsequent factors which serve to perpetuate, reinforce or modify developing patterns deserve closer analysis than they have received.

This examination is all the more important because the relation of the division of welfare to the division of labour is not invariable. Not only has it changed over time but differences in this relationship clearly exist between different societies.[10] The provision of both medical care and income support is now somewhat differently related to the division of labour in Britain than it was seventy, or even thirty, years ago. And neither then nor today does

7 Peter Townsend, *Sociology and Social Policy*, Allen Lane, London, 1975, p. 6.

8 Titmuss, *Essays on 'The Welfare State'*, p. 42. Titmuss's quoting of Durkheim on the social division of labour should not be taken to exclude any reference to the class structure by the former, despite the neglect of class conflict; see note 64 below.

9 R. M. Titmuss, *Income Distribution and Social Change*, Allen and Unwin, London, 1962; and his introduction to Richard H. Tawney, *Equality*, fifth edition, Allen and Unwin, London, 1964.

10 Harold L. Wilensky, *The Welfare State and Equality*, University of California Press, Berkeley, 1975.

the connection resemble that which exists in the provision of health care or social security for different categories of white- and blue-collar workers in many European countries,[11] let alone the many separate and stratified forms of medical care found in the majority of Latin American countries, where occupational, industrial and geographic, as well as straightforwardly economic, factors may determine access to particular delivery systems.[12] Again, despite the shared inheritance of what Jacobus Ten Broek described as 'the dual system of family law', including the Elizabethan Poor Law, and the frequent interchange of ideas since then, the organization of income support and family welfare in Britain and the United States corresponds in a different manner to the social division of labour in each country.[13]

The explanation of such differences presents an important and exciting challenge to the sociology of social policy. Attempts to explore the causes of such variations among for example basically capitalist societies will advance the understanding of not only the welfare systems but also the class structure of these societies. Indeed a major limitation in our knowledge of capitalism has been the failure to investigate more systematically its varying form in different societies. Equally we need studies of command as well as market economies, but there are clear dangers in comparison – generally very impressionistic – if we take one country from each group – usually the United States and the USSR. This seems particularly prone to the risk of reinforcing, rather than questioning and refining, stereotypes of different forms of society.

Even within any one society, however, a careful analysis of the distribution of resources, security, status and power through the social division of welfare would help us to understand much more thoroughly the operation of those mechanisms and systems of distribution and redistribution that generate and maintain social, political and economic inequality. And, in examining the relationship between the social divisions of welfare and labour, it is necessary to bear in mind that with increasing growth in all its systems welfare in turn has effects for the occupational structure and cannot simply be treated as a result, let alone a symptom, of a particular social and economic system.

[11] J. J. Dupeyroux, *Evolution et Tendances des Systèmes de Sécurité Sociale*, CECA, Luxembourg, 1966.

[12] Eleven systems are identified by Milton Roemer, 'Medical Care in Integrated Health Programmes of Latin America', *Medical Care*, July–September 1963.

[13] Jacobus Ten Broek, *Family Law and the Poor*, edited by J. F. Handler, Greenwood, Westport, 1971 (originally published as 'California's Dual System of Family Law: Its Origin, Development and Present Status'); and Samuel Mencher, *From Poor Law to Poverty Program*, University of Pittsburgh Press, Pittsburgh, 1969. Adrian Sinfield, 'Unemployment and Inequality', University of Essex, July 1976, presented at the annual conference of the Social Administration Association, compares income maintenance for the unemployed in Britain and the United States.

For example, the differential distribution of and access to economic and non-economic resources through the three systems of welfare may obviously enlarge or restrict the opportunities of different groups for maintaining their own class position or achieving upward mobility. At the same time the growth of the three systems has been a major factor in the proliferation of professional and administrative services with, for example, the greater employment of civil servants, accountants, tax lawyers, social workers and industrial relations and personnel management, with supporting clerical and many other lower-paid and lower-status workers, including cleaners, catering staff and porters. In ways such as these the social division of welfare has led to yet further differentiation and specificity in the division of labour, and any analysis of the impact of growing 'welfare state' employment alone will only give a limited and distorted picture of the changes that have occurred.

## THE GROWTH OF NEEDS AND 'MAN-MADE' STATES OF DEPENDENCY[14]

The major ways in which Richard Titmuss pursued the relationship between the two social divisions are to be found in his emphasis on the growth of needs with the division of labour and on the very different forms that recognition of these has taken in the three systems of welfare. More states of social dependency have both emerged and been recognized with the greater division of labour, and much of Titmuss's writing underlines the point that the ability to participate in society depends upon more and greater needs being met in increasingly complex and diversified industrial societies.

In attacking the myths of a 'welfare state' that massively reduced or even reversed existing inequalities, he argued that the proliferating benefits or services 'for many consumers. . .are not essentially benefits or increments to welfare at all: they represent partial compensations for disservices, for social costs and social insecurities which are the product of a rapidly changing industrial-urban society'.[15] Martin Rein put part of the problem very succinctly in 1970 – 'Growth creates dependency.'[16] Since then we have become more aware of the problems, and re-emergent or new needs, resulting from the lack of growth and economic decline.

The analysis of 'socially caused diswelfares. . .part of the price we pay to some people for bearing part of the costs of other people's progress' makes clear a very important policy distinction between the identification of

[14] Titmuss, *Essays on 'The Welfare State'*, p. 43.

[15] R. M. Titmuss, *Commitment to Welfare*, Allen and Unwin, London, 1968, p. 133.

[16] Martin Rein, *Social Policy: Issues of Choice and Change*, Random House, New York, 1970, ch. 5.

causal agents and the compensation of the bearer of social costs.[17] Helping the latter does not have to depend upon the tracking down and charging of the former; the two sets of action may be separated and costs not be left to 'lie where they fall'.[18] In establishing this point in the face of opposition from those defending the individualistic private market,[19] Titmuss and subsequent writers have not examined sufficiently rigorously and comprehensively the total impact of benefit and loss allocation together with the causes of diswelfares. They have tended to focus on the costs and those who bear them, and consideration of the causes has usually been limited to the policy implications of whether the individual is responsible for his position or whether it is 'socially caused' – for example, is he 'voluntarily' unemployed or redundant?[20]

If the individual is not seen as entirely to blame for his situation of dependency, then the concern has been with the appropriate method and extent of compensation. The causes of his predicament have generally been somewhat vaguely assumed to be the inevitable results of economic growth or decline, or the workings of the industrial process. These have generally been taken as given, and there has been little attempt to examine why the greater division of labour has taken a particular form or how it has been brought about, or to consider the influence of business or governmental decisions. In consequence discussion has come closer to the 'industrialism' thesis, with its implications of technological determinism, than anyone would, I think, care to admit.[21]

The implication for policy has been a relatively unquestioning acceptance of the transfer of many industrial or production costs to society with a consequent growth in the public welfare system to meet them. The socialization of the costs of industry reduces financial burdens upon employers, investors and shareholders, while they and their supporters tend to be among the strongest critics of any expansion in public expenditure. The particular significance of this for analyses of the social division of welfare will be discussed in the final sections of this paper.

[17] Titmuss, *Commitment to Welfare*, p. 133; and K. William Kapp, *The Social Costs of Business Enterprise*, Asia Publishing House, New York, 1963, especially chs 10 and 14.

[18] Titmuss, *Commitment to Welfare*, p. 117.

[19] In many states in the United States recipients of unemployment insurance benefit may be disqualified for long periods, if not the duration of their unemployment, if the cause of their leaving is not 'connected with the work or attributable to the employer'. Sinfield, *op. cit.* p. 15.

[20] Michael J. Hill, 'Can we Distinguish Voluntary from Involuntary Unemployment?', G. D. N. Worswick (ed.), *The Concept and Measurement of Involuntary Unemployment*, Allen and Unwin, London, 1976, ch. 9; and Sinfield, *The Long-Term Unemployed*, OECD, Paris, 1968, pp. 38–46.

[21] Clark Kerr, John T. Dunlop, Frederick H. Harbison and Charles A. Myers, *Industrialism and Industrial Man*, Harvard University Press, Cambridge, Massachusetts, 1960.

THE DIFFERENTIAL RECOGNITION OF NEEDS

The growth of states of dependency with the continuing social division of labour becomes all the more significant when similar needs are identified, recognized, defined and met differently in the separate systems of the social division of welfare. This point was not pursued as vigorously as others in 1955 because Titmuss was more concerned to establish the similarity of the different systems to a generally unreceptive audience than to reflect on their differences. Since then this argument has become more widely, though by no means universally, accepted.

A persisting example of differential recognition of need is the variety in form and extent of help available through the three systems to workers losing their jobs, and this shows too the overlap and integration of aid through these systems.[22] National insurance unemployment benefit for one year, increased for any dependants, is intended to be the basic public scheme, but for many years it has supported little more than half of those registered as unemployed at any one time and has now fallen well below this. Its earnings-related supplement, intended to ease the hardship of the first six months out of work, continues to be received by a fifth or less of those in the official counts of the unemployed.

Supplementary allowances are available when these benefits cease or fall below scale rates; also increased for dependants, they generally include a payment for rent and rates. Together with any other means-tested benefits for which they are eligible and a possible tax rebate, this is the extent of any entitlement for workers with less than two years' continuous service with the same employer. Their benefits may be reduced, and until mid-1975 a low-paid worker with a wife and children to support might have found that he was wage-stopped beneath the supplementary allowance scale rates.

Occupational welfare has provided redundancy payments for many years, and since 1965 there has been statutory provision financed jointly by individual employers and a fund to which all employers contribute. The amount received is determined by past earnings, age and length of service, with a maximum of £2,400, and it is payable whether or not the recipient finds another job at once or leaves the labour force. In addition many, and

22 For much of the material here and below I am drawing on a working paper, 'Transmitted Deprivation and the Social Division of Welfare', prepared for the Department of Health and Social Security and Social Science Research Council Working Party on Transmitted Deprivation in November 1976, which I hope to publish as a book. Some of this material has been included in Alan Deacon and Adrian Sinfield, 'The Unemployed, Policy and Public Debate: The Significance of the Scrounging Controversy', SSRC Workshop on Social Security, London, 18 March 1977; and Adrian Sinfield, 'Inequalities Beyond the Fringe', *Low Pay Bulletin*, no. 9, June 1976. For discussion of the experience of unemployment see Adrian Sinfield, 'The Social Meaning of Unemployment', in Kathleen Jones, Muriel Brown and Sally Baldwin (eds), *The Year Book of Social Policy in Britain 1976*, Routledge and Kegan Paul, London, 1977.

possibly most, firms pay higher amounts to certain groups of employees or staff and allow the retention of various fringe benefits, including for example the purchase of a company car on favourable terms. Some payments may be quite substantial, but we have only very limited data on the amounts involved and the number of recipients.

The benefits through fiscal welfare may also be considerable but again are only partially known. All national insurance, supplementary allowances and statutory redundancy payments are tax-free; this may bring not only a significant direct gain but also a bonus in terms of an income-tax rebate because of the cumulative PAYE (pay-as-you-earn) system over the tax year, which is unaffected by any benefits received. Less well known is the fact that 'payments on retirement or removal from office or payment' are tax-free up to £5,000; in addition the spreading of payments over a number of years, 'top-slicing', may substantially reduce the amount of tax payable.

Unlike the public benefits and allowances, this exemption applies even if the recipient has been sacked and not made redundant. It may act as an incentive, or even a bribe, to leave of one's own accord rather than being fired, and of course in either case a worker would probably be disqualified from national insurance benefits and would have any supplementary allowance reduced. But so long as the employer's payment on leaving is *not* for services rendered, it is tax-free; and of course all such costs may also be set against a company's liability to corporation tax on any profits, leaving the taxpayer to subsidize this operation in two ways.

For some senior executives and company directors protection is so great that they may be regarded as virtually 'fireproof'. Service contracts and agreements in the occupational system reflect a perception of the needs of those made redundant which is very different to the recognition given in the public programmes. One agreement in 1970 would have provided £450,000 among eight executive directors if they had been replaced, another gave a director £9,000 a year until he was sixty-five and £3,500 a year until his death, and many include provision for a percentage share in profits and some automatic protection against inflation.[23] With care a considerable subsidy of such costs can be arranged through the fiscal system of personal and company taxation. Yet our knowledge of the provision, let alone the subsidies, is even more limited than our knowledge of those already mentioned. These contracts do not have to be approved by, or even drawn to the attention of, the shareholders of a company, let alone made public.

The inequality in the visibility of benefits is an important and integral part of the social division of welfare. The hierarchy of benefits moreover is clearly considerable, providing very different amounts, under a wide range

[23] For further illustrations, see Sinfield, 'Inequalities Beyond the Fringe'.

of conditions that may reinforce or strip the recipients of their status. Even the official reports of the Supplementary Benefits Commission now draw attention to the relatively greater poverty among unemployed families dependent on their support, and the very limited extent of discretionary help that they receive.[24] 'The very poorest', as Robert Pinker has observed, 'will become the founder members of the fourth division of the new welfare league',[25] and there is a strong temptation to introduce the idea of 'social security classes' to make more evident the ways in which particular benefits may affect the resources and social status of recipients.[26]

## VARIATIONS IN THE PRIMARY OBJECTIVE OF WELFARE

The substantial differences in the extent and form of help and the ways in which needs are recognized in large part reflect the wide variation in the primary aims of provision both among and within the different systems, and this may occur even when the states of dependency recognized are remarkably similar. The sharpest contrast is probably between selective or means-tested public provision and the 'fringe benefits' of occupational welfare.

With the much greater growth of these, which Titmuss described as the 'concealed multipliers of occupational success',[27] there has been increasing awareness of the opportunities provided for just that. Today employers are much readier and staff more willing to use fringe benefits to maintain or even increase inequalities for executives and other salaried workers when pay differentials are too conspicuous or are being narrowed, and these benefits have been used more and more to retain managers or key workers tempted by offers of higher pay elsewhere. These developments have become increasingly important during wage or income freezes and have gained further significance as inflation has eroded wages faster than some provisions in kind. Although the very limited evidence indicates that such advantages are generally more available and more valuable for the better paid, they are also being extended to some manual workers.[28]

24 For example Supplementary Benefits Commission, *Annual Report 1976*, Cmnd 6910, HMSO, London, September 1977; and David Donnison, reported in *Social Work Today*, 20 September 1977.

25 Pinker, *op. cit.* p. 14.

26 See the attractive idea of 'housing classes' in John Rex and Robert E. Moore, *Race, Community and Conflict*, Oxford University Press, Oxford, 1967; but see also the important critique by Roy Haddon, 'A Minority in a Welfare State Society', *The New Atlantis*, 2:1 (1970), 125–33.

27 Titmuss, *Essays on 'The Welfare State'*, p. 52.

28 'Never Mind the Pay, Feel the Perks', *The Sunday People*, 8 December 1974. The widening of inequalities by fringe benefits is documented and analysed in Philippa Bevan, *The Growth of Fringe Benefit Provision: Causes and Consequences for Social Inequality and Social Integration*, D.Phil. thesis, Oxford University, submitted in August 1977. Jill

There are of course other reasons for occupational welfare, many of which have a greater or more overt element of control in them – for example, to introduce or extend benefits to maintain good relations in the industry; to promote company loyalty or at least reduce staff turnover; to resist trade unions and increase support for staff associations or clubs; to bring about greater productivity or to buy support for other measures calculated to achieve that, including changes of work routines and shifts, a switch to payment or piece-work rates and staff reductions by redundancy or natural wastage.

The variety of functions which benefits and services may perform was often emphasized by Titmuss, perhaps most forcefully in an American journal in 1965: 'Welfare can serve different masters. A multitude of sins may be committed in its appealing name.'[29] Although the first example he then offered was 'a form of social control', he gave relatively little attention to this function in any of the systems and appeared to play it down in some of his later writings on public means-tested benefits and services.[30] Curiously, his brief but vivid consideration of the controls exerted on worker and family in one of the more neglected of his essays on 'the welfare state', 'Industrialisation and the Family', does not explore the ways in which welfare may mitigate or sustain the tensions engendered by the industrial process and the social division of labour.[31]

The current debate on public welfare as control has gained most momentum from experiences outside the professional study of social policy. Those academics and others who have taken part have tended to learn of the controlling role of much public welfare from personal experience and participation in political and pressure group activities. This marks a belated shift away from the tendency to see social policies as something for 'them' rather than 'us', and a reaction to the 'corridors of power' role that has often lapsed into a position remarkably similar to that of the colonial administrator's expert and aide.[32]

The study of our activities as 'welfare colonialism' needs more careful attention than it has received and should include, amongst others, a con-

---

Bernstein at the University of Columbia is at present studying the growth of non-wage employment benefits in Britain and the United States. See also note 22 above.

[29] R. M. Titmuss, 'Poverty versus Inequality: Diagnosis', *Nation*, February 1965, p. 132; see also Titmuss, *Commitment to Welfare*, chs V and XI.

[30] For example R. M. Titmuss, 'The New Guardians of the Poor', in Shirley Jenkins (ed.), *Social Security in International Perspective*, Columbia University Press, New York, 1969. One major question for any biographer of Titmuss must be the effect on his writing of his work with the Supplementary Benefits Commission.

[31] Titmuss, *Essays on 'The Welfare State'*, ch. 6.

[32] Jean-Pierre Launay catches one aspect of this nicely in his description of the absolute poverty measure as 'la définition patronale' (the bosses' definition), in *La France Sous-développée*, Dunod Actualité, Paris, 1970, p. 1.

sideration of the influence of the optimistic proponents of the 'convergence' and 'end of ideology' theses on those who are engaged in policy and planning.[33] While such views have become the 'Aunt Sallies' of many undergraduate sociology courses, they have continued to serve as legitimators of the growth-before-welfare argument that treats all public welfare as beneficent and egalitarian. Much of the functionalist school's teaching diverted attention from the issues of welfare, conflict and control, probably because those who wrote of welfare policies were generally striving to establish the legitimacy of an 'institutional' system of welfare against the liberal economists who would only accept its 'residual' role.[34] Subsequent consideration of the regulation of the poor by public welfare[35] still needs to be related to controls in the other systems, and more widely to the social division of labour and welfare, in order to become more firmly located in the study of 'social power and advantage'.[36]

## THE INTERRELATIONSHIP OF THE SYSTEMS OF WELFARE

In many respects the different systems are 'separate and distinctive attempts to counter and to compensate for the growth of dependency in modern society. . .simultaneously enlarging and consolidating the area of social inequality'.[37] Their independence can be seen in the ways in which over the years governments have acted to strengthen one system while restricting another. One major effect, for example, of the last Conservative government was to encourage growth in fiscal, and even more in occupational, welfare at the same time as it held still or even ran down the public provision. The function of the *Housing Finance Act* 1972, with its complete disregard of the revenue forgone by tax subsidies to owner-occupiers, and the boost to private and occupational pensions offered by the *Social Security Act* 1973 are more obvious examples of measures which had considerable implications for the reallocation of resources between the different systems.[38]

33 See for example Daniel Bell, *The End of Ideology*, Collier, New York, 1961; Seymour Martin Lipset, *Political Man*, Heinemann, London, 1960; and Kerr *et al.*, *op. cit.*; and, for a more carefully qualified statement, Gunnar Myrdal, *Beyond the Welfare State*, Bantam Books, New York, 1967.

34 See for example Harold L. Wilensky and Charles N. Lebeaux, who introduced these two terms, in *Industrial Society and Social Welfare*, revised edition, Free Press, Glencoe, 1965. For a critique of the functionalist influence on trends in social policy in the public system, see John H. Goldthorpe, 'The Development of Social Policy in England, 1800–1914', *Transactions of the Fifth World Congress of Sociology*, Vol. IV, 1962.

35 See for example Frances Fox Piven and Richard A. Cloward, *Regulating the Poor: The Functions of Public Welfare*, Tavistock Publications, London, 1972. For a vigorous critique, see Joan Higgins, 'Regulating the Poor Revisited' (pp. 189–98 below).

36 John H. Goldthorpe, 'Social Inequality and Social Integration in Modern Britain', in Dorothy Wedderburn (ed.), *Poverty, Inequality and Class Structure*, Cambridge University Press, Cambridge, 1974, p. 218.

37 Titmuss, *Essays on 'The Welfare State'*, p. 55.

Recently the interaction of the systems has become much greater. As tax thresholds, particularly for families, have not been adjusted sufficiently for inflation, the income tax system has become a 'mass tax' including many on low incomes who are receiving or eligible for public means-tested benefits, and the poverty trap has been sharpened by the ending of reduced tax rates.[39] Concern over the 'wealth trap' of the managers who regard high taxation as a disincentive to business initiative has led to greater support through occupational welfare and pressure for more favourable tax treatment of these benefits. These are only limited illustrations of the ways in which today the systems may overlap, conflict or even cancel each other out, but until relatively recently their separate impact was easier to identify.

A historical analysis of the social division of welfare is long overdue, but even the patchy picture currently available underlines the separate origins of the systems. Although there may now be increasing overlap and sometimes planned integration, public welfare has often been the latest to be developed or expanded. Its role has consisted of extending to new groups some limited support of a kind which others have already been receiving through fiscal or occupational benefits. One instance already mentioned is the extension of redundancy payments, which existed in the occupational sector and were supported by special concessions through the fiscal system well before they were introduced in a state scheme.

In one comparative review of industrial welfare the development of many facilities appeared to have followed much the same pattern across a number of countries. First, larger companies, often multinational and generally based on capital-intensive technologies with highly trained personnel, or geographically isolated from any provision in cities, introduced services for their own workers, or special categories of them. Often as a result of tax incentives from the government, the benefits were gradually extended by these and other firms to more workers, their dependants, and even other members of the community. Specific legislative requirements applying to a wider range of employers and industries generally came at a later stage, and actual public provision last of all.[40]

Attempts to explore such patterns more systematically, however, come

38 See for example Michael Meacher, 'The Coming Class Struggle', *New Statesman*, 4 January 1974; and, for a case study of pensions, see Titmuss, *Social Policy*, ch. 8. Less evident examples can be found in certain aspects of the tax credits proposal and many other areas of policy, not only from 1970 to 1974 but also during the Labour administrations of 1964–70; see Peter Townsend and Nicholas Bosanquet (eds), *Labour and Inequality*, Fabian Society, London, 1972.

39 Titmuss, *Social Policy*, p. 126; see also Frank Field, Molly Meacher and Chris Pond, *To Him Who Hath* (a study of poverty and taxation), Penguin Books, Harmondsworth, 1977.

40 See United Nations, Department of Economic and Social Affairs, *Industrial Welfare*, United Nations, New York, 1971, ch. 3, for summary and references.

up against the social construction of the division of welfare and the differentiation and segmentation which have occurred. Comparing the provision of personal social services through industrial and occupational welfare with the public system illustrates these difficulties well. Although often recognizing the same states of dependency, the services may meet needs very differently, employing different categories of staff who have separate training and professional associations. Furthermore, the histories of these services have been written from very different and often conflicting perspectives by writers who appear to have little awareness of programmes in the other systems of welfare. Differential treatment, support and control of separate groups with often very similar needs become all the more difficult to identify.[41]

It is important to point out that these factors are not simply methodological irritants for the would-be researcher. They are part of the social division of welfare which serves to constrain our perceptions of the distributive and redistributive mechanisms of all resources in society. In general the analysis of the public system has been most systematically carried out. One outstanding example is the wealth of discussion and documentation of the development of subsidies for local authority housing as compared with the very limited account of aid to house-buyers through fiscal concessions, which have been taken so much for granted that Sabine's history of the tax system only very briefly mentions their introduction at the very beginning of taxation and treats it as apparently non-controversial.[42] The very fact that one measure should be so accepted and another so hotly disputed is an important part of the political reality of the social division of welfare which will be given further consideration below.[43]

## WELFARE AND THE LEGITIMATION OF INEQUALITY

The social division of welfare not only has considerable impact upon the resources and support that individuals, families and groups receive and the costs that they have to pay. It is itself an important element of society as a whole. In consequence it significantly affects perceptions of society, helping to legitimate and not just reflect the existing social structure with its current patterns of visible and concealed allocation and reallocation of resources. The social construct of 'the welfare state', as Richard Titmuss frequently emphasized, depends on 'a stereotype of social welfare which represents only the more visible part of the real world of welfare. The social history of our times inevitably becomes. . .sadly distorted.'[44] Some aspects of this have

[41] See note 22 above.
[42] B. E. V. Sabine, *A History of Income Tax*, Allen and Unwin, London, 1966.
[43] See pp. 148–9 below.
[44] Titmuss, *Essays on 'The Welfare State'*, p. 53.

already been mentioned but its significance goes much further and underlines the importance of what has been one of the most neglected arguments in the original essay. For any consideration of the total effects of social policy on society it is quite crucial, and its relevance even greater today.

Writing in 1955, Titmuss was particularly concerned that 'something akin to a stereotype or image of an all-pervasive Welfare State for the Working Classes. . .may, paradoxically, widen rather than narrow class relationships'.[45] There was the danger that 'If the upper classes monopolise the means of communication and fill the several mass media with the idea that all those at the bottom are there because they are lazy, unintelligent, and in general inferior, then these appraisals may be taken over by the poor and used in the building of an image of theirselves.'[46]

In their study of the psychology of social institutions Gerth and Mills go on to say that poor self-images, 'if impressed early enough and continually enough by all persons who are significant to these children, may cripple their chances to better their social position and thus obtain economic and social bases for more favourable self-images'.[47] Whether or not one accepts the values expressed here, there seems little doubt that the effects of the current division of welfare in reinforcing or even helping to shape perceptions of self and society deserve more systematic attention than they have received. While the social psychology of poverty remains undeveloped, there is a growing body of evidence of the impact of poverty and 'the demoralising effect of cumulative social rejection' on the perceptions of the poor.[48] In the United States the work of Robert Coles provides vivid evidence of the inferior self-images developed by black as opposed to white, or migrant as opposed to local, children and suggests how these are sustained by the inequalities of relationships between them.[49]

Self-images are likely to be affected by the services people receive – this of course is at the heart of the debate about the stigmatizing effect of means-tested services. Many have written about the meanness, even squalor and poverty, of much public provision and have argued that many services only help to keep the poor in poverty.[50] Appraisals of the services by the poor help to shape not only an image of self but also one of the wider society and

[45] *Ibid.* p. 37.

[46] *Ibid.* quoting Hans Gerth and C. Wright Mills, *Character and Social Structure*, Routledge and Kegan Paul, London, 1954, pp. 88–9.

[47] Gerth and Mills, *op. cit.* p. 89.

[48] R. M. Titmuss, 'The Irresponsible Society', in *Essays on 'The Welfare State'*, second edition, Allen and Unwin, London, 1963, p. 221.

[49] Robert Coles, *The Children of Crisis*, Delta, New York, 1967, ch. 3 and Part III.

[50] For example Peter Townsend, *The Social Minority*, Allen Lane, London, 1973; Muriel Brown, 'Inequality and the Personal Social Services', in Townsend and Bosanquet, *op. cit.*; and Adrian Sinfield, 'Poverty and the Social Services Department', in Malcolm Brown (ed.), *Social Issues and the Social Services*, Charles Knight, London, 1974.

its institutions, and in this way they help to legitimate the existing social structure. But there has generally been less explicit discussion of the wide range of ways in which many poor people come to feel inferior and even 'undeserving' for being poor.[51] Labelling theory has more recently made some contribution to this issue but seems very often to have had the effect of reinforcing, rather than refining, conventional social policy wisdom on means tests and other forms of 'separate and unequal' treatment.[52]

It is not of course the images of the poor alone that are shaped in this way: all of us are affected. People see the poor services of the public system with their limited rewards, their social controls and their maintenance of incentives and may come to think that the programmes are as they are because the poor are as they are. And so they come to accept as 'reality' the social division of welfare as seen through the eyes of the better off, the elites, the experts, and the 'rule-enforcers' of the public welfare system. In neglecting the effects of the distributive processes of the other systems of welfare, we are liable to blame the poor for being poor.[53] And, as the blinkered perceptions of both the poor and the non-poor act to increase the feelings of guilt for being poor, the non-poor have their complacent faith that their own achievements entitle them to a better standard of living falsely reinforced.[54]

## THE 'WELFARE STATE' IN AN ANTI-WELFARE SOCIETY[55]

So far I have tried to set out and develop some of the points that can be found explicitly or implicitly in the original essay. In selecting particular themes, I have been influenced partly by their growth in relevance, given developments over the last two decades, especially since the beginning of the cuts in public expenditure, and particularly by their importance for assessing the significance of these changes, which Peter Townsend summarized at one stage as 'the social underdevelopment of Britain'.[56]

The themes outlined have in my view considerable implications for both specific research and more general analysis. They demand that we examine more comprehensively the degree of inequality which results from the social

[51] Pinker, *op. cit.* p. 9.

[52] See Richard A. Cloward and Frances Fox Piven, 'Notes Toward A Radical Social Work', in Roy Bailey and Mike Brake (eds), *Radical Social Work*, American edition, Pantheon Books, New York, 1975. For consideration of what could be done, see Ken Plummer, 'In Defence of the Labelling Perspective', Paul Wiles (ed.), *Criminological Critiques*, Martin Robertson, London, forthcoming.

[53] William Ryan, *Blaming the Victim*, Orbach and Chambers, London, 1971.

[54] 'People with advantages are loath to believe that they just happen to be people with advantages' – C. Wright Mills, *The Power Elite*, Galaxy Books, New York, 1959, p. 14.

[55] See William A. Robson, *Welfare State and Welfare Society: Illusion and Reality*, Allen and Unwin, London, 1976, ch. 1.

[56] Peter Townsend, 'The Social Underdevelopment of Britain', *New Statesman*, 1 March 1974, p. 283.

division of welfare: concentration on 'the welfare state' alone, the traditional subject-matter of social administration, may only help to maintain or even increase the distortions resulting from the social division of welfare.

The analytical force of Richard Titmuss's work, however, has not always received the acceptance that has been accorded to his moral arguments. The criticisms are well caught by the leading review in *The Times Literary Supplement* some ten years ago which described Titmuss as 'essentially an impressionistic historian...[bringing] a combination of scholarship and broad intuitions, coupled with an attractive and subtle rhetoric'. His philosophy, the review concluded, 'is in no sense an engine of criticism'.[57]

Yet if any one essay makes the case for setting the sociological study of social policy at the centre of any analysis of British society today, it is in my view this contribution by Richard Titmuss. To establish it firmly as 'an engine of criticism' for a more dynamic analysis of change we need to integrate the themes set out so far with three other issues that received less attention from Titmuss – power and the state, time and security, and the institutions of capitalism.

### POWER AND THE STATE

The role of government in the division of welfare has become more important with increasing intervention. One crude and very formal measure of this is provided by the volume of legislation. 'In 1973 Parliament spewed out 64 new Acts and 2,229 mini-Acts' (that is, statutory instruments). These acts and their annotations take up 2,000 pages in Halsbury and the instruments more than 7,000 pages without the annotations. 'The courts and tribunals of England made their contribution with a myriad of precedent cases. And then there were the bye-laws promulgated with the authority of Parliament by local authorities and statutory authorities (such as British Rail)', and finally the regulations from Brussels.[58] However technical, limited or recondite, each decision involves the allocation of resources, power or discretion amongst different groups.

Much of this wide variety of government intervention, major or minor, may occur in one or other of the welfare systems, directing, restraining, promoting, modifying or even innovating. Building on Titmuss's analysis requires that we consider very carefully in whose welfare decisions are taken; that we take a closer look at the role of government in creating, shaping and reinforcing the social division of welfare; and that we examine the ways in which its actions are influenced and directed by particular groups or classes in society.

[57] 'Welfare and Diswelfare', *The Times Literary Supplement*, 15 August 1968.
[58] Andrew Phillips, untitled article in *The Guardian*, 2 January 1975.

Most references to government in the literature of social administration and social policy have tended to suggest that the state is seen as an institution for introducing greater fairness and equity and for mediating conflict. In the limited consideration of the state, policy and the class structure, the tendency has been to ask 'Given a class structure, how can the classes get along?' rather than 'How did a particular class structure come into being and by what means is its continued existence guaranteed?' These two questions distinguish what Sweezy describes as the classic liberal and progressive 'class-mediation theory of government' from the Marxist structural 'class-domination theory', where the state is seen 'as the guarantor of a given set of property relations'.[59] More recently the absence of any explicit theory of the state in writings on 'the welfare state' has been very correctly emphasized by many writers. But published work has tended to underline the significance of this neglect and does not appear to have developed any analysis or theory of the state which is sufficiently specific to be systematically applied.[60]

Much of the discussion on the state and welfare comes ironically close to committing the errors of 'misplaced aggregation' and 'illegitimate isolation' with which Gunnar Myrdal charged orthodox (bourgeois) development economists.[61] Either the state is treated as an unquestionably indistinguishable part of capitalism, a fixed wheel in the cycle of private profit, or as the autonomous and inflexible 'ideological state apparatus' of capital when no evidence has been provided of the form or extent of relations with business or industry. In addition the activities of 'the welfare state' tend to be 'illegitimately isolated' from the other systems. Too much of the work falls foul of the charge of argument by conflation which may be levelled against this article. There has been much illustrated theorizing, but as yet no sustained critique of the role of the state in the development of the social division of welfare, let alone any attempt to examine this across different societies.

Titmuss's concern with these issues in his writings seems to have been

59 Paul Sweezy, *The Theory of Capitalist Development*, Monthly Review Press, New York, 1942, p. 61; see also Ralph Miliband, *The State in Capitalist Society*, reprinted by Quartet Books, London, 1973. For the United States, see on 'the big rich' and the civil rights movement G. William Domhoff, *Fat Cats and Democrats*, Prentice-Hall, Englewood Cliffs, New Jersey, 1972, pp. 124–36; and G. William Domhoff, *The Higher Circles: The Governing Class in America*, Vintage Books, New York, 1971, ch. 6 ('How the Power Elite Shape Social Legislation').

60 See for example James O'Connor, *The Fiscal Crisis of the State*, St Martin's Press, New York, 1973, chs 1 and 5; Ian Gough, 'State Expenditure in Advanced Capitalism', *New Left Review*, 92 (1975); and also the papers being produced by the Conference of Socialist Economists.

61 Gunnar Myrdal, *Asian Drama*, Penguin Books, Harmondsworth, 1968, Appendix 3, sections 5 and 6.

fitful. In his analysis of the social division of welfare and the irresponsible society he does draw attention to 'the play of powerful economic and political forces, the strength and tenacity of privilege. . .behind the development' of the three systems leading to 'the new division of equity'.[62] Elsewhere he showed himself well aware of the power of the professional, especially in the health service, to influence both legislation and its implementation and also to control or at least affect expectations and demands in the rest of society.[63] But he did not sustain this analysis by examining the power, political and economic, of the different classes in society and the many ways in which its distribution influences the form and outcome of state intervention or inaction.

Dorothy Wedderburn's criticism therefore must stand: Richard Titmuss neglected any 'notion of class conflict as crucial in creating the overall balance of political forces which determines whether or not social legislation is enacted, or as an influence upon the final form of that legislation'.[64] Whatever government or reformers may initially intend, the power of certain groups may ensure that measures to redistribute resources downwards may have only symbolic rather than real effect.[65] Overt decisions may provide 'symbolic reassurance' to those who expect to benefit,[66] but actual experience indicates the powerful resisting-power of many of those who are intended to pay the costs. The American tax system, with its concessions to the wealthy, and the British one, 'treating "businessmen and professionals with great caution". . .and offering a rich reservoir of "loopholes"', illustrate Murray Edelman's thesis well, but some comparison with the Federal Republic of Germany suggests that such practice is not invariable and that the relations between government and business in market economies need more detailed examination.[67]

Similarly, the establishment of Wages Councils and the Wages Inspectorate provided symbolic reassurance that at least some previously low-paid workers were protected. But the actual effect was to weaken trade union vigilance and commitment and remove the plight of these workers from public and political debate. Not only did wage rates for apparently pro-

[62] Titmuss, *Essays on 'The Welfare State'* (1958), pp. 54–5.

[63] *Ibid.* especially in the second half of the book; and Titmuss, *Commitment to Welfare*, chs XIX and XX.

[64] Dorothy Wedderburn, 'Facts and Theories of the Welfare State', in Ralph Miliband and John Saville (eds), *The Socialist Register 1965*, Martin Press, London, 1965, p. 138.

[65] Vic George and Paul Wilding, *Ideology and Social Welfare*, Routledge and Kegan Paul, London, 1976, pp. 18–19.

[66] Murray Edelman, *The Symbolic Uses of Politics*, University of Illinois Press, Urbana, 1964.

[67] Arnold J. Heidenheimer, Hugo Heclo and Carolyn Teich Adams, *Comparative Public Policy: The Politics of Social Choice in Europe and America*, Macmillan, London, 1976, p. 237.

tected workers fall behind, but as a further consequence the efforts of the government's Wages Inspectorate became seriously undermined. Between 1970 and 1975 it 'recovered less than one sixth of an estimated underpayment of £8.6 million' to workers who will have been among the lowest paid in the whole labour force.[68]

The government's activities, or lack of them after the establishment of limited machinery, have therefore served to provide considerable control and some minimal welfare for these workers, while making larger benefits possible for the employers, the shareholders and maybe the consumers of the product – or at least enabling them to absorb increased costs in materials and production more easily. What was claimed to provide a floor for many wages came to act as more of a ceiling; meanwhile the slow and still uncertain gains of a seven-year campaign to encourage simply a more determined stance by the Wages Inspectorate bear out the difficulty of changing from symbolic to real support: 'Policies severely denying resources to large numbers of people can be pursued indefinitely without serious controversy.'[69]

The effect of such policies becomes even more inegalitarian when the growing security and welfare of the fiscal and occupational system, for which these workers are rarely eligible, is set against the much more limited and conditional advances in public welfare. This once again emphasizes the need for a more critical examination of the role of government and the differential influence of the classes on changes in the three systems. Here power may be more concerned with 'non-decision-making':[70] it is 'more a matter of successfully excluding policy alternatives from consideration than of determining the choice of alternatives among those considered'.[71]

The debate between universal and selective policies of redistribution in the public system provides one illustration of the significance of the social division of welfare in 'agenda-setting'.[72] If resources were not already available for significant and powerful groups of the population through fiscal or occupational welfare, it is likely that many more services and benefits would be demanded from the public system than is currently the case, and there would be much greater pressure for improved universal schemes. What

68 Steve Winyard, *Policing Low Wages*, Low Pay Pamphlet no. 4, London, March 1976, p. 1. There is a more detailed discussion in Steve Winyard, *Minimum Wage Enforcement: The Wages Council Inspectorate*, M.A. thesis, Department of Sociology, University of Essex, 1974.

69 Edelman, op. cit. p. 28.

70 The term made familiar by Peter Bachrach and Morton S. Baratz, *Power and Poverty*, Oxford University Press, New York, 1970.

71 John Westergaard, 'Sociology: The Myth of Classlessness', in Robin Blackburn (ed.), *Ideology in Social Science*, Fontana, London, 1972, p. 160.

72 Glasgow University Media Group, *Bad News*, Routledge and Kegan Paul, London, 1976.

many policy analysts, especially selectivists, who take part in the well-established public policy debate have failed to recognize is that the basic questions change when they are set in the wider context. The central concern shifts from asking why universal services are not enough for those who are seeking additional selective help, as they may appear to be to the rest of the population, to examining why those who are dependent on selective benefits are excluded from the resources and services available through the other two systems. This raises further questions about the equity and justice of the different extent, type and means of subsidy through the three systems, and the significance of the concepts of legitimacy, merit and need.[73]

The more successful the social construction of 'the welfare state' in disguising who really benefits, the less likely we are to accept the need for changes that will help to reduce inequalities. As Corwin and Miller have said of the United States, if with 'a selective vision we focus on how well the poor seem to be doing, we are diverted from realising that others are doing much better'.[74] We become, as Titmuss said, 'mesmerised by the language of the Welfare State',[75] and the social construction that results forms an even more important and integral aspect of the language of inequality itself. This has become more subtle as well as more blatant in recent years but it seems to have received very little study.[76]

It becomes one part of 'the larger structural phenomenon' described by Colin Crouch as 'the essential invisibility of class structure in capitalist society, especially a liberal capitalist society in which institutions of universal citizenship have been established'.[77] Corwin and Miller observe that 'The political genius of those who benefit [from government expenditures] lies in creating the impression that it is others who profit.' American society 'has one set of rules for corporations and another for individuals, one set of rules for the rich and another for the poor'.[78] They cite 'the oil depletion allowance, non-recoverable drilling cost write-off and foreign tax credits',

[73] See the thought-provoking discussion of stigma and legitimacy by Julia Parker in *Social Policy and Citizenship*, Macmillan, London, 1975, ch. 9; Robert Pinker in *Social Theory and Social Policy*, Heinemann, London, 1971, ch. 4; and Dale A. Tussing, quoted in note 94 below.

[74] R. D. Corwin and S. M. Miller, 'Taxation and its Beneficiaries: The Manipulation of Symbols', *American Journal of Orthopsychiatry*, 42:2 (1972), 200 and 213.

[75] Titmuss, *Income Distribution and Social Change*, p. 188, quoted in Wilding, *op. cit.* p. 163.

[76] For a brief exception, though not on social policy as such, see Philip Toynbee, 'The Language of Inequality', in Robin Blackburn and Alexander Cockburn (eds), *The Incompatibles*, Penguin Books, Harmondsworth, 1967.

[77] Colin Crouch, 'The Drive for Equality: Experience of Incomes Policy in Britain', in Leon N. Lindberg, Robert Alford, Colin Crouch and Clause Offe (eds), *Stress and Contradiction in Modern Capitalism*, Lexington Books, Lexington, Massachusetts, 1975, p. 216.

[78] Corwin and Miller, *op. cit.* pp. 200 and 207.

which, in the view of Peter Barnes, 'make the American oil industry one of the largest welfare recipients in the world'.[79]

Elliot Liebow makes much the same point, tongue in cheek, when he suggests that, if it is stigmatizing for the low paid to receive government hand-outs, the payments should be made to the employers to pass on, for they have never been prevented by pride or anything else from accepting government money.[80] Selective help by transfers or fiscal allowances to industry is justified in different terms and channelled in more acceptable ways than selective assistance to individuals and families classified as 'needy' or 'dependent'; yet both are transfers of public money and both affect the availability of revenue and expenditure for other groups in society. Paul Wilding is correct in saying that 'Titmuss lacks "a political sociology" of social policy and social deprivation',[81] but this criticism can also be applied to most contemporary writing on the subject. The greater power of certain classes or organizations to influence the allocation of scarce resources is a central issue for any analysis of the social divisions of labour and welfare.

## TIME, SECURITY AND POWER

The further consideration of power must also take particular account of the dimension of time. This is not simply to make the obvious but still neglected point that a sound historical base is lacking, or is restricted to too short a scale, in much social policy analysis. It is rather to stress that the value of time as a resource, different patterns of time and time-scales, and the differential ability of individuals, families, classes and organizations to plan or make arrangements over time are issues that we must aim to explore more systematically in analysing the social division of welfare and its distribution of benefits, services, status and power.[82] In *Income Distribution and Social Change* Richard Titmuss examined the different 'command over resources-in-time' of families with different forms and quantities of income and other assets, and this is probably still the most detailed investigation of the relations between time, class and policy.[83]

79 Peter Barnes, 'Oil Everywhere', *New Republic*, 6 November 1971, 22–3, quoted in Corwin and Miller, *op. cit.* p. 207.

80 Elliot Liebow, 'No Man can Live with the Terrible Knowledge that He is Not Needed', *New York Times Magazine*, 5 April 1970.

81 Wilding, *op. cit.* p. 164.

82 For a very brief discussion, see Titmuss, *Social Policy*, pp. 63–4; and, somewhat impenetrable but provoking, Georges Gurvitch, *The Spectrum of Social Time*, Reidel, Dordrecht, 1964, chs V and VI; also Michael Young and John Ziman, 'Cycles in Social Behaviour', *Nature*, 229 (1971), 91–5.

83 Titmuss, *Income Distribution and Social Change*, p. 68, even if the examination of class is sometimes limited.

Power, status, and security, or the lack of them, derive from *and* lead to differing time perceptions with varying degrees of predictability and certainty. In the United States at least, the non-poor not only receive more but 'even more striking, they receive their subsidies in a way that facilitates the creation of wealth'.[84] This is closely related to the very different time period over which different groups are able to manage and redeploy their resources. The senior trustee of the three hundred prime acres of Belgravia and Mayfair which form the Grosvenor estate of the Duke of Westminster has said 'Our ability is to look far, far ahead. Fifty years is nothing to us, and one hundred years is normal.'[85] Evidence so far available would suggest that the workings of the fiscal system may support and encourage the wealthier in long-term planning, and annual analyses of income tax units mislead us on the extent of taxation of both income and wealth.[86]

Those who derive most of their income from public benefits may depend upon intra-family transfers of child benefits mid-week until their weekly insurance benefit arrives. Most means-tested benefits, except perhaps for the retired, offer less guarantee of support with less predictability than resources from other systems. However, the meagreness of many occupational pensions, especially for manual workers and their widows, becomes more evident over time when their value has not been maintained during inflation. The exploration of the support and security over a substantial period of time offered by different benefits or allowances across the three systems would help us to examine the ways in which they enable groups to maintain or strengthen their economic position in the long term, or find themselves locked into some version of the 'poverty trap' by the interaction of payments and deductions.

To dismiss the effects of public policy as simply non-egalitarian, or at best neutral in effect and so irrelevant to the analysis of structural inequalities, is to miss the significance of the time dimension and fail to understand the options for change. In studying the full impact of the social division of welfare, we need to pay more attention to the length and predictability of payment, the extent of need met, the full or limited rights provided, and the different human relationships entailed by different schemes. The variations in these are likely to have a marked influence over time on the

[84] Corwin and Miller, *op. cit.* p. 213.

[85] Quoted in Oliver Marriott, *The Property Boom*, Hamish Hamilton, London, 1967, p. 112; and in Counter Information Service, *The Recurrent Crisis of London*, London, 1973, p. 22.

[86] Titmuss, *Income Distribution and Social Change*; A. B. Atkinson, 'Income Distribution and Social Change Revisited', *Journal of Social Policy*, 4:1 (1975), 57–68; and, for a discussion of the real extent of any shift from land-ownership to renting, see David Rose, Howard Newby, Peter Saunders and Colin Bell, 'Land Tenure and Official Statistics: A Research Note', *Journal of Agricultural Economics*, January 1977.

differential distribution of not only economic resources, but also security, status and power;[87] these become part of 'the hidden injuries of class'.[88]

THE DYNAMICS OF THE SOCIAL DIVISION OF WELFARE

The political economy of the social division of welfare has changed in both scale and form since 1955. Despite the growing amount of transfers within the three systems and among them, there is still no clear evidence on the exact and full extent of the movement of resources over time away from public revenue available for spending in the public system. The costs of occupational welfare which most benefit the securely employed and higher-status staff are borne to a significant extent by all who pay any revenue to the government. So much of this provision is tax deductible that in 1973 Titmuss estimated that probably about one-half of the cost fell 'on the whole body of taxpayers'.[89]

The extent of redistribution upward has probably grown since; in 1976 the Engineering Employers' Federation told the Chancellor that 'the proliferation of fringe benefits of recent years has been entirely due to the excessive and unreasonable rates of British personal taxation'.[90] Quite apart from the other reasons for increased occupational welfare discussed above,[91] the impact of the systems upon each other and the effect of this interaction on their beneficiaries is assuming increasingly greater significance.

The 'tax efficiency' industry, with its tax lawyers and accountants, its offices and swiftly increasing number of periodicals and newsletters advising on 'fiscal mitigation' or 'tax minimization' opportunities, seems to have increased at much the same time as the attacks on public expenditure. Preliminary research would suggest that its scale has greatly enlarged since Titmuss's comments in the early 1960s and since *The Economist*, no radical critic of our business system, lamented in 1969 the 'huge and swelling drain of talent, energy, working time and spare time being burned up in the wasteful process of tax avoiding and tax planning'.[92]

The social policy analyst may obtain a vicarious thrill from observing the tax-dodging of scroungerphobic businessmen and industrialists that he and his colleagues have so long dismissed or neglected, but the real significance

87 David Donnison, *An Approach to Social Policy*, National Economic and Social Council, Dublin, 1975, para. 27 provides very useful working definitions of these terms for application in social policy.

88 Richard Sennett and Jonathan Cobb, *The Hidden Injuries of Class*, Vintage Books, New York, 1973.

89 Titmuss, *Social Policy*, p. 139.

90 See their memorandum to the Chancellor of 19 May 1976.

91 See pp. 137–8 above.

92 Titmuss, *Income Distribution and Social Change*; 'Taxing in the Dark', *The Economist*, 31 May 1969, p. 54, quoted in Heidenheimer *et al.*, *op. cit.* p. 241. See also notes 22 and 23 above.

of these developments goes much further. However admirable or evasive the reason, any reduction of tax revenue benefits some at the expense of others, while at the same time it intensifies the highly visible and much debated public expenditure crises. Since taxable income is well below half total personal income, the implications are clearly considerable.[93]

In the recent years of high inflation the dramatic effects of 'fiscal drag' (where direct and indirect tax revenues increase as incomes and prices rise during the year, even when real living standards fall) have very largely obscured the counter-effects which act to reduce revenue. But even this politically convenient aspect of inflation may be accompanied by similar increases in transfers to tax units through the fiscal system. Owner-occupiers paying interest on mortgages receive a larger subsidy in tax not collected if their incomes reach a higher tax band or tax rates are raised. In contrast tenants receive no gain, and any rent rebate is reduced by increases in gross, not post-tax, income. A rise in mortgage interest rates is automatically partially compensated for through the fiscal system, but any council rent increase can only be eased by an explicit decision to help. This may be made very evident by the vigorous debate it tends to create and it may fuel further demands for restraint in public expenditure.

Even though many more workers are reaching the tax threshold and gaining some relief through fiscal allowances, most of these and the occupational benefits go to those with more pay, greater security and higher status. The losers in any relative reduction of resources available for public revenue are those excluded from most or all of the benefits of the occupational and fiscal systems.[94] Such people are likely to be found in the groups most vulnerable to poverty and already growing in number – the retired, the sick and disabled, one-parent families, the unemployed and the low paid.

The narrowing of the tax base, for whatever reason, does have wider political and economic implications. Governments wishing to maintain existing public services need to raise the tax rate to obtain as much revenue from the same total income because the proportion of that income actually subject to tax has diminished. Any increase in service costs for capital,

[93] Figures cited in Heidenheimer *et al.*, *op. cit.* p. 239 show taxable income as 43 per cent of total personal income in the United Kingdom, 45 per cent in the United States, 24 per cent in France and 79 per cent in West Germany at the end of the 1960s. My own impression is that this percentage will have fallen in the United Kingdom.

[94] A. Dale Tussing, 'The Dual Welfare System', *Society*, January–February 1974: 'The legitimacy of one's income and, especially, one's position in the overall distribution of income, are central preoccupations. No welfare programs are inherently legitimate where the dominant ideology of individualism still appears to reject the welfare state in principle (while applying it in practice – a conflict of some significance). In the view of many people, job-holders are members of and contributors to society; non-job-holders are not. Job-holding legitimates one's political role, as well. In local, state and national politics, more is heard today about "taxpayers" than about "citizens".'

labour or other current expenditure makes it even more difficult to maintain current public provision.

Yet the dynamic effect of the interaction of the three systems is occurring while the cost of much public provision is forced up by increasing demand resulting from more poverty with the far-reaching effects of the fourfold increase of unemployment in the last decade; from declining services, delays, increased inefficiency, and other social costs resulting from the cutbacks in public expenditure; and from increasing complexity and additional staff with the rising number of means-tested schemes and applicants for them. The shifts in the social division of welfare therefore deserve much closer attention from economists and political scientists than they have so far received.[95]

## THE DIVISION OF WELFARE IN A CAPITALIST SOCIETY

By drawing attention to the importance of power and the dynamic effect of changes over time in the political economy of the social division of welfare, one is forced to consider again the relation between welfare and the particular form and structure of the society under study. Is there a single welfare ethic, as George and Wilding suggest, which is at odds with capitalist society?[96] Perhaps this lies behind the much greater weight that Titmuss placed on altruism in his later work;[97] it certainly fuels much of the opposition to public expenditure cuts, the defence of 'the welfare state' in an anti-welfare society. But the preceding discussion would suggest that this view indicates an acceptance of a particular social construction of both welfare and government intervention and ignores fundamental questions about the causes of the differing characterization and legitimation of help and support to certain groups in certain ways.

For at least a generation most studies of social policy in a societal context tended to emphasize the need for the adaptation of programmes and policies to major changes within and across societies. But generally these changes were seen as functional and inevitable, the role of social policy being to counteract any ill effects, and, as I argued above, there were few attempts to identify the causes more precisely.[98] The consequence was an end-of-ideology view of both policy and the wider changes which so often, apparently, frustrated policy intention. With the assumption of government as a

95 Economists should not feel deterred by Titmuss's firmly held conception of social as opposed to economic markets. It does not in my view obstruct the analysis of the political economy of welfare, but there are other problems that have received little attention here such as the exact distinction between wages and non-wage benefits in employment.

96 George and Wilding, *op. cit.* p. 129.

97 See especially R. M. Titmuss, *The Gift Relationship*, Allen and Unwin, London, 1970.

98 See p. 134 above.

referee, if not Robin Hood, planning or just intervention meant a reduction of inequality and poverty. Change in much the same way was equated with progress, which needed no clearer definition in an apparently consensual political climate.[99] Economic growth provided the resources for and legitimated further beneficent government activity whose success depended largely on the skills of administrators and the wise judgements of professionals – two groups who have been among the main beneficiaries of the social division of welfare.[100]

In the last few years we have all become more aware from the news media, general discussion and some research that the operations of capitalism have considerable significance for social policy. The clamour for, as well as the manner, form and extent of, public expenditure cuts into the very fabric of the social services known as 'the welfare state' has made this much clearer than any academic treatise on social policy, capitalism and the state. The predominance in Britain of the economic burden view of the public system over the human capital approach with investment in social policy as a handmaiden to economic growth has reinforced the lesson.

There has also been recognition that in the last decade high or rising unemployment has been allowed, sometimes encouraged, to bring about trade union acceptance of control over labour in industrial relations or acquiescence in incomes policies. While the failure to pick up the full social and economic costs of the greater joblessness, and to defend those out of work against the accusation of scrounging when very few jobs are available, has led to the charge that unemployment is being used as a class weapon, there is certainly clear evidence that an unequal burden is borne by certain groups, and this is accompanied by a persistent tendency to deny the legitimacy of those claiming help.[101]

Greater awareness of the unequal impact of many social costs has been reinforced by the many debates over 'shake-out', 'hoarding' and 'overmanning', and by the loss of many jobs due to greater capital investment. There has also been closer examination of the human impact of many planning decisions and much property development since the return or greater visibility of those whom Pahl and Winkler have called 'hard' capitalists.[102]

[99] For a lively analysis of the varying roles of planning, see S. M. Miller, 'Planning: Can It Make a Difference in Capitalist America?', *Social Policy*, September–October 1975, p. 22. Hugh Heclo and Aaron Wildavsky, *The Private Government of Public Money*, Macmillan, London, 1974, ch. 2, would suggest that this view may persist in the conventional wisdom of the Treasury.

[100] T. H. Marshall, *Sociology at the Cross-Roads*, Heinemann, London, 1973, pp. 158–64 ('Professionalism in Relation to Social Structure and Social Policy') illustrates the optimistic perceptions of altruism in the new professional strength resulting from the 'welfare state'.

[101] See Deacon and Sinfield, *op. cit.*

[102] R. E. Pahl and J. T. Winkler, 'The Economic Elite: Theory and Practice', in Philip

Reports from the Community Development Project (CDP) and the Counter Information Service have emphasized these points[103] and illustrated ways in which companies have left both direct and indirect social costs in the areas in which they are located. The substantial problems of technological and economic change are very evident in CDP areas, but their impact stretches far more widely, creating a demand for more services to meet new or greater needs which are to be provided by local authorities and a central government under increasing pressure to restrain and cut back expenditure. The structural issues that these developments raise are reinforced by the changes in the social division of welfare since Richard Titmuss first discussed it.

Given the ways in which for many years Marxism was put down, caricatured or simply presented as 'something nasty in the woodshed' by now discredited authorities, it is hardly surprising that the basic structural arguments have often come to be associated with various forms of Marxism as if they can only be found there. Yet there are many possible sources for further discussion on these issues including the work of alleged conservatives such as Thorstein Veblen. In 1904 he argued that in a capitalist society 'industry is carried on for the sake of business, and not conversely; and the progress and activity are conditioned by the outlook of the market which means the presumptive chance of business profits. . .the economic welfare of the community at large is best served by a facile and uninterrupted interplay of the various processes which make up the industrial system at large; but the primary interests of the business men in whose hands lies the discretion in the matter are not best served by an unbroken maintenance of the industrial balance. . .Gain may come to them [and especially 'those greater business men'] by disturbance of the system whether the disturbance makes for heightened facility or for widespread hardship.'[104]

## CONCLUSION

Throughout this paper I have sought to argue with brief illustrations that the conceptual framework embodied in Richard Titmuss's discussion of the social division of welfare is not only a useful one, but has much greater value for analysts today than in 1955. There is no claim that a fully and explicitly developed design exists, let alone a formulated theoretical position; but I have attempted to indicate ways in which we might advance in

Stanworth and Anthony Giddens (eds), *Elites and Power in British Society*, Cambridge University Press, Cambridge, 1974, p. 119.

103 See especially Community Development Project, *The Costs of Industrial Change*, CDP Inter-Project Editorial Team, London, January 1977; and Counter Information Service, *op. cit.*

104 Thorstein Veblen, *The Theory of Business Enterprise*, first published in 1904 and reprinted by Mentor Books, New York, 1965, p. 19.

refining the ideas and developing a more rigorous and consistent critical apparatus. I am very conscious of the work that remains to be done, but this should be considered as more a wealth of exciting and challenging opportunities than a burdensome area for laborious examination.[105]

It is tempting to advance the trinity of welfare still further and speak of three divisions – economic, political and social – of the three systems. Given the persistence of the disciplinary fragmentation of the social sciences and the lack of sustained dialogue and interchange, this might be the quickest way to encourage more systematic analyses by those working in these three different traditions, who have tended to neglect or overlook the growing significance of developments in the division of welfare. But a basic argument of this paper has been the need to escape the traditional disciplinary and professional blinkers which have already functioned to advance a particular social construction of 'the welfare state' in for example the separate study of economic and social policy or public and fiscal welfare.

Of all the options for further work I believe that the most rewarding lie in greater explication of the dynamics of the social division of welfare and in comparative analyses of the relation between the division of welfare and labour, not only over time, but among different countries and different types of society. These too are probably among the most testing, but it is in work of this kind that we shall finally be able to judge whether the provocative insights and ideas of the original essay can be harnessed to provide 'an engine of criticism'.[106]

[105] As an indication of good faith in making such a challenge, I am attempting to respond to it myself in one way (see note 22 above), while becoming ever more aware of the wide range of opportunities that exist.

[106] See p. 144 and note 57 above.

# [6]

*Acta Sociologica* 1987 (30), 3/4:237–254

# Welfare States and Capitalist Markets

*Göran Therborn*
Institute for Political Science, Catholic University, Nijmegen, The Netherlands and Department of Sociology, University of Gothenburg, Sweden

In spite of an impressive expansion predominant welfare state research suffers from five important weaknesses: a linear conception of welfare state growth, a neglect of welfare state efficiency, an excessive quantification of variables, a Social Democratic bias, and an underdevelopment of theory. While the first four are held to be untenable undercurrent societal circumstances, the paper concentrates on theoretical problems. Welfare states are conceptualized as social systems of human reproduction, and a theory of market failures and market conflicts is sketched to account for the development of welfare states. A combination of economic and sociological theory is used to lay out a theory of welfare states as providers of public goods and of different kinds of private goods. Economic theory and socio-political theory are used to outline determinants of the supply and demand for state contributions to human reproduction.

## 1. Four reasons why welfare state research cannot remain as it is, and one more reason why it shouldn't

The most obvious limitation of the recent wave of welfare state studies is their non-problematized notion of *linear growth*, a notion summed up in the frequently used summary 'from the poorhouse to the welfare state', the title of Jens Alber's (1982) excellent book. This tends to preclude a systematic attention to options, dilemmas, social costs, contradictions. Empirically, it means a neglect of the contributions of studies of welfare professions, above all the medical (Foucault 1973; Navarro 1976; Larson 1977; Starr 1982; Geison 1984; Göckenjan 1985), of educational history (Katz 1975; Bowles & Gintis 1976; Archer 1979; Frijhoff 1983; Boli et al. 1985), of social discipline (Foucault 1977; Frykman & Löfgren 1979; Frevert 1984; Sachsse & Tenstedt 1986), of labour history (Hatzfeld 1971; Tenstedt 1983; Therborn 1986a), of business history (Hatzfeld 1971; Fischer 1978; Berkowitz & McQuaid 1980), of Feminist critiques (Wilson 1977; Kickbusch & Riedmüller 1984; Hernes 1984). The prevailing Whig interpretation of the welfare state is the one most likely to be discredited and surpassed in the near future.

Implicit in the growth syndrome has been the assumption that the bigger the better. This has precluded any central and systematic attention to welfare state *efficiency*. Whereas we have innumerable studies trying to show that the growth of welfare states is due to this or that factor, we have few studies geared to assessing the efficiency of welfare states in providing health, security, and equality or in preventing poverty. For some rare comparative exception, see Maxwell (1981) and

Walker et al. (1984). This situation cannot remain for very long. Everywhere, strong political pressure is building up for evaluating the efficiency of welfare states. Some detailed national studies of the redistributive effects already exist (e.g. Wiebrens 1981; LeGrand 1982; Rainwater et al. 1986).

A natural part of the linear growth orientation, but per se a separate dimension, has been a predominant *over-quantification* of the welfare state. This has been expressed in an overwhelming focus on social expenditure and on quantitative dimensions of social insurance, such as coverage percentages, income replacement ratios, days of waiting and of entitlement. These data lends themselves easily to capitalization on investments in quantitative methodological training, but the marginal utility of correlational and regression analyses diminishes rapidly. Their main usefulness is a selection of hypotheses worth pursuing, i.e. those which get some statistical support. The description of the development of social insurance systems and of comparative current ones is, of course, an important contribution to social knowledge in which the research teams of Peter Flora have been prominent (another important contribution, with regard to the most important social insurance scheme, pensions, has been made by John Myles (1984). However, the questions raised by the present conjuncture are likely to call for much more qualitative analyses, of social services, of forms of management and control, of implications of participation, etc.

In the course of the past ten years, the convergent industrialism–economic wealth–economic growth paradigm has been largely discredited among comparative empirical welfare researchers. Instead, a *Social Democratic paradigm* has become dominant, if not uncontested. In a linear quantitative growth perspective, Scandinavian and, in particular, Swedish Social Democracy has been presented as a state of culmination. This neglects extremely generous welfare states such as the Dutch, coming largely out of confessional party politics. It has little to say either about the forms of welfare states taken in countries low on labour mobilization and labour party government control or about current options in countries with weak Social Democracies. Furthermore, it is outside ongoing post-classical Social Democratic discussions about the welfare state (Opielka 1983; Theory and Society, Vol. 15 (5), 1986), centred on a decoupling of social entitlements and the labour market. The Scandinavian Social Democratic perspective is already being powerfully challenged (Amenta & Skocpol 1986), and it is most likely to disappear or to be marginalized as a general yardstick for evaluating problems of welfare.

With regard to the four weaknesses of contemporary welfare state research mentioned above, the non-problematic linear growth notion, the non-concern with goal-attainment, the quantitative preoccupation, and the Social Democratic ideal type, ongoing developments of economy, society, and politics are likely to bring about a change in academic research. A remedy for the fifth, and from a scientific point of view most serious, weakness, will depend much more on intra-scientific efforts. This refers to the *lack of theory* in welfare state studies. Lots of theories have been used to try to explain the rise of welfare states, but little theoretical effort has been used to capture the various meanings and structural implications of welfare states. Still the unsurpassed theoretician of welfare state studies is the great representative of the most empirical of social disciplines (social administration), the late Richard Titmuss (1963, 1974). When major contemporary social theorists turn to the welfare state, their contribution turns out unusually thin and jejune (e.g. Luhmann 1981; Habermas 1985).

The lack of any significant body of welfare state theory – of what welfare states mean and how they affect contemporary social life – is amazing. Here is a major, in its current scope very recently established, institution, which, for good or for bad, occupies a central role in the everyday life of people in the countries of advanced capitalism. In 1983, 43 per cent of all Dutch households received their primary income from public transfer payments, including income from public and para-public employment about 60 per cent received their main income from the state (own calculations on the basis of official statistics). In developed Western Europe in 1981 between 50 and 57 per cent of income recipients had their primary income from the state, in USA 42 per cent (Rose 1985:43). But this institution is still outside major social and political theorizing. On this point, there is relatively little external social pressure for remedy, but as a non-disputable anomaly this lack of theory is not very likely to persist, once pointed out.

If the above diagnosis is in any way to the point, a major turn of social policy studies is both likely to occur and to be painfully controversial. Of the five weaknesses listed above, only one – the Social Democratic bias, the least important one – is explicitly treated, together with a methodological scepticism of large-scale quantification, in the latest mainstream sociological summing up (Amenta & Skocpol 1986).

## 2. The welfare state as a social system of human reproduction

What is conventionally referred to as the welfare state constitutes a social system of human reproduction. Human reproduction has two elementary meanings, both to be found in what is called welfare state arrangements, maintaining alive already living human beings and maintaining a given population by creating new generations of humans. The latter is, of course, above all a sexual act, but human sexuality and procreation may be, and often are, regulated or subjected to intended affectation by social policy, by child allowances and other forms of family and parenthood support, by family planning. The connotation of the other meaning of human reproduction indicates that maintaining people alive is not only a question of providing subsistence, but also, often, of care, of health care, of the broad range of helping and supporting activities usually called social care. And this may be an enduring process. In actually existing human history, these tasks have usually befallen women, and it is Feminist theory and politics which have brought human reproduction and reproductive work into intellectual focus, a focus still to be recognized by mainstream welfare state research.

As an analytical concept, reproduction was first developed and applied in economics. It was a central concept of Marx' analysis, but it is no Marxist patent. From its origins in political economy, reproduction refers to two kinds of processes, both of which are useful for an understanding of welfare states, i.e. simple and expanded reproduction. The former refers to the maintenance of a given set of endowments, the latter to accumulation and growth. Applied to human reproduction, this distinction would entail, on the one hand, maintaining a stable population over time and keeping existing human beings alive during their life-span with necessary subsistence and care, and, on the other, provisions for population growth and for the broadening and bettering of human existence. To a, by time and place, varying extent, welfare states involve both simple and expanded human reproduction.

At this point we will leave it open whether the insights and assertions of systems theory (cf. Luhmann 1985) will prove useful economic tools for welfare state understanding. Anyway, however, bringing 'social system' into the definition has the advantage of drawing attention to the system/environment and identity/difference problems of the interdependent elements of welfare state institutions and policies in a wider socio-economic world. The word 'social' has primarily the function of distinguishing the kind of processes of human reproduction in which welfare states are engaged from biological ones.

Summing up somewhat more concretely, we may say that welfare states consist of state institutions and state arrangements for the simple and the expanded human reproduction of a given state population. These institutions and arrangements entail provisions for procreation, subsistence, education, housing, health, care, income guarantees, income maintenance, social services.

As a social system of human reproduction, the welfare state is part functional alternative to, part supplement of other social systems and institutions, above all the economic system and the family, but also others, such as local communities, associations, patron-clientele relationships. The best way of opening up an analysis of these relations and of the structure and functioning of welfare states seems to be to start from the economic system.

## 3. The exclusion principle and market failures

'The market can function only in a situation where the "exclusion principle" applies, i.e., where A's consumption is made contingent on his paying the price, while B, who does not pay, is excluded. Exchange cannot occur without property rights and property rights require exclusion' (Musgrave & Musgrave 1976:50). This formulation, from an eminent authority on public finance, brings us immediately to the core of the relationship between human reproduction and the market economy. Within normatively and/or politically bounded populations, human reproduction, human survival, has rarely been strictly and only regulated by the 'exclusion principle'. Here we have a theoretical key to the double historical economic process in which the modern welfare state emerged, a process of market expansion and a countermovement of protection against the market (cf. Polanyi 1957). As the establishment and expansion of markets, in land and labour, extended the exclusion principle, new arrangements for ensuring human reproduction were developed to compensate for the extension of exclusion.

However, the conflict between human reproduction and the market economy per se is not that clearcut. Before going further into the problems of the market economy, we should introduce a distinction seldom made by liberal economists. That is, between capitalist and non-capitalist market economies. The former implies a double exclusion, the exclusiveness of property rights and the exclusion of a large part of the population from property. Massive propertylessness in a market economy heightens the human reproduction problem. This is particularly the case under three conditions: (a) to the extent that going wages yield little discretionary income above what is necessary for day to day survival; (b) to the extent that labour markets are incapable of absorbing all the propertyless population; (c) to the extent that a restricted family system has confined non-market exchange and sharing to within households, defined by one (the 'breadwinner's') position with regard to property and the labour market. All three conditions applied to the time and place, when and where the modern welfare state developed in nineteenth early twentieth century.

The effects of propertylessness entail that access to property may be seen as an alternative to social policy and welfare state arrangements in the usual sense. In the first half of the 1920s the top reform priority of the Swedish labour movement was agrarian reform, second to disarmament as a political task. The trade union movement saw the solution to unemployment in the (urban, industrial) unemployed turning to agriculture, and in public support for the acquisition of small agrarian property by the unemployed. Social Democratic party secretary Gustav Möller, later to become the architect of Swedish social policy, in a programmatic speech at the 1920 party Congress saw the solution to the problem of poverty in socialization and in the abolition of capitalist 'waste of the productive forces' (Therborn 1986a:20, with references to primary sources).

Let us return to the market around which the socio-political conflicts about the welfare state have de facto centred and are centred today. Modern welfare states emerged and grew out of market failures, market problems, and market conflicts. The first two may be grasped with the help of market economic theory, the third first of all by looking into the social and political context and dynamics of market economies. Market-devoted economists usually recognize that there are two things for which markets provide suboptimal solutions – public goods (which Musgrave calls social goods) and externalities.

The theory of public goods was developed by Paul Samuelson, who defined them as 'goods which all enjoy in common in the sense that each individual's consumption of such goods leads to no subtraction from any other individual's consumption of the good (Samuelson 1954:387). This characteristic has later been spelled out in two dimensions, one of pure theory, i.e. the rival or non-rival character of consumption, and a pragmatic one of the feasibility or not of excluding non-paying consumers. Markets fail in all situations where consumption is non-rival and where it is rival but non-feasible or too costly to exclude non-paying consumers (Musgrave & Musgrave 1976:51–53). Non-paying free-riders prevent the market mechanism from providing such goods (adequately).

Externalities may be either beneficial or costly, and consist of non-compensated or non-charged effects upon others of actions by an individual market actor. Here again the market fails, underproviding beneficial externalities and overproviding costly ones, 'social bads'. An amelioration of the social situation of the 'lower' classes may provide external benefits to the 'higher' ones from amenity in public places and safety in the streets to political stability and extended markets, and a feeling of ruling achievement. The prevailing conditions of the lower class in Edwardian England were, according to the Majority Report of the Royal Commission on Poor Laws (1909), 'a discredit and a peril to the whole community' (quoted from Bruce 1968:154).

It is a thesis of this paper that a large part of welfare state provisions and arrangements consists of public goods and of coping with externalities. In this sense, the welfare state has developed as an institution for dealing with inherent market failures. The Musgraves (1976:65–66) introduce an ad hoc notion to deal with a number of state activities and expenditures of welfare state relevance. They call them 'merit goods', certain goods held meritorious or desirable by public decision-makers. By and large, they see them as an expression of 'paternalism'. This is an ad hoc, non-theorized notion – although they do refer to incompleteness of consumer information – because it is not related to any theory of why 'merit goods' are supplied and why they are accepted in democratic societies.

Gunnar Persson (1985) has here offered some very valuable hints from the perspective of problems of consumer choice. An important problem of market choice in the field of human reproduction is that many choices are *irreversible* while having long-term and possibly fatal effects. If you once choose not to go to (a higher) education, to disregard occupaional risks, to leave your sickness untreated or treated by a quack, or to neglect when you are young to provide for your support when old and infirm, this may have irreversible consequences which may later make you deeply but helplessly regret your previous choice. The irreversibility of your choice or simply the infrequency of many vital decisions impede or make impossible a learning by trial and error. In some opposite cases addiction will be a learning too.

## 4. Market conflicts with state, class and citizenship

The socio-political context of markets gives rise to conflicts about, as well as within, markets, both of which have been crucial to the development of welfare state systems of human reproduction. Three parameters of market economies have been particularly important in shaping welfare states and their relationships to markets – the state, class, and citizenship.

Markets require states, if for no other reason then for upholding the exclusion principle and the property rights on which they rest. In fact, states have another location as well, spatial as well as functional, in the territorial delimitation of supreme rule-making, of sovereignty. This means that market economies are always faced with a separate institution, the state, to which rationality is something different from that of market actors. Different, however, is of course not the same as superior, and from their different angles both Marxism and Public Choice theory have directed heavy artillery, and not without hits, against notions of 'general' or 'national' interests as guides of state behaviour.

State actions may be seen as inserted in three kinds of non-market logic – but it should not be assumed that the latter exhaustively define the former (or actions by states of capitalist market societies), because states are also affected by the other two sorts of market conflict, of citizenship and class – one is functional, following from the state's function to provide a framework for market action. This is a holistic rationality, in the sense that the state – its politicians and bureaucrats – act rationally to the extent that they safeguard and promote the accumulation and the legitimacy of the capitalist market economy as a whole. Another is geopolitical, ensuing from the territorial divisions of the world market – or of the world – according to which a given state has to maintain and, if possible, enhance its power and status, and those of its population in relation to those of other states. The third is positional, the individual rationality of state members and aspirant members – politicians out of office – in protecting and increasing their wealth, power, and status. These may be the same goals as those of market actors, but the positional difference is that they have to be reached by state, and not by market, action. As such, the individual state position rationality is at least to some extent related to the two systemic rationalities of the state. You tend to be more successful as a politician and as a bureaucrat to the extent that you succeed in stabilizing and promoting the economy as a whole and to the extent that you maintain or achieve a geopolitical upper hond. But there is no mechanism necessarily uniting the three rationalities.

Part of the payment for ensuring, more or less successfully, the pursuit of these state rationalities, is conventionally included in welfare state accounts, special insurance schemes and social benefits for public employees, payments and services to veterans and war victims.

Capitalism divides people into *classes*, around the poles of capital and labour. It also gives rise to class action and class conflict, (see further Therborn 1986d). Class action by the disadvantaged/exploited has a re-distributive and re-forming (revolutionary or reformist) drive, in other words a rationality directed against the given endowments and outcomes of the market, although not necessarily incompatible with an acceptance of capital as well as of the market (cf. Przeworski 1985: chs. 4–5).

In contrast to class, citizenship is not a necessary universal feature of capitalist market economies. You can be a market actor without being a citizen, either as an immigrant worker or as a foreign firm or investor, and you can be a citizen, also in the political sense, without being a fully capable market actor, such as a married woman, in France until 1965 (Dhavernas 1978:98–104). Nevertheless, there is an inherent tension giving rise to conflicts between citizenship and markets. In the latter you act and succeed according to your endowments, but as a citizen on the basis of equal rights – in both cases your actual success depends on your usage of your endowments or your rights. The conflict between markets and citizenship has perhaps best been formulated by the American economist Arthur Okun (1975:6): 'An obvious feature of rights – in sharp contrast with economic assets – is that they are acquired and exercised without any monetary charge. Because citizens do not normally have to pay a price for using their rights, they lack the usual incentive to economize on exercising them.' The conflictual relationship of citizenship and inequality (class as he saw it) and the conducive relationship of citizenship to the welfare state and social rights was laid out by the British sociologist T. H. Marshall in a famous lecture in 1949 (Marshall 1965). Bluntly put, citizens may use their rights to question and to change the endowments of market actors and the returns to different kinds of endowments.

Market conflicts, with state, class, and citizenship, have contributed to the development of the modern welfare state not only according to their own, specific redistributive and reforming lines. They also constitute the avenues along which remedies to market failures and solutions to market problems have asserted themselves. The latter could only be generated by forces and institutions outside the market. The distinction between, on one hand, market failures and market problems, and, on the other, market conflicts is not one of causality, but of consequences and implications. The former are market rational, the latter are open to market controversy.

By way of summary, welfare states are social systems of human reproduction which provide *public goods* and four kinds of private goods: regulations and/or provisions/prohibitions of market *externalities*; provisions or promotion of *merit goods* following from *problems of market choice* with regard to certain goods for human reproduction; *extra state wages* (special payments for services rendered to the state, including loyal suffering because of state actions, such as wars); *state supply of other private goods*. Public goods and the first two kinds of private goods derive from intrinsic failures and deficiencies of markets. The last two sorts of private goods from markets coming into conflicts with the different rationalities of states, classes, and citizenship.

## 5. Human reproduction as a public good

### 1. *The quantity and the quality of the population*

Simple human reproduction, in the sense of the sheer survival of a given socio-politically or ideologically bounded population, has of old been regarded as a public good in itself. It is inscribed in the prescription of alms and charity by all the world religions. From the feudal princes and the medieval town burghers (see, e.g., Lis & Soly 1979) to contemporary rightwing liberals such as, for instance, Milton Friedmann (1962:190 ff.) and his negative tax proposal, some kind of public obligation to provide in some ways at least for the incapacitated and socially abandoned indigent has been recognized. At issue has been and is how to distinguish natives from aliens, the deserving from the non-deserving, the requirements of securing labour supply, the conditions, the forms, and the terms of public intervention.

Expanded human reproduction may be regarded in qualitative as well as quantitative terms. Both are of old origins. The preamble to the Elizabethan Poor Law of 1598 stated that 'a good part of the strength of this realm consisteth in the number of good and able subjects' (Bruce 1968:36).

Population as an important source of national and state wealth was established in German political discourse in mid-eighteenth century by Johan Peter Süssmilch, Heinrich Gottlob von Justi and others, and adopted by the Elector of Brandenburg-Prussia. 'The number of people make the wealth of states' (Frevelt 1984:24–25).

Lots of public regulations are also geared to ensuring the quality of the population, from the prohibition of child labour to that of narcotic drugs, from housing norms to enviromental pollution control and, increasingly, regulation of smoking. The establishment of the British National Health Service is a major modern example of social policy geared to increasing the quality of the population. The 1946 Act which legislated the arrangement for England and Wales, somewhat different than from the rest of the UK, stated it to be the duty of the Minister of Health 'to promote the establishment in England and Wales of a comprehensive health service designed to secure improvement in the physical and mental health of the people of England and Wales and the prevention, diagnosis and treatment of illness' (Titmuss 1963:136).

The most important expression of state arrangements for ensuring the quality of the total population is, of course, compulsory education. A number of considerations coincided and combined in different mixtures pushing compulsory education in the course of the nineteenth century: nation-making and concerns with political loyalty, attention to moral order and social discipline, economic progress, human enlightenment, military capacity. Also the provision of higher education constitutes a public good in so far as a certain amount of higher education was regarded and instituted as a resource of the population as a whole and of its state organization.

2. *Expanded reproduction and the imbrication with the economic system*

Expanded human reproduction as a public good may also mean that the population should be able to live and reproduce itself under certain conditions above the level of survival. With regard to the welfare state, this would entail that the state undertakes a responsibility to provide for or to guarantee a supra-minimum maintenance and reproduction of human life. In economic terms, this could mean ensuring *security* against (the negative effects of) risks and hazards, a certain kind of *distribution*, and *growth*.

State commitment to ensuring economic growth constitutes a major change in political and economic history, the development of which has not yet been properly studied. It is clearly a post-World War II phenomenon, and theoretically an outflow of Keynesian economics, though hardly part of the post-war settlement. For instance, a commitment to promoting economic growth does not seem to have been included in any of the otherwise socio-economically very specific and intervention-ambitious constitutions of the West German provinces [Länder] in 1948–49 (Hartwich 1978:28 ff., 40 ff.). Rather, it seems to have developed out of the actual boom experiences under the changed political parameters. Mosley (1984:89) singles out the anti-recession budgets of the conservative Churchill and Eisenhower governments in 1953 and 1954, respectively, as a historical policy turn to growth stabilization in advanced capitalist countries. In the developmentalist perspective of Socialist as well as Third World countries, state commitment to economic growth has become a central aspect of policy.

Security may be assured in two fundamentally different ways. Either through prevention (including mechanisms for re-equilibrating disturbances) of or through compensation for negative outcomes. For many risks of human life there is no prevention, those of the life-cycle for example, or little effective, accidents, many kinds of illness. Compensation is therefore a major welfare state principle of above-minimum human reproduction, the prevailing feature of contemporary social insurance schemes. As a principle of state policy income compensation was first instituted by the Bismarck social insurance legislation. But we have already seen above that this does not warrant Luhmann's (1981:8) idea of a 'compensatory principle' constituting the 'logic of the welfare state'. And in one field of securing a life above subsistence, a major alternative has been developed, i.e. with regard to maintaining full employment.

Large-scale public job creation was propagated as early as the end of the Ancien Régime in France and was put into effect (albeit not very successfully, due to a still little competent state apparatus) during the Revolution (Forrest 1981: ch. 6). Its role and its bloody end in the 1848 revolution are well known. But the institutionalization of full employment as a public good for which the state has the ultimate responsibility is a post-World War II phenomenon. Most clearly and consensually this institutionalization took place in Norway. Also in Sweden, Switzerland, Japan, and Austria, full employment developed as an unconditional goal of policy and the economy.

In other countries it became established at least as one, of a few, major public policy goals. Other countries, notably Belgium and the Netherlands, opted for generous compensation of unemployment, while refraining from any commitment to full employment as part of their post-war settlement (Therborn 1986c: 110 ff., 149 ff.).

To what extent may growth and security, whether through compensation or prevention, be regarded as a public good? As such, the growth of national income is not a public good. Its benefits are divisible, rivally consumable, and parts of the population may feasibly be excluded from enjoying them. Only to the extent that economic growth is also regarded as an attribute of the nation, an attribute in which all members can take pride and draw some benefit, does it take on the character of a public good.

Security through compensation is mostly a state-provided private good. But it would make up a public good to the extent that a general above-subsistence income is guaranteed everybody in the given population in case of market income loss or non-availability. What is 'above subsistence' has no very clear boundary downwards. But the Netherlands makes up a clear case.

The most extensive above-subsistence system of general income maintenance was established in the Netherlands in 1974 – legally codified in 1979 but nevertheless partly eroded in the 1980s – when social assistance was made equal to the legal minimum wage, net of taxes (see further Roebroek & Therborn 1988).

To the extent that the supply of full employment is elastic to demand, it is a public good. Then A's 'consumption' of full employment does not subtract from B's. By and large for Japan and, more clearly, Norway and Sweden this holds true in the sense that in the 1974–85 crisis not only was full employment maintained – labour force survey-measured unemployment never going above 3.5 per cent of the labour force (OECD 1986:185) – the employment/population ratio also increased.

Distribution may refer to opportunity/access or to outcomes. Both have at least a class and territorial aspect, sometimes an ethnic one as well. Equality of opportunity with regard to post-elementary education seems to be a widespread general social norm, and thereby a public good, expressed in systems of economic support. Territorial equality of access was a most important reason for the establishment of the British National Health Service (Titmuss 1983:143).

The extent to which an egalitarian income distribution enters into individual welfare functions and come to constitute a public good is difficult to establish empirically. Looked at from the angle of the supply of welfare state policies, it appears clear that achieving a certain overall distribution of income has rarely been of any importance – in contrast to bettering the distributive outcome of particular groups and categories. On the whole, the welfare state has not been and is not about equality. Progressive income taxation seems to have emerged more out of pragmatic concerns of state revenue raising – more taxes could be got out of higher income earners – than with any redistributive aims in mind. This was clearly the case in Sweden, for example (Rodriguez 1981:25 ff.). A more ethically formulated variant of the revenue-raising perspective is the common Dutch political norm, that 'the strongest shoulders should carry the heaviest burdens'. Neither is directed towards a specific distributive outcome, and part of the finance of Dutch social insurance is in fact income regressive, with ceilings to contributions (see further Roebroek & Therborn 1988).

This being said, it should be added that the extensive Norwegian and Swedish welfare states, having both a relatively egalitarian pre-tax income distribution and apparently the strongest amount of tax redistribution (Sawyer 1976:16–17; Ringen 1986) – features which have hardly been affected by the changes of government incumbency in the past decade – seem to involve some kind of egalitarian income distribution as a public good in these countries. They would then constitute an exception among welfare states.

## 6. The demand for state welfare as a public good

In sociological terms, what economists call a public good presupposes a community and a community norm. A community in the minimal sense of a finite population making up one set of consumers, and (an internalized) community norm in the sense of a common element of individual utility functions. It is not necessary that this norm is internalized in every single individual of a given population, the public good may entail a cost to some part of the population, which has to be included in the social welfare function (cf. Thurow 1971:330–2). After all, the public good character of defence is not regarded as nullified by the existence of a pacifist minority. In the impure world of empirical reality there are forced riders as well as free riders (cf. Merman 1980). Likewise, sociological theory allows for deviance alongside norms. Thus, the boundary may be blurred, but a predominant community norm, a predominant common element of individual utility functions is required. The stronger the norm, the more important the common element(s) of the individual utility functions, the more important the public good.

For the provision of public goods to be invested in the state, at least one more condition is necessary. The community has to be coextensive with the state. Non-market provision is the best provision of public goods, but the state is not the only conceivable non-market provider. Supra- as well as sub-state non-market organizations of all kinds are equally conceivable. Churches, ethnic and class organizations – international, national, and subnational – generally 'clubs' of whatever sort (cf. Buchanan 1965) may provide public goods for their members. Vast social processes have contributed to the development of national communities, what Marx called the socialization of the productive forces – the extension of transport, communication and of general economic interpendence – the growth of state forces of administration, the industrialization of warfare, the political strivings of citizens exercising their equal rights, the challenge and the struggles of disadvantaged classes, secularization.

In brief, state-coextensive national communities should be expected to tend to develop state-invested public goods provisions. Ethnically, religiously or class divided or state-transcending communities not, or less, or less, so. Countries of ethnically heterogeneous immigration we should expect to have less of a state-coextensive national community and therefore of state-provided public goods than those of homogeneous immigration; Catholic less than Protestant countries or in countries with other national religions; religiously divided – whether by religions or by religion and secularism/atheism – countries less so than religiously homogeneous ones; sharply class-divided and stratified societies less than mildly class-divided and relatively egalitarian societies; nationalist or religiously committed national communities more than little nationalist and secularized ones.

Three determining and structuring mechanisms of public goods politics may be singled out – *power, learning, and strategic action and exchange.*

Sociologists and political scientists have good reasons for not just regarding human populations as interacting aggregates of individuals, but also as systems of power relations among individual and collective actors. We can then assume that the community norms established express the power relations, the hegemony, within a given community at a given point in time – without excluding the possibility of the limiting case in which the community distribution of power is absolutely equal.

There are many bases and forms of power relationships, but in this context we are only concerned with national communities, with the extent to which state-bound populations constitute national communities, a sociological prerequisite for the emergence of national public goods. Under these circumstances, inter-ethnic and inter-religious power relations are by definition of secondary importance. (If they were not, there would be no national community). Whereas ethnicity and religion belonging are inclusive/exclusive – the Other, those not belonging, being of indifferent character, or principally irrelevant. Otherness – class and gender are positional, one class or gender always having to relate to the other in a common mode of production and sexuality, respectively (see further Therborn 1980:22 ff.). In other words, in (class-structured) national communities, class tends to be a major aspect of power relations. On the basis of capacity for collective action, classes are also more powerful actors than genders (cf. Korpi 1983:23–24; Therborn 1986d: part III).

From class interests within a given mode of production, class perspectives on social policy can be deduced, and also empirically corroborated (Therborn 1984:20–30, 1986b:154 ff.). But these rational interests are not enough. There is also a process of historical learning from experiences with having to adapt to contingent historical parameters (cf. Heclo 1974). Out of processes of historical learning from handed-down institutions and conditions of state and society and from confrontations with crises, challenges, and problems potential community norms emerge, to be fed into the game of power and influence.

A special case is when and where the number and/or the quality of the population weigh upon inter-state and inter-national rivalry and conflict. Under such circumstances, we should expect the ruling powers to push for public provisions for expanded human reproduction. Perhaps has this point been nowhere as frankly put officially as in the final conclusion of the 1909 British Majority Report on the Poor Law: 'No country, however rich, can permanently hold its own in the face of international competition, if hampered by an increasing load of this dead weight;

or can successfully perform the role of sovereignty beyond the seas, if a portion of its own folk at home are sinking below the civilization and aspirations of its subject races abroad' (Bruce 1968:156).

Finally, power and goals are not sufficient for the realization of the latter. The translation of ends into reality is hardly ever an automatic process, however powerful. In between is the process of strategic action turning intentions into reality. Strategic action implies timing, definitions of possible partners and opponents, choice of moves. Furthermore, a community norm and a public good is not something imposable by the fiat of brute force. Sociologists would see it develop in a process of internalization, economists in one of exchange (of compensation for costs). Having to be made under conditions of uncertainty, we have no reaon to expect that strategic action and exchange should always be optimal, under given relations of power. From the transaction costs of replay, however, we should expect strong discontinuities in settlements of social contracts and of public goods. The community norm/public good game is not all the time instantly re-playable.

## 7. Schedules of state supply

An important contribution of both Public Choice theory and the so-called state-centred approach to social studies has been to highlight the political supply and offer of state-provided welfare as a correction to an exclusive focus on the societal demand for it. But neither has paid much systematic attention to the relations of both schedules. The supply schedule of state welfare should be seen as a function of the price in terms of pecuniary and non-pecuniary benefits – power, support, deference, etc. – that state leaders and administrators expect to obtain from it, and of the costs of effort and of possible loss of support. The shape of the supply schedules will basically depend on the character of the historical state formation and on the type of welfare goods.

Strong bureaucratic states, in the strict Weberian sense, coming out of Absolutism, should be expected to have a relatively inelastic supply of welfare, because such states have both relatively large fixed costs and have as an institutionalized apparatus little extra benefits of popular support to expect. The opposite holds for patronage-clientelistic states, having low fixed costs and being strongly dependent upon the support of (smaller or larger) clienteles.

With regard to the supply of public goods, of corrections for externalities, of merit goods, and of welfare to the state personnel itself, we should expect to find the supply schedule of bureaucratic states to be the right of that of clientelistic states. That is, for a given price, bureaucratic states should provide a larger quantity of welfare. In the first three cases mainly because of lower costs of effort in issuing regulations, providing services, organizing payments, and in raising revenue, due to the already existing organizational capacity of bureaucracies. With regard to the provision of extra state wages for itself, a strong bureaucracy faces less risk of loss of crucial public support.

On the other hand, less bureaucratic and more clientelistic states should be expected to be more generous in providing other private goods, welfare for societal pressure groups, because of low fixed administrative costs and crucial benefits to be reaped from clientelistic support. State supply of the latter kind of private welfare goods will also tend to be more inelastic to the extent political representation is based on equal citizens rather than on inegalitarian societal patterns of dependence, and to the extent that it is based on stable programmatic parties, rather than a fragmented and volatile electorate.

From the above we should expect the American state, at all levels, to be a major provider of private goods. This seems also to have been the case, above all in the post-Civil War period and in the times of the urban political machines. Around 1900, American pensions to Civil War veterans comprised four times as many beneficiaries (one million) as the famous German pensions insurance, to a younger population only one third larger than that of the German Reich (Orloff 1985:69; Ritter 1983:55; Maddison 1982:248, 258; see further Skocpol & Ikenberry 1983).

## 8. The demand for state-provided private goods

The demand schedule is a function of the benefits to be received, income, status, security, and of the price to pay, of taxes, loyalty, deference, of alternatives foregone. With regard to externalities, the popular demand schedule would tend to be rather inelastic, and actual supply should be mainly dependent on the character of the state and its supply schedule.

The same considerations will hold for merit goods, but here another relationship becomes important. The regulation of fatal (or at least problematic) choices with regard to human reproduction may very well take a non-state form. A classical alternative to the state is the institution of a self-governing profession. Both require a cost of deference and obedience from the public, and a complex interaction and exchange between state, the aspiring profession, and the public of citizens settled the terms. For the key case of medical practice, see Ramsey (1984), Starr (1982: ch. 3), Göckenjan (1985: ch. 5.3), cf. Navarro (1976). However, state medical care developed out of public asylums for the poor – which was the main pre-modern meaning of the 'hospital' – and failed to develop where the latter were insignificant, thus determined by the supply schedules of states (cf. Abel-Smith 1972).

Demand for state provision of pure private goods, without externalities and problems of choice, will be redistributive. It is rational for individuals of group A to demand state provision of a benefit for which B will pay or contribute. Demands for redistribution will come from actors who are disadvantaged in the primary income distribution. However, actual democratic history contains much less of redistributive efforts, and still less of unambiguously redistributive outcomes, than classical liberal political theory and its fears of democracy should lead us to expect.

There are two potential major costs, to the beneficiary, of state provision. One is state control – which may be stronger or milder, and at the limit even non-existent – over entitlements, use of funds and other resources. The other is loss of identity into a state-defined aggregate. These costs will tend to be higher the more distant one is from the centre of political power, which usually means the more disadvantaged one is in the primary distribution of income.

Contrary to liberal beliefs about democracy, the strongest demands for state provision of private goods should be expected to come from rather advantaged groups in the face of challenges and adversities. This also seems to be the case with means for direct human reproduction, here disregarding industrial and agricultural tariffs. The most extensive state funding of private services and privately distributed benefits have resulted from demands by powerful religious denominations. Particularly in Belgium and the Netherlands, both weak states, state funding or contributions to private religious schools, health services, social insurance schemes have developed on a large scale (for an overview of the history of social security in the Low Countries, see Veldkamp 1978: ch. 2). In neither case has there been any significant cost of state control and loss of identity, probably rather an enhancement of self-control and self-identity through state back-up.

Cases where successful demands for state provision of social insurance was used for establishing a separate social identity of a relatively well-off social category are the German and Austrian special white collar employee schemes of social insurance (Kocka 1981: 134 ff.; Otruba 1981). The ethnically based US political machines seem to have provided similar benefits for relatively established new immigrant ethnicities.

In contrast to this demanding activity of churches, of white collar employees, and of relatively resourceful immigrants, the passivity and often lack of interest, sometimes outright hostility of working-class organizations to state-provided welfare (Therborn 1986a: 5–7; Hatzfeld 1971: ch. IV) is remarkable, but understandable. The working class had a lot to lose. Its own cultural and organizational identity was established apart from the state, but was not likely to remain untouched by provisions and, to be expected, control from a hostile state. Once social insurance was set up or about to be passed in one form or another, the working class and the labour movement obviously had specific interests to pursue with regard to organization, coverage, finance, and level of benefits. To the extent also that the character of the state changed into being governed by labour parties, the costs lowered.

Two further important conditions have affected labour demand for state-provided private goods. To the extent that workers are organized as a class, and not just as an aggregate of workers, class unity and unifying alliances, with other low income earners, and general class conditions, enter into the utility function of working-class organizations. This unity is impossible to achieve in separate small-scale mutual aid societies, with their lack of competence, their accumulation of risks, tendencies of exclusion, their high probability of failure (de Swaan 1986; Köhler 1979:58–59), as well as in collectively bargained 'occupational welfare'. Such a kind of class organization is a political party of the 'Germanic' type, which has a political perspective transcending trade unions' representation but which is more rooted in everyday class concerns than a parliamentary party or one of notables (cf. Buci-Glucksmann & Therborn 1981:30 ff.; Kocka 1983; Castles 1985). In case such a party was not available, for pre-determined historical reasons, nor a friendly state capable of provision, working-class strategy had to be directed elwewhere. Samuel Gompers was not a working-class politician, but a (skilled worker, by origin a cigar-maker) trade unionist. But his notorious hostility to state provisions was not just an American or a personal aberration. His idea of union-provided social benefits (see further Taft 1957) is still embraced and practiced today by the strongest labour movement of the Capitalist world, the Swedish one, in the system of unemployment insurance (mainly state-paid for though, the same holds for unemployment insurance in Belgium, Denmark, and Finland), if only as part of a much wider welfare system. The problem is, however, that once the parameters are set against a unifying class strategy, the rational pursuit of a second-best stretegy may divide the class even more, which may be fatal the day the positive-sum game of capital-labour relations is over (for the background to the post-World War II concentration on enterprise welfare by American unions, see Stevens 1985).

Secondly, to the extent that workers and their organization grow strong enough to have a realistic chance of using the state for class redistribution, they will tend to demand a democratization of employer-controlled welfare, such as enterprise insurance funds at the employer's discretion, and an equalization of fringe benefits with white collar employees. In both respects collective bargaining is an alternative to demands upon the state, and from a unionized working-class point of view the latter will be a second option dependent upon the character of the state and the bargaining relations of power. The struggle for a working-class second-tier pensions system in Sweden in the late 1950s is a classical case.

Summarily put, workers' demands of state-provided private welfare goods is a positive function of class strength, class unity, and the friendly character of the state. It is not inherent in working-class rationality. Under opposite circumstances, workers' best strategy is a non-welfare state one.

Historically, the supply and effective demand of state goods, whether public or private, has been male. But to the extent that women assert their equal rights as citizens and their resources as market actors, a woman's demand for state services is likely to develop as a means of emancipation from patriarchal authority, demanding paid and secure maternity leave, daycare centres, publicly provided care of the elderly. Paid, public provision of care constitutes a major emancipation of women from unpaid, patriarchally controlled labour. The demand schedule for state-provided private goods has to include the independence and the market strength of women as well.

## References


Abel-Smith, B. 1972. The History of Medical Care. *In* E. W. Martin (ed.), *Comparative Development in Social Welfare*. London: Allen & Unwin.

Alber, J. 1982. *Vom Armenhaus zum Wohlfahrtstaat*. Frankfurt: Campus.

Amenta, E. & Skocpol, T. 1986. States and Social Policies. *Annual Rev. of Sociology* 12. In press.

Archer, M. 1979. *Social Origins of Educational Systems*. London and Beverly Hills: Sage.

Arrow, K. 1963. Uncertainty and the Welfare Economics of Medical Care. *Am. Economic Rev.* 53: 941–973.

Berkowitz, E. & McQuaid, K. 1980. *Creating the Welfare State*. New York: Praeger.

Boli, J. et al. 1985. Explaining the Origins and Expansion of Mass Education. *Comparative Education Review* 29: 145–170.

Bowles, S. & Gintis, H. 1976. *Schooling in Capitalist America*. New York: Basic Books.

Bruce, M. 1968. *The Coming of the Welfare State*. 4th ed. London: Batsford.

Buchanan, J. 1965. An Economic Theory of Clubs. *Economica* 32: 1–14.

Buci-Glucksmann, Ch. & Therborn, G. 1981. *Le défi social-démocrate*. Paris: Maspero.

Castles, F. 1985. *The Working Class and Welfare*. Wellington and London: Allen & Unwin.

Dhavernas, O. 1978. *Droits de femmes, pouvoir des hommes*. Paris: Seuil.

Fischer, W. 1978. Die Pionierrolle der betrieblichen Sozialpolitik im 19. und beginnenden 20. Jahrhundert. *Zeit-schrift f. Unternehmensgeschichte*, Beiheft 12.

Forrest, A. 1981. *The French Revolution and the Poor*. Oxford: Blackwell.

Foucault, M. 1973. *The Birth of the Clinic*. New York: Pantheon.

Foucault, M. 1977. *Discipline and Punish.* New York: Pantheon.
Frevert, U. 1984. *Krankheit als politisches Problem 1770–1880.* Göttingen: Vandenhoeck & Ruprecht.
Friedmann, M. 1962. *Capitalism and Freedom.* Chicago: Univ. of Chicago Press.
Frijhoff, W. (ed.) 1983. *L'offre d'école.* Paris: Publications de la Sorbonne.
Frykman, J. & Löfgren, O. 1979. *Den kultiverade människan.* Lund: Liber.
Geison, G. (ed.) 1984. *Professions and the French State, 1700–1900.* Philadelphia: Univ. of Pennsylvania Press.
Göckenjan, G. 1985. *Kurieren und Staat machen.* Frankfurt: Suhrkamp.
Gough, I. 1978. *The Political Economy of the Welfare State.* Basingstoke: Macmillan.
Habermas, J. 1985. Die Krise des Wohlfahrtstaates und die Erschöpfung utopischer Energien. Pp. 141–63 in idem, *Die neue Unübersichtlichkeit.* Frankfurt: Suhrkamp.
Hartwich, H. 1978. *Sozialstaatspostulat und gesellschaftlicher status quo.* 3rd ed. Opladen: Westedeutscher Verlag.
Hatzfeld, H. 1971. *Du Paupérisme à la sécurité sociale 1850–1940.* Paris: Armand Colin.
Heclo, H. 1974. *Modern Social Politics in Britain and Sweden.* New Haven: Yale Univ. Press.
Hernes, H. 1984. Women and the Welfare State: The Transition Private to Public Dependence. Pp. 26–45 in H. Holter (ed.), *Patriarchy in Welfare Society.* Oslo: Universitetsforlaget.
Katz, M. 1975. *Class, Bureaucracy and Schools.* New York: Praeger.
Kickbusch, I. & Riedmüller, B. (eds.) 1984. *Die armen Frauen.* Frankfurt: Suhrkamp.
Kocka, J. 1981. *Die Angestellten in der deutschen Geschichte.* Göttingen: Vandenhoeck & Ruprecht.
Kocka, J. 1983. Die Trennung von proletarsicher und bürgerlicher Demokratie im europäischen Vergleich. Pp. 5–20 in idem (ed.), *Europäische Arbeiterbewegungen im 19. Jahrhundert.* Göttingen: Vandenhoeck & Ruprecht.
Larson, M. S. 1977. *The Rise of Professionalism.* Berkeley: Univ. of California Press.
LeGrand, J. 1982. *The Strategy of Equality.* London: Allen & Unwin.
Lis, C. & Soly, H. 1979. *Poverty and Capitalism in Pre-Industrial Europe.* London: Harvester Press.
Luhmann, N. 1981. *Politische Theorie im Wohlfahrtsstaat.* München: Olzog.
Luhmann, N. 1985. *Soziale Systeme.* Frankfurt: Suhrkamp.
Maddison, A. 1982. *Ontwikkelingsfasen van het kapitalisme.* Utrecht: Het Spectrum.
Marshall, T. H. 1965. Citizenship and Social Class. Pp. 71–134 in idem *Class, Citizenship and Social Development.* Garden City, N.Y.: Anchor Books.
Maxwell, R. 1981. *Health and Wealth.* Lexington, Mass.: Lexington Books.
Meerman, J. 1980. Are Public Goods Public Goods? *Public Choice* 35:45–57.
Merton, R. 1957. *Social Theory and Social Structure.* Glencoe III: The Free Press. Rev. ed.
Mosley, P. 1984. *The Making of Economic Policy.* Brighton: Wheatsheaf Books.
Murray, Ch. 1984. *Losing Ground.* New York: Basic Books.
Musgrave, R. & Musgrave, P. 1976. *Public Finance in Theory and Practice.* New York: McGraw-Hill.
Myles, J. 1984. *Old Age in the Welfare State: The Political Economy of Public Pensions.* Boston: Little Brown.
Navarro, V. 1976. *Medicine under Capitalism.* New York: Neale Watson.
OECD 1986. Economic Outlook no. 39. Paris.
Okun, A. 1975. *Equality and Efficiency.* Washington: The Brookings Institution.
Opielka, M. (ed.) 1983. *Die Zukunft des Sozialstaats.* Stuttgart: Die Grünen. 2nd ed.
Orloff, A. 1985. The Politics of Pensions. PhD Diss. Dept. of Sociology, Princeton University.
Orloff, A. & Skocpol, T. 1984. Why not Equal Protection? *Am. Sociol. Rev.* 49:726–750.
Otruba, G. 1981. Privatbeamten, Handlungsgehilfen und Angestelltenorganisationen. Pp. 240–256 in J. Kocka (ed.), *Angestellte im europäischen Vergleich.* Göttingen: Vandenhoeck & Ruprecht.
Persson, G. 1985. A Theory of the Welfare State. Inst. of Economics, University of Copenhagen.
Polanyi, K. 1957. *The Great Transformation.* Boston: Beacon Press.
Przeworski, A. 1985. *Capitalism and Social Democracy.* Cambridge: Cambridge Uiversity Press.

Ramsey, M. 1984. The Politics of Professional Monopoly in Nineteenth-Century Medicine: The French Model and Its Rivals. Pp. 225–305 in G. Geison (ed.), *Professions and the French State, 1700–1900*. Philadelphia: Univ. of Pennsylvania Press.
Ringen, S. 1986. *Difference and Similarity*. Stockholm: SOFI.
Ritter, G. 1983. *Sozialversicherung in Deutschland und England*. München: Beck.
Roebroek, J. & Therborn, C. 1988. Netherlands. *In* P. Flora (ed.), *Growth to Limits*, Vol. IV, Berlin: De Gruyter, forthcoming.
Rodriguez, E. 1981. *Den svenska skattehistorien*. Lund: Liber.
Rose, R. 1985. *Public Employment in Western Nations*. Cambridge: Cambridge University Press.
Rothstein, B. 1986. *Den socialdemokratiska staten*. Lund: Arkiv.
Sachsse, Ch. & Tenstedt, F. (eds.) 1986. *Soziale Sicherheit und soziale Disziplinierung*. Frankfurt: Suhrkamp.
Samuelson, P. 1954. The Pure Theory of Public Expenditure. *Rev. of Economics and Statistics* 36:387–389.
Sawyer, M. 1976. Income Distribution in OECD Countries. *OECD Economic Outlook Occasional Studies (July)*: 3–36.
Schmidt, M. 1982. Wohlfahrtstaatliche Politik unter bürgerlichen und sozialdemokratischen Regierungen. Frankfurt: Campus.
Skocpol, T. & Ikenberry, J. 1983. The Political Formation of the American Welfare State in Historial and Comparative Perspective. *Comparative Social Research* 6:87–147.
Starr, P. 1982. *The Social Transformation of American Medicine*. New York: Basic Books.
Stevens, B. 1985. Blurring the Boundaries: How Federal Social Policy Has Shaped Private Sector Welfare Benefits. Dept. of Sociology, New York University.
Strasser, J. 1981. *Grenzen des Sozialstaats?* Köln: Europäische Verlagsanstalt.
Swaan, A. de. 1986. Workers' and Clients' Mutualism Compared: Perspectives from the Past in the Development of the Welfare State. *Government and Opposition* 21:36–55.
Taft, Ph. 1957. *The A. of L. in the Time of Gompers*. New York: Harper and Row.
Tenstedt, F. 1983. *Vom Proleten zum Indusatriearbeiter. Arbeiterbeweung und Sozialpolitik in Deutschland 1800 bis 1914*. Köln.
Therborn, G. 1980. *The Ideology of Power and the Power of Ideology* London: Verso.
Therborn, G. 1984. Classes and States: Welfare State Developments 1881–1981. *Studies in Political Economy* no. 14: 7–41.
Therborn, G. 1985. The Coming of Swedish Social Democracy. Pp. 527–593 in E. Collotti (ed.), *L'Internazionale operaia e socialista tra le due guerre*. Milano: Feltrinelli.
Therborn, G. 1986a. The Working Class and the Welfare State. *In* P. Kettunen (ed.), *Det nordiska i den nordiska arbetarörelsen*, Helsinki: Finnish Society for Labour History and Cultural Traditions.
Therborn, G. 1986b. Karl Marx Returning. The Welfare State and Neo-Marxist, Corporatist and Statist Theories. *Internat. Pol. Sc. Rev.* 7:131–164.
Therborn, G. 1986c. *Why Some Peoples Are More Unemployed Than Others*. London: Verso.
Thurow, L. 1971. The Income Distribution As A Pure Public Good. *Quarterly J. of Economics* LXXXV:327–336.
Titmuss, R. 1963. *Essays on 'the Welfare State'*. London: Allen & Unwin. 2nd ed.
Titmuss, R. 1974. *Social Policy*. London: Allen & Unwin.

# [7]

# Vulnerabilities and Responsibilities: An Ethical Defense of the Welfare State

ROBERT E. GOODIN
*University of Essex*

*We all acknowledge strong special responsibilities towards families, friends, clients, and compatriots. The moral basis of these responsibilities is traditionally analyzed in terms of self-assumed obligations. That analysis substantially restricts their scope, because we voluntarily commit ourselves to only a limited range of people. In this article I argue that it is the beneficiary's vulnerability rather than any voluntary commitment as such on the part of the benefactor that generates these special responsibilities. This analysis provides an argument for broader notions of responsibility, because there are many more agents vulnerable to us (individually or collectively) than to whom we have made commitments, in any sense. The welfare state is one particularly apt way of discharging at least some of these further responsibilities. Unlike more individualized responses, the welfare state can satisfy the criteria of a morally acceptable dependency relationship.*

The aim of this article is to broaden our sense of social responsibility. It is first and foremost an argument in favor of state welfare services. The basic strategy is to try to put them morally on a par with the services we render—and which we firmly believe we *should* render—to family and friends. The method of discharging these other responsibilities differs but, I will argue, their moral basis is the same. A parallel argument, which here I have space only to sketch baldly, generates analogous international and intergenerational responsibilities and responsibilities for protecting animals and natural environments. Thus this approach promises to provide a unified analysis of a great many of our moral responsibilities.

The argument employs the method of the "reflective equilibrium," in which the goal is to bring our general moral principles and our "settled intuitions" about what is right and wrong in any particular case into line with one another, striving all the while for coherence within our set of general principles and for concordance between those principles and our various other "background theories" (Daniels, 1979; Rawls, 1971, sections 4 and 9).

In such a procedure, we must always be prepared to reject some of the moral duties and responsibilities that untutored intuition lays upon us. By the same token, the reflective equilibrium can also carry us well beyond ordinary moral instincts by showing us that we have moral duties and responsibilities that intuitively we might deny having. This is the side of the reflective equilibrium that interests me here.

The moral theory that best explains those intuitions that we do have will, typically, also commit us to moral judgments about what we should do in situations that are strictly analogous but about which we have no strong intuitions. By showing us what lies hidden within our ordinary moral sentiments, the reflective equilibrium can thus drive us to acknowledge commitments we would pre-analytically have shunned.

## Special Responsibilities

My argument starts from what I take to be one of our firmest moral intuitions, one that we would be loath to sacrifice in this process of reflective equilibrium. That is the intuition that we have especially strong responsibilities toward our families, friends, clients, and compatriots. Charity, we seem strongly to believe, not only does but *should* begin at home. Our primary responsibilities are toward those who stand in some special relationship to us. Strangers get, and are ordin-

Received: February 14, 1984
Revision received: October 5, 1984
Accepted for publication: December 19, 1984

This essay draws on work done while I was attached to the Social Justice Project at the Australian National University (Goodin, 1985a). Earlier versions were read there and at the Universities of Auckland, Otago, Canterbury, Melbourne, and Essex. I am grateful for comments, then and later, from Annette Baier, Brian Barry, Stanley Benn, Ted Benton, Derek Browne, Tom Campbell, Jim Fishkin, Jim Flynn, Diane Gibson, John Kleinig, David Miller, David Novitz, Onora O'Neill, Carole Pateman, Philip Pettit, Val (Routley) Plumwood, Wojciech Sadurski, Marian Sawer, Christine Swanton, Richard (Routley) Sylvan, David Tucker, Patricia Tulloch, Jeremy Waldron, Hugh Ward, and this *Review*'s anonymous referees.

arily thought to deserve, only what (if anything) is left over.

An example from Bernard Williams effectively evokes this intuition. Suppose you were in a fiery air crash and able to pull out only one other victim before the entire plane exploded. On one side of you is a distinguished surgeon, black bag at hand, who could save the lives of several other passengers thrown clear of the airplane when it went down. On the other side is your son. It would, according to the intuition Williams shares with so many others, be morally reprehensible for you to save the surgeon in preference to your own son.[1]

Now, of course, such favoritism would be perfectly understandable from any number of perspectives. Both psychologically and sociologically, it is easy to see why our affections should extend principally to those "of our own kind" rather than to the unknown strangers the surgeon might save. Sociobiologists would point out that saving your son increases the chances of your own genes surviving in the next generation. There is no shortage of adequate explanations for why you would, in fact, favor your own flesh and blood. The question is whether morally you should.

A long tradition in moral theory says firmly you should not. Indeed, any universalistic theory—be it Kantian or utilitarian—would take just that stand. But that, say many philosophers and even more laypersons, is precisely what is wrong with all universalistic ethics. Sir David Ross (1930, p. 21) insists that "the essential defect of the . . . utilitarian theory is that it ignores . . . the highly personal character of duty"; he is outraged that, for example, act-utilitarians are incapable of distinguishing between my giving $10 to my benefactor and my giving the same sum to someone who needs it just as badly but "to whom I stand in no special relation." In a continuing stream of articles, Williams (1973, p. 110; 1981) has been arguing for the moral importance of respecting people, which entails among other things respecting their "projects," including their special commitments to their families and friends. For Parfit (1984, p. 95), "common-sense morality largely consists" in "special obligations" owed to "the people to whom we stand in certain relations—such as our children, parents, pupils, patients, members of our own trade union, or those whom we represent." Or, for a final example, a central theme in Walzer's (1983, p. 31) *Spheres of Justice* is that, "The idea of distributive justice presupposes a bounded world, a community within which distributions take place, a group of people committed to dividing, exchanging and sharing, first of all, among themselves."

Our firm moral intuitions go further still. Not only do we feel that we have these special duties to family and friends, alongside our other, more general moral duties. We also feel that "carrying out these obligations has priority over helping strangers," as Parfit (1984, p. 95) goes on to say. Perhaps those special obligations are not quite strong enough to override negative duties not to harm others. It would be thought wrong for us to commit murder, even if that were necessary for us to feed our own children. But apparently those special duties are quite strong enough to override any duties we might have to render positive assistance to others in general. In *Bleak House*, Dickens ridicules Mrs. Jellyby's "telescopic philanthropy," that is, her tendency to aid distant Africans while neglecting her own family. No doubt most of us are intuitively inclined to say that it is right to satisfy our own children before giving food to needy neighbors. The consequence of acting on such intuitions, however, is that our duties to those with whom we enjoy some special relationship ride roughshod over our duties to help others at large. That, obviously, is an outcome that any theory of social justice, or even of simple humanity, would dearly hope to avoid.

In what follows, I shall *not* be arguing that we lack any such responsibilities toward family and friends. Neither shall I be denying the strength of such claims. What I shall be arguing is that there is *nothing special* about those responsibilities. There are many others with precisely the same basis—and, depending on circumstances, perhaps even the same strength—as those responsibilities that we have always regarded as particularly binding. The upshot of this argument, if it is successful, is that we are not justified in our present practice of serving one set of claimants systematically to the exclusion of the other.

### Alternative Bases of Special Responsibilities

The theory ordinarily offered to account for the moral importance of these intuitively appealing special responsibilities deals in terms of self-assumed obligations. That analysis figures most famously in H.L.A. Hart's classic essay, "Are There Any Natural Rights?" which first introduced the concepts of special rights and duties into modern moral philosophy. "I think it is true of all special duties," Hart (1955, p. 185) wrote,

[1]This is just updating and inverting Godwin's (1793, bk. 2, chap. 2) infamous example of being forced to choose between saving your mother or some greater public benefactor (Archibishop Fenelon) from a house fire. William's air crash example is related by Hare (1981, p. 138), who is highly critical of the conclusions reached by Williams there and elsewhere (Williams, 1981, pp. 17-18). See similarly Gorovitz (1977), Blum (1980), Oldenquist (1982), and Winkler (1982).

"that they arise from previous voluntary acts." Hart's own discussion is characteristically cagey, abounding with qualifications, exceptions, and ambiguities. His general principle, however, has passed into the philosophical conventional wisdom pretty well shorn of equivocation. Thomson (1971, p. 65), for example, asserts quite baldly, "Surely we do not have any . . . 'special responsibility' for a person unless we have assumed it, explicitly or implicitly" (see similarly Rawls, 1958, p. 158).

The great appeal of the model of self-assumed obligations is that it explains so neatly what is "special" about our special rights, duties, obligations, and responsibilities. Special obligations are distinguished from general ones in two ways. First, whereas everyone has the same general duties, special obligations vary from person to person: I have special responsibilities that you do not. Second, whereas general duties are owed to everyone equally, special obligations are owed to specific others: I have different responsibilities to different people. The analysis of special obligations as self-assumed obligations accounts for both features beautifully. According to that analysis, I have some obligations that others do not because I have assumed them and others have not; my obligations vary because I have assumed obligations with respect to some people but not others.

The paradigm case of a special obligation is, for Hart (1955, pp. 183-184) as for all advocates of this model, a promissory or contractual obligation. A promissor, through a voluntary act of will, imposes upon himself an obligation that is peculiarly his own, not shared by the world at large, and his obligation is owed to a specific individual, the promisee, rather than to the world at large. Various other special responsibilities—of businessmen to their customers and employees (Atiyah, 1979), of professionals to their clients (Fried, 1974, p. 78), of all of us to our families (Hart, 1958, p. 104) and friends (Montaigne, 1580/1958, p. 137)—are, within this model, seen as more-or-less attenuated instances of this same basic promissory pattern.

Perhaps the most important practical consequence of analyzing special responsibilities as self-assumed obligations is to reinforce our intuitions about their restricted scope. After all, most of us voluntarily assume responsibility in any way whatsoever for only a very limited number of people. On this account, we have no special responsibilities (but only, at most, much weaker general responsibilities) that have not been voluntarily self-assumed.

The model I want to counterpose to that traditional one traces our special responsibilities to the peculiar vulnerabilities of specific others to our actions and choices. It is their vulnerability, not our promises or any other voluntary act of will on our part, that imposes upon us special responsibilities with respect to them. The promissory obligations that figure so centrally in the traditional account are, on this analysis, just a special case of vulnerability. If I promised and others are depending on me in consequence, then I am obliged to do as I promised—not because I promised, but merely because they are depending on (i.e., are vulnerable to) me.[2]

Whereas the paradigm of self-assumed special obligations is the promise or contract, the paradigm for the vulnerability model is family responsibilities. Hart (1955, p. 187) himself admits the difficulty of assimilating these rights and duties to his model of self-assumed obligations. And well he should. You do not enter into families voluntarily. You do not ask to be born; you do not choose your parents or siblings. In the first instance, anyway, you make them no promises and extract none from them.

Even areas of family life that appear on first brush to be contractual turn out not to be completely so. The standard "marriage contract," for example, deviates crucially from the legal ideal of a contract. The authors of the *Second Restatement of the Law of Contracts* are at pains to emphasize that fact: "Although marriage is sometimes loosely referred to as a 'contract,' the marital relationship has not been regarded by the common law as contractual in the usual sense" because "many terms of the relationship are seen as largely fixed by the state and beyond the power of the parties to modify" (Braucher & Farnsworth, 1981, sec. 90; see further Pateman, 1981). Even if marriage partners were to write their own contract, there would be certain duties (such as the duty of support) that would be regarded legally as "essential features" of the marital relationship and which the two parties involved would be legally unable to alter, even by mutual consent. That, of course, violates a fundamental precept of contracting.[3]

To see how completely ill-suited a model built

[2]Hence, I basically have no obligation to keep a promise when the promisee is not depending on me in any way to do so. The only reason I then would is that everyone in society depends on the maintenance of the institution of promising, which is vulnerable to being undermined (however slightly) by my breach. That fact explains why the courts award damages, but only nominal ones, in cases where one party suffers no loss from the other's breach of contract. See Braucher and Farnsworth (1981, sec. 346) and, more generally, Atiyah (1979), Gilmore (1974), and Kronman (1981).

[3]Champions of the voluntaristic model might reply that the parties have at least voluntarily assumed their roles and the concomitant (albeit unalterable) duties.

around contractual or quasi-contractual notions of reciprocity is to the analysis of family responsibilities, consider just two of its more absurd conclusions. First, on that account, a child who lived at home until age 21 would have incurred a debt to his parents 16.6% greater than that of his sister, who left home at 18. But surely the children's obligations to aid their ill and aged mother depend merely on her present needs and their relative capacities to meet them, and not on their past performances. It would be absurd to suggest that the son who remained at home longer should pay 16% more, even though he is now earning 50% less than his sister. (If it really were a case of debt, notice, it would not be absurd: our business obligations are invariant with respect to our capacities to meet them, at least until we declare bankruptcy.) Second, it would be equally absurd to suggest that the debt children owe their parents might at some point be fully repaid, and the children relieved of any further obligation to help parents, however ill they may be. Once contractual debts have been met, any special relationship between creditor and debtor dissolves. The two parties then stand in exactly the same relationship as before the debt was incurred. That is simply not how families or friendships work. A favor and a return-favor do not cancel each other out and dissolve the relationship; instead, they strengthen it (English, 1979, p. 345; Heath, 1976, pp. 59-60).[4]

What most fundamentally underlies the reciprocal duties of family life—of spouses to one another, of parents to their children, of children to their aged parents—is the vulnerability of those parties to one another. The protracted dependency of the human infant is, biologists tell us, one of the most striking features of the species. Much vulnerability is material in nature. Wageless members of the family depend on the wage-earner(s) to bring home the bacon; children depend upon their parents to feed, clothe, and shelter them; in the absence of adequate collective provision, ill or infirm parents are often dependent upon their children for care of a very material sort.[5] But we must not focus exclusively upon these material forms of vulnerability. Much of the vulnerability, in family life and friendships more generally, is of an emotional sort. That fact provides a crucial link in the argument explaining why the material support in question has to come from the particular person it does (for example, the parent, child), instead of some unrelated other who might be in an objectively better position to provide it.[6]

One way to demonstrate the superiority of the vulnerability model would be to survey systematically those "special relationships" that we so readily acknowledge. Among the cases that might be discussed, in addition to the family responsibilities just mentioned, are the special responsibilities of businessmen for the safety of their employees and customers, of professionals (especially doctors and lawyers) for their clients, of friends to one another, and of beneficiaries to their benefactors. The aim would be to show that the vulnerability model can offer a plausible account of all features of all these special responsibilities, whereas the model of self-assumed obligations can at best account for only a few features of a few of them. Such a case-by-case demonstration is, however, beyond the bounds of the present essay and is conducted elsewhere (Goodin, 1985a, chap. 4) instead.

The best quick demonstration of the superiority of the vulnerability model is this. Imagine someone who is utterly helpless. The model of self-assumed

Although that may explain why marriage partners have special responsibilities, no such voluntaristic analysis can explain what they are; for that, a separate account must be given. The vulnerability model, in contrast, provides a unified account of both the fact and the content of those duties.

[4]Where families and friendships are concerned, reciprocal favors create bonds transcending the simple sort of trust that underlies long-standing commercial relationships, which amounts to little more than "trust to honor your debts and to keep your word" (Hardin, 1982; Macneil, 1980).

[5]I treat these as "social facts" which should, at least provisionally, be taken as given. In these and many other cases, people end up being vulnerable to certain particular individuals merely because society happens to assign those particular people responsibility for caring for them (for example, parents for children). The only reason that this social allocation of responsibility matters morally is, I would argue, because of the vulnerability and dependency that it engenders. If it is regarded as your job, and no one else will do it if you do not (and if furthermore it is a job that really ought be done by someone), then there is a strong argument for you to do it. That is not to say that it should be your job, or that you (or we) should not try to get someone else to accept responsibility for doing it. It is merely to say that until and unless they do, you should keep on performing it. This is a topic to which I return in discussing collective responsibilities.

[6]Thus, although the courts are committed to doing whatever is in "the best interests of the child," children are not removed from marginally less suitable natural parents whenever marginally more suitable foster parents can be found, and the reason given (the risk of "separation trauma") points, just as my argument here suggests it should, to the emotional vulnerabilities of the child. See Mnookin (1973) and, more generally, Parfit (1984, p. 96) and Blum (1980, p. 56).

obligations says you have only such responsibilities with respect to that person as you voluntarily assume. You might agree to do all sorts of nice things for that person. It would be terribly kind of you to do so, and of course once you have assumed responsibilities it would be obligatory at that point for you to discharge them. But, within this model, you are initially under absolutely no obligations to agree to do all (or any) of those favors. You are morally at liberty to press your bargaining advantage to the hilt, and to exploit mercilessly the other's weakness. You can, and morally you *may,* force that person to agree to arrangements that are highly inequitable, to say the least. For examples, if any are needed, reflect upon the classic cases of "unconscionable contracts": peddling useless drugs to desperately ill patients at inflated prices, or charging $1000 for a hamburger when you find yourself enjoying a monopoly on food at some disaster site.

Now, according to the model of self-assumed obligations, parties in strong bargaining positions like these would be violating none of their moral responsibilities by pressing their advantage to the hilt. The vulnerability model, in contrast, regards it as the height of immorality for them to exploit the other's weakness in this way. The same thing that would enable the stronger to drive a hard bargain with (and, within the model of self-assumed obligations, to evade altogether any responsibility for) the weaker would, within the vulnerability model, impose a heavy responsibility upon the stronger to look after the weaker. In such cases, the implications of the two models diverge clearly. And surely our considered moral judgments, backed up by all our "background theories," side with the vulnerability model on this score. As Green (1881, p. 372) remarked, "There is no clearer ordinance of that supreme reason, often dark to us, which governs the course of man's affairs, than that no body of men should . . . be able to strengthen itself at the cost of the other's weakness."

## Protecting the Vulnerable

In spelling out the details of this vulnerability model of special responsibilities, I shall confine myself to three general remarks. The first concerns definitions of key terms: vulnerability, dependency, and responsibility. I use "vulnerability" and "dependency" interchangeably to refer to the following situation: *A* is vulnerable to *B* if and only if *B*'s actions and choices have a great impact on *A*'s interests. Here I equate "interests" with "welfare," following Barry (1965, p. 176; see also Reeve & Ware, 1983) in reading "*x* is in *A*'s interests" to mean "*x* increases *A*'s opportunities to get what *A* wants." Protecting the vulnerable is thus morally desirable because, *ceteris paribus,* it is morally desirable that people's interests and welfare should be furthered.[7]

Central to the concepts of "vulnerability" and "dependency" is the fact that they are relational. You are always vulnerable *to* or dependent *upon* some individual or group of individuals who have it within their power to help or to harm you in some respect(s). This relational character of the concepts is an enormous help in deciding where to settle responsibility for rendering assistance. If vulnerability gives rise to moral claims, then those moral claims must be principally against those agents to whose actions and choices one is vulnerable. Thus, this might be characterized as a "directed needs" model. Saying merely that "*A* is in need" leaves unspecified who should be responsible for meeting those needs. Saying that "*A* is vulnerable to *B*" provides a ready answer to that question.

Vulnerabilities are also relative. *A* would be more vulnerable to *B* than to *C* if *B*'s actions and choices make a greater impact on *A*'s interests than do *C*'s actions and choices. Those to whom one is relatively more vulnerable have relatively greater responsibilities. Anyone to whom *A* is uniquely vulnerable (no one else will help if that person does not) has the greatest responsibilities of all.

Although primary responsibility falls to whomsoever is in the best (or, in the limiting case, the unique) position to protect the vulnerable, that does not relieve others of responsibility altogether. Those who could help, albeit not as well as those with primary responsibility, retain a residual responsibility to do so should the others default, and they also have a continuing responsibility to monitor the situation to see whether or not their

[7]My principle is more catholic than it might appear. Although the definition of "interests" is recognizably liberal, the slippage between what people want and what is objectively best suited to satisfying their desires allows substantial scope for Marxian notions of false consciousness to operate. Similarly, although my principle is welfare-consequentialistic in form, deontologists can embrace it just so long as the *ceteris paribus* clause is understood to include their cherished rights-based constraints on action. Notice also that my principle treats acts and omissions symmetrically. Glover (1977, p. 94), Goodin (1982b, pp. 14-15), and Bennett (1983) show that, once other morally relevant correlates are factored out, not helping when you could have done so is morally indistinguishable from causing harm when you could have avoided doing so. That argument applies with particular force to bearers of standard special responsibilities (e.g., bodyguards and firemen), and would by extension apply equally forcefully to all vulnerability-based responsibilities that I have here argued are analogous.

assistance is in fact required (Feinberg, 1970, p. 244).[8]

Let us consider next the definition of responsibility. There are various forms, among them: causal responsibility (you produced this result); moral responsibility (you are to blame for it); and task responsibility (it's your job). Often we slide carelessly from one sense to another. To employ a pun that has frequently been mistaken for an argument, it is commonly said that those who are responsible should be made responsible. That is to say, (task) responsibility should be settled on those who are (causally) responsible. If *A*'s actions have caused some unfortunate situation, then according to this rule it should be *A*'s job to correct it. Most especially, if *A* got himself into a jam, it should be *A*'s responsibility to get himself out of it.

My argument is that task responsibility and causal responsibility are separable, logically, and should often be separated in practice. On my analysis, how *A* got into his present state is irrelevant. All that matters now is who is best able to get him out.[9] Sometimes—maybe even typically, for all I know—the person causally responsible for producing a state of affairs will be best able to reverse it. If so, then the pun will point us in the right direction. But in a great many cases, the agent best able to get a person out of a jam might well be someone other than the agent who got that person into it. Then, I would argue, task responsibility should be settled upon the former, even though that agent is in no way causally responsible. When the wake from a passing speedboat capsizes my sailboat, it must be the responsibility of other nearby sailors rather than the long-gone speeder to pull me out of the water.

That rule might, admittedly, tend to encourage improvident behavior. People could always rely on others to clean up their messes or get them out of jams they got themselves into. But providing appropriate counters to those perverse incentives is a practical rather than a moral matter. Incentives, as Rawls (1971, sec. 48) and Feinberg (1970, p. 94) rightly emphasize, are nothing more than socially necessary bribes; they do not necessarily have anything at all to do with moral deserts. On this nonmoralized view of incentives, encouraging people to get others out of bad situations is, in principle, just as important as discouraging those people from getting themselves into those situations in the first place. Where the emphasis should fall, in any particular instance, is simply a technical optimization exercise: we should just choose the most cost-effective method, or combination of methods, for avoiding suffering all around. This typically leads us to assign responsibility largely (and, on some analyses, almost exclusively) to people who were in no way causally responsible for the situations they are now being asked to remedy.[10] Furthermore, there are in any case clear limits on the use of incentives. They must be effective in accomplishing their desired goal; they must be no larger than strictly necessary to do so; and they must be no more costly than the goal itself is worth. All this combines to suggest that incentive considerations will not lead us to deviate often or largely from the course of action recommended by my principle of protecting the vulnerable.

The separate question of moral deserts remains.[11] It presents itself as a counterargument to my vulnerability model in two respects. One argument concerns those who find themselves in

[8]Notice an important asymmetry. When those with primary responsibility have acted, those with subsidiary responsibilities are relieved of any obligation to do so. But when those with subsidiary responsibility have, owing to the inability or especially the unwillingness of those with primary responsibility, been forced to act in their stead, that in no way relieves the latter of their obligations or excuses their defaulting.

[9]This saves my principle from the counterintuitive consequence that we have stronger responsibilities for protecting the rich than the poor, because, *ceteris paribus,* people are more vulnerable, the more they have to lose. But of course the more you have to lose, the better able you are to protect yourself from loss: the rich can protect themselves; it is the poor who need our help.

[10]The incentive problem posed here is discussed more fully by economists concerned with allocating the costs of accidents between those whose negligence created a dangerous situation, on the one hand, and those with the "last clear chance" to avoid the accident, on the other. Wittman (1981) has shown that the optimal incentives there require us to impose the bulk of the charges on the latter party rather than the former one. This is consistent with my suggestion that task responsibility should be predominantly forward-looking (who can remedy the situation?) rather than backward-looking (who caused the situation?).

[11]As a kind of hybrid between the incentive and desert arguments, there is a third proposition, which holds that it is our moral responsibility to protect the long-term interests of the profligate poor (or their or our successors, who would otherwise have to pay their bills) by creating appropriate incentives in the present to encourage them to do what they (or their or our successors) will at some future time wish they had done. But the same limits apply to this argument as the earlier incentive argument: it justifies incentives only insofar as they are necessary, effective, and entail less overall harm than benefit to the interests they are designed to protect. Thus, if the arguments of footnote 19 below are correct, the issue will simply not arise. Even if it does, this duty to be "cruel to be kind in the long term" might be counterbalanced by our duty not to be cruel in the short term.

difficulty through their own improvidence: some would say that they had it coming, that is, they deserve whatever they got and it would actually be *wrong* for anyone to help them out of their difficulty. The other argument concerns those who have done nothing to cause another's distress but are (perhaps uniquely) in a position to help relieve it: some would insist that they have done nothing to deserve this burden, and that it would be wrong to impose it on them although of course it would be terribly nice of them if they chose to assume it.[12]

Both claims, however, extend the notion of "deserts" beyond its proper bounds. Take the second counterargument first. Incurring a duty or a responsibility is not necessarily, nor even characteristically, something that you deserve. More often than not, it is something that just happens to you. When walking along a deserted beach, you see a child floundering in shallow water. Nothing in your background or character suggests that you deserve to bear the burden of effecting the rescue. It would, however, be absurd to say that you are therefore morally at liberty to leave the child to drown.

The notion of "deserts" is ordinarily equally out of place in the first counterargument as well. By and large, the improvident should be regarded as foolhardy people whose recklessness is to be discouraged through appropriate disincentives, not as evil people whose wickedness deserves to be punished. In dealing with people in precarious situations, questions of fault, blame, and desert are simply out of place. When two victims of a traffic accident are brought into the hospital emergency room with similar injuries, surely they should be treated with equal care and attention, even though one caused the accident while the other was its innocent victim. The need, dependency, or vulnerability of the victims, not their deserts, is what dictates physicians' responsibilities (Goodin, in press).

The third and final general point about my vulnerability model is that the "agents" to whom these responsibilities fall might be either individuals or collectivities. Consider the problem of famine relief. Millions of people are starving daily. But realistically what could I do to help? There are millions of them and only one of me. In such cases it may make little sense to hold anyone individually responsible; maybe, in my terms, those in need are just not very vulnerable to any single other individual.

Such invulnerability would, on my argument, relieve us individually of any responsibility for helping with famine relief efforts. Excuses of that sort, however, typically serve merely to get us out of the fire and into the frying pan (Austin, 1956). The price of letting individuals off the hook in that way is to put collectivities there in their place. The starving people of the world certainly *are* vulnerable to the actions and choices of those of us in rich nations, taken collectively. Hence we collectively have heavy responsibilities in respect of them.

Collective responsibilities are laid, in the first instance, upon the group as a whole to organize and to implement a scheme of coordinated action to protect the vulnerable agent or agents' interests. But these group responsibilities ultimately devolve onto individuals constituting the group. Each member of the group is responsible, so far as that person is able consistently with that person's other moral responsibilities: 1) to see to it that the group organizes a scheme of coordinated action that protects the vulnerable agent or agents' interests as well as it can; and 2) to discharge fully and effectively the responsibilities allocated to him or her under any such scheme that might be organized, just so long as it protects the vulnerable agent or agents' interests better than no scheme at all would protect them.[13]

In many ways, making something a collective responsibility only complicates things. In one important respect, however, it simplifies them. Making something a collective rather than an individual responsibility removes any objection to the social enforcement of that responsibility. Individuals have many moral duties which, for one reason or another, we think society ought not compel them to discharge. Where the duty is a collective one from the outset, however, collective action is clearly appropriate. Then the collectivity

[12]The most famous counterexample of this sort is Thomson's (1971, p. 48) of a dying violinist, who can survive only if plugged into your circulatory system. My principle does indeed require you to give the violinist's interests serious consideration; but they may of course be outweighed by the other responsibilities, including responsibilities to yourself, on which you would have to default to save the violinist's life. In this way my principle can wriggle out of Thomson's counterexample. Here it is to the credit of my theory that it requires some squirming: they simply answer, "It's my body, and that's that," surely makes far too short work of what truly is a terrible moral dilemma.

[13]Philosophers (McKinsey, 1981) tend to recognize the latter duty but not the former; for more details see Goodin (1985a, chap. 5). There is obviously some scope for trading off these two duties for one another, with political action designed to alter the scheme being preferred to cooperation under the scheme whenever it is likely to be sufficiently effective in instituting a scheme that is sufficiently better at promoting the vulnerable agent or agents' interests sufficiently quickly to justify the short-term damage to those interests.

is fully justified in compelling each of its constituent parts to play its full, appointed role in discharging those obligations, duties, and responsibilities.

## Broader Implications

The aim of this essay is to demonstrate that we have a broader range of social responsibilities than we traditionally acknowledge. What I hope to establish here is essentially a point of principle. The practicalities—how best to discharge these broader responsibilities—largely remain as open questions, although at the end of this essay I shall offer reasons for believing that the welfare state is a good way of discharging at least some of them.

The argument for broader responsibilities goes like this. We all acknowledge strong responsibilities toward our own families, friends, and certain others. Once we start examining the sources of those responsibilities, we discover there is nothing "special" about them. It is the vulnerability of the others, rather than any voluntary act of will on our part, that generates those responsibilities. There are many more people vulnerable to us, individually or especially collectively, than stand in any of the standard "special relationships" to us. If my analysis of the true basis of those standard responsibilities is correct, then we have strictly analogous (and, potentially, equally strong) responsibilities toward all those others as well. Aid to vulnerable strangers is thereby justified on the same basis as aid rendered to our own parents or children.

To see what all is at stake in this argument, its ramifications must be sketched, however briefly and unsatisfactorily. First and foremost, notice that state welfare services are essentially mechanisms whereby we attempt collectively to protect vulnerable members of our own society. They may or may not be the best mechanisms available for so doing, and I shall return to that issue presently. But for now, just note that the welfare state, as a device for protecting the vulnerable, can claim at least *prima facie* moral justifiability on my principle.

The vulnerability model, in its collective form, might also underwrite far stronger international obligations than are ordinarily acknowledged (Singer, 1972). People in very poor countries are enormously vulnerable to the actions and choices of people in very rich ones. Again, how we might best go about discharging these responsibilities is an open question and turns heavily upon various matters of empirical fact. It seems very likely, however, that the responsibility imposed on the rich will turn out to be a collective rather than an individual one.[14]

Yet another potential application concerns our obligations to future generations. Intergenerational transfers, especially spanning several generations, are singularly one-way affairs. We can do whatever we like to our distant successors without fear of retaliation. Future generations are enormously vulnerable to the actions and choices of present people, both individually and especially collectively. The things we destroy or use up will be unavailable for them to enjoy. Their extraordinary vulnerability to our actions and choices seems to be the best basis for assigning strong responsibilities to present generations to provide for the further future.

Finally, this model might entail responsibilities to protect animals and natural environments. "Dumb animals," delicate coral reefs, and ecosystems more generally have proven enormously vulnerable to the actions and choices of human agents, both individually and especially collectively. Whether or not that gives rise to any responsibilities on our part to protect them depends on whether this constitutes "vulnerability" in the relevant sense. Earlier, "vulnerability" was defined in terms of the impact of our actions and choices on the *interests* of those who are affected. The question thus becomes one of whether animals and other nonhuman entities can have genuine interests. This is not the place to enter into that debate.[15] It is enough to say that if (and insofar as) we see sentient creatures, ecosystems, or the natural environments upon which they depend as having "interests" at all, then their vulnerabil-

[14]Glover (1975) points out that, although none of us acting alone could eliminate world poverty, virtually any of us acting entirely alone could lift at least several starving Asians out of poverty. The essential flaw with individualistic programs such as "adopt-a-child," though, is that they work on a child-by-child basis; consequently they can end up doing as much harm as good, both for the putative beneficiaries and for those around them. To be sure our well-intentioned gifts have the desired effects, they must be set in the context of some reasonably comprehensive and well-integrated scheme for restructuring the recipient community as a whole. That requires a kind of coordination well beyond anything isolated donors—or even relatively large-scale voluntary charities—could reasonably hope to accomplish. Nozick (1974, pp. 266-267) makes just such a case for organized collective action.

[15]Feinberg (1980, pp. 159-206) persuasively argues that animals, at least, do have interests and hence interest-based claims; and since Routley and Routley (1979) are right to insist that the burden of proof must fall upon anyone who proposes to treat different agents' interests differently, animals' interests must at least presumptively enjoy the same status as our own.

ity will once again generate *prime facie* responsibilities on our part to protect them.

Of course, we will have to balance off one set of responsibilities against others. How much should we allocate to our collective responsibilities for social welfare, as against our private responsibilities for the well-being of our families and friends? How much to foreign assistance, as against domestic social services? How much to future generations, as against present people? How much to the protection of animals and environments, as against humans?

Some might regard these responsibilities as utterly incommensurable and therefore deny that any such balancing can ever be done. Recall Sartre's example of "the young man who is torn between remaining with his ailing mother and going off to join the Resistance. Sartre's point is that there is no way of adjudicating between these two strong claims on his moral allegiance through reason. . . ." But, as Taylor (1976, pp. 290-291) goes on to say, if there really were no bases for comparing the claims of kin and country, then the moral dilemma itself would disappear: the son should just "throw himself" one way or the other, as Buridan's ass in choosing between two equally good haystacks; since neither choice would be right or wrong, there would be no point agonizing over the choice. But that cannot be a correct analysis. We may find it hard to say which is the right choice, but we are quite confident that, whatever else, it is rightly to be regarded as a hard choice. That fact is conclusive evidence that the responsibilities cannot really be incommensurable, after all.

Here I suggest that the notion of "vulnerability," cashed out in terms of the notion of "interests," can not only account for the force of these dilemmas but can also help us resolve them. The dilemmas arise because discharging our responsibilities with respect to some of those who are vulnerable to us entails defaulting on our responsibilities with respect to some others who are also similarly vulnerable to us. Which we should favor depends, I suggest, upon the relative vulnerability of each agent. We must determine 1) how strongly that agent's interests would be affected by our alternative actions and choices, and 2) whether or not that agent would be able to find other sources of assistance or protection should we fail to provide it.[16]

On balance, it seems likely that those relatively near to us in space and in time probably will be rather more vulnerable to us in these ways. Hence my argument is saved from the traditional *reductio* of requiring us to give everything we have to starving Asians, or always to be saving everything for the ever-receding infinity of future generations, or to have our own lives and projects constantly interrupted to serve others. My argument would seem to allow—indeed, to require—us to show *some* bias toward our own kind, however defined. But that bias must not be absolute. The vulnerability of others—be they needy fellow-citizens, foreigners, heirs or hares—to our actions and choices may well be sufficiently large, and how we (and perhaps we alone) can help sufficiently clear, to require us to give their interests some substantial weight in reckoning our own responsibilities. Charity may indeed begin at home, but morally it must not stop there.

## Reducing Immoral Vulnerabilities

Up to this point, my argument has taken vulnerabilities and dependencies as given. I have argued that, if people are vulnerable to us, then it is our responsibility to protect them. Sometimes, however, it might be even better to try to eliminate the conditions making them vulnerable and dependent. A few of these conditions may be naturally fixed, inevitable and immutable. But most vulnerabilities will turn out to have been created, shaped, or sustained at least in part through certain social arrangements (Titmuss, 1958). In some respects, this is true of even those dependencies that would seem at first brush to be the most natural, such as those connected with childhood (Marks, 1975; Skolnick, 1975) or old age (Walker, 1980; 1982).

It is obviously immoral to hold people in an unnecessarily dependent status against their will. Moral theories built around notions of free choice, self-respect, or autonomy all yield that same conclusion. But in some cases people willingly do—and it seems morally and prudentially desirable that they should—render themselves vulnerable to a variety of other people for a variety of purposes. In personal relationships, love can plausibly be analyzed as putting yourself in one another's power. "A world in which no one had power over another, and in which no one was vulnerable, a world in which people could be moved to action by force or reason alone, would be a world without love, an inhuman world"

[16]We also need to decide how to weight one agent's interests relative to another's. Where human beings are concerned, I am firmly inclined to weight everyone's interests equally (Goodin, 1975). I am just as firmly inclined to weight future generations' interests the same as our own (Goodin, 1982a). But where animals or inanimate objects are concerned, I am far less certain what the appropriate weighting should be.

(Wilson, 1978, p. 315). In commercial relations, interdependence is the essence of trade and hence of all mutually profitable business ventures. Similarly in politics, interdependence forms the basis of all kinds of alliances and coalitions (Baldwin, 1980). Objectionable though we might find the particulars of any specific arrangement, there is surely nothing wrong with exchanges or alliances as such merely because they engender vulnerabilities of this sort.

Our moral theories must, then, allow for vulnerabilities, some of which are inevitable and some of which are self-selected. Yet at the same time we must recognize that such relationships are subject to abuse, and we must insist upon certain conditions to guard against that kind of abuse. The standard proposal is that, insofar as vulnerabilities or dependencies are within our power to create or alter or eliminate, they should be reciprocal or mutual. The real objection, various commentators observe, is not to dependency as such. It is instead to *unilateral* dependency, to *asymmetrical* power relations. That asymmetry is what creates opportunities for the strong to exploit the weak. Were each party equally dependent upon the other, there need be no fear of such behavior (Wilson, 1978, p. 315; see similarly Held, 1974; Pateman, 1981; Thompson, 1825; and Wollstonecraft, 1792).[17]

It is, however, wildly unrealistic to demand that dependencies or vulnerabilities be completely symmetrical, that is, that each depend on the other in exactly the same measure. That condition is satisfied in virtually no trading relation, in virtually no alliance, and probably in very few personal relationships. Neither is complete symmetry strictly necessary for a morally acceptable dependency relationship. There are, in fact, two acceptable alternatives.

The first is described by a pair of conditions. One is interdependency: each party must get something out of the relationship; or, alternatively, each must stand to lose something if it were terminated. The other condition is that neither party is so heavily dependent upon the other that the dependent party would cease to meet basic needs were the relationship terminated (Baldwin, 1980; Shue, 1980). The latter condition could be waived in cases of perfectly symmetrical vulnerabilities but becomes increasingly important the greater the asymmetry.[18]

The second alternative would permit monopoly suppliers of needed resources to exist. What it would crucially demand is merely that they have no discretionary control over the disposition of those resources. *B*, who needs the resource, would still be dependent upon *A*, the monopoly supplier of that resource. But *A* cannot *exploit B*'s dependency unless *A* can withhold the resource at will. And it is exploitable dependencies which we find morally most offensive.

## An Application: The Welfare State

The *raison d'etre* of the welfare state clearly is to discharge in part the responsibility I have here been discussing, namely, to protect vulnerable members of society. The early British initiatives—old-age pensions, health and unemployment insurance, minimum wage policies, and the like—were all aimed explicitly at "protecting the weakest and most vulnerable elements in society, such as the aged poor, the unemployed workman, the sweated worker" (Robson, 1976, p. 21). The subsequent history of the welfare state has similarly consisted in the increasing recognition of and response to "states of dependency" (Titmuss, 1958, pp. 42-43). Contemporary arguments for the expansion of the welfare state are all likewise couched in terms of dependency and vulnerability (van Lennep, 1981, p. 9; Australian Royal Commission on Human Relationships, 1977, vol. 1, p. 63).

Assuming my earlier arguments have proven persuasive, it is clear that we have a strong moral responsibility to protect those who are vulnerable to our actions and choices. The only remaining question is whether the welfare state is the best way of doing so. Of course, any particular welfare state may fail for reasons peculiar unto itself. It is important, therefore, to separate out and concentrate on what is generic to the welfare state as such.

For purposes of this discussion, I shall assume the defining features of the welfare state—and the features that must therefore be justified in any defense of it—are as follows. The welfare state necessarily entails *compulsory, collective provision for certain basic needs as a matter of right.* Welfare state provision is said to be compulsory and collective to distinguish it from private, voluntary charity; as distinct from more thoroughgoing egalitarian regimes, it provides only for people's basic needs; and as distinct from

[17]"Symmetry" must be subjectively defined: what one party gains from the relationship (or would lose were it terminated) must occupy as important a role in that party's overall life plan as what the other party gains or would lose plays in that other's.

[18]Symmetrical dependencies, even very great ones, admit of no abuse. If each party depends equally upon the other for the satisfaction of basic needs, then neither could exploit the other through a credible threat to terminate the relationship.

the old Poor Law, the welfare state allows beneficiaries to claim their entitlements as a matter of right.

The principal challenge facing any defense of the welfare state must surely be to show why protecting these vulnerable people should be a collective rather than an individual responsibility. There are basically two individualistic options available here. The first focuses upon the responsibilities of needy individuals themselves, while the second focuses upon the responsibilities of their families and friends.

Certainly it is true that people are even more vulnerable in even more ways to their own actions and choices than they are to those of the collectivity. For that reason, they should indeed bear primary responsibility for attending to their own needs. The state's responsibility is in the nature of a secondary, back-up responsibility, activated only when those with primary responsibility have failed to discharge it. Why they have failed, I have argued, is morally irrelevant: my analysis of responsibilities is, recall, forward-looking (asking only "Who is best able to help now?") rather than backward-looking (asking "Who is to blame for this situation?").[19] All that matters is that these individuals are now at risk of failing to have their most basic needs satisfied. That in itself is quite enough to activate secondary responsibility on the part of others to protect them.

The second individualistic option is to admit any need for someone to bear second responsibilities in such a case, but to lodge those responsibilities with some other private individuals rather than with the state. Specifically, this approach suggests that if people are unable to provide for themselves, it should be left to their families and friends to do so. That, curiously, is what "self-reliance" has come to mean in contemporary social policy debates (Goodin, 1985b). No doubt families and friends do, on my account, have strong moral responsibilities to provide assistance in such situations, and at its best, this system is no doubt preferable to state provision: material assistance from families and friends might betoken a deeper affection, in a way that state assistance necessarily cannot. The question is not whether families and friends should help out those in need. It is instead whether those in need should be forced to rely upon their families and friends for such support.

At this point, there is a strong case to be made for welfare-state provision as a kind of back-up to the back-up. An important part of this case is brutally empirical. One of the primary obstacles to an effective system of family responsibility for needy members is that needy people are ordinarily found in needy families, who are in no position to make any great sacrifices (Goodin, 1985b; Steiner, 1981, p. 114). There is also a principled objection to such policies, however, which would prove decisive even if these empirical facts were otherwise.

This principled objection harks back to the standards of an acceptable dependency relationship laid down above. Dependency might be acceptable if: 1) it were symmetrical; or 2) basic needs were not at stake; or 3) no one were to enjoy discretionary control over needed resources. *Ex hypothesi,* we are here discussing an asymmetrical relationship where the subordinate's basic needs are indeed at stake.

The only thing that could make such a relationship morally acceptable would be for the agent upon whom the subordinate depends not to have discretionary control over those needed resources. Where that agent is a person's family or friends, that condition cannot possibly be met: family and friends must inevitably enjoy discretionary control over resources that are, in the final analysis, still their own. Where the subordinate is dependent instead upon the state, however, it is possible to vest that person with a legal entitlement to assistance. Once such laws have been enacted, state officials (unlike families, friends, or private charities) lack any discretion in deciding whether or not to honor claims of needy petitioners (Goodin, 1985b; Smith, 1949, 1955; Titmuss, 1971).[20] The welfare state, defined as an institution which meets people's basic needs as a matter of right, is therefore a morally necessary adjunct

[19]Backward-looking considerations are relevant only insofar as, through incentive effects, they might have future consequences. But there is a substantial body of evidence suggesting that the poor tend to be poor planners and hence are largely impervious to incentives whether these are positive (e.g., incentives to slack off work when guaranteed a minimal income) or negative (e.g., incentives to avoid hazardous jobs); see Danziger, Haveman, and Plotnick (1981), Viscusi (1979), and Goodin (1985b). It is perfectly reasonable that the poor should be unresponsive to incentives: marginalist calculations are a costly business, and the poor have more pressing demands on their time and attention. Given that, however, restricting welfare benefits would probably amount to no more than bringing a gratuitous disincentive to bear on a group that is largely impervious to incentives of any kind.

[20]Discretion disappears only after such laws have been enacted; state officials are left with discretionary control over what laws they enact. But it is the exploitation of dependencies that worries us, and it is in the administration rather than in the enactment of welfare policies that the greatest danger (although certainly not the exclusive one) of such exploitation arises.

to other more individualistic responses to the problems of vulnerability and dependency in our larger community.

## References


Atiyah, P. S. *The rise and fall of freedom of contract.* Oxford: Clarendon Press, 1979.

Austin, J. L. A plea for excuses. *Proceedings of the Aristotelian Society,* 1956, *57,* 1-30.

Australia, Royal Commission on Human Relationships. *Final report.* Canberra: Australian Government Publishing Service, 1977.

Baldwin, D. A. Interdependence and power: a conceptual analysis. *International Organization,* 1980, *34,* 471-506.

Barry, B. *Political argument.* London: Routledge & Kegan Paul, 1965.

Bennett, J. Positive and negative relevance. *American Philosophical Quarterly,* 1983, *20,* 185-194.

Blum, L. A. *Friendship, altruism and morality.* London: Routledge & Kegan Paul, 1980.

Braucher, R., & Farnsworth, E. A. *Restatement (second) of the law of contracts.* St. Paul, Minn.: American Law Institute, 1981.

Daniels, N. Wide reflective equilibrium and theory acceptance in ethics. *Journal of Philosophy,* 1979, *76,* 256-282.

Danziger, S., Haveman, R., & Plotnick, R. How income transfer programs affect work, savings and income distribution. *Journal of Economic Literature,* 1981, *19,* 975-1028.

English, J. What do grown children owe their parents? In O. O'Neill & W. Ruddick (Eds.), *Having children.* New York: Oxford University Press, 1979.

Feinberg, J. *Doing and deserving.* Princeton, N.J.: Princeton University Press, 1970.

Feinberg, J. *Rights, justice and the bounds of liberty.* Princeton, N.J.: Princeton University Press, 1980.

Fried, C. *Medical experimentation.* New York: American Elsevier, 1974.

Gilmore, G. *The death of contract.* Columbus: Ohio State University Press, 1974.

Glover, J. It makes no difference whether or not I do it. *Proceedings of the Aristotelian Society (Supplement),* 1975, *49,* 171-190.

Glover, J. *Causing death and saving lives.* Harmondsworth, Mddx.: Penguin, 1977.

Godwin, W. *Enquiry concerning political justice.* London: G. G. J. & J. Robinson, 1793.

Goodin, R. E. How to determine who should get what. *Ethics,* 1975, *85,* 310-321.

Goodin, R. E. Discounting discounting. *Journal of Public Policy,* 1982a, *2,* 53-72.

Goodin, R. E. *Political theory and public policy.* Chicago: University of Chicago Press, 1982b.

Goodin, R. E. *Protecting the vulnerable: A re-analysis of our social responsibilities.* Chicago: University of Chicago Press, 1985a.

Goodin, R. E. Negating positive desert claims. *Political Theory,* in press.

Goodin, R. E. Self-reliance versus the welfare state. *Journal of Social Policy,* 1985b, *14,* 25-47.

Gorovitz, S. Bigotry, loyalty and malnutrition. In P. Brown & H. Shue (Eds.), *Food Policy.* New York: Free Press, 1977.

Hardin, R. Exchange theory on strategic bases. *Social Science Information,* 1982, *21,* 251-272.

Hare, R. M. *Moral thinking.* Oxford: Clarendon Press, 1981.

Hart, H. L. A. Are there any natural rights? *Philosophical Review,* 1955, *64,* 175-191.

Hart, H. L. A. Legal and moral obligation. In A. I. Melden (Ed.), *Essays in moral philosophy.* Seattle: University of Washington Press, 1958.

Heath, A. *Rational choice and social exchange.* Cambridge: Cambridge University Press, 1976.

Held, V. Marx, sex and the transformation of society. *Philosophical Forum,* 1974, *5,* 168-183.

Kronman, A. T. A new champion for the will theory. *Yale Law Journal,* 1981, *91,* 404-423.

Macneil, I. R. *The new social contract.* New Haven, Conn.: Yale University Press, 1980.

Marks, F. R. Detours on the road to maturity. *Law and Contemporary Problems,* 1975, *39* (Summer), 78-92.

McKinsey, M. Obligations to the starving. *Nous,* 1981, *15,* 309-323.

Mnookin, R. H. Foster care—in whose best interests? *Harvard Educational Review,* 1973, *43,* 599-638.

Montaigne, M. Of friendship. In D. M. Frame (Trans.), *The complete essays of Montaigne.* Stanford, Calif.: Stanford University Press, 1958 (originally published 1580).

Nozick, R. *Anarchy, state and utopia.* Oxford: Blackwell, 1974.

Oldenquist, A. Loyalties. *Journal of Philosophy,* 1982, *79,* 173-193.

Parfit, D. *Reasons and persons.* Oxford: Clarendon Press, 1984.

Pateman, C. The shame of the marriage contract. Mimeo, University of Sydney, 1981.

Rawls, J. Justice as fairness. *Philosophical Review,* 1958, *67,* 164-194.

Rawls, J. *A theory of justice.* Cambridge, Mass.: Harvard University Press, 1971.

Reeve, A., & Ware, A. Interests in political theory. *British Journal of Political Science,* 1983, *13,* 379-400.

Robson, W. A. *Welfare state and welfare society.* London: Allen & Unwin, 1976.

Ross, W. D. *The right and the good.* Oxford: Clarendon Press, 1930.

Routley, R., & Routley, V. Against the inevitability of human chauvinism. In K. Goodpaster & K. Sayre (Eds.), *Ethics and problems of the twenty-first century.* Notre Dame, Ind.: Notre Dame University Press, 1979.

Shue, H. *Basic rights.* Princeton, N.J.: Princeton University Press, 1980.

Singer, P. Famine, affluence and morality. *Philosophy and Public Affairs,* 1972, *1,* 229-243.

Skolnick, A. The limits of childhood. *Law and Contemporary Problems,* 1975, *39* (Summer), 38-77.

Smith, A. D. Public assistance as a social obligation. *Harvard Law Review,* 1949, *63,* 266-288.

Smith, A. D. *The right to life.* Chapel Hill: University of North Carolina Press, 1955.

Steiner, G. Y. *The futility of family policy.* Washington, D.C.: Brookings Institution, 1981.

Taylor, C. Responsibility for self. In A. O. Rorty (Ed.), *The identities of persons.* Berkeley: University of California Press, 1976.
Thompson, W. *Appeal of one half of the human race.* London: Longman, 1825.
Thompson, J. J. A defense of abortion. *Philosophy and Public Affairs,* 1971, *1,* 47-66.
Titmuss, R. M. The social division of welfare. In R. M. Titmuss, *Essays on "the welfare state."* London: Allen & Unwin, 1958.
Titmuss, R. M. Welfare "rights," law and discretion. *Political Quarterly,* 1971, *42,* 113-132.
van Lennep, E. Opening address. In *The Welfare state in crisis.* Paris: Organisation for Economic Co-operation and Development, 1981.
Viscusi, W. K. *Employment hazards.* Cambridge, Mass.: Harvard University Press, 1979.
Walker, A. The social creation of poverty and dependence in old age. *Journal of Social Policy,* 1980, *9,* 49-75.
Walker, A. Dependency in old age. *Social Policy and Administration,* 1982, *16,* 115-135.
Walzer, M. *Spheres of justice.* New York: Basic Books, 1983.
Williams, B. A critique of utilitarianism. In J. J. C Smart & B. Williams, *Utilitarianism, for and against.* Cambridge: Cambridge University Press, 1973.
Williams, B. *Moral luck.* Cambridge: Cambridge University Press, 1981.
Wilson, J. R. S. In one another's power. *Ethics,* 1978, *88,* 299-315.
Winkler, E. R. Utilitarian idealism and personal relations. *Canadian Journal of Philosophy,* 1982, *12,* 265-286.
Wittman, D. Optimal pricing of sequential inputs: last clear chance, mitigation of damages and related doctrines in the law. *Journal of Legal Studies,* 1981, *10,* 65-91.
Wollstonecraft, M. *A vindication of the rights of women* (2nd ed.). London: J. Johnson, 1792.

[8]

*B.J.Pol.S.* **18**, 415–443
*Printed in Great Britain*



# *Citizenship, Social Citizenship and the Defence of Welfare Provision*

DESMOND S. KING and JEREMY WALDRON

This article analyses the normative status of claims to the social rights of citizenship in the light of New Right criticisms of the welfare state. The article assesses whether there is any normative justification for treating welfare provision and citizenship as intrinsically linked. After outlining T. H. Marshall's conception of citizenship the article reviews its status in relation to: traditional arguments about citizenship of the polity; relativist arguments about the embedded place of citizenship within current societies; and, drawing upon Rawlsian analysis, absolutist arguments about what being a member of a modern society implies. Each argument has some strengths and together they indicate the importance of retaining the idea of citizenship at the centre of modern political debates about social and economic arrangements.

From the Second World War until very recently, most Western societies have treated an expanding public sector as the norm. Citizens in these countries have grown used to a consistent expansion in the state's provision of goods and services, in particular goods and services associated with the welfare state like education, health, social security and employment.[1] The 1945 election of the Labour party in Britain is often seen as a watershed in this regard – an emphatic popular endorsement of state planning as a promoter of the collective good through the pursuit of welfare policies and creation of welfare institutions like the National Health Service.[2] It is striking how universal this process has been amongst advanced industrial democracies: in most OECD countries, including the United States, the proportion of national income allocated to social welfare services has

Department of Politics, University of Edinburgh; Jurisprudence and Social Policy Program, School of Law, University of California, Berkeley, respectively. This is a joint work, authorship is listed alphabetically. The authors wish to thank the following for comments upon an earlier draft: Mike Adler, Ruth Adler, Nigel Bowles, Vinit Haksar, Neil MacCormick, Peter Morriss, Kim Scheppele, Janet Siltanen, Albert Weale and participants in the University of Edinburgh's Department of Politics seminar. They are also grateful for the advice and suggestions of Robert Goodin, co-editor of this Journal.

[1] See, for example, Peter Taylor-Gooby, *Public Opinion, Ideology and State Welfare* (London: Routledge & Kegan Paul, 1985). The 1986 British social attitudes survey revealed growing support for the institutions of the welfare state: see Nick Bosanquet, 'Interim Report: Public Spending and the Welfare State', in Roger Jowell, Sharon Witherspoon and Lindsay Brook, eds, *British Social Attitudes: The 1986 Report* (Aldershot: Gower Publishers, 1986). For an alternative view, and criticisms of these opinion polls, see Ralph Harris and Arthur Seldon, *Welfare Without the State: A Quarter-Century of Suppressed Choice* (London: Hobart Paperback No. 26, Institute of Economic Affairs, 1987).

[2] See: John Dryzek and Robert E. Goodin, 'Risk-Sharing and Social Justice: The Motivational Foundations of the Post-War Welfare State', *British Journal of Political Science*, 16 (1986), 1–34; Desmond S. King, *The New Right: Politics, Markets and Citizenship* (London: Macmillan, 1987); and Kenneth O. Morgan, *Labour in Power* 1945–1951 (Oxford: Oxford University Press, 1984).

increased steadily (in some instances dramatically) since the late 1940s, frequently absorbing as much as 50 per cent of GDP, and there has been a dramatic expansion in public employment and in the number of citizens receiving their primary income from the state in one form or another.[3]

However, since the mid-1970s this orthodoxy has suffered a serious material and ideological challenge. Materially, the post-1973 economic crisis rapidly undermined any expectation that economic growth would continue to supply the wealth necessary to sustain extensive public provision of welfare services. As a result, most developed countries have had to initiate some control of welfare spending (however modest or unsuccessful), and in many of them 'bringing welfare spending under control' has become a major political imperative. In the United States and Britain particularly, such policies have received ideological support from the major political development of the late 1970s and 1980s, the so-called 'New Right'. The New Right has many forms (both intellectual and political) but the core features of the movement include: a critique of the economics of state interventionism, particularly Keynesianism; an economic and moral critique of the welfare state; and an advocacy of free market mechanisms in all areas of public policy including the meeting of welfare needs in society. New Right theorists and politicians have sought to bring about a reversal in the post-1945 expansion of the public sector, as manifested primarily in the growth of the welfare state.[4]

New Right theorists are troubled by the welfare state for both economic and moral reasons. Economically, the provision of public welfare is thought to erode market incentives, for it provides people with a guaranteed source of income during difficult circumstances, making their search for work (especially for low-paying jobs) less diligent than it would be if such income protection were not available. Further, the welfare state is said to be economically damaging by virtue of its size (for example, crowding out private investment) and by virtue of its negative impact on individual savings as a basis for investment.[5]

In addition, the welfare state has regularly been cited as a source of moral corruption through its effect on the family: it provides support when families break down and therefore encourages their disintegration or encourages some people not to enter into them at all. Some New Right theorists complain that it saps the authority of the male breadwinner and encourages feminism.[6] As well as the

[3] See chapters in Richard Rose, ed., *Public Employment in Western Nations* (Cambridge: Cambridge University Press, 1985).

[4] See, for example: Milton Friedman, *Capitalism and Freedom* (Chicago: University of Chicago Press, 1962); F. A. Hayek, *The Road to Serfdom* (London: Routledge & Kegan Paul, 1944); and Hayek, *The Constitution of Liberty* (London: Routledge & Kegan Paul, 1960).

[5] See David G. Davies, *United States' Taxes and Tax Policy* (Cambridge: Cambridge University Press, 1986) regarding the United States.

[6] See George Gilder, *Poverty and Wealth* (New York: Basic Books, 1981). For a similar, but more effectively developed, thesis see Charles A. Murray, 'The Two Wars Against Poverty: Economic Growth and the Great Society', *The Public Interest*, 69 (1982), 3–16. Murray attributes the drop in husband–wife family units in the United States during the 1960s to the federal anti-poverty programmes associated with the Great Society: during the 1960s, he argues, 'fundamental changes

effect on morals, there is also the effect on values such as liberty. New Right theorists claim that the bureaucracy of welfare institutions reduces individual freedom and enhances state power. Collective provision limits the role of market processes, which are the most powerful guarantors of political liberty and economic prosperity, according to writers like Friedman and Hayek.[7] And, being financed out of taxation, it involves interference with private property and direct coercion of those individual taxpayers who would rather not contribute to 'compulsory charity' in this way.[8]

Despite the influence enjoyed by the New Right challenge (for example, in the public policies of the Thatcher and Reagan administrations), it is striking how little the welfare state has actually been eroded. There have certainly been cuts, and there are disputes about how welfare spending should be measured. In part, the maintenance of high levels of welfare spending reflects the impact of the economic recession: high unemployment has obviously raised the volume of direct income support from the state. But on the whole the main institutions – in Britain, the National Health Service, the education system and the benefit system – remain largely intact, and it is noticeable that politicians (even those on the Right) still feel constrained to assure the electorate that these institutions are 'safe in our hands'; for example, the stance of the Conservative party in the 1983 and 1987 elections. Some commentators argue that this is not just a superficial whim of the electorate; it is an indication of the extent to which welfare provision is now conceived of as a core element of citizenship in Western society.[9]

One way of putting the point is to say that the publicly guaranteed provision of welfare goods and services associated with the post-1945 expansion of the welfare state is no longer seen as a contingency of public policy, as something which might be changed whenever the administration changes its political hue. Instead, collective provision for welfare is associated now with an idea of social citizenship, and is taken to be comparable in status and importance to other aspects of citizenship such as the right to own property and the right to vote. Such a perception implies that if governments try to cut the welfare state, they will confront resistance based upon a belief that people have rights embedded in welfare services which no one ought to tamper with: such welfare 'rights' are integral to the contemporary sense of citizenship – so the argument goes – and therefore cannot simply be abrogated or whittled away at the whim of a particular government.

occurred in the philosophy, administration, and magnitude of social welfare programs for low-income families, and these changes altered – both directly and indirectly – the social risks and rewards, and the financial costs and benefits, of maintaining a husband–wife family' (p. 15).

[7] Friedman, *Capitalism and Freedom*; Hayek, *Road to Serfdom* and *Constitution of Liberty*.

[8] See, for example, Robert Nozick, *Anarchy, State and Utopia* (New York: Basic Books, 1974), Chaps 7–8.

[9] See figures in: King, *New Right*; Desmond S. King, 'The State and the Social Structures of Welfare in Advanced Industrial Democracies', *Theory and Society*, 16 (1987), 841–68; and Ray Robinson, 'Restructuring the Welfare State: An Analysis of Public Expenditure, 1979 80–1984 85', *Journal of Social Policy*, 15 (1986), 1–21.

That this is a widely held opinion cannot be doubted. But in this article we are going to attempt to *evaluate* it. We want to consider whether there is any normative justification for treating welfare provision and citizenship as linked in this way. Such provision should constitute more than a simple safety-net; it refers to the universal provision of education, health, social security and welfare benefits (financed through a system of redistributive taxation), available as attributes of citizenship and not granted as a residual fund to help the least well-off cope with excessive hardship as Hayek and Friedman would accept.

We should perhaps emphasize that there are other defences of the welfare state apart from those that can be developed through the citizenship idea.[10] The focus of the present article does not, of course, imply any disparagement of these other approaches. But it is the citizenship argument with which we are concerned. It is one which has enjoyed considerable prominence recently, in Britain and elsewhere.[11] Moreover, the claim that social provision is an attribute of citizenship is an important and interesting one, and it warrants a more thorough and searching examination, particularly in normative theory, than it has received up till now.

## I. T. H. MARSHALL AND SOCIAL CITIZENSHIP

The principal theorist of the 'social citizenship' idea is the British sociologist, T. H. Marshall. In an essay entitled 'Citizenship and Social Class', published originally in 1949, Marshall contended that social provision constituted one of three sets of rights associated with citizenship in modern Britain, the others being civil and political rights.[12] He began by defining citizenship in the following general terms:

> Citizenship is a status bestowed on those who are full members of a community. All who possess the status are equal with respect to the rights and duties with which the status is endowed. There is no universal principle that determines what those rights and duties shall be, but societies in which citizenship is a developing institution create an image of an ideal citizenship against which achievement can be measured and towards which aspiration can be directed. The urge forward along the path thus plotted is an urge towards a fuller measure of equality, an enrichment of the stuff of which the status is made and an increase in the number of those on whom the status is bestowed ... Citizenship requires a ... direct sense of community membership based on loyalty to a civilization which is a

[10] Robert E. Goodin, *Reasons for Welfare* (Princeton, NJ: Princeton University Press, forthcoming 1988); Raymond Plant, *Equality, Markets and the State* (London: Fabian Tract no. 494, 1984); and Plant, 'Needs, Agency and Rights' in C. J. G. Sampford and D. J. Galligan, eds, *Law, Rights, and the Welfare State* (London: Croom Helm, 1986).

[11] See, for the general argument, Gosta Esping-Andersen, *Politics Against Markets* (Princeton, NJ: Princeton University Press, 1985) and 'Power and Distributional Regimes', *Politics and Society*, 14 (1985), 223–56; and, for Britain, King, *New Right*, and recent publications of the Fabian Society, for example, Michael Mann, *Socialism Can Survive* (London: Fabian Tract no. 502, 1985).

[12] T. H. Marshall, 'Citizenship and Social Class', *Class, Citizenship and Social Development* (New York: Doubleday, 1964). This essay was first published in 1949.

common possession. It is a loyalty of free men endowed with rights and protected by a common law. Its growth is stimulated both by the struggle to win those rights and by their enjoyment when won.[13]

What are these rights and how have they evolved? In his 1949 essay Marshall differentiated between three layers of citizenship rights and the institutions which supported them. The first layer comprised *civil rights*: that is, those rights concerning individual freedom which were associated with the sphere of 'civil society': 'liberty of the person, freedom of speech, thought and faith, the right to own property and to conclude valid contracts, and the right to justice.'[14] Civil rights are associated principally with the institutions of legal justice, such as the courts; they are rights held by discrete individuals which they may come to law to vindicate. The second layer comprised *political rights*, that is, democratic rights of participation: 'the right to participate in the exercise of political power, as a member of a body invested with political authority or as an elector of the members of such a body.'[15] The institutions of representative democracy (Parliament and the electoral system) are central to the realization and maintenance of these political rights. Thirdly, there are *social rights*. By these, Marshall meant economic and welfare rights, rights to a minimum standard of welfare and income: 'the whole range from the right to a modicum of economic welfare and security to the right to share to the full in the social heritage and to live the life of a civilised being according to the standards prevailing in the society.'[16] Welfare state policies and institutions – the educational system and the social services – are the main expression of this third layer. The idea is that by providing civil rights, society mitigates the impact of force and violence in relations between people. By providing political rights, it ensures that power is not confined to an elite. And by providing minimum standards in these areas the state offsets the vagaries of market processes and corrects the gross inequalities of distribution arising from the market.

Now the first thing to note about these three types of citizenship rights is that they are not rigid or mutually exclusive as categories. Free speech, for example, can be regarded both as a civil right and as a political right. This point has particular importance for some of the items on the social agenda. Take, for instance, the case of education. Education is a facility important both for individual life-chances and for participation in other citizenship activities, such as voting or seeking redress through the courts.[17] This view is consonant with many

[13] Marshall, 'Citizenship and Social Class', pp. 84, 92.

[14] Marshall, 'Citizenship and Social Class', p. 71.

[15] Marshall, 'Citizenship and Social Class', p. 72.

[16] Marshall, 'Citizenship and Social Class', p. 72.

[17] As Marshall himself notes, 'education ... is a service of a unique kind' since 'the education of children has a direct bearing on citizenship, and, when the State guarantees that all children shall be educated, it has the requirements and the nature of citizenship definitely in mind. It is trying to stimulate the growth of citizens in the making. The right to education is a genuine social right of citizenship, because the aim of education during childhood is to shape the future adult ... Education is a necessary prerequisite of civil freedom'. Marshall, 'Citizenship and Social Class', pp. 81, 82.

traditional opinions in political theory about citizenship, as we shall show below. Like many citizenship arguments, it establishes a tight reciprocity between the duties individuals owe to the community and the duties the community owes to them. As Marshall notes, 'we have here a personal right combined with a public duty to exercise the right'.[18]

In other words, one and the same good can have several different aspects. In its contribution to a person's own well-being, free education is a social good; in its contribution to her or his political status and capabilities, it is a political right and, indeed, a political duty. And much the same can be said about the other aspects of social provision like health, social security and employment. The fact that Marshall's categories are not rigid should not worry us. Indeed, sometimes it is the very fluidity of the boundaries that provides the best case for the idea of social citizenship. One of the strongest arguments in favour of welfare provision is the empirical one that securing basic social standards does in fact promote the existence and exercise of other citizenship rights. We will explore this argument in section 3.

Consideration of the way in which these various aspects of citizenship have evolved plays an important part in Marshall's argument. In each case the evolution can be considered in two ways: in relation to its content; and in relation to its status as something which is universally enjoyed in a society. For example, when the concept of political citizenship emerged, it was first confined to a minority of the members of the polity: only recently has it been extended to all. Of these two aspects of evolution, it is the second which is of interest to us in this article – the gradual universalization of social provision, to the point where it is available equally to all.

Marshall suggests that the three kinds of citizenship right were originally part and parcel of a single core: 'in early times these three strands were wound into a single thread', in which there was a

> fusion of political and civil institutions and rights. But a man's social rights, too, were part of the same amalgam, and derived from the status which also determined the kind of justice he could get and where he could get it, and the way in which he could take part in the administration of the affairs of the community of which he was a member.[19]

However, this earlier notion of citizenship is by no means a direct equivalent of citizenship according to contemporary conceptions. Modern citizenship began in the twelfth century, according to Marshall, but it is the eighteenth, nineteenth and twentieth centuries which are crucial for the transformation of civil, political and social rights successively into universal rights.

*Civil rights* were established, in Britain, between the Revolution and the first Reform Act. During the eighteenth century the rule of law was established, mainly through the 'work of the courts, both in their daily practice and also in a series of famous cases in some of which they were fighting against parliament in

[18] Marshall, 'Citizenship and Social Class', p. 82.
[19] Marshall, 'Citizenship and Social Class', p. 72.

defence of individual liberty.'[20] There also developed a civil right in the economic sphere, the right to work, that is, the right to economic freedom as a complement to the rule of law, resultant, in no small degree, upon the development of markets. Thus individual freedom, as embodied in civil rights, became a universal feature of citizenship with the emergence and growth of the bourgeoisie. *Political rights* emerged in the nineteenth century, according to Marshall, as the franchise was steadily extended (to some extent as a consequence of working-class pressure for equal citizen rights) and the status of citizenship expanded to include rights of democratic participation. It was not until the present century, however, that political rights were universalized through universal franchise based on the equality of individuals as an attribute of citizenship. Thus by the 1920s in Britain civil and political rights reflected the position each person enjoyed as implicit in the status of citizen. All citizens enjoyed equal rights in civil and political spheres, and these rights were understood to be part and parcel of what it was to be a member of a society like our own.

*Social citizenship* is largely a twentieth-century phenomenon. Twentieth-century rights to education, health and an assured income are in many ways diametrically opposed to earlier practice in this area. For example, the 1834 Poor Law implemented an exclusionary principle of citizenship, since it

> treated the claims of the poor, not as an integral part of the rights of the citizen, but as an alternative to them – as claims which could be met only if the claimants ceased to be citizens in any true sense of the word. For paupers forfeited in practice the civil right of personal liberty, by internment in the workhouse, and they forfeited by law any political rights they might possess.[21]

Likewise, the Factory Acts initially narrowed the meaning of citizenship by applying to children and women exclusively, though 'by the end of the nineteenth century, such arguments had become obsolete, and the factory code had become one of the pillars of the edifice of social rights.'[22] In the twentieth century these social rights have undergone enormous expansion as state responsibility for education, health, welfare and employment has been increasingly expanded and taken for granted. For Marshall this expanded responsibility constitutes social or welfare rights and thus transforms them into legitimate attributes of citizenship. These developments were stimulated, in part, by growth in money incomes (unequally distributed), the introduction of direct taxation, and mass production or consumerism which fuelled demands for reductions in inequality.[23] Welfare state institutions directly counter market processes by

[20] Marshall, 'Citizenship and Social Class', p. 75.

[21] Marshall, 'Citizenship and Social Class', p. 80.

[22] Marshall, 'Citizenship and Social Class', p. 81.

[23] As another scholar argues, 'welfare statism is the twentieth century's response to the demands of citizens – however articulated – for material protection from contingencies that are beyond their privately organized capacity to resist'. Kathi V. Friedman, *Legitimation of Social Rights and the Western Welfare State: A Weberian Perspective* (Chapel Hill, NC: University of North Carolina Press, 1981), p. 15.

providing citizens with a minimum income, a basic standard of social services (health and education) and respite against economic uncertainty.[24]

Marshall's account of the development of the rights of citizenship has been the subject of controversy in two ways: there have been disputes about its descriptive plausibility and disputes about its normative claims. The second set of issues are our central concern, and we will deal with them in the sections that follow.[25]

## 2. IS THERE AN ARGUMENT FOR SOCIAL RIGHTS?

In saying that welfare provision was part and parcel of citizenship in the modern state, Marshall was describing how it had evolved and how it was viewed by the people who enjoyed it. But we think he was also doing more than this: we think he was talking about the way in which welfare provision *ought* to be viewed, and intimating an argument about how it might be defended.

At the minimum, to associate welfare provision with citizenship is to make a proposal about how welfare should be handled in society. For example, as we have seen, it is to endorse the replacement of the Poor Law approach to welfare with provision for need that is given universally, that is provided without supplication or stigma, and that avoids as far as possible the invidious operation of official discretion.[26] But associating it with citizenship is not just a way of making this proposal: it is also a way of defending it. The suggestion may be that

[24] See also King, *New Right*, and Julia Parker, *Social Policy and Citizenship* (London: Macmillan, 1975).

[25] With regard to the first set of issues, much of the debate has occurred within stratification studies, where Marshall's essay was 'one of the seminal works which resulted in the reorientation of the whole discussion of the class structure in capitalist societies' according to David Lockwood, 'For T. H. Marshall', *Sociology*, 8 (1974), 363–7. Arguments about citizenship informed Ralf Dahrendorf's *Class and Class Conflict in Industrial Society* (Stanford, Calif.: Stanford University Press, 1957) in which he considers the accuracy of Marshall's claims about the equalizing impact of social rights. The argument here is about empirical accuracy not normative validity. Dahrendorf contends that Marshall's thesis neglects the social distribution of power: though greater equalization through citizenship rights has certainly occurred, it has not resolved the conflicts centred on class. More recently, Giddens considers also the utility of Marshall's claims as a possible refutation of the centrality of class conflict. He argues that citizenship rights cannot be separated from the contradictory forms of modern capitalism, and more specifically, since the rights of citizenship do not extend to the workplace – where class conflict is most persistent according to Giddens – Marshall's thesis is an inadequate account of contemporary Western democracies: see Anthony Giddens, *A Contemporary Critique of Historical Materialism* (London: Macmillan, 1981), pp. 226–9. A more sympathetic treatment of Marshall's arguments is contributed by Turner who argues that the pursuit and establishment of citizenship rights has altered the nature of capitalist society in a fundamental and positive way: Bryan S. Turner, *Citizenship and Capitalism* (London: George Allen & Unwin, 1986).

[26] Such a proposal is advanced by Parker when she observes that, 'the idea of citizenship implies that there should be no stigma attached to the use of public services, either because of popular attitudes condemning dependency or as a result of deterrent administrative procedures or poor standards of provision'. Parker, *Social Policy and Citizenship*, pp. 145–6. In this regard, the provision of education and health services in Britain conforms more closely to the model of citizenship rights than, say, the provision of supplementary benefit. We will examine such distinctions in a little more detail in section 4.

we *ought* to associate welfare with citizenship because our concept of citizenship will be radically impoverished if we do not. Citizenship, on this account, *demands* welfare provision; we cannot have an adequate or attractive notion of citizenship without it.

Is there any justification for this claim? In normative terms, does our concept of citizenship provide us with a reason for continuing to assure health, education, social services and income support to everyone in our society? To put it another way, is there anything in the idea of social citizenship to trouble the theorists of the New Right in the normative arguments that they are making against the welfare state?

One way into these questions is through Marshall's focus upon equality. We have already mentioned that, for Marshall, citizenship seems to be about expanding and enriching society's notion of equality by extending its scope through civil, political and social rights. The development of universal rights of citizenship has pushed forward the meaning of equality by broadening the scope of its application. Marshall stresses that it is not 'absolute equality' he is aiming at nor is it any rigid equality of wealth:

> The extension of the social services is not primarily a means of equalizing incomes. In some cases it may, in others it may not. The question is relatively unimportant ... What matters is that there is *a general enrichment of the concrete substance of civilized life, a general reduction of risk and insecurity, an equalization between the more and the less fortunate at all levels* ... Equalization is not so much between classes as between individuals within a population which is now treated for this purpose as though it were one class. Equality of status is more important than equality of income.[27]

To talk about equality in the context of citizenship is to talk about a progressive enlargement and enrichment of people's life chances. Citizenship does this principally by altering existing patterns of social inequality, and making it less likely that extremes can be sustained: 'the preservation of inequalities has been made more difficult by the enrichment of the status of citizenship. There is less room for them and there is more and more likelihood of their being challenged'.[28] But, again, what if someone simply denies that this is an *enrichment* of the notion of equality, or that the value of equality, so enriched, is attractive? Does the notion of citizenship give us any basis for rebuttal?

There are two ways in which it might help. First, we might be able to show that citizenship as it has been traditionally understood is a concept which requires social provision and enriched equality for its effective realization. Or secondly, even if this is not the case, we might be able to show that a new concept of citizenship which *does* include a guarantee of social provision is nevertheless more attractive as an ideal than one which does not. The first line of argument takes us from a familiar value to one that is in dispute, asserting an empirical connection between welfare provision and the possibility of effective participation by everyone as a citizen. The second line of argument challenges us directly

[27] Marshall, 'Citizenship and Social Class', pp. 102–3, our emphasis.

[28] Marshall, 'Citizenship and Social Class', p. 117.

to adopt the disputed conception of citizenship as our modern social ideal. Instead of asserting an empirical connection between welfare and citizenship, it challenges us to adopt a new account of citizenship of which the guarantee of welfare rights is partly constitutive.[29]

We will explore the first line of argument in section 3. But most often it seems to be the second line of argument that Marshall is hinting at. His thesis seems to be that social rights derive from a widely shared notion of ideal citizenship within a given society – that is, there is a historically based public conviction in the appropriateness of social welfare as a characteristic of the status of equal citizenship. Certainly his evolutionary argument seems to advance such a position. He contends that 'societies in which citizenship is a developing institution create an image of an ideal citizenship against which the achievement can be measured and towards which aspiration can be directed'.[30] The image of ideal citizenship emerges in the struggle for rights. Given that this process has involved the extension of citizenship rights to more and more members of society – their universal application – through processes of conflict and demand (for example, working-class pressure for universal suffrage), then it would seem that at least those to whom those rights have historically been denied share a sense of the sort of citizenship they aspire to enjoy. It would not be remarkable if such a conception of the rights of citizenship expanded historically from civil through political to social rights as Marshall depicts.[31] Indeed, citizenship remains a dynamic process likely to expand into other areas in the future.

The limitation of such a view is that it requires us to impose some sort of teleology or purpose on what may be in fact a purely accidental and contingent process of evolution. It also makes social provision vulnerable to the course that social evolution happens to take. What if society lurches away from the welfare state, under the impact of New Right policies and ideologies? Does that show that the ideal of citizenship now no longer involves social rights? Or does it show that, as a society, we have abandoned this idea of citizenship? And how might we decide between these interpretations?

In sections 4 and 5, we explore two different ways in which social citizenship might be vindicated as an ideal. One of the arguments is relative to the actual course of development in our society, while the other purports to be more absolute. In section 4, we argue that – whether we like it or not – Marshall's idea of social citizenship captures something that has as a matter of fact become embedded in the expectations of ordinary people, and that it is not now something which can easily be done away with without grave disruption to people's lives. In section 5, we develop a Rawlsian argument about what it is to be a *member* of a modern society. Whatever course social development has taken so far, it cannot claim to treat its citizens equally as members unless it provides socio-

[29] We are grateful to Robert Goodin for drawing this distinction to our attention. See Goodin's *Reasons for Welfare*, Chap. 4 on 'Community'.

[30] Marshall, 'Citizenship and Social Class', p. 84.

[31] This is the view which Giddens appears to ascribe to Marshall's analysis. See Anthony Giddens's *Profiles and Critiques in Social Theory* (London: Macmillan, 1982).

economic structures that they could all have agreed to live under. We argue that a society without welfare provision would not be a structure that satisfied this condition.

But before we explore these arguments for the ideal of social citizenship, let us see how far we can get with the notion of citizenship as it has been traditionally understood.

## 3. CITIZENSHIP AND POLITICAL PARTICIPATION

Marshall, it will be remembered, distinguished between the political rights and the social rights associated with citizenship. But we know that these are not rigid categories, and an obvious starting point for our inquiry is to ask whether there is any deep or important connection between the two.

The most familiar notion of political citizenship that we have is of the citizen as a participator – particularly a participator in republican or democratic politics. In classical political thought, a citizen was a full member of a city, a *polis*, or a republic. He was not merely subject to its laws and under its protection – these were often characteristics of non-citizens as well (resident aliens, for example). His citizenship consisted in the fact that he could hold public office, that he could join in the determination of the laws and (as a juror) in their application, and that he could be called upon to discharge patriotic duties such as the defence of his polity against external attack. The classic definition was that of Aristotle. 'A citizen is one who has a share in both ruling and being ruled. Deliberative or judicial, we deem him to be a citizen of that state.'[32] The idea of citizenship is connected, then, with the view that political power should be exercised, not by a specialist elite who have made politics their vocation, but by ordinary members of the polity, acting either together or in rotation. Citizenship does not necessarily imply democracy: roughly, a democracy is a republic in which all adult men and women are citizens. In ancient Athens slaves and women were excluded from citizenship, and in the ideal polity that Aristotle proposed, workers and artisans would be excluded as well. In Britain (to the extent that we have ever had a genuine notion of the citizen, as opposed to the subject) citizenship was restricted until the late nineteenth century to men, and to men who held more than a specified amount of property. But citizenship in Britain is now universal: every adult participates in ruling to the extent that each can vote for representative legislators in elections, and any adult may be called to serve on a jury.

It may be thought that this idea of citizenship is *simply* a matter of political rights and that no conclusions can be drawn about the social or economic position that the citizen, as such, ought to be in. But, in fact, the tradition of Western political thought about political citizenship completely contradicts this. Almost all the great theorists of citizenship – Aristotle, Cicero, Machiavelli, Burke, de

[32] Aristotle, *Politics*, trans. T. A. Sinclair (Harmondsworth, Middx: Penguin Books, 1962), Bk III, Chaps 1, 13.

Tocqueville, Mill and, in the twentieth century, Hannah Arendt – have believed that in order to be a citizen of a *polis*, in order to be able to participate fully in public life, one needed to be in a certain socio-economic position. Or they certainly believed that a *well-ordered* city or republic would be one in which political participants were in a certain socio-economic position. People, it was said, could not act as citizens at all, or could not be expected to act well in the political sphere and to make adequate decisions, unless some attention was paid to matters of their wealth, their well-being and their social and economic status.

Two things have always been thought particularly important in this connection: the absence of great inequality, and the possession by all of some modicum of wealth (for example, a property qualification). We want to discuss them both.

Among theorists of citizenship, there has always been a consensus that some sort of rough equality among citizens is desirable. We find this in the Greek thinkers. While Plato did not develop a theory of citizenship in *The Republic*, he did stress there the danger of the struggle between rich and poor as a source of political instability, and in his later and less Utopian work, *The Laws*, he suggested that no citizen should be permitted to own an amount of wealth above a norm set at a level five times greater than the property of the poorest citizen.[33] Aristotle agreed that extremes of riches and poverty were likely to be a destabilizing factor, though he shied away from the imposition of any egalitarian norm.[34]

In later political thought, Machiavelli argued in the *Discourses*, that political solidarity was greatest among those who shared a reasonably austere style of life (the image was Sparta), and he suggested that republican institutions could survive in a territory only if the richer members of the gentry were eliminated.[35] Rousseau, too, insisted that extreme inequality was dangerous: it was the cause 'of mutual hatred among the citizens, of indifference to the common cause, of the corruption of the people, and of the weakening of all the springs of government'.[36]

We are not citing these writers because we think they are sages to whose authority we should submit on matters of citizenship; their works are not, as it were, sacred texts. But there is a long tradition of thinking about citizenship, and in our thought about modern institutions and practices we should take advantage of whatever insights and arguments they offer. The theme linking inequality and instability is an important one: if those who are radically unequal share in the exercise of political authority and the determination of the laws, there will be a constant and understandable tendency for one group of citizens to challenge the existing distribution of property, for another group of citizens to defend that distribution, and for both the challenge and the defence to be fired up by con-

[33] Plato, *The Republic*, trans. Desmond Lee (Harmondsworth, Middx: Penguin Books, 1974) and *The Laws*, trans. T. J. Sound (Harmondsworth, Middx: Penguin Books, 1980).

[34] Aristotle, *Politics*, Bk II, Chap. 7.

[35] N. Machiavelli, *The Discourses* (Harmondsworth, Middx: Penguin Books, 1970).

[36] J. J. Rousseau, *Discourse on Political Economy*, trans. and ed. G. D. H. Cole (London: Dent, 1966), p. 134.

siderations of intense personal advantage as well as, and perhaps at the expense of, whatever sense of justice there is on either side. In modern terms, reductions in inequality may enhance social integration and therefore promote stability.

Put more positively, the suggestion may be that there is a need for a certain spirit of fraternity to exist among citizens; they must regard one another as friends and work on a basis of goodwill and mutual understanding. That goodwill and understanding are required if civic politics is to be undertaken in good faith, and if debate and disagreement are to be possible without suspicion and paranoia creeping in. But that sort of solidarity and mutual trust may depend upon rough equality as well as on a sense of community and belonging, for the more inequality there is, the more cleavages there are likely to be in things like consumption patterns and life-style, and in a sense the less comprehensible citizens are likely to be to one another. (It is partly these ideas that are being appealed to, when concern is voiced about 'two nations' in British society.)

Besides stability and solidarity, other arguments for equality in the civic tradition have focused on the need for citizens to be economically independent of one another; as Rousseau put it, no one must be rich enough to be able to purchase the dependence of another, and none poor enough to be bought in that way. The argument rests on the premise that a citizen should be one who is in a position to bring his or her *own* judgement to public issues, rather than one who responds as a member of a faction or retinue or as a mere mouthpiece for another. As independent individuals, citizens can have some hope of reaching agreement on the common good; and no citizen would ever be interested in purchasing the vote or opinion of another unless he or she wanted to promote some sectional or peculiar interest of his or her own. There are, therefore, good civic reasons for ensuring, on the one hand, that no one is in a position to do this, and, on the other, that no one is so economically vulnerable that he or she would be tempted to sell his or her civic obligations for the food and shelter he or she needs to live. These concerns have been amplified in modern political theory, with an awareness of how easily the opinions, preferences and perceived interests of the poorer groups can be manipulated by those who have economic power over them – those with whom they must come to terms if they are to secure a living.[37]

So far we have presented this in terms of an attack on inequality. It does not follow that citizens should be rigidly equal in their wealth and income; these are arguments against extremes of inequality, arguments for narrowing the range between rich and poor, not arguments for making everyone the same or levelling all differences. Moreover, though extreme inequality undermines civic life *qua* inequality, because of the lack of fraternity between rich and poor, it also corrupts the citizens at either end of the social scale. Luxury and wealth corrupt the rich – that was Machiavelli's concern about the gentry. And poverty and vulnerability corrupt the poor. Now, a defence of welfare provision in terms of citizenship will naturally focus mainly on this last concern; the predicament of poverty,

[37] See Steven Lukes, *Power: A Radical View* (London: Macmillan, 1974) and Herbert Marcuse, *One-Dimensional Man* (London: Sphere, 1964).

and the insistence, by almost every writer in this tradition, that those who are poor cannot be citizens, that, in Aristotle's words, 'you could no more make a city out of paupers than out of slaves'.[38]

The view that the poor cannot be citizens is based in part on the way in which desperate need is conceived to interfere with the processes of reflection and deliberation that civic politics requires. It is trite to say that hunger is something of a distraction so far as politics is concerned. Perhaps it is more telling to reflect that people who are completely unsure about food and shelter in the coming days for themselves and their families will be worried sick and, as it were, understandably obsessed with this issue all the time, in a way which leaves little room, very little mental space, for any general and long-term reflection on issues that go very far beyond their present predicament. Similar concerns were voiced by the English Idealists (T. H. Green and others) when they argued that political participants could not develop into moral citizens, capable of contributing to the common good, if they were absorbed all the time by the pressure of material need.

Now, of course, we should take care not to exaggerate the point. We do not need to agree with Hegel that such a situation is one of 'savagery and unfreedom', nor do we need to go as far as Hobbes who suggests that the drive for elementary survival is psychologically irresistible and simply short-circuits all the apparatus of rational deliberation and consent on which political structures depend. We do not need to agree even with Hannah Arendt that the domination of politics by questions of need signals the entrance of violence and terror into the political realm. But there is something to Arendt's conviction that civic politics in a republic cannot be expected to survive for very long if there is constant clamouring for bread and constant demands for 'action now, not words' to meet the predicaments of those who may perish while the politicians talk. To clamour for 'action now, not words' to meet the social problem is, in effect, to dismiss as instantly irrelevant any articulate consideration of the means whereby the social problem may be addressed and any reflective discussion of the way in which those means might fit with the other goals and priorities of the republic. It is, in other words, to dismiss as irrelevant politics as the civic tradition understands it. Need, then, and the urgency of the demands that it generates, can radically undermine the possibility of civic politics and distort the contribution that an individual participator can make.

Another way of putting this is to note that Plato and Aristotle more or less took it for granted that the poverty of the masses, if given a political voice, would drive them to rapacious greed rather than to a genuine concern for justice. The hidden assumption of that view is, not that the masses are inherently depraved, but that poverty itself blocks and interferes with the articulate and deliberative reflection that a genuine concern for justice necessarily involves. Those who are in desperate need cannot be expected to take time to reflect on the issue of what resources they are justly entitled to: they are too taken up with the business of literally getting a living to concern themselves with that. But if articulate reflec-

[38] Aristotle, *Politics*, Bk III, Chap. 13.

tion about justice is, as Aristotle believed, the essence of political activity, need must somehow be banished from the forum before political activity can take place.

The point is one that can be taken conservatively or liberally. At the very least, it seems to imply that hungry people must not be let loose in the political forum, for their needs will impel them to make demands that subvert and short-circuit the leisurely course of citizens' deliberations. This implies that citizenship should be the privilege of those who are economically secure. But that may not be enough to meet the concern, for, as Arendt quite rightly points out, the compassion which desperate need kindles in others can often be as violent and anti-political in character as the original needs themselves. This sometimes leads her to the odd suggestion that citizens must steel themselves to resist the siren charms of compassion, and that they must blind themselves to any concern with the economic predicament of those languishing in poverty outside the doors of the assembly. Politics, she sometimes claims, must not concern itself with the life process. But that is fatuous, first, because people cannot always succeed in distancing themselves in that way, and secondly, because it implies that citizens should be unconcerned with the conditions that make their civic life possible. A more sensible and liberal solution is to say that the removal of need *from society* is one of the great and urgent issues of civic life, for as long as it remains, whether the poor are admitted to citizenship or not, there is always the danger that – directly or relayed through compassion – the clamour for bread *now* will subvert the processes of political debate.

Apart from the threat posed by need itself, there is also concern amongst civic theorists about the sort of life the poorest members of society are likely to lead. Aristotle wrote that 'the best state will not make the labourer a citizen',[39] and Plato spoke in *The Republic* of the 'stunted natures' of the working classes – 'their minds being as cramped and crushed by their mechanical lives as their bodies are deformed by manual trades'.[40] In ancient thought the concern was that the long hours of work necessary to secure a living for those who had no independent means would not leave them time or leisure to acquaint themselves with and deliberate upon the issues that citizens ought to be addressing. In modern political thought, this has combined with concern about the effects of the division of labour and the way that it contracts a person's mind and strength to the performance of just one task.[41]

[39] Aristotle, *Politics*, Bk III, Chap. 5.

[40] Plato, *The Republic*, Bk VI, 495e.

[41] As de Tocqueville puts it, once the workman becomes habituated to the concerns of, say, his particular place on the assembly line, 'he no longer belongs to himself, but to the calling which he has chosen ... In proportion as the principle of the division of labour is more extensively applied, the workman becomes more weak, more narrow-minded, and more dependent'; Alexis de Tocqueville *Democracy in America*, ed. J. P. Mayer and Max Lerner (New York, Harper & Row, 1970), Bk II, Chap. 20. This seems to mean then that the workman lacks the necessary qualities for citizenship: an open and broad mind, an independent point of view, and sufficient experience of the world beyond his own hovel or workshop to allow him to address himself intelligently to the great and general issues of politics.

Inevitably, these lines of thought direct the civic tradition towards the idea of a property franchise. The property-owner is independent of others, and he or she can hold independent views. Unlike the propertyless members of the proletariat, he or she does not have to come to terms with and submit himself or herself to the members of another class in order to secure a living. He or she can live off his or her own resources or the income which they generate.[42] To get a living he or she does not have to work long hours and preoccupy himself or herself exclusively with one task; his or her independent income gives the time and leisure to reflect on broader political issues.

As well as these considerations, there are several other arguments for restricting the class of citizens to property-holders. One is the narrow, pragmatic view favoured by Locke, that the tasks of the citizen in the modern state may not necessarily involve much more than periodic consent to taxation; and consent to taxation is morally required only from those on whom the burden of taxation falls. But Locke had an impoverished notion of citizenship. More interesting are the arguments of Edmund Burke, that only property-holders have something solid and permanently at stake in the commonwealth, or (if one is unconvinced by that argument, thinking perhaps that *everyone* has something solid at stake in the commonwealth, namely their lives and well-being), only property-holders can be expected to have a proper sense of caution, prudence, responsibility and permanence in their thought and action in public affairs.[43]

The theme of the ethical importance of property-owning is also taken up by Hegel in the *Philosophy of Right*. Owning property, he said, allows the individual's will to transcend and supersede 'the pure subjectivity of personality'.[44] People have all sorts of schemes and good ideas whizzing about in their heads, constantly changing and replacing one another. But once they have property to work on, the objects themselves start to register and embody the effects of their schemes and purposes in a more or less inerasable form, and so they have to start taking the business of settling upon some particular purpose or project seriously; you cannot always be changing your mind once you are working on external objects, for you will soon learn that the whimsicality of subjective thinking can wreck and undermine everything when it is applied in the real

[42] As John Stuart Mill puts it: 'those whose bread is already secured, and who desire no favours from men in power, or from bodies of men, or from the public, have nothing to fear from the open avowal of opinions'. *On Liberty* (London: Dent, 1972), Chap. 2, para. 19.

[43] 'We receive, we hold, we transmit our government and our privileges, in the same manner as we enjoy and transmit our property', Burke claimed, as an inheritance from the past and a responsibility for the future (Edmund Burke, *Reflections on the French Revolution* (Harmondsworth, Middx: Penguin Books, 1969), p. 120). He insisted therefore that 'by the spirit of philosophic analogy', we should conclude that the skills which are developed in those who are used to handling landed property are the very skills which we should want the citizen to exercise. These are skills which are unavailable to the common masses, who 'immersed in hopeless poverty, could regard all property ... with no other eye than that of envy. Nothing lasting, and therefore in human life nothing useful, could be expected from such men' (Burke, *Reflections*, p. 134).

[44] G. W. Hegel, *The Philosophy of Right*, ed. T. M. Knox (Oxford: Oxford University Press, 1967), para. 4.

world. Along Burkean lines, then, there is an emphasis on a sense of permanence, a sense of responsibility, and a stable sense of purpose which property-owners can be expected to have, and which those who are propertyless are likely to lack.

Enough has been said, we hope, to indicate that the traditional notion of citizenship is not independent of considerations of social and economic concerns. Everyone in the civic republican tradition of Western political thought – that is, everyone who has ever thought seriously about citizenship in a political sense – has reached certain conclusions about what the economic situation of the citizen ought to be. But one may still think that we are miles away from social citizenship in Marshall's sense. Indeed, if anything we seem to be going in the opposite direction: instead of just taking welfare rights away from the poor, the tendency of the civic tradition seems to be that we should take political rights away from them too!

The interesting thing, though, is that each of the arguments we have been considering can be pushed in either of two directions. On the one hand, as we have seen they can be used as arguments for restricting citizenship to those who happen to be in a certain socio-economic position – those who own property, those of independent means, or those who are economically secure in some other sense. But on the other hand, they can be used as a basis for exactly the opposite conclusion: if we are going to have universal citizenship, in a political sense, for our society, then we should do it properly and see to it that *everyone* is put in the socio-economic position that we have reason to believe citizens ought to be in. In other words, if we take the idea of universal suffrage seriously, then we should not be content simply to give everybody a vote: we should set about the task of giving them the economic security, which, on the arguments we have been considering, is the necessary precondition for good citizenship.

It is true that the arguments we have been considering are not in themselves arguments for universal suffrage. In the modern democratic age, we think we have independent arguments for that: ethical ideas about equal respect; utilitarian ideas about the necessity to get goverments to promote the general interest; Aristotlean ideas about participation being part of human nature, not just the nature of a few; arguments about what political obligation presupposes; and so on. Our thesis is a conditional one. *If* we accept any of these independent arguments for universal suffrage, *then*, taking seriously the arguments we have been outlining about fraternity, economic independence and security, we will have powerful reasons for associating political citizenship with at least some of the welfare rights that Marshall spoke about when he referred to citizenship in a social sense.

## 4. BELONGING TO OUR SOCIETY

So far we have explored the connections that there might be between what Marshall calls political citizenship and what he calls social citizenship. The other arguments we want to discuss appeal, however, to a broader notion of citizenship than this. Often when we say 'X is a citizen of the United Kingdom', what we mean is that he or she is a fully-fledged *member* of this community, entitled to live here and make a life here. We may not be implying any theory about political participation; we may be saying, rather, that this is where he or she belongs. What is the normative force of this idea? Is there anything in the concept of membership or belonging that lends support to Marshall's idea of social citizenship?

Let us start modestly with a discussion of what it is to belong to a society *like our own*. Then in section 5, we will consider whether any normative argument can be drawn out of the concept of belonging itself, quite apart from the history of the particular community with which it is associated. The argument we want to consider in this section goes roughly like this.

Over the last fifty years in Britain, we have taken it upon ourselves collectively to provide for much of the basic welfare of the members of society. Over that period, people who live here have become familiar with that provision: they are familiar with the way welfare is provided and they are familiar with the way it is paid for, out of taxation. Both taxpayers and potential recipients have taken all this on board, and organized their expectations and the way they run their lives, accordingly. Of course, there is disagreement at the margins: the precise array of goods and services that are on offer, and about the precise extent and incidence of taxation. But the broad idea that this is what our society does for its members and this is how, has caught on, and is used as a primary point of reference for the way people organize their lives. To launch an attack, then, on *the very idea* of welfare provision, in the way that some New Right thinkers suggest, would be to challenge the way people have grown accustomed to think about themselves and the planning of their lives. For that reason, it is to attack their basic sense of what it is to live here, to make a life here, to belong here. It is, in that way, to attack their sense of citizenship.

Notice a few things about this argument. It does not proceed, as the previous argument did, from an antecedent notion of citizenship to the demand that there should be welfare provision. Instead it proceeds from the contingent fact that welfare guarantees have been established in this society (for whatever reason) to the claim that they are now part of what we understand by citizenship. The suggestion is that what it is to be a member is not something fixed in stone for all time, but is expandable, as new ways develop in which the state can offer various benefits that accrue from collective organization, and in which members can participate in those arrangements to make benefits available to each other.

Secondly, the concept of citizenship here is somewhat broader than that used in the previous discussion. Now it means not only political participation, but all aspects of what it is to be a *member* of a society. Many political scientists argue that political participation is not what people think is most important about their lives (though some regret that this is so). The present argument is realistic, then, in focusing on a sense of citizenship which connects more comprehensively with people's sense of their social selves, and of the organization of their lives.

The third thing to note is that, in so far as it has any normative force, this argument is primarily a conservative one, with a small 'c' (and we shall have to consider shortly whether it is not *too* conservative). According to this conservative approach, the reasons for keeping welfare guarantees in existence once they have become established are not confined to the reasons there were for establishing them in the first place. Once a certain form of provision is established, people build their expectations around it, in a way that they would not build their expectations around a mere demand that welfare provision *ought* to be established. But when people do start building their expectations, the fact of establishment takes on a moral significance of its own.

The point can be put as one about security. When Jeremy Bentham wrote about security as one of the ends of law, he said that 'security consists in receiving no check, no shock, no derangement to the expectation founded on the laws, of enjoying such and such a portion of good: the legislator owes the greatest respect to this expectation which he has himself produced'.[45] Security of expectation, he argued, is the basis of people's ability to plan their lives: 'It is hence that we have the power of forming a general plan of conduct; it is hence that the successive instants which compose the duration of life are not like isolated and independent points, but become continuous parts of a whole'.[46] Similar points have been made in the New Right context itself by F. A. Hayek and others, stressing the need for stable and predictable laws.[47]

As Bentham stated it, the point was mainly about property law. Though there are good utilitarian reasons for redistributing property (utilitarianism favours equality on the basis of the law of diminishing marginal utility of resources), there are also powerful utilitarian reasons for resisting redistribution on the ground of security of expectations. Bentham believed it was possible to calculate in advance that the property-owner who suffers a shock to his or her expectations and those who are frightened or made anxious by the example of what is happening to him or her, will suffer more, directly and indirectly, than the beneficiaries of redistribution could possibly gain, even taking into account diminishing marginal utility. But everything that Bentham says about property expectations can be applied to welfare expectations, once they too have become established. Indeed, once they are established there is as much of a case for regarding them as part of the overall property scheme as there is for regarding, say, home-ownership in this way. In each case, someone has a recognized legal claim over certain of the resources available in society, and that claim forms the basis of his or her expectations and his or her ability to plan his or her life. (This is why a number of American writers have argued, for example, that welfare entitlements should be given protection under the Fifth Amendment to the US Constitution, which prohibits the taking of private property for public use without just compensation.)

Of course, many welfare benefits are awarded on a discretionary basis and this

[45] Jeremy Bentham, *The Theory of Legislation*, ed. C. K. Ogden (London: Routledge & Kegan Paul, 1931), p. 113.

[46] Bentham, *Theory of Legislation*, p. 111.

[47] See F. A. Hayek, *Law, Legislation and Liberty* (London: Routledge & Kegan Paul, 1973, 1976 and 1979), 3 vols.

raises issues about whether it is possible to describe them strictly speaking as rights. Though Marshall uses the terminology of rights, there is not space to consider here in any detail the issue of whether welfare provision is a matter of rights or even whether the idea of welfare rights makes sense. That is a subject for another paper.[48] Our point is about the morality of discontinuing or dismantling welfare provision (however this is described in the terminology of meta-ethics). Some welfare benefits are in fact distributed as a matter of legal right (for example, education and child benefits) but even those that are discretionary are still capable of giving rise to strong expectations amongst the members of a community. In other words, the fact that some aspects of social welfare are discretionary does not prevent people from forming expectations about it, and organizing their lives in often quite important ways on the basis of those expectations. Though people know that there is discretion in the award of these payments, still they expect that discretion to be exercised in their favour, at least if they become a clearly needy case, and they will be shocked, taken aback and outraged if it is not. That is the key to our argument.

To violate these expectations is not merely to disappoint people; it is also to radically disrupt their personal planning. In particular, there is one very important aspect of the way people run their lives which is bound up with the integrity of their social security expectations. Social security expectations radically affect the risks people think they can take in making their decisions. We have in mind here things like forming and breaking marital or quasi-marital relationships, conceiving children, moving away from close-knit communities, employment decisions, taking certain attitudes to one's employment on the shop floor, starting a small business, opting for higher education and so on, across a wide array of areas. In all these areas, people are taking chances, entering into gambles if you like, on certain assumptions and against the background of certain conditions. Now attitudes to social risk are crucial in establishing social identity, and beliefs about welfare provision are crucial to that. My sense of what it is to be a member of this community is going to be centrally linked to my awareness of the conditions under which I am to think about making a life for myself in this community and taking the various risks that that involves.

It is clear that people are willing to take much greater risks when they know that there is a safety net – a limit to the catastrophic losses that they may incur. They can say to themselves, 'I will go into this new relationship, or I will take the risk of university education rather than a secure school-leaver's job, or I will start this new business, knowing that if things work out badly at least I will not starve.' We should stress too that many of these risks are long-term, and the willingness to undertake them is based therefore on long-run expectations. We can see then immediately the force of the argument that would say it is wrong or unfair to, as it were, change the terms of the gamble – by abolishing the welfare safety net – half-way through.

[48] Some of these points are discussed in T. H. Marshall, *The Right to Welfare* (London: Heinemann, 1981), pp. 83–4. For the motion of a *right* to welfare, see Jeremy Waldron, *Nonsense Upon Stilts: Bentham, Burke and Marx on the Rights of Man* (London: Methuen, 1987), pp. 156–60.

Some New Right theorists have seized on this aspect of welfare provision as the very thing they are objecting to: welfare provision, they say, encourages people to run irresponsible risks, so that people become less prudent in their decisions about families, industrial action, education and so on. As we mentioned at the beginning of this article, they claim that the mitigation of risk undermines market discipline and other forms of discipline in the society. We do not want to get into that argument except to say attitudes towards risk in *any* society are going to be relative to institutional expectations: and so the New Right view presupposes already that there is some other good argument for choosing markets-without-safety nets as the baseline in terms of which personal responsibility is to be assessed. We should say, too, that there are arguments on the other side – particularly feminist and modernist (as well as economic) arguments – for increasing mobility and choice in modern society for everyone in it. Mitigating the risks of choice and mobility is one way of doing this.

But eventually we have to come back to the point about conservatism. Suppose the New Right theorists are even half right, and we do suffer harm as a society — in terms of unemployment and erosion of incentives — because this social security is on offer. Is it our argument that no expectations can *ever* be overturned no matter how socially harmful they are?

The question is a good one, and the argument we have put forward should not be regarded as absolute. There are all sorts of traditional privileges in society, which are the centre of people's established expectations, but which nevertheless are socially harmful and ought to be abolished. For example, one of the issues at stake in the American Civil War was not whether slavery was wrong but whether it was right to violate all the expectations and life-plans that had become bound up with this (admittedly undesirable) institution. The danger is that people can organize their lives around harmful systems as well as good ones; and then the force of a conservative argument would be to perpetuate the evil. Indeed, if this had been accepted as a general argument in 1945 social provision in its modern form might never have been established.

The force of this objection, however, should not be exaggerated in the present context. It is important in the case of social citizenship that we are talking, not about an institution like slavery, but about benefits and privileges that are universal – that is part of the significance of drawing attention to their status as aspects of 'citizenship'. Since this is so, we need to be quite clear about what is being said when it is alleged they are socially harmful. Is it the case that *everybody* would be better off if welfare benefits were withdrawn, if the risks people run were not socially underwritten, and if unmitigated market discipline were allowed to operate? Or is it merely that *some* would be be better off and their gains would outweigh others' losses? We may be dealing here with a clash between the common good and the greatest good, familiar to all involved in the modern discussion of utilitarianism. The fact that a conservative argument protects a universal entitlement in the face of aggregate social utility is hardly a devastating objection, unless more is said.

Secondly, a conservative argument does not imply absolute and slavish adherence to the expectations of the past. It implies rather that if one wants to make changes in the basis of people's expectations, one must do so slowly, over decades or even generations, rather than (say) in the space of one parliament. Otherwise one is not sufficiently respecting the people one is dealing with – the people who have to live their lives in the environment one is manipulating – and the need that they have to get a settled sense of the basis on which they can make their plans and choices.

Thirdly, it should be noted that, though the objection is an important one, it does nothing to diminish the *concern* which is at the basis of our argument: it does not deny that people do form expectations, and that their lives may be disrupted and disoriented if these are shattered, by even well-intentioned reform. The present argument is not a cast-iron defence of welfare provision. But it uses the notions of citizenship, membership and belonging – as they relate to our society – to sound a serious note of caution about any attempt to roll back the welfare state. The virtue of the social citizenship argument, or this interpretation, is to draw attention to certain costs, which might otherwise be underestimated, attendant upon any such anti-welfare initiative. That cost is not merely the material loss to the people concerned: it is also the disruption of a whole array of plans and decisions about how to organize their lives, and therefore a loss of people's social sense of themselves as members of this community, living and choosing within its social structures. We must bear in mind that the argument to be made here is not necessarily an argument for a massive welfare state or a welfare state expanding inexorably toward socialism. The argument we are making is for public provision of a minimum level of welfare as a universal entitlement, defining a threshold below which people will not be allowed to fall without diminishing their sense and their capacities of citizenship. That is something one ought to be very wary about disrupting, for it is most unlikely that the alienation, disappointment and disorientation that results would have no effects on other aspects of social action and social integration. If the idea of citizenship can be associated with that of membership, then we can say what is disrupted is people's whole sense of what it is to be a citizen in Britain.

## 5. MEMBERSHIP IN GENERAL

The argument we have just made is a relative one: the set of welfare provision that has been established in Britain helps to constitute citizens' sense of what it is to be a member of this society. Some writers however have taken the citizenship–membership–welfare link even further, and argued that provision for welfare is not just an incident of particular conceptions of community and membership in particular countries, but partly constitutive of *the very concept* of community and membership. If there is any force to this argument, then it provides a universal rather than a merely relative case for welfare based on citizenship. Though some of Marshall's arguments seem oriented towards the relative approach – this is where *we* have got to in the evolution of citizenship – some of his arguments, as we have seen, seem to imply that a more absolute case can be made: that there is, in some sense, an ideal of social citizenship towards which the evolution of modern citizenship is taking us.

To make this case, it is not sufficient to establish merely that welfare provision is, in fact, a characteristic of all modern societies. In Humean terms, the 'constant conjunction' of citizenship and welfare in the modern world does not establish that one is *implied* by the other. It may be mere coincidence; or it may be that all societies have accepted other arguments for welfare provision that have nothing to do with citizenship. (We did not want to say that the arguments we are considering are the only arguments for welfare.) Moreover, we should remember that the New Right proposal, that universal practice should be altered in this regard, is one which is also made in all modern societies. One does not have to be a firm believer in the fact/value gap to see that a normative argument for resisting that proposal cannot simply be inferred from the very state of affairs that New Right critics are proposing to challenge.

Nor are we likely to get very far with purely conceptual or linguistic analysis of ideas like 'citizenship', 'membership' and 'community'. We can stare at the words for as long as we like, but the dictionary will not do our moral thinking for us. Anyone who thinks that these terms can be linked *definitionally* to the pursuit of certain ends, such as the provision of welfare, needs to bear in mind Max Weber's dictum that 'the state cannot be defined in terms of its end. There is scarcely any task that some political association has not taken in hand'.[49] Equally one might say with Weber that there is no task that has not sometime been neglected by some political association or community. Political societies have neglected welfare provision in the past, and there are proposals from people on the Right that they should neglect welfare provision in the future. One can make the move of insisting that such societies are not really entitled to be called '*communities*' in some defined sense; but that is simply rhetoric and happy talk, and begs the morally much more important question of why people should be interested in the application of *that* definition, rather than some other.

In a recent book, *Spheres of Justice*, Michael Walzer has suggested that 'every political community is in principle a "welfare state"',[50] and insisted that the very idea of a community connotes some distribution according to need: 'Every political community must attend to the needs of its members as they collectively understand those needs; ... the goods that are distributed must be distributed in proportion to need; and that distribution must recognize and uphold the underlying equality of membership.'[51] If Walzer is right about this, then citizenship in the sense of membership has a direct implication of welfare provision. Unfortunately, his argument for these assertions falls into both the traps we have mentioned. First, he takes the fact that welfare provision is a universal feature of all

[49] Max Weber, 'Politics as a Vocation' in *From Max Weber*, ed. Hans Gerth and C. Wright Mills (London: Routledge & Kegan Paul, 1948), p. 77.

[50] Michael Walzer, *Spheres of Justice* (Oxford: Martin Robertson, 1983), p. 62.

[51] Walzer, *Spheres of Justice*, p. 84.

societies as a basis for his normative claim that proposals to end welfare provision are misguided:

> There has never been a political community that did not provide, or try to provide, or claim to provide, for the needs of its members as its members understood those needs. And there has never been a political community that did not engage its collective strength – its capacity to direct, regulate, pressure and coerce – in this project.[52]

Now, that fact, if it is true, is no doubt interesting; but it does not in itself imply any reason not to try something new in this regard. As it happens, Walzer's factual claim is false. He himself cites the example of Athens as a society which recognized and understood a much wider range of poverty-related needs than it attempted to cater for; it was well understood, for example, that all widows were potentially in need of economic assistance, but there was state provision only for the widows of fallen soldiers. Athens certainly recognized the importance of economic support for political citizenship; public money was paid out to make it possible for poorer citizens to miss a day's work to come to the Assembly or serve on juries, and this charge often amounted to more than half the public revenue of the city. This was in recognition of some of the arguments we mentioned in section 3. But beyond that, it is simply untrue to say that Athens catered for all the needs, or even all the pressing needs, that it recognized its members to have.

There are two moves Walzer uses to deal with such counterexamples. On the one hand, he argues that certain societies do not count as communities in the appropriate sense. Thus, for example, 'the indifference of Britain's rulers during the Irish potato famine is a sure sign that Ireland was a colony', not part of the British community; and he says also that his principles, such as the principle that if distribution *is* undertaken it is distribution according to need, 'probably don't apply to a society organized hierarchically, as in traditional India, where the fruits of the harvest are distributed not according to need but according to caste'.[53] But the question then arises: what moral reason is there for having a Walzerian community rather than a colony or caste society in this sense? Walzer gives no answer.

Secondly, and connected with that, Walzer stresses the vagueness of welfare provision as a concept which applies to all communities: 'the idea of need and the commitment to communal provision do not by themselves yield any clear determination of priorities and degrees'.[54] That is something, Walzer believed, every society works out for itself, in terms of its own history, its politics and its social understandings. (It is not for the philosopher to second-guess from his or her armchair the process of the evolution Marshall has described.) But then, Walzer is moving back towads the relativist position we have already considered in section 4:

52 Walzer, *Spheres of Justice*, p. 68.
53 Walzer, *Spheres of Justice*, p. 84.
54 Walzer, *Spheres of Justice*, p. 66.

The ancient Athenians, for example, provided public baths and gymnasiums for the citizens but never provided anything remotely resembling unemployment insurance or social security. They made a choice about how to spend public funds, a choice shaped presumably by their understanding of what the common life required. It would be hard to argue that they made a mistake. I suppose there are notions of need that would yield such a conclusion, but these would not be notions acceptable to – they might not even be comprehensible to – the Athenians themselves.[55]

In fact the main interest of Walzer's book has been in his relativist suggestion that different standards of distribution are morally appropriate to the social understandings established in different societies. For our purposes the important point is that there is no longer any sense of an argument that membership and community, as such, imply a commitment to welfare provision, in anything other than a notional sense.

Are there then no substantive conclusions we can reach about membership as such, only the relativist conclusions with which we ended the previous section? We think that there is one other approach that may be promising.

The work of John Rawls has been very influential in political philosophy, for its revival of contractarianism as a method of argument, and for the liberal egalitarianism of its conclusions.[56] Rawls's argument is usually considered in terms of justice and injustice. A just society, he argues, will be one in which people enjoy equal basic liberties and in which inequalities of wealth and power are tolerated only if they contribute positively to the well-being of the least advantaged group of society. Though Rawls is agnostic about whether these principles are capable of legitimating a market economy and the institutions of capitalism, there is no doubt at all that they require social redistribution and the establishment of a welfare state.[57] Rawls's theory has been subject, of course, to many criticisms by New Right philosophers. Some, like Anthony Flew, accuse him of distorting the very notion of justice;[58] others, like Nozick, take him to task for ignoring the primacy of property and for assuming that society simply has at its disposal goods it may distribute in accordance with Rawlsian principles;[59] and still others, like Hayek, extend a cautious welcome to Rawls's work mainly because they misunderstood its tendency.[60]

For our purposes, the interest lies not only in the welfarist and redistributivist *conclusions* of Rawls's discussion, but also in the way they are presented. We believe Rawls's work can be understood as a discussion of what it is to be a citizen or member of a given society. A person is a mere *subject* of a regime and not

[55] Walzer, *Spheres of Justice*, p. 67. See Goodin, *Reasons for Welfare*, Chap. 4, for a general critique of 'community' in arguments of this sort.

[56] John Rawls, *A Theory of Justice* (Cambridge, Mass.: Harvard University Press, 1971).

[57] Rawls, *Theory of Justice*, pp. 275–84. Minimum provision in this context is discussed in Jeremy Waldron, 'John Rawls and the Social Minimum', *Journal of Applied Philosophy*, 3 (1986), 21–34.

[58] Anthony Flew, *The Politics of Procrustes: Contradictions of Enforced Equality* (London: Temple-Smith, 1981).

[59] Nozick, *Anarchy, State and Utopia*.

[60] F. A. Hayek, *Law, Legislation and Liberty* (London: Routledge, Kegan & Paul, 1976), p. 100.

a citizen, if its rules and policies will be applied to him or her whether he or she likes it or not and whether they serve his or her interests or not. They are applied without reference to his or her consent. But, since Locke, the liberal tradition has always been that we should try and think of subjects as though they were founding members of the society in which they live. Even though they cannot actually choose the regime they live under, nevertheless in our attempts to evaluate and to legitimize such a regime, we should at least ask what sort of order they would have chosen if they had had the choice. This is the tradition Rawls pursues. For Rawls, being a member of a society is not just a matter of living in and being subject to a social framework, it is also a matter of how that framework is justified. A person is a *member* of a society if and only if the design of its basic institutions fairly reflects a concern for his or her interests along with those of everyone else.

As everyone knows, the way Rawls chooses to express this idea is through the myth of the social contract. A society is just, and the people living in it are members rather than subjects, if we can show that its institutions satisfy certain principles that people would have agreed to as basic terms of co-operation, had they been given the opportunity to decide. If its institutions do not satisfy such principles, or if they are based on principles that would not or could not have been agreed to in advance by those who have to live with them, then they cannot be regarded as just, for they do not embody sufficient respect for the persons they apply to. Thus understood, the social contract myth attractively expresses the idea of a veto. You cannot be voted into a contract; everyone has to agree, everyone has to be convinced, and everyone has to gain. Now, of course, Rawls is the first to concede that in fact nothing like the 'original position' ever takes place: it is a moral perspective or a thought-experiment, not a historical speculation:[61]

> No society can, of course, be a scheme of co-operation which men enter voluntarily in a literal sense; each person finds himself placed at birth in some particular position in some particular society, and the nature of his position materially affects his life prospects. Yet a society satisfying the principles of justice comes as close as a society can to being a voluntary scheme, for it meets the principles which free and equal people *would assent to* under circumstances that are fair. In this sense, its members are autonomous and the obligations they recognize self-imposed.[62]

If people learn to think about their society in this way, then they can say to one another 'that they are co-operating on terms to which they would agree if they were free and equal'[63] or, if they are critical, they can say that what is wrong with their society is that it would *not* pass this test of agreement by everyone under conditions of fairness. The terms that would be agreed to can be used then as a basis for evaluating both present arrangements and proposals for change in the future.

Rawls argues that people in his 'original position' would choose a mix of principles. They would choose a principle of equal political liberty and they would

[61] Rawls, *Theory of Justice*, pp. 138–9.

[62] Rawls, *Theory of Justice*, p. 13, our emphasis.

[63] Rawls, *Theory of Justice*, p. 13.

choose a principle of fair equality of opportunity and what he calls 'the Difference Principle' to govern the distribution of social and economic goods. The Difference Principle is our concern here. Rawls argues that it would be impossible in the 'original position' to secure general agreement for a set of social institutions that did not make collective provision for the plight of the members of the worst-off group. Social institutions that did not include the securing of a social minimum, the familiar apparatus of welfare provision, and perhaps more substantial methods of redistribution as well, would not command unanimous agreement in the original position. People would not be willing to accept an economic system or a system of property unless it had all this built into it. Those who feared they might fall into the worst-off group in the community would be reluctant to accept anything less than this, because they would be unsure of their ability to *live with* anything less. Agreeing to terms of co-operation that did not include such gurantees would impose what Rawls refers to as 'strains of commitment' on the parties:

> they cannot enter into agreements that may have consequences they cannot accept. They will avoid those that they can adhere to only with great difficulty. Since the original agreement is final and made in perpetuity, there is no second chance. In view of the serious nature of the possible consequences, the question of burden of commitment is especially acute ... Looking at the question from the standpoint of the original position, the parties recognise that it would be highly unwise if not irrational to choose principles which may have consequences so extreme that they could not accept them in practice.[64]

In other words, the Rawlsian argument takes us from what he refers to as 'a general knowledge of human psychology' to conclusions about the sort of social arrangements people could live with. Faced with great deprivation and inequality, people cannot be expected to live quiet and satisfied lives. They therefore cannot in good faith undertake or agree to live with such deprivation and inequality. So a political theory which gives any weight to the question of what people would agree to has an argument against the acceptability of such arrangements.

His argument connects with our concerns then in two ways. First, a political theory treats people as citizens and members (as opposed to subjects) only if it concerns itself with what social arrangements those people would agree to. Secondly, Rawls argues that people would agree only to principles which focused concern on the plight of the poorest members of society. His principles certainly require a welfare state; indeed they may require much more. They therefore provide the backbone of a powerful argument connecting citizenship or membership as such with at least basic welfare provision.

As Rawls presents it, *no one* would sign up for an economic system without welfare provision. That is because one of the features of his 'original position' is that the people taking this perspective must pretend to be ignorant of their wealth, class and talents, and Rawls argues that no one would want to take the risk of turning out to be poor and untalented in a society that lacked a safety net.

[64] Rawls, *Theory of Justice*, pp. 176–8.

But it is worth noting that the argument can be made out even without Rawls's controversial 'veil of ignorance'. All one needs is a veto and the requirement of unanimous agreement. Those who happen to be poor or untalented may be expected to veto the adoption of any social system that does not attempt to ameliorate their plight. If they have to live under such a system, they will be unable to give it their support and they will be driven by their need to subvert it where they can. Knowing this, they wll be unable in good faith to agree to such a system from the standpoint of the original postion. If nevertheless they find themselves in a society which lacks a safety net, or which lacks a basic welfare system, they are perfectly entitled to say to themselves, 'This society does not treat us as members, as citizens, or as people who belong here, for it is operating a system which could not possibly have commanded our consent'. So once again, the warning of the social citizenship argument, on this interpretation, is that the cost of rolling back welfare provision may be the acceptance of this sort of alienation.

If an argument like this can be made, then there is a reason for having welfare rights in a society whether it has a tradition of such institutions or not. Social rights of citizenship are a necessary condition for genuine and meaningful consent to social and political arrangements. It is true that in his more recent work Rawls has drawn back a little from the apparent universalism of *A Theory of Justice*: he now maintains that the principles of justice and the reasoning that leads to them do not represent moral conclusions valid for all times and places but rather moral conclusions whose validity is in some sense relative to the 'social and historical conditions' which have produced what he calls 'an overlapping consensus' about the basic values of a democratic society.[65] Rawls appears to be adopting a very deep and general relativism about social and political thought here. But the relativism which distinguished our argument in section 4 was more concerned with existing institutional arrangements like the welfare state and their effect on people's expectations. It is therefore a more 'surface-level' relativism than that to which Rawls has recently committed himself. The argument we have made in this section may be relative in Rawls's terms – that is, it only makes sense to people who have been brought up in a certain sort of culture with a certain sense of history. All the same, some of the societies with this history have had welfare arrangements, others have not. The Rawlsian argument reaches very deeply into the underlying values of our culture to show that welfare arguments are necessary if we are to keep faith with those values.

## 6. CONCLUSION

In this article we have sought to explore different arguments which might underlie, and give normative substance to, the notion of citizenship. Our analysis has

[65] J. Rawls, 'The Idea of an Overlapping Consensus', *Oxford Journal of Legal Studies*, 7 (1987), 4; see also Rawls, 'Kantian Constructivism in Moral Theory', *Journal of Philosophy*, 77 (1980), 515–72. For a critique of this relativism, see Waldron, *Nonsense Upon Stilts*, pp. 166–72.

been framed with reference to two possible views of the relationship between welfare provision and citizenship: an idealistic argument whereby social welfare is presented as an attribute of citizenship in a statement about the most desirable form of social organization,and an empirical argument about the necessity of welfare for effective citizenship in a traditional sense. The first branch of the argument in turn divides in two: one branch arguing from the impact of expectations of existing welfare provision, the other not being so directly relative to actual social institutions. The arguments are separate but they are not meant to be mutually exclusive: we have presented them here as partially overlapping, partially complementary ways of teasing out the normative implications of social citizenship.

The importance of this discussion lies in its relevance to contemporary political and social discourse. In an effort to rebut New Right arguments and policies, some scholars and politicians have drawn upon social right and citizenship arguments to defend the policies and institutions of the welfare state. We have tried to evaluate the strength of such claims through examination of their analytical basis and to suggest various ways in which those claims might be understood. Above all, we think it important that the idea of citizenship should remain at the centre of modern political debates about social and economic arrangements. The concept of a citizen is that of a person who can hold her or his head high and participate fully and with dignity in the life of her or his society. Although, as we have seen, there are many competing conceptions of what it is to be a citizen in the modern state, and although, as our argument has shown, none of these conceptions is particularly straightforward, nevertheless the underlying idea is one that must not ever be lost sight of when we are considering in our political discussions what life in this society is to be like.

# Part III
# The Political and Economic Context of Welfare

*Jnl Soc. Pol.* I, 1, 15–32 

# Value problems of Welfare-Capitalism

T. H. MARSHALL*

I have borrowed this term from Richard Crossman. When he wrote his contribution to the *New Fabian Essays* in 1952 he took stock of the present state of socialism, as the original Fabians had done in 1889. He hoped to discover 'a philosophy of Socialism' with life in it. But he failed. An obvious place to look for it was in the Welfare State, as it had emerged from the hands of the post-war Labour government. But the Welfare State, he decided, was not socialist; it was 'the climax of a long process, in the course of which capitalism had been civilised and to a large extent reconciled with democracy'. Later on he referred to the product of this process as 'welfare capitalism'.[1] He ought to have called it 'democratic-welfare-capitalism' because, as I shall argue, democracy deserves to have a position as a third party of independent status, not just to be taken for granted.

Crossman was not alone in finding it impossible to describe society at about that time without the help of a hyphen, either written or implied. Others had the same experience. In fact one might say that, from the 1930s onwards, the social systems of Europe, except when Communist, Fascist or 'Nazi' (*Nationalsozialist* was always one word in German), were hopelessly hyphenated, because they were essentially composite. Evan Durbin, on the eve of the war, set out to show how one could convert 'democratic capitalism' into 'democratic socialism' and he envisaged the latter, not simply as a partnership of two familiar systems but, in Tawney's words, as 'a new social order'.[2] He believed a genuine fusion of the two was possible because, he said, 'there is a complex and important sense in which socialism is necessary to democracy – the sense in which capitalism is incompatible with democracy. But there is a simple and much more obvious sense in which democracy is necessary to socialism.'[3] It was the 'indispensable means' of achieving that great end. Schumpeter, in a well-known book,[4] took up the same question. Capitalism, he believed, was destroying itself by

* Emeritus Professor of Sociology, University of London.

[1] R. H. Crossman (ed.), *New Fabian Essays*, London: The Turnstile Press, 1952, pp. 6 and 25.

[2] E. F. M. Durbin, *The Politics of Democratic Socialism*, London: Routledge, 1940; the comment by R. H. Tawney was on the dust cover.

[3] *Loc. cit.* p. 271.

[4] Joseph A. Schumpeter, *Capitalism, Socialism and Democracy*, London: Allen and Unwin, 1947, especially pp. 296–302.

16 *T. H. Marshall*

its own success (shades of Rolls Royce!), so we should be left with socialism and democracy. Could they be fruitfully combined together? Was 'socialist democracy' a viable political system? He was not as certain about this as Durbin. We find a third example of this hyphenated political terminology used about Sweden by Professor Tingsten; he calls it a 'welfare democracy'.[5]

This substitution of 'welfare' for 'socialism' is significant. Socialism, as seen by Durbin and Schumpeter, was the antithesis of capitalism, an antagonist with whom there could be no fusion or compromise. Neither of them said anything much about welfare, and Durbin made it quite clear that what he called 'further ameliorative measures' must be kept in their proper order of priority, 'after, and not before, the socialization of industry'.[6] He believed, like the original Fabians, that once the socialist system had been established, the rest would follow. Schumpeter also examined socialism as a system for the management of a country's economic affairs rather than as a way of life. In the 1950s a new emphasis became apparent. Hugh Gaitskell described socialism in terms of its ideals, the first of which was equality – 'social equality, which to us is substantially the same as social justice', greater equality (or reduced inequality) of incomes, and 'equal opportunity for the pursuit of happiness'.[7] This had become the end, and the 'socialization of industry' the means, or even only one of the means. And Gaitskell risked his position as leader of the party in his attempt to impose this view by deleting from the constitution of the party the famous Clause 4 which pledged it to total nationalization. He failed, and opinion on this issue was divided. One of the strongest advocates of the new emphasis was Anthony Crosland, who wrote, after Labour's failure in the 1959 election: 'Socialism denotes a belief in the pre-eminence of certain values, such as equality or co-operation or collective welfare or internationalism. But such values are not absolute.'[8] With socialism redefined in this way, and nationalization demoted to the status of a means, the hyphenated democratic-welfare-capitalist society became possible, or even inevitable.

This movement of ideas extended over most of western Europe and was christened, I believe by Edward Shils, the 'end of ideology?' – with a question mark. The phrase has been current ever since to describe the abandonment of the state of mind which automatically treats every party political issue as a matter of principle on which it would be treachery to

[5] Herbert Tingsten, 'Stability and Vitality in Swedish Democracy', *Political Quarterly*, XXVI, no. 2, 1955, p. 141.

[6] Durbin, *op. cit.* p. 298.

[7] Hugh Gaitskell, *Socialism and Nationalisation*, Fabian Tract 300, London: The Fabian Society, 1956, pp. 3–4.

[8] C. A. R. Crosland, *Future of the Left*, Encounter Pamphlets no. 4, March 1960, p. 7.

yield an inch. Most of those who noted the change at the time applauded it. They saw it as a victory for rationalism and sensible co-operation. They believed, as Gunnar Myrdal put it, that political attitudes were converging and the area of inter-party consensus extending,[9] though others saw in it a sad loss of vitality and political faith.

Since the focal point of this essay is social policy, the most significant fact here is that the position of 'welfare' within the hyphenated democratic-welfare-capitalist system was not challenged in the countries of continental Europe; on the contrary it was steadily reinforced, and it is being built into the economic structure of the Common Market, although the process is slow and is not yet completed. Even in the United States, the democratic-capitalist society *par excellence*, events were moving in the same direction, towards acceptance of the basic principles of the Welfare State. 'We move toward the Welfare State, but we do it with ill grace, carping and complaining all the way', wrote Harold Wilensky in 1965.[10] In 1969 President Nixon assured his audience that he would not allow America to become 'a garrison state, or a welfare state, or a police state',[11] having in mind, no doubt, the saying that you can tell a man by the company he keeps. But in his State of the Union Message of January 1971 he gave top priority to welfare reform, declaring that 'the present welfare system has become a monstrous, consuming outrage'.[12] So it is odd that Britain, which invented the Welfare State, should be the one country that has expressed grave doubts about some of its basic principles. The attacks of the 1950s[13] were warded off, but the Conservative government has reopened the issues in a manner likely to provoke an outbreak of ideological warfare.

I cannot attempt here to explain this difference between British and European experience. It would not be easy to do so, and it is not my purpose. I am concerned in this essay with the general – the structural type – rather than with the particular case. I will make just two observations. The British were the only people who idolized the Welfare State from the first, when it was still very imperfect and incomplete. It is not surprising that out of debates over its further development there should emerge a reaction against this idolatry which, in turn, provoked an ideological backlash. Secondly, Britain, having emerged victorious from a long and exhausting war, passed from voluntary self-denial, via imposed austerity, through apparent affluence to near-bankruptcy; this made it harder for her than for,

[9] Gunnar Myrdal, *Beyond the Welfare State*, London: Duckworth, 1960, p. 53.
[10] Harold L. Wilensky and Charles N. Lebaux, *Industrial Society and Social Welfare*, Introduction to 1965 edition, New York: The Free Press, p. xvii.
[11] The *New York Times*, 4 June 1969.
[12] *The Times*, 25 January 1971.
[13] E.g. Iain Macleod and J. Enoch Powell, *The Social Services – Needs and Means*, 1952.

18 *T. H. Marshall*

say, Germany, in which almost total destruction was followed by an 'economic miracle', to take in her stride the high costs of top-grade social services and social security. So the problems which beset this composite type of society come out more strongly and, I believe, more clearly in Britain than elsewhere.

In choosing to study these problems in terms of the relations between the three components which, following Crossman, I am calling democracy, welfare and capitalism, I am not suggesting that these are the only potential sources of trouble. It is just that I find the structural approach interesting and fancy it might be pursued further with advantage. The terminology I am using is, of course, not at all precise. It refers to the elements we may assume to be present when a country with a *capitalist* market economy develops *democratic* political and civil institutions and practices out of which emerge a mixed economy including both private and public capitalism similarly organized and using the same calculus, together with that complex of public social services, insurances and assistances which is the eponymous element in what all the world knows as the *Welfare* State.

I shall begin at the macro-political level, and consider how the three components of the hyphenated democratic-welfare-capitalist social system approach the task of taking policy decisions. Kenneth Arrow has said that 'in a capitalist democracy there are essentially two methods by which social choices can be made: voting, typically used to make "political" decisions, and the market mechanism, typically used to make "economic" decisions'. And a little later he defines the central problem of welfare economics as that of 'achieving a social maximum derived from individual desires'.[14] The democratic and the economic process are alike in that they both take a mass of individuals, process them through institutions – the ballot and the market – which register and react to their desires, and produce a single body of answers, a set of prices or a Houseful of Members. But, whereas the market gets its result by combination, by discovering the combined effect of the expressed wishes of everyone and so arriving at what Arrow calls the 'social maximum', the ballot reaches its conclusion by division, by sorting out the expressed wishes so as to identify the majority, and then accepting *their* wish as the decision. The case of welfare is different again. Although it must take careful note of expressed desires, it does not simply react to or obey them. Its responsibility is to satisfy needs, which is a different undertaking.

In contrast to the economic process, it is a fundamental principle of the

[14] Kenneth Arrow, *Social Choice and Individual Values*, London: Chapman and Hall, 1951, pp. 1 and 3.

Welfare State that the market value of an individual cannot be the measure of his right to welfare. The central function of welfare, in fact, is to supersede the market by taking goods and services out of it, or in some way to control and modify its operations so as to produce a result which it would not have produced of itself. The life-history of a policy decision in welfare, as in any other sphere of democratic government, begins in a general election and is marked at various stages by the use of the political instrument of the majority vote. But this in all cases is only a part of the process by which vital choices are made, and in some cases it is less in tune with the true nature of those choices than in others. Some political decisions, that is to say, could more appropriately be submitted to a plebiscite than others. The relation between majority voting and policy decisions in welfare is very equivocal. Democratic voting is egotistic; most voters voice what they believe to be their own interests. The more comprehensive the franchise, the more legitimate this seems to be, because everybody can speak for himself. Welfare decisions depend on altruism – both concern for others and mutual concern for one another. In Victorian bourgeois democracy this was obvious, because the enfranchised were persons of property and the needy were voteless. Not that the former were conspicuously altruistic, but it was only to their social conscience that reformers could appeal in support of measures which were not vote-catchers. Dicey was convinced that if pensioners were allowed to vote – if, that is, the beneficiaries could put pressure on their benefactors – government would be corrupted and the foundations of democracy undermined.

That idea no longer holds, and the appeals of politicians to the self-interests of voters are frank and loud. Is it possible that the legitimacy of democratic egotism partly, at least, accounts for the obstinate blindness of total democracy to the urgent needs of minorities which, for various reasons, are not psephologically significant? When everybody is represented, it is easy to assume that everybody has been taken care of. This myopic inability to focus on things outside one's own circle can be, and to an important extent is, counteracted by the mass media, which are an integral part of the political apparatus of mass democracy. Television has had some remarkable successes, but it has its limitations. A case can rarely be argued to its conclusion, a subject run for too long becomes boring, and shock tactics may only produce the familiar sequence – distortion, sensation, oblivion.

But even egotism is often a poor judge of its own interests, because, in the sphere of welfare, provision is being made at the expense of one set of people for the immediate needs of others, and for what may seem remote or hypothetical contingencies, as far as they themselves are concerned, to those who are paying. It is a general habit to identify earnings with 'take-home-pay', to treat what has been taken off as a dead loss, and to pay little or no account either to the employers' insurance contributions or to the credits which are being built up and may be drawn on in the future. Demands for increased earnings are not consciously related to concurrent increases in social income. A similar short-sighted egotism prevails at the moment in the industrial counterpart of political democracy, the trade union movement, and is threatening to disrupt it. A union which is pressing a wage claim often pays scant attention to the position of other unions except as an index of 'relative deprivation', to possible ulterior effects on the trade union population as a whole (including itself), or even to the special claims of its own low-paid members. In Sweden today, says Dr Kurt Samuelsson, the unions 'fight not only over the total pay available and the aggregate amount of fringe benefits, but also with equal intensity over how much one group can carve out for itself at the expense of the others'.[15] My purpose here is to stress the way in which the ethos of the normal processes of political and industrial democracy is out of harmony with the spirit required for taking policy decisions at operational level in the field of welfare.

Welfare decisions, then, are essentially altruistic, and they must draw on standards of value embodied in an autonomous ethical system which, though an intrinsic part of the contemporary civilization, is not the product either of the summation of individual preferences (as in a market) or of a hypothetical majority vote. It is impossible to say exactly how these ethical standards arise in a society or are recognized by its members. Total consensus with regard to them is unthinkable, outside a devout religious community, but without a foundation of near-consensus, no general social welfare policy would be possible. Those who acclaimed the 'end of ideology' imagined we had arrived at a happy mean between hopeless conflict and dead unanimity – that 'middle way' which Daniel Bell thought could satisfy none but the middle-aged.[16] However that may be, it would be dishonest to pretend that there is not about welfare policy decisions something intrinsically authoritarian or, to use a less loaded but rather horrible word, paternalistic. Dahrendorf, for example, writes that 'in a certain sense the authoritarian State is always a Welfare State, just as, the other way round, the Welfare State always contains authoritarian elements'.[17] For one thing, welfare policy would be of little use if it did not actively help to create standards of value in its field and promote consensus on them. It is by

[15] Kurt Samuelsson, *From Great Power to Welfare State*, London: Allen and Unwin, 1968, p. 272.
[16] Daniel Bell, *The End of Ideology*, Illinois: The Free Press, 1960, p. 375.
[17] Ralf Dahrendorf, *Gesellschaft und Freiheit*, Munich: Piper, 1964, p. 238.

nature educational, not only in schools and colleges, but in its health service and welfare centres, and in everything it does to impress upon the public and the politicians the true significance, in real terms, of the disabilities under which many categories of citizen suffer. In all this it is creating and, quite frankly, inculcating concepts and standards of welfare which are not yet universally accepted. This, no doubt, is what Gunnar Myrdal is referring to when, looking ahead to the 'next phase', he speaks of 'the coming into existence of a "Welfare Culture" within the structure of the Welfare State.'[18]

The three components of my hyphenated social system differ also as to the agencies through which basic policy decisions are translated into operational programmes and put into effect. Each has, I suggest, one type of agent particularly associated with its characteristic methods of procedure, though all of them make some use of all three. They are, for economic policy (the 'capitalist' component) the social scientist and technician, for welfare the professional, and for general political administration the bureaucrat. Many students of social policy are suspicious of those who think progress lies in making more use of scientific methods, such as cost-benefit analysis and model-building. 'We tend,' says Martin Rein, 'to over-estimate the contribution of social science disciplines, and to accept "technical decisions" in place of value judgements and political choices.'[19] The same point was made more recently by critics of the Roskill Committee Report on the third London airport. This is one source of potential conflict within the hyphenated social structure. Comparison of professionalism with bureaucracy reveals another.

The professional is in a special position with regard both to public policy and to its execution at the level of the individual case. When on the job he (or she) enjoys a certain autonomy which is the complement of the personal responsibility of which, at that stage, he cannot be relieved. Within the limits set by his professional skills and his official function he takes personal, that is to say original, decisions in the light of the character of the case. The bureaucrat has much less freedom and is much more tightly bound by rules; he must apply them equally and impartially; he must be fair. The professional, on the job, does not have to think of being fair, but only of doing what is best. Impartiality for him does not consist in treating all cases in the same way, but in treating them with equal devotion. But at the same time the professional has the right and the duty to criticize policy and contribute to its improvement, and his association has the right and

[18] *Beyond the Welfare State, op. cit.*, p. 67.

[19] Martin Rein, *Social Policy: Issues of Choice and Change*, New York: Random House, 1970, p. 10.

22 T. H. Marshall

the duty to act as a pressure group in national and local politics. The bureaucrat cannot do this either. Social policy must make use both of the professional and of the bureaucrat, and they do not always run happily in double harness. The severest test of their compatibility occurs in those hybrid cases where a cut-and-dried official decision must be given on a welfare claim in an area not governed by rules. A discretionary judgement must be given which is at least as much a bureaucratic as a professional one. Obvious examples are the administration of non-contractual benefits in cash and in kind and the allocation of housing – and especially, perhaps, the handling of appeals against such decisions. The findings of recent research on appeal tribunals are disquieting, but the very fact that one uses that word implies that, once the facts are fully understood, the problem should be soluble. For 'disquiet' signifies awareness that a value is being violated.

In passing from this general comparison of the three components of democratic-welfare-capitalism to look at some specific areas in which incompatibilities might be expected to reveal themselves I can do no more than take a few examples, and I shall begin with that authoritarian or paternal character of welfare of which I have already spoken. Its potentialities as a creator of conflicts with both the democratic and the capitalist principles are obvious. These may involve either the producers or the consumers of welfare services. Beginning with the former, let us look first at the question of the respective roles of public and private enterprise in the welfare field. As things are now, we have a spectrum extending from those services in which a large or even a dominant part is played by voluntary organizations or private enterprise to those in which the State has a near-monopoly, as in the running of hospitals, or a total monopoly, as in probation. This seems to indicate that the Gaitskell view on the nationalization issue, namely that to treat it as a battle between good and evil is ideological nonsense, applies as much to welfare services as to industries. There is room for both public and private enterprise, and the criterion on which to determine their respective roles is efficiency in achieving the desired result. But this is too simple; there are some important qualifications to be made.

First, the responsibility of government in the field of welfare is more immediate and compelling than it is, generally speaking, in economic affairs. One of the virtues claimed for capitalist private enterprise is that it can take risks, and it earns a considerable part of its substantial rewards by doing so. But a government cannot allow risk-taking in welfare – or only minimally. It cannot leave any important part of its overall responsibilities in the hands of private agencies unless it takes steps to limit risk by regulation, supervision, inspection or safety-nets, as when a basic State pension underpins private ones. It was, in fact, the disastrous effects of the frequent failure of private savings and pension schemes that forced European governments to intervene in this field in the nineteenth century. Thus the distinction between public and private enterprise in welfare is not as sharp as one might imagine; it is a matter of degree.

My second qualification starts from this and leads on to a new point. Where there is in a major service like health or education a division or, if you like, a partnership between the public and the private sectors, with the State taking very much the larger share, the public service must be potentially comprehensive. By this I mean that it must make its service accessible to all by spreading it nation-wide, and it must be ready to provide for anybody who comes back to it from the private sector (for financial or other reasons), and also to cater for a possible shift of the balance of demand in its direction in the rising generation. The larger the private sector, the more difficult it is to meet this responsibility, especially in the case of personal service. On this rests one objection to the proposal to allow people to 'opt out' of the national health and education services, taking with them part of their contribution to their cost. In the circumstances I have described 'fair competition' between the public and the private sectors is not possible, since the transfer of clients from the former to the latter would reduce the income of the public service without permitting a corresponding economy of expenditure, and, by splitting resources, would lower the standard of efficiency attainable in it.

But it is not only a question of efficiency. Two major issues of value are involved. First, quantitative change would inevitably lead, very rapidly, to qualitative change. A point would soon be reached at which the whole conception of a community dedicated to providing for the vital needs of its members by systems of mutual aid would be lost, and the balance between the elements constituting the democratic-welfare-capitalist society destroyed. Secondly, it is beyond dispute that medical care and education, which enter into the lives of all citizens, are areas in which differences of opportunity and experience, and particularly an institutionalized dual standard (which would inevitably follow), do more to create and sustain class distinctions than any other. It proved possible to establish a democratic Welfare State in this country without abolishing or drastically altering the status of the Public Schools, but the two cannot coexist indefinitely in their present form. Any deliberate enlargement or extension of this kind of social distinction by a democratic policy decision would signify not so much a conflict between the elements of the hyphenated society as an abandonment by the majority of the very concept itself.

But without envisaging such a debacle, it is easy to see that disputes and

24 T. H. Marshall

conflicts over the design and administration of the personal social services will be continuous and they will not all be technical, value-free disputes about the best means of achieving agreed ends. It is, I think, true that a very high degree of consensus exists about the aims of the welfare services; without this there could be no Welfare State. But two things must be remembered. First, while in the case of a health service ends and means can be fairly clearly distinguished, this is not true of a service like education. Whereas in medicine one may be able to test alternative treatments and eliminate those that are least successful, the relative value of different educational systems or methods may be matters of opinion which are not testable in that way. It is therefore all the more important that room for variety be provided both within the public system and in a private sector of acceptable size and scope. Secondly, means, as well as ends, raise value problems. A system which could be shown to make the optimum use of scarce resources could be rejected because it involved a means-test of a kind that is offensive to human dignity, just as a policy deemed likely to bring economic prosperity in the long run might be rejected because it would cause an unacceptable level of unemployment on the way.

I have been speaking about the personal social services. The case of social insurance (as distinct from 'assistance') is different. This is so because it does not belong wholly to the welfare component, but has become virtually part of the conditions of employment. The right to social income in the periods when employment is interrupted or is terminated by retirement is derived from work done in accordance with those conditions, which include deductions from the wages paid for it. The employer's contributions are also part of those conditions. The welfare element in the system – which varies from country to country – can consist in arrangements for drawing on tax revenue (as Beveridge did) or varying the ratio between contributions and benefits in such a way as to bring about a transfer of income from the higher to the lower paid, and for linking the level of benefits to the cost of living or, more logically, to the standard of living, or average earnings. Finally, the practice is well established of making contributions and benefits reflect the scale of differential earnings arrived at in the labour market, up to a limiting ceiling, thus subordinating welfare to some extent to market value. Social insurance is thus a hybrid of welfare and capitalism and a bridge between them. So tightly integrated a structure cannot be left floating at large. Whether it is run wholly by the State or, as often, by some kind of partnership between the State and private firms, it must be consistent in all essentials, and therefore controlled and enforced. If such a system is adopted, then the kind of saving which Arthur Seldon describes as 'an intimate, elemental, personal decision' with which 'a free society will not lightly tamper'[20] will have to function on top of it, where there will be room enough for those who value this liberty and have the means to make use of it.

I must now look at the matter, very briefly, from the point of view of the consumer of welfare services. There are two main ways in which it may be thought that the authoritarian, or paternal, character of welfare must do him injury, namely by limiting his scope for the exercise of choice, and by weakening his initiative and self-reliance. Obviously there are values at stake here, the values of freedom and independence, both of which have a crucial role to play in the democratic and the 'capitalist' components of the composite society. So there is bound to be conflict, but at what level? It is not, as I see it, in the nature of a head-on clash between irreconcilable beliefs or of a contest seen by each side as a battle between good and evil. Welfare recognizes the values of freedom and independence, not only in the abstract but in its daily work, and the champions of these values know that without some curtailment of them welfare could not meet its responsibilities. You cannot make the optimum use of scarce skills and resources in a nation-wide service open to all if you allow every applicant for its help to pick and choose as he pleases. In some cases, like primary schools, choice is geographically limited; in others the knowledge on which a rational choice can be made is lacking. So the issue is one of balance and proportion, of deciding how much freedom of choice can be provided for, both by arrangements within the public services and by the operation of a private sector in co-operation, or at least in harmony, with the public one. As to the exercise of the faculty of choice itself, there is probably more scope for this in our contemporary civilization than there has ever been before. It is not likely to atrophy.

The question whether paternalist welfare enfeebles the virtuous and valued properties of initiative, independence and, if you will, self-help is a difficult one to answer honestly. It would be dishonest to rule out the possibility that this may happen to a significant extent. On the other hand it is absurd to argue that free medical care and free schooling undermine the sense of personal responsibility for the health and education of oneself and one's family. It must also be remembered that the need for welfare services provides one of the great incentives to social action of the kind which is most effective in integrating the diverse elements in a community. But there are ways in which over-paternalism in welfare can do social harm. It may encourage the assumption that, if something needs doing, it should be done by public authority, and that all the citizens have to do is to

[20] Quoted in G. L. Reid and D. J. Robertson, *Fringe Benefits, Labour Costs and Social Security*, London: Allen and Unwin, 1965, p. 189.

protest and demonstrate. This may stifle initiative in fields in which much can be achieved by individual, or still more by co-operative, effort. It may nourish the closely related assumption that the required service must be provided free of charge to users. For example, I understand that the 'Women's Lib' movement demands free contraceptives and free abortion on request. But if birth-control advice and contraceptives are made available, the case for free abortion in all cases is not self-evident. It may also increase the possibilities for 'scrounging' on public funds. I am not thinking only, or even mainly, of deliberately fraudulent claims on social security, since these are relatively rare, but rather of the readiness to extract the last legitimate penny with complete disregard of the general community interest and the effects upon it of such self-seeking action, if extensively practised. Some student spokesmen, when putting the case for higher grants, do not seem to realize that taxpayers whose sons and daughters have failed to get into a university have to be convinced it is right that they should pay in full for the education and maintenance of other people's sons and daughters who have succeeded in getting in. But the distinction I made between fraud and mere scrounging reminds us that, in discussing this in relation to welfare, we are touching the fringe, only, of a much wider and more general problem, for its counterpart at a higher economic level is the distinction between 'tax avoidance' (which is deemed respectable) and 'tax evasion' (which is not, but is nevertheless extensively practised). My point is only that welfare has some responsibility in the matter, which it should recognize.

I want to turn now to an aspect of welfare at the micro-level of the individual case, and again I start by quoting an economist, this time Adam Smith. He began his discussion of value by distinguishing between 'value in use' and 'value in exchange', and then devoted his whole attention to the latter, because it was the only kind with which an economist was concerned. But for welfare, value in use is vital. Smith referred to it also as 'utility', but not in the modern sense (to quote Jacob Viner) of 'an attempt to explain price-determination in psychological terms'.[21] It was not subjective in this individual sense. For, in his famous illustration he said that, in contrast to water, diamonds had 'scarce any value in use'. This must refer, not to their value in the eyes of those who wear them, which is great, but to some common estimation of their capacity to satisfy a real human need, which is negligible. Welfare, as I have already said, must base its action on value of this kind, and cannot simply react directly to individual, subjective desires. When the discrepancy between these two kinds of value is insuper-

[21] Quoted in Alfred N. Page, *Utility Theory: a Book of Readings*, New York: Wiley, 1968, p. 123.

able and the consequences intolerable, welfare steps in and takes over from the market. My example is housing. A house is a commodity to the landlord but to the occupant it is a home, and these are two quite different objects. When houses are scarce and incomes low, governments of all countries have stepped in to assert what we might call the welfare value of a home over the market value of a house, by controlling or freezing rents and by suspending the normal rights of property and contract so as to guarantee security of tenure. The methods were crude, devoid of any principle of valuation, subjective or objective, and operated unilaterally for tenant against landlord. The result was a mess.

The invention by the Labour government of the 'fair rent' standard of value is extraordinarily interesting. Looking back over the past five years or so *The Times* remarked that 'considering that the "fair rent" formula in the 1965 Rent Act is theoretically nonsensical...it has worked remarkably well to bring about a sort of rough justice between landlords and tenants'.[22] Quite apart from the fact that this is much better than the rough injustice which prevailed before, I do not agree that the formula is nonsensical. It provides a means of arriving at a bilaterally conceived evaluation through which the different types of value can be reduced to a common denominator. What it does is to strike an acceptable balance between 'value in use', or welfare value and 'value in exchange', or market value through the intermediary concept of the value of the thing itself seen in terms of its physical properties – size, structure, accommodation, equipment, etc. – estimated, not objectively as a commodity in the market nor subjectively as a home in use, but as a thing *for* use, which can be classified and valued in relation to others of its kind. The formula took account of the interests of both parties, as must be done if the State continues to depend in part on a private housing sector to meet its responsibilities towards its citizens and their families.

For my last illustration I take the subject of poverty and inequality. There has been evident for some time past a reaction against the idea of the 'poverty line' in favour of the view that the concept 'poverty' has no meaning except in a relative sense, whereas the 'poverty line' implies that it can be conceived in absolute terms. This has been accompanied by the contention that the real problem is not poverty, but inequality. If this means that poverty is relative to the standard of civilization of the country concerned, it is beyond dispute. If it means that I may not say that A is poor, but only that he is poorer than B, I cannot accept it. If it means that inequality is a major social issue of which poverty is a part, that is beyond dispute. But if it means that the problems of poverty and inequality are

[22] *The Times*, 3 March 1971, Leading Article.

28 *T. H. Marshall*

identical and inseparable, so that one could not eradicate poverty without solving the problem of inequality, then I cannot accept that either. What I said above about welfare value and welfare standards implies the belief that it is possible and necessary, in the present state of society, to envisage a state of destitution or deprivation which must be condemned as intolerable and, even though no exact measurement or definition of this condition can be given, we may refer to it as 'poverty'. The poor remain a category, and the fact that its boundaries would be different in another place or age does not make it any the less absolute for the country in which it exists. Nor does the recognition of poverty as a problem and the poor as a category imply that all forms of poverty are the same; on the contrary, it emphasizes the value of making subtle studies of its distinguishing features. The common factor in the state of the poor is the urgency of their need.

At this point the complexity of the subject obliges me to adopt an 'ideal type' approach and ask what place poverty and inequality would occupy in a democratic-welfare-capitalist society which had, so to speak, fulfilled itself. The simple answer is that in such a society poverty is a disease, but inequality is an essential structural feature. We, who are now enmeshed in this composite social system, have long ago rejected the theory of the necessity of poverty, as expressed by Patrick Colquhoun when he described poverty as 'a most necessary and indispensable ingredient in society', because 'it is the source of wealth'.[23] We have abandoned belief in the evolutionary benefits of poverty, as a weeder-out of the unfit. We no longer accept poverty as the inevitable and perpetual deposit of personal failures in the competitive struggle, and we do not even rely greatly on the fear of poverty as an incentive to work, as witness unemployment benefits and redundancy payments. It has no logical place in the system, but it obstinately remains with us, so we relieve it – when we notice it. Not very long ago it became almost invisible, but now it has reappeared. The invisibility of poverty has been a recurrent phenomenon in the western world.

The task of banishing poverty from our 'ideal type' society must be undertaken jointly by welfare and capitalism; there is no other way. Not only is there no evidence in history or in contemporary affairs to suggest that conflict between these two components must frustrate any effort at a joint solution but, on the contrary, it is clear that our particular type of social system has got nearer to achieving this objective than any that has gone before or now exists – unless one takes a totally relative view and asserts that poverty has been abolished in societies in which everybody is poor. Furthermore, the mechanics of the process are understood, the instru-

[23] Patrick Colquhoun, *A Treatise on Indigence*, London: Hatchard, 1806, pp. 7–8.

ments have been forged or are on the drawing-board, and all that is needed is the will to use them and a period of economic calm and stability long enough to allow the complexities of the problem to be mastered and the large variety of exceptional and abnormal cases to be brought within the scope of the operation. It is not necessary for me, nor have I the space, to give an exposition of these mechanics and instruments, the range and potentialities of which are well known in this country, thanks to the writings of Peter Townsend and others. So I will press on to my final problem, that of inequality, an area in which the different principles and pressures of the three components of the hyphenated society are most difficult to reconcile with one another.

Democracy stands for equality of citizenship rights. The aim of welfare services is to give equal care to similar cases. 'Capitalism' – or the market – lives by recognizing and rewarding inequalities, and depends on them to provide the motive force that makes it work. When this process was given free rein and welfare picked up the casualties, there was no problem. The shape of inequality was rough-hewn by the market. But two things have happened since then. Democracy took a hand. First, it made collective bargaining possible and this led in turn to the formal recognition of differentials, both within and between units of labour. Then it developed, somewhere in the socio-economic atmosphere, the notion that, by correctly reading the cultural signs, one could tell what a certain sort of man ought to be paid, especially if he was in the civil service or one of the professions. Differentials were given an ethical flavour. Thirdly it made a show of cutting inequalities down to the ethical scale, as far as money incomes were concerned, by heavy progressive taxation. Democracy, one might say, legitimized inequality (since you do not tax stolen goods), with the help of the trade unions.

The second thing that happened was that social security in the typical affluent western countries tied itself to the inequalities of the market by relating its whole system of contributions and benefits to differences in earnings, up to a limiting ceiling. Since social security contains, as I have said, a welfare element and forms the bridge between 'capitalism' and welfare, one may say that welfare, like democracy, legitimized inequality. There was nothing conspiratorial in all this. It represents the convergence without which the composite social system would have had little chance of stabilizing itself, and there could have been no 'end of ideology'. It certainly does not imply approval of any particular scale of inequality.

So we have a position where all three components accept inequality, but without agreement as to its pattern in any detail. Obviously there could not be any fixed pattern, or the whole economic system would be ossified.

30 T. H. Marshall

But there is no agreement even about the principle to apply in drawing a pattern, or any clear idea where to look for such a principle. A high growth-rate can cover a multitude of sins, but with our low rate, the confusion is patent and the disruption of life serious. Prestige, politics and bargaining-power overlay the simpler facts of relative productivity, creating a state of uncertainty in which jealousy and 'relative deprivation' flourish – not only at the bottom, but right up the scale, and probably least of all among the poor. That is why I said that poverty and inequality were different problems, when viewed structurally. Poverty is a tumour which should be cut out, and theoretically could be; inequality is a vital organ which is functioning badly.

This malfunctioning of the system of legitimate inequality is probably the most deeply-rooted threat to the viability of the hybrid or hyphenated social structure. This is not just another way of saying that the most disturbing factor in society is the class struggle. Of course the reaction to economic differentials is coloured by the power structure of industry and, in British society, by the peculiar persistence of historic forms of class-consciousness. But these are not indispensable features, as Dr Samuelsson argues in the case of Sweden. The trouble is that no way has been found of equating a man's value in the market (capitalist value), his value as a citizen (democratic value), and his value for himself (welfare value). But that is not all. The democratic and welfare components have each its own internal, unsolved problem – how to find a balance, so perfect as to silence all discontent, between equality of persons and their circumstances on the one hand and equality of opportunity, that great architect of inequality on the other. Militating against a resolution of this dilemma is the ebullience of that subjective and wholly individual assessment of social injustice which sociologists call 'relative deprivation', but which our ancestors classed (under a simpler name) among the seven deadly sins. In these circumstances it is futile to imagine that differentials can be made acceptable simply by scaling them down, however necessary this may be. It can be done only by changing the attitude towards them. The problem is structural in origin, but there is no purely structural solution to it.

The failure to solve the problem of economic inequality is evidence of the weakness of contemporary democracy. Since the task of maintaining the balance between the component elements of the system falls on democracy, this weakness is dangerous, but it is not critical nor, one hopes, irremediable. The outstanding needs are for better two-way communication to remedy the lack of contact and understanding between politicians, bureaucrats and the public, and for a reconciliation of the roles of the two competing democracies, the political and the industrial, in the power structure. At the moment it may seem that, in our own country, the spirit of pre-Welfare-State capitalism is gaining ascendancy over the democratic component and, through it, threatening the status of welfare in the system. But this, too, has all the appearance of being a transitory aberration, the reaction to which is already showing itself in the deep recesses of the popular conscience. Capitalism is most dangerous when it is weak and frightened, not when it is strong and confident, and recent measures taken to economize on welfare are in large part a hasty response to capitalist alarmism and, as such, unlikely to be built into the system. I firmly believe that the main effect of thinking of school meals only as an expense item will be to initiate a study of the real function of school meals in relation to the health of the children and the social life of the school and the family. One might almost say that this has already begun.

In conclusion, to see these rather fragmentary observations in perspective we must go back to the beginning, to that 'end of ideology' which ushered in the democratic-welfare-capitalist society. It was expected to bring with it consensus over basic issues and values. Even the most cursory glance at the history of western Europe during the last ten or fifteen years shows that it did not. But the disturbances of those years did not arise, in my view, from the incompatibility of the three components I have been examining. Of course there was conflict between them. But conflict is a normal feature of every healthy society. The unrest which struck a new note in recent years was something other than this. It was in part a fulfilment of a prophecy made by Shils in 1955 when he wrote that, if you ban ideology altogether, it 'will creep in through the back door, or more particularly, through a rebellious younger generation'.[24] And it was in part an expression of the disillusionment of many people in the older generations with the dominant values of their societies. But, though the principles and practices of democracy, capitalism, and welfare were the objects of much criticism, this did not reflect battles being waged between them, but dissatisfaction with the whole of which they were the parts. Materialism, profit-seeking, quantity-worship and growth-mania are not characteristics of capitalism alone, but permeate the whole of modern technological mass society. Bureaucratic excesses and rigidities are not a political malady only but are found also in the economy, the universities and even in welfare. The transformation sought by the more purposeful and less destructive sections of those voicing our present discontents is one of attitudes and values rather than of basic structure, though institutional changes are sought as a means to this end, as is also the protection of the physical environment. I see no reason why their aims should not be achieved – if they can be achieved at

[24] E. A. Shils, 'The End of Ideology', *Encounter*, vol. 5, November 1955, p. 57.

32 T. H. *Marshall*

all – within a social framework that includes representative government, a mixed economy and a Welfare State. The only alternative is something more totalitarian and bureaucratic, and that is not at all what the more novel and significant elements in the movement of protest are seeking.

# [10]

## The Positive Functions of Poverty[1]

Herbert J. Gans
*Columbia University and Center for Policy Research*

Mertonian functional analysis is applied to explain the persistence of poverty, and fifteen functions which poverty and the poor perform for the rest of American society, particularly the affluent, are identified and described. Functional alternatives which would substitute for these functions and make poverty unnecessary are suggested, but the most important alternatives are themselves dysfunctional for the affluent, since they require some redistribution of income and power. A functional analysis of poverty thus comes to many of the same conclusions as radical sociological analysis, demonstrating anew Merton's assertion that functionalism need not be conservative in ideological outlook or implication.

I

Over 20 years ago, Merton (1949, p. 71), analyzing the persistence of the urban political machine, wrote that because "we should ordinarily . . . expect persistent social patterns and social structures to perform positive functions which are at the time not adequately fulfilled by other existing patterns and structures . . . perhaps this publicly maligned organization is, under present conditions, satisfying basic latent functions." He pointed out how the machine provided central authority to get things done when a decentralized local government could not act, humanized the services of the impersonal bureaucracy for fearful citizens, offered concrete help (rather than law or justice) to the poor, and otherwise performed services needed or demanded by many people but considered unconventional or even illegal by formal public agencies.

This paper is not concerned with the political machine, however, but with poverty, a social phenomenon which is as maligned as and far more persistent than the machine. Consequently, there may be some merit in applying functional analysis to poverty, to ask whether it too has positive functions that explain its persistence. Since functional analysis has itself taken on a maligned status among some American sociologists, a

[1] Earlier versions of this paper were presented at a Vassar College conference on the war on poverty in 1964, at the 7th World Congress of Sociology in 1971, and in *Social Policy* 2 (July-August 1971): 20–24. The present paper will appear in a forthcoming book on poverty and stratification, edited by S. M. Lipset and S. M. Miller, for the American Academy of Arts and Sciences. I am indebted to Peter Marris, Robert K. Merton, and S. M. Miller for helpful comments on earlier drafts of this paper.

secondary purpose of this paper is to ask whether it is still a useful approach.[2]

II

Merton (1949, p. 50) defined functions as "those observed consequences which make for the adaptation or adjustment of a given system; and dysfunctions, those observed consequences which lessen the adaptation or adjustment of the system." This definition does not specify the nature or scope of the system, but elsewhere in his classic paper "Manifest and Latent Functions," Merton indicated that social system was not a synonym for society, and that systems vary in size, requiring a functional analysis "to consider a *range* of units for which the item (or social phenomenon H.G.) has designated consequences: individuals in diverse statuses, subgroups, the larger social system and cultural systems" (1949, p. 51).

In discussing the functions of poverty, I shall identify functions for *groups* and *aggregates*; specifically, interest groups, socioeconomic classes, and other population aggregates, for example, those with shared values or similar statuses. This definitional approach is based on the assumption that almost every social system—and of course every society—is composed of groups or aggregates with different interests and values, so that, as Merton put it (1949, p. 51), "items may be functional for some individuals and subgroups and dysfunctional for others." Indeed, frequently one group's functions are another group's dysfunctions.[3] For example, the political machine analyzed by Merton was functional for the working class and business interests of the city but dysfunctional for many middle class and reform interests. Consequently, functions are defined as those observed consequences which are positive *as judged by the values of the group under analysis*; dysfunctions, as those which are negative by these values.[4] Because functions benefit the group in question and dysfunctions

[2] The paper also has the latent function, as S. M. Miller has suggested, of contributing to the long debate over the functional analysis of social stratification presented by Davis and Moore (1945).

[3] Probably one of the few instances in which a phenomenon has the same function for two groups with different interests is when the survival of the system in which both participate is at stake. Thus, a wage increase can be functional for labor and dysfunctional for management (and consumers), but if the wage increase endangers the firm's survival, it is dysfunctional for labor as well. This assumes, however, that the firm's survival is valued by the workers, which may not always be the case, for example, when jobs are available elsewhere.

[4] Merton (1949, p. 50) originally described functions and dysfunctions in terms of encouraging or hindering adaptation or adjustment to a system, although subsequently he has written that "dysfunction refers to the particular inadequacies of a particular part of the system for a designated requirement" (1961, p. 732). Since adaptation and

hurt it, I shall also describe functions and dysfunctions in the language of economic planning and systems analysis as benefits and costs.[5]

Identifying functions and dysfunctions for groups and aggregates rather than systems reduces the possibility that what is functional for one group in a multigroup system will be seen as being functional for the whole system, making it more difficult, for example, to suggest that a given phenomenon is functional for a corporation or political regime when it may in fact only be functional for their officers or leaders. Also, this approach precludes reaching a priori conclusions about two other important empirical questions raised by Merton (1949, pp. 32–36), whether any phenomenon is ever functional or dysfunctional for an entire society, and, if functional, whether it is therefore indispensable to that society.

In a modern heterogeneous society, few phenomena are functional or dysfunctional for the society as a whole, and most result in benefits to some groups and costs to others. Given the level of differentiation in modern society, I am even skeptical whether one can empirically identify a social system called society. Society exists, of course, but it is closer to being a very large aggregate, and when sociologists talk about society as a system, they often really mean the nation, a system which, among other things, sets up boundaries and other distinguishing characteristics between societal aggregates.

I would also argue that no social phenomenon is indispensable; it may be too powerful or too highly valued to be eliminated, but in most instances, one can suggest what Merton calls "functional alternatives" or equivalents for a social phenomena, that is, other social patterns or policies which achieve the same functions but avoid the dysfunctions.

## III

The conventional view of American poverty is so dedicated to identifying the dysfunctions of poverty, both for the poor and the nation, that at

adjustment to a system can have conservative ideological implications, Merton's later formulation and my own definitional approach make it easier to use functional analysis as an ideologically neutral or at least ideologically variable method, insofar as the researcher can decide for himself whether he supports the values of the group under analysis.

[5] It should be noted, however, that there are no absolute benefits and costs just as there are no absolute functions and dysfunctions; not only are one group's benefits often another group's costs, but every group defines benefits by its own manifest and latent values, and a social scientist or planner who has determined that certain phenomena provide beneficial consequences for a group may find that the group thinks otherwise. For example, during the 1960s, advocates of racial integration discovered that a significant portion of the black community no longer considered it a benefit but saw it rather as a policy to assimilate blacks into white society and to decimate the political power of the black community.

first glance it seems inconceivable to suggest that poverty could be functional for anyone. Of course, the slum lord and the loan shark are widely known to profit from the existence of poverty; but they are popularly viewed as evil men, and their activities are, at least in part, dysfunctional for the poor. However, what is less often recognized, at least in the conventional wisdom, is that poverty also makes possible the existence or expansion of "respectable" professions and occupations, for example, penology, criminology, social work, and public health. More recently, the poor have provided jobs for professional and paraprofessional "poverty warriors," as well as journalists and social scientists, this author included, who have supplied the information demanded when public curiosity about the poor developed in the 1960s.

Clearly, then, poverty and the poor may well serve a number of functions for many nonpoor groups in American society, and I shall describe 15 sets of such functions—economic, social, cultural, and political—that seem to me most significant.

*First*, the existence of poverty makes sure that "dirty work" is done. Every economy has such work: physically dirty or dangerous, temporary, dead-end and underpaid, undignified, and menial jobs. These jobs can be filled by paying higher wages than for "clean" work, or by requiring people who have no other choice to do the dirty work and at low wages. In America, poverty functions to provide a low-wage labor pool that is willing—or, rather, unable to be unwilling—to perform dirty work at low cost. Indeed, this function is so important that in some Southern states, welfare payments have been cut off during the summer months when the poor are needed to work in the fields. Moreover, the debate about welfare—and about proposed substitutes such as the negative income tax and the Family Assistance Plan—has emphasized the impact of income grants on work incentive, with opponents often arguing that such grants would reduce the incentive of—actually, the pressure on—the poor to carry out the needed dirty work if the wages therefore are no larger than the income grant. Furthermore, many economic activities which involve dirty work depend heavily on the poor; restaurants, hospitals, parts of the garment industry, and industrial agriculture, among others, could not persist in their present form without their dependence on the substandard wages which they pay to their employees.

*Second*, the poor subsidize, directly and indirectly, many activities that benefit the affluent.[6] For one thing, they have long supported both

[6] Of course, the poor do not actually subsidize the affluent. Rather, by being forced to work for low wages, they enable the affluent to use the money saved in this fashion for other purposes. The concept of subsidy used here thus assumes belief in a "just wage."

the consumption and investment activities of the private economy by virtue of the low wages which they receive. This was openly recognized at the beginning of the Industrial Revolution, when a French writer quoted by T. H. Marshall (forthcoming, p. 7) pointed out that "to assure and maintain the prosperities of our industries, it is necessary that the workers should never acquire wealth." Examples of this kind of subsidization abound even today; for example, domestics subsidize the upper middle and upper classes, making life easier for their employers and freeing affluent women for a variety of professional, cultural, civic, or social activities. In addition, as Barry Schwartz pointed out (personal communication), the low income of the poor enables the rich to divert a higher proportion of their income to savings and investment, and thus to fuel economic growth. This, in turn, can produce higher incomes for everybody, including the poor, although it does not necessarily improve the position of the poor in the socioeconomic hierarchy, since the benefits of economic growth are also distributed unequally.

At the same time, the poor subsidize the governmental economy. Because local property and sales taxes and the ungraduated income taxes levied by many states are regressive, the poor pay a higher percentage of their income in taxes than the rest of the population, thus subsidizing the many state and local governmental programs that serve more affluent taxpayers.[7] In addition, the poor support medical innovation as patients in teaching and research hospitals, and as guinea pigs in medical experiments, subsidizing the more affluent patients who alone can afford these innovations once they are incorporated into medical practice.

*Third*, poverty creates jobs for a number of occupations and professions which serve the poor, or shield the rest of the population from them. As already noted, penology would be miniscule without the poor, as would the police, since the poor provide the majority of their "clients." Other activities which flourish because of the existence of poverty are the numbers game, the sale of heroin and cheap wines and liquors, pentecostal ministers, faith healers, prostitutes, pawn shops, and the peacetime army, which recruits its enlisted men mainly from among the poor.

*Fourth*, the poor buy goods which others do not want and thus prolong their economic usefulness, such as day-old bread, fruit and vegetables which would otherwise have to be thrown out, second-hand clothes, and deteriorating automobiles and buildings. They also provide incomes for

[7] Pechman (1969) and Herriott and Miller (1971) found that the poor pay a higher proportion of their income in taxes than any other part of the population: 50% among people earning $2,000 or less according to the latter study.

doctors, lawyers, teachers, and others who are too old, poorly trained, or incompetent to attract more affluent clients.

In addition, the poor perform a number of social and cultural functions:

*Fifth,* the poor can be identified and punished as alleged or real deviants in order to uphold the legitimacy of dominant norms (Macarov 1970, pp. 31–33). The defenders of the desirability of hard work, thrift, honesty, and monogamy need people who can be accused of being lazy, spendthrift, dishonest, and promiscuous to justify these norms; and as Erikson (1964) and others following Durkheim have pointed out, the norms themselves are best legitimated by discovering violations.

Whether the poor actually violate these norms more than affluent people is still open to question. The working poor work harder and longer than high-status jobholders, and poor housewives must do more housework to keep their slum apartments clean than their middle-class peers in standard housing. The proportion of cheaters among welfare recipients is quite low and considerably lower than among income taxpayers.[8] Violent crime is higher among the poor, but the affluent commit a variety of white-collar crimes, and several studies of self-reported delinquency have concluded that middle-class youngsters are sometimes as delinquent as the poor. However, the poor are more likely to be caught when participating in deviant acts and, once caught, to be punished more often than middle-class transgressors. Moreover, they lack the political and cultural power to correct the stereotypes that affluent people hold of them, and thus continue to be thought of as lazy, spendthrift, etc., whatever the empirical evidence, by those who need living proof that deviance does not pay.[9] The actually or allegedly deviant poor have traditionally been described as undeserving and, in more recent terminology, culturally deprived or pathological.

*Sixth,* another group of poor, described as deserving because they are disabled or suffering from bad luck, provide the rest of the population with different emotional satisfactions; they evoke compassion, pity, and charity, thus allowing those who help them to feel that they are altruistic, moral, and practicing the Judeo-Christian ethic. The deserving poor also enable others to feel fortunate for being spared the deprivations that come with poverty.[10]

[8] Most official investigations of welfare cheating have concluded that less than 5% of recipients are on the rolls illegally, while it has been estimated that about a third of the population cheats in filing income tax returns.

[9] Although this paper deals with the functions of poverty for other groups, poverty has often been described as a motivating or character-building device for the poor themselves; and economic conservatives have argued that by generating the incentive to work, poverty encourages the poor to escape poverty. For an argument that work incentive is more enhanced by income than lack of it, see Gans (1971, p. 96).

[10] One psychiatrist (Chernus 1967) has even proposed the fantastic hypothesis that

*Seventh*, as a converse of the fifth function described previously, the poor offer affluent people vicarious participation in the uninhibited sexual, alcoholic, and narcotic behavior in which many poor people are alleged to indulge, and which, being freed from the constraints of affluence and respectability, they are often thought to enjoy more than the middle classes. One of the popular beliefs about welfare recipients is that many are on a permanent sex-filled vacation. Although it may be true that the poor are more given to uninhibited behavior, studies by Rainwater (1970) and other observers of the lower class indicate that such behavior is as often motivated by despair as by lack of inhibition, and that it results less in pleasure than in a compulsive escape from grim reality. However, whether the poor actually have more sex and enjoy it more than affluent people is irrelevant; as long as the latter believe it to be so, they can share it vicariously and perhaps enviously when instances are reported in fictional, journalistic, or sociological and anthropological formats.

*Eighth*, poverty helps to guarantee the status of those who are not poor. In a stratified society, where social mobility is an especially important goal and class boundaries are fuzzy, people need to know quite urgently where they stand. As a result, the poor function as a reliable and relatively permanent measuring rod for status comparison, particularly for the working class, which must find and maintain status distinctions between itself and the poor, much as the aristocracy must find ways of distinguishing itself from the *nouveau riche*.

*Ninth*, the poor also assist in the upward mobility of the nonpoor, for, as Goode has pointed out (1967, p. 5), "the privileged . . . try systematically to prevent the talent of the less privileged from being recognized or developed." By being denied educational opportunities or being stereotyped as stupid or unteachable, the poor thus enable others to obtain the better jobs. Also, an unknown number of people have moved themselves or their children up in the socioeconomic hierarchy through the incomes earned from the provision of goods and services in the slums: by becoming policemen and teachers, owning "Mom and Pop" stores, or working in the various rackets that flourish in the slums.

In fact, members of almost every immigrant group have financed their upward mobility by providing retail goods and services, housing, entertainment, gambling, narcotics, etc., to later arrivals in America (or in the city), most recently to blacks, Mexicans, and Puerto Ricans. Other Americans, of both European and native origin, have financed their entry into the upper middle and upper classes by owning or managing the illegal institutions that serve the poor, as well as the legal but not respectable ones, such as slum housing.

the rich and the poor are engaged in a sadomasochistic relationship, the latter being supported financially by the former so that they can gratify their sadistic needs.

American Journal of Sociology

*Tenth,* just as the poor contribute to the economic viability of a number of businesses and professions (see function 3 above), they also add to the social viability of noneconomic groups. For one thing, they help to keep the aristocracy busy, thus justifying its continued existence. "Society" uses the poor as clients of settlement houses and charity benefits; indeed, it must have the poor to practice its public-mindedness so as to demonstrate its superiority over the *nouveaux riches* who devote themselves to conspicuous consumption. The poor play a similar function for philanthropic enterprises at other levels of the socioeconomic hierarchy, including the mass of middle-class civic organizations and women's clubs engaged in volunteer work and fundraising in almost every American community. Doing good among the poor has traditionally helped the church to find a method of expressing religious sentiments in action; in recent years, militant church activity among and for the poor has enabled the church to hold on to its more liberal and radical members who might otherwise have dropped out of organized religion altogether.

*Eleventh,* the poor perform several cultural functions. They have played an unsung role in the creation of "civilization," having supplied the construction labor for many of the monuments which are often identified as the noblest expressions and examples of civilization, for example, the Egyptian pyramids, Greek temples, and medieval churches.[11] Moreover, they have helped to create a goodly share of the surplus capital that funds the artists and intellectuals who make culture, and particularly "high" culture, possible in the first place.

*Twelfth,* the "low" culture created for or by the poor is often adopted by the more affluent. The rich collect artifacts from extinct folk cultures (although not only from poor ones), and almost all Americans listen to the jazz, blues, spirituals, and country music which originated among the Southern poor—as well as rock, which was derived from similar sources. The protest of the poor sometimes becomes literature; in 1970, for example, poetry written by ghetto children became popular in sophisticated literary circles. The poor also serve as culture heroes and literary subjects, particularly, of course, for the Left, but the hobo, cowboy, hipster, and the mythical prostitute with a heart of gold have performed this function for a variety of groups.

Finally, the poor carry out a number of important political functions:

*Thirteenth,* the poor serve as symbolic constituencies and opponents for several political groups. For example, parts of the revolutionary Left could not exist without the poor, particularly now that the working class can no longer be perceived as the vanguard of the revolution. Conversely,

[11] Although this is not a contemporary function of poverty in America, it should be noted that today these monuments serve to attract and gratify American tourists.

political groups of conservative bent need the "welfare chiselers" and others who "live off the taxpayer's hard-earned money" in order to justify their demands for reductions in welfare payments and tax relief. Moreover, the role of the poor in upholding dominant norms (see function 5 above) also has a significant political function. An economy based on the ideology of laissez faire requires a deprived population which is allegedly unwilling to work; not only does the alleged moral inferiority of the poor reduce the moral pressure on the present political economy to eliminate poverty, but redistributive alternatives can be made to look quite unattractive if those who will benefit from them most can be described as lazy, spendthrift, dishonest, and promiscuous. Thus, conservatives and classical liberals would find it difficult to justify many of their political beliefs without the poor; but then so would modern liberals and socialists who seek to eliminate poverty.

*Fourteenth*, the poor, being powerless, can be made to absorb the economic and political costs of change and growth in American society. During the 19th century, they did the backbreaking work that built the cities; today, they are pushed out of their neighborhoods to make room for "progress." Urban renewal projects to hold middle-class taxpayers and stores in the city and expressways to enable suburbanites to commute downtown have typically been located in poor neighborhoods, since no other group will allow itself to be displaced. For much the same reason, urban universities, hospitals, and civic centers also expand into land occupied by the poor. The major costs of the industrialization of agriculture in America have been borne by the poor, who are pushed off the land without recompense, just as in earlier centuries in Europe, they bore the brunt of the transformation of agrarian societies into industrial ones. The poor have also paid a large share of the human cost of the growth of American power overseas, for they have provided many of the foot soldiers for Vietnam and other wars.

*Fifteenth*, the poor have played an important role in shaping the American political process; because they vote and participate less than other groups, the political system has often been free to ignore them. This has not only made American politics more centrist than would otherwise be the case, but it has also added to the stability of the political process. If the 15% of the population below the federal "poverty line" participated fully in the political process, they would almost certainly demand better jobs and higher incomes, which would require income redistribution and would thus generate further political conflict between the haves and the have-nots. Moreover, when the poor do participate, they often provide the Democrats with a captive constituency, for they can rarely support Republicans, lack parties of their own, and thus have no other place to go politically. This, in turn, has enabled the Democrats to count on the votes of the poor, allowing the party to be more responsive to voters who might otherwise switch to the Republicans, in recent years, for example, the white working class.

IV

I have described fifteen of the more important functions which the poor carry out in American society, enough to support the functionalist thesis that poverty survives in part because it is useful to a number of groups in society. This analysis is not intended to suggest that because it is functional, poverty *should* persist, or that it *must* persist. Whether it should persist is a normative question; whether it must, an analytic and empirical one, but the answer to both depends in part on whether the dysfunctions of poverty outweigh the functions. Obviously, poverty has many dysfunctions, mainly for the poor themselves but also for the more affluent. For example, their social order is upset by the pathology, crime, political protest, and disruption emanating from the poor, and the income of the affluent is affected by the taxes that must be levied to protect their social order. Whether the dysfunctions outweigh the functions is a question that clearly deserves study.

It is, however, possible to suggest alternatives for many of the functions of the poor. Thus, society's dirty work (function 1) could be done without poverty, some by automating it, the rest by paying the workers who do it decent wages, which would help considerably to cleanse that kind of work. Nor is it necessary for the poor to subsidize the activities they support through their low-wage jobs (function 2), for, like dirty work, many of these activities are essential enough to persist even if wages were raised. In both instances, however, costs would be driven up, resulting in higher prices to the customers and clients of dirty work and subsidized activity, with obvious dysfunctional consequences for more affluent people.

Alternative roles for the professionals who flourish because of the poor (function 3) are easy to suggest. Social workers could counsel the affluent, as most prefer to do anyway, and the police could devote themselves to traffic and organized crime. Fewer penologists would be employable, however, and pentecostal religion would probably not survive without the poor. Nor would parts of the second- and third-hand market (function 4), although even affluent people sometimes buy used goods. Other roles would have to be found for badly trained or incompetent professionals now relegated to serving the poor, and someone else would have to pay their salaries.

Alternatives for the deviance-connected social functions (functions 5–7) can be found more easily and cheaply than for the economic functions.

Other groups are already available to serve as deviants to uphold traditional morality, for example, entertainers, hippies, and most recently, adolescents in general. These same groups are also available as alleged or real orgiasts to provide vicarious participation in sexual fantasies. The blind and disabled function as objects of pity and charity, and the poor may therefore not even be needed for functions 5–7.

The status and mobility functions of the poor (functions 8 and 9) are far more difficult to substitute, however. In a hierarchical society, some people must be defined as inferior to everyone else with respect to a variety of attributes, and the poor perform this function more adequately than others. They could, however, perform it without being as poverty-stricken as they are, and one can conceive of a stratification system in which the people below the federal "poverty line" would receive 75% of the median income rather than 40% or less, as is now the case—even though they would still be last in the pecking order.[12] Needless to say, such a reduction of economic inequality would also require income redistribution. Given the opposition to income redistribution among more affluent people, however, it seems unlikely that the status functions of poverty can be replaced, and they—together with the economic functions of the poor, which are equally expensive to replace—may turn out to be the major obstacles to the elimination of poverty.

The role of the poor in the upward mobility of other groups could be maintained without their being so low in income. However, if their incomes were raised above subsistence levels, they would begin to generate capital so that their own entrepreneurs could supply them with goods and services, thus competing with and perhaps rejecting "outside" suppliers. Indeed, this is already happening in a number of ghettoes, where blacks are replacing white storeowners.

Similarly, if the poor were more affluent, they would make less willing clients for upper- and middle-class philanthropic and religious groups (function 10), although as long as they are economically and otherwise unequal, this function need not disappear altogether. Moreover, some would still use the settlement houses and other philanthropic institutions to pursue individual upward mobility, as they do now.

The cultural functions (11 and 12) may not need to be replaced. In America, the labor unions have rarely allowed the poor to help build cultural monuments anyway, and there is sufficient surplus capital from other sources to subsidize the unprofitable components of high culture.

[12] In 1971, the median family income in the United States was about $10,000, and the federal poverty line for a family of four was set at just about $4,000. Of course, most of the poor were earning less than 40% of the median, and about a third of them, less than 20% of the median.

Similarly, other deviant groups are available to innovate in popular culture and supply new culture heroes, for example, the hippies and members of other counter-cultures.

Some of the political functions of the poor would, however, be as difficult to replace as their economic and status functions. Although the poor could probably continue to serve as symbolic constituencies and opponents (function 13) if their incomes were raised while they remained unequal in other respects, increases in income are generally accompanied by increases in power as well. Consequently, once they were no longer so poor, people would be likely to resist paying the costs of growth and change (function 14); and it is difficult to find alternative groups who can be displaced for urban renewal and technological "progress." Of course, it is possible to design city-rebuilding and highway projects which properly reimburse the displaced people, but such projects would then become considerably more expensive, thus raising the price for those now benefiting from urban renewal and expressways. Alternatively, many might never be built, thus reducing the comfort and convenience of those beneficiaries. Similarly, if the poor were subjected to less economic pressure, they would probably be less willing to serve in the army, except at considerably higher pay, in which case war would become yet more costly and thus less popular politically. Alternatively, more servicemen would have to be recruited from the middle and upper classes, but in that case war would also become less popular.

The political stabilizing and "centering" role of the poor (function 15) probably cannot be substituted for at all, since no other group is willing to be disenfranchised or likely enough to remain apathetic so as to reduce the fragility of the political system. Moreover, if the poor were given higher incomes, they would probably become more active politically, thus adding their demands for more to those of other groups already putting pressure on the political allocators of resources. The poor might continue to remain loyal to the Democratic party, but like other moderate-income voters, they could also be attracted to the Republicans or to third parties. While improving the economic status of the presently poor would not necessarily drive the political system far to the left, it would enlarge the constituencies now demanding higher wages and more public funds. It is of course possible to add new powerless groups who do not vote or otherwise participate to the political mix and can thus serve as "ballast" in the polity, for example, by encouraging the import of new poor immigrants from Europe and elsewhere, except that the labor unions are probably strong enough to veto such a policy.

In sum, then, several of the most important functions of the poor cannot be replaced with alternatives, while some could be replaced, but almost always only at higher costs to other people, particularly more affluent ones. Consequently, *a functional analysis must conclude that poverty persists not only because it satisfies a number of functions but also because many of the functional alternatives to poverty would be quite dysfunctional for the more affluent members of society.*[13]

V

I noted earlier that functional analysis had itself become a maligned phenomenon and that a secondary purpose of this paper was to demonstrate its continued usefulness. One reason for its presently low status is political; insofar as an analysis of functions, particularly latent functions, seems to justify what ought to be condemned, it appears to lend itself to the support of conservative ideological positions, although it can also have radical implications when it subverts the conventional wisdom. Still, as Merton has pointed out (1949, p. 43; 1961, pp. 736-37), functional analysis per se is ideologically neutral, and "like other forms of sociological analysis, it can be infused with any of a wide range of sociological values" (1949, p. 40). This infusion depends, of course, on the purposes—and even the functions—of the functional analysis, for as Wirth (1936, p. xvii) suggested long ago, "every assertion of a 'fact' about the social world touches the interests of some individual or group," and even if functional analyses are conceived and conducted in a neutral manner, they are rarely interpreted in an ideological vacuum.

In one sense, my analysis is, however, neutral; if one makes no judgment as to whether poverty ought to be eliminated—and if one can subsequently avoid being accused of acquiescing in poverty—then the analysis suggests only that poverty exists because it is useful to many groups in society.[14] If one favors the elimination of poverty, however, then the analysis can have a variety of political implications, *depending in part on how completely it is carried out.*

If functional analysis only identifies the functions of social phenomena without mentioning their dysfunctions, then it may, intentionally or otherwise, agree with or support holders of conservative values. Thus, to say that the poor perform many functions for the rich might be interpreted or used to justify poverty, just as Davis and Moore's argument

[13] Or as Stein (1971, p. 171) puts it: "If the non-poor make the rules . . . antipoverty efforts will only be made up to the point where the needs of the non-poor are satisfied, rather than the needs of the poor."

[14] Of course, even in this case the analysis need not be purely neutral, but can be put to important policy uses, for example, by indicating more effectively than moral attacks on poverty the exact nature of the obstacles that must be overcome if poverty is to be eliminated. See also Merton (1961, pp. 709-12).

American Journal of Sociology

(1945) that social stratification is functional because it provides society with highly trained professionals could be taken to justify inequality.

Actually, the Davis and Moore analysis was conservative because it was incomplete; it did not identify the dysfunctions of inequality and failed to suggest functional alternatives, as Tumin (1953) and Schwartz (1955) have pointed out.[15] Once a functional analysis is made more complete by the addition of functional alternatives, however, it can take on a liberal and reform cast, because the alternatives often provide ameliorative policies that do not require any drastic change in the existing social order.

Even so, to make functional analysis complete requires yet another step, an examination of the functional alternatives themselves. My analysis suggests that the alternatives for poverty are themselves dysfunctional for the affluent population, and it ultimately comes to a conclusion which is not very different from that of radical sociologists. To wit: *that social phenomena which are functional for affluent groups and dysfunctional for poor ones persist; that when the elimination of such phenomena through functional alternatives generates dysfunctions for the affluent, they will continue to persist; and that phenomena like poverty can be eliminated only when they either become sufficiently dysfunctional for the affluent or when the poor can obtain enough power to change the system of social stratification.*[16]

## REFERENCES

Chernus, J. 1967. "Cities: A Study in Sadomasochism." *Medical Opinion and Review* (May), pp. 104–9.

Davis, K., and W. E. Moore. 1945. "Some Principles of Stratification." *American Sociological Review* 10 (April): 242–49.

Erikson, K. T. 1964. "Notes on the Sociology of Deviance." In *The Other Side*, edited by Howard S. Becker. New York: Free Press.

[15] Functional analysis can, of course, be conservative in value or have conservative implications for a number of other reasons, principally in its overt or covert comparison of the advantages of functions and disadvantages of dysfunctions, or in its attitudes toward the groups that are benefiting and paying the costs. Thus, a conservatively inclined policy researcher could conclude that the dysfunctions of poverty far outnumber the functions, but still decide that the needs of the poor are simply not as important or worthy as those of other groups, or of the country as a whole.

[16] On the possibility of radical functional analysis, see Merton (1949, pp. 40–43) and Gouldner (1970, p. 443). One difference between my analysis and the prevailing radical view is that most of the functions I have described are latent, whereas many radicals treat them as manifest: recognized and intended by an unjust economic system to oppress the poor. Practically speaking, however, this difference may be unimportant, for if unintended and unrecognized functions were recognized, many affluent people might then decide that they ought to be intended as well, so as to forestall a more expensive antipoverty effort that might be dysfunctional for the affluent.

Gans, H. J. 1971. "Three Ways to Solve the Welfare Problem." *New York Times Magazine*, March 7, pp. 26–27, 94–100.
Goode, W. J. 1967. "The Protection of the Inept." *American Sociological Review* 32 (February): 5–19.
Gouldner, A. 1970. *The Coming Crisis of Western Sociology*. New York: Basic.
Herriot, A., and H. P. Miller. 1971. "Who Paid the Taxes in 1968." Paper prepared for the National Industrial Conference Board.
Macarov, D. 1970. *Incentives to Work*. San Francisco: Jossey-Bass.
Marshall, T. H. Forthcoming. "Poverty and Inequality." Paper prepared for the American Academy of Arts and Sciences volume on poverty and stratification.
Merton, R. K. 1949. "Manifest and Latent Functions." In *Social Theory and Social Structure*. Glencoe, Ill.: Free Press.
———. 1961. "Social Problems and Sociological Theory." In *Contemporary Social Problems*, edited by R. K. Merton and R. Nisbet. New York: Harcourt Brace.
Pechman, J. A. 1969. "The Rich, the Poor, and the Taxes They Pay." *Public Interest*, no. 17 (Fall), pp. 21–43.
Rainwater, L. 1970. *Behind Ghetto Walls*. Chicago: Aldine.
Schwartz, R. 1955. "Functional Alternatives to Inequality." *American Sociological Review* 20 (August): 424–30.
Stein, B. 1971. *On Relief*. New York: Basic.
Tumin, M. B. 1953. "Some Principles of Stratification: A Critical Analysis." *American Sociological Review* 18 (August): 387–93.
Wirth, L. 1936. "Preface." In *Ideology and Utopia*, by Karl Mannheim. New York: Harcourt Brace.

# [11]

Ian Gough

# State Expenditure in Advanced Capitalism

The current stage of 'neo-capitalism' or 'state monopoly capitalism' is characterized by a qualitatively expanded role of the state in capitalist social formations.[1] One expression of this huge politico-economic weight of the modern state is the prolonged expansion in state expenditures, such that they now exceed one half of gross domestic product in contemporary Britain.[2] Yet despite this, there have been only isolated studies by Marxists which systematically examine the causes and consequences of this unprecedented growth. In the following sections we propose to outline the patterns and trends in state expenditure in the major capitalist economies; briefly to analyse the nature of the modern capitalist state and its socio-economic setting; in the light of this to attempt an explanation of the growth and composition of state expenditures; and finally to consider briefly some of the major economic and political consequences of this phenomenon. Beforehand, however, it is incumbent on us to consider current theories and state why we regard them as unsatisfactory or incomplete. To this end, the recent studies of O'Connor, Yaffe and Barratt Brown will be singled out for attention.

## I. Introduction: Critique of Existing Theories

*The Fiscal Crisis of the State* by James O'Connor[3] is an important book representing the first systematic attempt by a Marxist to come to grips with the explosion of state expenditure since the Second World War. Its complexity means that any brief discussion will necessarily do it an injustice, and the reader is referred elsewhere to an extended review of it.[4] Briefly, the growth of the state is, for O'Connor, both a cause and consequence of the expansion of monopoly capital. The growing socialization of production necessitates greater state intervention to ensure private accumulation and profitability; hence *social capital* expenditures on roads, education, research and development, etc. This stimulates the development of productive capacity, notably in the monopoly sector of the economy, but demand for its products rises less fast bringing about tendencies to surplus capacity and surplus population. This in turn generates a further round of *social expenses* designed to generate demand but not add to capacity: surplus capital necessitates military expenditure and the surplus population requires an expansion of state functions in welfare relief, etc.[5] The result is a two-fold growth of state expenditure: on indirectly productive social capital and on unproductive warfare-welfare expenses. This growth tends to a structural gap between state revenue and expenditure, or a fiscal crisis of the state. The outcome of this can take a variety of forms, the major one of which is inflation, the solutions to each creating further problems.

Whilst the first part of the argument (concerning the growth of social capital) is sound and whilst the whole is embellished with many powerful insights, the second part rests on two false 'laws' of Marxist political economy: the tendencies to immiseration of the working class and to underconsumption.[6] The first is nowhere seriously entertained today, but the second continues to flourish, most notably in the USA where the influence of Baran and Sweezy's *Monopoly Capital* continues strong.[7] It thus represents in this respect a sophisticated version of their argument,

---

* My thanks are due to Robin Blackburn, Norman Geras, John Harrison, Geoff Hodgson and Bob Rowthorn for comments on an earlier draft.

1 The term 'state monopoly capitalism' is more precise than 'neo-capitalism' but suffers from the emphasis sometimes given to the 'fusion' of big monopolies and the state (see N. Poulantzas, *Political Power and Social Classes*, London 1973, p. 273) and from the connotations of the 'anti-monopoly' alliance.

2 There are many other areas of intervention which do not entail direct state expenditure. For an attempted classification see R. Murray, 'Internationalization of capital and the nation state', NLR 67, 1971; and for an excellent survey Bill Warren, 'The state and capitalist planning', NLR 72, 1972.

3 J. O'Connor, *The Fiscal Crisis of the State*, New York, 1973.

4 I. Gough, 'The fiscal crisis of the state', *Bulletin of the Conference of Socialist Economists*, 11, Summer 1975.

5 The result of this tendency is the Marcusian warfare-welfare state. Cf. 'The welfare-warfare state is one single phenomenon, and military and civilian expenditure cannot be reduced significantly at the expense of one another' (O'Connor, op. cit., p. 236; also p. 151)—a prognostication long since falsified even in the USA (see Section II below).

6 On underconsumption: O'Connor, op. cit., pp. 24–5, 29; on immiseration: pp. 162, 236–7.

7 At least on the evidence of O'Connor's book. P. Baran and P. Sweezy, *Monopoly Capital*, Harmondsworth 1968.

and indeed of associated theories of the permanent arms economy.[8] For Baran and Sweezy it was not the economic nature of arms spending which made it ideal for offsetting tendencies to underconsumption, but its political nature. Given the power structure of US monopoly capitalism there were powerful forces opposing the growth of Federal spending on civilian items,[9] but there were no established private interests opposed to the expansion of the military establishment, which moreover had other functional consequences for monopoly capital. O'Connor on the other hand correctly recognizes the productive contributions of many other state activities today. But for him, precisely because they augment productivity in the monopoly sector, they exacerbate the gap between this and the demand for its products, thus furthering the need for state *expenses* (welfare relief, etc.) to cope with the resulting surplus population. A dynamic interplay thus occurs as a result of the two contradictory functions of the state—to aid private capital accumulation and to legitimize its social relations—but this is premised on the existence of tendencies to overproduction in the monopoly sector.

## Functional Theories of the State

The errors of Marxist underconsumption and associated breakdown theories have been exposed elsewhere.[10] These errors undermine all attempts to explain the growth of modern state expenditure as an offset to lack of demand elsewhere in the economy. The theory of the permanent arms economy—the most popular variant of underconsumptionism—is not even in tune with the facts, since military spending has continually declined as a share of the total in all western countries since the early 1950s.[11] Kidron's attempt to resurrect it by demonstrating that military spending acts instead as an offset to the falling tendency of the rate of profit has been refuted.[12] More generally, all such theories suffer from two related weaknesses: the lack of a historical approach and a mechanistic distinction between the economic base and the superstructure, between objective and subjective factors. Purdy argues well against the first (in connection with the arms economy theory): 'Attention is focused on the *function* of arms spending within an ongoing capitalist economy. The historical genesis of the arms economy is ignored . . . . The arms race is a historically specific feature of a particular stage of capitalist development. To confine analysis to an account of its functional role in modern capitalism is to fall into one of the basic methodological faults of bourgeois social science: the complete failure to understand the present as history.'[13]

[8] e.g. T. Cliff, 'Perspectives of the permanent war economy', *A Socialist Review*, London 1965.

[9] Specifically: private and professional interests threatened by state intervention (e.g. real estate, the medical profession), the need to protect the existing benefits of the oligarchy (e.g. in education), and the danger of undermining the work ethic with social security schemes. Baran and Sweezy, op. cit., pp. 163–75, and P. Baran, *The Political Economy of Growth*, Harmondsworth 1973, pp. 231–3.

[10] Lenin long ago attacked the underconsumptionism of the Narodniks in *The Development of Capitalism in Russia*, 1964, ch. 1. For a recent critique see G. Hodgson, 'The permanent arms economy', *International*, vol. 1, no. 8, 1973, pp. 56–8.

[11] See section II below.

[12] M. Kidron, *Western Capitalism since the War*, Harmondsworth 1970, p. 56. The best critique is D. Purdy, 'The theory of permanent arms economy—a critique and an alternative', CSEB Spring 1973.

[13] Purdy, p. 23.

The same argument applies to all theories of the state premised on 'breakdown' theories of the economy. The associated error is a false polarization of the economy and the superstructure. The former is seen as an autonomous 'factor' leading, if unchecked, to some form of economic breakdown, whereas the latter is interpreted as a passive instrument in the hands of the bourgeoisie whose functions are determined by the offsetting action required in order to avoid or check the tendencies to breakdown. We shall argue below that the capitalist state is characterized by a relative autonomy from the economic structure and is responsive to the ongoing struggle between and within the dominant and dominated classes. All this is in fact recognized by O'Connor,[14] and this is the real merit of his book, but it coexists uneasily with a functionalist view of the state stemming from his underlying analysis of the economy.

The same fundamental criticisms can be made of those analyses of state expenditures recently put forward by David Yaffe.[15] For him, the growth of state expenditure represents part of the attempt to solve the crisis of profitability, brought about by the falling tendency of the rate of profit under late capitalism. 'It is precisely the crisis of profitability that makes a growing state expenditure necessary.'[16] More specifically, state expenditure has been functional in maintaining social and political stability since the war, in supplementing private investment and in maintaining full employment. But this state intervention has a contradictory impact for it subsequently (a) reduces private accumulation and (b) fuels inflation. The first results because all or most state expenditure (including that on the purchase of goods and services from the capitalist sector) is 'unproductive'. It constitutes a deduction from the surplus value produced by 'productive' workers and reduces the amount available for private capital accumulation. The second follows from both the 'unproductiveness' of the expenditure and the way it is financed: 'government expenditure requires, indeed necessitates, deficit financing and increased borrowing which leads to inflation.'[17]

There are many errors in this argument. First, it gives insufficient weight to the role of class struggle in shaping state- especially social-expenditures, and erroneously regards them all as 'unproductive'. Many can better be regarded as a part of the value of labour power collectively provided rather than a 'cost that capital must pay for social stability etc.'[18] which is deducted from surplus value already produced. If this is so these services are not luxuries, but part of Marx's department II (producing the material elements of variable capital) as O'Connor correctly emphasizes, and are indirectly productive of sur-

[14] See O'Connor, op. cit., p. 2 and ch. 9 on the role of class struggle, and ch. 3 for a profound analysis of the state and budgetary control.

[15] D. Yaffe, 'The Marxian theory of crisis, capital and the state', CSEB Winter 1972, and 'The crisis of profitability', NLR 80, 1973.

[16] Yaffe, NLR 80, p. 51ff.

[17] Ibid., p. 52. Which of these two factors crucially determines the inflationary impact of state expenditure is not clear. Mandel, with whom on many points Yaffe's analysis shares a lot in common, recognizes that if the expenditure were entirely financed by taxation it would not be inflationary. Unfortunately he concludes: 'Such a case is practically unknown in the epoch of the decline of capitalism,' E. Mandel, *Marxist Economic Theory*, London 1968, p. 527.

[18] Yaffe, NLR 80, p. 57, fn. 42.

plus value.[19] Second, as we show in the next section, it is not the case that the great expansion of state spending since the Second World War has been financed by government borrowing; instead taxation has grown in parallel. This does not reduce its inflationary impact but it does mean that inflation cannot be explained solely by the intervention of the capitalist state as a *deus ex machina* isolated from the class struggle. Third, and most fundamentally, the 'law' of the falling tendency of the rate of profit has been subject to definitive criticism following advances in Marxist political economy in recent years.[20] It follows that the role of the modern capitalist state can no longer be explained as a functional response to the profitability crisis of late capitalism.[21]

## Class Struggle and the State

Once again we find here the false polarity between objective economic laws and the subjective political response to them, the 'divorce of materialism and history' in Colletti's words,[22] and a conception of the modern state as determined by these functions. A Marxist theory of crisis must situate the class struggle at its heart. This is not to argue that there are no general laws of capitalist development (the laws of the concentration of capital or combined and uneven development are examples), but that all laws which mechanically posit a tendency to 'breakdown' of whatever nature must no longer be given credence. Nor is it to deny that the actions of the modern state are not shaped by these material forces; merely that they are not determined by them without remainder.

Against this functional approach may be set those who emphasize the role of class struggle in the development particularly of social services since the Second World War. This was stressed by Wedderburn writing in 1965, though it must be recognized that the view of the welfare state as a repressive agency continues to flourish especially in much American writing.[23] The most recent British attempt to analyse objectively the developments in state expenditure is by Barratt Brown,[24] who provides an excellent summary of the major trends. However part of his explanation is weakened by a quite un-Marxist over-emphasis on the autonomy of the state from the dominant class(es) in the context of growing working class power. Quoting Engels, that 'when the warring classes so nearly attain equilibrium that the state, ostensibly appearing as a mediator, assumes for the moment a certain independence in relation to

---

[19] For a demonstration of this see section V below.

[20] G. Hodgson, 'The theory of the falling rate of profit', NLR 84, 1974, and I. Steedman, 'Value, price and profit', NLR 90, 1975.

[21] This is not to deny the inevitability of crises under capitalism, nor that profitability is the basic determinant of the current crisis. See section V below.

[22] L. Colletti, *From Rousseau to Lenin*, London 1972, p. 66. Pp. 62–72 present an excellent critique of breakdown theories.

[23] D. Wedderburn, 'Facts and theories of the welfare state' in *The Socialist Register 1965*, ed. R. Miliband and J. Saville. Even Piven and Cloward in their informative study write: 'The key to an understanding of relief-giving is in the functions it serves for the larger economic and political order . . . . Expansive relief policies are designed to mute civil disorder, and restrictive ones to reinforce work norms,' F. Piven and R. Cloward, *Regulating the Poor*, London 1972, p. xiii.

[24] M. Barratt Brown, *From Labourism to Socialism*, Nottingham 1972, especially ch. 3.

both,'[25] he suggests that British working-class organizations in the 1970s could be moving in this direction. In other words, anxious to reject the crude Marxist view of the state as a passive representative of the interests of the bourgeoisie, he goes too far and effectively denies the structural link between the state and the dominant class.[26]

In section III we shall attempt a synthesis of these two views based on the recent works of Poulantzas and Miliband and in the light of that will propose a general theory to explain the growth and composition of state expenditures. But beforehand, we must consider those trends in some detail, since part of the confusion in this area rests on simple factual errors as to what has actually happened.

## II. The Growth of the Capitalist State

Tables 1 and 2 summarize the structure and trends of total state expenditure in the UK and the five other major OECD countries.[27] In 1972 it amounted to 37–40 per cent of GDP in the major European economies, 34 per cent in the USA and perhaps 20 per cent in Japan. Since the war, state spending has grown faster than GDP in every OECD country. From 1955 to 1969 it rose 23 per cent faster in all countries taken together, with only France and Japan among the major economies exhibiting a slower relative growth (see bottom half of Table 1). This trend has continued up to 1972. Of course the divergent rates of growth of these economies has meant that the *absolute* growth of state spending has varied enormously. On this count it has grown most rapidly in Japan: 50 per cent faster than the EEC and twice as fast as the UK.[28] Taking the growth of public expenditure in the UK over a longer time period, it can be seen there have been three major periods of expansion. The first occurred during the First World War when its share of GNP (at factor cost) doubled to between 25 per cent and 30 per cent in the inter-war period. During the Second World War, the economic role of the state rose to record levels (three quarters of GNP in 1943), but at the end of

[25] F. Engels, *The Origin of the Family, the State and Private Property*. Moscow 1940, p. 194.

[26] Barratt Brown quotes in this context a remark by Miliband concerning a 'secondary view' of the state in Marx and Engels as 'independent from and superior to all social classes, as being the dominant force in society rather than the instrument of a dominant class', despite Miliband's clear critique of the passage by Engels quoted above: 'For Marx, the Bonapartist state, however independent it may have been *politically* from any given class, remains, and cannot in a class society but remain, the protector of an economically and socially dominant class', R. Miliband, 'Marx and the state', *The Socialist Register 1965*, pp. 283, 285.

[27] The two tables are not comparable. Table 1 excludes capital expenditure of state productive enterprises, i.e. it measures total government rather than public expenditure. It also excludes capital transfers. In Table 1 the items are expressed as a percentage of GDP at purchasers' values, in Table 2 of GNP at factor cost. The purchasers' values/factor cost distinction is crucial since the latter excludes the artificial inflation of national output brought about by the imposition of indirect taxes, notably on consumer items, which raises their market price. Since the burden of indirect taxes on government expenditure is small, the procedure in Table 2 gives a more accurate impression of the relative weight of state expenditure. Gross National Product differs from Gross Domestic Product by including net property income paid or received from abroad; but the difference is slight.

[28] OECD, 'Public expenditure trends' (by M. Garin-Painter) in *Occasional Studies*, July 1970, Table 1, p. 45.

## TABLE I

*State Expenditure[1] in Major OECD Countries*

| | UK | FRANCE | WEST GERMANY | ITALY | USA | JAPAN |
|---|---|---|---|---|---|---|
| *Per cent of GDP[2] in 1972:* | | | | | | |
| Military | 4·9 | 3·5 | 3·0 | 2·4 | 6·7 | |
| + Health and education | 7·7 | 8·8 (Health and education + Other civilian) | 14·7 (Health and education + Other civilian) | 5·7 | 7·1 | |
| + Other civilian | 6·1 | | | 6·7 | 7·0 | |
| = Current real expenditure | 18·7 | 12·3 | 17·7 | 14·8 | 20·8 | 9·1 |
| + Capital expenditure | 4·7 | 3·1 | 3·7 | 2·6 | 3·2 | |
| = Total real expenditure | 23·4 | 15·4 | 21·4 | 17·4 | 24·0 | |
| + Social security | 8·9 | 17·2 | 13·0 | 14·6 | 8·0 | 4·7 |
| + Debt interest | 3·8 | 0·8 | 1·0 | 2·9 | 1·9 | 0·8 |
| + Other transfers and subsidies | 3·7 | 3·3 | 2·6 | 5·1 | 0·4 | |
| = TOTAL EXPENDITURE[3] | 39·8 | 36·7 | 38·0 | 40·0 | 34·3 | |
| TOTAL REVENUE[4] | 37·9 | 38·0 | 39·0 | 34·7 | 31·4 | 22·6 |
| State borrowing[5] | 1·8 | −0·5 | 0·1 | 6·5 | 0·3 | |
| *Ratio of growth rates to growth of GNP, 1955–1969:[6]* | | | | | | |
| Military | 0·62 | 0·44 | 0·84 | 1·22 | 0·80 | |
| All civilian | 1·36 | 1·20 | 1·34 | 1·13 | 1·65 | |
| Current real expenditure | 1·09 | 0·92 | 1·22 | 1·15 | 1·23 | 0·92 |
| Capital expenditure | 1·41 | 1·51 | 1·22 | 0·71 | 1·15 | |
| Social security | 1·59 | 1·32 | 1·19 | 1·37 | 1·47 | 1·10 |
| TOTAL EXPENDITURE | 1·24 | 1·14 | 1·24 | 1·20 | 1·23 | |
| Current expenditure at *constant* prices: | 0·62 | 0·58 | 0·85 | 0·74 | 1·06 | 0·55 |

[1] Excluding state productive enterprises.

[2] At market prices.

[3] Excluding capital transfers.

[4] All taxation, including social security contributions and local taxes, government trading income and current transfers.

[5] Equals expenditure − revenue ± capital transfers.

[6] France 1959–69, West Germany 1960–69.

SOURCES: OECD, *National Accounts 1961–1972*, 1974; OECD, *Expenditure Trends in OECD Countries, 1960–1980*, 1972.

## TABLE 2

*State Expenditure[1] in the UK, 1910–1973*

<table>
<tr><th></th><th>1910</th><th>1937</th><th>1951</th><th>1961</th><th>1971</th><th>1973</th></tr>
<tr><td>Per cent of GNP[2] in each year:</td><td></td><td></td><td></td><td></td><td></td><td></td></tr>
<tr><td>Social security</td><td></td><td>5·2</td><td>5·3</td><td>6·7</td><td>8·9</td><td>8·7</td></tr>
<tr><td>Health and welfare</td><td></td><td>1·8</td><td>4·5</td><td>4·4</td><td>5·8</td><td>5·9</td></tr>
<tr><td>Education</td><td></td><td>2·6</td><td>3·2</td><td>4·2</td><td>6·5</td><td>6·8</td></tr>
<tr><td>Housing</td><td></td><td>1·4</td><td>3·1</td><td>2·3</td><td>2·6</td><td>3·5</td></tr>
<tr><td>Total social services</td><td>4·2</td><td>10·9</td><td>16·1</td><td>17·6</td><td>23·8</td><td>24·9</td></tr>
<tr><td>Environment[3]</td><td rowspan="2">0·7</td><td rowspan="2">1·0</td><td>1·5</td><td>1·6</td><td>2·4</td><td>2·5</td></tr>
<tr><td>Transport and communications</td><td>2·1</td><td>3·2</td><td>3·9</td><td>3·9</td></tr>
<tr><td>Commerce and industry[4]</td><td>1·8</td><td>2·8</td><td>6·9</td><td>4·9</td><td>6·5</td><td>5·6</td></tr>
<tr><td>Justice and law[5]</td><td>0·6</td><td>0·7</td><td>0·6</td><td>0·8</td><td>1·3</td><td>1·4</td></tr>
<tr><td>Military and external</td><td>3·5</td><td>5·0</td><td>10·8</td><td>7·6</td><td>6·6</td><td>6·4</td></tr>
<tr><td>Debt interest and other</td><td>1·9</td><td>5·2</td><td>6·9</td><td>6·3</td><td>5·9</td><td>5·8</td></tr>
<tr><td>TOTAL PUBLIC EXPENDITURE</td><td>12·7</td><td>25·7</td><td>44·9</td><td>42·1</td><td>50·3</td><td>50·5</td></tr>
<tr><td>Total taxation</td><td>11·0</td><td>22·5</td><td>37·5</td><td>32·8</td><td>41·8</td><td>37·7</td></tr>
<tr><td>Trading surpluses, rent, interest</td><td></td><td>1·3</td><td>5·2</td><td>5·7</td><td>6·8</td><td>6·9</td></tr>
<tr><td>TOTAL REVENUE</td><td>11·0</td><td>23·8</td><td>42·7</td><td>38·5</td><td>48·6</td><td>44·6</td></tr>
<tr><td>Borrowing requirement[6]</td><td>1·7</td><td>1·9</td><td>2·2</td><td>3·6</td><td>1·7</td><td>5·9</td></tr>
</table>

[1] Including capital expenditure of public corporations.

[2] At factor cost.

[3] Water, sewerage and refuse disposal; public health, clean air, parks, town and country planning etc.

[4] Employment services, research and development, investment grants, agricultural support, and certain public corporations' investment.

[5] Police, prisons, law courts and Parliament.

[6] Plus other financial transactions (a residual item).

SOURCES: A. Peacock and D. Wiseman, *The Growth of Public Expenditure in the UK*, London 1961; London and Cambridge Economic Service, *The British Economy: Key Statistics 1900–1970*; CSO, *National Income and Expenditure* and *Social Trends*.

hostilities it settled down to a much higher plateau than before, accounting for about two-fifths of GNP. The third period of expansion did not begin in the UK until the early 1960s (during the 1950s its share fell somewhat), but since then it has proceeded without interruption to take the share of total public expenditure over 50 per cent of GNP in the late 1960s.

This rapid expansion since the Second World War has *not* been financed by a secular increase in state borrowing, with the crucial exception of the USA. From the mid 1950s to the late 1960s taxation in all OECD countries combined rose by 4·7 per cent of GNP—faster than the rise in all *current* expenditure if the USA is excluded, and not much below the rise in *total* expenditure including capital investment.[29] In this context it should be remembered that some state capital expenditure provides assets which yield a trading income, for which therefore loan finance is not necessarily inflationary: hence, it is reasonable to expect taxation to cover only part of capital spending. Data for the UK in Table 2 shows that up to 1971 taxation plus trading surpluses rose roughly in line with expenditure. Since 1971 deficits have mushroomed in the UK, Italy and several other countries but this in no way disturbs our conclusions on the long run trend in state finance: there are specific conjunctural explanations of this new 'fiscal crisis of the state'.[30] Alongside this long-run growth in tax revenues there has been a marked shift in their burden away from corporations and onto households in all countries:[31] an important point to which we return later.

## Trends

Turning to the composition of state expenditure, certain trends are clearly discernible in all advanced capitalist countries. These are: the growth in expenditure on the social services, certain infra-structure items and aid to private industry, and the decline in the share absorbed by armaments. Of these 'the most striking feature is the extent to which education, health and social security were responsible for the rising share of government expenditure over this period' according to an OECD report.[32] In the UK the social services (including housing) have expanded continuously since the beginning of the century, with the exception of the 1930s, and today account for one half of public expenditure. In the US they increased from 9 per cent of GNP in 1955 to 15 per cent in 1969. In the EEC social expenditure rose as a percentage of private consumption from 1962–70; in the Netherlands a huge increase from 22 per cent to 35 per cent.[33] Parallel with this expansion has been

---

[29] Current spending rose by 4·4 per cent of GNP (4·9 per cent including the USA) and total spending by 5·0 per cent (5·5 per cent including the USA). OECD, *Expenditure Trends in OECD Countries 1960–1980*, 1972, Tables 16, 19. In these and subsequent calculations, countries are weighted by their aggregate GNPs at current exchange rates. In 1967–9 this gave the USA a weight of 51 per cent and the other five major countries a weight of 34 per cent of the OECD total.

[30] And for the aberrant behaviour of the US. O'Connor (p. 43) attributes the growing government deficit in the 1960s to the unpopularity of the war in South East Asia which prevented the imposition of tax increases to finance it.

[31] OECD, 1972, p. 56.

[32] OECD, 1970, p. 48.

[33] OECD, 1972, pp. 72–81 for a detailed comparative analysis.

the ubiquitous decline in military spending relative to GNP. From the mid 1950s to the late 1960s its share fell from 7·1 per cent to 6·2 per cent of GNP in all OECD countries combined; from 4·1 per cent to 3·2 per cent if the US is excluded.[34] Since then this tendency has if anything intensified with a major drop in the US from 9 per cent to below 7 per cent in 1972 and in Italy, from 4 per cent to 2½ per cent. Other major developments since the Second World War have been a growth in 'environmental' and infra-structure expenses, transport and roads, and a relative decline in agricultural support. Comparable data on these and other items is harder to come by but the trends in the UK revealed in Table 2 are probably common to all advanced capitalist economies.[35] Two further notable increases also occurred in the 1960s: a growth in state economic aid to the private sector and a growth in state expenditure on its legal and coercive apparatus. The decline in expenditure on 'commerce and industry' since 1971 does not represent a real decline in the former item. Instead direct investment grants have been replaced by tax allowances to corporations, a change which leaves unaltered the impact on total state finances, and which reveals the pitfalls in extrapolating figures on expenditure to reveal the total economic impact of the modern state.

By no means does all state spending pre-empt resources and reduce the total available for the private sector. This is only the case with real (current and capital) spending, such as on arms or education services. The remaining money transfers do just that: they merely transfer the ability to purchase resources to other groups, whether individual households (e.g. pensions or family allowances) or private firms (e.g. investment grants). They thus add to private purchasing power, just as the taxes to finance them subtract from it. Table I shows that for the major OECD countries real expenditure accounted for between 42 per cent of total spending in Italy and 70 per cent in the USA. In most OECD countries it was transfer expenditure which rose most rapidly between 1955 and 1969. For all OECD countries combined it grew 42 per cent faster than GNP, whereas real state expenditure rose only 16 per cent faster (8 per cent faster if the US is excluded) and total state spending 23 per cent faster.[36] Almost everywhere this has been due to the decline in arms spending, since real civilian expenditure continued to grow throughout this period. In the UK, total real expenditures actually fell as a share of GNP in the 1950s, and this trend has continued since then in France and Japan (see bottom half of Table 1). So the rapid growth of the state since the Second World War has not significantly reduced the share of growing resources available for private consumption, investment or exports. Rather it has been utilized to raise the share of the last two in particular—noticeably so in the last few years as profit rates have been squeezed.

### Structures

Of course, despite the similarity in *trends*, the *structures* of state expenditure still differ substantially between the major OECD countries. In

[34] Ibid., table 16.
[35] See OECD, 1970, p. 53.
[36] OECD, 1972, table 17.

general one can distinguish three groups of countries: the US and UK, the EEC countries and Japan. The US and UK are characterized by higher military and lower social security spending than the EEC. Partly because of this the share of public expenditure which pre-empts real resources is higher in the US and UK, accounting for almost one quarter of GDP (Table 1). Since interest on the National Debt is also more burdensome there, the total of 'war related expenditure' is also higher than in the EEC, and total social spending is markedly lower (especially in the USA until recent years).[37] Japan is in a category of its own, the state spending less than any other OECD country with the exception of Spain and Portugal. These differences are matched by variations in the structure of state revenues. Not surprisingly the high social security benefits in the EEC are matched by higher social security contributions, though in France especially these are mostly paid by employers. In the UK and US personal income taxation is higher and in the US corporation tax is still significant; social security contributions are much lower. In Japan taxes of all kinds are very low: less than two-thirds of the OECD average.[38] These different patterns of expenditure and revenue reflect of course the very different historical antecedents and processes in each nation state (the high war-related expenditures of the UK even today reminding us of its past global role). On the other hand the similarity in *trends* mean that these differences are diminishing and the structures of expenditure are 'converging' in all advanced capitalist countries.

Two further points should be emphasized when interpreting data on state spending. First, part, even of real expenditure, consists of purchases of goods and services from the capitalist sector, for example arms, drugs, books, building construction etc. In the UK at the present time this amounts to one third of current real expenditure, the remaining two thirds representing the wages of state employees, whether soldiers, teachers or doctors. Ten per cent of the output of UK manufacturing industry (and a much higher proportion in certain sectors, e.g. aerospace) is purchased by the central government alone.[39] Not all state *expenditure* represents state *production*.

Secondly, trends in productivity in the state sector must also be considered, for it is well known that this rises less fast than in the capitalist sector, due to the predominance of low productivity, labour-intensive services in the former, particularly the social services. As a result the cost index of state services has risen faster than the average and a greater level of expenditure is required year by year in all countries just to maintain the level of services in real terms. Thus state consumption expenditure, which in *money* terms has risen faster than GNP in the OECD as a whole has in constant price terms risen more slowly (see Table I, last line). Excluding the USA (where it was boosted by military spending in the 1960s) state consumption rose by 3·9 per cent p.a. in real terms in all OECD countries from 1955–69, whilst GNP rose by

[37] T. Hill, 'Too much consumption', *National Westminster Bank Review*, November 1969.
[38] OECD, 1972, Table 19, and CSO, *Social Trends No. 5*, 1974, Table 210.
[39] T. Chester, 'Public money in the private sector', *National Westminster Bank Review*, May 1973, p. 24.

5·7 per cent.[40] In other words *real* state consumption expenditure has fallen as a share of GNP over the last two decades. Admittedly this is more than accounted for by the decline in military spending, and social transfers have continued to rise, but the point remains. For slow growing economies such as the British, it can mean that a rising proportion of GNP must be expanded each year in order merely to protect the social services against the inflation in their costs.[41] As we shall see, this phenomenon has contributed to the recent crisis of social expenditure in the UK and elsewhere.

## III. The Capitalist State and Capitalist Economy

In this section we shall attempt to present the essential characteristics of the capitalist state and to situate it in the current stage of the capitalist world economy. For the first task we shall draw heavily on the recent major studies of Poulantzas and Miliband.[42] Though there are very important differences indeed between their analyses,[43] it is the common area of agreement in their work which is of most significance for the purposes of this essay. The state, as institutionalized political power, consists of the interrelationship of the following six institutions: the executive, legislature, administration, military and police, judiciary and 'sub-central' government.[44] For both Poulantzas and Miliband the capitalist state is a relatively autonomous entity representing the political interests of the dominant classes and situated within the field of class struggle. Let us consider each of these characteristics in turn.

### Autonomy of the State

First, the capitalist state is *relatively autonomous*, *both* from the economic structures of capitalist social formations and from the politically dominant classes in those social formations.[45] The latter point is crucial: not since the patriciates of Venice and Lübeck have businessmen governed directly as a class.[46] This has been so because of the structural position of the state within capitalist social formations. It is the incapacity of the capitalist classes to organize itself as a political force which requires the state to step in and realize its political hegemony, to act as a class conscious political directorate.[47] This incapacity

[40] OECD, 1972, Tables 2, 3. 'State consumption' refers to current real expenditure in Table 1.

[41] For example, expenditure on the National Health Service in the UK which rose as a share of GNP at current prices (see Table 2) actually fell at constant prices from 3·9 per cent in 1951 to 3·4 per cent in 1971.

[42] N. Poulantzas, *Political Power and Social Classes*, London 1973; R. Miliband, *The State in Capitalist Society*, London 1969.

[43] See the debate in NLR 58 (1969) and 59 (1970). In particular the criticisms by Miliband in 'Poulantzas and the capitalist state', NLR 82, 1973 are persuasive.

[44] Miliband, 1969, pp. 49–54.

[45] e.g. Poulantzas, p. 282; Miliband, 1973, p. 85.

[46] Miliband, 1969, p. 53.

[47] Poulantzas, pp. 284–5, 188–9. See also O'Connor, p. 67ff. Miliband (1973, pp. 88–9) has criticized Poulantzas for ignoring the effective role played by bourgeois political parties (themselves outside the state system proper) in organizing and articulating the interests of the dominant class and its supporting classes. This is correct, but does not preclude the various institutions of the state, in particular the civil service, aiding the parties in this role, as Miliband himself demonstrates (1969, ch. 5).

is due to two major factors. First, the existence of different factions within the dominant class, for example industrial and financial capital in the UK, and/or of different classes within the dominant bloc (landlords and capitalists), necessitates the existence of an 'external' institution representing the common, longer term, political interests of the dominant class(es) as a whole.[48] Without this they would degenerate into special-interest lobbying. Second, and more important, political unity is essential in the political conflict with the dominated classes particularly in the context of bourgeois democracy, the most pervasive form of class rule particularly since the Second World War. To this end, the state plays a crucial role in politically disabling the dominated classes by setting itself up as the representative of 'national unity', of the 'general interests' of 'the people' as a whole.[49] This of course is powerfully legitimized by the existence of universal suffrage and the attendant bourgeois 'freedoms' in all major advanced capitalist countries, particularly when social democratic governments are in office. These two factors, then, mean that the capitalist state simultaneously acts to organize the dominant classes as a political force and to politically disorganize the dominated classes. Both these functions however necessitate its autonomy from the dominant class itself: the first in order to realize its common interest, the second in order to effectively pose as the representative of national unity. The relative autonomy of the capitalist state is thus a structurally determined characteristic; it does not depend on an equilibrium of class forces, either within the dominant class(es), or between the dominant and dominated classes,[50] as much contemporary political analysis suggests.

Second, given this autonomy, the capitalist state does constitute itself as the 'unambiguous political power of the dominant class'. But it can only effectively represent its *political* interests by means of this relative autonomy, which requires it continually to challenge the short-term and even long-term *economic* interests of *particular* sections of capital. 'This relative autonomy allows the state to intervene not only in order to arrange compromises vis-a-vis the dominated classes, which, in the long run, are useful for the actual economic interests of the dominant classes or factions; but also (depending on the concrete conjuncture) to intervene against the long-term economic interests of *one or other* faction of the dominant class: for such compromises and sacrifices are sometimes necessary for the realization of their political class interests.'[51]

This 'unstable equilibrium of compromise' provides the basis for the whole series of social and economic reforms extracted by the working class in the post-war 'welfare states' of advanced capitalist societies, which yet leaves untouched the political power of capital and the repressive apparatus of the state on which it is ultimately based. This introduces at the centre of the analysis of the capitalist state the third

[48] Poulantzas, pp. 284, 287; Miliband, 1973, p. 85, fn. 4.

[49] Poulantzas, pp. 132–7, 277–9, 287, 288–9; Miliband, 1969, pp. 72–6; O'Connor, p. 69. For a lucid though brief exposition of the advantages and risks of bourgeois democracy for the capitalist class, see N. Geras, 'Rosa Luxemburg after 1905', NLR 89, 1975, pp. 13–16.

[50] Poulantzas, pp. 260, 274, 287.

[51] Poulantzas, p. 285, also p. 193; Miliband, 1969, p. 102.

feature noted above: the political class struggle. This essentially determines the degree of autonomy which any particular state exhibits.[52] The basic struggle at both the economic and political level today is of course that between capital and labour. In the political sphere the role of social democracy (and at particular conjunctures of communist parties) has been important especially since the Second World War. Social democracy is always involved in a tightrope act—balancing the concessions it can offer to its mass base on the one hand with the need to serve the political interests of capital on the other hand.[53] So long as the concessions are there to be given, 'it can walk quite a way along this tightrope without actually falling off';[54] when the economy is in a downturn however its political survival is considerably more precarious. But all governments of whatever political complexion depend for their survival under bourgeois democracy on their ability to offer *certain* reforms and concessions to the struggles of the dominated classes.[55]

### Concentration of Capital

These states are operating within a determinate socio-economic context: it would be quite antithetical to historical materialism to deny that there are objective laws of capitalist development which, within limits, operate independently of men's will. These laws of development also impose certain functions on the capitalist state, though the response to these will depend on the individual social formation and state. Two have had a major impact on the role of the modern state: the accumulation and centralization of capital, and the law of combined and uneven development which follows from it.

The inbuilt tendencies for capital to accumulate and to be concentrated in fewer and larger units are central aspects of Marx's analysis of capitalist society. Capitalist competition in the context of rapid technological development ensures the continued concentration into fewer and larger corporations and units of production.[56] The direct consequences of this include a growth in the ratio of means of production to direct labour, the 'deepening' of capital, an increasing span of time separating the original decision to produce and the final output, greater inflexibility of capital commitment, a massive infusion of technology into the productive process, and more and more complex corporate organization and planning.[57] These trends have numerous consequences for the modern capitalist state, ranging from research and development to guarantees of profitability, financial aid for investment and the attempt to provide a 'total favourable environment' for monopoly capital by means of capitalist planning.[58]

---

[52] Poulantzas, p. 289.
[53] For an excellent analysis of social democracy see Miliband, 1969, p. 96ff and his book *Parliamentary Socialism*, London 1972.
[54] J. Harrison, 'British capitalism in 1973 and 1974: the deepening crisis', CSEB Spring 1974, p. 55.
[55] Miliband, 1969, pp. 102, 187.
[56] For a good international survey see Mandel, op. cit., ch. 12.
[57] This list is adapted from that in J. K. Galbraith, *The New Industrial State*, Harmondsworth 1974, ch. 2. For Galbraith they are all the results of the 'imperatives of technology' not of capitalist social relations of production.
[58] Warren, NLR 72, and Mandel, op. cit., pp. 498–507.

But accumulation and concentration of capital has, ever since the Industrial Revolution, brought in its train other upheavals in the socio-economic structure of an epochal nature. Three are crucial for an understanding of the role of the state in advanced capitalist countries. First, the continuous proletarianization of the population as capital spreads its influence to all sectors of the economy is a feature of every capitalist society. As a result, the proportion of the self-employed, peasants and small farmers, independent professionals, etc., continues to fall in every capitalist economy whilst the share of employees continues to rise.[59] This trend towards a common proletarian status, whatever the income differentials and despite the high absolute living standards especially of certain salaried workers, has important consequences especially in the field of welfare provision. For the security provided by family production and the possession of a minimum quantum of means of production is no longer present. As a result collective provision often by the state is more and more necessary, especially since industrialization creates new 'diswelfares' (industrial diseases) and further sources of insecurity (redundancy and shake-out).[60] Second, the quality of labour power must necessarily be raised in all capitalist economies to match the increased sophistication of production and of its attendant social processes. Side by side with investment in instruments of production, investment in labour power has grown apace especially in the twentieth century,[61] and this has again necessitated the intervention of the capitalist state. Lastly, the urbanization process is, in the capitalist epoch, a major consequence of the tendencies to capital accumulation and concentration. In all countries conurbations and other urban areas (including their suburbs) continue to grow, whilst regional and sub-regional areas expand and contract in an uneven way. This historic process has major implications for state intervention. It necessitates on the one hand state physical planning: land use, town and country planning, regional programmes, etc.; and on the other hand a rapid growth in infrastructural investment in housing, roads, transport, water, sewerage, gas, electricity, parks, city centres, clean air, etc., etc., most of which can again only be undertaken directly by the state or indirectly by its agencies.[62]

Accumulation and concentration of capital, proletarianization and education of the labour force and the population generally, and urbanization: these then are the major ongoing trends in the socio-economic structures of capitalism. Together they are all aspects of the socialization of production—the inevitable corollary of the development of the capitalist mode of production. As we shall see, in all advanced capitalist countries, they have resulted in a growing socialization of the *costs* of production in the shape of growing state expenditures.

## Combined and Uneven Development

The 'law' of combined and uneven development begins from the fact

[59] See A. Glyn and B. Sutcliffe, *British Capitalism, Workers and the Profits Squeeze*, Harmondsworth 1972, appendix G for post-war data.
[60] O'Connor, p. 124ff. Also R. M. Titmuss, *Commitment to Welfare*, London 1968, chs. 5, 10, 11.
[61] J. Sheehan, *The Economics of Education*, London 1973, ch. 1.
[62] O'Connor, chs. 4–6.

that capitalism is a world system, based on international division of labour and world-wide development of productive forces. Nation states are not totally autonomous entities but elements of this system, and the destiny of any individual country cannot be considered in isolation from developments elsewhere. 'The historical dialectic knows neither naked backwardness nor chemically pure progressiveness. It is all a question of concrete correlations. The present day history of mankind is full of "paradoxes", not so colossal as the arising of a proletarian dictatorship in a backward country, but of similar historical type.'[63] One might restate the law by saying that nothing in history is a 'paradox': everything is explicable historically. How then has the operation of this law revealed itself since the Second World War, and what are the implications for the capitalist states of today?

On a world scale three developments have been crucial. First the expansion and strengthening of the Soviet bloc, followed in 1949 by the successful Chinese revolution. These developments have narrowed the global base for capitalist exploitation, and resulted very soon after the end of hostilities in the Cold War and the arms race. Second, the appearance of liberation struggles throughout the Third World which have further challenged imperialist domination. These have gained strength from the existence of the Soviet and Chinese states who have objectively been driven to support them even though their policies have often worked against them. The third factor is the total hegemony of the United States amongst the capitalist nations emerging from the aftermath of the Second World War.[64] But recently this is being challenged, on the economic and political if not the military plane, as inter-imperialist rivalries intensify. The rapid recovery and growth of Germany, the other EEC countries and Japan, is leading to a situation where there are three centres of imperialism in the contemporary world, not one.[65] The prolonged period of US hegemony was a contributory factor in the growth and stability of the post-war era, providing for example a stable international monetary framework within which progressively liberalized trade could take place. The economic challenge to the US has already disrupted this system and has contributed to the first synchronized boom and the deepest recession since the war.

It is the resonance of these global trends on the nature of advanced capitalist societies and in particular on the nature and role of their states with which we are chiefly concerned here. Here the major consequence has undoubtedly been the absence of massive unemployment (and of internecine trade warfare and zero or slow growth) since the Second World War. This is *primarily* due to the *political unacceptability* of a reversion to the capitalism of the thirties given the example of the Soviet economies and the unfavourable (for capitalism) shift in the balance of world forces. The experience of full employment and wide-

[63] L. Trotsky, *The History of the Russian Revolution*, London 1967, vol. 3, p. 350. For his statement of the 'law' see vol. 1, ch. 3 and vol. 3, appendix II.

[64] D. Horowitz provides a concise summary and percipient analysis of the post-war world in *Imperialism and Revolution*, Harmondsworth 1971, chs. 9–12. However he fails to note the challenge to US hegemony posed by the growing strength of other capitalist powers: pp. 246–7.

[65] E. Mandel, *Europe versus America?*, London 1970, and B. Rowthorn, 'Imperialism: unity or rivalry?', NLR 69, 1971.

spread state planning during the Second World War contributed to these rising expectations among the western working class. In the same way the greater security enjoyed by many during wartime, despite the absolute fall in living standards, made demands for extended state intervention in the field of social welfare irresistible. To this the high peace-time level of arms expenditure brought about by the Cold War and wars of liberation added a further stimulus. But the primary cause was the political necessity for capitalist states to avoid a return to slumps of the interwar scale, and their ability to implement this by means of Keynesian policies.[66]

## Class Struggle since the War

This change in trajectory occurred despite the international defeat of working-class struggles after the Second World War. Unlike the turbulent years following 1918, this struggle took a bourgeois political form with the entry of social democratic or communist parties into government in several major countries, but because of this the movements were more open to, and soon weakened by, their reformist leadership. The ejection of communist ministers from the French and Italian post-war coalitions and the defeat of the British Labour Party in 1951 were paralleled by the defeat of the Japanese general strike of 1947, the West German defeats of 1947–52 and the victory of McCarthyism in the US (where an upsurge of strike activity took place in 1946). But despite these setbacks, the political constraints on the capitalist class in the west were, (if loosened somewhat) not removed: the underlying world balance of power had not 'improved', indeed in 1949 it 'worsened' considerably. A 'post-war settlement' between capital and labour was essential to lay the basis for (what later transpired to be) the unprecedented boom of the next two decades. In this the social democratic and communist parties in power played a crucial role. By defusing militant pressure from below, by laying the basis for economic growth with selective nationalization and economic aid to private industry and by granting certain important welfare reforms, they ensured the re-generation of capitalist social relations in the aftermath of war.[67] Of course these 'concessions' reflected the relative strengths of the labour movements in these countries (by contrast with West Germany, for example) and undoubtedly they sometimes went further than the dominant class would have wished. Each nation experienced a unique combination of circumstances. In Britain, the experience of collective mobilization and widespread sacrifices brought about by modern total war, combined with the absence of military occupation, subsequent victory but economic weakening resulted in a landslide majority for the Labour Party, and gave to the British 'Welfare State' its unique ideology, one which persists in the British Labour movement to the present day. But this is not to deny that the policies of the 1945 Labour government should be seen primarily as (a culturally specific) part of the world wide 'post-war settlement' between capital and labour brought about by the changed international balance of class forces, and not as concessions forced from the state by militant working-class struggle.[68]

[66] Purdy, op. cit., pp. 24–9.

[67] Miliband, 1972, ch. 9; A. Calder, *The People's War*, London 1971.

[68] Glyn and Sutcliffe, op. cit., ch. 2.

The relative strength of the labour movements has increased *subsequently* over the years with experience of prolonged full employment. Not until the 1960s did the labour movements in the major European countries begin utilizing the bargaining power derived from full employment substantially to raise the share of wages in national income.[69] This in turn stimulated greater intervention by the state via incomes policies, planning, etc. 'High employment policy . . . was a product of the fear of the political repercussions of a repetition of the mass unemployment of the 1930s. Capitalist planning was, on the contrary, designed to deal with the economic, as much as the political, consequences of high employment policies after the Second World War.'[70] The changed balance of power on a world scale brought about a commitment to full employment and greater state intervention on the part of all capitalist states, (though, as noted above at different *tempos* in individual countries). This 'post-war settlement' has subsequently strengthened the bargaining power of labour vis-a-vis capital. The shift in the internal balance of power is therefore the *result* of the changed state policies, rather than their *cause*. The ultimate cause was the international outcome of the Second World War, product of the operation of the law of combined and uneven development. Some implications of this for a theory of crisis are investigated in section V.

## IV. Categories of State Expenditure

We shall now seek to apply the analysis of the capitalist state and capitalist world economy outlined in section III to explain the trends in state expenditure noted in section II. In general they can be viewed as the response of the state to the long-term trends within advanced capitalism, in combination with the international and internal balance of class forces. But to explain national differences and changes in the composition of expenditures we must first attempt to classify them.

O'Connor has provided the only serious and comprehensive Marxist attempt to categorize state expenditures, by allocating them to Marx's departments of production.[71] On this basis he discerns three categories:
1. '*Social investment* consists of projects and services that increase the productivity of a given amount of labour power and, other factors being equal, increase the rate of profit.' This is 'social constant capital'.
2. '*Social consumption* consists of projects and services that lower the reproduction costs of labour and, other factors being equal, increase the rate of profit.' This is 'social variable capital'.
3. '*Social expenses* consist of projects and services which are required to maintain social harmony'[72] (including here, rather oddly, warfare expenses).

It is apparent that these correspond to Marx's three departments, producing respectively the material elements of constant capital (means of

69 For a comparative survey, Glyn and Sutcliffe, ch. 4.
70 Warren, op. cit., pp. 3–4.
71 K. Marx, *Capital*, vol. II, 1967, pp. 406–15. O'Connor makes no direct reference to Marx's analysis, but it is apparent from his definitions.
72 O'Connor, p. 7. The language is extremely imprecise: 'labour power' should read 'labour' in category 1 and vice versa in category 2.

production), variable capital (wage goods) and luxuries. Hence social investment and social consumption expenditures are indirectly productive of surplus value whereas social expenses are not (this will be precisely demonstrated in section V below). O'Connor immediately notes the problems in actually classifying expenditures in this way, since 'nearly every state expenditure is part social investment, part social consumption, and part social expense'. However, he notes that in each case a 'preponderant set of social forces' determines the size and nature of that particular state intervention, and this enables us to classify the expenditure accordingly.[73] Certainly, only on rare occasions can one allocate any particular expenditure unambiguously to one department. Water or transport services, for example, are a means of production when utilized by industry, but consumption goods when utilized by households. Social security and health services are elements of variable capital when consumed by the productive workforce, but luxuries when consumed by the elderly or other unproductive groups (excepting children, who are the future workforce). Ultimately, there is no alternative to dividing each expenditure into the different categories on this basis, but this exercise is presently beyond us. The basis, however, will be not so much the forces instrumental in setting up the project etc., as a material input-output analysis of their predominant use-value.

In what follows we shall simply group expenditures very roughly into these three categories, according to what we estimate to be their predominant material characteristic, but no pretence at accuracy is made. In each we shall try to account for the trends and differences we have previously observed. No attempt will be made at an historical explanation for each country: that is something beyond the scope of this essay, yet ultimately nothing short of a concrete analysis of the development of each social formation will suffice. Instead we shall concentrate on the impact of the common elements discussed in section III on the state spending of the major OECD countries. We have already seen that certain trends are common to all; and this method also gives us some understanding of the national variations still observable. No more than that is claimed for it. We shall consider the three groups in reverse order, since this roughly corresponds to the historical sequence of their appearance.

### 1. Military and associated services

Included here are external services, the police and judiciary and interest on the National Debt. These are the classic functions of all states, not only capitalist but also, for example, feudal. Expenditure to meet them has risen (as a share of GNP) in the long term since the nineteenth century, reflecting the growing costs of expanding and later on protecting the interests of national capitals, and, since 1917, of capitalism as a world system. The major item here—military expenditure—is thus high by the standards of the past century, but as we have seen, has been falling in all countries since the war. This high 'peace-time' level reflects precisely the armed nature of this 'peace': the Cold War and the

[73] O'Connor, p. 105; also p. 7.

continual struggles for national liberation. The declining trend reflects the semi-successful détente with the Soviet bloc, the colonial withdrawal plus the move to other forms of imperialist domination, and other pressing claims on government expenditure. Another feature of this expenditure is the wide variation between countries. The dominant position of military spending in the US is to be expected given its world hegemony; the relatively high level in the UK, on the other hand, testifies to its past hegemony and the attempt until recently to pursue an 'international' policy beneficial to British finance capital. In both countries too the existence of large professional armies is expensive.

The high ratio of National Debt interest in the UK also derives from its past policy, both directly and indirectly via the higher domestic interest rates it entailed. Though these state interest payments are a financial transfer and not a claim on real resources, they do require additional taxation to finance them. Consequently, taxation equivalent to 10 per cent GNP is pre-empted in Britain (and the US) simply to finance military and debt, i.e. war-related, expenditures, thus considerably restricting these states' room for manoeuvre. This has led to calls for the other members of NATO to assume a more equal share of the burden, but so far this appears to have been unsuccessful (see Table 1, figures on growth rates in various countries). Expenditure on the police and judiciary is the only item in this category to have consistently increased since the war, at least in Britain (Table 2). This is a response both to the growing need for regulatory functions given the complexity of modern urban life (e.g. traffic control) and to the growing class and other antagonisms in these societies particularly since the mid-1960s. It is significant that in the UK, expenditure on police and prisons is planned to increase faster than average over the next five years.[74]

These then are the major items of state expenditure which can be categorized as luxury production: services entering neither directly nor indirectly into the value of labour power, but required because of the antagonistic nature of capitalism and all other forms of class society. Even here, however, there are problems of delimitation: some such services (e.g. law and order) may well be indirectly productive for capital. But a distinction must be drawn for the purpose of analysis between those state goods and services which provide a favourable framework for the operation of the capitalist sector and those which directly constitute its *inputs*.

## 2. The social services

By this term is meant state expenditure on income maintenance, education, health and welfare and certain aspects of housing. It covers several economic categories: direct spending on current goods and services (education, health), capital expenditure (municipal housing, schools), transfers (pensions, family allowances, student grants) and subsidies (on food, housing). It is also difficult to separate out their material characteristics, since a substantial proportion benefit the 'unproductive' members of society, indeed the Welfare State can be seen primarily as a

[74] *Public Expenditure to 1977–78*, Cmnd. 5519, 1973, Table 1.

redistribution within the working class as a whole from workers to dependents. However, the bulk of such expenditure clearly benefits those of working age or their children, whose cost of subsistence must be regarded as part of the value of labour power.[75] We shall demonstrate below that housewives are also indirectly productive for capital, so that services benefiting them should also be included here.

For these reasons, we analyse all social services as inputs into the production of labour power. The question which then arises is, why does the state collectively provide an increasing proportion of wage goods in every capitalist society today? The answer to this question, essentially querying the origin of the' Welfare State', is necessarily complex. Broadly it reflects the impacts of both sets of factors discussed in our previous analysis: the 'demands' of contemporary capitalism and the state of the class struggle. For the purposes of exposition, we shall analyse each in turn, before considering their interrelation.

## Social Needs under Capitalism

First, the role of the capitalist state in ensuring the adequate reproduction and maintenance of labour power, the *sine qua non* of capitalist production, has been apparent since the earliest Factory and Public Health Acts in Britain. Since then, the trend towards more wage-labour, greater urbanization, the geographical movement of the population and the break-up of the extended family have all intensified the need for collective provision against insecurity.[76] Furthermore, capitalist industrialization increases the sources of insecurity and dependence (for example, unemployment, industrial injury and disease) and necessitates the state provision of certain services to compensate the casualties for their suffering.[77] Sanitary conditions which would be acceptable in rural areas are a danger to public health in the towns. Wars have often provided a stimulus to these services, throwing light on the condition of recruits and social conditions generally, and raising fears about 'national efficiency'. The poverty of the working class revealed in the Boer War and the campaign for 'national physical efficiency' was instrumental in introducing school meals and medical inspection of school children in 1906 and 1907.[78] Of decisive importance in the twentieth century, of course, has been the state's active role in improving the *quality* of labour power, not only by means of education, but also via health services, housing policy, family allowances and other social policies. This has followed, first, the growing complexity of the production process and its need for skilled labourers, scientists, technologists, planners, administrators and so forth. And second, often overlooked, the growing complexity of all aspects of social life: everything from travel to filling in tax forms demands a greater degree of knowledge and adaptability.

[75] The most recent data on the UK is to be found in D. Wedderburn, ed., *Poverty, Inequality and Class Structure*, London 1974, chs. 2, 3.

[76] O'Connor, pp. 124–5.

[77] Titmuss, op. cit., chs. 5, 10, 11

[78] B. Gilbert, *The Evolution of National Insurance in Great Britain*, London 1966, chs. 2, 3; J. Hay, *The Origins of the Liberal Welfare Reforms 1906–1914*, London 1975. On the role of the two world wars see R. Titmuss, *Problems of Social Policy*, 1950; A. Peacock and D. Wiseman, *The Growth of Public Expenditure in the UK*, London 1961, Introduction and ch. 2.

Furthermore, many of these needs are complementary, so that developments in education for example lead to demands for improved housing or health.

Since the Second World War, there has occurred a dislocation of many aspects of social relations in the advanced capitalist countries, which has thrown new burdens on the state. To take just one example, there are in Britain today over one million children living with only one parent as a result of increasing marriage breakdown.[79] These new social needs reflect the great change in values and life-styles occasioned by the post-war boom.[80] Ultimately they are determined by the central contradiction within capitalist societies between the forces and relations of production. Within the framework of capitalism they can only be ameliorated by the wider penetration of the state into domains previously the exclusive preserve of the family.[81]

The reasons for greater *state* intervention are several. Partly it is essential in the nature of the service: some are collective or semi-collective goods which it pays no individual capitalist to supply since the benefits will be derived by his competitors (e.g. industrial training). Even then one must distinguish state *provision* and state *finance* of private providers. The latter maintains the capitalist sector, indeed by providing secure finance and an assured demand, often enhances its profitability. But this often leads to escalating costs, due both to fraud and private profit-taking and to the inefficiency and wastefulness of unregulated production. For this reason the state, representing the interests of capital as a class, may step in against the interests of that specific capital and provide the service directly at a lower cost (see section V below). An example of these alternatives is provided by a comparison of health services in the US and UK. In the US a part-private service is increasingly funded by the Federal government: it provides a poorer service at much greater cost than the centralized National Health Service in the UK. The extent to which this will result in a growing state intervention and expenditure will depend on the relation of class forces and the nature of the state: in particular the extent to which the parties, the executive and the administration can act in the interest of the class as a whole, and how far the state (in particular the legislature) is susceptible to pressure groups representing the interests of specific sections of capital.[82] We would expect it to be greater in centralized states, such as Britain or France, than in Federal states like the US. Even in the former, however, powerful interests, such as the pensions lobby in the UK, can prevent any serious inroads by the state. These account for some of the international differences we observe, but everywhere the process of the socialization of production results in a growth of social expenditure.

### Role of Labour Movements

The second factor in this trend has been the effect of the 'post-war

[79] *Report of the Committee on One-Parent Families*, 1974.

[80] E. Hobsbawm speculates on the effects of the post-war boom on consumption patterns and popular culture in *Industry and Empire*, Harmondsworth 1969, pp. 164, 281–4.

[81] See E. Wilson, *Women and the Welfare State*, London 1974, p. 27.

[82] O'Connor, op. cit., ch. 3.

settlement' between capital and labour in the wake of the Second World War and the balance of class forces since then. Since the last century the threat of popular discontent and mass struggle has led to important social concessions being made—for example unemployment insurance in the UK in 1911.[83] At other times, social policies have been introduced by forward looking representatives of the dominant class to head off anticipated revolutionary demands. Many in Edwardian Britain were impressed by the success of the Bismarck model, among them Churchill, Chamberlain, Lloyd George and Balfour.[84] This was particularly important in the reform of the 1940s: it must be remembered that the Beveridge Report, the White Paper on Full Employment and the Butler Education Act were all drawn up during war-time by a Coalition government. They were consciously seen as a necessary part of the war effort by integrating all classes and alleviating discontent.[85] The need to secure working-class co-operation in rebuilding capitalism in the war-devastated countries of Europe led to the introduction of similar policies.

This however is not to deny the role of particular labour movements in extracting significant concessions from the state, over and above what it would wish to have granted. The relationship of class forces in Britain and the war-time radicalization must account for certain of the post-war social legislation: in particular the National Health Service and the comprehensive coverage of the National Insurance scheme.[86] Since then the social services have increasingly been viewed by labour movements as an integral part of wages, to be defended and increased in the same way as money wages. They are a *social wage* provided collectively by the state or some other body. There is an important difference here between countries relying on state vis-a-vis occupational provision. Many of the social security benefits in the EEC are provided by industry-wide semi-autonomous bodies with whom trade unions can directly negotiate, whereas in the UK, despite the growing importance of occupational pension schemes, it is via its political relation with the state that the TUC and the labour movement exerts pressure.[87] But whatever the administration of the scheme, the strength of working-class pressure can roughly be gauged by the *comprehensiveness* and the *level* of the social benefits. The partial, haphazard and extremely unequal system of benefits in the US reveals the *relative* lack of power of its labour movement (and the absence of a party based on the trade unions) as much as the Federal nature of its state. On the other hand, the marked improvement in recent years reveals that both factors are changing.

Having established the role of these two major determinants of social policy, it is essential to point out that their interrelation in any particular policy decision is complex. For example, the original pressure for free secondary education for all in Britain undoubtedly originated in

[83] Gilbert, op. cit., chs. 1, 5; Hay, op. cit., pp. 47–54.
[84] In 1895 Balfour declared: 'Social legislation is not merely to be distinguished from Socialist legislation, but it is its most direct opposite and its most effective antidote.' Quoted in V. George and P. Wilding, 'Social values, social class and social policy', *Social and Economic Administration*, vol. 6, no. 3, 1972.
[85] Calder, op. cit., pp. 607–29.
[86] Wedderburn, op. cit., pp. 142–3.
[87] See for example T. Lynes, *French Pensions*, London 1967.

the labour movement and among progressive educationalists. But what Maynard and Miliband call the 'bias of the system' ensured that these pressures were modified and deflected to suit the interests of the capitalist class. The tripartite system was consolidated and the raising of the school-leaving age repeatedly postponed until 1973.[88] This bias operates in many ways even after legislation has been passed: its administration always offers great scope for discretion, benefits can fail to be adjusted for inflation, above all, the state determines what finance is available. At certain conjunctures the interests of the dominant and dominated classes appear to converge, as for example with the expansion of higher education throughout the capitalist world in the 1960s. But even then the 'class alliance' is a temporary one based on quite different goals and quickly dissipates. Another development is for the state to use certain social policies as a *quid pro quo* for wage restraint —the most open expression of this strategy being the present Labour government's 'Social Contract'.

So the interaction of long-term socio-economic trends, the political strategy of the capitalist state and the ongoing class struggle rule out any simple, single-factor explanation of social policies. Above all, it is essential to distinguish their concrete historical *origins* from the ongoing *function* they play within that particular social formation. Social policies originally the product of class struggle will, in the absence of further struggle, be absorbed and adapted to benefit the interests of the dominant classes. On the other hand, whatever their particular function for capital at any time, the fact that social services are also an integral part of the real wage level of the working class means that they are fought for in much the same way as money wages, in economic and political class struggle.

### Escalating Costs

Once established, two important forces at work increase the *costs* of providing a given level of service or set of benefits over time. The first is the 'relative price effect': the tendency already noted for the costs of state services to rise faster than average. Though this is in part due to the 'technical' problems in raising productivity in the service sector, it is undoubtedly exacerbated in the case of state services by the absence of competitive pressure to reduce costs. The second has been the tendency for the dependent population to expand as a proportion of the total, raising the demand for many social services—from maternity allowances to geriatric services. In every OECD country without exception, for instance, the share of the elderly rose from 1955–69. This has given a powerful impetus to expenditure on social security benefits and education in particular.[89] Population structure is not determined by socio-economic structure,[90] but these trends have constituted an im-

[88] D. Rubinstein and B. Simon, *The Evolution of the Comprehensive School 1926–1972*, London 1973.

[89] OECD, 1972, Tables A11, A12.

[90] But neither are they entirely unrelated: the low inter-war birth rate which stemmed from the depressed economic conditions is an important factor accounting for the low proportion of adults of working age since the war. J. Thompson, 'The growth of population to the end of the century', *Social Trends no. 1*, 1970. G. Hawthorn ('Pop-

portant parameter for the last two decades and they will continue for at least another decade. These two factors account for much of the increase in social expenditure—but not all. The OECD concluded: 'These factors explain only part of the changes and inter-country differences observed. In most of the Common Market countries social security provisions in the fields of minimum old age pensions, survivor allowances, finance or direct provision of medical services, medical provisions and income maintenance of the disabled have been improved considerably in substance and coverage.'[91] The growth of social expenditure is due to growing needs and costs *and* to real improvements in services.

### 3. Infrastructure services and economic aid

Collected together in this category are those expenditures which either (a) finance state provided means of production, or (b) directly assist private profitability and accumulation. The first group can be further divided into infrastructure expenditures and public corporation investment.

State expenditure on social infrastructure — posts, roads, water and sewerage, industrial estates, environmental and pollution control services, urban renewal etc.—is increasing in all countries. This is predominantly a response to the increasing scale and concentration of economic activity, to the accompanying urbanization and to the effect of the 'cumulative causation' mechanism on the growth and decline of regions.[92] Many of these services are collective or quasi-collective, that is they cannot be sold in discrete units to individual purchasers, and so must be provided by the state or a semi-autonomous state body. Furthermore many such expenditures are large-scale and indivisible, requiring large sums of risk capital (e.g. the development of water supplies)—another reason for state provision or state aid to private providers. Lastly, the 'highway lobby' has clearly been important, at least in the US, in securing ever-growing road-development plans. In all, much of this is 'complementary' investment: whenever private development takes place a whole range of public infra-structure services must be provided in order for it to function. But here too the initiative of the state manifests itself, for increasingly governments are using this social investment as part of physical planning or regional policy to help determine the location of economic activity rather than passively react to it.[93] Of course, all these services are also utilized directly by households, which relates them to the social services as elements of variable capital, and some, such as pollution control, may be regarded as an unavoidable expense of private production and thus akin to luxury expenditures. But the absolute dependence of private production on transport, water supplies, waste disposal etc., is testified by

ulation policy: a modern delusion', *Fabian Tract* 418, 1973) discusses the effects of economic conditions on the birth rate.

[91] OECD, 1972, p. 77. It is far more difficult to assess whether they kept pace with the growing *needs* per head of the population.

[92] For the analysis of the latter, see G. Myrdal, *Economic Theory and Underdeveloped Regions*, London 1963, chs. 2, 3.

[93] J. Cullingworth, *Problems of an Urban Society*, vol. 1, London 1972.

their use of it; for example industry and agriculture consume over three quarters of the US water supply, and private consumers less than a quarter. In Japan, two thirds of public investment is in 'industry support services'.[94] It is for this reason that these expenditures are best analysed as the costs of social constant capital.

The nationalized industry sector differs from social infrastructure in that it produces commodities for sale: non-collective goods and services, which *could* be produced by capitalist enterprise. The degree of public ownership varies between the major capitalist nations, from the US at one extreme to perhaps Italy (with the IRI and ENI) at the other, but in many countries rail and air transport, communication, coal, gas and electricity are now part of the public sector.[95] These commodities are distinguished materially from many others by their character as *basic inputs*, that is goods and services which enter into the production of every other commodity. The role of many nationalized industries is to provide these basic inputs as cheaply as possible, thus aiding each national capital in its competition with other capitals. If the resulting deficits are financed from general taxation the cost is passed on to the working population whilst the benefits are reaped by the capitalist sector. But once again, we must distinguish the ongoing functions of any state activity from its origins. In the case of nationalization, several factors led to its extension in particular during the inter-war period and after the Second World War. Several basic industries such as railways and coal-mining were for various reasons unprofitable, yet their essential nature meant that state subsidy or control was necessary in the interests of the national capital as a whole. Generous compensation payments meant that the previous owners often benefited from nationalization. Last, and very important, social democratic governments were pressured from below to include some nationalization schemes in their legislation.[96] These factors explain the virtual absence of nationalization in the USA: its economy emerged from the war strong and physically undamaged, there was no party organizationally based on the labour movement and the Federal system precluded, except at times of crisis such as the New Deal, the state independently initiating policies opposed to the interests of powerful sections of capital.

Public corporations are in most capitalist countries semi-autonomous bodies, typically relying on trading income to finance their operations, with or without generating a surplus. But capital expenditure is normally under the control of and partially financed by central government, and it is this item which is included in our wider definition of state expenditure. The growth of this expenditure will clearly depend on investment policies in fuel, transport and other areas, and on any increase or contraction in the nationalized sector as a whole. For these reasons no clear trend is evident in this item. In the UK, public corporation investment has fluctuated little below one fifth of total investment since the war, but since 1968 it has declined year by year, partly as a

94 O'Connor, p. 175; J. Fujiwara, 'Japan: the end of the miracle', *Inprecor*, 16–17, January 1975, p. 41.

95 A. Shonfield, *Modern Capitalism*, London 1965; O'Connor, ch. 7.

96 Miliband, 1969, pp. 107–9.

result of government financial and price-restraint policies.[97] Trends in other countries will depend on the scope of the public sector: in France, where one half of the car industry is under public control, it is more dynamic than in West Germany. The Italian state holding companies of IRI and ENI permit greater flexibility and expansion of productive state investment, but in many ways this is more akin to state subsidized private activity, the third area of expenditure to which we now turn.

### State and Private Capital

State aid to private industry takes many forms and has grown apace particularly in the post-war period. Certain activities here are similar to infra-structure expenditures, for example state research and development work, employment services etc. These constitute direct inputs to firms and reflect partly the increased scale and technical advance of production, necessitating state financial aid even for some of the largest corporations in the world. But another form of state aid is perhaps of greater importance: these are a whole range of financial transfers to firms to raise profits and/or private investment. Examples include investment grants and other incentives, capital transfers, export incentives, subsidies to agriculture and declining industries, etc.,—the range of mechanisms by which the state acts as the 'guarantor of monopoly profits.'[98] These benefits must not be separated from the effects of the tax system, which can also aid profits and investment in many ways: a corporation-tax allowance can have the same effect for the firm as an investment grant, but will not figure as an increase in state expenditure. In some countries, such as the UK and Japan, pension funds are an important source of investment capital for industry, but are increasingly subject to state control. Thus state requirements that all workers belong to an approved pension scheme in effect raises the rate of 'forced savings' from the working class in a way no different to a rise in social security contributions, but again they will not figure in statistics on state revenue and expenditure.[99] Lastly, the state's role as purchaser of goods (notably armaments) produced in the capitalist sector gives it great scope to aid private profitability. It can offer guaranteed profit mark-ups to the supplying industries, give generous allowances for research and development costs (themselves often financed by the state), discriminate in favour of domestic concerns and in many other ways indirectly boost private profitability and capital accumulation.[100]

For these and other reasons it is exceedingly difficult to quantify the amount of state financial aid to the capitalist sector. Different states rely on different methods. The immense government orders for the products of US industry, for example, permit the US state to channel public money to the private sector without the aid of special institutions such as the IRC (and now the NEB) in Britain. But in all countries such aid is undoubtedly large and increasing, particularly over the last

97 B. Sutcliffe, 'Britain: free fall', *Inprecor* 16–17, p. 18.
98 Mandel, *Marxist Economic Theory*, op. cit., pp. 501–7.
99 This was the purpose of the Conservative government's proposed State Reserve Pension scheme—see *The Economist*, 11 May 1974, p. 85. On Japan: Fujiwara, p. 41.
100 Baran and Sweezy, ch. 7.

decade. This has predominantly been caused by the decline in the rate of profit in many capitalist countries over this period, resulting from the raised tempo of the class struggle and intensifying competition between the capitalist economies. As a result, France is now subsidizing the Citröen car firm, Japan is subsidizing its ship-building industry and the UK is setting up the National Enterprise Board.[101] When capitalist enterprises are unable to retain sufficient of their earnings to permit further capital accumulation, they must look to the state to supply these funds. The result is the complex series of arrangements by which the capitalist state today taxes money from the working class and transfers it to profits. The battle over the burden of taxation and the composition of state expenditure is now as much a part of the class struggle as the ongoing battle over wages.

We have attempted above to categorize state expenditures according to their use-value in the productive process and to explain the variations in their size and the trends in their growth. The single most important conclusion which emerges is that an increasing proportion of the total (constituting therefore a fast-growing share of GNP) are *productive* expenditures, producing inputs for the capitalist sector. The share of social services, infrastructure and accumulation expenditure is growing whilst that of unproductive luxury expenditure is declining. *It is quite wrong therefore to regard the growth of the state as an unproductive 'burden' upon the capitalist sector: more and more it is a necessary precondition for private capital accumulation.* The implications and further contradictions of this growth will be considered in section V below.

Lastly, it should be noted that we have adopted a disaggregated approach in explaining this growth. But this does not mean that the state exerts no control over expenditure *in toto*. On the contrary, the very size of the state sector necessitates an overall policy on state expenditure and taxation. During the 1950s this chiefly took the form of anti-cyclical policies, using the budget to raise or lower total demand and economic activity. But in the 1960s attention shifted to longer-term forward planning of public expenditure by national governments.[102] This was a response to the inefficiency of traditional stop-go methods of economic management and the shift towards greater state planning.[103] It signified a growing awareness of the long-run productive contribution of state expenditure and of the consequent inefficiency of using it in particular as a weapon of short-term demand management. As a result, most governments now frame plans for the major components of public expenditure three to five years ahead.

## V. State Expenditure and the Current Crisis

The essential characteristic of the current world capitalist crisis is a combination of rampant inflation and a decline or absolute fall in the rate of accumulation and economic growth; a combination accurately labelled 'slumpflation'. This crisis is *not* caused by the growth of state

[101] *Inprecor*, 16–17, pp. 37, 43.
[102] On the US, O'Connor, ch. 3; on the UK, P. Clayton, 'Accountability in government expenditure', *National Westminster Bank Review*, November 1971.
[103] Warren, op. cit., p. 4.

expenditure: it has far more fundamental roots. But the growing role of the state both reflects and exacerbates the present crisis. In order to elaborate on this interrelation, this section is divided into three parts: first, the view that this crisis is predominantly caused by the growth of state expenditure is criticized; second, the general nature and causes of the crisis are analysed; and third, the specific nature of the crisis of state expenditure in the UK is elaborated.

### Unproductive labour and the State

The theory that 'the growth of state expenditure must be seen as one of the key factors in an explanation of inflation' rests upon the assertion that all or the greater part of state employees are 'unproductive'.[104] It is not intended to discuss Marx's concept of productive and unproductive labour in detail here,[105] but some comments are necessary to rebut this theory. For Marx, all labour which produces a use-value and surplus-value is productive. State workers (excepting today those in nationalized industries) do not produce a commodity for exchange, hence do not produce surplus value (even though they perform surplus labour) and are therefore 'unproductive'. They are supported out of the surplus value produced in the capitalist sector and transferred to them by taxation. Hence the greater are their numbers, the less surplus value remains to expand capital accumulation in the 'productive' sector. Recently, however, it has been appreciated that not all production workers in the capitalist sector contribute to the reproduction and accumulation of capital: those in Marx's department III produce luxuries which do not enter as inputs into further rounds of production. A massive increase in armaments workers, for example, would lead to a contraction of capital accumulation in the economy as the material basis for further production is whittled away.[106] Whilst one cannot agree that arms workers, etc., are for this reason unproductive from Marx's viewpoint[107] (they still labour to produce surplus value for their employer), this material distinction between workers producing elements of constant and variable capital on the one hand, and luxuries on the other, is crucial. It holds the key to discovering the productive contributions of state workers.

Rowthorn has recently demonstrated that state education workers may contribute to relative increases in surplus value in a way materially

---

104 Yaffe, NLR 80, pp. 50–2.

105 See I. Gough, 'Marx's theory of productive and unproductive labour', NLR 76, 1972; J. Harrison, 'Productive and unproductive labour in Marx's political economy', CSEB Autumn 1973; P. Bullock, 'Defining productive labour for capital', CSEB Autumn 1974; I. Gough and J. Harrison, 'Unproductive labour and housework again', CSEB February 1975.

106 Gough, NLR 76, pp. 64–7 (following Blake); Bullock, op. cit. See Mandel, 1968, ch. 10 on contracted reproduction.

107 The view of Bullock and Yaffe. Excluding circulation workers, with whom we are not here concerned, we are left with four groups of labourers, each of which plays a different role in the production process (see Gough and Harrison, op cit. p. 7):

| | *Departments I and II* | *Department III* |
|---|---|---|
| Capitalist sector | 1 | 2 |
| Other sectors | 3 | 4 |

In our view it is preferable to specify each category separately rather than indulge in further debates on which group is 'really' productive.

identical to capitalist sector workers in departments I and II.[108] The mechanism is as follows. So long as the labour they perform exceeds the labour embodied in the wage goods they consume, state employees perform *surplus labour*.[109] However the taxes levied to pay teachers, etc., cover only their necessary, paid labour. In terms of embodied labour, there is a net flow from the state to the capitalist sector equivalent to their unpaid labour. 'Surplus labour performed in education may be transferred to the capitalist sector where it appears as surplus value, apparently originating there. In reality, however, this surplus value is merely the converted form of surplus labour performed outside of the capitalist sector.'[110] As a result, all state workers producing either components of the real wage, for example social services, or elements of constant capital, for example research and development work, are indirectly productive for capital. Thus increases in their productivity benefit the capitalist sector: taxes on capital can be reduced, or taxes on the working class, and hence their pre-tax wages, can be reduced. Either way post-tax profits rise. The labour-time to (directly or indirectly) maintain and reproduce labour power will have been lowered, and hence capital can appropriate more surplus labour.[111]

We arrive at an important conclusion: the growth of state employment and expenditure, much of which has been in social or 'economic' services, has undoubtedly contributed to the production of surplus value and profits in the capitalist sector. In this sense their growth is not antagonistic to private capital accumulation; on the contrary, it is increasingly a necessary prerequisite.[112] Nor is it *per se* inflationary. We have already criticized the view that state expenditures cannot be entirely financed from taxation and must necessarily involve inflationary borrowing. The recent growth of public sector deficits is a conjunctural phenomenon *following from* the present slumpflation, not precipitating it (see below).

### Growth of State Employment

On the other hand, Rowthorn does point out that growing public employment may inhibit capital accumulation in another way, by reducing the supply of labour available to the capitalist sector at times

---

[108] B. Rowthorn, 'Skilled labour in the Marxist system', CSEB Spring 1974. Also Gough and Harrison, op. cit.

[109] This is likely given the national determination of wage levels for a particular skill and norms on average intensity of labour.

[110] Rowthorn, CSEB 1974, p. 31.

[111] Capital as a whole will also benefit from state provision of department III services (e.g. police): it will pay only their necessary labour costs compared with full labour time cost if the service were provided by private capital. The crucial difference is that the labour expended in this department will not augment surplus value in further rounds of production.

[112] We have already mentioned the role of the Welfare State in buttressing the family. Since it has also been demonstrated that surplus labour performed by housewives can augment surplus value and profits in the capitalist sector, it would appear that state social services also aid capital accumulation in this way. (See J. Harrison, 'The political economy of housework', CSEB Winter 1973.) However the same competition over scarce labour applies—see below and Gough and Harrison, p. 5.

of full employment.[113] The continual expansion of such a low productivity, labour-intensive sector will in any case steadily reduce the remaining supply of labour, unless new sources, e.g., married women, continually replenish it. The alternative—of raising productivity in the state sector by means of speed-ups, performance targets, dilution of skills, etc.,—is increasingly tried but is unlikely to reduce its demand for labour appreciably. Does not this growing state service sector create an objective barrier to profitable accumulation of private capital? To answer this question it is necessary to divide state expenditure into transfer payments, purchases of goods and services from the capitalist sector, and the wages of state workers. We have already seen in section II that growing state transfers do not directly pre-empt resources available to the capitalist sector. State purchases of private output may well boost profits by providing secure, risk-free, high-profit markets for domestic firms. Only the last category of expenditure—wage payments for state employees—directly reduces the sphere of capitalist operations, though, in the case of indirectly productive workers, at the same time 'subsidizing' the capitalist sector. In the UK and probably elsewhere the share of the state sector in total 'value added' has risen since the war: over one quarter of the labour force is employed in the public sector. Now such a trend will clearly reduce the *share* of profits in national income *ceteris paribus*: if the profit share in the capitalist sector remains constant, but the relative size of this sector declines, this is inevitable. However this does not mean that the *rate* of profit will be reduced by this fact alone—it may even rise. If the rate of growth is substantial, then the absolute size of the capitalist sector and, *ceteris paribus*, of the mass of profits will also increase. A threat to capital accumulation will only materialize when either the rate of growth in the economy as a whole is low or the 'relative price effect' (the relative rate of cost inflation in the state sector) is high. In this situation a growing share of state GNP may be necessary simply to maintain standards of service, and an absolute decline in private production may be needed for them to improve.[114] The growth of the state sector will contribute, it is true, to a secular slowdown in the rate of growth, but this effect is attributable to the growing share of services in all advanced economies, and is not a problem specific to the state sector.

To conclude then, state transfers and purchases from the capitalist sector may well have a net beneficial effect on its demand and profit levels, whilst State services in departments I and II will indirectly augment surplus value and private profit. At the same time during an economic upswing state employment may exacerbate labour shortages which inhibit private production. The slower growth of productivity in the state sector will necessitate a steady transfer of labour from the capitalist sector, but while this will tend, *ceteris paribus*, to a declining share of profits in national income, the rate of profit need not be affected. Only where the national rate of productivity growth is so low and/or the rate of growth of state employment is high will taxes on the private sector reduce absolutely wages and profit levels and thus threaten accumulation and exacerbate inflation. But in this case, as we shall

[113] Rowthorn, CSEB 1974, pp. 35–6.

[114] See I. Gough, 'Inflation and social policy', in *The Yearbook of Social Policy*, ed. K. Jones, 1975.

argue below, these pressures reflect rather than cause the phenomenon of slumpflation.

## Political Consequences

This is not to argue of course that the interests of specific capitals are not threatened by a growth of state employment, or that there are no political consequences of the growth in state expenditure. The range of services performed by governments in advanced capitalist countries promises rich pickings to capitalist enterprises, whether health insurance companies, private schools or Securicor guards. We have already argued that the balance struck between direct state *provision* of a service, state finance of private provision or untrammelled private operation will depend on the balance of class forces and the political structure of each individual state. The above analysis demonstrates why the state, acting in the political interests of national capital as a whole, may decide to overrule the economic interests of specific capitals and directly provide certain services itself. The competitive position of that capitalist class may benefit in two ways: from the unpaid labour of state employees (whereas purchases from other capitalists would necessarily include a profit element), and from the greater rationalization of production which state provision often entails. For these reasons there is as yet no concerted campaign to dismantle the NHS in Britain. Nevertheless, at certain conjunctures there will be some who would argue in favour of greater private provision, especially in the social services. The development of such a 'social-industrial' complex, with wide government subsidies for private provision, may yet develop outside the USA.[115]

The growth of state expenditure *has* led to a marked political centralization within the modern capitalist state, as O'Connor has observed in the US. Trends such as the removal of functions from local government and its reorganization into large areas, greater control over its current expenditure, centralization of public sector debt management, the setting up of new unelected *ad hoc* bodies, the growth of regional planning institutions and the centralization of control over public expenditure within the executive: all these trends are observable within the UK as much as the US.[116] Many of these are responses to a profound crisis afflicting local government, squeezed between expanding services and fast growing costs on the one hand, and a static local revenue on the other. At both local and national level growing state expenditures have thus led to important shifts in the institutions and processes of bourgeois democracy.[117] But here, as in the economic sphere, they are reflections of more profound changes.

## The Current Crisis

It is not possible here to present a comprehensive account and analysis of the current crisis: instead we shall concentrate solely on what we

---

115 O'Connor, pp. 51–8.

116 See for example H. Page, 'Local government in decline', *Three Banks Review*, 90, 1971.

117 Warren, NLR 72, p. 29; O'Connor, ch. 3.

believe to be its key determinants. The inflationary crisis of the world capitalist economy is the cumulative result (a) of the changed balance of class forces on a world scale since the Second World War, and (b) of the uneven development of the capitalist nations since then. We shall deal with each of these in turn, since the fundamental cause is the heightened bargaining power (economically and politically) of the Western labour movements following a prolonged period of near full employment. The generation of inflation under these circumstances has been well analysed by Devine.[118] In brief, capitalists cannot prevent workers from obtaining money wage increases in excess of the rate of productivity growth and workers cannot prevent capitalists from raising prices. The result is chronic inflation. The growth of state expenditure superimposes on this fundamental conflict between capital and labour a further conflict which gives an added impetus to inflation. 'The competing claims of private consumption, investment, public provision, military expenditure, the foreign balance, have exceeded the availability of resources. Efforts to commandeer resources for one use, if not acquiesced in by those from whom the resources are to be taken, call forth responses designed to frustrate them which for the most part manifest themselves in higher prices. Thus, if the state increases direct taxation on personal incomes or indirect taxation, in order to increase social provision or to stimulate private investment via reductions in corporate taxation or to make room for a shift of resources into the balance of payments, workers will seek to offset the effect of this on their private consumption through higher money wages; if capitalists raise prices in order to raise profits to finance increased investment or if the terms of trade deteriorate and prices rise, workers will again seek to offset this through higher money wages; if workers obtain higher money wages, in order to offset increased taxes or increased prices or simply to assert their claim to a higher standard of living and a larger share of what is produced, they will commandeer a larger proportion of resources for private consumption than would otherwise be the case and the state or capitalists will seek to offset this through higher taxes or higher prices. Chronic inflation is the result of a situation in which available resources are insufficient to meet claims on them and claimants cannot be prevented from bidding—workers via higher money wages, capitalists via higher prices, the state via higher taxes or borrowing from the banking system.'[119]

This model of contemporary capitalism does not of course imply that the state is independent of capital; rather it is premised upon that relative autonomy that we emphasized in section III. Finally, against arguments that this theory puts the 'blame' for inflation on the working class, we may agree with Devine: 'It is unscientific to attempt to attribute "blame" or "responsibility" to different classes . . . . Inflation is a product of the capitalist *system* in its present stage of state monopoly capitalism.'[120]

Thus structural conflict within advanced capitalism explains the chronic inflation experienced since the Second World War. Together

[118] P. Devine, 'Inflation and Marxist theory', *Marxism Today*, March 1974.

[119] Ibid., pp. 85–6. Mandel and Warren suggest the same analysis in their recent debate, NLR 87–8, 1974.

[120] Devine, op. cit., p. 92.

with the growth of the power of labour movements and of state expenditure, it explains the acceleration of inflation in the late 1960s. But we have yet to discover the link between this and the current world recession. This has followed the steady decline in investment expenditure over each cycle since the early 1960s, so that in the 1970–73 cycle investment for the first time ever rose less rapidly than output in the OECD countries.[121] This followed the fundamental decline in profitability which occurred in several countries in the 1970s, itself a reflection of growing labour strength at a time of heightened international competition.[122] The fundamental factor determining whether capitalists will advance money capital and expand output is their view of the expected rate of profit. If the past rate of profit has been falling and if they hold a pessimistic assessment of the balance of class forces, then the rate of private investment will fall. This is precisely what has happened since 1973 in several major capitalist countries, and this defines the current inflationary recession as a qualitative crisis of capitalist production.

Of course, the separate nation states can intervene in this situation to boost the rate of investment. If the rate of exploitation is being reduced the state can indirectly raise it by reducing post-tax wages and funnelling the money back to the capitalist sector. The share of taxes paid by corporations was reduced in the OECD area between 1955 and 1969, and the burden of rising state expenditure shifted onto the working class by means of direct and indirect taxes. Direct state aid to private industry has also risen over the long term, but in 1974 it rose precipitately in many countries.[123] However this state aid will in turn fuel the rate of inflation. Given the balance of class forces a rise in taxes on wages or on goods and services will lead to higher, pre-emptive wage claims, whilst attempts to reduce the 'social wage', by means of cuts in state social spending, will also be resisted. As a result, in all major countries state borrowing and public sector deficits have mushroomed in 1974 and 1975.[124] (However the rising unemployment in all countries suggests this has not been sufficient to offset falling private investment and consumption.) The twin characters of the current crisis—rampant inflation and worldwide slump—thus both reflect the balance of class forces and the attempts of the state to help rectify the resulting contradictions.

## Uneven Development

But if this is the most general explanation of the current crisis, its particular national manifestations are circumscribed by the second factor: the operation of the 'law' of uneven development. The extent to which the class conflict results in inflation and/or pressure on profits will depend on the underlying strength of each economy. In the post-

[121] By less than 4 per cent and 4½ per cent respectively: J. Harrison, 'Capitalist crisis and economic recession', unpublished.
[122] See the analyses in *Inprecor*, 16–17, January 1975; by Wolf on Germany, p. 30, Valentin and Leucate on France, p. 36. For a comparative survey Glyn and Sutcliffe, op. cit., chs. 2, 3 and appendix G.
[123] *Inprecor*, 16–17, pp. 37, 43.
[124] *The Economist*, 15 March 1975, p. 77; 29 March 1975, p. 81; 5 April 1975, p. 65.

war epoch this uneven development has predominantly taken the form of differences in productivity growth and in the balance of payments. Capitalist states with high rates of growth and a strong payments position (such as Japan and West Germany) have been in the strongest position to reconcile conflicting claims on resources without incurring high rates of inflation. Weak countries, notably the UK, have much less room for manoeuvre. But these differences are in part determined once again by the relative strengths of the national labour movements: for example, their ability to resist redundancies, changes in work practices etc. The uneven strength of different economies is indicated by national data on profitability. Only in the US, Benelux and Italy did the rising share of wages in the 1950s and 1960s have the same adverse effect on profits as in the UK—elsewhere it did not even match the movement of the self-employed into wage employment.[125] The delay in recovery of the labour movements in Germany and Japan postponed any decline in profitability there till the 1970s.[126] The relative weakness of labour movements in several countries may permit the rate of exploitation to be raised in 1975 under the threat of high unemployment: in the US real wages have fallen for over two years in succession, current wage increases in Germany are down to 7 per cent, in France and Japan important public sector strikes have been defeated.[127] In all these countries the rate of inflation is being reduced, profitability restored and the basis laid for further expansion. Only in Italy and the UK among the major OECD countries is this not the case. The strength of the labour movement and the weakness of the economy are intimately related in both cases, though in Italy it is the moderation of the trade unions and the Communist Party on which the state mainly relies.[128] For this reason, one should strictly-speaking refer to a generalized *recession* of the international capitalist economy, but not of a generalized *crisis*. This term should be reserved for Britain, Italy and any other country where the balance of class forces prevents the rate of exploitation being raised and the dynamic of capitalist accumulation re-established, unless their labour movements are first seriously weakened.

However if there is not yet a generalized world economic crisis, the consequences of uneven development may already be laying the basis for one. One manifestation of this has been the decline of US hegemony (in the economic and political, if not the military, sphere), the growth of regional economic groupings, and the growing challenge of the EEC and Japan. Already these trends have severely dislocated the Bretton Woods international monetary system, and have hindered decisive leadership of the world capitalist economy.[129] A further consequence has been the synchronization of the world trade-cycle following the large US trade deficits and the wages explosions of the late 1960s. Instead of a boom in some countries offsetting a recession in others, all major OECD countries are now moving together and the

[125] Glyn and Sutcliffe, op. cit. appendix G.
[126] Ibid., pp. 98–9. For Germany see E. Altvater et al, 'On the analysis of imperialism in the metropolitan countries: the West German example', CSEB Spring 1974, pp. 6ff.
[127] *The Economist*, 29 March 1975, p. 81; 5 April 1975, pp. 64, 69, 80–2.
[128] *The Economist*, 29 March 1975, pp. 69–75
[129] E. Mandel, 'The generalized recession of the international capitalist economy', *Inprecor*, 16–17, pp. 13–14.

trade cycle is becoming dangerously destabilized.[130] This accounted for the commodity and oil price explosions during the 1971–73 boom, and this is now accounting for the severity of the 1974–75 slump. The consequent under-utilization of capital has been a further factor depressing profits and inhibiting investment. So the operation of the law of uneven development within the post-war context is creating fresh contradictions which will tax (but not necessarily defeat) the bourgeois political order in the coming years. But the underlying factor, and one which has thrown up an open economic and political crisis today in at least Britain and Italy, is the economic strength of the working class in the post-war epoch.

## State Expenditure and the British Crisis

The share of profits in Britain fell from 21 per cent in 1964 to 12 per cent in 1970 to 4 per cent in the second quarter of 1974, whilst the rate of pre-tax profit fell from 14 per cent to 10 per cent to 5 per cent.[131] The urgent necessity to raise the rate of exploitation has been clear to capital for several years. This is not the place to go into the alternative strategies adopted.[132] The victory of the 1974 Miners' strike and the election of a Labour government in this context represented a strategic defeat for the British state and the capitalist class. The attempt to restrain wages via the Social Contract is now in ruins. Britain has entered its most critical post-war crisis with the organizational and political strength of the working class at a new height and the bourgeois political order in a state of unprecedented disarray: indeed this combination defines the contemporary crisis in Britain. With this framework in mind let us now consider the economic and political role of state expenditure.

State expenditure continued to grow during the years of the 1970–74 Conservative government, but due to a recognition of the origins of the 1969–70 wages explosion and a need to reduce the rate of inflation, this was accompanied by a reduction in taxation. The fast growth in public expenditure projected in 1971 and 1972 was predominantly to reduce unemployment and raise investment and to restrain price rises by letting nationalized industry deficits grow.[133] But at the same time, as part of its general offensive against labour (the Industrial Relations Act, the 1972 pay freeze and stage 2), the government attempted to cut back the growth of social expenditure, notably via the Housing Finance Act and the cuts of £500 million and £1180 million in May and December 1973. Nevertheless the growth of social spending up to then was considerable and contributed to the unprecedented rise in real incomes from 1971–73. This attempt to stimulate the economy by means of public investment resulted in a rapid growth of the public sector borrowing requirement to over £4 billion in 1973. It is likely

[130] *The Economist*, 12 April 1975, pp. 79–80.

[131] The most recent survey is by A. Glyn, 'Notes on the profit squeeze', CSEB, February 1975.

[132] See A. Jones, 'The economic impasse of British imperialism', *Inter-Continental Press*, 5 August 1974; and J. Harrison, 'British capitalism in 1973 and 1974: the deepening crisis', CSEB Spring 1974.

[133] *White Papers on Public Expenditure*: Cmnd. 5178 (1972), p. 9; Cmnd. 5519 (1973), p. 7.

then that the government's attempts to combat inflation only led to its regeneration by another route. In the absence of any wholly successful reduction in real wages (via money wages and/or the 'social wage') this was inevitable.

But even this partial success was destroyed by the 1974 Miners' strike. The incoming Labour government extended social benefits as its part of the Social Contract with the trade union movement. The major elements here were food subsidies, the freeze on rents and pension increases,[134] although the cuts in health and education spending were not restored. Grants to local authorities were raised to offset rate increases. Militant action among public sector workers, traditionally low paid and less under the control of union bureaucracies, gained large wage rises and further raised public expenditure.[135] With the sudden onset of the international recession the government intervened to channel aid towards the capitalist sector by reducing payments of corporation tax, relaxing price controls, setting up the National Enterprise Board, etc. All this has resulted, in a massive growth in public expenditure to £54 billion in 1975–76 equivalent to 60 per cent of GNP. Despite the operation of 'fiscal drag' this has opened up an enormous public sector borrowing requirement equal to 10 per cent of GNP.[136]

Budget deficits of this size are not of themselves inflationary in a deep recession. Measured in terms of its effect on aggregate demand the public sector deficit has risen from 9 per cent of GNP in 1971 to 12 per cent following the November 1974 Budget. 'In real terms the budget is not increasing the pressure on real resources in the economy—a fact which is in any case obvious from the unemployment figures.'[137] On the contrary, the first Labour Budget in March 1974 was savagely deflationary. In any case large public sector deficits are inevitable at the present time given the large oil deficit in the balance of payments of most OECD countries. The inability of the corporate sector to run a financial deficit for any length of time (the November 1974 Budget in the UK was designed to correct this) means that balance of payments deficits must be offset by government deficits if the economy is not to move into a cumulative recession.[138] This is further revealed by the low rate of increase of the money supply at the present time: in the UK at a rate less than half that of price increases. As the National Institute remarked, the budget deficits 'do however *reflect* the serious problems of inflation and the balance of payments situation—but we think these problems have other causes.'[139] The basic cause is the underlying balance of class forces in Britain and the inability of the Labour government so far decisively to challenge the trade union movement. Given the need to channel aid to the capitalist sector to prevent a total

[134] See Gough, *Inflation and social policy*, op. cit., for a detailed study.
[135] The *National Institute Economic Review* (February 1975, p. 16) calculates that this added £400–700m to public expenditure in 1974–75.
[136] £7½ billion in 1974–75 and £9 billion in 1975–76. *The Economist*, 19 April 1975, p. 80 ff.
[137] NIER February 1975, pp. 14–15. This was before the big upward revision revealed in the April Budget.
[138] NIER February 1975, p. 15. For a good general analysis see D. Kern, 'Public sector deficits', *National Westminster Bank Review*, May 1974.
[139] NIER, ibid., p. 15.

collapse of investment, to maintain public investment, to raise certain social benefits as part of the Social Contract, and to avoid any further increases in taxation for fear of their repercussions on inflation and profitability, the result is inevitably a growing gap between state expenditure and revenue. The present Budget deficit passively reflects the alignment of class forces which have generated the current inflationary crisis: it is not itself an active cause of that crisis.

## The Struggle over Social Expenditure

The only solution for the capitalist class and for the state representing its political interests, is a decisive rise in the rate of exploitation. This would permit a reduction in the rate of inflation, a rise in profit expectations and would release resources for investment and exports. To achieve this two separate strategies are identifiable, though in practice both are normally used in combination. The first is some form of wages freeze, which would directly achieve the three objectives above. The second is to deliberately allow unemployment to rise in order to indirectly bring down the rate of wage increases, though the unemployment level necessary would probably need to be extremely high by post-war standards. To achieve this without fuelling inflation, large cuts in public expenditure would be essential. Within the total of public spending, aid to private capital would need to be maintained and cuts in military spending, though they cannot be ruled out, would not suffice. The burden would necessarily be borne by the social services, and this for two reasons. First, they constitute the most dynamic area of state expenditure. Second, they comprise the 'social wage' of the working class, and a cut in this would be interpreted by capitalists at home and abroad as a deliberate government decision to reduce living standards and raise the rate of exploitation. An integral component of this second strategy would therefore be an attack on social expenditure. In fact, this has already begun with a sharp cutback in planned local authority expenditure announced in early 1975.[140] But this 'crisis of social expenditure' has no autonomous dynamic: it is an element of the general crisis analysed above.

There are then powerful pressures on the British state to raise the rate of exploitation and thus permit the extended reproduction of capital. But of course precisely what *defines* the crisis is the powerful opposition of contradictory pressures: the ability and determination of the working class to resist such a rise.[141] This is not the place to analyse the strengths and weaknesses of the British labour movement: its tremendous economic power is intimately related to its reformism and economism. What is clear is that any attempt to impose a wage freeze or substantial unemployment will be vigorously resisted. However the specific strength of opposition to any cuts in social expenditure should be noted, for the growth in the numbers of state employees has itself created a new force within the working class of all advanced capitalist countries. The organization of public sector workers has proceeded apace in recent

---

[140] *Public Expenditure to 1978–79*, Cmnd. 5879, 1975, p. 9 and the Chancellor's April Budget statement, *The Economist*, 19 April 1975, p. 11.
[141] J. Harrison, 1975, unpublished.

years; and it is likely that the rate of pay rises they have obtained have exceeded those in the private sector. Perhaps more important, state employees by the very nature of their employment tend to inject qualitative, political issues into their struggle to protect and improve their terms and conditions of service.[142] Thus in the UK the public sector union NUPE has been to the forefront in the attempt to end private pay beds within the NHS. This is related to the traditional autonomy enjoyed by certain professions, for example doctors, lecturers and social workers. Questions of the content of education, the aims of social work, the structure of medical practice are increasingly fused with day-to-day trade-union struggle within the State sector. Other factors at work here include the growing relation with organizations of state clients (claimants unions, education pressure groups), the direct political control periodically exercised by governments over public sector pay levels, and the weaker control of the trade union bureaucracy over some of these newly organized groups. These forces mean that public sector workers will form an increasingly important and effective bloc opposing cuts in social expenditure as a solution to the contemporary crisis in the UK. At the same time, the increasing recognition of the importance of the social services within the real wage has prompted other sections of workers to take action in their defence. In 1974 miners in the Yorkshire coalfields struck in support of an increase in nurses' pay, in order to protect the NHS. These actions have been echoed at the base of the Labour Party, the most notable struggle being the long-standing refusal of the councillors at Clay Cross to implement the Housing Finance Act. To summarize then, the forces opposed to cutbacks in social expenditure as a solution to the British crisis would appear to be gaining strength over time.

If our analysis of the current crisis in Britain is correct, we cannot at the time of writing predict its outcome. Though at some stage there will be a decisive test of strength, it is possible that beforehand state policies will contain simultaneously concessions to the labour movement plus attempts to weaken it. The political reflection of these conflicts will have a semi-autonomous impact on their outcome. The crisis will impose tremendous strains on the Labour government, caught as it is between the contradictory need to raise living standards in order to maintain credibility with its political base, and the need to lower them in order to work towards solving the crisis. The crisis of social expenditure will exacerbate this fundamental contradiction, for a distinguishing feature of social democratic reformism since the war has been the Welfare State itself: the offer of social reforms and services in exchange for a certain measure of trade union co-operation with the state. At the present time this *quid pro quo* is institutionally enshrined in the Social Contract. The depth of the British crisis probably requires the simultaneous adoption of wage controls, deflation and cuts in social expenditure: all of which will precipitate an internal crisis within British social democracy. The outcome will thus depend not only on the reaction of the working class in mass struggle, but also on the political reflection of these conflicts. The outcome of the current crisis, no less than its origins, turns on the total *class* struggle: a fusion of economic, political and ideological struggle.

[142] For a fruitful discussion see O'Connor, op. cit., ch. 9.

# [12]

# THE WELFARE STATE: A SELF-INFLICTED CRISIS?

RUDOLF KLEIN

If I had sat down to write this article 20 or even 10 years ago, and taken as my theme the development of Britain's Welfare State, the result would almost certainly have been the celebration of a national achievement. Naturally I would have qualified my enthusiasm with a few criticisms, but I do not think that I would have had any fundamental doubts about the appropriateness of the underlying structure and policies. Today, it seems mildly eccentric to suggest even two cheers for the Welfare State. Its natural allies on the Left have made an industry of analysing its shortcomings: in particular, there is disillusion because poverty, far from having been eradicated, appears to be as prevalent as ever. Its natural critics on the Right are in the ascendant: there is widespread acceptance of the argument that welfare spending is parasitic on the economy, threatening the prospects of resumed growth. This assumption is not only embodied in the public expenditure policies of the present Conservative Administration but was already reflected in those of the previous Labour Government.

One possible reaction to both the disillusionment and the criticism is to point out that much of it is exaggerated or misplaced. The National Health Service may indeed be shabby and threadbare by the standards of many advanced industrial countries. But, then, Britain is a poor nation by the standards of these same countries, and it is hardly surprising that her public services mirror this fact; additionally, it can be argued that the NHS remains the best instrument yet devised for rationing inadequate resources equitably. Poverty, as it was defined in absolute terms when the Welfare State was created in the post-war era, has virtually disappeared.[1] When people lament the persistence of poverty, they are mostly talking about the persistence of inequalities in incomes—an equally important, but very different, issue. Moreover, Britain devotes a smaller proportion of her national income to welfare expenditure than such successful and virtuous economies as Germany, Sweden

* The author is Professor of Social Policy at the University of Bath.

[1] G. C. Fiegehen, P. S. Lansley and A. D. Smith, *Poverty and Progress in Britain 1953–1973* (Cambridge University Press, Cambridge, 1977).

and the Netherlands.[2] So there is clearly no simple, causal link between high welfare spending and poor economic performance.

The case for the defence is therefore strong. But proclaiming the very real achievements of the Welfare State is not necessarily enlightening in trying to think about the future evolution of policy. Nor does it really help, in the present climate of opinion, to produce a shopping list of things that ought to be done to remedy the gaps in welfare provision. My purpose in this article is therefore to try to tease out the reasons for the disillusion and criticism: to identify the likely constraints on social policy in the coming decade. In doing so, I shall suggest that the disillusion of the Left is largely self-inflicted: it rests on an inadequate analysis of the political and economic framework of social policy. Similarly, I will try to show that the criticisms of the Right, while based on a more realistic assessment of the political and economic framework, contain some wrong-headed assumptions.

## The Politics of Social Policy

Social policy is about coercion. Its very essence lies in compelling people to do what they would otherwise not do, either for their own good or for what is conceived to be the good of society as a whole. Thus people may be compelled to go to prison or to mental hospital. More centrally to my argument, social policy involves parting people from their money through the tax system. If we are interested in the Welfare State, we are therefore necessarily concerned about the political and economic factors which either facilitate or hinder the use of coercion by the State.

In the context of a debate about the role of the State, this might seem a fairly trite remark. In the context of the British debate about social policy over the past decades, however, it is likely to raise some eyebrows. For the British tradition of social policy has been conspicuously strong on prescription but short on any theory of power: significantly one of Richard Titmuss's most popular books [3] was devoted to the central role of altruism in social policy. Yet a framework of State coercion may well be a necessary condition for encouraging altruism: even if we are altruistically inclined, even if we are ready to see a part of our income transferred to the elderly, the disabled and the sick, we are more likely to do so if we know

[2] OECD, *Public Expenditure Trends* (OECD, Paris, 1978).

[3] Richard M. Titmuss, *The Gift Relationship* (George Allen & Unwin, London, 1970). For a highly relevant discussion, see also David Collard, *Altruism and Economy* (Martin Robertson, London, 1978).

that others will not be "free riders"—exploiting our good impulses by not contributing. In other words, altruism may grease the wheels of social policy but it is no substitute for a machinery of coercion.

It is the failure to appreciate this simple but central point which explains, I think, the widespread disillusion with the achievements of the Welfare State. Let me illustrate this by looking at the debate about poverty. As already pointed out, this is a debate essentially about inequalities of income (and opportunity). But as soon as we define it in these terms, it becomes apparent that when we ask why inequalities have persisted so stubbornly, we are asking why it is politically so difficult to re-distribute income: a question not about the design of specific social policies but about the political feasibility of achieving certain policy aims.

In defining the problem in this way, I am of course echoing the Marxists.[4] Their analysis is simple: given the inequalities in the distribution of power within a capitalist society, it follows that inequalities of income will be perpetuated. But while I share their "political economy" approach to the analysis of the Welfare State, I draw very different conclusions. The paradox of the modern Welfare State, I would argue, is that it has become more difficult to make any further progress in achieving a more equal distribution of income precisely because both power and income have become more diffused: indeed if Britain were still a classic "capitalist" society, the task would be very much easier. Putting the same point more forcibly still, I would argue that the successful redistribution of power and income in itself creates the strongest impediment to further progress; and that it is precisely this fact which explains why not only Britain but other advanced industrial societies (Communist as well as capitalist) have found it so difficult to change the pattern in recent decades.

For, looking at the long-term evolution of income distribution, a seemingly odd phenomenon is noticeable. This is that the major shifts in income distribution took place *before* the major expansion of the Welfare State in Britain and elsewhere: over the past two decades rising welfare expenditure has failed to make much of a dent on the pattern of income inequalities. But this seemingly puzzling and perverse phenomenon makes a great deal of sense if we examine the politics of income distribution.

The distribution of incomes is, as is well known, diamond shaped. That is the bulk of incomes is concentrated around the middle.

[4] For the best Marxist analysis, see Ian Gough, *The Political Economy of the Welfare State* (Macmillan, London, 1979).

THE WELFARE STATE: A SELF-INFLICTED CRISIS?

The implication of this is that, as Welfare States expand, it becomes progressively difficult to finance extra expenditure by soaking the rich. It is easy enough to finance the first steps towards the Welfare State by increasing taxes on the well-to-do (however defined). But such a policy becomes progressively less feasible in a mature Welfare State. Similarly, in the early days of a Welfare State the benefits of spending tend to be concentrated selectively on the very poorest at the bottom of the diamond: a considerable income distribution impact can thus be achieved at a relatively low cost. But as the Welfare State becomes more universalised, so the cost of changing the distribution of income becomes higher. The paradox of the mature Welfare State is therefore that more people have to be coerced into paying higher taxes in order to make what will be inevitably less of an impact on the distribution of incomes. Hence the well-known downward creep of taxation: as public expenditure rises as a proportion of national income, so increasingly average and even below average wage-earners are drawn into the tax network.

At the same time, the task of coercion becomes more difficult. For when public expenditure starts to nudge up towards 50 per cent. of the national income (and when a high proportion of that expenditure is devoted to welfare policies in their widest sense), it is inevitable that Governments will come face to face with those organised interests in society whose members have to foot the bill: the trade unions. If income redistribution is difficult, it is not so much because we live in a capitalist society but because we live in a society with powerful trade unions—precisely because, to return to my earlier assertion, because power is diffused.

### The Collapse of the Social Contract

The point is illustrated by the experience of the Labour Government between 1974 and 1979. The Labour Government came to office committed to expanding the Welfare State and in fact did so by increasing pensions and taking other measures designed to change the redistribution of income in favour of the least-favoured sections of the population. The concept of the " social wage " (or " social contract ") was invented to justify such an approach: the idea that trade unionists would restrain their wage demands in return for improved welfare benefits and social services.

The policy, as we all know, collapsed in ruins—as did attempts to introduce similar policies in Norway, Sweden and the Netherlands. The unions insisted on maintaining their net-of-tax take-home-pay. The Government was forced to reverse its policies, and to offer tax *cuts* (which, in turn, implied expenditure reductions) in return for wage restraint. The " social wage " was not, in other words, perceived by union members as equivalent to money in their own pockets: they voted, in their wage bargaining, against a policy of redistribution to the elderly and others via the State. Further, they also voted, by their tactics, against the redistribution of income within the trade union ranks themselves: they fought to maintain traditional relativities as between different occupations, as had the miners in 1974. Attempts to change the distribution of income are, it seems, seen as threatening by a majority of the people—and, most importantly, by the best organised sections of the population. The rhetoric of soaking the rich does not persuade those who would really have to finance the expansion of the Welfare State, *i.e.* the unions, to pay up their inevitable share. As the results of the 1979 General Election showed, the backlash phenomenon is not limited to the middle classes.

One long-term implication of this is that those who are concerned about the future of the Welfare State should also be concerned about Britain's trade union movement. For there would appear to be two necessary conditions for even attempting to pursue a " social wage " strategy. First, there has to be a central trade union body capable of getting the agreement of all the member organisations. Secondly, within each union, the leadership must be able to carry its rank and file within it. In other words, there has to be both the organisational capacity and the leadership ability required to translate official commitment to such an approach into the bargaining arena. In the years after 1974, the Trades Union Congress made the commitment —but was unable to deliver the goods. And the Labour Government, consequently, came unstuck. Unless there are fundamental changes in the nature of Britain's trade-union movement, there would seem to be little point in trying to repeat the experiment of trying to solve the problem of financing higher welfare spending with the help of the TUC.

There is a further reason why those concerned about the problems of the mature Welfare State ought to be preoccupied with the role of the trade unions. The Welfare State is more than a metaphor. It is a set of institutions employing a large number of people: the NHS alone employs some 1,000,000 men and women. The Welfare State provides welfare not only for its nominal beneficiaries but also for those who work for it. Increasing expenditure on the Welfare State cannot therefore automatically be equated with increasing the amount of welfare provided to society: the distinction between

Welfare State and Welfare Society is crucial.[5] Rising spending may in part at least reflect the fact that, given the constituencies for the *status quo* represented by organised labour (whether the BMA or NUPE) it is extraordinarily difficult to liquidate existing, perhaps no longer relevant, commitments in order to meet new demands: that there is a built-in inertia, which means that all change tends to be additive. In short, organisational impediments to redistributing resources (whether geographically or by population groups) are built into the structure of the Welfare State.

All this underlines, I think, the inadequacy of what might be called the " moral " tradition of British social policy writing and thinking over the past few decades: it is a tradition which, by ignoring the political context of social policy, invites disillusion and a sense of betrayal. More dangerously, perhaps, the sense of betrayal can all too easily lead to a feeling that unless society as a whole is transformed, it will never be possible to pursue the ideal social policy. This, of course, is perfectly true in the trivial sense that in utopia it is possible to pursue utopian policy. But in practice the demands for fundamental change in the political and economic structure are often another way of saying that if the State's coercive powers were to be strengthened it would be easier to compel people (whether trade unionists or capitalists) to do what the moralists believe ought to be done. In thinking about the future evolution of social policy, it may therefore be more sensible to analyse further what might be called the " enabling conditions " which have allowed the Welfare State to expand over the past 30 years.

## Dividends of Economic Growth

The Welfare State is the residual beneficiary of the Growth State.[6] If there has been a steady expansion in both services and cash benefits, until recently, the reason is simple. Economic growth made it possible to finance improvements in the Welfare State while also permitting private consumption to increase: the dividends of economic growth could be shared out among various competing societal aims in an exercise from which everyone emerged as a winner—so easing the problem of coercion. The most successful Welfare States—such as Sweden's and Germany's—tended to develop precisely in those countries with the best growth record, while Britain predict-

[5] William A. Robson, *Welfare State and Welfare Society* (George Allen & Unwin, London, 1976).

[6] For an earlier elaboration of this point, see Rudolf Klein, *Inflation and Priorities* (Centre for Studies in Social Policy, London, 1975), p. 1.

ably began to discover that her social services and provision were falling behind those of other nations, in line with her economic performance. It is only in the last few years of worldwide stagflation that financing the Welfare State has become, particularly in no-growth economies like Britain's, a zero sum game. The need for political coercion, through the tax system, inevitably rises as economic growth declines.

Again, all this is reasonably self-evident.[7] Yet this very obvious insight has been massively neglected in the debate about social policy, except by the Right-wing critics of the Welfare State. Caricaturing only slightly, the industrial system has been seen as parasitical on the Welfare State by the Left while the Welfare State has been seen as parasitical on the industrial system by the Right. Specifically, the Left—and the central tradition of social policy thinking which found its inspiration in the works of Titmuss—tended to stress the damaging side-effects of economic growth: the fact that the Welfare State had to cope with the social dislocation, ill-health and the casualties generated by the industrial system. The Right, in contrast, tended to see the Welfare State as a burden on the industrial system: undermining incentives (whether directly through high social benefits or indirectly through taxation), weakening the work ethos and discouraging self-help.

It is difficult to avoid the conclusion that, in this debate, the Right at least asked the right questions—although, as I shall argue, it reached the wrong conclusions. Of course, the process of economic growth imposes considerable costs on society, for which the Welfare State often has to pick up the bill. This is why an increase in the GNP does not necessarily indicate an equivalent increase in national well-being: ironically, the costs of dealing with the disbenefits of economic growth may themselves help to swell the total national income. But assuming that economic growth has made at least some real improvements in welfare possible—such as higher living standards for old-age pensioners—it follows that those concerned about the Welfare State should also be concerned about its relationship with the industrial system in a positive sense: that they should be asking themselves to what extent social policies can contribute to economic growth.

In practice, social policies are largely and inevitably shaped by economic considerations. The principle of lesser eligibility—*i.e.* that

[7] For a cross-national discussion of the relationship between public expenditure and taxation, see Richard Rose and Guy Peters, *Can Government Go Bankrupt?* (Macmillan, London, 1978).

those receiving public support should be treated less generously than those in work—remains central to social policy, even though the 1834 Poor Law report is held out as an example of the heartless excesses of *laissez-faire* principles in most textbooks. The preoccupation with maintaining work incentives still dominates thinking about social policy, even though we have realised that the level of taxes may be as crucial as the level of benefits. Much of Welfare State expenditure also reflects direct economic priorities: for example, spending on education is often explicitly justified on the ground that Britain needs a well-trained labour force.

Unfortunately, those who perceive the Welfare State as an instrument of social justice above everything else find it difficult to proclaim the case for investment in social policy on grounds of economic and political expediency. The field therefore tends to be left wide open to those on the Right who argue that Welfare State spending is parasitical on the economy: a case which appears to have been largely accepted by the present Conservative Government.

Central to the case against Welfare State spending is the argument—put forward by Robert Bacon and Walter Eltis in one of the most influential books published in the last decade [8]—that the social services suck up the labour which would otherwise swell Britain's productive capacity. If Britain's economic performance has been poor, so runs the argument, it is because too many workers have been drawn into the "unproductive" public sector. This line of reasoning is based on some questionable figures and dubious assumptions. It is perfectly true that the numbers employed in the public sector have shot up sharply: but the figures usually given do not allow for the fact that many of those working in the public sector are part-time women—for whom the choice is often not between employment in the public sector and in the "productive" sector, but between employment in the public sector and staying at home. More crucially, perhaps, the assertion that the social services are "unproductive" needs to be challenged: as already argued, much of social expenditure can and should be seen as a necessary condition for maintaining the performance of the economy.

Further, the Bacon and Eltis type of reasoning confuses two quite different arguments. There is the argument that particular *kinds* of service are unproductive: in which case, they represent a waste of national resources, whether provided in the public or the private sector—yet those who support this line of reasoning rarely criticise

[8] Robert Bacon and Walter Eltis, *Britain's Economic Problem: Too Few Producers* (Macmillan, London, 1976).

the provision of social services (*e.g.* health) in the private sector. Alternatively, the services may be viewed as desirable in themselves, but it can be argued that problems of economic management may be caused by the difficulties of financing them in the public sector through taxation: a point which has more substance but which leads to the conclusion that such "unproductive" services actually ought to be encouraged, but within the private sector.

Lastly, it is worth stressing that the growth of the Welfare State manpower can—rather more plausibly—be seen as an attempt to fill the vacuum left by the failure of British industry. British industry is in trouble not because the State taxes away its profits in order to finance the Welfare State but because of its failure to make enough profits in the first place.[9] The Welfare State can therefore be seen as an essential instrument for making the consequences of economic decline socially and politically acceptable. The paradox would seem to be that it is the development of the Welfare State which has made it possible for successive Governments—Labour as well as Conservative—to pursue economic policies which, until recently, would have been seen as threatening to the entire social and political order.

A two-fold conclusion would seem to follow if this analysis is accepted. First, the role of the Welfare State in promoting economic growth should be recognised more explicitly when discussing specific policies: which might, for instance, suggest that more emphasis requires to be placed on encouraging mobility in housing policy (particularly local authority housing) and that the possibility of using NHS resources to give priority to active members of the labour force should be considered (which might be more sensible than protesting about the growth of the private sector, which fulfils precisely this function). Secondly, and more generally, it should not be left to the Right to stress the relationship between social and economic policies: here there would surely seem to be a case for stealing the clothes of the Right, but wearing them with a difference—and using their arguments to make out the case *for* the Welfare State.

## Implications of Stagnation

So far my analysis has implied that economic growth is still possible, and that renewed growth will once again be the solvent of conflicts about the distribution of incomes and national resources. This may, however, turn out to be a wildly optimistic assumption—and certainly would seem to be inappropriate in the present economic

[9] Mervyn A. King, "The United Kingdom Profits Crisis: Myth or Reality", *Economic Journal* (March 1975), p. 33.

climate. In thinking about the future of the Welfare State it is therefore essential to contemplate the possibility that the age of economic growth may be over. If I am right in my assertion that the Welfare State was largely the product of the Growth State, what would be the implications of the No-Growth State for the Welfare State?

One answer, in such circumstances, might be to see the Welfare State as a system for job-creation in a no-growth society: as I have suggested, it is this function which may already help to explain some recent developments. If there is permanent unemployment—fluctuating between one and two millions—the cost of creating jobs in the public sector diminishes: it effectively becomes the difference between the cost of unemployment benefits and the wages or salaries paid. But such an approach raises a crucial question. If the expansion of public sector jobs is not to create problems of finance (and, by definition, the problems of raising extra funds through the tax system become more acute in a no-growth economy), then it means that those jobs will have to be designed to employ unskilled, low-paid workers—*i.e.* those where the margin of income as between being in or out of work is lowest. In turn, this would mean a deliberate policy of designing social services which can be delivered by a large force of unskilled workers—a process of deskilling, thus reversing the trend of the past decades towards greater professionalisation.

This point illustrates what I take to be the main conclusion to be drawn from assuming that the era of economic growth is over. This is that we can no longer sensibly think about the future of the Welfare State by simply extrapolating from the past. If there is a crisis of the Welfare State it is self-inflicted to the extent that the reaction to a new situation has been to assume that we must demand more of what we have had in the past. The Welfare State should be seen not as an historic monument—to be defended at all costs—but as a set of institutions and policies which have to be adapted to changed circumstances. To conclude, let me therefore suggest three areas where we could be exploring the scope for change.

First, the conventional definition of Welfare State policies is far too rigid. As Titmuss pointed out a long time ago, a great deal of welfare is supplied by the market sector of the economy, *e.g.* through occupational pension schemes. But the tendency has been to see such developments as somehow second-best to State provision. This proposition is, to put it mildly, not self-evident—if (to pursue the example of occupational pensions) such problems as transferability and inflation-proofing can be dealt with. More neglected still, most analyses of the Welfare State leave out of account those governmental decisions whose costs are carried by the private sector: yet, looking to the future, it may be that the aims of public policy should be to internalise the social costs now generated by the private sector —by regulatory policies designed to improve health and safety at work or to reduce the amount of atmospheric pollution. Such measures are obviously not costless, but they do not have to be financed out of taxation. If we cannot manage politically to increase the budget of the NHS, we might yet be able to limit the demands on the service if only at the margins.

Secondly, and following on from this point, the demarcation line between the public and the private sectors is much too firm in another respect as well. One of the most interesting developments in the field of social care has been the growth of the " grey sector " [10]: smudging the usual distinction between paid and voluntary work, there has been the development of paid volunteers, such as child minders and foster parents. In future, welfare support could increasingly be provided by expanding this sector, rather than by a policy of simply extending the public services we have already got.

Thirdly, we should recognise that some of the existing institutions of the Welfare State may be becoming disfunctional in terms of organisational complexity and resistance to change. The task of administrative co-ordination—as the experience of the NHS shows—may be generating more costs than benefits. This might suggest experiments with new institutional patterns: for example, with the Yugoslav model (echoes of G. D. H. Cole) of services run by co-operatives of producers who negotiate both the financial costs and the level of provision with co-operatives of consumers—the creation of a kind of social market, as it were.

Any movement in these directions would mean abandoning some of the aims of the founding fathers of the Welfare State. It would imply a less tidy system, with more diversity and variation. It would mean less emphasis on national planning and national priorities. But, as I have tried to suggest, the costs of such adaptive changes might be less than the costs of insisting on travelling along the same rail track, even though we know that the bridges have broken down.

[10] I am indebted for this point to Roy Parker's paper on " The future of the personal social services ", given at the Seminar at the University of Bath to mark the 10th anniversary of the Seebohm report, September 1978.

# [13]

*Geraint Parry*

## Welfare State and Welfare Society*

'CRISIS? WHAT CRISIS?', THE CHANCELLOR OF THE EXCHEQUER was reported to have replied to a question concerning the alleged crisis in sterling. In the case of the welfare state it might seem that the appropriate response would be '*Which* crisis?' since there are several on the menu – fiscal crisis, legitimacy crisis, crisis of ungovernability. Left, Right and Centre have become convinced that there is a crisis. This is after a period of history which had seen an unprecedented rise in the standard of living of the vast majority of the population living in what are normally regarded as welfare states.

This period of economic growth sustained the commitment to welfare spending financed by increased taxation and by budget deficits. Although there was some awareness that the benefits of both economic growth and of social services were unevenly spread, there was little sense that this was a zero-sum game. It is significant that talk was of *relative* deprivation or poverty rather than absolute. Demands for welfare support to satisfy 'needs' – itself a term widely seen as relative or as belonging in a hierarchy – were translated into legal entitlements

*The articles published in this special issue are based on papers presented to a Workshop on the Politics of the Welfare State held at Holly Royde College, Manchester on 13–14 September 1984. The Workshop was jointly sponsored by *Government and Opposition* and the Department of Government, University of Manchester. The sponsors gratefully acknowledge the assistance of the Nuffield Foundation.

In addition to the contributors the following participated in the Workshop: Digby Anderson (Social Affairs Unit); S. E. Finer (All Souls, Oxford); Ian Gough (University of Manchester); Julius Gould (University of Nottingham); Ghiţa Ionescu (*Government and Opposition* and University of Manchester); John Kay (Institute of Fiscal Studies); Sir Arthur Knight (Business History Unit, London School of Economics); Isabel de Madariaga (University of London); Abram de Swaan (University of Amsterdam). The authors and the issue editor would like to thank all the other participants in the Workshop for their contributions. Geraint Parry also thanks Mrs Lynn Dignan for her secretarial and administrative assistance.

and hence into spending commitments which were assumed to be virtually non-negotiable.

The sharp decline in economic growth during the 1970s was significant not only for the obvious reason that high expenditure commitments continued despite the failure of the forces which would sustain its financing. Equally striking was the apparently rapid loss of confidence in the welfare state among its erstwhile supporters. Libertarian and market theories, on the sidelines during the period of consensus, came to dominate the terms of debate about the welfare state in the 1970s and 1980s.

Why should there have been such an abrupt reversal of intellectual positions? One persuasive explanation is offered by Heclo in his perceptive essay on the future of the welfare state.[1] Fundamentally the victory of the welfare state had been too easy. Politics is about conflicts over priorities. But economic growth had made it unnecessary to choose between evils or to agonize excessively over sacrificing one goal for another. It was not necessary to mobilize political forces behind the welfare state or behind one particular conception of a welfare state which would entail a choice between that conception and some other with a differing hierarchy of values. With so many benefiting whilst none were required to make a positive or agonized decision in its favour, the welfare state might seem to rest on a Rousseauian will of all rather than a general will.

The decline of the welfare state's economic base brought out into the open the previously concealed divergent interests beneath the consensus. If, indeed, the growth of the welfare state rested to any considerable degree on the facts of economic growth rather than on a considered political judgment it is less surprising that the crisis of the welfare state was seen as arising from what was often presented as another stubborn irreducible 'fact' – that the welfare state had reached its limits. There was a limit to the proportion of GNP which could be devoted to public expenditure with the consequential effects on taxation. There should be a reversal of outlook, summarized in the British

1 H. Heclo, 'Toward a New Welfare State', in P. Flora and A. Heidenheimer (eds), *The Development of Welfare States in Europe and America*, New Brunswick and London, Transaction books, 1981, p. 395.

Treasury's aphorism 'finance must determine expenditure not expenditure finance'.[2]

This may carry the authoritative stamp of 'realism' but it does in fact conceal significant judgments which are in the final resort 'political'. Throughout the twentieth century, as Bernard Cazes points out, economists have proclaimed that the limits have been attained. The virtue of the recent analyses of the fiscal crisis or the overload crisis is not that they have established any clear upper limits on welfare spending but that they have forced a reconsideration of political objectives. Underlying many of the most penetrating attacks have been new, or the revival of older, conceptions of society and the individual.

The welfare state is one in which society organizes to take collective responsibility for provision of services to relieve the effects of ill-health, poverty, unemployment, old age, etc. One major approach is to view provisions as a response to 'needs' which some have seen as presenting a firm, even an objective, claim on resources. Notoriously, however, need is a much disputed concept – relative rather than absolute. Indeed, its alleged relativity has been seen by some critics as at the centre of some of the supposed excesses of the welfare state. Need is said to be insatiable. Even a sympathetic commentator will accept this. Rosanvallon in his penetrating study on *La crise de l'État-providence* rejects the notion that the welfare state can have a 'programme' which can be 'fulfilled'. Rather the 'dynamic of the welfare state rests on an illimitable programme: to liberate society from need and risk'.[3] For the severer critics this is indeed the problem. By some standard or other the needy will always be with us. Assessing the exact numbers of the needy and the quantitative estimation of needs has become one of the major welfare state industries. In the view of some critics this industry, staffed by an intellectual elite, is noted more for the imprecision rather than the accuracy of its figures, which

[2] H.M. Treasury, *The Next Ten Years: Public Expenditure and Taxation into the 1990s*, Cmnd 9189, HMSO, 1984, p. 21.

[3] P. Rosanvallon, *La crise de l'État-providence*, Paris, Éditions du Seuil, 1981, pp. 33–4. See also G. Ionescu, *Politics and the Pursuit of Happiness*, London, Longman, 1984, ch. 9 and *passim*.

does not preclude bold attempts at policy recommendations. As Digby Anderson put it during the Workshop:

> What can we call an institution which is, and is likely to remain, ignorant about the needs and wishes of its clients, relies on a discipline, 'social policy', which cannot be relied on, is served by a bureaucracy which is not its servant and relies for accountability on a mechanism, 'debate', which is, in fact, rhetoric and discord?

To challenge the aura of precision surrounding some estimates of needs is not of course to deny that the needy exist. Nevertheless, just as Burke argued that no political system could implement abstract natural rights conceived outside political society, so it could also be argued that no state can be committed to the satisfaction of need. To the degree that existing welfare spending is predicated on need and that the needy, as defined in present policy (e.g. aged, unemployed) are growing, the crisis of the welfare state is precisely that it has permitted itself to be need-driven rather than resource-driven.

Raymond Plant's paper seeks to restore the concept of need to its place in the discourse concerning welfare state and welfare society. He first expounds the critique of the concepts underlying the welfare society mounted classically by Hayek – social justice, need, coercion. Plant then attempts a rebuttal which in large part acknowledges the centrality of the idea of individual moral agency upon which Hayek insists, but argues that there exist basic needs the provision of which are necessary to the very possibility of agency itself. These needs go well beyond physical survival to include 'well-being' – not only life but the good life. Some writers who have argued along comparable lines explicitly proceed in an overtly socialist direction.[4] For Plant welfare goods are, to a degree, culturally relative and their extent and distribution are disputable. There is no non-politicized manner of settling such disputes. This firm assertion of the essentially political and contestable nature of judgments concerning welfare provision and, consequently, expenditure in many respects set the terms of much of the Workshop discussion. Did not, it was objected, economic performance set

[4] e.g. L. Doyal and I. Gough, 'A Theory of Human Needs', *Critical Social Policy*, 10, 1984, pp. 6–38. This paper was also presented at the *Government and Opposition* Workshop.

outer limits to political decisions? Or could it be instead that 'performance is all about politics'?

The more standard notion of basic need suggests that there will be a common thrust in all advanced states towards a very similar pattern of welfare provision. An alternative view of the welfare state regards it as an expression of the community's concern for certain values which it seeks to promote or defend. It would be expected that the pattern of distribution of benefits would vary from one community to another according to that community's particular cultural values. Michael Walzer has recently argued[5] that the type of welfare provision, its extent and what citizens will regard as fair shares will be relative to some common understanding of the character of the political community. In Walzer's terms 'every political community is in principle a "welfare state"'.[6] Needs are related to some collective view about the character of the community. The needs which are to be satisfied and those which must have lower priority will reflect this conception.

That there are significant differences between the welfare states in their patterns and institutions of provision is clear. Catherine Jones opens her article by suggesting that to talk of the welfare state being in crisis begs the question as to whether there is such a standard phenomenon. Central terms such as social policy or social spending are used in differing ways in different countries reflecting in part alternative views as to the objectives of commitments to welfare. Nevertheless, she argues that a difference of orientation exists between those countries which pursue a 'society-first' social policy, aimed at supporting a capitalist system, and those which follow an 'individuals-first' policy which places non-market criteria at the head of their hierarchy of values and where capitalism is merely a means to this end. These differences of emphasis are indicated by her designations of the two orientations as, respectively, 'welfare *capitalism*' and '*welfare* capitalism'.

There is a sense in which these distinctions reflect, as Walzer believes, a kind of general will of the communities – a disposition to place certain values as a priority. Equally striking is

5 M. Walzer, *Spheres of Justice: A Defence of Pluralism and Equality*, Oxford, Martin Robertson, 1983. See especially ch. 3.

6 ibid., p. 68.

that the differences display the extraordinary inertial forces which carry a society in a certain direction once set in motion, e.g. the West German society-first system owes as much to its Wilhelmine origins as to any more recent reaffirmation.[7] Governments are of course prone by the nature of policy-making to build incrementally on what is already established and to handle new problems in large part by methods familiar to them. Few, if any, welfare systems will accurately translate political theory into practice even were that possible.

Indeed, another way of viewing national variations in welfare systems is as the result of the particular conjuncture of social forces which prevailed at the crucial stages of the formation of the welfare state. The bias of the system is the result of the changing configuration of forces and of the ideology which legitimizes them.

Whatever the reason, several contributors point to the ways in which welfare systems display a particular national bias. In Britain the Beveridge Report is used, in a normally most un-British manner, rather like a constitutional document to which politicians, academics and practitioners variously pay lip service, cite as holy writ or construe according to need. (Richard Titmuss's works stand as the first Ten Amendments to the original Constitution and Jones can refer to the British 'Titmuss-fortified tradition'). Walters points out that the Swedish Social Democrats have sought to insist on an equitable distribution of resources as the central and distinctive feature of their welfare state at whatever level of expenditure. Jean-Pierre Jallade assesses the successes and failures of the Socialists in impressing an egalitarian stamp on the French social security system which has traditionally had protection against risk rather than equality as its main objective. In a crisis, he suggests, it will be the traditional conservative, consensual features which will come to the fore. The article by Francis Castles, arising out of reflection on his study of the pioneering but neglected welfare states of Australasia, is a criticism (and a self-criticism) of the whole enterprise of explaining the welfare state in specifically political

[7] For a discussion of the influence of type of regime on the development of the welfare state, see P. Flora and J. Alber, 'Modernization, Democratization, and the Development of Welfare States in Western Europe', in P. Flora and A. Heidenheimer, op. cit., pp. 37–80.

terms. His proposed 'contextual' strategy would not only re-introduce political actors to the explanation but also, presumably, the political formulae they profess or adopt, whether unique to the particular community or more widely shared between the advanced nations of either hemisphere.

If a welfare state is, as Walzer would hope, a reflection of community values there must be appropriate means whereby these values can be articulated and expressed in procedures and institutions. Albert Weale argues that to call for a more egalitarian welfare system or to criticize it for failure to achieve equality (supposing that to be its objective) is to be insufficiently precise. He detects two contrasting conceptions of equality – of resources and of welfare – whose achievement would, taken singly, result in different distributions of welfare goods. They also have alternative implications for the centralized or decentralized control of welfare institutions and for the processes of welfare delivery. To the degree, however, that *both* conceptions of equality are embedded in liberal thinking about the person and about a welfare society, the political issue for the pluralist welfare state would be to decide which principle of equality should prevail in which areas of welfare.

The impact of market and libertarian theories has similarly been to question both ends and means. As well as being allegedly costly and wasteful, the welfare state has been seen as paternalist and inimical to individual autonomy and responsibility. The real beneficiaries, it is sometimes suggested, are the welfare professionals themselves for whom welfare delivery is not an entirely altruistic or communitarian matter.[8] The scepticism about the quality of professionalized welfare has not been confined to the Right but has also spread to writers on the Left who perceive that those who look to the market in place of the state system may not necessarily have totally lost their socialist virtue. Colin Crouch employs Hirschman's concepts of exit and voice in an attempt to redress the acknowledged defects in much state welfare provision and delivery by calling in an element of the market. Arguing from an explicitly socialist position which typically favours voice over exit, Crouch proposes

[8] See N. Glazer, 'Towards a Self-Service Society', *The Public Interest*, Winter, 1982, pp. 66–90 for a discussion of decentralizing tendencies in welfare systems.

a market element within the public sector which would cover certain less basic services and provide a signal to welfare producers about changes in demands. The purely private sector would remain small and even superfluous. Such mild concessions to the 'New Right' would not of course answer the question which many of them would pose – whether there can be justifications for attempts to restrict exit rather than merely making it a less advantageous option. On what grounds, some Workshop participants asked, can the individual's right to private provision be denied?

How far privatization combined with decentralization can go without undermining the most basic objectives of welfare states is a central political dispute.[9] Claus Offe remains sceptical of the scope for change in this direction:

> most social needs can no longer be absorbed by arrangements that have fallen victim to the process of modernisation, for instance, the extended three-generation family, community networks, or some version of the 'American dream' of self-help.[10]

For Offe the welfare state is, in its essentials, irreversible. At the Workshop Abram de Swaan presented a case study which provided qualified support for both Crouch's view on the one side and for Offe on the other. He displayed the logic whereby state provision took over from mutual arrangements to repair the deficiencies of mutual help in insurance and other money transfers. The same logic would not apply to many benefits in kind which may best be provided by local groupings aware of the needs and the sensitivities of the recipients.

In fact, as Richard Rose has insisted, welfare is already provided by multiple agencies and in particular by the market and the household as well as by the state.[11] Rose points out that it does not follow that total welfare is cut as a result of a fall in state expenditure. In many cases the cost is transferred elsewhere, often to the household in the case of care for the elderly or the provisions of lunches for schoolchildren. Offloading is one answer to overload. But this is not a mere technical solution;

9 Rosanvallon, op cit., third part.

10 Offe, op cit, p. 288. See also the comments by Cazes on this option.

11 R. Rose, *Getting by in Three Economies: The Resources of the Official, Unofficial and Domestic Economies*, Glasgow, University of Strathclyde Studies in Public Policy, No. 110, 1983.

it involves shifts of burdens which should require clear decisions. More in the way of the extended family and community networks may survive than Offe supposes, but one suspects that many women would like to express a view on any shift in welfare obligations which threatens to burden them again with *Kinder* and *Küche*, if no longer *Kirche*.

Obtaining consent, Rose has also declared, is the first priority of government.[12] In liberal thought and liberal regimes political and civil rights preceded welfare rights and there is reason to think that they may still do so in the minds of many citizens. Nevertheless modern states are now irreversibly enterprise associations and not simply civil associations, to use Oakeshott's terms. They pursue goals of economic growth and welfare. To the degree that both governments and regimes rely on specific as well as more diffuse support, the estimation of their performance in welfare provision must be a matter of some concern. Peter Taylor-Gooby's new survey of opinion in Britain shows that the support for the welfare state conceals a complex set of beliefs. Very strong support for state services goes hand in hand with a high degree of support for private equivalents. People are indeed at ease in the two economies. The poor believe the better off benefit and the wealthy see the poor as gaining most. Take away the pluses and the minuses, as Rousseau might have said, and the welfare state retains the favour of the population – but whether one can speak of a general will is highly doubtful.

Perhaps such evidence means that the fundamental reassessment of the political priorities of welfare states discussed here and elsewhere is not after all necessary. Policies on welfare, as in other areas, are incremental and the results ramshackle. As John Kay put it during the Workshop, 'government committees are rarely the progenitors of major original thought'. Committees, he argued, can improve a system whose basic essentials are accepted and functioning well. Where, as at present, such consensus is lacking, radical reappraisal is unlikely and all one can hope for is some modest and pragmatic reform of a mixture of

12 R. Rose, *Understanding Big Government*, London and Beverly Hills, Sage Publications, 1984, p. 235.

benefits which, in Britain at least, owes as much to political history as to national analysis.[13]

There will also always be those who still believe that a small adjustment in expenditure and a modest increase in economic growth will solve all problems. Participants in the Workshop were, however, sceptical of what Bernard Cazes called the 'Welfare State as Usual' option. He rejects the possibility of returning to the conditions of the great period of growth in the welfare state (a point echoed by Sir Arthur Knight in introducing a session when he pointed to the particular and probably unrepeatable social trends of the postwar era). The two main structural remedies of budget constraint and market incentive should, Cazes argues, be pursued in combination if they are to be at all effective and acceptable. However the combination of economic and demographic trends must mean that unpopular 'political' decisions will have to be taken. The 'political' choices to be made about the welfare system (however much they may be supposed to embody the conception a national community may have of itself) can only be brought to fruition if they take account of, and contribute to, the performance of the system since this will be a necessary condition for progress towards *any* objectives. This is to spell out the implications of Ghiţa Ionescu's comment on the greater appropriateness of Beveridge's term 'welfare society' over 'welfare state': 'For it was not the political institution which provided the welfare, but the social and economic forces of society . . .'.[14]

But there is a dialectic here: the welfare may be provided by society's forces but it is in large part through choices made in the political realm that welfare is decided upon – including decisions to withdraw the state and leave more to personal initiative. The crisis of the welfare state has been presented too often as a financial or economic crisis. However, there is, as Rosanvallon again rightly says,[15] a deeper crisis: it is the relation of society to state which is in question. The proper relations between state, society and individual, between public, social and private, are moral and political questions and deserve reinstatement as priorities.

[13] John Kay contributes to a full discussion of the development of social security and of the rival proposals for reform in A. W. Dilnot, J. A. Kay and C. N. Morris, *The Reform of Social Security,* Oxford, Oxford University Press, 1984.

[14] G. Ionescu, op. cit., p. 169.

[15] Rosanvallon, op. cit., p. 31.

# Part IV
# Rights, Discretion and Welfare

# [14]

# INDIVIDUAL RIGHTS AND SOCIAL WELFARE: THE EMERGING LEGAL ISSUES

CHARLES A. REICH*

THE time has come for lawyers to take a major interest in social welfare, and for the welfare profession to concern itself with the rapidly growing relevance of law. Although welfare has always existed within a structure of law, until recently there has been little recognition or study of the basic legal issues underlying decisions affecting recipients of public assistance and other welfare beneficiaries. These issues will lie quiet no longer; they urgently demand our attention.

The New Deal undertook a far-reaching experiment in social welfare, with the rapid enactment of new legislation in the fields of social security, unemployment compensation, public housing, and other forms of public aid. Since that time the experiment has been accepted as a fundamental and permanent aspect of our society. But although thirty years have passed, and a vast amount of experience has accumulated, there has been little in the way of critical examination of the legal issues in these welfare statutes — least of all by those who support the general principles of social welfare, and least of all with respect to issues concerning the substantive and procedural rights of individual beneficiaries. It is not surprising, then, that the legal status of these individuals' rights requires critical reexamination.

The law of social welfare grew up on the theory that welfare is a "gratuity" furnished by the state, and thus may be made subject to whatever conditions the state sees fit to impose. A corollary legal theory holds that since all forms of welfare represent the expenditure of public funds, the public may properly interest itself in these funds even after they have reached the hands of beneficiaries. With these justifications at hand, recipients have been subjected to many forms of procedure and control not imposed on other citizens. No one will deny that fair and reasonable eligibility standards and effective protection against fraud are necessary when benefits are handed out. But the poor are all too easily regulated.[1] They are an irresistible temptation to

*Professor of Law, Yale University. The author wishes to thank Mrs. Elizabeth Wickenden for invaluable help both on the general philosophy of this article and on its discussion of specific issues; also Brian Glick and David Pittinsky for their assistance on legal research.

1. "Paradoxical though it may seem, the most serious threat to freedom in our programs of public services and public benefits is to the freedom of the recipient. The original Agricultural Adjustment Act was once described, rather harshly, as government by bribery. The power of the purse is great; it is sometimes possible, by paying people to do things or not to do them, to control their actions as effectively as by threatening to send them to jail. It behooves us to be constantly on our guard lest, out of zeal to better people's lot, we impose on them patterns of behavior in matters in which, under our scheme of things, government ought not to meddle."

Willcox, *Patterns of Social Legislation: Reflections on the Welfare State*, 6 J. OF PUB. L. 3, 7 (1957).

moralists, who want not only to assist but to "improve" by imposing virtue. They are subject to social workers' urges to prescribe "what is best."[2] And they are necessarily caught up in the workings of large organizations which by their nature are rigid and dehumanizing.

The Social Security Act represented a departure from this general welfare philosophy. The framers of the Act had a clear concept concerning the "right" to public assistance, and provided devices to protect these rights. Thus, in the program for aid to families with needy children, the Act requires that states afford an opportunity for a fair hearing to any individual whose claim is denied or not acted upon with reasonable promptness, provide safeguards which restrict the use or disclosure of information concerning recipients, and ensure that all individuals wishing to make application for aid have opportunity to do so.[3] Despite these and other statutory safeguards, problems have grown up with respect to federal as well as state programs. In part, these are the outgrowth of difficulties in administration.

Welfare is surrounded by the processes of administrative procedure. The procedures of the New Deal regulatory agencies were looked upon with high hopes by the reformers of thirty years ago, who sought fair and simplified alternatives to the cumbersome methods of the courts. But the administrative process has developed its own abuses and oppressiveness. These abuses are harmful whatever the work of an agency, but their impact on people as individuals is perhaps greatest in the welfare field. The clients of many government agencies are large organizations; those who deal with the Federal Communications Commission or the Civil Aeronautics Board are usually well able to protect themselves. Welfare clients are often ignorant of their rights, lack adequate representation by counsel, and lack the resources to fight a large public agency. If even our biggest corporations sometimes find government (no matter how well-meaning) to be arbitrary and oppressive, we may expect to find that the welfare beneficiary often suffers far more from heavy handed governmental regulation. There is mounting evidence to confirm this expectation.

## A Sampling of Issues

Although there has as yet been no systematic effort to uncover legal issues involving welfare beneficiaries, some problems have, particularly in recent months, forced themselves upon persons working in the social welfare field.[4] These problems arise in many different welfare programs, federal and state, including aid to families with needy children, other forms of public assistance,

2. See Schorr, *The Trend to Rx,* Social Work, January, 1962.

3. 42 U.S.C. § 602 (1962).

4. See generally Wickenden & Bell, Public Welfare — Time for a Change (1961); U.S. Dept. of Health, Education and Welfare, The Extension of Legal Services to the Poor (1964); Wickenden, Memorandum: Poverty and the Law, The Constitutional Rights of Assistance Recipients, March 25, 1965; U.S. Advisory Commission on Intergovernmental Relations, Statutory and Administrative Controls Associated With Federal Grants for Public Assistance (1964).

unemployment insurance, job retraining, public housing, and the new Economic Opportunity Act. They are most readily sorted out, however, in terms of the impact on the recipient or his family.

*Morals.* Some welfare regulation attempts to impose a standard of moral behavior on beneficiaries. Louisiana cut off aid to needy children in all cases where the mother gave birth to an illegitimate child after going on the relief rolls, except where she could prove that she had subsequently "ceased such illicit relationships." Twenty-three thousand children, a large proportion of them Negro, were removed from assistance before the Secretary of Health, Education and Welfare ruled Louisiana's plan invalid under the Department's own standards.[5] In other states mothers of illegitimate children may be dissuaded from applying for assistance by threats of neglect proceedings leading to loss of custody of the child or children.[6] Sometimes mothers who, while receiving assistance for their children, give birth to an illegitimate child are subjected to the charge that the latest pregnancy constitutes "neglect" of the previous children.[7] In California, if a mother receiving aid to dependent children uses any portion of the grant to support a man "assuming the role of spouse" to whom she is not married she may be charged with the crime of misusing the grant,[8] despite the fact that such grants may be used to support a lawful husband or other caretaker-relatives. She is also in danger of being charged with grand theft if she receives assistance and fails to disclose that she is living with a man deemed capable of rendering financial support, although he may be far less than a full time member of the family;[9] thus illicit relationships are hazardous. In the District of Columbia, the courts were faced with the question whether the mother of nine must be denied aid because her estranged legitimate husband visited her too frequently.[10] In no other area of entitlement, such as social security or veterans' benefits, are there similar pressures to impose a moral code.

*Privacy.* In order to administer public welfare funds, investigation of eligibility and extent of need are both normal and necessary. Merchants may be asked for information, financial data is checked, the whereabouts of relatives

5. Memorandum for The Commissioner of Social Security from Secretary Flemming, January 16, 1961. See Wickenden, The Indigent and Welfare Administration, in U.S. Dept. of Health, Education and Welfare, Conference Proceedings: The Extension of Legal Services to the Poor, 42 (1964).

6. Wickenden, Memorandum: Poverty and the Law, The Constitutional Rights of Assistance Recipients (March 25, 1965) p. 6.

7. *Ibid.* at 5.

8. See OPINION OF ATTORNEY GENERAL OF CALIFORNIA 64/63, 44. A.G.O. 155; CALIF. WELFARE AND INSTITUTIONS CODE § 1508, 1575.

9. People v. Shirley, 360 P.2d 33, 55 Cal. App. 2d 521 (1961). See CALIF. WELFARE & INSTITUTIONS CODE § 508. 42 U.S.C. § 605 sanctions the use of state criminal penalties to punish relatives who do not use aid for the benefit of the children on whose behalf it is received.

10. Simmons v. Simmons, Civil No. D 2545-61, D.C. Ct. of Gen. Sessions, Domestic Relations Branch, June 12, 1964; See Washington Post, Nov. 10, 1964, p. C 1.

sought.[11] Investigation is, however, inevitably an invasion of privacy, and all the more so if steps are not taken to keep the findings confidential.[12] One specific invasion of privacy that seems both illegal and unwarranted is the widespread practice of conducting "midnight raids" on homes receiving aid to dependent children, to see if there is a "man in the house" who is or should be contributing to the family's support.[13] Investigators may burst in, frighten the children, and threaten the mother with loss of assistance. Several states have halted this practice, but elsewhere it continues unchecked.[14]

*Responsibility.* Welfare laws sometimes seek to impose duties of financial responsibility for relatives beyond those required by the general law.[15] The concept of relatives' responsibility is a survival from the Elizabethan poor laws, which attempted to compel relatives to support indigent members of their families.[16] Controversy over such requirements is active today; California's highest court recently held unconstitutional the requirement that children be compelled to support the care of aged parents in mental institutions.[17] Under aid to families with dependent children programs in many states, a "man in the house," although not married, may be presumed to be responsible for contributing to the support of the woman's children.

*Residence.* Another survival of the Elizabethan poor laws is the doctrine that public assistance is basically a matter of local concern, and the corollary that only residents of the states are entitled to be assisted.[18] Many states have statutes denying assistance to persons who do not qualify as residents, and making it difficult to become a "resident."[19] Many laws now on the books are designed to hinder the migration of indigents. Some of these laws have been held unconstitutional,[20] but New York has a law disqualifying one who comes to the state for the purpose of obtaining welfare,[21] South Dakota has a law making

11. *E.g.*, N.Y. SOCIAL WELFARE LAW § 132, 143(a); CALIF. WELFARE & INSTITUTIONS CODE § 1523, 1572.

12. See, *e.g.*, CAL. WELFARE & INSTITUTIONS CODE § 1552.6.

13. Reich, *Midnight Welfare Searches and the Social Security Act*, 72 YALE L.J. 1347 (1963); U.S. COMPTROLLER GENERAL, REPORT ON THE ADEQUACY OF THE NATIONWIDE REVIEW OF ELIGIBILITY IN THE AID TO FAMILIES WITH DEPENDENT CHILDREN PROGRAM WELFARE ADMINISTRATION, DEPARTMENT OF HEALTH, EDUCATION, AND WELFARE JANUARY-JULY 1963, 18-22.

14. See, *e.g.*, Baltimore Sun, January 19, 1964, p. 1, 20; N.Y. Times, August 23, 1964, p. 66; AMERICN CIVIL LIBERTIES WEEKLY BULLETIN No. 2209, (1964) p. 1.

15. CALIF. WELFARE & INSTITUTIONS CODE § 2181, 2224, 2576, 2881; N.Y. SOCIAL WELFARE LAW § 101. See generally Mandelker, General Assistance in the United States, Ch. III 1955 (unpublished thesis in Yale Law School Library).

16. ten Broek, *California's Dual System of Family Law: Its Origin, Development and Present Status:* I, 16 STAN. L. REV. 257, 283 (1964).

17. Department of Mental Hygiene v. Kirchner, 60 C.2d 716, 36 Cal. Rptr. 488, 388 P.2d 720 (1964), vacated and remanded, 380 U.S. 194 (1965).

18. tenBroek, *supra* note 16, at 262-65 (1964).

19. N.Y. SOCIAL WELFARE LAW § 117-21, 149 (McKinney Supp. 1964); N.Y. SOCIAL WELFARE LAW § 148.

20. Edwards v. California, 314 U.S. 160 (1941).

21. N.Y. SOCIAL WELFARE LAW § 139-a (Supp. 1964).

it virtually impossible for migrants to receive general public assistance,[22] and many states have laws authorizing the "removal" of indigents back to their state of origin.[23] The removal statutes seem plainly unconstitutional, but remain on the books and are indirectly enforced by the threatened withdrawal of assistance. In one New York case, assistance was denied because the authorities deemed it "socially valid" for the applicant to return to her family in a southern state from which she had departed.[24] Settlement and removal laws, and more recent reciprocal agreements concerning the settlement of children, may also hinder the interstate placement of children in foster homes or for adoption, making it difficult for a court or agency to send a child to a family in a state which demands assurances that the child will not become a public charge.[25]

*Employment.* Whether a welfare recipient must work to obtain assistance, and what work he may be compelled to do, have also been issues since the days of the Elizabethan poor laws.[26] "Work relief" still exists.[27] Recently several men in upstate New York challenged the power of St. Lawrence County to compel them, subject to criminal penalties, to work cutting brush in deep snow.[28] Fathers refusing work relief have been criminally prosecuted for nonsupport. An even more difficult problem concerning employment arises in connection with vocational retraining programs which are part of some state schemes for unemployment compensation,[29] and an important part of the new federal poverty programs.[30] Here an individual is put under pressure to

22. South Dakota Code § 50.0102(6).

23. See generally Mandelker, *Exclusion and Removal Legislation,* 1956 Wisc. L. Rev. 57; Note, *Depression Migrants and the States,* 53 Harv. L. Rev. 1031 (1940); Note, *Interstate Migration and Personal Liberty,* 40 Colum. L. Rev. 1032 (1940).

24. *Preliminary Statement,* in Brief for Appellant, In the Matter of the Appeal of Minnie Lee Nixon, State of New York, Department of Social Welfare (1964).

25. Matter of Anonymous, Docket No. 1146/64, New York County Court, May 12 1965. The Uniform Transfer of Dependents Act (U. C. A. 9 C, p. 218) provides that states may enter into reciprocal agreements with corresponding states regarding the interstate transportation of indigent persons and the acceptance, transfer and support of persons receiving public aid in other states. See, e.g., Virginia Code § 63-114. Under § 63-244 of the Virginia Code no nonresident child may be placed in a foster home in Virginia without the consent of the Welfare Commissioner. The State Welfare Board is authorized to require any placing agency to agree to remove a child from the state at any time at the Commissioner's request, and the Commissioner may require any placing agency to post a bond not in excess of $2500 conditioned on fulfillment of the agreement.

26. tenBroek, *supra* note 16, at 270-79 (1964).

27. N.Y. Social Welfare Law § 164. See also § 131(4) (1964 Supp.) See generally, Mandelker, *supra* note 15, at 36-42. See also 42 U.S.C. § 607, sanctioning State plans for aid to families with dependent children under which parents may be required to seek employment.

28. See N.Y. Times, July 30, 1964.

29. See Calif. Welfare & Institutions Code § 1523 and Note, *Charity versus Social Insurance in Unemployment Compensation Laws,* 73 Yale L.J. 357, 382, n. 94 (1963). See also N.Y. Social Welfare Law § 131(4) and 131(5)(b) (Supp. 1964).

30. See the Area Redevelopment Program, 75 Stat. 57 (1961), 42 U.S.C. § 2513 (Supp. V, 1963) (occupational retraining) and the Manpower Development and Training Program, 76 Stat. 25 (1962), 42 U.S.C. § 2582 (Supp. V, 1963).

undergo retraining in a new occupation, not necessarily of his own choosing. The issues are sharpest where a proposed retraining program involves work that is foreign to a man's prior skills, requires acceptance of a lower status, demands transfer to a new locality, or presents the risk that no jobs will be available even after retraining.[31]

*Housing.* Public housing authorities have the power to select tenants, and also to oust them.[32] Within the limits set by family income qualifications this power can be exercised in a way that is largely discretionary, based in part upon officials' intangible impressions from interviews and home visits. In deciding to admit initially or to terminate a lease, housing authorities are apparently free to use such criteria as whether any member of the family has a police record, keeps undesirable company, or engages in immoral conduct.[33] The standards are generally vague, and there are no clearly articulated methods of proof. There may be little in the way of procedure to make certain that the authorities' information is true. Month-to-month leases maintain tenants in a state of insecurity.

*Loyalty Oaths.* Legislators apparently have a great urge to impose loyalty tests which neither the general public nor the legislators themselves are required to meet. For a time several states required a loyalty oath of applicants for public housing,[34] and Ohio still has a loyalty oath for unemployment compensation.[35] These instances might be dismissed as the irrational residue of the vindictive McCarthy years, were it not for the shocking fact that President Johnson's new poverty program contains the requirement that every recipient of aid thereunder take a loyalty oath.[36]

*Criteria of Eligibility.* Many of the forms of assistance contained in present-day social welfare programs, and particularly those under the Economic Opportunity Act, are, like public housing, available only on a selective basis. The

31. Strauss, *Retraining and Unemployment Compensation: New Wine in Old Bottles* (1964) (unpublished paper in Yale Law Library).

32. See N.Y. PUB. HOUSING LAW § 156.

33. New York City Housing Authority Resolution No. 53-3-185, Article II, Section 2.01(g) provides that tenancy in an authority project may be terminated for: "*Non-Desirability.* The conduct or behavior of the tenant which is objectionable, or which imperils the health, safety or morals of his neighbors or the community, or is a source of danger or causes damages to the premises or to the property of the Authority or to the peaceful occupation of the other tenants, or constitutes a nuisance, or violates accepted social norms."

34. See Reich, *The New Property,* 73 YALE L.J. 733, 747 n. 81 (1964).

35. Note, *Charity versus Social Insurance in Unemployment Compensation Laws,* 73 YALE L.J. 357, 379 n. 87 (1963).

36. Economic Opportunity Act, 78 Stat. 508, 533, 42 U.S.C. § 2701, 2966:

"No part of any funds appropriated or otherwise made available for expenditure under authority of this chapter shall be used to make payments to any individual unless such individual has executed and filed with the Director an affidavit that he does not believe in, and is not a member of and does not support any organization that believes in or teaches, the overthrow of the United States Government by force or violence or any illegal or unconstitutional methods."

list includes the Manpower Development and Training Program,[37] Child Welfare Services,[38] The Maternal and Child Health Program,[39] The Crippled Children Service,[40] as well as the programs of the Office of Economic Opportunity.[41] The problem here is what criteria of eligibility are employed by the various agencies having the power of choice. A major difficulty is that in many cases the governing statutes supply no criteria at all, and the criteria actually employed by administrators are not easily discovered. For example, no regulations have been published in the Federal Register spelling out standards for the programs of the Economic Opportunity Act. The new federal job corps is reported to refuse automatically all youths with police records. In other areas standards may exist on paper but are not readily enforced.

*Independence.* Programs for the relief of poverty raise basic issues over how much independence is to be allowed the recipients. Under nonfederal general assistance programs "supervision" of beneficiaries by authorities is permitted.[42] When such welfare is administered under a means test, the welfare agency may gain detailed control over the family budget.[43] A specific type of supervision results from relief in kind, such as direct payment of rent under general assistance programs; this limits recipients' freedom of choice.[44] Beyond the question of specific supervision lies a broader question — an issue which will become increasingly troublesome as programs to combat poverty grow. How much shall individuals be supervised from above, and how much by themselves?[45] This fundamental issue furnishes a fitting place to halt the present sampling. Next it is important to consider what general legal problems are raised by these many issues.

### The Underlying Questions of Law

Although the issues discussed in the previous section are diverse in nature and fortuitous in selection, they do have in common some underlying legal questions. Broadly speaking, these involve matters of procedure, of constitutional law, and questions relating to the nature of the individual rights created by public welfare legislation.

By way of prologue, it should be noted that the interpretation of the applicable welfare statutes provides a series of additional important legal questions.

37. 78 Stat. 23, 42 U.S.C. § 2571 (1964).

38. 78 Stat. 182, 42 U.S.C. § 721 (1964).

39. 77 Stat. 273, 42 U.S.C. § 701 (Supp. V 1963).

40. 77 Stat. 273, 42 U.S.C. § 711 (Supp. V 1963).

41. 78 Stat. 508 (1964), 42 U.S.C.A. § 2701 (1958).

42. See N.Y. Social Welfare Code § 134, 214, 215, 350; Schorr, *Policy Issues in Fighting Poverty,* 11 Children 127 (1964); Schorr, *The Trend to Rx,* Social Work, January 1962.

43. tenBroek & Wilson, *Public Assistance and Social Insurance — A Normative Approach,* 1 U.C.L.A.L. Rev. 237, 264-67 (1954). On the means test generally see Mandelker, *supra* note 15, Ch. IV.

44. *E.g.,* Calif. Welfare & Institutions Code § 1552.2.

45. See Cahn & Cahn, *The War on Poverty: A Civilian Perspective,* 73 Yale L.J. 1317 (1964).

Because welfare clients seldom have legal assistance, statutory interpretations by administrators have generally gone unchallenged. But when a real challenge is made, a significant change in prevailing practice may result. Absent challenge, welfare administrators are permitted broad areas of discretion in which they make the law by administrative interpretations under the pressures of current public opinion — interpretations that may be neither consistent from one jurisdiction to another nor in accord with the original purposes of the legislature. Each statutory question is, however, a distinctive legal problem in itself; the present discussion will be limited to the more general questions already listed.

*Procedure.* In the sampling of issues already given there were many instances of welfare decisions capable of having a major impact on the lives of individuals. Many of these decisions are made in a manner that is lacking in basic safeguards.[46] In the case of a decision removing a family from public housing, or a decision denying aid to families with dependent children, generally the matter is finally determined at some level within the appropriate agency, after investigation by the agency, and with comparatively informal procedures, if any, available to the persons affected. In the welfare area procedures often exist on paper, but are not pursued in practice. This contrasts sharply with what happens in agencies dealing with business regulation, where lawyers have made paper procedures a practical reality.

In the past thirty years a large body of experience and law has grown up with respect to the procedures of government agencies which undertake regulation of economic affairs, or dispensation of benefits such as airline routes or television licenses. In a general way, the standards which have developed are as follows. (1) The rules which are to furnish the standard of decision should be clearly formulated in advance of any action; (2) the rules should be available to the public; (3) every action should begin with actual notice of the proposed action and a full statement of the basis for it; (4) the relevant facts should be determined in a proceeding at which the person or company affected can know the evidence and have an opportunity to rebut it; factual findings should not be based on hearsay or secret evidence known only to the agency; (5) the person or company should have the right to be represented by counsel; (6) there should be a distinct separation between those officials who investigate and initiate action and those who find the facts and make the decision; the latter officials should be subject to different authority than the former and free of any of the atmosphere in which the action was begun; (7) the decision, once made, should be accompanied by findings and reasons; (8) there should be opportunity for review of the decision within the agency, and, ultimately, in the courts.[47]

46. See generally Mandelker, Judicial Review in General Assistance, 6 J. of Pub. L. 100 (1957). Some of the most recent legislation on poverty has provisions for "finality" of determinations designed to preclude challenge and review. 75 Stat. 59 (1961), 42 U.S.C. § 2514(e) (1958); 76 Stat. 26 (1962), 42 U.S.C. § 2583(g) (1958).

47. A fairly complete administrative procedure is found in New York City Housing Authority Resolution No. 53, 3-185. Article III of the Resolution sets up a Continued

These procedures, however cumbersome they may seem, have come to represent a fundamental standard of fairness in administrative process. They may be exaggerated and misused until they produce inordinate delay and expense, but they represent effective checks on the characteristic evils of proceedings in any large public or private organization: closed doors, Kafka-like uncertainty, difficulty in locating responsibility, and rigid adherence to a particular point of view. They are fundamental safeguards for those who must deal with government.

In a society where a significant portion of the population is dependent on social welfare, decisions about eligibility for benefits are among the most important that a government can make. By one set of values the granting of a license to broadcast over a television channel, or to build a hydroelectric project on a river, might seem of more far-reaching significance. But in a society that considers the individual as its basic unit a decision affecting the life of a person or a family should not be taken by means that would be unfair for a television station or power company. Indeed, full adjudicatory procedures are far more appropriate in welfare cases than in most of the areas of administrative procedure. In the licensing of television or hydroelectric dams, policy-making and planning are so mixed with fact-finding as to severely limit the possibility of reaching "objective" decisions. Welfare cases rest on comparatively objective statutory criteria, are less subject to ad hoc policy-making, and demand high standards of fairness and equitable treatment for large numbers of individuals. At a minimum, there should be notice to beneficiaries of regulations and proposed adverse action, and fact finding should be carried on in a scrupulous fashion. There is much to be said for a genuine separation of the functions of investigator and judge, so that welfare workers are not put in the psychologically impossible position of having to evaluate their own actions, or those of their colleagues. And a clear statement of reasons, plus some form of review, would give a beneficiary one more opportunity to argue his side of the case. Procedures can develop gradually and pragmatically, but as welfare grows in importance in our society, it will be necessary to give increasing attention to the procedures by which welfare rights are granted or refused. Here the experience of lawyers can be of great assistance; whatever the outcome of particular decisions, adequate procedure gives a sense of fairness that is vital to community acceptance of a welfare program.

*Constitutional Questions.* The welfare issues discussed earlier present a number of important constitutional questions. Some of these, like the previously mentioned questions of statutory interpretation, relate to only one specific issue. Midnight searches appear to violate the Fourth Amendment. Settlement and removal statutes seem an invasion of liberty to travel and to choose one's place of abode. Relatives' responsibility laws may present issues of due process

Occupancy Board consisting of three Authority Officials empowered to hold hearings to review findings of ineligibility for continued occupancy. See also the provision for departmental appeal in the case of denial of assistance, N.Y. SOCIAL WELFARE LAW, §§ 139(a), 353.

in imposing financial responsibility without adequate basis. But aside from these individual questions at least two problems cut across the welfare field. They involve personal liberty and equal protection of the laws.

(a) *Personal Liberty.* The most difficult and challenging constitutional question presented by welfare programs relates to invasions of personal liberty and privacy. "Liberty" is protected in the Fifth and Fourteenth Amendments, but nowhere defined. For many years it was used as a protection against various forms of economic and business regulation; this view is now largely discredited. But if liberty has any remaining meaning in the constitutional sense, it must at least cover the management of personal and family affairs — the sort of things that are, to the average person, nobody else's business, certainly not government's.[48] Hence undue interference with the private lives of welfare beneficiaries may present serious constitutional issues.

Closely related to liberty is the concept of privacy. Privacy is not protected by any specific provision of the Constitution. But many sections of the Bill of Rights involve aspects of a right to privacy, centering on home and family. This right was expressly affirmed by the Supreme Court in the recent case of *Griswold v. Connecticut,* holding unconstitutional a state statute barring the use of contraceptive devices.[49] Although this is a major forward step, the law has not yet developed a constitutional theory of privacy fully adequate to the present-day interdependent world. The rise of the welfare state would seem to demand that this development be delayed no longer.

(b) *Equal Protection.* Another developing constitutional problem is the degree to which it is valid to impose different standards of behavior upon people because they happen to receive some form of public assistance. The constitutional concept of equal protection has never been that everyone should be treated exactly the same; women may be treated differently from men, children from adults, and so forth; the guiding principle is that classifications must be reasonable. But the status of being a welfare beneficiary does not necessarily justify all of the differential forms of treatment which now exist under the law. Why should recipients of aid under the poverty program be required to take a special loyalty oath? Why should the relatives of indigent people have a greater financial responsibility than is applicable generally? As noted above, the Supreme Court of California has ruled that it violates equal protection to

48. See Griswold v. Connecticut, 33 U.S.L. WEEK 4587 (1965); see also Harlan, J., dissenting in Poe v. Ullman, 367 U.S. 497 (1961), 522, 543:

"This 'liberty' is not a series of isolated points pricked out in terms of the taking of property; the freedom of speech, press and religion; the right to keep and bear arms; the freedom from unreasonable searches and seizures; and so on. It is a rational continuum which, broadly speaking, includes a freedom from all substantial arbitrary impositions and purposeless restraints . . . and which also recognizes, what a reasonable and sensitive judgment must, that certain interests require particularly careful scrutiny of the state needs asserted to justify their abridgment."

49. 33 U.S.L. WEEK 4587 (1965). See Brief for Appellants, pp. 79-90, Griswold v. Connecticut, No. 496, U.S. Supreme Court, Oct. Term, 1964.

make children responsible for the care of aged parents in mental institutions.[50] Again, why should welfare recipients have less freedom to take up residence in any part of the country? The test of each discrimination is that it be *reasonably* related to a proper object of legislative policy. And if a discrimination has come into being by administrative practice, without a basis in legislation, it should be open to much more severe questioning by the courts.

*Entitlement.* Beyond the procedural and constitutional problems already considered lies a further legal problem that embraces large issues of public policy. This is the question of entitlement.[51]

Society today is built around entitlement. The automobile dealer has his franchise, the doctor and lawyer their professional licenses, the worker his union membership, contract, and pension rights, the executive his contract and stock options; all are devices to aid security and independence. Many of the most important of these entitlements now flow from government: subsidies to farmers and businessmen, routes for airlines and channels for television stations; long term contracts for defense, space, and education; social security pensions for individuals. Such sources of security, whether private or public, are no longer regarded as luxuries or gratuities; to the recipients they are essentials, fully deserved, and in no sense a form of charity. It is only the poor whose entitlements, although recognized by public policy, have not been effectively enforced.

Perhaps at one time we could have justified this discrimination by arguing that the poor are to blame for their poverty. But today we see poverty as the consequence of large impersonal forces in a complex industrial society — forces like automation, lack of jobs and changing technologies that are beyond the control of individuals. It is closer to the truth to say that the poor are affirmative contributors to today's society, for we are so organized as virtually to compel this sacrifice by a segment of the population. Since the enactment of the Social Security Act, we have recognized that they have a right — not a mere privilege — to a minimal share in the commonwealth.

Even were this not so, the experience of thirty years has shown how much danger there is to society as a whole when any group in the population lacks entitlements and hence chronically suffers from insecurity and dependence. These same years have also shown how dangerous it is to permit government to have widespread discretionary powers over business or individuals; how

---

50. It is established in this state that the mere presence of wealth or lack thereof in an individual citizen cannot be the basis for valid class discrimination . . . .

> Section 6650 by its terms imposes absolute liability upon, and does not even purport to vest in, the servient relatives any right of control over, or to recoup from, the assets of the patient. A statute obviously violates the equal protection clause if it selects one particular class of persons for a species of taxation and no rational basis supports such classification. . . . Such a concept for the state's taking of a free man's property manifestly denies him equal protection of the law.

Department of Mental Hygiene v. Kirchner, 60 C.2d 716, 721-23; 388 P.2d 720, 723-24 (1964).

51. See generally tenBroek and Wilson, *Public Assistance and Social Insurance — A Normative Evaluation,* 1 U.C.L.A.L. Rev. 237 (1954).

abuses and oppressions grow, and how the very structure of bureaucracy causes a constant reaching out for new power.

The idea of entitlement is simply that when individuals have insufficient resources to live under conditions of health and decency, society has obligations to provide support, and the individual is entitled to that support as of right. To the greatest degree possible, public welfare should rest upon a comprehensive concept of actual need spelled out in objectively defined eligibility that assures a maximum degree of security and independence. The concept of equal treatment also inheres in entitlement, and argues against basing eligibility on special statuses, such as maternity.

The evils of any public welfare system consist, to a large degree, in subjecting large numbers of people to bureaucratic discretion, in making their source of livelihood insecure by uncertain or changeable standards of eligibility, and in keeping their benefits constantly subject to the visitorial powers of the state, so that there is an excess of supervision and a lack of sufficient independence of action. The concept of entitlement attempts to meet these evils. It means objective eligibility safeguards against revocation or loss of benefits, and it means that the individual's rights, whatever they may be, should be known to him and enforceable through law. Thus entitlement is a problem for lawyers, for while the policy of entitlement is one developed by philosophers of welfare, effectuating it (particularly when the ideal must be approached pragmatically) is within the professional competence of lawyers alone.

## Conclusion

The field of social welfare has developed for thirty years with relatively little attention to the protection or clarification of the legal rights of beneficiaries, especially in programs operating with a large degree of discretion. Where other fields have seen the steady growth of rights through the processes of litigation, rights that might have been developed out of existing welfare statutes have atrophied from disuse. In point of fact, the legal profession does not even know enough about agency practices in the welfare field to be able to identify possible denials of rights. There has been no systematic effort to find out what statutes, rules, administrative regulations or institutional practices may now be causing unnecessary or unjustified injury to beneficiaries or giving rise to discrimination against some of them. The sampling of problems given above was uncovered largely by fortuity; it is impossible to tell what might be revealed by a systematic search. The clients of welfare themselves are rarely in a position to know whether they are being wrongly treated.

We need a radically new approach to the field of social welfare. Today the nation's poor stand as far from the enjoyment of basic rights as did the Negro at the beginning of the Civil Rights movement. As in the case of the Negro, the avenue of reform must be through law. In a society that is highly organized, institutional and bureaucratic, law is the essential means by which individuals are protected; law alone can ensure the fairness and lack of oppression that is essential to individual independence.[52] The field of social welfare has grown up with virtually no participation by lawyers at the level where individual rights are at stake. Lawyers are desperately needed now.[53]

We need organized legal research to examine statutes, regulations, manuals and practices to determine where changes are needed. We need institutions capable of financing both legal research and test cases to determine the extent of rights in given areas. And we need lawyers to represent individual clients who cannot pay for help or secure that help from any existing organizations; it is only through individual cases that the law comes into being and keeps on growing.

The condition of the field of social welfare is an indictment of the present day legal profession. Lawyers have simply not been available when help was needed. There are virtually no organized sources of legal aid to assist persons with welfare problems, law schools have no courses designed to prepare lawyers for such service, and the need for lawyers is rarely recognized by the agencies themselves or the individuals concerned. Today, as law increasingly becomes our central instrument of social policy, we can no longer afford this form of neglect.

By the same token, decisions concerning human rights are too important to be left to public welfare workers and public administration officials without the aid of law. Law is needed to help them to see issues clearly, to guide them, and to strengthen their good intentions. In a constructive alliance of law and social welfare there lies hope for a fundamental change in the status of the disadvantaged of our society — a bill of rights for the disinherited.

52. Jones, *The Rule of Law and the Welfare State,* 58 COLUM. L. REV. 143 (1958).

53. See *The Availability of Counsel and Group Legal Services: A Symposium,* 12 U.C.L.A.L. REV. 279 (1965), especially Sparer, *The Role of the Welfare Client's Lawyer,* 12 U.C.L.A.L. REV. 361 (1965); Carlin & Howard, *Legal Representation and Class Justice,* 12 U.C.L.A.L. REV. 381 (1965).

# [15]

# THE SUPREME COURT
## 1968 TERM

### FOREWORD: ON PROTECTING THE POOR THROUGH THE FOURTEENTH AMENDMENT

*Frank I. Michelman* *

IN the end, no doubt, a victorious War on Poverty will have somehow attacked and conquered relative deprivation. In the end, we may believe, the real problem will be found lurking in people's responses to "the disparity between the low access of the poor to resources and the observable large control over resources of the elite," [1] or in the poor's felt "lack of [the] opportunity viewed as being available to the major part of members of society." [2] "[I]n a hyperbolic way," it can respectably be said that "poverty is inequality," and that this, rather than "hardship," is the problem to be solved.[3]

No unflattering portrait of the human psyche — as beset with envy and spite — is necessary to the belief that relative deprivation can be a great evil, especially where the inequalities are neither marginal in significance nor randomly distributed. One need believe only that a socially assigned position of noticeably inferior command over resources and influence is gravely prejudicial to one's chances for a decent life — that, as Lawrence Haworth puts it,

> One is poor not because he has no money, but because, possibly owing to lack of money, he lacks also access to the social instrumentalities that make humanly significant action possible. In part, it is a simple matter of not having the price of admission . . . . But in larger part it is a matter of not having the character or competence (*e.g.* lack of verbal facility, lack of motivation, destructive orientation) that establishes one's capability of taking up an opportunity that is formally open.[4]

---

* Professor of Law, Harvard Law School. B.A., Yale, 1957; LL.B., Harvard, 1960.

This article was prepared, in part, in connection with research supported by The Harvard Center on Law and Education with funds provided by The U.S. Office of Economic Opportunity.

[1] Ornati, *The Spatial Distribution of Urban Poverty*, in POWER, POVERTY, AND URBAN POLICY 49, 50 (W. Bloomberg & H. Schmandt eds. 1968).

[2] Goodpaster, *An Introduction to the Community Development Corporation*, 46 J. URBAN LAW 603, 625 (1969).

[3] *Id.* at 626.

[4] Haworth, *Deprivation and the Good City*, in POWER, POVERTY, AND URBAN POLICY, *supra* note 1, at 27, 39.

On such a view, it would be natural for one's vision of the target evil to transcend, say, the specific inadequacy of an education or diet, and to see poverty inhering in all demoralizing vestiges of institutionalized subjugation — or, less heatedly, institutionalized preference. One would, accordingly, take umbrage at any significant — and especially at any officially sponsored — relative deprivation. The ultimate goal would be an end to significant inequality respecting power, resources, standing, and the tokens thereof.

But it is not less sane to approach the evil of poverty as if it were composed of a complex of absolute, not relative, deprivations — a syndrome of particularly poignant hardships and particularly crushing denials of opportunity. Indeed, this is Haworth's own view of the matter. To be sure, it is not the grosser, materialistic deprivations of food and shelter on which he concentrates, but rather "severe deprivation with respect to capability to act in humanly decent ways." [5] The point is that cause for concern is found not in some repugnant discrimination which may accompany a deprivation, but in the severe deprivation itself; and this is true even though such deprivations may take the form of, or be known through the observation of, particular kinds of "extreme inequalities." [6]

Even on Haworth's terms, an anti-poverty grand strategy which focused exclusively on a catalogue of severe deprivations would probably have to be construed as an attack on symptoms rather than on the disease itself. But treatment of symptoms is not always a thing to disparage: to hide the signs of measles under a layer of cosmetics is unworthy; to treat the symptomatic suffocation of a pneumonia patient is not. Indeed, to refer to the suffocation as mere symptom is so misleading that we ought to find another term for it — "quasi-symptom" perhaps. Prima facie, it would seem that the role of courts and other rights-enforcing agencies in an anti-poverty war would be restricted almost entirely to the treatment of quasi-symptomatic, specific and severe deprivations. Since this is a worthy endeavor, the restriction need not chafe. Indeed, it might be welcomed on the ground that alleviating specific deprivations is a much more manageable task than closing the general inequality gap to acceptable dimensions. In any event, a court solicitous of its own accuracy and credibility should perhaps try to avoid suggesting that its anti-poverty role might go much beyond the alleviation of those severe deprivations of which Haworth speaks. I wish to raise a question about whether the Supreme Court, and those

[5] *Id.* at 38.

[6] *See id.* at 44; pp. 18–19, 49 *infra*.

who chronicle its doings and sayings have been as careful about this matter as they ought. My question implies no criticism of the Court's past holdings which could be said to compose its contribution to the great War. Yet the question does suggest possibilities for future departures which the Court's accustomed rhetoric has left obscure.

## I. Equality or Minimum Welfare?

Let me then suggest that the judicial "equality" explosion of recent times [7] has largely been ignited by reawakened sensitivity, not to equality, but to a quite different sort of value or claim which might better be called "minimum welfare." In the recent judicial handiwork which has been hailed (and reviled) as an "egalitarian revolution," [8] a particularly striking and propitious note has been sounded through those acts whereby the Court has directly shielded poor persons from the most elemental consequence of poverty: lack of funds to exchange for needed goods, services, or privileges of access. I hope to show how these events in particular can, with profit to the understanding, be approached through systematic resistance to the notions that economic inequality as such is repugnant to constitutional values (if the state is in any manner implicated by its activities in that inequality), and that the Court's interventions are mainly designed to move us towards a condition of economic equality.[9] Certainly these notions are uneasy ones, given a society which on the whole continues to be individualistic, competitive, and market-oriented.

Of course, the Court's "egalitarian" interventions are often occasioned by problems which would not exist but for economic inequality. *Yet I hope to make clear that in many instances their purposes could be more soundly and satisfyingly understood as vindication of a state's duty to protect against certain hazards which are endemic in an unequal society, rather than vindication of a duty to avoid complicity in unequal treatment.*

In elaborating upon this theme, I shall be treading where others have trod before. Especially with respect to a hypothe-

[7] *See, e.g.*, Cox, *The Supreme Court, 1965 Term, Foreword: Constitutional Adjudication and the Promotion of Human Rights*, 80 Harv. L. Rev. 91 (1966); Kurland, *The Supreme Court, 1963 Term, Foreword: "Equal in Origin and Equal in Title to the Legislative and Executive Branches of the Government,"* 78 Harv. L. Rev. 143 (1964).

[8] The phrase may first have been applied to the Court's recent work by Professor Kurland, a reviler. *See* Kurland, *supra* note 7, at 144.

[9] A refreshing note of skepticism has been sounded in Lewis & Levy, *Family Law and Welfare Policies: The Case for "Dual Systems,"* 54 Calif. L. Rev. 748 (1966). There are several points of tangency between the present article and the first half of that one.

sized state duty to protect actively against certain risks associated with membership in a minority race, related ideas have been well-ventilated.[10] The principal focus here will be on a different class of risks, those associated with paucity of income or wealth.

The instances of actual or potential judicial intervention of which I speak are, characteristically, not such as involve a "de jure" discrimination, in which complaint is made of some official decision to "classify" a population for purposes of extending different treatments to the classes officially distinguished. They comprise, rather, cases of "de facto" discrimination in which the state is charged with responsibility for disadvantage suffered by members of some group, even though that group is not one which state officials are supposed to have identified or treated as such in the actions giving rise to state liability — for example, a case in which the state is held responsible for disadvantage suffered by "the poor" as a result of its decision to "classify" the population into those who do and do not pay, say, a tuition fee or poll tax.

We shall, in short, be chiefly interested here in cases involving claims that a government must spend its revenues in order to satisfy certain wants felt by its impecunious citizens, or otherwise render those wants satisfiable even though the claimant has no money to spare. I confess to some ambivalence between two possible meanings of my argument about the preferable way of "understanding" judicial responses in these situations. On the one hand, I do not limit myself to speculations about the ethical outlooks or inchoate theories of social justice which might lie at the roots of judicial behavior (although I shall advance for consideration a particular — albeit not quite choate — theory of social justice). On the other hand, I do not campaign for explicit recognition or adoption of some novel legal theorem. As will presently appear, I am more interested in ways of thinking about certain legal problems, and in ways of saying what the significant factors are, than I am in doctrinally formulated summaries or predictions of outcomes. Perhaps the best description of what ties these paragraphs together is provisional adoption, as inchoate legal doctrine, of a theory of social justice which prima facie seems capable of rationalizing an important group of equal protection decisions without positing equality or evenhandedness as the guiding value (or discrimination as the target evil). The

---

[10] *See, e.g.*, Black, *The Supreme Court, 1966 Term, Foreword: "State Action," Equal Protection, and California's Proposition 14*, 81 HARV. L. REV. 69 (1967); Karst & Horowitz, *Reitman v. Mulkey: A Telophase of Substantive Equal Protection*, 1967 SUP. CT. REV. 39; Sager, *Tight Little Islands: Exclusionary Zoning, Equal Protection, and the Indigent*, 21 STAN. L. REV. 767 (1969).

purpose is to see what insight can thus be gained into the doings and sayings of courts and commentators. Whether any dissonances thereby exposed should be ascribed to the constitutional text or to the judicial and scholarly interpretations thereof seems to me a fairly separable question on which I shall also offer some views.

These purposes, of course, suggest that differences of consequence may ensue from a theoretical distinction between a duty to protect against certain severe consequences of economic inequality and a duty to avoid hyper-offensive inequalities in treatment. Two obvious differences are that a duty to extend protection against certain hazards need not entail or suggest any "equalization" of treatment or circumstances beyond that necessary to obviate the hazard and, more important, that such a duty may obtain even where the state would choose to remain quiescent and to "treat" everyone equally by not according any relevant treatment whatsoever.[11] If offensive and demoralizing discrimination generally be taken as the target evil, and if an empirical assumption be made that the affairs in which government is visibly involved are ipso facto likely to be popularly invested with special meaning, then there is a certain kind of sense in a "state action" qualification upon government's duties to relieve against hazards of poverty. But it is less easy to be reconciled to the "state action" notion when alleviation of certain, specially poignant hardships or crushing disadvantages is thought to be the object. If we can see and feel that the hardship is poignant or the disadvantage dire, the government's noninvolvement then may come not as relief but as reproach.

The equal protection clause is the constitutional text which most naturally suggests itself to one who would claim a legal right to have certain wants satisfied out of the public treasury, insofar as he means to found his argument upon a comparison of burdens and opportunities which must otherwise accrue to the relatively rich and the relatively poor. And equal protection is, of course, the text which the Supreme Court has preferred in upholding such claims with respect to criminal defense needs[12]

---

[11] In addition to the two differences in consequence mentioned in the text, I shall also be suggesting that the initial choice between formulation of the duty as one of minimum protection or as one of avoidance of "discriminatory" treatment may result in differences in intellectual strategy which will sometimes issue in different results — even assuming active state complicity, as well as agreement on all questions of value except such as may be implicit in the initial choice of how to formulate the duty. *See* pp. 33–39 *infra*.

[12] *See, e.g.*, Douglas v. California, 372 U.S. 353 (1963) (state must provide counsel to criminal accused on first appeal as of right, irrespective of court's assessment of probable merits).

and voting rights.[13] Yet it could well be thought paradoxical to infer from a general statement of duty on the government's part to treat all persons "equally" a more particular duty to satisfy certain wants irrespective of the recipient's readiness to pay the associated costs.

The paradox and its resolution are most clearly seen by noting first that when a government's practice of, say, charging tuition fees or otherwise requiring persons to pay for their (or their dependents') education out of their own means is challenged,[14] there may be ambiguity about the intended scope and focus of the attack. The target might consist of the government's assertedly "discriminatory" actions in setting conditions of access to that education which it is visibly engaged in providing. Alternatively, the attack might concentrate on the poor person's predicament of being unable to afford a certain amount of education. Now, given a prevalent assumption that the "proper" allocation of resources results when consumers of goods[15] are required to pay a "market" price for goods consumed — one which fairly reflects and reconciles the cost of providing those goods and the felt benefits of consuming them — it would seem that *if the "treatment" immediately at issue is the setting of conditions under which a person will be granted access to a good*, "equality" would normally reside in access to goods at the same market price which everyone else must pay, while "discrimination" would consist of price discrimination.[16] Bringing the claim within the locutions of the equal protection clause thus involves obvious strains on usage, *as long as the focus of attack is the official act of setting conditions of access.*

Of course, we remain free to say that there is a list of select goods which are "properly" rationed according to need rather than according to a consumer's readiness to purchase at market prices, and that for *these* goods "equality" (the norm) consists of a compensatory assurance of access to universally "needed" amounts, while "discrimination" (departure from the norm) ex-

---

[13] *See* Harper v. Virginia State Bd. of Elections, 383 U.S. 663 (1966) (state may not condition franchise on payment of fee or tax); pp. 24–25 *infra*.

[14] *Cf.* McInnis v. Ogilvie, 394 U.S. 322 (1969), *aff'g mem.* McInnis v. Shapiro, 293 F. Supp. 327 (N.D. Ill. 1968); pp. 47–48 *infra*.

[15] As used here "goods" means not only material commodities, but also services and privileges of access to valued activities.

[16] The Supreme Court's "typical" approach to equal protection questions has been said to incorporate a "presumption" that laws which accord "numerically" or "formally" equal treatment — that is, apply a uniform rule to all persons irrespective of possibly relevant differences in their attributes or situations — are valid. *See Developments in the Law — Equal Protection*, 82 HARV. L. REV. 1065, 1171 (1969).

ists wherever access to the universally needed portion is so straitened, by a uniform price or other impediment, that some persons are effectively deprived of it. But our undoubted freedom to state the matter in this fashion does not lead to any Lewis Carroll punch line, because that linguistic freedom is significantly burdened: *in shaping the statement of our claim so as to fit it to the locutions of the equal protection clause, we must find an "inequality" to complain about; and the only inequality turns out to be that some persons, less than all, are suffering from inability to satisfy certain "basic" wants which presumably are felt by all alike.* But if we define the inequality that way, we can hardly avoid admitting that the injury consists more essentially of deprivation than of discrimination, that the cure accordingly lies more in provision than in equalization, and that the reality of injury and need for cure are to be determined largely without reference to whether the complainant's predicament is somehow visibly related to past or current governmental activity. A focus on a government's access-determining practices implies, or at least is consistent with, an overriding concern with the moral and psychological harms uniquely associated with official nonevenhandedness. But a focus on the predicament of nonaccess is consistent only with an overriding concern for the impairments of welfare or effectiveness flowing from the exclusion — which seem the same no matter whether the government is or is not actively engaged in satisfying the want in question. And that, Dear Reader (plus a suggestion that the Court has not been as clear on the point as seems desirable), is in essence my story. All that follows is a scramble of restatement, development, and recapitulation.

### *A. An Imperfect Theory of Social Justice*

Before proceeding to an examination of the Court's work, and that of some of its scholarly kibitzers, it will be helpful to dwell briefly on a proposition about social justice which I shall call "minimum protection against economic hazard."

As applied to economic hazards, a claim to "minimum protection" would mean that persons are entitled to have certain wants satisfied — certain existing needs filled — by government, free of any direct charge over and above the obligation to pay general taxes (and perhaps free of conditions referring to past idleness, prodigality, or other economic "misconduct"). Wants to which this claim applies we shall call "just wants." The claimant does not, except in a quite limited sense, try to show that an overall distributional configuration is improper. He claims a right to have *a specific, existing want* provided for, rather than to have a generally larger or more equal income.[17]

It is crucial for the minimum protection claimant that the question of present entitlement to certain goods "free" be discussable separately from that of the overall justice of practices governing the general pattern of distribution. Otherwise the minimum-protection claim is misdirected: every claim to have a specified want satisfied "free" will be convertible into a claim that the practices which eventuated in the existing distribution [18] are improper because they have left some persons unable to "afford" the cost of satisfying that want. The latter proposition will be much harder to sustain in any forum, legal or popular — especially when account must be taken of contingencies of exertion, moderation, judgment, and planning — than the simple assertion that there is presently a want conjoined with a lack of personal means to satisfy it. Thus it is not enough for the minimum protectionist, who entertains some hope of vindicating his claims through legal action, to produce a theory of distributive justice which is both incisive enough in its criteria and convincing enough in its correspondence to prevailing sentiments to yield a persuasive catalogue of just wants. For one could concede that a distributional system is unjust unless it takes account of certain basic needs and somehow provides for their fulfillment, but still deny that this must be done through any commitment to fulfillment of needs as and when they materialize. One might, rather, say that justice is satisfied as long as the prevailing social and economic institutions afford every one a fair opportunity to derive an income sufficient over time to provide for whatever needs are considered "basic." The argument for minimum protection as applied to specific needs and occasions must, then, depend on the proposition that justice requires *more* than a fair opportunity to realize an income which can cover these needs or insure against them — requires, to be sure, absolute assurance that they will be met when and as felt, free of any remote [19] contingencies pertaining to effort, thrift, or foresight.

We might take our cue from Professor Rawls' idea of "jus-

[17] The argument is not, of course, that an item-budget approach is generally required or desirable in the fashioning of legislative schemes for income maintenance or public assistance, but simply that a person may repair to the courts in quest of particular items when whatever legislative programs exist have failed him.

[18] Including not only explicit taxes and income transfers but also basic organization and manipulation of the economy — matters such as protectionism, immigration and inter-regional migration policies, and trading off between price stability and full employment.

[19] "Remote" is intended to save the possibility that a person might deliberately and effectively waive his claims by informed and proximate choice. Such choice could, conceivably, assume a variety of forms — monastic vows, perhaps, or deliberate waste of publicly provided food or shelter.

tice as fairness."[20] Rawls grants that social institutions and practices may be just, even though they produce unequal incomes and accumulations. Yet for an unequal system to be just, it must be the case that a rational person, hypothetically ignorant of what particular place in society awaits him, would find the inequalities acceptable. To Rawls this means that inequalities of wealth and income are unjust unless they are necessary to a system which assures to those who turn out to occupy society's least advantageous positions a better situation than they could reasonably expect under a system which distributed the net social product in equal shares. In particular, such inequalities might be just insofar as they were necessary to incentives and market allocations thought to make the economy more efficient and productive than it could otherwise be. But a just arrangement would be grudging in its allowance of such inequalities and would go as far as possible in the direction of channeling the additional outputs generated by an incentive system into a generous guarantee of a minimum welfare for all (entailing, very likely, redistributions which to some extent limit incentive effects). Accordingly, an arrangement would not be just insofar as it overlooked means whereby persons could be insured against the risk of relatively grave need with relatively little damage to efficiency and incentives.

The identity of "just wants" would then be determined according to a judgment arrived at through the following process of reasoning. Assume that a man has no idea what his social and economic station in a predominantly competitive society is to be and that he fully recognizes the role of income incentives and free markets in maximizing social productivity. Will he nevertheless wish to have each person insured against the risk that certain needs will remain unfulfilled as and when they accrue — and what specific risks of that sort, if any, will he say should be insured against?[21] Might he, for example, say that insofar

---

[20] *See* Rawls, *Distributive Justice: Some Addenda*, 13 NAT. L. FORUM 51 (1968); Rawls, *Constitutional Liberty and the Concept of Justice*, in NOMOS VI: JUSTICE 96 (C. Friedrich & J. Chapman eds. 1963); Rawls, *The Sense of Justice*, 72 PHIL. REV. 281 (1963); Rawls, *Justice as Fairness*, 67 PHIL. REV. 164 (1958), in JUSTICE AND SOCIAL POLICY 80 (F. Olafson ed. 1961). *See also* J. BUCHANAN & G. TULLOCK, THE CALCULUS OF CONSENT: LOGICAL FOUNDATIONS OF CONSTITUTIONAL DEMOCRACY 190–97 (paper ed. 1965).

[21] Here we may briefly note some possible reasons for insisting on such assurances, over and above insistence on a system of economic rewards and transfers which would tend generally to assure each household head of an income adequate to his household's important needs. Assurances may be desired against the risk that one — or the family head upon whom one is dependent — will not measure up to generally reasonable minimum standards of active participation in the economy, or against the risk that a generally fair system of judging the quality of one's

as the society provides for "democratic" political participation through such means as voting and standing for office, access to these activities should never be blocked by economic vicissitude? Or that persons must at all times be assured of effective access to some impartial and remedially competent forum for the peaceful settlement of bona fide legal disputes? Or that everyone at all times must be assured of facilities for a modicum of privacy, intimacy, confidentiality, self-expression? Or that each child must be guaranteed the means of developing his competence, self-knowledge, and tastes for living?

Our immediate purpose is not to try to answer these or any cognate questions. It is, rather, a much more limited one: to show that the judicial and scholarly literature of constitutionally guaranteed economic "equality" is increasingly instinct with such questions, and that this literature itself suggests (indirectly and sometimes unconsciously) that the questions above are necessary, pertinent, and by some means or other answerable. Putting it slightly differently, our purpose is to show how the possibility of propounding such questions might affect the elaboration of constitutional rights pertaining to the status of being poor.[22]

### *B. The Magnetism of Equality*

It is not difficult to imagine reasons why a court, even if we supposed that it was inspired to its interventions by notions of minimum protection and just wants, might nevertheless be given to clothing its decisions in the verbiage of inequality and discrimination. There is, to begin with, the language of the Con-

participation, or the extenuating force of one's disabilities, will in a particular case miscarry. More generally, assurance may be desired against the chance that the sincerest attempts to devise and maintain a generally fair system of rewards and transfers will nevertheless leave some persons on some occasions desperately unprovisioned. Most generally, flat assurances concerning just wants may upon reflection seem a desirable way of simplifying (and thus cheapening) the continuing task of adjustment of the reward/transfer system, either because this method obviates any need to place a dollar value from time to time on the whole catalogue of just wants (a composite we may call the just minimum) or because it assures society that transferred purchasing power will not be dissipated on other wants, leaving just wants unfulfilled and, accordingly, an unsatisfied claim still outstanding. The latter point, I suspect, will eventually turn out to be the key to the argument. It provides a reason why persons in a just system would agree to receive their guaranteed minimum in kind rather than in cash. *Cf.* Musgrave, *The Role of Social Insurance in an Overall Program for Social Welfare*, in THE AMERICAN SYSTEM OF SOCIAL INSURANCE: ITS PHILOSOPHY, IMPACT, AND FUTURE DEVELOPMENT 23, 25–28 (W. Bowen *et al.* eds. 1968).

[22] This article is part of a continuing study which has as one of its aims the discovery or development of criteria for answering such questions, in a form suitable for judging. I do not warrant that it can be done.

stitution. The due process clause inveighs only against certain "deprivations" by the "state," occurrences which seemingly cannot occur by mere default. On the other hand, the equal protection clause's injunction against "denying" the "equal protection of the laws" is not so clearly void of a requirement that the quiescent state must "act" (*i.e.*, cease denying protection) in certain circumstances when it would choose not to.[23] Moreover, possibly because of unhappy connotations associated with "substantive due process" as well as because equal protection remains an empty conundrum without some frank infusion of judicially "sculpted" values,[24] the Court seems currently more comfortable in staking out and valuing "fundamental" interests under the aegis of equal protection than it could well feel under due process.[25]

But to the extent that the Court were disposed to exploit the equal protection clause to enforce some affirmative duties of protection, it could hardly help noticing that it would be "equal," not minimum protection which had to be extended. *X*, it seems, would be entitled to protection only insofar as *Y* was protected. By the same token, *X* would be entitled to just as much protection as *Y* enjoyed. Therefore, if the situation were one which obligated the state to extend protection to *X* at all, it would also be one which required that *X*'s "treatment" be made "equal" to *Y*'s. The rhetoric of equality would be injected by the preferred constitutional text.

But apart from the texts, there is an independent problem of standards which would be likely to induce reliance (even if

---

[23] *See* P. KAUPER, CIVIL LIBERTIES AND THE CONSTITUTION 128–29 (1962).

[24] *See* Coons, Clune, & Sugarman, ***Educational Opportunity: A Workable Constitutional Test for State Financial Structures***, 57 CALIF. L. REV. 305, 335 (1969) [hereinafter cited as Coons].

[25] *See* Ferguson v. Skrupa, 372 U.S. 726, 731–32 (1963); Goldberg, ***Equality and Governmental Action***, 39 N.Y.U.L. REV. 205, 211–12 (1964); ***Developments in the Law***, ***supra*** note 16, at 1131–32. If any doubts remain that the "new" equal protection method — that of demanding a compelling state interest to justify measures which are "invidious" and/or which encroach upon "fundamental" interests — involves the Court in a sculpting and ranking of values not essentially different from what occurs under "substantive due process," it is a purpose of this Foreword to dispel such doubts. The Court itself seems not inclined to deny that its selections of favored interests are inspired at least in part by a higher law; it eschews, in any event, the wistful suggestion of Justices Stewart and Black that the complete catalogue is somehow inferable from the written constitutional text. *See* Kramer v. Union Free School Dist., 395 U.S. 621, 634 (1969) (Stewart, J., dissenting); Shapiro v. Thompson, 394 U.S. 618, 642 (1969) (Stewart, J., concurring). The suggestion seems not overly compelling anyhow, and certainly exegesis does not explain the Court's performance. And I shall hope to show that the presence in these favored-interest cases of offensive classifications is not an autonomously significant factor.

spurious) on equality. How could the Court, which presumably has not forgotten Holmes' "Mr. Herbert Spencer" jibe,[26] defend in suitably judicial terms the abstract proposition that some particular risk associated with poverty is one of those relatively few risks against which the state must protect? Even after the risk had been so identified, how could the Court say when "enough" protection had been furnished? "As much as" seems to provide just the certainty of measure which "enough of" so sorely lacks. Is it not much more comfortable for a court, in explaining why *X* is entitled to, say, legal assistance on his appeal from a criminal conviction, to adopt as a benchmark what *Y* in fact has rather than what justice requires? [27] If in fact *X* doesn't need as much or as good assistance as *Y* has; or if the Court's remedy in fact doesn't assure him of that much or even seriously try to; or if the fact that *Y* also has a lawyer to handle his divorce suit does not now and may not ever induce the Court to hold that *X*, too, must be provided with a divorce lawyer — it remains that all of those truths are, thankfully, not such as need to receive any explicit attention (except from Mr. Justice Harlan and an occasional dissenting ally [28]) in the course of rendering a decision whose real, practical effect is precisely to get a tolerable, minimum amount of criminal lawyering for *X*.

Finally, it must be noted that while the idea of "just wants" or "severe deprivations" expresses an ethical precept distinct from that of "equality," detecting a failure to provide the required minimum may nonetheless depend in part upon the detection of inequalities; and elimination or reduction of inequality may be entailed in rectifying such a failure, insofar as the just minimum is understood to be a function (in part) of the existing maximum. Such an understanding could grow out of a residue of indissoluble interpenetration of the felt evils of relative deprivation and poignant hardship. Thus if the extent of society's obligation to tax itself for support of the needy depends in part upon its overall level of affluence, widening inequalities become increasingly suggestive of failure to furnish the just minimum. Or again, insofar as the components of the required (or "a decent") minimum are affected by what others have — by prevailing tastes and expectations, or by emulation — then extremity of inequality is suggestive. Standing on a quite different ground is

[26] *See* Lochner v. New York, 198 U.S. 45, 75 (1905) (Holmes, J., dissenting).

[27] *Cf.* Lewis & Levy, *supra* note 9, at 748–49.

[28] See his dissenting opinions in Douglas v. California, 372 U.S. 353, 363 (1963), and Griffin v. Illinois, 351 U.S. 12, 34–36 (1956). I shall forbear to cite the *Griffin* dissent at every point of correspondence between its argument and that offered herein. My inclination to agree with Mr. Justice Harlan is qualified mainly by the fact that he dissented in the *Griffin-Douglas* line of cases.

the relevance of what others have when the want in question is deemed specially significant — as education, for example, might be — because of its importance for success in competitive activities.[29]

## II. Discrimination Against the Poor — Pecuniary Circumstance as an "Invidious" or "Suspect" Classifying Trait

A notable feature in the Court's "egalitarian revolution," many commentators suggest, is the emergence of special judicial hostility towards official discrimination, be it de jure or de facto, according to pecuniary circumstance.[30] (It is important to bear in mind from the beginning that the data from which this thesis is induced consist exclusively of decisions requiring states to see to the satisfaction of certain wants when a general requirement of payment would prevent a destitute person from satisfying them out of his own means.[31]) If the commentators are right, relative impecuniousness appears to be joining race and national ancestry to compose a complex of traits which, if detectible as a basis of officially sanctioned disadvantage, render such disadvantage "invidious" or "suspect."

In this Foreword, I shall use the words "invidious" and "suspect" in the following somewhat specialized fashion: "Invidious," a term of opprobrium, refers generally to legislative or adminis-

[29] *See Developments in the Law, supra* note 16, at 1168–69.

[30] *See, e.g.*, Coons at 348, 358–71; *Developments in the Law, supra* note 16, at 1124; Note, *Discriminations Against the Poor and the Fourteenth Amendment*, 81 Harv. L. Rev. 435 (1967); *cf.* Sager, *supra* note 10, at 779–80.

[31] The decisions said to support the thesis are discussed at text later in the present section. Edwards v. California, 314 U.S. 160 (1941), presented the Court with a case of de jure wealth discrimination; but, despite Justice Jackson's concurring eloquence, *id.* at 181, the Court chose to rest its opinion there upon the invalidity of the state's interference with interstate commerce, rather than upon either the protected status of the interest in interstate travel or the invidiousness of the wealth classification. Cipriano v. City of Houma, 395 U.S. 701 (1969), involved a de jure classification by property ownership, which might be thought to partake of the same invidiousness which characterizes wealth classifications, a point certainly not lost on the Court if only because highly visible in the opinions below. *See* Cipriano v. City of Houma, 286 F. Supp. 823 (E.D. La. 1968), and especially Judge Wisdom's dissent, *id.* at 828. The Supreme Court's decision, quite understandably, was predicated on the fundamental quality of the voting interest, and not on any possible invidiousness in the classification. As for decisions by lesser courts, there are a few cases dealing with minimum-cost zoning requirements cited in Sager, *supra* note 10, at 781 n.67. The most prominent decision placing any weight on a de facto wealth classification other than a payment requirement is Hobson v. Hansen, 269 F. Supp. 401 (D.D.C. 1967), *aff'd sub nom.* Smuck v. Hobson, 408 F.2d 175 (D.C. Cir. 1969).

trative behavior as reflected in an act of classifying, and specifically to certain obnoxious tendencies or implications which the classification is thought to harbor. "Suspect," a neutral term, refers to judicial behavior, and specifically to certain variations in that behavior which are supposed to result from a classification's invidiousness. An "invidious" classification or trait is one which combines, in greater or lesser degree and in varying proportions, three qualities: (1) a general ill-suitedness to the advancement of any proper governmental objective; (2) a high degree of adaptation to uses which are oppressive in the sense of systematic and unfair devaluation, through majority rule, of the claims of certain persons to nondiscriminatory sharing in the benefits and burdens of social existence; (3) a potency to injure through an effect of stigmatizing certain persons by implying popular or official belief in their inherent inferiority or undeservingness.[32] A law requiring racial segregation epitomizes the idea of "invidiousness." The operational meaning of "suspect" is, roughly, that a court will invalidate the classification unless it is shown to be "necessary" in the service of some "compelling" state interest (rather than merely "rationally related" to some "permissible" governmental objective).[33] This form of "special judicial scrutiny" is said to be due when invidious classifications are employed, particularly if certain "fundamental" interests are also at stake. Since there are, obviously, degrees of invidiousness, it would seem to follow that there are also degrees of suspectness — that is, of judicial stringency in the evaluation of the "compellingness" of state interests and the "necessity" in their pursuit of certain classifications.[34] Of these related continuums, more anon.[35]

A limited assimilation of impecuniousness to membership in a racial, ethnic, or national minority is not lacking in plausibility. The convincing reasons which can be offered for extremely skeptical judicial inspection of official acts which explicitly classify by race (or have the obvious purpose of doing so, although not explicitly) seem applicable to statutes which explicitly or de-

[32] *See Developments in the Law, supra* note 16, at 1124–27, 1173–76.

[33] The diction has evolved in cases involving classifications bearing upon "fundamental interests" such as those in voting and free travel. *See* Kramer v. Union Free School Dist., 395 U.S. 621 (1969); Shapiro v. Thompson, 394 U.S. 618 (1969).

[34] "Strict review" or "close judicial scrutiny" seems to entail (a) a requirement that the challenged classification be strictly relevant to whatever purpose is claimed by the state to justify its use, and also that it be the fairest and least restrictive alternative evidently available for the pursuit of that purpose ("necessity"); and (b) a requirement that the infringement of fundamental interests resulting from the classification's use be outweighed by the claimed state purpose ("compellingness"). *See Developments in the Law, supra* note 16, at 1101–04.

[35] *See* pp. 33–35 *infra.*

signedly classify by wealth or income, *in the sense of deliberately subdividing the population according to a wealth or income criterion for the purpose of extending different treatment to the groups so distinguished.* For if money is power, then a class deliberately defined so as to include everyone who has less wealth or income than any person outside it may certainly be deemed, as racial minorities are by many observers deemed, to be especially susceptible to abuse by majoritarian process; and classification of "the poor" as such may, like classification of racial minorities as such, be popularly understood as a badge of inferiority. Especially is this so in light of the extreme difficulty of imagining proper governmental objectives which require for their achievement the explicit carving out, for relatively disadvantageous treatment, of a class defined by relative paucity of wealth or income.

But if there are good reasons for treating de jure wealth classifications as specially suspect irrespective of the interests particularly involved, there are also good reasons (to which we shall presently turn) for doubting whether a doctrine has yet emerged or ought to be encouraged which would draw pecuniary circumstance into an "inner circle"[36] of invidious and therefore suspect classifying traits insofar as de facto classifications are concerned. One danger in such a doctrine — though not the one in which we shall be chiefly interested — is that it demonstrably exerts some temptation to equate de facto "wealth" cases with de facto race cases.[37] But governmental actions which are accidentally, even if systematically, linked with comparative disadvantage to the relatively impecunious, while not always entirely free of invidiousness, so clearly tend to be less freighted with it than do de facto racial classifications that assimilation of the two effects, for purposes of fixing the appropriate degree of judicial skepticism, seems bound to mislead.[38]

---

[36] *See* Coons at 346.

[37] *See* Karst & Horowitz, *supra* note 10, at 75.

[38] For an intuitive testing of the proposition in text, consider the following hypothetical cases: (1) A municipal government refuses to budge from its historic policy of "assigning" residents to public swimming pools according to their respective neighborhoods of residence. Plaintiff *B* challenges his exclusion from a "white" area's pool, complaining of segregation by race. Plaintiff *P*, who is white and native, challenges his exclusion from a "rich" area's pool on grounds of de facto segregation by income. All facilities, however separate, are admittedly "equal." Who has the stronger case? (2) Plaintiffs are being dislocated from their homes by a municipal development project. Relocation housing of suitable price, quality, and proximity to work places is admittedly available. Plaintiff *B* alleges that the effect of the project is to break up the town's only racially integrated neighborhood and force him into a black ghetto. Plaintiff *P* alleges that the effect is to force him out of an economically integrated area and into public housing. Who

A suggestion that the Supreme Court is developing a hostile stance towards de facto "discriminations against the poor" is, to say the least, understandable in view of the rhetoric which the Court has repeatedly employed in decisions upholding demands that the state relieve a person of poverty-related inability to satisfy an important want.[39] Commentators who make the suggestion are usually astute enough to rush on to a major qualification: they observe that de facto pecuniary classifications are not per se invalid, but rather will result in (or tend towards) invalidity only when they bear adversely upon "fundamental" interests. Even so, it seems fair to characterize this line of scholarly distillation of the raw judicial product as one which shares the Court's penchant for making a distinct issue of the "discriminatory" connotations said to inhere in the condemned payment requirements, over and above their objective effect of preventing impecunious persons from satisfying certain wants.

It will be helpful, before discussing why this instinct for "discrimination" is unfortunate, to present a taxonomy of possible meanings for "no discrimination by wealth" doctrines. A doctrinal form of statement which isolates for special treatment all official action involving de facto wealth discriminations could, it seems, have any of at least four meanings: (1) all such action is invalid; (2) all such action is suspect and will be held invalid in the absence of special justifications; [40] (3) such action is invalid when it infringes a "fundamental" or "favored" interest; (4) such action, when it infringes a fundamental or favored in-

---

has the stronger case? (3) A municipal government has recently introduced the policy of constructing neighborhood swimming pools only in those areas whose residents by majority vote agree to special assessments to pay for the pool. It happens that the only area left in town without a pool is relatively poor and almost exclusively black. In his complaint seeking provision of the last swimming pool out of general revenues, should counsel allege the latter fact?

[39] *E.g.*, McDonald v. Board of Election Comm'rs, 394 U.S. 802, 807 (1969) (dictum), discussed at pp. 26–27 *infra*; Roberts v. La Vallee, 389 U.S. 40, 42 (1967) ("differences in access to the instruments needed to vindicate legal rights, when based upon the financial situation of the defendant, are repugnant to the Constitution"); Anders v. California, 386 U.S. 738, 745 (1967) (provision of counsel "would merely afford [the indigent accused] that advocacy which a non-indigent defendant is able to obtain" and thereby satisfy requirement of "substantial equality"). Perhaps the most prominent example is Douglas v. California, 372 U.S. 353, 355, 357, 358 (1963): "There is lacking that equality demanded by the Fourteenth Amendment where the rich man . . . enjoys the benefit of counsel's [assistance] . . . while the indigent . . . is forced to shift for himself. . . . [T]he evil is . . . discrimination against the indigent. . . . [A]n unconstitutional line has been drawn between rich and poor."

[40] *See* McDonald v. Board of Election Comm'rs, 394 U.S. 802, 807 (1969) (dictum), discussed at pp. 26–27 *infra,* for the Supreme Court's most recent utterance on the subject.

terest, is suspect and will be held invalid in the absence of special justifications.[41] I shall hope to show that, especially in view of the predominance of payment requirements in the whole collection of practices called "de facto wealth discriminations," meanings (1), (2), and (3) are clearly false if taken as descriptive of judicial behavior, wrong if taken as descriptive of popular attitudes, and, accordingly, generally harmful if uttered by or plausibly ascribed to courts; [42] that meanings (2) and (4) are lacking in utility, adding nothing helpful to forms of statement which focus on the "fundamental interest" notion while avoiding mention of "wealth discriminations"; [43] that statements perhaps intended to convey harmless meaning (4) inevitably tend to suggest one of the harmful meanings, (1) or (2); [44] and that meanings (2) and (3), which are perhaps the most natural ones, in part because they can coexist compatibly and are mutually reinforcing, have a tendency to mislead thought and impair judgment.[45]

---

[41] Even the most distinguished opinions and scholarly essays display some ambivalence between meanings (3) and (4). In the classic judicial example of the method, Hobson v. Hansen, 269 F. Supp. 401, 506–08 (D.D.C. 1967), *aff'd sub nom.* Smuck v. Hobson, 408 F.2d 175 (D.C. Cir. 1969), Judge Wright begins by assigning cases of de jure invidious classification (by race or nationality) to category (2). He then states that infringement of a "critical personal right" is enough by itself to call for special justification, irrespective of any invidiousness in the classification. His next step is to state that an *even more* stringent review is in order when infringement of critical rights and de facto disadvantage to a judicially favored class, such as the poor, coincide in the same case. This looks like category (4) leaning strongly towards category (3). Judge Wright at this point drops a footnote (269 F. Supp. at 507 n.197) which suggests that in his discussion he has not distinguished between de jure and de facto discrimination against judicially favored groups; but if de facto wealth discrimination, accordingly, falls within category (2) irrespective of the interest involved, then when a fundamental interest is added to the mix the resulting stringency of review would seem somewhat understated by rule (4), even if somewhat overstated by rule (3). Coons, Clune, and Sugarman, in what will certainly become the classic scholarly discussion of this material, are obviously susceptible to the allure of rule (3) and flirt openly with "the principle . . . that wealth classifications — explicit or de facto — may not determine the state's disposition of fundamental personal interests." *See* Coons at 361. While in general their argument is characterized by a particularism more in keeping with rule (4) than rule (3), they do repeatedly intimate that, once they can establish that the interest in education comes within the "fundamental" category, the argument will be complete that the state must avoid implication in any de facto wealth classification bearing upon that interest. *E.g.*, *id.* at 350. Perhaps what all this shows is that even conscious and determined ear-stuffing will not wholly shut out the siren song of rule (3). Professor Sager is one commentator who seems immune. *See* Sager, *supra* note 10, at 778–79.

[42] *See* pp. 29–33 *infra*.

[43] *See* p. 31 *infra*.

[44] *See* p. 35 *infra*.

[45] *See* pp. 36–38 *infra*

Cases involving de facto pecuniary classifications in which, it is suggested, the Supreme Court has intervened in order to forestall discrimination against the poor, have involved the interests in voting and in access to the machinery of justice in criminal cases. Such cases have, so far, apparently not involved any other interests.[46]

In the voting sphere, the crucial decision is, of course, that in *Harper v. Virginia State Board of Elections*,[47] invalidating Virginia's poll tax. It is true that the *Harper* plaintiffs sued on behalf of a class defined as including those prevented by poverty from paying the tax. But it is far from clear, upon a close reading of Mr. Justice Douglas' opinion for the Court, that the *Harper* decision rests mainly on the impropriety of a pecuniary classification or of discrimination against the poor. The opinion repeatedly indicates that *no* fee may validly be collected in exchange for admission to the vote and strongly suggests that deprivation of the vote may not validly be employed as a sanction for nonpayment of any fee or tax.[48] Thus we may imagine that a state imposes a steeply graduated income tax with ample personal exemptions at the foundation of its rate structure and refuses admission to the vote to any delinquent taxpayer. Or we may imagine that it invents a form of "fee" for the privilege of voting which is similarly adjusted to ability to pay. It cannot be said that such a practice would bear more harshly upon the poor than upon the rich. Yet the *Harper* opinion, rather clearly, forbids it. In short, the de jure classification and the judicially disfavored classification are in that case one and the same: the classification of potential voters into those who have and those who haven't paid the poll tax.

Just why the classification is forbidden is not made clear. At some points the opinion seems to say that forfeiture of the franchise for nonpayment of a fee or tax simply cannot be defended as a rational means to any proper state end. At other points the "fundamental" character of the right to vote and the absence of substantial justification for the poll tax's inhibitory effect on its exercise are made to seem crucial.[49]

---

[46] Shapiro v. Thompson, 394 U.S. 618 (1969), involving the interest in interstate migration, probably should not be treated as a case of de facto wealth classification. *See* pp. 40–42 *infra*.

[47] 383 U.S. 663 (1966).

[48] "[A] State violates the Equal Protection Clause . . . whenever it makes the affluence of the voter or payment of any fee an electoral standard. Voter qualifications have no relation to wealth nor to paying or not paying this or any other tax." *Id.* at 666. It should be noted that Virginia's "poll" (*i.e.*, "head" or "capitation") tax was a true tax payable irrespective of voting. *See* Harper v. Virginia State Bd. of Elections, 240 F. Supp. 270 (E.D. Va. 1964).

[49] The right to vote is said to be "too precious, too fundamental to be . . .

But let us grant, *arguendo*, that the search for a single *Harper* theme is misguided; that *Harper* is, rather, a symphony of holdings, among them the holding that a practice which systematically denies the vote to the poorest groups in a population, or makes its exercise specially burdensome for them, is ipso facto unconstitutional. Is it not, even so, a more natural and parsimonious ordering of the data to treat that holding as one of a family of statements about *the interest in voting* than as a statement about *poverty and special judicial protection linked with that status?* The Court, after all, is entitled to a presumption that it composes symphony, not random cacophony. A statement which calls unacceptable any liability to exclusion from voting because of inability to pay fees or taxes fits closely with similar statements about the relationship between race,[50] or military status,[51] and liability to exclusion from the vote. This group of statements, in turn, is evidently harmonious with a more varied collection, all of which treat the voting interest as deserving of special nurture.[52] Nowhere in *Harper* is there any occasion for inference that the poor are, in any more general sense, a judicially favored class or that de facto wealth discriminations are generally disfavored.

The same is true of the "criminal procedure" cases — *Griffin v. Illinois*,[53] *Douglas v. California*,[54] and their numerous spawn of decisions insisting that a state which subjects a man to criminal prosecution must make sure that he is not prevented by want of means from defending himself with full vigor, perseverance, and effectiveness.[55] These can easily be explained as belonging to a family which treats as meriting special support the interest in strong opposition to the state's prosecutorial thrusts.[56] There is, again, no need to fabricate a no-pecuniary-discrimination doctrine.[57]

burdened or conditioned" by a "payment" requirement. Harper v. Virginia State Bd. of Elections, 383 U.S. 663, 670 (1966).

[50] *E.g.*, Nixon v. Herndon, 273 U.S. 536 (1927).

[51] *See* Carrington v. Rash, 380 U.S. 89 (1965).

[52] *See, e.g.*, Kramer v. Union Free School Dist., 395 U.S. 621 (1969).

[53] 351 U.S. 12 (1956).

[54] 372 U.S. 353 (1963).

[55] Williams v. Oklahoma City, 395 U.S. 458 (1969); Anders v. California, 386 U.S. 738 (1967); Swenson v. Bosler, 386 U.S. 258 (1967); Long v. District Ct., 385 U.S. 192 (1966); Draper v. Washington, 372 U.S. 487 (1963); Lane v. Brown, 372 U.S. 477 (1963); Smith v. Bennett, 365 U.S. 708 (1961); Burns v. Ohio, 360 U.S. 252 (1959); Eskridge v. Washington State Bd., 357 U.S. 214 (1958).

[56] Other members are Ferguson v. Georgia, 365 U.S. 570 (1961), and Chandler v. Fretag, 348 U.S. 3 (1954).

[57] *See* Coons at 370–71. One simply has to ask: Does the Court, by laying the emphasis on inequality, mean to imply that indigent defendants might constitutionally be left to their own devices, as long as privately employed counsel were also excluded? *Cf.* Lewis & Levy, *supra* note 9, at 748–49.

It is true that the remedy usually adopted in the *Griffin-Douglas* line of cases — furnishing "free" to those classed as "indigent" something for which the more affluent must continue to pay — may suggest that the grievance must have consisted of some form of "discrimination against" the class of "indigents." But a little reflection will show that it makes at least as much sense to speak of an obligation on the part of organized society to ensure that everyone's just wants are fulfilled — which obligation is, in these instances, carried out by free provision to those and only to those who cannot satisfy their just wants out of their own means. Moreover, the common practice of limiting special assistance to those claiming indigency or inability to afford a lawyer, rather than employing a graduated schedule of partial subsidies geared to ability to pay, suggests strongly that fulfillment of just wants exhausts the system's concern. The "equality" which infects judicial rhetoric is not reflected in the social practice which courts have so far deemed acceptable; [58] with respect neither to the quality of legal services provided nor to the degree of financial sacrifice required is an equality goal seriously pursued.

We should not leave this topic without taking note of the decision last Term in *McDonald v. Board of Election Commissioners*.[59] The Court there rejected a challenge to Illinois statutes authorizing absentee ballots for certain classes of persons not including that to which petitioners belonged, to wit, persons detained in Illinois prisons prior to any disqualifying conviction of crime. The Court noted that close review is required where the voting interest is affected, and then added that

> a careful examination on our part is especially warranted where lines are drawn on the basis of wealth or race, *Harper v. Virginia* [*State*] *Board of Elections*, . . . two factors which would independently render a classification highly suspect and thereby demand a more exacting judicial scrutiny. *Douglas v. California*, . . . *McLaughlin v. Florida*.[60]

(The Court went on to decide that "[s]uch an exacting approach is not necessary" on the facts of *McDonald*.[61])

The quoted dictum would be of little interest were it not for the citation of *Douglas v. California*. Heightened judicial skep-

[58] *See* Goldberg, *supra* note 25, at 223–24.

[59] 394 U.S. 802 (1969).

[60] *Id.* at 807.

[61] *Id.* While one of the petitioners was detained on election day solely because of his inability to make bail, the Court felt that no wealth classification was involved because the record did not show that the state had refused to provide a jailhouse polling station.

ticism about statutes which explicitly isolate an economic class for special treatment — *i.e.*, the cases "where lines are drawn on the basis of wealth" — is, as I have already noted, obviously justified.[62] It is true that *Harper* was not technically such a case, since the line there was drawn on the basis of payment, not wealth. But in citing *Harper* to support its dictum, the Court might be telling us nothing more than that it stands ready to interpret a "payment" line as a "wealth" line when it feels justified in concluding that isolation of the poor was an impelling statutory purpose. It might be saying that the lines in *Harper* *were* drawn on the basis of wealth, just as the lines in *Gomillion* were drawn on the basis of race.[63]

But in *Douglas v. California*, state officials drew no lines at all which resulted in disadvantage to the poor. Through its citation of *Douglas*, the *McDonald* dictum becomes perhaps the clearest statement yet made by the Court to the effect that de facto pecuniary discriminations, arising out of payment requirements, are invidious and suspect. Yet it remains true that in no decision of the Court has any such doctrine been needed.

Such a doctrine is not only gratuitous insofar as an ordering of the data is concerned. It is also endemically troublesome as a matter of principle. The trouble is that, unlike a de facto racial classification which usually must seek its justifications in purposes completely distinct from its race-related impacts, a de facto pecuniary classification typically carries a highly persuasive justification inseparable from the very effect which excites antipathy — *i.e.*, the hard choices it forces upon the financially straitened. For the typical form assumed by such a classification is simply the charging of a price, reasonably approximating cost, for some good or service which the complaining person may freely choose to purchase or not to purchase. A de facto pecuniary classification, that is, is usually nothing more or less than the making of a market (*e.g.*, in trial transcripts) or the failure to relieve someone of the vicissitudes of market pricing (*e.g.*, for appellate legal services).[64] But the risk of exposure to markets and their "deci-

[62] *See* p. 21 *supra*.

[63] *See* Gomillion v. Lightfoot, 364 U.S. 339 (1960).

[64] That this was not the case in *Harper* — or, putting it a little differently, that the state's interest in allocating scarce resources through market pricing was obviously not at stake in *Harper* — might explain how the Court could have felt free to treat that case as one of quasi de jure wealth discrimination. The same observation, of course, further impugns reliance on *Harper* as an example of judicial hostility towards payment classifications which *do* serve a resource-allocating function. It is interesting to compare petitioner's claim in Davis v. Denham, Civil No. 69–683–WM (S.D. Fla., filed June 6, 1969), a habeas petition for relief from a sixty-day jail sentence imposed in lieu of a $500 fine which went unpaid because of the petitioner's indigency. The situation resembles *Harper* in that freedom from incar-

sions" is not normally deemed objectionable, to say the least, in our society. Not only do we not inveigh generally against unequal distribution of income or full-cost pricing for most goods. We usually regard it as both the fairest and most efficient arrangement to require each consumer to pay the full market price of what he consumes, limiting his consumption to what his income permits.[65] Exceptions, of course, exist. The point is precisely that such "commodities" as a vote, an effective defense to criminal prosecution, perhaps education, conceivably some others, *are* exceptional, and that the exceptions depend on the special qualities of the excepted commodities. It is uninformative at best, and very likely misleading as well, to defend such exceptional holdings through formulas of disparagement ("invidious" or "suspect classification"; "lines . . . drawn on the basis of wealth"; "discrimination against the indigent") which apply nonselectively to the pricing practice and refer not at all to any exceptional attributes in the excepted commodities.

The disparaging phraseology seems aptly designed for instances of de jure wealth discrimination, and also, perhaps, for instances of de facto wealth discrimination (should the Court ever meet up with one) other than those implicit in payment requirements. Most typically, these latter might be cases of unequal provision of municipal services to neighborhoods significantly segregated (though without official complicity) by wealth or income.[66] If a resident of the north side of town complains

---

ceration, like admission to the vote, has no natural scarcity value. Thus no resource-allocating purpose can be served by conditioning such freedom on the payment of money. The only other imaginable purposes for the condition would be to induce payment of validly levied fines, or to provide a substitute punishment for convicted offenders who are currently fine-proof. But a firm insistence on resort to less restrictive alternatives when basic liberties are at stake would lead rather clearly to a holding of invalidity inasmuch as the state has available alternative, nondiscriminatory solutions such as scaling the fine to the offender's ability to pay, or collecting it in the form of a debt to be repaid out of the offender's future income. *Cf.* Note, *Discriminations Against the Poor and the Fourteenth Amendment, supra* note 30, at 447–48. In view of these alternatives, sentencing an indigent to jail in default of involuntary nonpayment of a fine seems rather clearly a deprivation of liberty without due process of law, and there is no occasion to contend, as petitioner did in *Davis v. Denham,* that "the equal protection clause requires the state to equalize as much as is reasonably possible the inherent inequality which exists between rich and poor defendants in criminal cases."

[65] This norm, it must be noted, extends to the purveying of goods and services by government. Such devices as special assessments for local improvements or "betterments," admission fees, tolls, college tuition fees, and other user charges covering all or a part of the costs of a good or service are generally accepted as natural and appropriate. *See, e.g.,* R. MUSGRAVE, THE THEORY OF PUBLIC FINANCE 48 (1959).

[66] *See generally* Ratner, *Inter-Neighborhood Denials of Equal Protection in*

that police, sanitation, or recreational services are inferior to those provided on the south side, no doubt his complaint is significantly strengthened by an allegation that the relatively poor are disproportionately concentrated on the north side, while the richer citizens congregate on the south side. The situation is visibly suggestive of oppression and stigma, and may have a high invidiousness quotient, to the point where convincing justifications ought to be required to dispel one's irrepressible suspicions. In fact, it seems to me questionable whether these cases should be classed together with those of payment requirements, in a collection labeled "de facto," rather than along with cases of explicit discrimination against the poor under the "de jure" label. Although the official lines (if any) were supposedly drawn with reference to geography rather than income, the geographical distinctions in themselves seem prima facie random and purposeless. It is precisely the *wealth* distinctions which strike an observer as probably nonrandom and purposeful. Thus we should perhaps call this an instance of quasi de jure wealth discrimination, subject to possible dissolution of the de jure inference by adequate justification.[67]

But this treatment seems wholly inappropriate for cases involving payment requirements. No doubt we could conceive of such cases as having historically presented state officials with a choice between requiring and not requiring payment. Then, noting that decisions to require payment are always specially burdensome to the poor, we could say that such decisions always come freighted with intimations of oppression and stigma which demand special justification. But this line of thought seems unhelpful, since in every such case *except for those involving just wants (or "fundamental interests") or nonscarce values*, a convincing justification is present. The proper conclusion, then, seems to be not that it is helpful to emphasize and weigh invidiousness factors in disposing of payment-requirements cases, but that one ought to be appropriately cautious about equating the set of such cases with the set of cases involving de facto wealth discriminations.

The emphasis on invidiousness, I have said, is not only distracting and uninformative, but positively misleading. My reasons for thinking so are perhaps best approached through acknowledgement that a qualified disparagement of pricing practices may sometimes be quite in order.

When objection is made to a state's allowing some want to go

*the Provision of Municipal Services*, 4 HARV. CIV. RIGHTS-CIV. LIB. L. REV. 1 (1968).

[67] *Cf.* Hobson v. Hansen, 269 F. Supp. 401 (D.D.C. 1967), *aff'd sub nom.* Smuck v. Hobson, 408 F.2d 175 (D.C. Cir. 1969).

unsatisfied because of the subject's inability to pay the cost of satisfaction, that objection must depend on an argument to the effect that even (or especially) in a society as prevalently individualistic and competitive as ours is, certain wants can be identified which justice requires shall not go involuntarily unfulfilled.[68] For convenience, we style these "just wants." For the most part, we can proceed on the assumption that once a want has been identified as a just want, the mere fact of its involuntary nonfulfillment constitutes an injustice.

But perhaps we should not categorically exclude the possibility that some collective practices will promise such large benefits to society as a whole, at the cost of such a slight risk of nonfulfillment of just wants, that the practices should be deemed just. Pricing practices come to mind. Their virtues are (1) that they more or less faithfully carry out whatever income distribution has otherwise been arrived at, and (2) that they assure us that resources will be efficiently employed. But the first phenomenon is no virtue insofar as the distribution it enforces prevents satisfaction of just wants. And the latter virtue lacks its normal force because, insofar as it is at all possible to identify just wants, it must also be appropriate to act as if every person would rank those wants higher on his personal list of priorities than any others he may have.[69] But if a want is such that (a) justice requires that everyone be enabled to satisfy it, and (b) everyone presumably would choose to satisfy it if he but had the means, then there is no legitimate "efficiency" objective to be served by the pricing of resources needed for the satisfaction of that want.[70]

---

[68] *See* pp. 13–16 *supra*.

[69] This is so because the reason for treating a want as a just want must be either that persons urgently desire satisfaction of the want or that society as a whole urgently desires that it not go unsatisfied. *Cf.* Draper v. Washington, 372 U.S. 487, 495 n.4 (1963), where the Court observed that "[i]t defies common sense to think that a moneyed defendant faced with long-term imprisonment and advised by counsel that he has substantial grounds for appeal . . . will choose not to appeal merely to save the cost of a transcript" — this in response to the state's contention that its practice of conditioning an indigent appellant's right to a free transcript on a judicial finding of nonfrivolity was justified by its effect of allocating resources away from frivolous (*i.e.*, wasteful) appeals.

[70] The argument as given in the text is, of course, overly categorical. The degree to which a want is a just want — and to which we are entitled to act as if it ranks at the top of everyone's list — seems to lie along a continuum. Likewise, there seems to be a continuous gradation in the intensity of the state's interest in efficient resource allocation — as affected, *e.g.*, by the fraction of GNP which would have to be allocated in order to satisfy the want in question to the point of universal satiation. Accordingly, a balancing act rather than a categorical assay of the want will be in order. But the argument in its categorical form leads to maximum disparagement of the state's "efficiency" interest, which correlates in turn with maximum coolness to de facto wealth classifications. The conclusions in text,

And so we arrive at a kind of disparagement of pricing practices: their characteristic virtues offer a superficially tempting, but upon examination insufficient, reason for tolerating the nonsatisfaction of just wants. Just so might truth-telling be disparaged: its virtues offer a tempting, but ultimately inadequate, justification for otherwise actionable invasions of privacy.[71] It would be an odd way of announcing the latter conclusion, though not quite a falsehood, to say that "when they are true, damaging revelations about the private affairs of another tend to be tortious." One would either omit the reference to truth altogether, or else take care to use an adversative conjunction like "even though" in place of the limiting "when." Precisely analogous would be a statement that encroachments upon fundamental interests are suspect when they result from a payment requirement. In both statements the dependent clauses turn out to be operationally meaningless, because disclosures of intimacies and deprivation of fundamental rights tend towards liability — that is, are suspect — all by themselves. But in their meaninglessness, these clauses convey totally misleading messages about prevailing attitudes towards truth-telling and pricing.

The miscarriage of meaning is aggravated, of course, by the free use of opprobrious diction such as "invidious classification" and "discrimination." The total effect is to treat the pricing practice, rather than nonsatisfaction of a particular want, as chiefly constituting the evil to be curbed. What results finally is a palpable, if vague, impression that the ledger of occasions when the Court will intervene against a pricing practice is not only pregnant [72] but fecund and that an evolutionary series of future deliveries waits only upon lawyerly fertilization. Conceivably [73] the Court is prepared to contemplate just such a process. If not, then surely nothing good can come of intimations that it is. Some harm, of the sort generally associated with mistakenly heard promises, might result.[74] Moreover, the suggestion that the target

---

therefore, are only strengthened by introducing the refinements suggested in this footnote.

[71] *See* W. PROSSER, HANDBOOK OF THE LAW OF TORTS 834–37, 842–43 (3d ed. 1964).

[72] *See* Coons at 361.

[73] Law students of a decade ago played at thinking up anti-epithets for Rose II of Aberlone, the miraculous cow of Sherwood v. Walker, 66 Mich. 568, 33 N.W. 919 (1887). The list, as I recall, included at least the following: impregnable, inconceivable, unbearable, insurmountable, unfathomable, and inscrutable. As for lawyerly fertilization, it should perhaps be noted that Coons *et al.* speak (unforgettably) of a *judicial* bull. *See* J. COONS, W. CLUNE, & S. SUGARMAN, PRIVATE WEALTH AND PUBLIC EDUCATION ch. 8 (forthcoming, 1969).

[74] In the case of utterances by the Supreme Court, the popular audience is in all likelihood tuned to a different station. But the poverty bar is all ears; and the

evil resides in the act of "discriminating" induces a restriction of concern to cases in which such an act can fairly be ascribed to a government, lulling us into a kind of legal torpor with respect to all those cases in which the government's "only" implication in the nonsatisfaction of just wants is its failure to come forward and satisfy them.[75]

If the relevant insight concerning payment requirements must be given a doctrinal form of statement, the appropriate construction would seem to be something like: "It is no justification for deprivation of a fundamental right (*i.e.*, involuntary nonfulfillment of a just want) that the deprivation results from a general practice of requiring persons to pay for what they get." Such a construction focuses the inquiry on the crucial variable — the nature and quality of the deprivation — and thereby avoids the distractions, false stirring of hopes, and tunneling of vision which results from a rhetorical emphasis on acts of "discrimination" that consist of nothing more than charging a price.

It must of course be conceded that one might find inaccurate or intolerable the premise, implicit in the foregoing remarks, that significant income disparities look to be a long-term fixture in American society.[76] One might even believe that judicial action can be made an effective instrument of income equalization (though surely it is not easy to imagine how courts could hasten the demise of relative deprivation in general except through treatment of severe deprivations in particular).[77] Those who so believe may be justified — though I suspect they would be tactically ill-advised — in arguing whenever possible that a government's challenged refusal to fulfill some want is unconstitutional because, among other vices, it "discriminates against the poor." But other participants in the process of social reform through litigation ought, I believe, to be more discriminating. They might, at any rate, consider the possibility that judges specially sensitive to the overbreadth of that formulation will be deterred by its recital from recognizing claims which might have been acceptable if presented without invoking it.

In sum, I believe we ought to hear the teachings of *Harper*

---

poverty bar (a) litigates on behalf of the poor and (b) talks to them. Moreover, its members communicate intensively among themselves, in the process inevitably amplifying messages of hope which may initially have been audible only through sensitive antennae. The suggestibility of hopeful lawyers may be illustrated by the remark that "The principle of [*Griffin v. Illinois*] . . . will constitute a new charter of freedom for the poor." Willcox & Bloustein, *The Griffin Case — Poverty and the Fourteenth Amendment*, 43 CORNELL L.Q. 1, 26 (1957).

[75] *See* pp. 37–39 *infra*.

[76] *But see* B. SELIGMAN, PERMANENT POVERTY (1968).

[77] *See* pp. 8–9 *supra*.

and the *Griffin-Douglas* line with an ear resolutely deaf to superfluous rhetoric. We do better by the Court to regard it, not as nine (or seven, or five) Canutes railing against tides of economic inequality which they have no apparent means of stemming, but as a body commendably busy with the critically important task of charting some islands of haven from economic disaster in the ocean of (what continues to be known as) free enterprise.

## III. Classification and "Discrimination" in the New Equal Protection

We have been considering a legal problem — a set of circumstances giving rise to legal claims — which can be stated in the following general form: a person is denied access to certain goods or activities because of some trait or situation which he is powerless to change currently and which is not the result of any decision freely made by him in the proximate past. A special case of the general problem, in which we have a particular interest, is that of the impecunious person denied access because of inability to pay a price. Two different strategies for thought about the problem, and the legal claim against the state which arises from it, may be sketched and compared. The first somewhat resembles that which has become associated with litigation under the equal protection clause, and I shall label it "equal protection." The second is the one which I have styled "minimum protection." [78]

"Equal protection" radar is sensitized to governmental implication in systematic inequality. It blips whenever a government seems (a) to be "classifying" persons so as to extend to them unequal treatments, or (b) otherwise to be acting in a way which results in systematic inequality in treatments received by definable groups of persons. Here we are primarily concerned with cases in category (b). When a blip — a warning signal — occurs, the ensuing inspection focuses first upon the criteria which, explicitly or implicitly, are used to classify the affected population. If those criteria are free of invidiousness,[79] the case is to be treated, in effect, as one of "substantive due process." [80]

---

[78] In using the tags "equal protection" and "minimum protection" for convenience in differentiating the two conceptual strategies, I do not of course mean to forswear reliance on the equal protection clause as a textual base for litigation inspired or shaped by minimum-protection thinking.

[79] *See* p. 20 *supra*.

[80] That is, the challenged acts of government will be invalidated only if (i) not rationally related to any proper governmental purpose, or (ii) so damaging to some judicially favored interest as not (in the court's judgment) to be justified by whatever tendency they do have to advance a proper governmental end. Invalidation on either of these grounds is unconcerned with whether the govern-

If, however, they are in noticeable degree suggestive of oppression or stigmatization, that fact is to be borne in mind as attention shifts to the actual clash of interests involved in the case: the personal interests [81] which are adversely affected by unequal treatment and the interest of the government [82] in continuing the "unequal" practice. We are concerned about the degree of special importance (in some sense) which attaches to the unequally served personal interest; we factor this with the degree of invidiousness of the classifying trait. The resultant is a kind of "prejudice" variable which, if it exceeds a certain critical magnitude, we are to balance against the governmental interest — a procedure crudely described by the statement that in such cases the governmental interest can prevail only if it is "compelling." [83] (There are special or limiting cases in which the invidiousness factor is "1" — *i.e.*, neutrality of classifying trait — but in which the unaugmented personal interest factor is itself a prejudice variable weighty enough to call for balancing. Voting rights cases seem to be an example.[84] And there are converse limiting cases, notably involving de jure racial segregation, where the personal interest factor may be "1" — signifying no special importance — but the unaugmented invidiousness factor is of critical magnitude.[85])

At this point we may note that the foregoing articulation of thought process is useful in "wealth" cases only on the assumption that there will be a significant number of such cases in which a classification's rating on the *i* ("invidiousness") scale makes a crucial difference in the result. As we have seen, this will be so

mental acts in question entail any "classification" or disparity of treatment. *See Developments in the Law, supra* note 16, at 1129–32.

[81] "Personal" interest, as used here, refers to interests upon which individuals base claims against, and thereby differentiate themselves from, a *government*; but the usage does not imply adversity between the individual and the whole of society. Recognition of the claim must reflect a judgment that it is generally good for society that such claims be recognized. And so a "personal" interest is a kind of societal interest.

[82] In speaking of a "governmental" interest, I of course do not mean an interest which certain individuals have by virtue of occupying governmental office, but rather an interest pertaining to the society as a whole which is to be effectuated through that particular organ of its collective activities which we call government. A "governmental" interest is, then, also a societal interest.

[83] *See Developments in the Law, supra* note 16, at 1120–21.

[84] *See* p. 25 *supra*. If such cases can be distinguished at all from substantive due process cases, the distinction must lie in the notion that an equal protection case is one in which classification or inequality is a critical component of the grievance. Cases in which this is so although the classification is itself neither invidious nor irrational are not easy to dream up — but the Reapportionment Cases are enough to show that this is not a null set.

[85] *See Developments in the Law, supra* note 16, at 1088–91.

for cases in which the wealth classification is de jure. But on the evidence we have so far, it is far from likely to be so of de facto wealth classifications. *Hobson v. Hansen*[86] seems to be the notable instance in which a de facto wealth classification's positive *i* rating may have swayed the final outcome. Surely this was not the case in *Harper* or in the *Griffin-Douglas* line. Later on we shall examine some hypothetical de facto cases in which variations on the *i* scale might be thought to make a difference, and shall discover (as it appears to me) that the difference they make tends to be precious little.[87]

We should note also that while subtle equal protection theorists take care to avoid flat statements about the consequences of bringing an interest within the "inner circle" or of labelling a classifying trait as invidious or specially suspect, it does seem that if the suspect trait/favored interest approach is to have any special utility, any intellectual labor-saving potency, it should mean that the constitutional tilt sign flickers whenever there is a convergence in the same case of suspect classification and encroachment on a fundamental interest, suggesting a super-likelihood of invalidity.[88] If the meaning were merely that the convergence of suspect-trait and favored-interest triggers strict review, the extravagance of the method would be clear; for the favored interest or the suspect trait alone would have that effect.

"Minimum protection" radar scans, not for inequalities, but for instances in which persons have important needs or interests which they are prevented from satisfying because of traits or predicaments not adopted by free and proximate choice. Such instances, when located, are subject to inspection to see whether, in a just society, the hazard is tolerable that the trait or predicament in question will be burdened by nonsatisfaction of the want in question. If the Rawlsian conception of justice is accepted, the question will be whether a person would insist on the relevant assurances assuming that he was (a) deprived of knowledge about whether he personally will find himself in the relevant predicament, but (b) sufficiently informed about the organizing principles of the society to be able to appraise (i) the frequency of the predicament and (ii) the gravity, in such a society, of the particular unfulfilled want. On the answer to this question, the existence and content of governmental duties will depend.

[86] 269 F. Supp. 401 (D.D.C. 1967), *aff'd sub nom.* Smuck v. Hobson, 408 F.2d 175 (D.C. Cir. 1969), discussed in note 41 *supra*.

[87] *See* pp. 36–37 *infra*.

[88] But allowance could still be made for such extraordinarily exigent circumstances as were detected in Korematsu v. United States, 323 U.S. 214 (1944), where, with full awareness of the exceptional nature of what it was doing, the Court upheld a national ancestry classification imposing bodily confinement upon an unpopular minority.

In comparing the two conceptual strategies, it is well to begin by noting relationships of overlap and correspondence. The area of overlap, of common scanning and simultaneous blipping, may be described as that covered by equal protection except for (a) the area occupied by cases of "irrationally" imposed disadvantage not affecting specially important interests, and (b) the area occupied by cases of de jure classification so invidious as to require invalidation irrespective of the importance of the affected interest. The overlapped area may also be described, from an equal protection viewpoint, as that covered by the "new equal protection" method of cross-hatching the "invidiousness" of classifying traits with the "importance" of the affected interests to derive composite prejudice variables. Alternatively, the overlapped area may be described from a minimum-protection standpoint as including all cases which tentatively excite minimum-protection concern, except for those in which a clear absence of "state action" would turn off equal protection.

Within the overlapped area, the two strategies have some tendency to arrive, ultimately, at closely similar interest balancings to determine validity. An example may make this clear. Suppose that a government is charging admission fees as a condition of access to the golf course it operates in a public park or the grand opera being staged in a civic auditorium, thus making it difficult or impossible for poor persons to enjoy the facility. Equal protection might detect a degree of invidiousness in the implicit wealth classification, which it would factor together with the degree of importance (probably not exceeding "1") of the interest in golf playing or opera going. The resultant prejudice variable would probably be found less weighty than the governmental interest in optimizing the allocation of resources to the golf course or opera stage (for maintenance, improvement, expansion of facilities, etc.). Minimum protection would proceed directly to the question whether assurance would be consensually demanded against the risk that preclusion from golf or opera may be an accompaniment of a low income — taking into account the general social advantages of allocating resources in accordance with dollar-expressed demand, but also bearing in mind the possibilities of systematic oppression of the poor in the guise of admission fees and of harmful stigmatization by exclusion of the poor from public facilities. The determinative mental calculus (or should we say chemistry) seems hard to distinguish from that employed under equal protection.

But the two approaches do not always tend toward identical outcomes. Consider the following case. The average annual per-pupil expenditure in all of a state's public schools is $800. Two juvenile institutions, one of the protective and one of the corrective variety, are situated in a county which annually spends $1100 per child in attendance at its public schools. The institutions are state-operated and state-financed, but each serves a "constituency" defined by county boundaries. Each of the "homes" operates its own school program. The orphanage spends $900 per child per year, while the reform school spends $500. Suits are brought on behalf of children confined in each institution, complaining of unequal protection. The orphan plaintiff points to the $1100 standard established by "his" county. The delinquent points to that and also to the $800 state average and the $900 orphanage expenditures.

We have, I think, good reason to fear that the "new equal protection" will make a mess of these cases — especially if we imagine that the orphan's case is decided first with full appellate opinions. The orphan will argue, with great plausibility, that the effect of the combined state and county practices is to "classify" school-age children resident in the county into those who are and those who are not orphans. Indeed, the classification is de jure. He will then claim, quite convincingly, that orphanage is a distinctly invidious classifying trait. Since educational resource seems to be a "fundamental" good, the cross-hatching of suspect classification with damage to a favored interest is likely to yield a decision in favor of the orphan plaintiff.[89] The opinion, naturally, will lay great stress on the presence in the case of the invidious classification. The delinquent, when his turn comes, of course can argue to similar effect that he has been disadvantageously classified; but the argument that delinquency is an invidious classifying trait will be much harder to sustain, and he therefore may well find that his case will be distinguished.[90]

---

[89] That is, the argument will seem persuasive that the orphan is constitutionally aggrieved. The court may shrink from the straightforward remedy of ordering the state to increase per-pupil expenditure at the orphanage to whatever level is maintained by the county — either because of respect for the memory of the eleventh amendment (if it is a federal court) or because of other doubts about institutional competency.

[90] Coons, Clune, and Sugarman suggest a doctrinal appendage to the "new equal protection" which might forfend against such a disaster. To the categories of favored interests and suspect traits they would add a category of "preferred people" which has as its first (and conceivably only) member the class of children. *See* Coons at 389–95. This category would apparently serve, in the overall method of inquiry, an office analogous to that of the suspect trait. That is, whenever the governmental acts in question are prejudicial to the favored interests of a "preferred person" (*i.e.*, child), we would be in constitutionally active territory — even though children as an entire class are not disfavored, and even though the trait whereby the class of children is subclassified, and unfavorable treatment

Two elements in this fantasy are noteworthy. First, equal protection seems somewhat undiscriminatingly sensitized to any and all inequalities affecting "favored" interests. The quality of an inequality — in this case, the fact that orphans already receive an educational expenditure which is average for the state — does not seem to concern it. We might say that equal protection responds to relative deprivation, even though the presence of a quasi-symptomatic and severe absolute deprivation is doubtful. Second, once doctrinal reliance has been reposed in the "invidiousness" of some classification, issues are likely to be confused in subsequent cases which are somewhat analogous but which involve different, and noninvidious, classifications. A severe and quasi-symptomatic absolute deprivation may beget no response unless a "discrimination" suggestive of prevalent, institutionalized, relative deprivation is also present.

Minimum protection avoids both these effects. For each of the two cases it poses a custom-built question, eschewing equality as an end but focusing instead upon just what it is that institutionalized children seek but do not get. In a supposedly just society, it would ask, which risk is the more likely to be consensually deemed unacceptable: the risk that orphanage will entail deprivation of stratospheric educational expenditure (assuming a guaranty of at least that expenditure which is normal for the state), or the risk that conviction of delinquency will entail an educational expenditure as low as 63% of the state average?

In sum, it can be said that in the area of overlapping concern, where governmental action is somehow associated with a person's exclusion from an important good, minimum protection leads to inquiry at least as refined and sensitive to relevant factors as does equal protection, and that equal protection, conversely, cannot ultimately avoid reliance on judgments as complex, subjective, and ineffable as those arising under minimum protection. Yet there are, even in the overlapped area, differences between the two methods which seem to me quite significant. They are

dealt out to one of the subclasses, is not itself invidious. In sum, it is enough to trigger strict review that the important interests of a child are being disserved, and the presence of some invidious disparity in treatment is not deemed crucial. (That this is the meaning of Coons, *et al.*, may be inferred from their use of the "preferred people" notion to defend their proposition that "compensatory" educational spending by the state, which would vary expenditure *inversely* with family wealth, should be held unconstitutional.) The notion seems to me a sound one. But I cannot refrain from commenting that it seems also to give away the point that intolerable exposure to risk, rather than offensive inequality, is at the root of our unease about these cases (especially when one reflects upon the convincing reasons for special judicial skepticism about governmental acts which damage the important interests of any child).

that minimum protection goes about its work without pretension to general pursuit of an "equality" goal, that minimum protection does not employ, as a separate and doctrinally packaged step in the reasoning, any attempt to rank classifying traits according to their "invidiousness," and most particularly, that minimum protection avoids general declarations to the effect that inequalities in treatment are "specially suspect" or "discriminatory" when born of inequalities in wealth.

Minimum protection, in short, imports no doctrine, worthy of separate statement, which inveighs generally against "de facto discriminations against the poor." It thus answers the argument made earlier in this Foreword that recognition of any such general doctrine ought to be given grudgingly, if at all.

We may now summarize the theoretical and practical consequences of approaching the denial-of-access problem by way of a "minimum protection" thought process — one not regimented, as equal protection thinking has come to be, by categories of *governmental involvement* and *invidious discriminations* (including in the latter category discriminations bearing adversely upon the fundamental interests of some "judicially favored" class). These consequences fall under two major heads: (1) *Minimum protection is likely to demand correction of certain practices or conditions which equal protection would tolerate.* This may come about, most notably, under either of two interesting sets of circumstances: (a) when, although there is governmental complicity in an inequality which affects important interests, the disadvantaged class is deemed to have no special claim to judicial favor; or (b) when, although the important interests of a class meriting special protection are comparatively ill-served, no governmental action has occurred which proximately caused (or crystallized) the troublesome disadvantage. (2) *Minimum protection is likely to demand remedies which cannot be directly embodied in judicial decrees.* This may come about either because (a) justiciable standards are lacking whereby a court can say whether a government has done its duty, or (b) the remedy entails positive action, of a substantially discretionary or indeterminate character, by a legislative body.

I shall hope to illustrate these points further, and comment on their significance, through discussion of the problems tendered to the Supreme Court last Term in *Shapiro v. Thompson*[91] and *McInnis v. Ogilvie*.[92]

---

[91] 394 U.S. 618 (1969).

[92] 394 U.S. 322 (1969), *aff'g mem.*, McInnis v. Shapiro, 293 F. Supp. 327 (N.D. Ill. 1968).

## IV. Shapiro v. Thompson

In *Shapiro v. Thompson* the Court struck down as a violation of equal protection the requirement that an indigent have been a state resident for a year prior to claiming state public assistance benefits.[93]

Viewed in terms of the categories we have been using, *Shapiro* presents a rather complex situation. De jure, the classifying line is drawn between needy persons who are recent interstate migrants and other needy persons who are not. Inasmuch as the Court treated the personal and societal interest in free interstate migration as a "fundamental" one, any infringement of which warrants special judicial concern, the case seems to involve a classifying trait which is also a specially protected interest.[94] It is as if the state were to levy an excise on the "privilege" of voting, or of bringing a lawyer along to one's criminal trial. *Shapiro* thus bears a strong family resemblance to *Harper*. Where *Harper*, in effect, holds that no conceivable statutory purpose can justify the injury inflicted by levy of a toll upon the franchise, *Shapiro* carefully examines and rejects the adequacy of the reasons advanced by the state to justify its "toll" upon interstate migration.

But the "toll" in *Shapiro* falls with special weight upon the poor in a sense rather different than in *Harper* and *Griffin-Douglas*, for it is exacted in a currency — access to public assistance — which only the poor employ. One may thus tend to overlook the de facto classification between indigent and non-indigent wrought by the prior-residence requirement and see

---

[93] 394 U.S. 618 (1969). The case is described and discussed by the editors of this magazine at pp. 118–26 *infra*. The state schemes in question were Connecticut's and Pennsylvania's. A similar requirement imposed by the District of Columbia was held void in *Shapiro* under fifth amendment due process.

[94] In a second possible perspective, *Shapiro* might be said to involve the interest in subsistence. The classifying trait would, again, be recency of arrival. If both the interests in subsistence and in unfettered interstate movement are deemed "fundamental," then the case would involve a piling on of fundamentalities — an imposition requiring a person to trade off two fundamental interests against each other — not matched in any other case we have examined. And Mr. Justice Brennan's opinion for the Court does seem to get a little mileage out of this phenomenon. The waiting-period rule, he notes at the very outset of his discussion, is used to deny "welfare aid upon which may depend the ability of the families to obtain the very means to subsist — food, shelter, and other necessities of life." 394 U.S. at 627. On this view, not the least interesting facet of *Shapiro* is the suggestion that the interest in subsistence is in the inner circle. Mr. Justice Harlan, dissenting, true to his artless custom of drawing out and building up precisely those intimations in majority opinions which trouble him most deeply, draws our attention to this one at 394 U.S. at 661.

it as differentiating only between migrant and nonmigrant indigents.[95] Yet the statutes do clearly contribute to making migration more burdensome to the poor who are dependent on welfare than to the nonpoor; and so, de facto, "discriminate" between these two classes.

Viewing the case this way raises issues so intractable as to suggest, once again, that the notion of a general bias against de facto wealth classifications is not a very reliable or serviceable instrument of analysis. The pecuniary-discrimination effect depends upon the prior existence, in the state of former residence, of a public-assistance program to which the migrant had access. (That is, the special price the poor pay to migrate must consist of having to sacrifice access to one source of subsistence income without immediately being able to replace it with another, rather than simply of the unavailability of assistance in the state of destination. For to complain of the latter circumstance would be to unhinge the complaint from any deterrence of travel and thus, in effect, to make a constitutional grievance out of the very state of being poor.)

It is readily understandable, then, why the Court in *Shapiro* simply ignored its contemporaneous *McDonald* dictum [96] and declined to rest its decision even partly on the undeniable presence of a wealth discrimination. For to have done so would have been tantamount to saying that a destination state's duty is to equalize the choice situations confronting prospective affluent and indigent immigrants by standing ready to provide benefits not substantially less generous than those which had been available in the departure state — or, perhaps, that a departure state must continue providing benefits to all of its welfare-client emigrés. Either of these would have been a very queer saying, indeed.

But the Court's avoidance of these quiddities does not in itself dispel any drift in their direction which may inhere in the *McDonald* dictum or in the equal protection strategy for which it speaks. That some such drift is there seems hard to deny. If a destination state refuses to match a departure state's welfare benefits, we have an instance of de facto wealth discrimination (invidious according to *McDonald*) coupled with injury to the free-travel interest (fundamental according to *Shapiro*). It is true that the wealth classification has arisen without any official stigmatizing act, but that was also true of the *Douglas* case cited in *McDonald*. If a search be launched for justifying state policies, those would seem more likely to be found, say, in a state's

[95] And this, indeed, is precisely how Mr. Justice Brennan states the case. *See* 394 U.S. at 627.

[96] *See* pp. 26–27 *supra*.

flat refusal to provide criminal defense lawyers — which is clearly forbidden — than in its refusal to scale welfare benefits so that all needy immigrants can continue to live in the style to which they have become accustomed. The refusal to provide lawyers might (though pretty tenuously) claim justification by a pluralistic preference for private-bar responsibility or a distaste for governmental involvement in the demeaning features of any "handout" program; but even these weak reeds are beyond the grasp of the state which, already running a public assistance program, refuses benefit-level maintenance for new arrivals. And if it be suggested that there is no discriminatory state action in a mere refusal to furnish benefits up to some designated level, well, discriminatory state action in *Douglas* isn't so easy to find, either.[97]

Now of course I do not mean that new equal protectionists are in danger of conceding the welfare-dependent's claim to carry his latest benefit levels around with him from state to state. I mean only that their categorical style of thought and expression drifts toward that interpretation, and that the utility of that style is somewhat impugned by having to reject it. For rejection means that the states' duty to avoid unequal treatment of the poor not only does not apply to all the interests which poor people have, but also does not apply even to all their "inner circle" interests. What it comes down to, I believe, is that a state's duty to the poor respecting their inner-circle interests is not to avoid unequal treatment at all, but rather to provide assurances against certain hazards associated with impecuniousness which even a society strongly committed to competition and incentives would have to find unjust.[98] The risk of being deterred from interstate travel because of the relatively low level of public assistance benefits in the destination state seems not to be one of these hazards — at least if we assume that the benefits there meet whatever subsistence standards define our acceptable minimum.[99] But "travel" might still remain in the inner-circle in the basic sense that

[97] *See Developments in the Law*, *supra* note 16, at 1189. The demand for benefit maintenance fits amply within the "broadened" concept of state action there suggested, which would "require . . . government attention to those inequalities for which it is not directly responsible, but which nevertheless are concomitant features of the existence of the organized state" in that they result "from societal arrangements such as class structures, distribution of wealth, and group prejudices."

[98] *See* pp. 9–16 *supra*.

[99] To keep the issues clear, we must assume here that all states are meeting through their programs whatever minimum obligations the Constitution may impose to assure their residents of an acceptable standard of living — whether that be bare subsistence, or something more, or (so far as the Constitution is concerned) something less.

the acceptable minimum standard of living must include provision for a certain degree of mobility.

Let us now turn to the opinion which Mr. Justice Brennan wrote for the Court in the *Shapiro* case — or, more precisely, to selected aspects of it inasmuch as the ultimate holding is of no special interest to our thesis. Its purport is simply that subclassification of indigents according to time of arrival in the state, for purposes of determining eligibility for public assistance, violates the equal protection clause because (a) freedom to migrate from state to state being a "fundamental right," statutory classifications which bear adversely on its exercise are invalid unless necessary to advance a "compelling" state interest; and (b) as to every suggested purpose for the classification either (i) that purpose is itself not only not compelling, but is constitutionally improper, or (ii) the classification is functionally unrelated to the purpose or is unnecessarily restrictive in light of available alternatives for achieving it.[100]

The core of the state's argument can be so couched as to lack neither plausibility nor sympathetic appeal. Its welfare programs, the state would assert, offer generous benefits — at least by comparison with certain states and in certain categories of assistance. The state seeks nothing more than to preserve this commendable level of benefits for those who it feels have a prior claim upon its welfare budget and to protect that budget against the depredations of persons who would enter the state for no other reason than to avail themselves of what has been intended for the state's "natural" dependents. Unless such "raiding" can be stopped, the benefit shares available to long-standing residents and justifiably motivated immigrants will diminish (or, alternatively, the state's taxpayers will have to sacrifice additionally in shouldering some other state's proper burden); and a one year waiting period requirement will deter the "raiding."

Mr. Justice Brennan does not shrink from dealing with this argument. He pays it its due — but circumspectly. Rather than try to crack the nut with a single squeeze, his method is to hack away at it from several angles. He is able to expose vulnerable premises by positing for discussion various statutory purposes no one of which, alone, fairly and fully comprehends the sympathetic form of argument offered above. Here we shall discuss the opinion's handling of two supposed state purposes: that of inhibiting immigration by persons motivated solely by a desire for higher welfare benefits, and that of minimizing the cost to the

[100] The defects of functional unrelatedness and over-restrictiveness pertain to certain administrative interests advanced by the states. These will not be discussed.

state of achieving the general objectives of its public assistance programs.[101]

The first of these purposes is held to be constitutionally improper. A state, wrote Mr. Justice Brennan,

> may no more try to fence out those indigents who seek higher welfare benefits than it may try to fence out indigents generally. Implicit in any such distinction is the notion that indigents who enter a State with the hope of securing higher welfare benefits are somehow less deserving than indigents who do not take this consideration into account. But we do not perceive why a mother who is seeking to make a new life for herself and her children should be regarded as less deserving because she considers, among other factors, the level of a State's public assistance.[102]

Thus, insofar as the state means to claim that the welfare prospector, as such, has an inferior claim to assistance, the Court's answer is quite direct and utterly blunt: in terms neither of need nor of desert can the seeker after improved benefits be deemed to have a claim inferior to anyone else's.

The method here is worthy of study. Connecticut's claimed interest in conserving the fruits of Connecticut humanitarianism for persons substantially committed to or dependent upon Connecticut society or economy is not self-evidently negligible; and "balancing" it against the free-travel interest or the mother's interest in a better lot for her family does not seem to lead to any clear conclusion. The conclusion becomes clear only when the Court lays it down that Connecticut may not act on the premise that a person's deservingness of its taxpayers' humanitarianism is a function of his having some reason other than a welfare quest for being in Connecticut. The sources of this morality are left mysterious, but it is worth suggesting that the "risk" perspective which, I have argued, may imply duties of minimum protection, may also be at work here. Suppose that we know about a national society that its economy is essentially unitary and its people highly mobile, and further that it is, to some noticeable degree, undertaking to fulfill the minimum wel-

[101] Other purposes dealt with in the opinion were restriction of benefits to those who had made contributions to state welfare, and deterrence of immigration by those who might exert a continuing drain (through welfare needs) on state finances. It is immaterial to the discussion in text that the classifying line actually used (*i.e.*, time of arrival) may not have correlated very well with the motivational lines professedly aimed at. For, while Mr. Justice Brennan notes (and condemns) discrepancies between actual impacts and professed purposes, he chooses not to rest his decision solely on such grounds. In each significant instance he deliberately and explicitly rejects the purpose, as well as shows that the prior-residence requirement is ill-adapted to serving it.

[102] 394 U.S. at 631–32.

fare assurances which, given its predominantly competitive cast, justice probably requires. Given further the unlikelihood that any significant segment of the society would voluntarily sacrifice in support of a welfare program much in excess of the just minimum, might we not find unacceptable a decentralization of authority to decide how heavily to sacrifice for such programs, with its significantly increased risk that an unusually benighted faction could gain control of some of the decisions? If so, might it not be an appropriate judicial response to the political preference for decentralization to protect the ability of highly motivated welfare clients to avoid the untoward consequences of that preference? I sketch this argument not in order to suggest that *Shapiro* is a datum confirming the existence of a "minimum protection" doctrine, or that Mr. Justice Brennan should have included something like it in his opinion. The sketch is drawn in order to illustrate the earlier point that equal protection, once it gets beyond cases of sheer irrationality and blatantly invidious de jure discrimination, has no way of avoiding precisely the sort of judicial value-sculpting which a minimum-protection argument entails. It also anticipates a later point that a court's inability to enforce minimum protection duties directly (as by forbidding Congress to permit states to choose their own welfare-benefit levels) does not mean that minimum-protection thinking might not contribute to the issuance of a more regular judicial remedy.[103]

Let us now turn to Mr. Justice Brennan's handling of the "economizing" purpose ascribed to the welfare-residency requirement. Here is what he says:

> [A state] may legitimately attempt to limit its expenditures, whether for public assistance, public education, or any other program. But a State may not accomplish such a purpose by invidious distinctions between classes of its citizens. It could not, for example, reduce expenditures for education by *barring indigent children from its schools*. Similarly, in the cases before us, appellants must do more than show that denying welfare benefits to new residents saves money. The saving of welfare costs cannot justify an otherwise invidious classification.[104]

This is a noteworthy passage. It would have been quite sufficient, after all, simply to have made the indisputable point that the objective of controlling or reducing the size of public budgets, as any other governmental objective, must be pursued if at all by means which avoid discrimination among citizens whose situations vis-à-vis that objective cannot appropriately be differenti-

[103] *Cf.* pp. 51–52 *infra*.

[104] 394 U.S. at 633 (emphasis supplied).

ated. If analogy was to be employed in driving home the point, tradition would have dictated some such remark as that the state could not reduce expenditures for welfare by barring, say, red-headed children from its AFDC program. We are entitled, then, to be fascinated by Mr. Justice Brennan's remark about indigents and education. The remark is fascinating not only because of its suggestion of some relevant similarity between education and public assistance, but because it seems upon reflection to confirm the view that wealth classifications tend not to be notably invidious except when they are de jure.

The state, we are told, is free to reduce its public expenditures — that is, the volume of sacrifice it coerces through taxation — for public education. It may not, however, bring about such a reduction by "barring" indigents (*i.e.*, those whose families do not pay even a small fraction of their way) from the schools. Might the state, then, achieve its goal of reducing education's claims on its general revenues by imposing cost-related, full or partial, tuition charges as a condition of school attendance (thereby avoiding the use of statutory classifications)? A minimum protectionist would surely resist this conclusion, given the crucial importance of education and the unlikelihood that any cognizable misallocation of resources to basic education will result from public subsidization thereof. A more conventional equal-protectionist might accept it if only because discriminatory state action is not much in evidence under a tuition-fee dispensation. If not, he almost certainly would accept the distributionally equivalent choice of closing down the public schools altogether.[105] But would it not be reasonable, then, to press him on why he finds it acceptable to exclude indigents from education by throwing them and everyone else upon the mercy of the market, but not by "barring" them from publicly operated institutions on the ground that their families contribute nothing to the support of such institutions? [106]

He could respond that the de jure exclusion of indigents hypothesized by Mr. Justice Brennan is materially more obnoxious

---

[105] *See* pp. 54–56 *infra*.

[106] It is no answer to say that "the purpose" of a public school system is to treat education as a community good by financing it entirely out of general tax revenues, and that in light of such a purpose exclusion of indigents is "irrational." The state which bars from its schools those whose tax contributions fall below a certain line by that very act asserts a more complex — and by no means incoherent — purpose to treat education as in significant part a private good which should not be provided to those who will not or cannot pay a substantial share of its cost. The device of barring those whose tax contributions are negligible, while continuing to finance the system out of general taxes, is, however, pretty crude; and this, as indicated in the following text, is probably its undoing.

than a school shutdown by reason of its much higher individiousness content. The relationship of the de jure wealth classification to a proper governmental purpose is certainly tenuous. There are obviously unusual opportunities for majoritarian oppression through such measures (which can draw the wealth or income floor at any selected level so as to make certain that they isolate a politically impotent minority), as well as rather extreme stigmatizing tendencies. The oppressive and stigmatizing potential is much less in the case of full-cost tuition charges or a total school shutdown. Although one can imagine a delicately fashioned scheme of partial tuition charges (or of school shut-down accompanied by partial tuition grants) calculated to isolate the same impotent, "indigent" minority, the political frictions of working out the scheme (absent some immense provocation on the order of a desegregation decree) [107] are likely to be prohibitive. In short, Mr. Justice Brennan's dictum can be construed to avoid the minimum protectionist's inference that the state is duty-bound to provide free schooling for those who cannot afford to pay — but only, it seems, by sharply downgrading the invidiousness of payment requirements, thereby expressing disagreement with Chief Justice Warren's dictum in *McDonald*.

## V. McInnis v. Ogilvie

*McInnis v. Ogilvie* [108] was a suit brought on behalf of students in a number of Cook County school districts seeking revision of the Illinois system of public school finance. Briefly, Illinois relied heavily on resort by the several school districts to their own widely varying tax bases, the state supplementing their locally raised revenues by a state-financed system of "foundation grants." [109] The upshot was wide discrepancies among local dis-

---

[107] *See* Griffin v. County School Bd., 377 U.S. 218 (1964).

[108] 394 U.S. 322 (1969), *aff'g mem.* McInnis v. Shapiro, 293 F. Supp. 327 (N.D. Ill. 1968).

[109] A foundation plan "is essentially a guaranty to the district by the state that, if it will tax itself at a specified minimum level, the district will have a specified number of dollars available per pupil . . . ." Coons at 314. Unless the minimum rate is so high as to approach what the richer districts actually levy, and the guaranteed proceeds so high as to approach what the richer districts actually spend, the foundation plan does not eliminate wealth-determined inequalities in expenditures because it does not prevent richer districts from tapping their local reservoirs of wealth by taxing above the minimum level. Thus in Illinois in 1966–67, the guaranteed per-pupil yield was $350, assuming a one percent minimum effort level (plus a $50 flat grant received by every district irrespective of effort). District per-pupil expenditures ranged from $480 at the bottom to $1,000 at the top. *See* McInnis v. Shapiro, 293 F. Supp. 327, 330 & n.8 (N.D. Ill. 1968); Appellants' Jurisdictional Statement, McInnis v. Ogilvie, 394 U.S. 322 (1969).

tricts with respect to the amount of revenue which became available at equal levels of tax effort, as well as with respect to actual per-pupil expenditure levels. The complaint, while not free of ambiguity, appeared to pursue a relatively unrestricted equality goal. It could, at any rate, easily be interpreted to assert an obligation on the part of the state of Illinois so to order its arrangements for financing public education as to maximize the probability — insofar as having money available bears upon that probability — that each person, upon completion of his education, would be equally well prepared to play the game of Life.[110] Whether or not because of this radical implication in the complaint, the three-judge district court dismissed it with a thoroughly unsatisfying opinion.[111] At its 1968 Term, the Supreme Court affirmed summarily and without full briefs or arguments the direct appeal from the three-judge district court.[112]

Now the scandalously unequal distribution of school expenditures among local districts within the several states has been widely known and discussed for some years,[113] and is increasingly deplored in places high and low.[114] It is a condition which arises largely out of economic segregation — self-segregation by the rich often attended, it seems, by forced segregation of the poor — combined with decentralization to local districts of the main responsibility for financing public schools. Because taxable wealth varies so widely from district to district, wide expenditure variations are the inevitable result. No clearer or socially more significant case of wealth-related disadvantage is imaginable.[115] State involvement and responsibility are indisputable. It is a plausible hypothesis that education is one of those interests which will be categorized as "fundamental." [116] It would thus seem likely that persons situated as were the plaintiffs in *McInnis* could devise a claim for relief and supporting argument which would present very substantial constitutional questions. The Supreme Court will sooner or later have to say whether the proposition that de facto wealth classifications are disfavored, with or without support from the proposition that education is a "fundamental" in-

---

[110] *Cf.* Coons at 339–40.

[111] McInnis v. Shapiro, 293 F. Supp. 327 (N.D. Ill. 1968); *see* Coons at 344.

[112] Mr. Justice Douglas was of the opinion that probable jurisdiction should be noted and the case set for argument.

[113] *E.g.*, J. CONANT, SLUMS AND SUBURBS 2–3 (1961).

[114] *E.g.*, REPORT OF THE NATIONAL ADVISORY COMMISSION ON CIVIL DISORDERS 434–36 (Bantam ed. 1968).

[115] That the relevant wealth is that of a district, and not that of an individual or household, could be counted an aggravating factor. *See* Coons at 370.

[116] *See* Coons at 382–89; *Developments in the Law*, *supra* note 16, at 1129, 1183–87.

terest, means that states are duty-bound to "equalize" the fiscal determinants of educational quality for all their children; and to say also, with judicially enforceable precision, what such "equalization" might mean. Exhaustive discussion of the problem and all its ramifications, were I capable of it, would overflow the reader's cup, the capacity of this magazine, and the hospitality of its editors.[117] My comments here will be limited to a few, selected facets.

It will be necessary, before proceeding, to pause over two analytical matters. First, we must refine somewhat our distinction between the evils of relative and absolute deprivation, and observe that any given instance of objective inequality may partake of either, neither, or both kinds of evil. The peculiar evil of a relative deprivation (read "discrimination" or "nonevenhandedness") is psychic or moral; it consists of an affront; it is immediately injurious insofar as resented or taken personally, and consequentially injurious insofar as demoralizing. The evil of an absolute deprivation (or, simply, "deprivation") consists of pain, discomfort, disadvantage, or disability which arises and injures regardless of the interpretation which anyone "chooses to put upon" the deprivation.[118] Where a good (or privilege of access) is valued because of its relevance to competitive activity (voting, for example), inequality of access will entail evils of absolute deprivation — of practical disadvantage.[119] The inequality may also entail evils of relative deprivation, especially if it results visibly from some particular, positive act of discrimination.

Education seems to be valued in part for the benefits of having as much as or more than someone else has. Insofar as this is so, deprivation exists only where inequality exists; and conversely, inequality implies deprivation. Educational inequality may also, but need not, be associated with offensive discrimination. Whether the evils wrought by any given instance of educational inequality are predominantly those of discrimination or of disadvantage can be known only after investigation of the instance. Accordingly, it would seem foolhardy to decide in advance that educational inequalities generally are tolerable or not depending upon whether or not they arise with governmental complicity, inasmuch as the fact of governmental complicity pertains strictly to the psychic, demoralizing impacts of an inequality.

The other analytical matter is relatively simple. It is that

---

[117] It would also be presumptuous in view of the monumental efforts of Coons, Clune and Sugarman.

[118] Plessy v. Ferguson, 163 U.S. 537, 551 (1896).

[119] *See Developments in the Law, supra* note 16, at 1130, noting the bearing of inequality upon the identification of "fundamental" interests.

the school-finance cases are essentially, but not simply, payment-requirements cases. The core of the grievance is that states are forcing local districts to settle for whatever education they can afford out of their own means. To a considerable degree, therefore, earlier discussion concerning justifications for payment requirements is applicable here.[120] But it must be noted that the states' involvement transcends a mere payment requirement — though perhaps, when all is said, the transcendence will seem marginal. In any event, the states have done at least these other things: they have determined that there will be public education, collectively financed out of general taxes; they have determined that the collective financing will not rest mainly on a statewide tax base, but will be largely decentralized to districts; they have composed the district boundaries, thereby determining wealth distribution among districts; in so doing, they have not only sorted education-consuming households into groups of widely varying average wealth, but they have sorted non-school-using taxpayers — households and others — quite unequally among districts; and they have made education compulsory. At some point, we may expect, the question will arise whether these "extras" materially enhance the invidiousness of an inequality over what it would have been in their absence.

Substantial inequality in educational offering would seem a deprivation critical and singular enough to arouse at least tentative concern under either equal protection or minimum protection thinking. It seems reasonable to assume, also, that educational expenditure is a sufficiently important predictor of educational quality to warrant the excitation of equal protection sensors by any state-sanctioned differences therein.[121]

Suppose, now, that suit is brought on behalf of a child resident in District *A*, complaining of substantial disparity between that district's annual per-pupil expenditure and much larger annual per-pupil expenditures in most other school districts in the state. The state, let us imagine, disclaims liability on the ground that it has, through a statewide system of taxes and subventions, "equalized" the fiscal opportunities open to all districts by standardizing the expenditure yield for every permitted level of district fiscal effort. Under this "district power equalizing" dispensation, expenditures rise with district effort, but districts which tax at the same effort level spend the same amount per pupil. In short, the state's subsidies to (and tax withdrawals from) the local districts are calibrated so that equal "effort" levels in a rich and a poor district yield the same dollar ex-

---

[120] *See* pp. 29–30 *supra*.

[121] *See* Coons at 310.

penditure for public education. Expenditure outcomes are thus shielded from the effects of wealth disparities among districts.[122] The question for discussion is whether we ought to be satisfied with this response. (While it is true that no state, at present, could truthfully assert such a defense, discussion of it is not idle because "district power equalizing" is currently receiving persuasive and distinguished support as a desirable reform which will satisfy a state's constitutional obligations in the field of educational finance.[123])

One difficulty is that children whose families have identical (let us say rather low) incomes and identical (let us say rather avid) tastes for education, and who differ only in where they live, may under a district power equalizing system receive substantially unequal treatment depending upon the levels of sacrifice for education which are *collectively* (*i.e.*, politically) preferred by the voters in their respective districts of residence. Here is a systematic, state-sponsored discrimination among the possibly favored class [124] of children, affecting their almost certainly favored interest in education. Equal protectionists of surpassing craft, subtlety, learning, and integrity assure us that it is constitutionally inoffensive — virtually in the same breath with their magisterial argument that a like discriminatory result, when linked to inter-district wealth differences as in the Illinois of *McInnis*, is beyond the pale. The general theorem which they derive through equal protection argument, and would invoke against the Illinois arrangements, is that educational quality may not be a function of wealth other than the wealth of the state as a whole.[125] In arriving at this theorem (which is not offended by expenditure differences among power-equalized districts) they

---

[122] The essence of a power equalizing system is to develop a rational index of district revenue effort (say, the mill rate on real property, or total district school revenues expressed as a percentage of total district personal income) and then provide that equal effort yields equal dollars per pupil. A kind of "natural" system would give each district the per-pupil amount which would have been produced by applying its chosen effort level to the statewide average taxable property (or income, as the case may be) per pupil. But a marvelous group of variations, refinements, and qualifications are available to make the system respond to all manner of imaginable state policies. These are discussed at length in J. Coons, W. Clune, & S. Sugarman, Private Wealth and Public Education ch. 6 (forthcoming, 1969, Harvard U. Press). The essential requirement is that districts which tax themselves at the same intensity wind up spending the same amounts per pupil.

[123] *I.e.*, by Coons *et al.*

[124] *See* note 90 *supra*.

[125] *See* Coons at 311. The authors explicitly recognize that they are arguing by way of a generalization which will constrain state choices to certain outcomes, and not merely invalidate the particular arrangement under attack. *See id.* at 334–35, 344–45.

must, of course, succeed in distinguishing between place-determined and wealth-determined educational inequalities.

The thing is in part a feat of advocacy, achieved by dialectics of deceptive and alluring simplicity: wealth as a classifying trait is invidious; [126] place is not.[127] Therefore, it should come as no great surprise that exposure to relative educational deprivation by accident of location may be tolerated by the same equal protection clause which inveighs against such deprivations when traceable to wealth differences. But these advocates, delightfully, are also scholars, ready to expose the false simplicity of their own argument and to rehabilitate it complexly. Though enticed, they disdain reliance on the doctrinaire formula equating invidious-trait-plus-favored-interest with constitutional violation. For them the ultimately crucial points are (1) that education is terribly important and no convincing reason appears for tolerating the apparent injustice of wealth-determined inequality, while (2) there does exist a persuasive justification for place-determined inequality. To this justification the name "subsidiarity" is given. "Subsidiarity" encompasses a set of values roughly corresponding to what others often refer to as "federalism" or "decentralization" — "a policy preference for decisionmaking by the smallest unit of society competent to do so." [128] Clearly this ranks consensually as a prime objective; and, just as clearly, it will be significantly furthered through the decentralization of effort decisions permitted by district power equalizing.[129]

Perhaps a minimum protectionist would be satisfied with the District *A* situation. Having readily agreed that a just society cannot tolerate the risk that a child's educational needs will be severely disserved by accident of poverty, he would want to be shown how the risk of such disservice by accident of residence might be relevantly different. The promise of social benefits through subsidiarity might be enough to make the attendant personal exposure seem tolerable. But there is a good chance that it might not. Having never stopped to appraise the relative invidiousness of wealth and place discriminations, and therefore not in the least appeased by the neutrality of place discriminations as such, the minimum protectionist would almost certainly go on to inquire whether subsidiarity benefits could not be realized by means which do not expose children to the possibility of involuntary and severe educational deprivation. He would dis-

[126] *See id.* at 358–71. The authors say that "[t]hese cases which appear to thrust the classifying fact of wealth into the inner circle of equal protection may be the key to the establishment" of their theorem. *Id.* at 358.

[127] *See id.* at 352–55.

[128] *Id.* at 318.

[129] *See id.* at 319–21.

cover, as I shall explain presently, that they can. The devices by which subsidiarity can be reconciled with protection are not without problems, and it is by no means evident that the minimum protectionist would end by opting for them. But it is certain that he would worry about them at length.

Now the disturbing thing is that these devices are known to our equal protection theorists.[130] (It is they, in fact, who taught them to the minimum protectionist.) Yet they don't worry at all over the thought that the availability of such devices disqualifies district power equalizing as an acceptable solution. In equal protection lingo, they are surprisingly insensitive to the argument, latent in their own exposition, that exposure to place-determined inequality is not "necessary" to the concededly "compelling" state interest in subsidiarity. Perhaps it is not unfair, then, to suggest that in spite of conscientious defenses, they have as scholars fallen victim to the power of their own advocates' dialectics — that they have been unduly appeased by the dearth of invidiousness in place discriminations (comparing them with wealth discriminations), and that their appraisal of the case would have been sounder had they never gotten into the "classification" issue in the first place.

The devices through which protection can be extended, without prejudice to subsidiarity, are all variations on a theme which we may call "family power equalizing." To illustrate briefly: a plausible measure of family effort would be the percentage of family net income (perhaps after adjustment by exempting a "subsistence" amount) which the family determines to set aside for education. Families exerting an average effort but having per-child incomes below the state average would then receive subsidy payments (probably in a scrip form), while families with above-average per-child incomes would have to account to the state for the excess "yield" resulting from their chosen effort levels. Financial support of education could be exacted from childless families and nonfamily wealth, in any desired degree, by a general system of educational grants-in-aid to families or to public school systems (probably of a "matching" type), with the wherewithal to be raised by general state taxation.

Under such a "family power equalizing" system, wealthy households[131] in control of district politics could not avoid or limit their "subsidization" of other people's education by voting to abandon tax-financed education for privately marketed edu-

[130] "Family power equalizing" is briefly introduced in Coons at 321–22 and discussed at length in J. COONS, W. CLUNE, & S. SUGARMAN, *supra* note 122.

[131] Or households which for some other reason preferred private schooling in any event.

cation. Family educational expenditures would be determined by family effort, and any treasury deficits would be made good by general taxation. A functional, district-wide collective process of budgetary decisionmaking could be preserved under such a dispensation. District governing bodies could continue to operate public schools, stating their periodic revenue needs in the form of a per-pupil tuition cost rather than a district-wide general tax rate. Since a stated tuition cost would represent an identical effort level for every school user, there would exist a district-wide constituency sharing a common interest in the district governing body's expenditure decisions. This would be true even though the private-school option would now be practically open to all, assuming the continuation of a preference for "public" or "common" schooling on the part of a substantial segment of the population.

Let us return to our appraisal of the state's response to the complaint of the child in District *A*. It should be observed that in spite of district power equalizing the situation complained of entails the possibility of a wealth-determined inequality of educational resources. To take the extreme case, suppose that District *A* decides to reduce its effort to zero, thus exiting completely from the public education sphere.[132] The access of that district's children to education will then become dependent upon ability to pay private-school tuition fees. Thus a requirement of district power equalizing leaves open possibilities not only of serious *place*-determined inequalities among children in *different* districts, but also of serious *wealth*-determined inequalities among children in *the same* district.[133] Why is this not a crucial embarrassment to equal protectionists who would argue to the invalidity of existing state systems by way of a generalization about the invalidity of *all* wealth-determined inequalities in educational expenditure? [134] The answer, it seems, must lie in the arcana of "state action."

[132] That this is a real-life possibility is evidenced by Griffin v. County School Bd., 377 U.S. 218 (1964); Hall v. St. Helena Parish School Board, 197 F. Supp. 649 (E.D. La. 1961), *aff'd*, 368 U.S. 515 (1962). It is true that these instances arose out of desegregation agonies; but it is all too conceivable that like gestures could be motivated by other forms of vindictiveness, selfishness, or insularity.

[133] It should be noted that the "no wealth" theorem of Coons *et al.* does not, strictly speaking, require district power equalizing as a remedy. It would be content with a scheme of centralized state finance under which any variations in per-pupil expenditure were determined by factors other than wealth. *See* Coons at 340–45. But the important point here is that the theorem *would not insist on more* than district power equalizing.

[134] Of course, Coons *et al.* would not welcome the emergence of the wealth discrimination discussed in text. As legislators, indeed, they would forfend against it. *See* J. COONS, W. CLUNE, & S. SUGARMAN, *supra* note 122, at chs. 6–7. The point, again, is that their constitutional theorem would allow it.

The state appears to have made three choices leading to the situation which permits within-district wealth favoritism: (1) it has chosen to leave effort decisions to local districts; (2) it has chosen to "power equalize" those districts; and (3) it has chosen neither to require family power equalizing, nor to put a floor under district expenditures, nor otherwise to protect the poor against the risks of extremely low district effort. Choice (2) is plainly not a cause of any within-district wealth favoritism which may arise; its only effect is to purge choice (1) of wealth favoritism *among* districts. Choices (1) and (3) in combination could be said to be responsible for permitting within-district wealth favoritism — but only if we put away altogether any serious state action requirement when objection is made to government's failure to relieve poor persons of their inability to pay for things. For it cannot be maintained with any seriousness that the state's *having authorized* District *A* optionally to support a public school system is what makes District *A*'s withdrawal obnoxious to the Constitution. The authorization contributes absolutely nothing to the injury. Nor does its converse, the closing of schools by local option (rather than by statewide doom). For how would the complainant be better off if there were no public schools anywhere in the state? Would he be better off because then his sinking boat would have more poor persons in it? The only remaining possibility is that the injurious state action inheres in the very decision to decentralize to this particular set of districts — a decision which, it could be contended, inevitably affected the probabilities that some unit would opt for school shutdown. But this position is untenable because, while it may be arguable that a poor person's exposure is aggravated when these decisions are decentralized to districts rather than retained by the state, it is obvious that he is worse off still if the state simply dissolves its school districts and exits from public education. That is, if the injury wrought by decentralizing is reduction of the probabilities that adequate public subsidy will be forthcoming for some poor persons' educations, then the maximum possible degree of *that* sort of injury — reduction of the probability to zero — occurs in the case of utter state withdrawal, which is also the epitome of no state action.

One who chooses not to junk the state action doctrine in ability-to-pay cases is then forced to the conclusion that the injurious inequality within District *A* is a fruit of official choices entailing *inaction*, a thing deemed crucially different from *action*. The inaction is jointly District *A*'s in not supporting a school system and the state's in not forcing it to do so. If the Constitution be not offended, the reason seems to be precisely the one given by equal protectionists who have worried about the problem

— to wit, that the negative right not to be officially subjected to unfavorable treatment by reason of poverty does not encompass the positive right to be educated at public expense.[135]

"State action" then may rationalize the legal position that district power equalizing is a sufficient response to a constitutional prohibition against wealth-determined inequalities in public educational expenditure. But legal rationalization need not, and in this instance does not, fully satisfy. If we may, for the moment, pass by considerations of judicial role, it seems that to find inter-district educational wealth favoritism (as presently in Illinois) unacceptable because of state complicity, while educational wealth favoritism within a district (as in the District *A* case) is accepted because of state neutrality, can only mean that there is a detectable and crucial difference in the invidiousness of the two cases; and that view, in turn, implies that in one or both cases the evils are preponderantly those of discrimination rather than deprivation.[136] Yet both those implications seem very wrong to me. I submit that *disadvantage*, not demoralization or affront, is manifestly the principal source of grievance in both these cases, and that in any event, they are virtually indistinguishable in terms of invidiousness content. If this be accepted, then I submit further that unless considerations of judicial role intervene, the Constitution ought to be construed if at all possible so that it does not distinguish between these cases without a difference.

The availability of family power equalizing seems to make judicial role a problematical factor here, for family power equalizing would remove all possibility of wealth favoritism among or within districts [137] — or, as a minimum protectionist would have it, of blocked access resulting from poverty — without, perhaps, crucially escalating the degree of judicial interventionism beyond what equal protectionists are already seeking. The point is fairly debatable. Family power equalizing is, by comparison with district power equalizing, such a strange and radical departure from present dispensations that possibly district power equalizing is as far as a court ought to go.[138] But it remains an indictment of the best in equal protection thinking that it never gets quite far enough even to confront this issue; and it seems fair to say also

---

[135] *Cf.* Coons at 342, 373–74.

[136] *See* p. 49 *supra*.

[137] This assumes treatment of a household — parents and children — as a unitary moral entity. That is, it would impute to the child the parents' decision not to exert educational effort. There are considerations of personal liberty which may justify this assumption, though perhaps it is problematical.

[138] *Cf.* Coons at 324–25, 340–41, 343–44.

that the issue's existence furnishes only the most tenuous and remote of vindications for a state action doctrine.

Of course, it may be argued that "state action" needn't claim any vindication outside the four corners of the Constitution. I think that constitutional exegetes have shown the way to treating the doctrine as a moribund letter, by lines of argument which can be made serviceable here.[139] But that is a story for another day. For today's story, the important point is that minimum protection thinking would have achieved what equal protection thinking did not achieve: it would have carried us to the issue of judicial role as the determinative one in deciding whether family power equalizing ought to be the minimum acceptable remedy in cases like *McInnis*. To see how that is so will be our last gasp.

To a very large extent, the significant differences in principle between a complete legal duty of minimum protection and the duty of equal protection seem destined to remain practically inconsequential. In abstract discourse it is not uninteresting to observe that, in one important respect, minimum protection emerges as the more conservative formulation of the state's duty. For the demands of minimum protection can, in principle, be satisfied by a state-aid system of "flat" or "foundation" grants which assure to each district an acceptable minimum resource per pupil at a tolerable sacrifice level, but leave each district free to repair to its own unequalized tax base for some additional level of funding as long as the competitive-inequality gap does not grow too large. But this can never satisfy an equal protection doctrine which is offended by the state's involvement in any wealth-favoritism in the educational field.[140]

But this "advantage" of the minimum protection hypothesis (if we would so regard it) remains utterly theoretical until (if ever) we can develop a "justiciable" standard for specifying the acceptable minimum and the acceptable gap. Absent such standards, the supposed duty of minimum-protection cannot be directly enforced; in fact, its violation cannot even be coherently alleged.[141] Evidently, some notion of equality or nondiscrimination is needed to provide a foothold for litigants and judges intent upon defining a grievance and fashioning a remedy. Unless the

[139] *See* Black, *supra* note 10; Karst & Horowitz, *supra* note 10.

[140] *See* note 108 *supra* and accompanying text. Possibly an exception would be made for a system of per-pupil flat grants so luxurious that any local add-ons would be of trifling significance.

[141] This must be what Coons *et al.* mean when they say that a minimum protection duty (which they suggest can be inferred from *Douglas v. California*) would cut no ice in a state which already has any sort of flat-grant or foundation program. *See* Coons at 362, 365.

grievance can be rendered into the verbal and conceptual forms of inequality and discrimination, it will remain suspended — accusing, oppressive, and unresolved — in some moral heaven.

It happens that educational inequality and educational deprivation are so closely intertwined that minimum protection thinking about the educational-finance problem may lead to a statement of grievance in a justiciable form resembling that of more conventional equal protection disputation. The flow of thought might go something like this. First, in a market-oriented and technological society justice demands minimum educational assurances, and the minimum is significantly a function of the maximum and to that extent calls for equalization. Second, there are gross disparities in educational expenditure (which may correlate with other plausible indices of equality[142]), and also evidence of the relationships among these disparities and the other crucial factors of wealth and effort, sufficient to raise a strong suspicion that lack of money is resulting in severe educational deprivation. Third, a system of family power equalizing, if embracing all educational spending in the state, can provide assurances against such deprivation without trenching significantly on subsidiarity.

The crucial proposition is the third, and its most interesting aspect is the insistence on channeling all the state's educational expenditures into the common pool. Family power equalizing is here advanced in the guise of what in other contexts might be called a "prophylactic" remedy. Essentially, the idea is that we can be assured that each family has adequate access to no less than the just minimum, even if we cannot specify what constitutes that minimum, as long as we know that all resources throughout the state which are being devoted to education have been pooled in such a way that equal sacrifice levels give rise to equal withdrawals. Under such a regime, each family is guaranteed access to that level of educational spending which is "average" or modal for the state, if only that family exerts an average effort.

It thus appears that manifestations of minimum protection thinking in school finance litigation — in the definition of a grievance and fabrication of a remedy — will tend towards results similar to those contended for by a more familiar style of equal

[142] In addition to such inputs as teacher qualifications and such standard output measures as test scores, one might wish to concentrate on outcome discrepancies peculiarly suggestive of failure to meet the state's own notions of competitive adequacy — as reflected, *e.g.*, in civil-service examinations. There is, of course, a burgeoning literature on input-output relationships in public schooling, partially collected in Coons at 310–11 n.16.

protection argument, but will press harder on the question of family power equalizing.

An additional effect of minimum protection thinking may be to help the decisionmaker understand how to differentiate education from other goods, say opera and golf, which persons will have to continue to pay for out of their own means or do without. Evenhandedness tends to be an all-encompassing value, to become an end in itself, to be "not easily cabined" once loosed.[143] Education, golf, and opera may tend to seem but fungible objects upon which evenhandedness can work, or vehicles through which evenhandedness can realize itself. The distinctive psychic and moral evils of relative deprivation may not seem significantly less present when golf or opera is made available through a governmental facility, but only to those who can and will pay, than when schooling is similarly offered. What we may call the "Harlan syndrome" [144] is an indubitably real phenomenon. The notion of protection against severe deprivation may seem helpfully selective when laid beside that of evenhandedness. It is insistent upon getting what is basic, but is outspokenly explicit in claiming nothing more. It reacts more hospitably than evenhandedness to the question: why education and not golf?

---

[143] *See* Cox, *supra* note 7, at 91.

[144] *See* note 20 *supra*.

# [16]

# Legality, Bureaucracy, and Class in the Welfare System

William H. Simon†

When lawyers confronted the welfare system in the 1960's, they charged it with oppressive moralism, personal manipulation, and invasion of privacy. They focused attention on the "man-in-the-house" rules that disqualified families on the basis of the mother's sexual conduct and the "midnight raids" in which welfare workers forced their way into recipients' homes searching for evidence of cohabitation.[1]

When I represented welfare recipients from 1979 to 1981, the workers showed little interest in policing their morals or intruding on their private lives. The "man-in-the-house" rule and the practice of unannounced or nighttime visits had been repudiated.[2] Yet the pathologies emphasized by the lawyers of the 1960's seemed to have been mitigated at the cost of exacerbating others that were in some respects their mirror images: indifference, impersonality, and irresponsibility. The new pathologies were typified by cases in which newly arrived Cuban refugees were denied assistance because they could not produce appropriately certified copies of birth certificates for their children or in which people who sought assistance from the wrong worker were sent away without explanation, thinking mistakenly that they were entitled to nothing.

I have a particularly vivid memory of a woman whose grant was terminated when she failed to produce a recently dated letter from the school of one of her children verifying his enrollment. She had produced letters from the three other schools her children attended and had produced let-

† Assistant Professor of Law, Stanford University. This essay arises from my practice at the Legal Services Institute, Boston, Massachusetts, from 1979 to 1981 and from conversations with my colleagues there, especially Evelyn Brodkin, Duncan Kennedy, Michael Lipsky, and Teresa Nelson. Many other friends and colleagues gave valuable advice and assistance. Theodore Marmor, Deborah Rhode, and Richard Scott were especially generous. I am distinctively indebted to Jerry Mashaw and Joel Handler for their encouragement of my attempt to criticize (as well as to appropriate from) their work. Research for the essay was supported by the Stanford Legal Research Fund, made possible by a bequest from the estate of Ira S. Lillick and by gifts from other friends of the Stanford Law School.

1. *See* Reich, *Midnight Welfare Searches and the Social Security Act*, 72 YALE L.J. 1347 (1963); Sparer, *The Place of Law in Social Work Education*, 17 BUFFALO L. REV. 733, 734-37 (1968).

2. *See* King v. Smith, 392 U.S. 309 (1968); U.S. DEP'T OF HEALTH, EDUC. & WELFARE, HANDBOOK OF PUBLIC ASSISTANCE ADMINISTRATION pt. IV, §§ 2200(a), 2300 (1967). Some inquiry about personal matters still occurs. Establishing economic eligibility requires information about financial affairs, and this sometimes involves inquiry into sexual relations, for example, in connection with the establishment of paternity for the purpose of enforcing support obligations. But both the scope and frequency of such inquiries has sharply diminished.

ters from all four schools on three prior occasions within the preceeding six months. But this time she was unable to get the letter from one school because it was August, and the school office was closed. After the school office opened, she brought the letter to her worker, who responded that it was too late: "There is nothing I can do." What she meant (as she explained to me later after the woman's checks had stopped) was that there was nothing she, as an "ongoing" case worker, could do but that the recipient could have been immediately reinstated simply by filing an application with the "intake" unit. If the literary personification of the pathologies of the old regime was Dostoyevsky's Grand Inquisitor, with his relentless intimacy and psychological omnipotence, the personification of the pathologies of the new regime is Kafka's Doorkeeper, who stands, passive and inscrutable, before the door to the Law and announces only when it is too late, "this door was intended for you. I am now going to shut it."[3]

Of course, one should not appraise a system solely in terms of its worst cases. Such horror stories are merely the more dramatic and disturbing manifestations of a series of related developments I want to discuss. For better or worse (and I don't intend to argue it has been only for worse), the welfare system has been transformed in the past two decades. Lawyers and legal ideas have played a central role in this transformation. Since the 1960's, the social work profession has ceded to the professions of law and management both its ideological custody of the welfare system and its preeminent role in its administration. The concerns of law and management have converged in the three basic themes of the recent literature and practice of welfare administration: first, the formalization of entitlement, by which I mean the formulation of the eligibility norms as rules; second, the bureaucratization of administration, by which I mean the intensification of formally hierarchical organization; and third, the proletarianization of the work force, by which I mean the diminution of the status, skill, education, and reward associated with the frontline welfare worker's job.

This essay examines the relation of contemporary legal discourse to these institutional and social developments. Part I illustrates the developments with a discussion of the largest and most controversial cash public assistance program, Aid to Families with Dependent Children (AFDC). Part II discusses the legal doctrines with which these developments have been explained, promoted, and criticized. These doctrines take the form of a kind of sociological jurisprudence that proceeds by linking certain basic social goals with a particular style of legality and in turn with a particular form of organization. The version of this approach that has most influ-

3. F. KAFKA, THE TRIAL 269 (Vintage ed. 1969).

enced the welfare system holds that the goals of efficiency, freedom, and fairness require a legality of formality which in turn requires a hierarchical enforcement organization staffed at the lower tier by a proletarian work force. I argue that this doctrine is implausible, at least on the level of abstraction at which it has influenced welfare reform, and that it has tended to obscure some of the problems that have attended the transformation of the system. While the great virtue of recent legal writing on the welfare system has been to focus attention on the relation of legality to organization, its failing has been to blur important sociological and political questions by (often in spite of the expressed intentions of the authors) treating them as legal questions. Part III sketches an alternative account of the welfare system that attempts to do justice to social context and political contingency.

Although its primary purposes are historical and critical, there is a prescriptive theme running through this essay. I suggest that a vision of legality and organization opposed to the dominant vision is more plausible as an ideal and as a guide to reform in welfare administration. This opposed vision involves a legality of relative informality, a decentralized enforcement structure, and a corps of enforcers with some of the attributes of skill, education, and status associated with professionalism. This vision is in many respects similar to the understanding of welfare legality and enforcement of the New Deal social workers who founded the modern public assistance system.[4] Although the argument for the opposed vision remains speculative and inconclusive, it attempts to clarify the basic issues by linking the contest between the dominant and opposed visions to larger social and political issues. I argue that the choice between the competing visions depends on the resolution in theory and practice of a central tension in the understanding of class implicit in sociological jurisprudence and in much contemporary legal scholarship.

## I. The Transformation of Public Assistance

The trends of formalization, bureaucratization, and proletarianization in public assistance are exemplified by the recent history of the AFDC program. I use AFDC, and particularly the Massachusetts AFDC program, as my principal example for reasons of convenience—I've had personal experience with it, and it is described in a variety of available materials. But other considerations also make AFDC an appropriate focus. Despite anachronistic eligibility limitations that exclude most indigent

4. Although the social workers and their program have been blamed for the pathologies of welfare administration, the charge is unfair. In fact their approach has never fairly been tried. *See infra* pp. 1214-16; Simon, *The Invention and Reinvention of Welfare Rights*, 44 MD. L. REV. (1984) (forthcoming).

two-parent families, AFDC is the central pillar of the American public assistance system. It is the largest cash assistance program and the one on which intense and conflicting popular attitudes toward welfare tend to focus. At the level of initial determination, it is normally administered by the state welfare departments in close conjunction with one of the two other major cash assistance programs, General Assistance, and with the two major in-kind assistance programs, Food Stamps and Medicaid.[5] Most of the developments in AFDC have either directly affected these programs or correspond to analogous developments in them. There have also been analogous developments in Supplemental Security Income, the cash public assistance program for the aged, blind, and disabled administered by the Social Security Administration, and the two largest cash social insurance programs, Social Security, and Unemployment Insurance.

## A. *Developments*

Here are the more notable instances of the three overlapping trends of formalization, bureaucratization, and proletarianization in AFDC:

*The Reformulation of Substantive Norms.* The substantive eligibility norms have been revised to increase their substantive formality, that is, to give them the form of rules rather than of standards.[6] There are three aspects to this distinction.

First, rules are more explicit than standards. During the period from 1935 to the early 1960's, which I call the old regime, promulgated regulations and published norms of any kind were brief. Workers were expected to absorb some aspects of the eligibility criteria through experience on the job and to have learned other aspects previously through education or experience in the community. The reforms of the past two decades have sought to make the criteria as explicit as possible. Statutes and regulations have become more voluminous and detailed, and they have been supplemented by still more voluminous instructional manuals that attempt to explicate them.

5. AFDC is the creature of Title IV of the Social Security Act of 1935 and subsequent amendments. 42 U.S.C. §§ 601-615 (1976 & Supp. V 1981). The Act creates a system of federal grants to the states for programs formulated and administered by them but subject to federal statutory and regulatory restrictions and to the supervision of the Secretary of Health and Human Services (HHS). (For convenience, I refer throughout this essay to the agency's predecessors by its current name.) The federal government reimburses the states for expenditures under their programs at rates that average about 55%. In 1980, there were 11.1 million recipients, and expenditures totaled $12.5 billion. *Current Operating Statistics*, SOC. SECURITY BULL., Sept. 1982, at 43-44. For a history of the program up to 1974, see Lurie, *Major Changes in the Structure of the AFDC Program Since 1935*, 59 CORNELL L. REV. 825 (1974); for an overview of the American income maintenance system, see S. LEVITAN, PROGRAMS IN AID OF THE POOR FOR THE 1980S (3d ed. 1980).

6. On formality and the distinction between rules and standards, see Kennedy, *Form and Substance in Private Law Adjudication*, 89 HARV. L. REV. 1685 (1976).

Second, rules constrain judgment more than standards by limiting the number of factors to be considered in decisionmaking. Standards tend to declare a general social goal or value and direct the decisionmaker to take the action most consistent with it in the light of all relevant circumstances. They tend to permit an individualized assessment of how goals or values can be implemented in the circumstances of the particular case. Rules, on the other hand, tend to permit consideration of relatively few specified factors. They are over- and under-inclusive in regard to their purposes.[7] The trend toward formalization can be seen in the elimination of many norms that invoked general language and made relevant a wide variety of factors. The best known instances are the "suitable home" regulations and others that required in very general language determinations of the adequacy of the applicant as a parent and homemaker.[8] Other instances involve the consideration of the claimant's income and assets. For example, a provision that a car not be counted as a potentially disqualifying asset if it is "needed" by the applicant has been replaced by one providing that ownership of a car not be counted if its value is less than $1500. A provision requiring that earned income not be counted to the extent offset by expenses "reasonably attributable" to the earnings has been replaced by one requiring that $75 per month be disregarded as an expense allowance.[9]

In the late 1960's and early 1970's most states restructured their AFDC budgeting norms to eliminate many specific circumstances of need that were previously considered in determining eligibility. Prior to this "consolidation" of need standards, AFDC grants typically took some account of the actual cost to the particular applicant of items such as shelter and fuel (as opposed to making a uniform allowance to all applicants), of the age of the recipients (families with older children got higher grants), and of a variety of "special" recurring or non-recurring needs. For example, an applicant without a washing machine might receive a supplement for laundry expenses; a diabetic might receive a supplement for the extra food expenses of a restrictive diet; a new baby might receive a crib; a recipient whose check has been stolen might receive a replacement grant. Consolidation eliminated many such factors and moved state programs toward a uniform need standard based only on the size of the family.[10] Analogous

7. *Id.* at 1687-89.

8. *See* W. BELL, AID TO DEPENDENT CHILDREN (1965).

9. Chief, *Need Determination in AFDC Programs*, SOC. SECURITY BULL., Sept. 1979, at 11, 18 n.4 (prior automobile rules); 45 C.F.R. § 233.20(a)(2)(xiv)(A) (1983) (current automobile rule); Shea v. Vialpando, 416 U.S. 251 (1974) (prior earned income rule); 42 U.S.C. § 602(a)(8)(A)(ii) (Supp. V 1981) (current earned income rule).

10. URBAN SYSTEMS RESEARCH & ENGINEERING, AFDC STANDARDS OF NEED: AN EVALUATION OF CURRENT PRACTICES, ALTERNATIVE APPROACHES, AND POLICY OPTIONS 174-246 (report prepared

developments on the income side of the budget have eliminated consideration of factors regarding the applicant's living arrangements. For example, a variety of norms requiring consideration of the financial benefit to recipients of the income or expenditures of non-recipient household members has been eliminated.[11]

Another manifestation of this aspect of formalization is the development of various sub-legal instructional materials that purport to break down the prescriptions of the promulgated law into still more precise operations. For example, the instructions that operationalize a regulation providing that the applicant's monthly income be deducted from the need standard might set out a form and instruct the worker to enter the need standard on line *a* of the form, to enter the amounts shown on the applicant's pay stubs for the three most recent weeks on line *b*, to add these amounts and enter the total on line *c*; to divide the total on line *c* by 3 and enter the quotient on line *d*; to multiply the amount on line *d* by 4.3 and enter the product on line *e*, and to subtract from the amount on line *a* the amount on line *e*.[12]

The third aspect of the formalization of substantive norms concerns the style of judgment and the attitude prescribed for the decisionmakers. The old regime aspired to inculcate a capacity for complex interpretative judgment based on an understanding of the fundamental purposes of the program. Work was conceived as direct participation in the elaboration and implementation of important social goals. Mechanical judgment and literalistic interpretation were discouraged.[13] The formalization of recent years repudiates this ideal and embraces mechanical judgment and literalistic

for SSA, Aug. 1980); *see* Rosado v. Wyman, 304 F. Supp. 1356, 1365-69 (S.D.N.Y.), *rev'd*, 414 F.2d 170 (2d Cir. 1969), *rev'd*, 397 U.S. 397 (1970).

A variety of separate "special need" programs remain, but they are generally marginal both in coverage and funding. They have been strained in recent years as a consequence of both the elimination of specialized coverage in AFDC and funding cutbacks. *See* J. HANDLER & M. SOSIN, LAST RESORTS: MEETING EMERGENCY NEEDS IN PUBLIC ASSISTANCE (1983).

The trend toward formalization has been partially offset by the recent growth of "in kind" medical and education programs that require complex, informal judgments regarding the particular needs of the applicant. Within the welfare system, Medicare and Medicaid are the most important instances. However, these programs are structured so that such judgments are not made within the welfare administration but are delegated to medical professionals outside the administration.

11. *See* Van Lare v. Hurley, 421 U.S. 338 (1975); Lewis v. Martin, 397 U.S. 552 (1970). These cases have spawned a large body of litigation further restricting consideration of variations in living arrangements. *See, e.g.*, Leone v. Blum, 73 A.D.2d 254, 425 N.Y.S.2d 836 (1980), *aff'd sub nom.* Delmar v. Blum, 53 N.Y.2d 105, 423 N.E.2d 27, 440 N.Y.S.2d 604 (1981). The 1981 and 1982 AFDC amendments, which partially reintroduce factors eliminated by *Lewis* and *Van Lare*, are partial retreats from the trend toward simplification. 42 U.S.C. §§ 602(a)(31), 612, *as amended by* Pub. L. No. 97-35, § 2306(a) (1981), and Pub. L. No. 97-248, § 155 (1982).

12. The example is based on my memory of provisions of the Massachusetts *AFDC Worker Handbook* in effect in 1980.

13. *See* FEDERAL SECURITY AGENCY, COMMON HUMAN NEEDS: AN INTERPRETATION FOR STAFF IN PUBLIC ASSISTANCE AGENCIES 104-22 (1945).

interpretation. At the same time, it implicitly prescribes an attitude of impersonality. It seeks to alienate the worker from the purposes of the norms she enforces. There are two versions of this alienation; in one the worker is unaware of the purposes underlying the norms she enforces; in the other the worker feels bound to apply the norms in spite of their purposes. For example, consider a worker applying the instructions regarding income averaging in the preceding paragraph to an applicant who works only three weeks a month. The instructions, in effect, require the determination of a monthly average on the basis of the three most recent weekly pay stubs. If the immediate purpose of specifying three stubs is to spare the recipient the burden of having to produce more than three (or the welfare department the burden of having to store more than three) and the basic purpose of the entire set of instructions is to produce an estimate of the applicant's monthly earnings (which is what everyone interprets the regulations and statute to require), following the instructions literally in the case of a recipient who works only three weeks a month will result in violating the basic purpose by overstating the applicant's monthly income and thus understating the proper grant. When the client appeals to the basic purpose and argues that the grant is too low, the worker's response will depend on which version of alienation applies. Either he will feel that the client's claim is meaningless or irrelevant to his work or he will recognize the situation as one in which the system requires him to violate one of its basic purposes in the interest of formality.[14]

A cumulative effect of the three aspects of formality is that the system appears to require fewer and simpler substantive judgments and to require less information from the client about her personal circumstances. Another effect is that assistance is less sensitive to the circumstances of the applicant.[15]

*The Reconception of Proof.* Under the old regime, the dominant view of the fact-finding phase of the eligibility process focused on the worker's

14. This example comes from a case described to me by Duncan Kennedy, who represented the recipient. The worker was aware that his action violated the purpose and language of the regulation but believed he was constrained by the handbook instruction.

15. The second and third aspects of formalization are notably exemplified in recent developments in the disability components of the Social Security and Supplemental Security Income programs. The Social Security Administration (SSA) has always provided lengthy and explicit statements of eligibility norms to front line workers. However, these statements have tended to take the form of the elaboration of standards through general interpretative principles and illustrative hypotheticals rather than specific instructions. In recent years, the Administration has revised its instructions to restrict the considerations bearing on the determinations and to foster more simplified and mechanical judgment. As the Administration acknowledges, the new rules frequently require denial of claims that a purposive interpretation based on the more standard-like norms of the statute and regulations would allow. The intention to replace complex judgment with routine mechanical operations is expressed in the change of the title of the instructions from "Claims Manual" to "Program Operating Manual System." *See The Bellmon Report*, SOC. SECURITY BULL., May 1982, at 3, 8, 11-17.

Welfare System

assessment of the credibility of the claimant's oral statements. The worker was expected to make an extensive and active investigation through office interviews of the claimant and visits to her home. He was to accord the claimant a strong presumption of credibility. When doubts arose, the worker was expected to undertake inquiry of employers, friends, or relatives.[16] The presumption of credibility was often violated and states required applicants to document some statements prior to the 1960's. Nevertheless, as recently as 1969, the Department of Health and Human Services (HHS) proposed that states require workers to determine eligibility on the basis of the applicant's statements unless the statements were "incomplete, unclear, or inconsistent, or . . . other circumstances in the particular case indicate to a prudent person that further inquiry should be made, and the individual cannot clarify the situation . . . ."[17]

Since then, however, this view has been rejected in favor of one that emphasizes the claimant's responsibility for verifying eligibility through documents and that portrays the worker's role as passively policing the claimant's compliance with documentation requirements. Verification requirements have increased to require documentation of almost every factor bearing on eligibility. The Massachusetts welfare department gives applicants a list of thirty documents that they may be asked to supply. The typical applicant is required to produce about half that number and to do so must undertake dealings with about five or six bureaucracies other than the welfare department.[18] At the same time, the frequency with which recipients must re-establish eligibility and renew much of the documentation has been increased to at least two and occasionally as often as five times a year.[19] Many of the documents must meet stringent technical requirements. For example a letter verifying a child's enrollment at school

16. *See* FEDERAL SECURITY AGENCY, *supra* note 13, at vii, 22–23; 2 G. ABBOTT, THE CHILD AND THE STATE 238 (1938); Towle, *Social Work: Cause and Function*, in CHARLOTTE TOWLE ON SOCIAL WORK AND SOCIAL CASEWORK 31 (H. Perlman ed. 1969); Note, *Rehabilitation, Investigation and the Welfare Home Visit*, 79 YALE L.J. 746, 746–51 (1970).

17. Methods for Determination of Eligibility, 34 Fed. Reg. 1145 (1969); *see* Note, *Eligibility Determinations in Public Assistance: Selected Problems and Proposals for Reform in Pennsylvania*, 115 U. PA. L. REV. 1307 (1967).

18. For example, the applicant may have to deal with the Bureau of Vital Statistics to get birth certificates; the SSA to get Social Security numbers; the welfare department's office of child support enforcement, the prosecutor's office, and the courts in connection with her obligation to assist the state in collecting support payments from an absent parent; the employment security department in order to register for the Work Incentive (WIN) program; other welfare bureaucracies in order to verify applications for all benefits she may be eligible for; her children's schools in order to verify their enrollment; her employer in order to verify her wages; her landlord and utility company in order to verify rent and utility payments; and a variety of institutions in order to verify the absence of a parent from the home. *See* Guttman, *The Application Process*, in CONG. RESEARCH SERV. REP. TO HOUSE COMM. ON GOV'T OPERATIONS, 95TH CONG., 1ST SESS., ADMINISTRATION OF THE AFDC PROGRAM 30–84 (Comm. Print 1977).

19. Federal regulations require redetermination at least every six months. 45 C.F.R. § 206.10(d)(9)(iii) (1983). More frequent redeterminations are made for cases considered "error prone."

may be rejected if not signed by the right official or not dated within the appropriate number of days. The workers are encouraged through training and supervision to insist on strict compliance with the documentation rules, and they are discouraged from relying on the claimant's undocumented statements even when the rules do not expressly require documentation. (This does not invariably work to the disadvantage of the claimant. For a few months during 1980, Boston welfare workers believed—even though the regulations did not so provide—that they could not reduce or terminate a grant on the basis of an orally reported increase in wages until the increase had been documented by the pay stubs for three successive weeks.) Even a well-educated person (which most claimants are not) without specialized knowledge of the system would not be able to satisfy the documentation requirements without extensive explanation, and in some instances, active assistance.[20] Although many states purport to require the workers to provide such explanation and assistance, as we will see, relatively little effort is made to enforce these requirements.

The changed approach to proof has formalized fact-finding in a manner analogous to the way the substantive norms have been formalized. At the same time, it has increased the burden on recipients of paper-pushing and bureaucratic hoop-jumping.

*The Advent of Quality Control.* Another important development is the change in the character of organizational review and supervisory procedures. Under the old regime, two such procedures were emphasized. One was relatively constant and direct personal supervision of the worker by a supervisor in the same office. The relationship was conceived as a collegial one between professionals, albeit professionals of unequal experience and authority. Supervision involved both review of written case records by the supervisor and oral consultation in which the supervisor explained her judgments and the worker was encouraged to participate actively and respond to the supervisor's comments. The goal was an informal consensus regarding the appropriate disposition of the case. The process was supposed to involve an intense scrutiny of both the applicant's situation and the worker's response to it.[21] In practice, supervision appears to have been

20. An Urban Institute Study underscores the importance of advice and assistance to claimants by comparing a "client accessibility index" for each state with the average educational level of recipients in the state. The accessibility index is a function of the percentage of denials and terminations on "procedural" (including documentation) grounds, underpayment errors as a percentage of caseload and payments, and the percentage of applications processed late. The study finds, "the lower the average educational levels of AFDC clients, the lower was the index accessibility," and "the higher the proportion of Spanish-speaking clients in a state, the lower its accessibility." M. BENDICK, A. LAVINE & T. CAMPBELL, THE ANATOMY OF AFDC ERRORS 58-60 (1978).

21. *See* FEDERAL SECURITY AGENCY, *supra* note 13, at 95-122; V. ROBINSON, SUPERVISION IN SOCIAL CASE WORK (1936).

Welfare System

more authoritarian and summary than this ideal.[22] Nevertheless, as the basic method of organizational review, it made for relatively complex judgment and decentralized administration. Review was done by a person with extensive knowledge of the worker, the case, and the immediate context of decision, and it was done in a manner facilitating participation by the worker.

Supervision was supplemented by a variety of procedures, the most important of which was the federal audit. Periodically, HHS would review the records of a sample of the caseload. It would disallow reimbursement for the federal share of improper payments to the reviewed cases. When the review disclosed a pattern of mistake or lawlessness, HHS pressed the state to change its policy and instruct its workers appropriately. Efforts to affect the program through the audit appear to have been largely concerned with major policy matters.[23]

Beginning in the 1960's, the federal audit was supplemented and eventually replaced by procedures called Quality Control. Aside from their zealous invocation of the jargon of business management, the new procedures differ from the old in three respects. First, they use statistical methods to designate the sample of cases for review and to derive from the reviews an estimate of the total number of the state's cases and the total amount of its payments in "error." Second, since 1973, these estimates have been backed by the threat of "fiscal sanctions" in the form of withheld federal reimbursement for a portion of the estimated erroneous payments in the entire caseload, not just the cases reviewed. Third, Quality Control involves a more intensive and detailed review of the sample cases than the old procedures. In response to the federal system, the states have developed their own supplementary quality control processes, which make similar but less intensive reviews of larger samples of cases. These supplementary reviews are designed to lower error rates in advance of the federal reviews.[24]

22. *See* Scott, *Professional Employees in a Bureaucratic Structure: Social Work*, in THE SEMI-PROFESSIONS AND THEIR ORGANIZATION 82, 102–10 (A. Etzioni ed. 1969).

23. *See* M. DERTHICK, THE INFLUENCE OF FEDERAL GRANTS: PUBLIC ASSISTANCE IN MASSACHUSETTS (1970).

24. *See* Richardson, *Quality Control Efforts in Administration of the AFDC Program*, in CONG. RESEARCH SERV. REP. TO HOUSE COMM. ON GOV'T OPERATIONS, *supra* note 18, at 202–05; Pratt, *State Agencies Can Be Managed: The Massachusetts Experience with AFDC Error Rates*, NEW ENG. J. HUM. SERV., Spring 1981, at 20. The regulations governing AFDC Quality Control appear at 45 C.F.R. § 205.40 (1983). On the emergence of similar procedures in other programs, see *HEW Efforts to Reduce Errors in Welfare Programs (AFDC and SSI): Hearings Before the Subcomm. on Oversight of the House Ways & Means Comm.*, 94th Cong., 2d Sess. (1976) [hereinafter cited as *HEW Efforts*]; J. HANDLER, PROTECTING THE SOCIAL SERVICES CLIENT 101–16 (1979); M. MCDONALD, FOOD, STAMPS, AND INCOME MAINTENANCE 39–43 (1977); Chassman & Rolston, *Social Security Disability Hearings: A Case Study in Quality Assurance and Due Process*, 65 CORNELL L. REV. 801 (1980).

The new procedures have fueled both public and professional rhetoric about welfare in recent years, and in states with high error rates threatened with large fiscal sanctions, they have become the dominant influence on welfare administration. Reports of high error rates—federal Quality Control found 41% of all AFDC cases and 17% of all expenditures in error in 1973[25]—have confirmed hostile views among legislators, the media, and the public about the system's beneficiaries and the people who run it and have been taken as evidence warranting cutbacks.[26] At the same time, administrators, having committed large amounts of resources in response to Quality Control, have cited the consequent reductions in error as evidence of improvement in the system.[27]

There is, however, good reason to doubt these intepretations of Quality Control. To a large extent, Quality Control has obfuscated discussion of welfare administration by propagating a question-begging rhetoric of "error" to promote reforms that often could not survive reflective analysis. Many of the errors reported by Quality Control simply represent disagreements between reviewers and initial decisionmakers over the interpretation of ambiguous legal norms (is money paid for child care to a relative who would care for the child for free an "expense" deductible from earnings?) or ambiguous evidence (is a father reported by the recipient to be no longer residing at home but recently seen there on two occasions by a neighbor "absent" from the home?).

Many more of the error designations are undisputed but have been discovered only because the reviewer has used a different, more expensive procedure than the initial decisionmaker. A reviewer who makes more lengthy investigations is likely to discover errors, but such errors prove little about the reasonableness of the initial decisions, which depend in part on the ex ante appropriateness of devoting additional resources to the investigation. The fallacy of equating Quality Control errors with bad initial decisionmaking and error reduction with improved decisionmaking

25. *See* Richardson, *supra* note 24, at 218.

26. In 1978, Congressman Michel proposed to cut $1 billion from HHS on the ground that at least that amount represented erroneous payments under welfare programs. The amendment was enacted but proved inconsequential because HHS was able at year end to make up the deficiency through fiscal maneuvering. Since then, Congress has enacted a series of provisions mandating fiscal sanctions for states failing to meet designated error reduction targets. To date, no sanctions have been imposed, in part because the states have had success in meeting the targets, in part because the Secretary has exercised the power to waive the sanctions. *See* G. Mills, Quality Control in Welfare Administration: An Analysis of Payment Error in Aid to Families with Dependent Children 56–64 (unpublished Harvard University Ph.D. dissertation 1981).

The current provision, which denies reimbursement for erroneous payments exceeding 4% in fiscal year 1984, appears at 42 U.S.C. § 603(i) (Supp. V 1981). In 1982, the Reagan Administration proposed denying funds for the federal share of *all* payments found in error. *Reagan's Bid for Zero Error Rate Encounters Skepticism in the States*, AMERICAN PUBLIC WELFARE ASSOCIATION W-MEMO, Apr. 1982, at 1.

27. *See* Pratt, *supra* note 24.

Welfare System

has recently been emphasized by a study concluding that half of the decline in the national AFDC overpayment error between 1975 and 1977 from 11.2% to 8.7% is attributable to nothing more than an increase in the caseloads of quality control reviewers during this period: when cases increased, the reviewers spent less time on each case and hence found fewer errors.[28]

Still a further portion of Quality Control errors consists of "paper errors," formal procedural omissions that when remedied do not affect the amount of the grant and often provide little benefit to the program. For example, in 1978, HHS decided to count as erroneous all payments to recipients who appeared not to have applied for Social Security cards or registered for the Work Incentive Program, omissions of minimal practical consequence to the program.[29]

The Quality Control regime has tended to ignore the distinction between these kinds of errors and less controversial or more serious ones. It has often fallen into a crude formalism that ignores whether the program's purposes are served by the way it designates error or by the often frenzied remedial efforts such designations induce.[30]

28. G. Mills, *supra* note 26, at 165–70.

29. U.S. Dep't of Health, Educ. & Welfare, Action Transmittal SSA AT-78-31 (Aug. 4, 1978); Massachusetts Dep't of Pub. Welfare, AFDC Quality Control Statistical Analysis for Review Period April 1979–September 1979 (1980) (unpublished manuscript).

Aside from serving as a means of internal identification, Social Security numbers facilitate cross-checking of welfare files and Social Security wage reports to detect unreported recipient income that can be counted against the welfare grant. However, the majority of AFDC recipients are either pre-school children almost certain to be without earnings or students whose income was until 1981 exempt. If my observations in Massachusetts are typical, most of the Social Security card "errors" involve pre-school children.

The WIN program is supposed to provide job placement and training services, but it is notoriously underfunded and ineffective and has provided services to only a small fraction of registrants. Anderson, *WIN: From Both Sides Now*, 13 CLEARINGHOUSE REV. 584, 585 (1979). Increasing the number of registrants without increasing funding or improving administration merely adds to the number of unserved registrants and creates paper-pushing burdens for the program and the recipients.

30. For example, the reason HHS has given for counting "paper errors" in the payment error rate is that procedures such as Social Security application and WIN registration are required by statute as "conditions of eligibility." *See* 44 Fed. Reg. 12,581 (1979). Although the premise is correct, see 42 U.S.C. §§ 602(a)(19), (a)(25) (1976 & Supp. V 1981), the conclusion is a non sequitur. Legal scholarship and education have been devoted for decades to establishing that one cannot plausibly designate something a legal wrong or prescribe the consequences of such designation without reference to the purposes underlying the regulatory scheme. *See, e.g.*, Jacob & Youngs, Inc. v. Kent, 230 N.Y. 239, 129 N.E. 889 (1921) (failure of compliance with terms of contract not actionable if not detrimental to parties' expectations and purposes); Fuller & Perdue, *The Reliance Interest in Contract Damages*, 46 YALE L.J. 52, 77 (1936) (refuting notion that any particular remedy follows from the characterization of an act as a contractual wrong).

For critical evaluations of AFDC Quality Control, see Brodkin & Lipsky, *Quality Control in AFDC as an Administrative Strategy*, 57 SOC. SERV. REV. 1 (1983); E. Brodkin, The Error of Their Ways: Reforming Welfare Administration Through Quality Control (unpublished M.I.T. Ph.D. dissertation 1983). My understanding of Quality Control has developed in the course of many conversations with Evelyn Brodkin and Michael Lipsky.

While legislators and the media have tended to take the public assistance Quality Control data at face value, they have shown appropriate skepticism about such data in the Social Security disability

When different groups of decisionmakers using different procedures arrive at different conclusions in the same case, there is no occasion for surprise. When one group asserts that the other is in error, the question arises whether the assertion involves a process of measurement or a struggle for power. Whether or not AFDC Quality Control has made any contribution to the measurement of the welfare system's performance is still an open question, but it has clearly contributed to the system's transformation.

First, Quality Control has reinforced the trend toward formalization of eligibility norms. Relatively complex eligibility schemes relying on standards generate more quality control errors than relatively simple ones relying on rules. They do so, first, because they require a larger number of judgments on the part of the worker, and second, because these judgments are more susceptible to differences of interpretation between worker and reviewer. Much of the reduction in the error rate during the 1970's simply reflects the formalization discussed above. One study estimates that a third of the decline in AFDC case error rate between 1973 and 1976 (from 41% to 25%) is attributable to formalization during that period.[31] Another study advises that a state which has not yet consolidated its grants could achieve a reduction in its case error rate of 2.9 percentage points simply by doing so.[32]

Even when the norms are still expressed as standards susceptible to complex judgment, the review process encourages formalistic styles of interpretation. The reviewers are encouraged to adopt such styles. And where they adopt informalistic styles, they often fail to explain their judgments to the workers. Workers left without any understanding of the basis of reviewer judgment tend to adopt formalistic interpretations on the assumption that they are more likely to be correct than informalistic ones. For example, in 1979, one of the more frequently cited errors in the Massachusetts AFDC program was the failure to properly consider bank accounts in determining eligibility. Most of the errors were cited in situations in which a relative outside the home had opened and made deposits

insurance program. When Social Security Commissioner John Svahn invoked a prior finding of a 30% "error rate" as justification for the increased rate of terminations and denials in the Reagan Administration's "accelerated" disability review program, the House Select Committee on Aging responded: "[V]irtually the entire 'error rate' is accounted for by SSA's own findings on the use of standards stricter than the law and regulations, inadequate medical documentation, and simple disagreement between two sets of adjudications examining the same evidence." HOUSE SELECT COMM. ON AGING, IMPACT OF THE ACCELERATED REVIEW PROCESS ON CESSATIONS AND DENIALS IN THE SOCIAL SECURITY DISABILITY INSURANCE PROGRAM at vi (Comm. Print 1982); *see also* Mashaw, *How Much of What Quality?: A Comment on Conscientious Procedural Design*, 65 CORNELL L. REV. 823 (1980) (benefits of accurate disability claims decisions should be weighed against costs to other values).

31. Touche, Ross & Co., Evaluation of AFDC-QC Corrective Actions: Final Report (1977) (report to SSA) (unpublished manuscript on file with author).

32. M. BENDICK, A. LAVINE & T. CAMPBELL, *supra* note 20, at 82.

into an account on which the name of one of the children in the home appeared. According to the regulation, whether such a resource is countable depends on whether it is "actually and currently available" to a member of the assistance unit.[33] Although the regulations provide little further guidance, most lawyers would probably agree that deciding whether an account was "available" requires a sophisticated analysis involving banking and trust law and complicated factual judgments. Yet, the Quality Control staff apparently made their judgments summarily with minimal analysis and investigation and without communicating their interpretations to the workers. Some workers responded by counting *all* bank accounts.[34]

Second, Quality Control has intensified organizational hierarchy. It has created corps of elite officials charged with supervision of lower level decisionmaking. By prescribing detailed case reviews and using statistical techniques to generalize the results of such reviews, quality control has increased both the intensity and scope of review. The role of the relatively decentralized and collegial supervision process between worker and immediate supervisor has been correspondingly reduced. Both worker and supervisor now decide in the shadow of Quality Control, attempting to anticipate its judgments. Quality Control reviewers make judgments with little opportunity for participation by the worker or supervisor and with little or no explanation to them.

Third, Quality Control has reinforced the trend toward increased documentation requirements. The enforcement of some documentation requirements reduces error by providing more accurate information regarding substantive eligibility. However, a major portion of the documentation efforts of some states in recent years has been devoted to procedural or "paper" errors unrelated to substantive eligibility. Many administrators find increasing documentation requirements the most appealing way to reduce both paper and substantive errors because documentation requirements can be enforced by file checks, which are cheaper and require less judgment than investigations. Thus, in Massachusetts, for example, the state-initiated quality control procedures focus primarily on documentation and rely exclusively on file checks. Reviewers make little effort to determine whether substantive errors of judgment or fact have been made; their primary task is simply to see if the correct documents are in the file.[35]

The most notable instances of this tendency are consequences of HHS's

33. MASS. ADMIN. CODE tit. 106, § 304.010 (1982).

34. Interviews with Massachusetts welfare personnel (1981). The workers' response also reflects the fact that Quality Control creates incentives to resolve doubts against recipients. *See infra* pp. 1212-13.

35. Massachusetts Dep't of Public Welfare, Quality Assurance (1979) (unpublished manuscript on file with author).

The Yale Law Journal Vol. 92: 1198, 1983

decision to count payments to recipients who had not secured Social Security numbers or registered for the Work Incentive (WIN) Program as erroneous. In 1979, HHS announced that Massachusetts had a 14.9% payment error rate and was faced with sanctions of nearly $5 million for a portion of the preceding year. The announcement created a furor in the state government, and reducing error became the administration's top welfare priority. Forty-one percent of this error rate was due to Social Security and WIN "paper errors." Since these were both the largest source of errors and the most cheaply remediable, the welfare department responded with a campaign focused on them. It proceeded, not by contacting the Social Security or WIN agency to see if recipients had actually secured numbers or registered, but simply by pulling the file of every recipient and threatening to terminate those whose files lacked the official Social Security or WIN documentation unless they provided it promptly. (In many instances, the documentation was missing because the department had lost it or because the workers had assumed that they could accept less formal verification than the quality control reviewers insisted on.[36]) A major portion of the department's resources were devoted to this effort. Many recipients were inconvenienced by having to negotiate long lines at the welfare, Social Security, and WIN offices, and many who were confused or insufficiently prompt lost benefits at least temporarily. It is doubtful that these costs were offset by any substantial tangible benefit to the program.[37]

Fourth, by emphasizing "positive" errors (overpayments and payments to ineligibles) and de-emphasizing "negative" errors (underpayments and wrongful denials or terminations), Quality Control may shift costs of the transformed eligibility process to recipients. The 1973 federal regulations that first linked quality control to fiscal sanctions prescribed review only for positive case actions and sanctions only for positive errors.[38] The regulations were subsequently revised to prescribe review for negative actions, but negative review is more summary than positive review, and there are still no sanctions for negative errors.[39] This situation creates incentives for

36. HHS had found 71% of the Social Security errors and 96% of the WIN errors to be the fault of the welfare department, rather than of recipients. Massachusetts Dep't of Pub. Welfare, *supra* note 29.

37. *See supra* note 29.

38. Improvements in Quality Control System and Reduction of Payment Error, 38 Fed. Reg. 8744 (1973).

39. *See* 45 C.F.R. § 205.40 (1983); Richardson, *supra* note 24, at 249.

Positive review routinely involves both a file check and a field investigation. Negative review relies on only a file check except in unusual circumstances. U.S. Dep't of Health, Educ. & Welfare, *supra* note 29, at 4–5.

Informally, HHS officials have often explained their refusal to sanction negative errors by asserting that the Social Security Act authorizes withholding of reimbursement to the states only for improper payments. The Act, according to this view, gives no authority to withhold reimbursement of proper

Welfare System

states to behave in ways that simultaneously decrease positive errors and increase negative errors. This occurs when states resolve difficult or ambiguous issues against eligibility. It also occurs when states allocate enforcement resources toward the analysis and investigation of cases that initially appear eligible (but that upon further development may turn out to be ineligible) and away from cases that initially appear ineligible (but that on further development may turn out to be eligible).[40]

Perhaps the most important adverse impact on claimants arises from the fact that Quality Control does not measure failures of compliance with rules that provide important protections for claimants. These include rules that require workers to make timely responses to recipient requests for such things as grant increases, emergency benefits, replacements of lost or stolen checks, and changes of address. At the time Massachusetts undertook its major campaign to eliminate paper errors, it had recently settled a lawsuit charging it with routinely violating such rules. The consent decree enjoined the department to comply with these requirements.[41] Although the department did establish some procedures in response to the decree, the paper error campaign reduced the resources available for compliance with it. Workers who previously had had insufficient time to comply with the timeliness norms now had even less time to do so because of the greater pressure to enforce documentation requirements that were measured by Quality Control. The predictable result was continued noncompliance with the timeliness norms.

While the reforms have made it more complicated for recipients to establish eligibility, Quality Control has made no effort to review compliance with the rules that entitle clients to advice and assistance in the eligibility process. It thus increases incentives to shift resources away from the provision of such assistance.[42]

payments on account of the improper failure to make other payments. *See* 42 U.S.C. §§ 601, 603 (1976 & Supp. V. 1981). The explanation seems implausible and disingenuous. The Act gives HHS general regulatory authority with specific reference to "methods of administration," *id.* § 602(a)(5), and HHS has in the past successfully taken at least as broad a view of this authority as would be required to warrant a program of sanctions for negative errors. *See* Burns v. Alcala, 420 U.S. 575 (1975).

40. G. Mills, *supra* note 26, at 100–08, 149–51, presents an elaborate statistical analysis of overpayment and underpayment data for 1975 through 1977 suggesting a "fairly severe tradeoff" between positive and negative error correction.

41. The decree and subsequent contempt proceedings are discussed in Fortin v. Commissioner of the Massachusetts Dep't of Pub. Welfare, 692 F.2d 790 (1st Cir. 1982).

42. *Cf.* Pesso, *Local Welfare Offices: Managing the Intake Process*, 26 PUB. POL'Y 305, 310, 317–21 (1978) (analysis based on two months of observations at two Massachusetts welfare offices noting low levels of information and assistance).

The importance of advice and assistance arises, not only from documentation requirements, but from the increasingly long and technical application forms. An Urban Institute study that reviewed application forms and explanatory literature, as well as data on the educational levels of AFDC recipients, concluded, "the vast majority of these documents are difficult or impossible for most of their intended audience to comprehend." M. BENDICK, A. LAVINE & T. CAMPBELL, *supra* note 20, at 56.

*The Expulsion of the Social Workers, the Advent of the Clerks.* The principal personnel goal of the old regime was administration at both upper and lower levels by professional social workers. The old regime emphasized three aspects of the front-line worker's job which called for the abilities of a professional social worker. First, as we have seen, financial assistance was assumed to involve relatively complex, particularized judgment. Second, financial assistance was linked to counseling, a task requiring intimate and concrete knowledge of the client and her circumstances. AFDC was originally seen as a program to enable mothers to stay home with their children, and counseling was prescribed to improve the recipient's ability as a parent and homemaker. Later, the program's purposes were reconceived, and counseling was prescribed to enhance recipients' capacities for self-support in the labor market.[43] Third, an important part of the worker's job in this conception was the mobilization of community resources available outside the public assistance program to serve the particular needs of the recipient. The social worker was "among other things, a guide through a kind of civilized jungle, made up of specialized agencies and service functionaries the citizen can hardly name, let alone locate."[44] At a minimum, this involved advice and referral; more ambitiously, it involved active participation in securing assistance for the client from outside agencies. The social work profession developed an elaborate body of psychosocial and pedagogical theory to educate people for these tasks.

This personnel goal was never achieved. Only a small minority of front line workers under the old regime had any social work training, and only a handful had attained the basic professional credential, the master's degree in social work.[45] Nevertheless, social work professionalism had a significant influence on the sytem. From the 1930's through the 1960's, professional social workers dominated AFDC administration at the federal level and were substantially represented at higher administrative levels in

43. In 1956, 1962, and 1967, Congress expanded federal support for AFDC counseling in the hope that it would assist recipients to become self-supporting. Lurie, *supra* note 5, at 846–48; Rein, *Social Services as a Work Strategy*, 49 SOC. SERV. REV. 515, 516–19 (1975).

44. H. WILENSKY & C. LEBEAUX, INDUSTRIAL SOCIETY AND SOCIAL WELFARE 14 (1958); *see* Flexner, *Is Social Work a Profession?*, in NATIONAL CONFERENCE OF CHARITIES AND CORRECTIONS, PROCEEDINGS 576–90 (1915).

45. In 1960, only 1.2% of public assistance caseworkers had completed the two years of graduate training required for a M.S.W.; only 10.5% had any graduate social work education. U.S. DEP'T OF HEALTH, EDUC. & WELFARE, BUREAU OF FAMILY SERVICES AND CHILDREN'S BUREAU, PUBLIC SOCIAL WELFARE PERSONNEL—1960, at 86 (1962).

The social work model nevertheless did directly influence the practice of workers without professional training. One indication of this influence is the style of public assistance record-keeping, which involved a continuing and often astonishingly detailed description of the client and her background, together with speculations as to what kind of help would be appropriate. A good deal of Susan Sheehan's vivid portrait, S. SHEEHAN, A WELFARE MOTHER (1976), is based on the subject's AFDC case record. This style of record-keeping changed abruptly in the 1970's, when the detail and personal interest disappeared and AFDC records came to resemble business records.

the state public assistance departments.[46] During this period, the most prominent federal approach to administrative reform was to encourage professionalization of the lower level work force. Using informal pressures, regulations, and legislative proposals, federal administrators pushed for higher educational requirements for front line workers, subsidization of education at social work schools, and increases in in-service professional training for workers.[47]

In the 1960's and 1970's, the ideal of social work professionalism in public assistance administration was repudiated, and the actual influence of the social work profession was almost entirely eliminated. Social work lost prestige during this period as it came to be associated on the left with invasion of privacy and conformist manipulation and on the right with bleeding heart sentimentality and administrative laxity.[48] Congress turned away from counseling toward economic approaches (financial incentives and work requirements) to fostering recipient self-support.[49]

The most important event in this development was the administrative separation of social services from financial assistance, which HHS encouraged in the late 1960's through federally sponsored demonstration projects, and mandated by regulation in 1972.[50] Proponents explained this reform as a way of reducing the danger that services would be coercively imposed on the client as a condition of financial assistance and as a way of increasing administrative efficiency through specialization.[51] A consequence of this separation was that nearly all front-line workers with qualifications or aspirations as professional social workers left financial assistance to work in social services, which involved the professionally most prestigious and challenging jobs. Financial assistance jobs were then restyled as clerical. The titles "social worker" or "caseworker" were replaced with titles such as "eligibility technician" or "income maintenance worker."[52] Educational requirements were reduced and efforts were made to recruit people who did not aspire to status or responsibility beyond

46. A 1950 survey indicated that 57% of federal public assistance personnel had had two or more years of graduate social work study. M. DERTHICK, *supra* note 23, at 159. A 1960 study of state personnel indicated that 9.6% of all "executives" and 15.3% of all "supervisory staff" had had two or more years and 29.3% of all "executives" and 46.6% percent of all "supervisory staff" had had some graduate social work study. U.S. DEP'T OF HEALTH, EDUC. & WELFARE, *supra* note 45, at 86.

47. *See* M. DERTHICK, *supra* note 23, at 158-89.

48. *See, e.g.*, Glasser, *Prisoners of Benevolence*, in W. GAYLIN, I. GLASSER, S. MARCUS & D. ROTHMAN, DOING GOOD (1978); V. BURKE & V. BURKE, NIXON'S GOOD DEED: WELFARE REFORM 99 (1974) (Richard Nixon and Spiro Agnew on social workers).

49. *See* Lurie, *supra* note 5, at 833-34, 835-38, 848-51.

50. Separation of Services from Assistance Payments, 37 Fed. Reg. 11,060 (1972).

51. *See* U.S. DEP'T OF HEALTH, EDUC. & WELFARE, THE SEPARATION OF SERVICES FROM ASSISTANCE PAYMENTS: A GUIDE FOR STATE AGENCIES 5-8 (1972).

52. *See* U.S. DEP'T OF HEALTH, EDUC. & WELFARE, INCOME MAINTENANCE WORKER STUDY: A TWO-WAY TAXONOMY AND ANALYSIS III-3 to III-12 (1981).

clerical work. As the Director of Labor Relations of the Massachusetts welfare department explained to me, "We've been trying to get the people who think like social workers out and the people who think like bank tellers in."

Parallel changes occurred at higher administrative levels. Through a series of reorganizations and cutbacks, the Nixon Administration decreased the size and authority of the HHS offices traditionally staffed by career social work professionals. At the same time, it expanded the size and authority of offices with technocratic managerial missions and staffed them with people with backgrounds in business management.[53] Analogous changes in the upper tiers of state welfare administrations increased the influence of technocrats at the expense of social work professionals.

A critical result of these developments has been the expulsion from the system of people socialized to think of the frontline worker's role as involving complex, particularized judgments and direct responsibility to claimants as individuals.[54] They have been replaced by people socialized to think of the role as characterized by routine, unreflective judgment and responsibility only to hierarchical organizational authority.

*Division of Labor.* The old regime's conception of the welfare worker's job has been decomposed into many more specialized functions—"mini-jobs" as one management consultant puts it.[55] The separation of social services and financial assistance is merely one example of this trend. Within financial assistance the task of taking new applications ("intake") has been separated from the task of administering established cases ("ongoing payments"). Still further divisions have been implemented or proposed: "Intake" can be divided into the function of advising the applicant of eligibility requirements and that of actual eligibility determination. The latter function may be further divided into the function of securing information regarding the claimant and that of deciding whether the information indicates the claimant is eligible. The old regime emphasized the importance of continuity of relation between worker and claimant. The new regime encourages the assignment of work so that workers have no continuing relations with claimants and claimants see a different worker every time they come in. The old regime emphasized the importance of understanding the claimant in her environmental context. The

53. Randall, *Presidential Power Versus Bureaucratic Intransigence: The Influence of the Nixon Administration on Welfare Policy*, 78 AM. POL. SCI. REV. 795, 799-804 (1979).

54. Studies conducted of two midwestern welfare agencies in the 1950's indicate that a substantial portion of welfare workers did think of their job in these terms prior to separation. Blau, *Orientations Toward Clients in a Public Welfare Agency*, 5 AD. SCI. Q. 341 (1960); Scott, *supra* note 22. The latter study presents evidence that attitudes of direct responsibility to clients and to social norms, as opposed to organizational hierarchy, correlate with professional training.

55. U.S. DEP'T OF HEALTH, EDUC. & WELFARE, *supra* note 52, at III-3.

new regime is sympathetic to reforms such as Massachusetts' abolition of the system by which workers were assigned cases in accordance with the location of recipients' residences (which gave workers an opportunity to learn a neighborhood and its institutions) and began to assign cases in the alphabetical order of recipients' last names.[56]

The general tendency of these developments is to limit workers' understanding of the way the welfare system works and of claimants and their circumstances.

*Mechanization.* A variety of mechanical and computer systems have been introduced to mechanize the eligibility process. Eligibility is increasingly determined and checks are issued by computer. Welfare administrators use computers to search social insurance, employment, and bank records for evidence of unreported income and resources of recipients. The recently established Monthly Income Reporting system requires recipients to fill out and return every month an income report that a computer then uses to redetermine eligibility. Mechanization is designed to perform more efficiently operations previously done by hand and to facilitate the use of relevant but previously inaccessible information. Although some of these efforts are generally considered effective, many have been hampered by a panoply of problems attributed to inadequate design and implementation. Mass overpayments and underpayments have resulted from programming errors; poor analysis of Social Security data has triggered unwarranted fraud investigations and threats of prosecution; substantively eligible recipients have been terminated because they could not understand the monthly income report instructions.[57] For our purposes, the most significant effect of mechanization has been to reinforce or facilitate some of the trends described above.

First, mechanization requires formalization. Eligibility determination can only be automated when norms are explicit and judgment, constrained. Second, mechanization facilitates centralization. A variety of functions previously performed at the local office level have been centralized through computers. Previously checks were commonly issued at the local office in emergencies. It is now relatively rare for a local office to be able to issue a check in any circumstances; the office merely generates computer input which is reviewed centrally before the check is issued by the central computer. (In Massachusetts, this change has become, if not the cause, the excuse for the system's inability to respond to emergencies.

56. *See* M. GREENBLATT & S. RICHMOND, PUBLIC WELFARE: NOTES FROM UNDERGROUND 17 (1979) (workers' distress at alphabetization of cases in Massachusetts); S. SHEEHAN, *supra* note 45, at 84 (one recipient's distress at New York's change to a system in which workers have no continuing responsibility for cases).

57. *See* Baily, *Electronic Data Processing*, in CONG. RESEARCH SERV. REP. TO HOUSE COMM. ON GOV'T OPERATIONS, *supra* note 18, at 144-63; sources cited *infra* note 66.

Whereas previously a check could be issued immediately, it now takes ten days or more.) Another example concerns work assignments for case workers. In Massachusetts, the details of work assignments were previously determined at the local office, thus making it possible for workers to participate in the decision. Assignments are now prescribed centrally and in detail for each worker by computer. Third, mechanization has encouraged intensification of the division of labor, since the machinery brings new work roles with it. Existing work must be re-divided and reapportioned among the old and new roles.

*Productivity Enforcement.* Quality Control has been supplemented by productivity regimes designed to measure the quantity of work and facilitate the sanctioning of low producers. Under the old regime, appraisal of productivity was relatively informal and decentralized. It was integrally related to the appraisal of quality and was largely the responsibility of the local office supervisor. The basic measure of productivity was the caseload, the number of recipients or families for whom the worker was responsible. The managers of the new regime have rejected this approach for a number of reasons. For one thing, the caseload measure depended on the system of work assignment by which workers retained responsibility for particular claimants throughout their stay in the program. This system limited the flexibility of managers in assigning work. Second, the breadth of the caseload measure limited the possibilities of hierarchical control since it did not enable the manager to monitor specific activities within the case handling job. Third, the semi-collegial nature of the supervisor worker relation was thought to inhibit the supervisor from vigorous application of coercive sanctions.

The newer productivity measurement systems are more elaborate. In 1975, for example, the business consulting firm of Coopers & Lybrand, hired by the Massachusetts welfare department to formulate a measurement system, conducted a time-and-motion study of eligibility work. On the basis of observations of worker practices timed with stop watches, the consultants decomposed the work into more than 1000 activities and assigned to each a "reasonable" completion time based on observed averages. For example, the standards for the activities involved in redetermining eligibility include two minutes to "identify case requiring redetermination," one minute to "pull case folder," and one minute to "obtain necessary forms." These activity standards were then aggregated into various combinations to generate overall productivity standards for a wide variety of different work roles.[58]

58. MASSACHUSETTS DEP'T OF PUB. WELFARE, PRODUCTIVITY STANDARDS REPORT PREPARED BY COOPERS & LYBRAND 23 (1979).

Welfare System

The basic purpose of such regimes is to enhance centralization and limit worker and local office autonomy. As implemented in Massachusetts, the new system confirmed the tendency of Quality Control to allocate resources away from advice and assistance to recipients. At the time the consultants made their observations, the system was, as the department had conceded in response to a lawsuit, consistently violating the requirements regarding the timely processing of claimant requests for assistance.[59] Standards that merely codified the practices (as Coopers & Lybrand purported to have done) would have tended to perpetuate this situation. In fact, the standards implemented apparently allowed the workers even less time than before to respond to recipient requests and put greater emphasis on redetermination and policing documentation requirements. The productivity requirements contributed to the further attenuation of the worker's sense of responsibility to the client by encouraging workers to threaten clients in order to induce them to comply more promptly with documentation requirements and by implicitly penalizing time spent responding to client requests.[60]

### B. *Effects*

The task of assessing the effects of these reforms is encumbered by a poverty of both information and concepts. Information about the effects of welfare administration tends to come in the form either of system-wide data, which tend to be limited and ambiguous, or case histories (usually from aggrieved recipients), which tend to be of questionable representativeness. There are no generally accepted standards for using the information that is available for measuring or assessing the system's performance. Nevertheless, putting aside for the moment a variety of conceptual problems and acknowledging the limitations on information, two tentative generalizations seem plausible.

First, there is no reason to believe that the administrative transformation of the system has made any major contributions either to the liberals' goal of increasing the participation rate—the percentage of the substantively eligible population that actually receives benefits—or the conservatives' goal of reducing inappropriate expenditures.

There does seem to have been a substantial increase in the participation rates in public assistance programs, and particularly AFDC, in recent decades. Much of the increase, however, seems attributable, not to administrative reform, but to the increased availability of information and advo-

59. *See* Fortin v. Commissioners of the Massachusetts Dep't of Pub. Welfare, 692 F.2d 790 (1st Cir. 1982).

60. Massachusetts Dep't of Pub. Welfare, The Effects of Implementing Coopers & Lybrand's Productivity Measurement System (1977) (unpublished manuscript on file with author).

cacy resources outside the welfare system through informal transmission, community groups, and subsidized legal services and to declining cultural inhibitions about accepting welfare.[61] Administrative reform probably has made benefits more accessible in some ways, notably by reducing the capacity of the workers to deny benefits in conscious disregard of legal norms.[62] But to some extent, this effect seems to have been offset by other trends that have reduced accessibility, notably by making the eligibility process more complex and burdensome and by reducing advice and assistance to applicants.[63] As far as the participation rate is concerned, the reforms may simply have substituted one set of mechanisms of "disentitlement" for another. It is still the case that the system fails to deliver benefits to a substantial portion of people, including some of the most needy,

61. Statistics for New York City in the late 1950's and early 1960's indicated that the AFDC participation rate was not higher than 50%. Cloward & Piven, *A Strategy to End Poverty*, 202 NATION 510, 511 (1966). Studies in 1975 and 1976 estimated the participation rate at 87% and 74%, respectively; a 1970 study put the rate for female-headed families at 90%. *See* Bendick, *Failure to Enroll in Public Assistance Programs*, 25 SOC. WORK 268, 269 (1980) (summarizing studies). Rates for other programs appear to have increased as well, but generally to considerably lower levels than AFDC. *Id.*

The lowest participation rates reported in connection with the major public assistance programs are for those segments of Medicaid that provide partial medical reimbursement to non-welfare recipients. In the states that have this program, participation rates are estimated to run as low as 5%. This is explained in part by the relatively small benefits due to some eligible non-recipients and in part by the extraordinary complexity of its eligibility process. *See* URBAN SYSTEMS RESEARCH & ENG'G, EVALUATION OF MEDICAID SPEND-DOWN, at vii, x–xi, xvii (report to Dep't of Health, Educ. & Welfare, Feb. 15, 1976).

In order to consider the impact of administrative reform (formalization, bureaucratization, and proletarianization) on participation rates, one has to distinguish another phenomenon—the effect of changes in substantive eligibility norms on the amount of benefits and the number of beneficiaries. This is a difficult distinction in some instances. Many of the liberal welfare victories of the 1960's and 1970's took the form of judicial invalidation of state regulations under federal law. From the point of view of the judiciary, one might regard this type of reform as administrative (compelling compliance with existing substantive law). But from the point of view of the lower-tier bureaucracy, this type of reform involved a change in substantive eligibility norms rather than modes of administration. The discussion in the text adopts this latter perspective.

62. While reformers are probably correct to count the decrease in conscious disregard or indifference to law as a victory for claimants, it has not been an unmixed blessing for them. On the one hand, some of the harshest anti-recipient practices documented in the welfare reform literature seem to have arisen from such disregard. Mashaw, *Welfare Reform and Local Administration of Aid to Families with Dependent Children in Virginia*, 57 VA. L. REV. 818, 826, 836 (1971) (denial of benefits to illegitimates; refusals to take applications from mothers before they initiate criminal support proceedings: official explains "there's the law and there's how you do things"). On the other hand, disregard sometimes benefited recipients. Advocates and workers I have talked to in California and Massachusetts say that under the old regime workers often ignored legal requirements they considered pointlessly or excessively burdensome to claimants. *See* M. GREENBLATT & S. RICHMOND, *supra* note 56, at 29 (Massachusetts example). In a 1967 study of the Wisconsin AFDC Program, workers reported that "they do not bother to enforce responsible relative laws, or require the disclosure of the father of an unwed mother, or apply rules about [deductions for] earned income." J. HANDLER & E. HOLLINGSWORTH, THE "DESERVING POOR": A STUDY IN WELFARE ADMINISTRATION 199 (1971).

63. *See* Brodkin & Lipsky, *supra* note 30; Mendeloff, *Welfare Procedures and Error Rates: An Alternative Perspective*, 3 POL'Y ANALYSIS 357, 362–63 (1977); M. Vesely, S. McEntree & A. Schorr, Fair Play: A Report of a Study of the Administration of Aid to Families with Dependent Children in Several Midwestern States (unpublished manuscript, School of Applied Social Sciences, Case Western Reserve Univ., 1982).

who meet its substantive standards of need.[64]

The achievements of administrative reform with respect to cost reduction also remain to be demonstrated. Payment error rates have decreased substantially, but as we have seen, reducing payment error does not necessarily lower grant expenditures (as in the case of "paper" errors), and error reduction has been achieved only at substantially increased administrative expense. Efforts to compare these added expenses with savings from error reduction have been insubstantial and inconclusive.[65] And although a few specific reforms, such as some versions of periodic income reporting, appear to have reduced grant expenditures by more than their administrative costs, these savings have sometimes been achieved only by imposing large costs on eligible claimants.[66]

Second, the transformation of the system seems to have had an important effect on the way claimants and workers experience the system and their relation to each other. The reforms seem to have reduced the claimant's experience of oppressive and punitive moralism, of invasion of privacy, and of dependence on idiosyncratic personal favor. But they also have reduced their experience of trust and personal care and have increased their experience of bewilderment and opacity.

As far as the worker's role is concerned, the reforms have consistently reinforced experiences of alienation and subordination. Moreover, they appear to have encouraged the worker to view her own interests as in constant conflict with the claimant's. The worker's success depends on compliance with coercively enforced, intensely monitored rules that primarily require her to police the claimant's paper-pushing and bureaucratic hoop-jumping. She works in anxious awareness of pervasive but only par-

64. *See* Bendick, *supra* note 61, at 268-69; Menefee, Edwards & Brown, *Analysis of Non-Participation in the SSI Program*, SOC. SECURITY BULL., June 1981, at 3, 13-20.

65. Moran, *AFDC Administrative Costs*, in CONG. RESEARCH SERV. REP. TO HOUSE COMM. ON GOV'T OPERATIONS, *supra* note 18, at 126; Richardson, *supra* note 24, at 250. A study by Touche, Ross & Co. of 15 states with about half the AFDC caseload argues that savings from Quality Control between April 1973 and June 1976 in these states exceeded increased administrative costs by about $80 million, although only 9 of the states were found to have net savings. Touche, Ross & Co., *supra* note 31. This sum is substantial, though, in a program spending $7 to 10 billion annually during this period, far from the magnitude one would expect from the more ambitious pronouncements about Quality Control. *See* Pratt, *supra* note 24, at 20. The main problem with the study is that, although it tries to remove the effects of paper errors and eligibility changes, its savings estimates take the Quality Control error measurements at face value. But for the reasons indicated *supra* pp. 1207-09, this is a dubious procedure. For example, Mills' more recent study argues that half the error reduction during a period that overlaps that of the Touche, Ross study is attributable, not to any change in program performance, but to reduction in Quality Control reviewer caseloads. G. Mills, *supra* note 26.

66. *Compare* B. BERNSTEIN, THE POLITICS OF WELFARE: THE NEW YORK CITY EXPERIENCE 26-30 (1982) (former New York City welfare commissioner reporting savings from city-initiated income reporting) *with* Center on Budget & Policy Priorities, Research Findings on Monthly Reporting Systems and Their Implications for State Administrators (1983) (unpublished manuscript on file with author) (summarizing evidence that many federally required reporting procedures are not cost-effective and cause substantial benefit losses to eligible recipients).

tially predictable supervisory authority in circumstances that minimize her ability to respond to the claimant's particular needs either for benefits or for assistance in the enforcement process. In this situation, the worker encounters the claimant as either a threat or a nuisance—a threat to the extent the claimant is a potential source of damaging information to supervisors monitoring the worker's performance, a nuisance to the extent that the claimant makes requests that the system disables or penalizes the worker for responding to.

## II. The Sociological Jurisprudence of Welfare Reform

Some would argue that the defects of the new public assistance regime should be attributed, not to the general program of formalization, bureaucratization, and proletarianization, but to the specific ways the program has been implemented. Certainly, there are strong arguments for specific reforms that do not challenge the general program. For example, if the premises of the Quality Control and productivity measurement systems are to be retained, the systems should be overhauled to divert attention away from paper errors, to focus attempts to reduce improper payments on errors that are large and can be identified as errors without controversy, and to encourage compliance with rules that protect claimants, especially the rules entitling them to information and assistance and to the timely determination of claims.[67]

I propose to put aside this type of analysis of specific reforms in order to focus on the general program of formalization, bureaucratization, and proletarianization. Any discussion of specific reforms necessarily takes place against a background of assumptions about the limits and possibilities of change imposed by the legal system and the society. I want to discuss the set of assumptions that has dominated writing on the welfare system during the past two decades. This dominant vision is derived from a style of sociological jurisprudence that proceeds by linking certain fundamental characteristics of modern society with a particular type of legality and in turn with a particular type of enforcement organization.[68] In this manner, the dominant vision of contemporary welfare jurisprudence associates social goals such as efficiency, freedom, and fairness with a legality of formality and in turn with a bureaucratized enforcement organization staffed at the lower tier by proletarians.

67. *See* J. HANDLER, *supra* note 24, at 101–16; Mashaw, *The Management Side of Due Process: Some Theoretical and Litigation Notes on the Assurance of Accuracy, Fairness, and Timeliness in the Adjudication of Welfare Claims*, 59 CORNELL L. REV. 772, 810–23 (1974).
68. *See* R. UNGER, LAW IN MODERN SOCIETY: TOWARD A CRITICISM OF SOCIAL THEORY 23–37, 262–65 (1976).

Welfare System

### A. *Rules, Hierarchy, Proletariat*

In the early 1960's, the dominant vision was principally associated with liberals concerned with the interests of the poor; more recently it has been co-opted by conservatives concerned with cost-cutting and disciplining the public work force.[69] The rhetoric of both groups has converged on the term "discretion." The dominant vision contrasts legality with discretion and prescribes the elimination or minimization of discretion. The meaning of discretion in this literature, however, turns out to be elusive. Sometimes discretion is defined simply as the absence of formalization, bureaucratization, or proletarianization. Thus, discretion can mean informality in eligibility norms (standards rather than rules), decentralized administration, or administration by professionals. Sometimes, however, discretion is defined in two more general senses.

The first sense refers to decisionmaking without regard to norms, or more simply, arbitrariness.[70] Although the dominant vision frequently speaks of the problem as discretion in this sense, it seems unlikely that many of the phenomena to which it reacts are accurately characterized this way. It is extremely difficult for people to act in any setting without regard to norms, let alone in a public bureaucracy. As anthropologists have often shown in the context of primitive societies, and as Peter Blau and Michael Lipsky have shown in our context, when observers call behavior arbitrary it is usually because they either fail to perceive the norms involved or because they refuse to acknowledge them, perhaps because they conflict with the observers' own norms.[71] The moralistically punitive and racist conduct in the horror stories of the old regime was wrong, but it was not arbitrary.

The second general sense of discretion is the practical ability to make a

69. The main themes of what I call the dominant vision can be found to varying degrees in nearly all the lawyers' writing on the welfare system of recent decades. The most prominent exponents of the liberal version of the dominant vision are Charles Reich, Edward Sparer, Joel Handler, Kenneth Culp Davis, and Jerry Mashaw. *See, e.g.*, K. DAVIS, DISCRETIONARY JUSTICE (1969); Handler, *Controlling Official Behavior in Welfare Administration*, 54 CALIF. L. REV. 479 (1966); Mashaw, *supra* note 67; Reich, *The New Property*, 73 YALE L.J. 733 (1964); Sparer, *The Role of the Welfare Client's Lawyer*, 12 UCLA L. REV. 361 (1965). The most prominent exponents of the conservative version are Judge Friendly, Justice Rehnquist, and Robert Dixon. *See* Hansen v. Harris, 619 F.2d 942, 949–58 (2d Cir. 1980) (Friendly, J., dissenting), *rev'd sub nom.* Schweiker v. Hansen, 450 U.S. 785 (1981); Califano v. Boles, 443 U.S. 282 (1979) (Rehnquist, J.); R. DIXON, SOCIAL SECURITY DISABILITY AND MASS JUSTICE (1973).

These works include some of the most creative and interesting legal scholarship of recent years, and I am indebted to them for my understanding of the welfare system. Indeed, much of my criticism simply elaborates on problems that some of these writers have acknowledged in the course of developing their own approaches.

70. K. DAVIS, *supra* note 69, at 4–5; J. HANDLER, *supra* note 24, at 5–6; Sparer, *The Right to Welfare*, in THE RIGHTS OF AMERICANS 65, 71 (N. Dorsen ed. 1971) (discretion as "whim").

71. P. BLAU, THE DYNAMICS OF BUREAUCRACY (rev. ed. 1963); M. LIPSKY, STREET-LEVEL BUREAUCRACY 81–156 (1980).

decision that violates the applicable norm.[72] This is the most frequent use of the term, and much of the rhetorical power of the dominant vision derives from its tendency to associate discretion in this sense with informality, decentralization, and professionalism. Yet this general notion is often hard to apply. First, in order to identify discretion in this sense, one needs to know what the applicable norms are. But it is often, and perhaps typically, the case that there is basic disagreement over what the applicable norms are.[73] A further difficulty is that, on a formal level, discretion of this sort can never be reduced. There is a law of conservation of discretion: one limits the discretion of one set of actors only by increasing that of others.[74] Thus, while the dominant vision spoke generally of reducing discretion, its proposals tended to reduce only the discretion of lower level officials and to increase correspondingly the discretion of others. Conservative proposals tended to increase the discretion of upper level officials; liberal proposals tended to increase the discretion of the federal judiciary.

The rhetoric of discretion raises two related questions: the question of value and the question of trust. The question of value is how norms are to be derived to assess the conduct of public officials. The question of trust is under what circumstances officials can be relied upon to comply with applicable norms.

The dominant vision responds to these questions in terms of notions of society and law that resemble in important respects those of Max Weber.[75] The starting point is a vision of dissensus and distrust as basic

72. *E.g.*, K. DAVIS, *supra* note 69, at 12-14; Handler, *supra* note 69, at 493-95.

73. This problem does not arise where the decisionmaker acknowledges the applicable norm but refuses to follow it. *See supra* note 62. But this was probably not the case in most of the situations in which the dominant vision complained of arbitrariness.

74. Here I paraphrase Kennedy & Michelman, *Are Property and Contract Efficient?*, 8 HOFSTRA L. REV. 711, 759 (1980).

75. 1 M. WEBER, ECONOMY AND SOCIETY 217-25 (G. Roth & C. Wittich eds. 1968); 3 M. WEBER, *supra*, at 956-1001. Neither the rhetoric nor the ideas of the dominant vision fully coincide with Weber's sociology of law, and the primary influence on the dominant vision has been Anglo-American liberal legalism. Nevertheless, Weber is the preemminent exponent of a critical theme of the dominant vision—the interpretation of legality in terms of both formality and hierarchical bureaucracy—that departs from the main-stream of the Anglo-American tradition. *See* 1 M. WEBER, *supra*, at 217-25; A. DICEY, THE LAW OF THE CONSTITUTION 183-205 (10th ed. 1959) (emphasizing divergence in organizational premises of Anglo-American tradition from continental legal tradition on which Weber's views focus).

Neither Weber nor contemporary welfare jurisprudence speaks explicitly of a proletarian work force. (Indeed, Weber ascribes the attributes of professional status to the bureaucratic staff, 3 M. WEBER, *supra*, at 958-63.) Nevertheless, I think the term proletarian best expresses the limited autonomy and judgment, limited education, and low status and reward involved in the dominant vision's conception of the welfare worker's role. For example, the use by proponents of the dominant vision of the term "quality control" for administrative review procedure analogizes welfare workers to the industrial work force. Mashaw, *supra* note 67, at 810-23. And proletarianization is the negative implication of the often expressed hostility for social work professionalism, which the dominant vision tends to associate with illegitimate discretion. Sparer, *supra* note 1, at 733.

conditions of modern social life. In these circumstances, the central goals of social order are efficiency, freedom, and fairness. The goal of efficiency is to coordinate the activities of individuals so as to attain the greatest aggregate satisfaction; the goal of freedom is to enlarge each individual's autonomy to pursue her subjective goals; the goal of fairness is to protect people from the danger that collective activity will favor some citizens at the expense of others.

The Weberian view suggests that these goals are best furthered by insulating the legal system from the surrounding society and by insulating the process of enactment from the process of enforcement within the legal system. Both types of insulation are designed to minimize reliance on shared values and trust. The basic quality that insulates the legal system and the process of enactment is formality. Formality has two dimensions: one is substantive formality, which as we have seen means that law takes the form of rules with the characteristics of explicitness, constrained judgment, and impersonality. The other is procedural formality, which means that the validity of a law depends on its enactment by a specialized, unitary institution or sovereign. The Weberian view contrasts this type of legality to governance through undifferentiated or organic social norms and institutions that are informal, diffusely generated, and implicated in the conflict and dissensus of society.

The Weberian answers to the questions of value and trust are founded on this basic notion of the legal system insulated from the surrounding society by substantive and procedural formality.

The answer to the question of value is that official conduct is to be judged by the formal rules enacted by the sovereign. The basic goals of social order are thought to require this answer for several reasons. First, while organic social norms are implicated in the controversies and conflicts of the surrounding society, procedurally formal rules are generally considered fair. For reasons that vary depending on the form the sovereign takes (for example, legislature, monarch, party), it is understood (at least in the long run and relative to other social actors) to legislate in the interests of everyone. By marking off legal from other norms and establishing a link between legal norms and the sovereign, formality contributes to fairness. Second, formal rules involve consideration of fewer factors than organic social norms. This promotes efficiency because decision under rules takes less time and resources. It contributes to freedom to the extent that it limits the circumstances that trigger the sovereign's intervention in private affairs. And it is consistent with the conception of fairness that holds that the sovereign in dealing with citizens should take account of only a narrow range of broadly shared characteristics. Third, unlike organic social norms, formal rules are determinate. This is important for efficiency be-

The Yale Law Journal Vol. 92: 1198, 1983

cause it prevents confusion, which interferes with coordination. It is important for freedom because it enhances people's capacities to plan their activities so as to best attain their goals. It is important for fairness because it enables people to perceive a basis for official decision other than personal or group preference.

The argument proceeds from this notion of formal rules as the answer to the question of value to the notion of hierarchical bureaucracy and a proletarian work force as the answer to the question of trust. This conclusion is based on both the substantive and procedural dimensions of formality. Hierarchical bureaucracy is premised on the same mechanism of control as substantive formality: rules. Moreover, substantive formality is related to the low skill and education that are defining features of proletarianism because constrained judgment tends to require less skill and education. And constrained judgment is associated with the proletarian characteristics of low status and reward: work involving constrained judgment is thought to merit low status and reward, which in turn are thought to make people more willing to have their judgment constrained.

Bureaucratic, proletarian organization is also related to procedural formality. Procedural formality expresses a commitment to order society in accordance with the will of the sovereign. Hierarchical bureaucracy with the sovereign at the top and a proletarian work force at the bottom purports to maximize the sovereign's control over enforcement.

This Weberian view of legality and organization has provoked a critique that is as well developed as the view itself. This critique surely has not been unknown to the authors of the dominant vision, but the problems the critique points to are underemphasized or obscured in their writings. The influence of the Weberian view in the dominant vision takes the form of a tendency to presume that arrangements that satisfy the conditions of formality, bureaucracy, and proletarianism are more compatible with goals of social order than those that do not satisfy these conditions. I propose here to review some of the problems emphasized in the critique and to focus on a few that seem especially pertinent to the recent history of the welfare system. The general point is not that Weberian-style legality and organization have no role to play in a plausible conception of social order, but that the presumption in its favor in the dominant vision is unjustified. Its viability depends on contingencies that the dominant vision does not directly confront.

*Problems of Communication—Officials.* One set of problems arises from the limitations of the means available to the sovereign for communicating norms to officials.[76] From one perspective, the problems are rooted

76. *See* H. SIMON, ADMINISTRATIVE BEHAVIOR (2d ed. 1957); Ehrlich & Posner, *An Economic*

Welfare System

in the nature of the language. Language is too imprecise and indeterminate to play the role assigned to it in the Weberian view. From another perspective, the problem is rooted in the finitude of life. The sovereign does not have time to formulate precise norms for every case that may arise. Even if she did, her instructions would be so voluminous that officials and citizens could not possibly master them. These circumstances create problems of imprecision, overload, and indeterminacy.

The problem of imprecision is that rules are over- and under-inclusive in regard to their purposes. Constraining judgment has costs in terms of the purposes of the program. The consolidation of need standards and the reduction of special and emergency benefits in the reformed system exemplifies this sort of cost. Simplified need standards pay many people more than their needs (as measured by the normative premises of the program) and many less. From the point of view of efficiency, this is a cost that must be set against gains resulting from constrained judgment.

Imprecision may also impair the goals of freedom and fairness. From the point of view of freedom, the reduction in the number of personal contingencies on which assistance is predicated has increased the claimant's autonomy of the welfare system only at the cost of exacerbating his vulnerability to the oppressions and uncertainties of private life. The recipient need submit to less inquiry about the circumstances of her life (since fewer of them are relevant), but she has less protection against many types of misfortune arising in her private affairs. The elimination in some states of replacement benefits for lost or stolen assistance checks exemplifies this disadvantage. And to the extent that fairness requires not simply treating everyone the same, but taking account of relevant differences, imprecision jeopardizes fairness. The fact that people viewed as having similar needs are treated differently (because the rules ignore some aspects of need) may fuel a sense of unfairness.[77]

*Analysis of Legal Rulemaking*, 3 J. LEGAL STUD. 257, 267–71 (1974); Kennedy, *supra* note 6.

77. A longstanding theme in liberal welfare jurisprudence is the appeal to the Social Security retirement program as evidence of the virtues of formality and an inspiration for the reform of public assistance. *See* Handler, *Discretion in Social Welfare: The Uneasy Position in the Rule of Law*, 92 YALE L.J. 1270 (1983); tenBroek & Wilson, *Public Assistance and Social Insurance—A Normative Evaluation*, 1 UCLA L. REV. 237 (1954). I think this theme may exaggerate the degree of formality in Social Security. For one thing, the program does employ a variety of standards-type norms that require complex judgment. *See, e.g.*, UNEMPL. INS. REP. (CCH) ¶¶ 10,607 ("net earnings from self-employment"), 12,459 ("retired"), 12,335 ("dependent" child). Even where norms are formal, they may call for complex factual judgments where they deal with circumstances not susceptible to formal proof (replacement of lost or stolen checks) or where the usual formal proof is unavailable or suspect (immigrants who lack birth certificates). And some factual determinations, notably wage history, seem simple only because the government at great expense to itself and others has kept records (and has acquired a near monopoly of relevant information) about them. More importantly, what formality there is has been achieved only at the cost of spectacular imprecision in relation to both the goal of aiding the needy and the goal of paying recipients a fair return on their contribution. *See* THE CRISIS IN SOCIAL SECURITY 65–86, 125–45 (M. Boskin ed. 1977). The costs of underinclusiveness in relation

The Yale Law Journal Vol. 92: 1198, 1983

Overload is another liability of formality that has afflicted the reformed public assistance system. While the constrained judgment aspect of formality tends to simplify norms, the explicitness aspect tends to increase their volume. One of the most frequent complaints of public assistance workers these days is that they have neither the time nor sufficient memory to master the instructions the system generates so prolifically.[78]

While the problem of imprecision arises to the extent norms are determinate but fail to express their goals, the problem of indeterminacy arises to the extent that norms are ambiguous. It is a commonplace of contemporary jurisprudence that the most rigorously specified norms will have ambiguities that often require complex interpretive judgment and reference to social context.[79] To the extent such indeterminacy exists, formality simply fails to achieve its end.

Most discussion of the problem of indeterminacy has focused on ambiguity in substantive norms. However, there is another dimension of the problem that is especially important for the dominant vision. This dimension arises from the ambiguous relation between substantive and procedural norms. Substantive legal norms are mediated by a second order of legal norms that regulates the distribution of enforcement power and resources. This second order includes rules governing waiver and default, rules that confer or deny prosecutorial authority (public prosecutorial discretion, standing, private rights of action), and rules governing the allocation of enforcement expenses and the dissemination of legal knowledge. Even given a fully determinate substantive norm, this second order of legality often makes possible controversy over whether the norm should be enforced. It is often—perhaps typically—ambiguous whether instances of non-enforcement should be understood as violations of substantive norms or vindications of procedural ones. Low participation rates in welfare programs can be viewed as a matter of violation of substantive norms. (People are not getting benefits for which they are substantively eligible.) But they can also be viewed as a matter of enforcement of procedural rules governing waiver and default. (People are not getting benefits because they have not complied with the application requirements.) More generally, the way procedural norms limit substantive norms can be understood as

to need are tolerable only because a public assistance program more sensitive to the contingencies of need exists to serve those whose needs are overlooked by Social Security. The costs of overinclusiveness in relation to need are tolerable (though this tolerance has lately been strained) only because of the largely unwarranted belief that payments represent a return on contributions. If one did not have to exclude the non-needy from public assistance, one could design an otherwise adequate program with a high degree of formality, but this does not seem a plausible condition either politically or ethically.

78. M. GREENBLATT & S. RICHMOND, *supra* note 56.

79. *See* Fuller, *Positivism and Fidelity to Law: A Reply to Professor Hart*, 71 HARV. L. REV. 630, 661-69 (1958).

accommodating a variety of social goals not adequately specified in the substantive law. Thus, to some, low participation rates, even when they result from burdensome application procedures, indicate, not the failure of social order, but its vindication; they simply show that the system has worked to ration scarce public resources and serve the goal of fiscal economy.[80]

The Weberian view seems unable to come to terms plausibly with such views or the experiences from which they arise. It tends to conflate legality with substantive law and to see all substantive enforcement as a vindication of order.[81] But this is implausible. First, it simply ignores the extent to which law enforcement is experienced in the society as disorder. For example, an interesting development of the past two decades has been the emergence of a radical literature calling for law enforcement as a means of disrupting and weakening the established order. Some radical theorists embraced the liberal Weberian program of welfare enforcement in the hope of hastening the fiscal collapse of the state and the consequent egalitarian transformation of the society.[82] And in fact, the increased participation rates induced by the enforcement efforts of the 1960's did generate a sense of crisis consistent with some of the more modest of these predictions. A sociology of law incapable of distinguishing between what people experience as normal social practice and what they experience as crisis does not seem very satisfactory. Second, conflating substantive norm enforcement with order is inconsistent with the most plausible approach to substantive interpretation. The sovereign legislates particular substantive rules against a background of second order procedural rules and social practices that generally limit enforcement. Though it is rarely clear what impact the sovereign intended this regime to have on the enforcement of a particular rule, it usually seems likely that it did intend the regime to have *some* limiting impact. Third, almost all the Weberians acknowledge some areas of law in which limited enforcement is compatible with social order. For example, liberals generally approve of limited enforcement of the soft drug and prostitution laws; conservatives, of the desegregation and criminal defendants' rights laws. Yet nothing in the basic Weberian premises suggests any basis for such distinctions.[83]

The enforcement dimension of indeterminacy creates basic problems for the dominant vision. This vision answers the question of value by appealing to the substantive law as an uncontroversial basis for criticizing the

80. *See* H.R. Rep. No. 97-139, 97th Cong., 1st Sess., *reprinted in* 1981 U.S. CODE CONG. & AD. NEWS 454-55 (explaining elimination of requirement of Food Stamp statute that administering agencies engage in "outreach" activities).

81. *See* Abel, *Law Books and Books About Law*, 26 STAN. L. REV. 175, 184-89 (1973).

82. A. WOLFE, THE LIMITS OF LEGITIMACY (1979); Cloward & Piven, *supra* note 61.

83. I consider efforts to modify the Weberian view to permit such distinctions *infra* pp. 1250-69.

performance of public officials. But the problem of indeterminacy indicates that to criticize officials for not enforcing the substantive law either assumes a mistaken notion of social order (order equals substantive enforcement) or is question-begging (it fails to explain why particular rules should be enforced and others not). Moreover, the problem of indeterminacy undermines the Weberian answer to the question of trust in terms of bureaucratic control. If the Weberian denies that officials exercise discretion or judgment to resolve indeterminacies of enforcement, then he cannot explain how these indeterminacies are resolved; on the other hand, if he recognizes that officials exercise such discretion or judgment, he cannot explain why they can be trusted to do so. When the Weberians do recognize that officials exercise enforcement discretion, they can only deplore this fact and urge more formalization of procedural norms governing enforcement.[84] But, of course, this response exacerbates the problems of imprecision and normative overload.

*Problems of Communication—Citizens.* The problems of imprecision, overload, and indeterminacy limit even more severely the sovereign's capacity to communicate to citizens about their rights, since the citizens tend to have less ability to master the law than the officials.

As the enforcement process has become increasingly complicated in the reformed welfare system, the citizen has become increasingly dependent on legal knowledge. Most obviously, she needs to know what benefits there are in order to apply for them. She also needs to know what information she must provide in order to establish eligibility. Often, the relevant facts will be ambiguous, and her eligibility will depend on how she characterizes them.[85] Her eligibility may depend also on how she structures her private affairs prior to application.[86] She also needs to know what procedural steps she must take, for example, what documents she must procure. She cannot fulfill a requirement even as simple as a written application unless she knows of the requirement, knows how to secure an application, and knows how to fill it out.[87]

84. *See* K. DAVIS, *supra* note 69; Handler, *supra* note 69.

85. For example, whether a migrant worker will be found to satisfy the residence requirement for AFDC, 45 C.F.R. § 233.40 (1983), will depend on whether she is able to give the correct responses to often highly ambiguous questions concerning her travel and work plans.

86. For example, in some AFDC programs, whether a recipient who shares an apartment or who borrows money suffers a grant reduction depends on whether the rental or loan agreement satisfies specified formal conditions. *E.g.*, MASS. ADMIN. CODE tit. 106, § 304.510 (1982) (rent regulation); CALIFORNIA DEP'T OF SOCIAL SERVICES, MANUAL OF POLICIES AND PROCEDURES § 44-111.437 (loan regulation).

87. *See, e.g.*, Schweiker v. Hansen, 450 U.S. 785 (1980) (government not estopped to deny retroactive Social Security benefits to woman who was discouraged from filing an application by worker who wrongly told her she was ineligible); M. BENDICK, A. LAVINE & T. CAMPBELL, *supra* note 20, at 56 ("[T]he vast majority of [applications and other documents provided claimants] are difficult or impossible for most of their intended audience to comprehend.").

Welfare System

The citizen's dependence on such knowledge raises doubts about the capacity of the system to secure the goals of freedom and fairness. The system is supposed to safeguard the citizen's autonomy and insure even-handed treatment by binding officials to the rules. But even in a system of perfectly enforced rules, the officials will have power over the citizens and over the incidence of enforcement to the extent they have control over the distribution of enforcement resources such as information and assistance. While the public assistance reforms of recent decades have sought with some success to limit the kind of discretion that arises from informal norms and limited supervision, they have enlarged the kind of discretion that arises from the control of enforcement resources. Claimants' dependence on enforcement resources has grown with increased procedural requirements.

I suspect that many liberal lawyers underestimate this point because of their vocational perspective. The transformation of the system has increased its accessibility and responsiveness to people with rule knowledge and enforcement resources, in particular professional advocates. But very few recipients have the knowledge and resources of professional advocates and only a few more are able to get representation by professional advocates.[88] For the rest, formalization and bureaucratization have in many ways decreased accessibility and responsiveness.

Now it might be thought that this objection does not go to the Weberian project itself, but to the perverse implementation of it in the recent reforms. The reforms have notably failed to formalize and bureaucratize many of the critical aspects of the provision of enforcement resources. Thus, there are responses within the dominant vision to the failure of the current regime to secure information and assistance. Such responses would require workers to provide specified packages of enforcement resources that would differ from applicant to applicant only in terms of a small number of characteristics. The *Miranda* warnings given by policemen to those they arrest exemplify this kind of activity.

But such responses are plagued by imprecision, overload, and indeterminacy. In order to serve the goal of freedom, the enforcement activities must achieve a genuine understanding by the right-holder of her rights and what she has to do to enforce them and must provide her with the assistance she needs to do so. But the process of informing lay people about legal rights is complex and difficult. This is particularly so when it involves people who are relatively uneducated and with limited experience of the dominant culture, as both criminal defendants and welfare recipi-

88. Even among the small fraction of AFDC applicants and recipients who took appeals to administrative hearings, *see infra* note 124, only 11.5% had any kind of representation in fiscal 1980. U.S. DEP'T OF HEALTH & HUMAN SERVS., Q. PUB. ASSISTANCE STATISTICS, Jan.-Mar. 1981, at 25.

ents tend to be. As students of the *Miranda* warning have concluded, a plausible attempt to impart understanding to such right-holders must involve sensitivity on the part of the person providing the information to personal and social characteristics of the particular right-holder and an ability to shape communication and assistance in accordance with these characteristics.[89] Such an approach would seem to require informal, particularized judgment, lower-level autonomy, and sophistication and training to a degree incompatible with the dominant vision.[90]

*Problems of Supervision.* The Weberian view relies on each successive layer of administrative hierarchy, culminating in the sovereign, to superin-

89. Griffiths & Ayres, *A Postscript to the Miranda Project: Interrogation of Draft Protesters*, 77 YALE L.J. 300, 318-19 (1967); Note, *Interrogations in New Haven: The Impact of* Miranda, 76 YALE L.J. 1519, 1577-78, 1613-16 (1967).

Bendick concludes on the basis of studies of welfare "outreach" efforts that, "Because of the ineffectiveness of mass-media outreach campaigns, face-to-face interaction, patient communication with the client in his or her own terms, and follow-up assistance in the application process may be necessary elements of outreach for the recruitment of most needy nonparticipants." Bendick, *supra* note 61, at 271.

90. The problem of communication about rights and provision of enforcement resources exemplifies a basic dilemma of the dominant vision and of liberal legalism generally. It is a premise of liberal legalism that legally competent citizens must have the ability to know their rights and duties and to enforce and perform them. This imposes an obligation on the state to make the law known to citizens and to make performance and enforcement possible. Société Internationale pour Participations Industrielles et Commercials, S.A. v. Rogers, 357 U.S. 197 (1958); Lambert v. California, 355 U.S. 225 (1957); *see* L. FULLER, THE MORALITY OF LAW 49-51, 63-65, 70-79 (rev. ed. 1969). The problem is that liberal legalism does not have a satisfactory answer to the question of whether the state's obligations are measured by a subjective standard, which would require that each citizen be guaranteed an opportunity to know and enforce her rights, or an objective standard, which would require some uniform standard regardless of the capacities and circumstances of individual citizens. A subjective standard would undermine formality and bureaucracy by making enforcement depend on a multitude of personal characteristics of each right-holder. But an objective standard deprives a broad segment of the citizenry of the freedom promised by legality and makes enforcement turn on substantively irrelevant factors such as wealth and education. *Compare* Goldberg v. Kelly, 397 U.S. 254, 268-69 (1970) ("The opportunity to be heard must be tailored to the capacities and circumstances of those who are to be heard.") *with* Guerrero v. Carleson, 9 Cal. 3d 808, 512 P.2d 833, 109 Cal. Rptr. 201 (1973) (notice required by due process need not be in language understandable by non-English speaking claimant), *cert. denied*, 414 U.S. 1137 (1974).

These issues are rarely faced in the welfare area. With a few exceptions, welfare statutes do not attempt to require the provision of enforcement resources. *See* Note, *Outreach: Bringing the Eligible into Federal Assistance Programs*, 62 CORNELL L. REV. 1093 (1977). Judicially developed doctrine is sparse, vague, and inconsistent. On the one hand, it is often said that the burden of proof with respect to eligibility is on the claimant. Lavine v. Milne, 424 U.S. 577 (1976); Torres v. Schweiker, 682 F.2d 109 (3d Cir. 1982), *cert. denied*, 103 S. Ct. 823 (1983). And in a case holding the government not estopped to deny benefits to a woman who had failed to file an application because a Social Security worker erroneously told her she was ineligible, the Supreme Court apparently assumed that neither due process nor the substantive statute implicitly create a duty to provide information and facilitate application. Schweiker v. Hansen, 450 U.S. 785, 789-90 (1981). On the other hand, some cases explicitly or implicitly recognize the limited ability of claimants to secure evidence and shift the burden of proof to the government. *See* Krauss v. A. & M. Karagheusian, Inc., 13 N.J. 447, 456-57, 100 A.2d 277, 282 (1953) (Brennan, J.); Liebman, *The Definition of Disability in Social Security and Supplemental Security Income: Drawing the Bounds of Social Welfare Estates*, 89 HARV. L. REV. 833, 850-51 (1976). Still others recognize governmental duties to provide information and assistance to claimants, whether by virtue of due process, common law estoppel, or inferences from substantive statutes. *See* Jagow v. Child, 95 Idaho 830, 521 P.2d 654 (1974). Some use language suggesting a subjective standard. *See* Crowder v. Gardner, 249 F. Supp. 678, 680 (D.S.C. 1966).

tend the activities of the layers below it. A critical problem with this approach is that each level of the hierarchy receives a progressively narrower range of information regarding matters within the control of its subordinates. In important respects, the supervisors have less information than those they supervise. Thus, the sovereign and her supervisors may lack sufficient information to formulate enforcement norms or to detect willful non-compliance with the norms. Supervision may cause subordinates to focus their efforts on the activities most easily reviewed by supervisors even though such a focus may be inconsistent with the substantive goals of the program. In a famous illustration of this point, Peter Blau showed how the introduction of productivity standards based on the number of job referrals for officials in a public employment service caused the officials to devote their efforts to the most easily employable applicants, many of whom would have found jobs without their help, and to ignore more difficult cases that could have benefited more from help.[91] As we have seen, this pathology pervades the AFDC Quality Control system.

*Problems of Alienation.* A further set of concerns arises from the failure of the Weberian view to address the phenomenon of alienation.

One widely recognized problem is that the tendency of formality and bureaucracy to alienate the worker from the goals of the enterprise may jeopardize efficiency.[92] Workers who share the goals of the enterprise will contribute their efforts and comply with its norms voluntarily. Because the ability to induce effort and compliance through hierarchical supervision is limited by the problems of supervision, voluntary contribution and compliance enhance efficiency. Organizations modeled on the Weberian view thus may undermine efficiency by virtue of their impact on the workers' goals. Widespread impressions of high turnover and low morale in the public assistance system suggest this problem may be present there.

A more elusive but perhaps more important problem is that the tendency of the system to alienate the citizen undermines the goal of freedom. The Weberian view purports to secure freedom simply by insuring that the citizen is subject only to formally and bureaucratically constrained power. This view does not require that the system guarantee the ability to satisfy any particular goal or need or that it take into account any particular characteristic of the citizen. In contrast, an important tradition of criticism asserts that a plausible notion of freedom must make provision for some recognition of the concrete individuality of the person.[93] It suggests

91. P. BLAU, *supra* note 71, at 36–56.

92. *E.g.*, M. CROZIER, THE BUREAUCRATIC PHENOMENON 187–98 (1964); A. GOULDNER, PATTERNS OF INDUSTRIAL BUREAUCRACY 207–14 (1954).

93. G. HEGEL, PHILOSOPHY OF RIGHT 75–104 (T. Knox trans. 1953). Weber himself contributed to this tradition. M. WEBER, *Science as a Vocation*, in FROM MAX WEBER: ESSAYS IN SOCIOLOGY 129, 155–56 (1946).

that formalized, bureaucratized power may be perceived as arbitrariness or oppression. Whether in fact such power is perceived as freedom or as arbitrariness or oppression seems to vary with social and personal circumstances in ways that the dominant vision does not acknowledge. For example, some of the long-term welfare recipients I met in Boston expressed nostalgia for the old, unreformed system as one that "cared more" about them. They missed the special needs grants. Although I doubt that their total grants were larger before consolidation, they interpreted the particularized need standard as an expression of concern about them as individuals. They also missed the long-term relation with an individual worker. They missed the workers' expressions of interest in their lives. And they missed the sense that the office they dealt with was rooted in the community.[94] It would have been totally meaningless to them to suggest that this loss had been compensated by an enlargement of their freedom. Such feelings were not universal and perhaps not even typical. But a conception of freedom indifferent to such feelings seems inadequate.

Even if we ignore such feelings, the plausibility of the conception of freedom as subjection to formalized, bureaucratized power still depends on the assumption that the citizen exercises autonomous choice within the framework of such power. I mentioned above that the problems of communication cast doubt on this assumption. The doubt is intensified by the problems of alienation, since they suggest that the citizen's perception of her goals may be influenced by the legal system. Consider a recent study of the effects of the administrative separation of financial assistance and social services. One of the main arguments for this reform asserted that it would enhance the client's capacity for choice by limiting the ability of workers to force services on the client by tacitly conditioning financial assistance on acceptance of services.[95] The study suggests how problematical the notion of choice in this argument is. It reports on differences in requests for both financial assistance and social services by clients with similar information and background characteristics in different administrative settings and concludes that separation reduces requests, not only for social services, but for financial benefits as well. The authors speculate that in the combined function model the interest expressed by workers in the recipients' personal circumstances relaxes their shame-induced inhibitions

94. There are similar expressions of nostalgia in S. SHEEHAN, *supra* note 45, at 18-31, 83-85. Joel Handler's and Ellen Jane Hollingsworth's 1967 study of the Wisconsin AFDC program found a high level of recipient satisfaction in the personal aspects of the caseworker relation, although these aspects were more limited than the social work doctrine of the old regime prescribed. J. HANDLER & E. HOLLINGSWORTH, *supra* note 62, at 103-63.

95. U.S. DEP'T OF HEALTH, EDUC. & WELFARE, *supra* note 51, at 5-6; J. HANDLER & E. HOLLINGSWORTH, *supra* note 62, at 130-33.

about requesting financial assistance.[96] Whether or not this interpretation is correct, the study suggests that what people express as their goals is influenced by the organizational structure in which they express them. This suggestion undermines the claim of the Weberian regime to enhance freedom. In order to decide which of the different patterns of choices associated with different administrative arrangements more accurately represents the claimant's goals, one would need a conception of individual goals that did not depend on the claimant's choices. One would need a nonsubjective conception of needs or interests. But the Weberian view has no such conception.

*The Organizational Paradox of Formality.* A final problem with the Weberian view overlaps some of the problems of communication, supervision, and alienation. It arises from the indeterminate and paradoxical relation of substantive and procedural formality. It suggests that the Weberian answer to the question of trust (hierarchical bureaucracy) not only does not follow from the Weberian answer to the question of value (formal rules), but may not even be compatible with it.

Substantive formality requires that the sovereign's will be expressed as rules. This principle seems to *preclude* direct participation of the sovereign in enforcement because such participation leads to ad hoc decision based on unformulated criteria. Hence the notion that enforcers should be independent of the sovereign. On the other hand, procedural formality requires that enforcement comply with the will of the sovereign. This principle seems to *require* direct participation of the sovereign in enforcement because the problems of communication prevent rules from fully expressing the sovereign will. Hence the notion that enforcers should be subject to the control of the sovereign.[97] These conflicting implications exemplify

96. Piliavin & Gross, *The Effects of Separation of Services and Income Maintenance on AFDC Recipients*, 51 SOC. SERV. REV. 389, 403-04 (1977).

97. The fact that it is often difficult to identify a unitary sovereign in American legal culture is another difficulty with the Weberian view. Public law discourse influenced by the Weberian view usually presumes that the legislature is the relevant sovereign, that top level executive officials are closest (most directly accountable) to it, and that lower level officials become accountable to the legislature as they become subordinate to upper level ones. *See* V. OSTROM, THE INTELLECTUAL CRISIS IN AMERICAN PUBLIC ADMINISTRATION 23-47 (1973); Wilson, *The Study of Administration*, 2 POL. SCI. Q. 197 (1887). But this perspective often encounters difficulties from two traditions. First, the constitutionalist tradition holds that the sovereign people have divided power among the three branches and limited the power of each. In this view, it is sometimes hard to determine which branch has preeminence and to what extent the constitutional limitations on each of them can be enforced by lower level executive authority or citizen self-help. *See* M. KADISH & S. KADISH, DISCRETION TO DISOBEY 37-140 (1973). Second, the pluralist tradition holds that sovereignty should be and has been divided up by myriad private groups. In matters within the sphere of their interests, compliance is owed to the wills of such groups. *See* Stewart, *The Reformation of American Administrative Law*, 88 HARV. L. REV. 1667, 1760-90 (1975); Yeazell, *Intervention and the Idea of Litigation: A Commentary on the Los Angeles School Case*, 25 UCLA L. REV. 244 (1977). To the extent that legal doctrine portrays sovereignty as diffused in either way, it further undercuts the Weberian association of procedural formality and bureaucratic hierarchy.

a general instability in the liberal understanding of legality, which sees law as a means of both restraining the sovereign and extending its power.

For our purposes, the important aspect of the problem is that substantive formality contradicts the hierarchical implications of procedural formality. Procedural formality purports to limit discretion through hierarchical organization; it thus makes it possible for superior officials to argue that their organizational proximity to the sovereign gives their views authority. But substantive formality purports to limit discretion through the rules themselves; it thus makes it possible for subordinate officials to appeal beyond their superiors to the rules.

This possibility has been illustrated throughout modern history by the various struggles of judicial officers for autonomy from executive authority in particular and hierarchical authority in general. It is expressed in the principle of some European constitutions that "[j]udges are subject only to the law"[98] and in the civil law doctrine that a lower court judge is not bound (at least on first remand) by a judgment of reversal by an appellate court.[99] It is also expressed in the American doctrine of judicial review that permits lower court judges to enjoin the actions of the highest executive officials. ("A court that checks Uncle Sam's agents is not limiting Uncle Sam's will but is helping to carry out his will," Kenneth Culp Davis writes.)[100] And it is expressed in principles that recognize the right of citizens to appeal directly to the law over the heads of officials, for example, in the doctrines that allow juries to reject judicial instructions at trial and citizens to reject executive prohibitions regarding their conduct in the hope of subsequently establishing its legality in court.[101] Such doctrines are based on the belief, inspired by formalistic conceptions of legality, that people have an unmediated relation with the law itself. The defiant subordinate can claim the support of the sovereign by arguing that the sovereign's will is embodied in the rule (as she interprets it) and not in the superior's command.[102]

The Weberian perspective ignores the organizational paradox of for-

98. *See* Const. of Italy, art. 101, ¶ 2; M. CAPPELLETTI & W. COHEN, COMPARATIVE CONSTITUTIONAL LAW 330-57 (1979).

99. J. DAWSON, THE ORACLES OF THE LAW 403-05 (1968).

100. K. DAVIS, *supra* note 69, at 175.

101. *See* M. KADISH & S. KADISH, *supra* note 97, at 37-94.

102. *See* L. WHITE, THE FEDERALISTS 204 (1948):

> The extent of the Secretary of the Treasury's power of superintendence was challenged by some customs collectors, who alleged that their oath of office required them to execute their offices *according to the law*, and thus allowed them to follow the law as they understood it, not as it might be explained to them by Alexander Hamilton.

A more recent example is the refusal of some state welfare officials responsible for Social Security disability determinations to follow instructions from the Reagan Administration designed to limit favorable determinations on the ground that the instructions violate the Social Security Act. Lauter, *Disability-Benefit Cases Flood Courts*, Nat'l L.J., Oct. 17, 1983, at 1.

mality: It tends simultaneously to encourage the constitution of hierarchical enforcement authority and to encourage individuals to appeal beyond constituted authority to the sovereign will itself. To the extent that such appeals occur, they are often perceived as disorder.[103] To the extent they are inhibited by procedural norms, substantive norms often inspire a sense of oppression or unfairness.[104] The paradox means that the organizational implications of formality are more indeterminate than the Weberian view allows. There is no basis from which to presume that hierarchical bureaucracy maximizes compliance with the sovereign will or serves the goals of social order. In fact, most modern legal and administrative systems are a hodgepodge of centralization and decentralization, and even in the ones most committed to the Weberian view the paradox asserts itself in anomalous norms such as the civil law rule about the freedom of the trial judge on remand or the contemporary American concern with "whistle blowing" by subordinate executive officials.[105]

Two California cases are examples of such anomalies in the context of recent welfare reforms. In one, the California Supreme Court held that a welfare worker could not be discharged for disobeying her supervisor's order to engage in a search of a recipient's home that the worker asserted (and the court agreed) was unlawful.[106] In another, it held that a welfare appeals official has the authority and duty to ignore a welfare department regulation when she decides it is in conflict with a statute.[107] Neither decision has had a dramatic impact, and it is easy to formulate limiting interpretations of each. (The first decision concerns physical conduct rather than decisionmaking; the second concerns quasi-judicial officials rather

103. For example, see Dawson's discussion of the degeneration of nineteenth century French legal scholarship into a "chaos of clear ideas":

> It is strange and paradoxical that the supremacy attributed to the legislature should have maximized this individual self-assertion. Yet one can follow the reasoning that greatly influenced attitudes . . . . If the interpreter was to be faithful to his high mission he must fix his eyes on the authentic text and penetrate through the encasing words to the living thought of the legislature. He could take aid from others but the task was essentially for him alone.

J. DAWSON, *supra* note 99, at 395–96.

The organizational paradox of formality parallels a central paradox of Protestant theology. *See* D. LITTLE, RELIGION, LAW AND ORDER: A STUDY OF ELIZABETHAN ENGLAND 38–56 (1969).

104. *See* Walker v. City of Birmingham, 388 U.S. 307, 324 (1967) (Warren, C.J., dissenting) (criticizing majority's decision that Martin Luther King and others could be punished for violating unconstitutional injunction as oppressive and likely to undermine confidence in legal system).

105. *See* Damaska, *Structures of Authority and Comparative Criminal Procedure*, 84 YALE L.J. 480, 494–98 (1975); Vaughn, *Statutory Protection of Whistle Blowers in the Federal Executive Branch*, 1982 U. ILL. L. REV. 615.

106. Parrish v. Civil Serv. Comm'n, 66 Cal. 2d 260, 425 P.2d 223, 57 Cal. Rptr. 623 (1967).

107. *See* Woods v. Superior Court, 28 Cal. 3d 668, 680, 620 P.2d 1032, 1038-39, 170 Cal. Rptr. 484, 490 (1981). The counter-hierarchical implications of the decision are limited by the fact that the California appeals system permits the welfare department director to review the appeals official's decision before it becomes effective. CALIFORNIA DEP'T OF SOCIAL SERVS., STATE DEPARTMENT OF SOCIAL SERVICE MANUAL § 22-061.

than bottom tier administrators.) But the cases do not mention such interpretations; they rely on a premise with broadly counter-hierarchical implications: that invalid orders or regulations "have no force or life."[108]

The most notable expression of the decentralizing implications of substantive formality in welfare in recent years was the welfare rights movement. Even in some of its most defiant moments, the movement was animated by (usually very plausible) appeals to substantive legal rights. Some of its most successful efforts involved pressure by groups of recipients (often through threats of violence) on local offices to enforce rights to special need grants. There is some irony in the fact that the elimination of special need grants and of local office autonomy—reforms promoted by liberal lawyers in the name of recipient rights[109]—played an important role in killing this particular form of quality control.

*A Further Illustration.* The range of problems of the dominant vision is apparent in the current efforts of the Reagan Administration to come to terms with the widely varying but generally high reversal rates in disability appeals to Administrative Law Judges (ALJs) of the Social Security Administration. For many years, reversal rates have averaged around fifty percent or more, but they have varied widely among individual ALJs; some judges decide for claimants in a high percentage of cases; other judges applying the same substantive norms decide for claimants in a low percentage of cases. How does one decide whether either or both groups are performing improperly? The Reagan Administration responded to this challenge by having the Social Security Administration's Appeals Council review the files of a sample of cases decided by ALJs. The Reagan Administration reasoned that since by law the Appeals Council has the highest authority within HHS with respect to disability decisions, its decisions on review are presumptively correct. Because the Appeals Council disagreed with the ALJs' reversals more frequently than with their affirmances and with the high reversal rate ALJs more frequently than the low reversal rate ALJs, the Administration interprets the study to show that the ALJs are reversing too much. It has used the study to justify a series of reforms designed to decrease reversals, including instructing the

108. *Woods*, 28 Cal. 3d at 680, 620 P.2d at 1038-39, 170 Cal. Rptr. at 490.

109. *See* J. HANDLER & E. HOLLINGSWORTH, *supra* note 62, at 198–99, 208–11. When welfare departments initiated consolidation in response to the welfare rights movement, the reform was perceived as conservative and opposed by liberal advocates. The irony is that the liberals were answered with the Weberian arguments they themselves had developed. *See* L. BAILIS, BREAD OR JUSTICE 143 (1974).

The opposition to consolidation in the course of the welfare rights movement is one of numerous instances in which liberal advocates took positions inconsistent with the dominant vision. However, these positions were ad hoc and were never integrated into an alternative perspective to the Weberian view. That view did not inform every position the advocates took, but it was the dominant theoretical influence on their work.

ALJs to follow the voluminous and relatively formal rules of the Program Operating Manual System designed for front-line workers and focusing supervisory efforts on the high reversal rate ALJs.[110]

This program exemplifies the problems of the Weberian view. First, there are problems of communication, particularly imprecision. As the Administration admits, the Program Operating Manual System's instructions are substantially under-inclusive.[111] They deny eligibility to a large number of applicants with disabilities, such as psychiatric ailments or ailments that cause disabling pain, which cannot be established with simple physical observations or quantitative medical tests. They do this despite the fact that nearly everyone permitted to make a judgment on the matter believes that many of these claims are within the substantive legislative norm.[112]

Second, there are problems of supervision. Because the Appeals Council's review was conducted on a paper record, it lacked some information available to the ALJs who made the decisions under review: physical appearance and demeanor of the claimant. American law has always asserted the importance of this type of information in doctrines such as those limiting the scope of appellate review of trial court findings of fact and the right of confrontation. Appearance and demeanor are often dispositive in two of the largest categories of cases that come to the ALJs: cases involving psychiatric impairments and those turning on assessments of the degree of pain.

Third, there are problems of alienation. By reducing the capacity of the ALJ to respond to the contingencies of the particular case, the reforms reduce the capacity of the system to treat the claimant as a concrete individual. From the claimant's point of view, the reforms would make the appeal less an inquiry about whether he can legitimately be expected to earn his own living and more an inquiry about whether he fits a set of formal categories that have no perceptible relation to his experience and needs.[113]

And fourth, there is the organizational paradox of formality. The same factors that make the Administration doubt the authority of the ALJs—their administrative insulation from the immediate control of the

110. *The Bellmon Report*, *supra* note 15, at 3; SUBCOMM. ON OVERSIGHT OF GOVERNMENT MANAGEMENT, SEN. COMM. ON GOVERNMENTAL AFFAIRS, THE ROLE OF THE ADMINISTRATIVE LAW JUDGE IN THE DISABILITY ADJUDICATION PROCESS 22-24 (Comm. Print 1983).

111. *The Bellmon Report*, *supra* note 15, at 12–15.

112. *See* Bittel v. Richardson, 441 F.2d 1193 (3d Cir. 1971); Miracle v. Celebrezze, 351 F.2d 361 (6th Cir. 1965).

113. *See* Mashaw, *The Supreme Court's Due Process Calculus for Administrative Adjudication in* Mathews v. Eldridge: *Three Factors in Search of a Theory of Value*, 44 U. CHI. L. REV. 28, 49–52 (1976).

sovereign and their ethos of decisional independence—from another point of view inspire confidence in them. And the same factor that gives the Administration confidence in the authority of the Appeals Council—its proximity to the sovereign—raises questions about it. The Appeals Council's lesser independence and its closer association to policymaking executives associated with the Reagan Administration's budget cutting commitments undermines the claim to authority from its superior position in the hierarchy. These factors suggest that the review judgments may represent, not more accurate applications of the disability norms, but the betrayal of those norms to the Reagan Administration's ad hoc policy commitments.[114]

B. *Standards, Decentralization, Profession*

If the Weberian view were considered as one end of a spectrum of sociologies of law, the view at the opposite end would characterize society as founded on shared values and trust, and law as largely undifferentiated from organic social norms. There would be no distinction between enactment and enforcement; both sovereignty and enforcement powers would be diffused throughout the society and would involve extensive self-help, unspecialized decentralized institutions, and broad participation. Although this view is most readily associated with traditional societies, it bears some resemblance to the accounts of revolutionary America by recent historians and of early nineteenth century America by Alexis de Tocqueville.[115]

But of course the view of legality and society that competes in contemporary America with what I have called the dominant vision in welfare jurisprudence is not this vision of undifferentiated legality. The competing view aspires to synthesize the two polar views. This competing view resembles the program of the social work profession under the old regime of welfare administration, but in recent decades its most prominent influence has been in the literature on the judiciary. The competing view has been developed in theories of reasoned elaboration and irrebuttable presumptions, of due process and process values, of judicial administration, and of federal habeas corpus, class actions, and structural remedies.[116]

114. *See HEW Efforts*, *supra* note 24.

115. A. DE TOCQUEVILLE, DEMOCRACY IN AMERICA 213-26, 241-90 (J. Mayer & M. Lerner eds. 1966) (emphasis on enforcement through diffuse social pressures and the jury); G. WOOD, THE CREATION OF THE AMERICAN REPUBLIC, 1776-1783 at 319-28 (1969) (emphasis on self-help and enforcement through "The People Out-of-Doors"); Nader, *Styles of Court Procedures: To Make the Balance*, in LAW IN CULTURE AND SOCIETY 69 (L. Nader ed. 1969).

116. *See* J. DAWSON, *supra* note 99; P. FISH, THE POLITICS OF FEDERAL JUDICIAL ADMINISTRATION (1973); Chayes, *The Role of the Judge in Public Law Litigation*, 89 HARV. L. REV. 1281 (1976); Fiss, *The Supreme Court, 1978 Term—Foreword: The Forms of Justice*, 93 HARV. L. REV. 1 (1979); Neuborne, *The Myth of Parity*, 90 HARV. L. REV. 1105 (1977); Tribe, *Structural Due Process*, 10 HARV. C.R.-C.L. L. REV. 267 (1975); H. Hart & A. Sacks, The Legal Process: Basic

Welfare System

In the competing view, law is seen as both autonomous of society and a function of it. Substantively, legal norms are less formal than rules but more formal than organic social norms: their characteristic form is the standard, a norm that requires an individualized assessment of how a social goal can best be furthered in a particular case. Procedurally, the norms are legitimated through enactment by specialized institutions, but participation in enactment is broadened by delegation of power to social groups and by the incorporation of social norms into the promulgated law. The distinction between enactment and enforcement is attenuated; it is expected that substantive norms will be elaborated and developed in the process of enforcement.

The most characteristic feature of the organizational structure that the competing vision associates with this type of legality is the profession. The profession plays the role in the opposed vision that the aristocracy played in classical political theory and the civil service played in Hegel's political theory; it mediates between legality and society. This role is best expressed in Hegel's notion of the "universal class." The reference to class suggests that the profession is differentiated from other groups within organic society, but also that, to a far greater degree than the Weberian bureaucracy, it is immersed in society. On the other hand, the reference to universality suggests that the profession aspires to rise above the conflicting interests and particularistic orientations of other classes.

This organizational structure differs from the dominant vision in that it is more decentralized and prescribes a higher degree of education, skill, status, and reward for front-line decisionmakers. Decentralization is associated with the relatively diffused character of sovereignty in the opposed vision. Since sovereignty is not embodied in a unitary actor or institution, it cannot be organized as the apex of a hierarchical bureaucracy. Moreover, the commitment to relatively individualized judgment under standards requires autonomy on the part of the decisionmaker to respond to the contingencies of the particular case. Hierarchical review is limited by the inability of reviewers to know the full range of information on which the initial decisionmaker acts. In addition, decentralization is required to make possible meaningful participation by citizens affected by the decisions. The importance of such participation arises from the attenuation of the differentiation of law and of the distinction between enactment and enforcement. Since citizens have information and views that are valuable

Problems in the Making and Application of Law (1958) (unpublished manuscript). In the area of welfare this perspective has been applied to judicial review and administrative appeals, but rarely to the front-line administrative work force. *See* Mashaw, *supra* note 113; Rosenblatt, *Health Care Reforms and Administrative Law: A Structural Approach*, 88 YALE L.J. 243 (1978). Two broadly theoretical accounts of welfare administration which analyze some features of the opposed vision are J. MASHAW, BUREAUCRATIC JUSTICE (1983); P. NONET, ADMINISTRATIVE JUSTICE (1969).

to the decisionmaker, participation secures the benefit of this information and these views. Moreover, such participation gives the decisionmaker an opportunity to justify the decision to the citizen as an expression of legal norms rather than of individual will; it also enables the legal system to express a respect for the citizen that mitigates the socially centrifugal effects of adverse decisions. Such participation requires limited review because the more review restricts the decisionmaker whom the citizen actually confronts, the more attenuated becomes the citizen's participation in the decision.

The argument for the education, status, and reward associated with professionalism is that, first, since under a regime of standards decisions cannot be mechanized, they will require complex and reflective judgment for which extensive training is needed; second, given the impossibility of coordination and control through formal rules and hierarchical supervision, coordination and control must come through self-control instilled in the course of professional socialization, through the continuing collective elaboration and development of norms in the professional culture, and through collegial peer pressure; and third, high status and reward are needed to attract sufficiently able people and to maintain the confidence of the citizenry in the system.

Here then are the answers of the opposed vision to the questions raised by the issue of discretion. The answer to the question of value is that standards for the assessment of the conduct of public officials are those elaborated collectively by professional officials and developed in decentralized enforcement proceedings in which citizens participate. The answer to the question of trust is that public officials can be trusted to adhere to applicable standards when they are socialized through professional training to do so, when they are active participants in a vital professional culture, when they are subject to pressure from peers to do so, when they have a duty to justify their decisions to citizens affected by them, and when they receive relatively high status and reward.

The opposed vision sees a limited but important degree of shared values and relations of trust in the society. The common goals of order on which the society is founded are somewhat more concrete than in the dominant vision. Efficiency means, not only a general goal of coordination, but more specific goals (for example, high GNP, clean environment); freedom means not only a general autonomy to pursue subjective ends, but the social guarantee of specific personal interests (for example, privacy, access to justice, minimum needs); and fairness means, not only a general prohibition of favoritism, but also specific requirements of similar treatment and prohibitions of different treatment (for example, "suspect classifications"). The greater degree of shared values and trust in the society both requires and makes possible a greater degree of individuation and participation in the legal system.

The opposed vision responds to the first of the problems of communication—imprecision—by trying to achieve a tighter fit of decisions to goals through a legality of standards, through decentralized organization permitting flexible response to the contingencies of particular cases, and through professional decisionmakers who can be trusted to elaborate and apply the standards in accordance with their purposes. Its response to the problem of overload lies in its notion of professional doctrine as a manageable body of basic principles and methods that, once mastered, can generate decisions in an infinite number of particular cases. Professional doctrine thus obviates the need to provide explicit rules to govern every foreseeable case.

The response to the problem of indeterminacy is more complex. The opposed vision does not identify order with the enforcement of a differentiated set of formal substantive rules. It recognizes that substantive rules are indeterminate and holds that they must be elaborated progressively in individual cases. It also recognizes the enforcement dimension of indeterminacy and holds that the legal norms must be qualified and mediated by a variety of procedural norms and institutions, as well as by non-legal practices and institutions. It responds to the dialectic of legal and other social norms with theories about when legal norms should have priority (for example, where basic rights of discrete insular minorities are at stake, where a particular commercial group in its dealings with consumers or strangers has lagged behind the moral or technical standards of the rest of the society) and when non-legal social norms should prevail (for example, in dealings between businessmen), and with balancing methods for reconciling conflicts.

The opposed vision aspires to provide the citizen a genuine understanding of the norms that affect her. It purports to achieve this goal through the individual's direct participation in proceedings that affect her and through relatively individualized communication by decisionmakers or professional advocates.

The opposed vision responds to the problems of supervision by reducing supervision to a secondary role and relying on peer relations and socialization, supplemented by citizen participation, as its primary means of organizational control.

It responds to the problem of worker alienation by trying to engender official commitment to the purposes of the system through professionalism. It responds to the problem of citizen alienation by encouraging citizen participation in the elaboration of the norms of the system, by taking some account of concrete personal goals and characteristics in substantive norms, and by promoting reflective and informed citizen choice through the provision of enforcement resources. The opposed vision recognizes that the citizen's understanding of her own purposes may be affected by the legal system. Indeed, the legal system is designed to affect the litigant by encouraging a sense of solidarity. But the system is also designed to encourage autonomous decision through measures such as rules disfavoring specific types of superficially solidaristic choices (for example, guilty pleas) that seem unlikely to be genuinely autonomous, and procedures designed to provide information and assistance and to secure participation.

The opposed vision also aspires to mute the organizational paradox of formality. By diffusing sovereignty and attenuating the distinction between enactment and enforcement, the system tends to discourage appeal beyond constituted authority to the sovereign will, as the citizen herself interprets it. Citizen participation in a process involving both enactment and enforcement limits the sense of distance from the sovereign and the dangers of disorder and unfairness it creates.

Considered as an alternative to the dominant vision in welfare administration, the opposed vision is subject to at least two types of criticism. One type arises from within the literature of the opposed vision. Except for the relatively modest and supervised participation afforded citizens, the vision of public work arrangements premised on shared values and trust in the opposed vision is limited to a specific group, the professional class. The literature of the opposed vision generally assumes and occasionally (as in the recent writing expressing anxiety about the growth of the federal judiciary[117]) asserts that this group is necessarily a small one and that the possibilities for its expansion are limited. Some believe that the limit has already been exceeded; in any event, the expansion of professionalism that would be required to implement the opposed vision at the lower tier of the public work force would surely—the criticism asserts—exceed the limit.

A second set of criticisms arises from outside the opposed vision.[118] It denies that decentralized professional organizations can achieve controlled, coordinated enforcement in any manner that could be interpreted as expressing or implementing the goals of social order. It asserts that the doctrines and practices of those who appeal to the opposed vision express, not the interests of the larger society, but the group interests of the professionals themselves and/or their patrons and clients.

A related but more tentative criticism would suggest that the under-

117. *See* H. FRIENDLY, FEDERAL JURISDICTION: A GENERAL VIEW 28-31 (1973); McCree, *Bureaucratic Justice: An Early Warning*, 129 U. PA. L. REV. 777 (1981).

118. *See* Brest, *The Fundamental Rights Controversy: The Essential Contradictions of Normative Constitutional Scholarship*, 90 YALE L.J. 1063 (1981); Tushnet, *Truth, Justice, and the American Way: An Interpretation of Public Law Scholarship in the Seventies*, 57 TEX. L. REV. 1307 (1979).

standing of shared values and trust is, not so much implausible, as ambiguous. Sometimes the opposed vision speaks of shared values and relations of trust as if they were embodied in established social institutions and practices. In these instances, it tends to take hierarchy for granted or to interpret it as a social necessity. But at other times, it speaks of shared values and trust as if they were ideals to be realized through the transformation of established social institutions and practices. In these instances, it tends to be suspicious of hierarchy or to interpret it as a social failure.

Consider the response of the opposed vision to developments such as the welfare enforcement activities of the 1960's and 1970's, in which established institutions were strained by the large-scale assertion of previously unenforced norms. Unlike the Weberian view, the opposed vision does not assume that order depends uniquely on the enforcement of the norms. It can see in these developments a conflict between the redistributive and humanitarian goals expressed in the substantive norms on the one hand and a variety of other goals embodied in established institutions (for example, fiscal economy, preservation of labor incentives) on the other. At this point, the ambiguity appears. One tendency of the opposed vision is to suggest that officials limit substantive enforcement to moderate the strain on established institutions. But another tendency suggests that characteristics of the particular substantive norms involved—the fact that they concern basic needs of disadvantaged people—warrant enforcement even at the cost of strain on other social goals.

I want to postpone final assessment of these criticisms in order to turn now to a prominent set of arguments designed to reconcile the dominant and opposed visions in public law.

### C. *Separation of Powers/Combination of Functions*

I have been discussing the two visions of legality and organization as if they were mutually exclusive. In fact, however, most contemporary legal thought attempts to make room for them both. Indeed, the liberal legal scholarship of the 1960's and 1970's made notable efforts to develop both. At the same time that the liberals were arguing for the elimination of the discretion (informality, decentralization, professionalism) of welfare workers on the grounds that the rights they enforced were vital and the rightholders vulnerable, they were arguing for the expansion of the discretion of federal judges on precisely these grounds. While in the former effort they consistently conflated informality and decentralization with arbitrariness, in the latter, they produced an enormous literature vindicating the notion that a standards jurisprudence and a decentralized judicial organization could produce—indeed was required to produce—coherent, rational decisionmaking.

In this effort the two visions have been mediated by notions of separation of powers or combination of functions that suggest that they can be institutionalized so as to complement each other. The aspect of the separation of powers most pertinent here distinguishes between ministerial administrative tasks and judicial tasks; it associates the vision of rules, hierarchy, and proletarianism with the former, and the vision of standards, decentralization, and professionalism with the latter. This mediating project calls for an interpretation that permits the characterization of different enforcement decisions as ministerial or judicial. Such distinctions have never been stable; the understanding of the administrative-judicial distinction worked out early in this century has been repeatedly upset by the growth of the regulatory-welfare state.[119] For example, in important respects, the job of the welfare worker seems the same as that of the federal judge: both make decisions about claims of individual right which are governed by complex state and federal laws and involve potentially complex factual judgments.

There are two overlapping approaches to characterizing enforcement work for the purposes of separation and combination. One assumes that both modes of decision are applicable to all substantive areas but that within each area different decisions lend themselves to one or the other mode. The other assumes that certain substantive areas lend themselves generally to one or the other mode of decision.

*Internal Differentiation: Routine Cases v. Trouble Cases.* The first type of interpretation emphasizes the separation and combination of judicial and ministerial enforcement within the welfare system. It is reflected not only in the way the courts have defined their own roles in relation to administrators, but also in the internal development of administration.

One response of the welfare managers to the efforts of advocates and the courts to expand the procedural rights of recipients has been to increase the differentiation and separation of nominally ministerial from nominally adjudicatory functions within the system. The trends toward legalization, bureaucratization, and proletarianization have been accompanied by the promotion of small, marginal sub-bureaucracies with nominally judicial functions in which concessions are made to individualized judgment, decentralization, and professionalism. One manifestation of this structure is the codification of systems of dual law in which the "workers" are required to make decisions only on the basis of the voluminous sublegal instructional materials that purport to break down the prescriptions of the statutes and regulations into routine mechanical operations, while

119. *See* M. VILE, CONSTITUTIONALISM AND THE SEPARATION OF POWERS 29-32, 86-88, 280-90 (1967); Arnold, *The Role of Substantive Law and Procedure in the Legal Process*, 45 HARV. L. REV. 617, 624-31 (1932).

Welfare System

the hearing "officials" are expected to make decisions by directly referring to and interpreting the more general norms of the statutes and regulations.[120]

The system is designed so that adjudicatory decisionmaking has no effect outside of the particular cases appealed on the nominally administrative functions. For example, most programs repudiate the principle of stare decisis in the appeal procedure. The consequence is to limit collegiality among the hearing officials, and more indirectly but more importantly, to preclude the development of a sense of autonomy and responsibility among the workers. The workers are taught that a reversal of one of their decisions is not to affect their future conduct. They have no duty to consider or distinguish it; they may not regard it as a precedent; it is simply not a comment on their work. The message (well understood by the workers I have talked with) is that procedures in which decision depends on complex judgment, in which clients participate actively, or in which decisionmakers enjoy autonomy and status have nothing to do with the front-line worker's job.[121] A further instance of the segregation of nominally administrative and judicial functions results from a change in recruitment patterns. Under the old regime, hearing officers were recruited from front-line workers or from administrators. In the new regime, they tend to be recruited from outside the system, often from law schools.

This internal administrative differentiation of functions, as well as the parallel differentiation between the adminstration as a whole and the courts, seems to rest on a distinction between routine cases and "trouble" cases. Routine cases are appropriate for ministerial decision; trouble cases for judicial decision. All cases are determined ministerially first; trouble cases are identified and channeled into the judicial sphere when claimants initiate appeals.[122]

One variation of this distinction understands routine cases as those in which there is no dispute between the administration and the claimant and trouble cases as those in which there is a dispute. On this view, the primary enforcement role is ministerial; the function of judicial decision is to resolve disputes. This view explains the administrative design that min-

120. On the differences in the norms applied by eligibility workers and hearing officials, see *The Bellmon Report*, *supra* note 15, at 12–15; B. Hecker & T. Nelson, AFDC Fair Hearings: A Study of Administrative Due Process (Legal Servs. Inst. 1981) (unpublished manuscript on file with author); Lissner, *Escalating State Agency Denial Rates and Their Impact on OHA*, OHA L. REP., Apr. 1980, at 40.

121. A more extreme degree of separation is achieved in systems such as Social Security, Unemployment Insurance, and a few state welfare programs in which the worker does not even appear at the hearing. The administration's case is presented by a full-time representative, or the hearing officer undertakes to develop both cases.

122. *See* H. Hart & A. Sacks, *supra* note 116, at 312.

imizes the impact of judicial decision on unappealed cases: The judicial function has no role where there is no dispute. The problem with this view is that whether a case is disputed or not is a function of organizational structure. If the ministerial sphere encourages requests for benefits, effectively communicates to claimants about their rights, effectively enforces hearing rights, and provides advocacy resources, it will generate a great number of trouble cases. If the system maintains or exacerbates claimant inhibitions about requesting benefits, fails to communicate about rights, fails to enforce hearing rights, and provides no advocacy resources, it will generate few trouble cases. The critique of the Weberian view suggests that the factors that determine which cases are disputed will be to an important extent arbitrary in relation to the goals of efficiency, freedom, and fairness.

Another variation understands the routine/trouble distinction in terms of relative difficulty. Judicial decision is considered more reliable than ministerial decision, but in the ordinary or easy case, there is a relatively high probability that ministerial decision will reach the same result as judicial decision. Since judicial decision is thought more expensive, it is most expedient to reserve it for the more difficult cases. This view suffers from a problem similar to that of its predecessor. The system depends on claimant initiation of appeals to distinguish hard from easy cases.[123] Given the problems of communication and alienation, the factors that determine which cases are appealed may be to a significant extent arbitrary in relation to probability of reversal on appeal. In most public assistance programs, reversal rates for appealed cases tend to be substantial but appeal rates, low.[124] If one could believe that most hard cases were in fact channeled into the appeal process, one might interpret the low appeal rates as a vindication of the ministerial function and the substantial reversal rates as the normal consequence of review of hard cases. But both intuition and the scant data that bear on the question suggest that the premise is incorrect. It appears that a large but indeterminable number of cases that would be reversed are not appealed by claimants because they lack under-

123. A variety of administrative review or quality control procedures have been developed that seek ministerially to distinguish easy from hard cases in order to focus enforcement resources on the latter. *See* J. MASHAW, C. GOETZ, F. GOODMAN, W. SCHWARTZ, P. VERKUIL & M. CARROW, SOCIAL SECURITY HEARINGS AND APPEALS 14-15, 22-24 (1978). These methods are highly formal and hence suffer from the liabilities of formality. Nevertheless, they appear to have some promise, and I suggest below that they might supplement a variety of more fundamental reforms. *See infra* notes 176-77.

124. Mashaw estimates that in the first six months of 1971 only 2% of all appealable decisions in public assistance programs were appealed and that more than half of these appeals were in only three states. Mashaw, *supra* note 67, at 784 & n.33. Reversal rates vary widely but are usually substantial; for example, 42% of the AFDC appeals decided at hearing (that is, not settled or abandoned) in fiscal year 1980 were decided in favor of the claimant. U.S. DEP'T OF HEALTH, EDUC. & WELFARE, QUARTERLY PUBLIC ASSISTANCE STATISTICS, Jan.-Mar. 1981, at 22.

standing of the rules, because they are unable to negotiate the appeal procedures, or because the administration fails to enforce the appeal procedures.[125]

Another problem with the hard/easy case distinction is that the category of easy cases may not be large enough to justify the ministerial function. It may be that in many areas of welfare, most claims will look different under informal than under formal norms and that, given an appropriate degree of informality, most will look different when reconsidered by an autonomous and better educated decisionmaker under a procedure that affords more opportunity for claimant participation. This is one interpretation of the crisis of the Social Security Administration disability programs, which are among the few income maintenance programs with high appeal rates. Despite high appeal rates, the programs have also had high reversal rates. From 1975 to 1980, when, apparently as a result of increasing formalization and bureaucratization of the ministerial decision process, the appeal rate increased from 52% to 69%, the reversal rates also increased, from 49% to 58%.[126] If, as seems likely, the reversal rates would remain high at an even higher appeal rate, it seems questionable whether there would be enough easy cases to justify the ministerial role even if there were some ministerial way of distinguishing them from the hard cases.

*External Differentiation: Desert v. Efficiency.* The other approach to the separation of powers and the combination of functions is to try to assign claims to one or the other type of legality and organization in terms of the type of substantive norms they involve. Most frequently, the opposed vision is associated with norms implicating individual desert, while the dominant vision is associated with norms implicating social efficiency. And the claims characterized in terms of desert usually turn out to be private law claims, while those characterized in terms of efficiency usually include welfare claims.

125. The data include a survey of denied applicants in Virginia indicating that many who appeared eligible did not appeal, surveys of recipients showing that most appear to have insufficient knowledge of appeal rights to make effective use of them, and a 1972 study of New York indicating substantial failure to implement hearing rights for those who file appeals. *See* Handler, *supra* note 69, at 54–69.

Several studies of unappealed Social Security disability cases suggest that a substantial percentage would have been reversed if they had been appealed. S. NAGI, DISABILITY AND REHABILITATION (1969); Mashaw, *supra* note 113, at 44–45 (describing Government Accounting Office study); *The Bellmon Report*, *supra* note 15.

126. Lissner, *supra* note 120, at 44; *The Bellmon Report*, *supra* note 15, at 9. The appeal and reversal rates apply to denied claims appealed from the second stage of administrative determination (reconsideration) to the ALJs. The rates of claims denied at the initial administrative stage reaching and reversed by the ALJs are considerably smaller. The appeal rate figures apply to both Social Security and Supplemental Security Income disability claims; the reversal rate figures only to Social Security and concurrent claims.

The Yale Law Journal Vol. 92: 1198, 1983

Although few who invoke such distinctions these days try to defend them systematically, this type of argument has a long history. That history, however, does not suggest promise for current efforts to defend the distinctions. Distinctions between private law claims and claims by beneficiaries of public regulatory or welfare activities were fundamental to the classical liberal legalism of the substantive due process era. Private law claims were matters of individual right because they were defined by a basic social process—the self-regulating market—which could be deduced from a morally fundamental conception of individual autonomy. A claim of right asserted an infringement of individual autonomy; its vindication restored a preexisting distributive equilibrium. Since judicial enforcement was the paradigmatic mode of rights enforcement, it was the appropriate one for private law claims. On the other hand, claims by beneficiaries of regulatory or welfare programs were matters of policy. These government activities involved collective coercion to re-distribute wealth, which though not necessarily impermissible, was suspect because of its threat to individual rights. Since beneficiary claims were not rights, their enforcement raised only issues of social convenience.

Much of the liberal jurisprudence of this century has been devoted to dismantling this view, especially its emphasis on the distinction between private and public claims. First, liberals showed that the private law regime of the classicists did not follow from the classicists' concept of individual autonomy, that private law was in fact as riven with policy considerations and as coercively redistributive as any welfare activity. Second, they showed that a broad range of welfare beneficiary interests was as consistent with the classicists' notion (as well as with some more plausible notions) of individual autonomy as any private law claim. As a consequence of these efforts, almost every area of American legal culture is characterized by controversies involving the assertion of values of both individual desert and efficiency.[127]

Against this background, the project of vindicating some combination of the two models of legality and organization in terms of classification based on the private/public, individual/social efficiency distinction does not seem promising. Nevertheless, the project seems lately to have tempted both conservatives and liberals. The project is implicit in two types of arguments; one makes the distinction in terms of the underlying moral concerns of private and welfare claims; the other, in terms of the volume of claims.

An example of the first type is the suggestion that private law claims

127. Cohen, *Property and Sovereignty*, 13 CORNELL L. REV. 8 (1927); Pound, *A Survey of Social Interests*, 57 HARV. L. REV. 1 (1943); Reich, *supra* note 69.

Welfare System

tend to invoke concepts such as "fault," which express a judgment on the moral character of the litigants, while welfare claims, which are generally premised on need, do not involve such personal moral judgment. Judicial enforcement, with its greater capacity for individuation and litigant participation, is said to be more appropriate for decisions expressing personal judgment.[128] This suggestion seems factually mistaken. Private law is pervaded by non-fault deterrent and distributive principles that do not imply judgment on moral character.[129] (In the years since Roscoe Pound proposed negligence as the paradigmatic moral judgment norm, the law-and-economics writers have restated just about every variation on the negligence principle in social efficiency terms.) And even the reformed welfare system is pervaded by considerations of fault and moral character. (In some programs, the applicant must show "good cause" for not being self-supporting; in others, more formal criteria, such as disability or "absence of a parent from the home," stand as proxies for such determinations.)[130]

The second type of argument for external differentiation is less well formulated but far more pervasive. It is signaled by anxious concern with the volume of welfare claims. For some, this concern is so intense, and the factor of volume so dispositive, that the mere incantation of phrases like "mass justice," amplified, if at all, by recitations of the number of welfare applications or appeals and vague references to cost or efficiency, is sufficient to justify almost any measure of formalization or bureaucratization of a welfare program.[131] The argument underlying this rhetoric seems to be that (a) efficiency is a distinctively important concern with welfare claims because they have a relatively high volume, and (b) enforcement procedures characterized by formality, bureaucracy, and proletarianism are presumptively more efficient.

None of the recent expressions of this argument is persuasive. For one

128. Mashaw, *Conflict and Compromise Among Models of Administrative Justice*, 1981 DUKE L.J. 181; *see* R. POUND, AN INTRODUCTION TO THE PHILOSOPHY OF LAW 68–71 (rev. ed. 1958). Neither Mashaw's nor Pound's deservedness/efficiency distinctions coincide with the conventional private/public distinctions, but both draw their deservedness examples from private law, and Mashaw uses a public assistance program (food stamps) to exemplify social efficiency.

129. *See* Kennedy, *Distributive and Paternalist Motives in Contract and Tort Law, with Special Reference to Compulsory Terms and Unequal Bargaining Power*, 41 MD. L. REV. 563 (1982); *see also* R. WASSERSTROM, THE JUDICIAL DECISION: TOWARD A THEORY OF LEGAL JUSTIFICATION 98–105 (1961) (criticizing Pound's distinctions).

130. 42 U.S.C. § 5606(a) (1976) (absence of a parent in AFDC); Liebman, *supra* note 90 (elements of moral judgment implicit in disability standards).

Even where the legislative concern can be characterized unambiguously as efficiency, the values of the rule of law expressed in the due process clause and throughout the legal culture limit the extent to which a legislature may pursue efficiency at the expense of individual deservedness concerns. As Mashaw has observed, given these values, individual deservedness concerns are relevant to *any* legal issue. Mashaw, *supra* note 113, at 48–49.

131. R. DIXON, *supra* note 69; Califano v. Boles, 443 U.S. 282, 283–87 (1979) (Rehnquist, J.); Friendly, *Some Kind of Hearing*, 123 U. PA. L. REV. 1267, 1298, 1301 (1975).

thing, they do not specify the baseline to which the volume of welfare claims is being compared. If the focus is on initial welfare claims, the relevant comparison would seem to be the volume of initial private law claims (most of which of course are made to private parties), or perhaps some sub-category of welfare such as social insurance should be compared to a private law sub-category, such as private insurance. If the focus is on welfare appeals, then the appropriate comparison probably would be some set of private judicial claims. Neither intuition nor any data I know of suggests that, on any of these comparisons, welfare claims are more voluminous than private claims. Moreover, a plausible argument about efficiency should consider, not simply volume, but the magnitude of the stakes or benefits involved in the claims.[132] It is very hard to see on efficiency grounds why, for example, Justice Rehnquist should find enforcement expense a distinctively important concern in the Social Security system[133] (in which the average monetary value of a disability claim exceeds $30,000) when enforcement expenses in many private law areas are probably far higher absolutely and relatively to the stakes involved.[134] Of course, the dollar value of the average public assistance claim is far less than that of the Social Security disability claim and may well be less than that of the average private law claim (at least if we exclude "small claims"). But unlike most private law claims, most public assistance claims are a matter of basic subsistence to the claimant. If the comparison is made in terms of subjective value, magnitudes of stakes seem unlikely to justify emphasis on administrative cost in welfare.

More importantly, even if one accepts the premise that volume is higher and efficiency more important in the welfare area, it simply does not follow that formalization, bureaucratization, or proletarianization are more

132. Mashaw, *Administrative Due Process as Social-Cost Accounting*, 9 HOFSTRA L. REV. 1423 (1981).

133. Califano v. Boles, 443 U.S. 282, 283-87 (1979) (Rehnquist, J.) (because of volume, efficiency is basic concern in Social Security)

134. Mashaw, *supra* note 30, at 824, reports that in 1979 the monetary value of Social Security disability claims averaged $30,000 and enforcement costs averaged $500 per case.

I do not have either the data or the theoretical framework for a systematic comparison of welfare and private law claims, but the studies emerging from the Rand civil litigation research project tend to reinforce my intuition that the relative emphasis on efficiency in welfare, as opposed to private law, is unjustified. For example, the Cook County, Illinois, study concludes that "[t]he amount in dispute in most Cook County trials is almost certainly less than the combined costs to taxpayers and parties" of processing the claims. M. Shanley & M. Peterson, Comparative Justice: Civil Jury Verdicts in San Francisco and Cook Counties, 1960-1979, at 2 (Rand Inst. for Civil Justice, Working Draft, Mar. 1983); *see also* J. Kakalik and A. Robyn, Costs of the Civil Justice System, at xv (Rand Inst. for Civil Justice 1982) (average expenditures for jury trials in tort cases estimated between $2790 and $12,035, depending on jurisdiction and case type).

Despite such indications, the "mass justice" writers sometimes seem to be as indifferent to efficiency in private law as they are obsessed with it in welfare. *See* Parklane Hosiery Co. v. Shore, 439 U.S. 322, 338 (1979) (Rehnquist, J.) (expressing "nagging sense of unfairness" about Court's application of collateral estoppel to deny corporate defendant a *second* judicial trial on fraud defense).

appropriate. Whatever the resource constraints are, they will limit enforcement options, but at any given level of resources, there will be a spectrum of options that will range from relatively formal, bureaucratic arrangements to relatively informal, decentralized ones. Even at low levels of resources, there is no warrant for presuming that formality and bureaucracy will be more efficient.

It may often be true, as the argument from volume asserts, that accurate decisionmaking—that is, decisionmaking that conforms to the norms—takes less time when the norms are formal.[135] But the relevant measure of efficiency is not the extent to which decisions conform to the norms, but the extent to which they promote the purposes of the program. As I emphasized above, formal norms have built into them a substantial discrepancy with the program's purposes. As AFDC Quality Control illustrates, accurate decisionmaking is not necessarily efficient decisionmaking.[136] And it may also often be true, as the argument from volume emphasizes, that a given level of resources will support a larger number of clerical than professional workers. But if professionalism improves the quality and/or quantity of decisions, a smaller number of professionals may well be more efficient than a larger number of clerks.

To presume simply because of volume and scarcity that we should prefer clerks to professionals in welfare is no more rational than to presume because of these factors that we should prefer orderlies to doctors in a medical emergency. Indeed, the example of medical triage shows that volume and scarcity may *increase* the efficiency of complex, informal judgment, decentralization, and professionalism. Triage connotes a dimension of enforcement decisions that is quite pertinent to the job of welfare workers and other street level public servants such as police officers. The Weberian view tends to see enforcement decisions as simply distinguishing between valid and invalid claims. But in triage situations, there are insufficient resources to enforce all the claims that are recognized as valid. Triage decisions thus involve, in addition to distinguishing valid from invalid claims, deciding which claims among the valid ones will be enforced.[137] In the medical triage situation, the stakes involved in claims are high but vary widely in accordance with diverse circumstances. The imprecision costs of formality tend to be high; the information needed for supervision is costly or impossible to get; concerns about worker and claimant alienation are intense. The circumstances that make informality,

135. *But see supra* p. 1228 (on problem of normative overload).

136. *See supra* pp. 1210-13, 1226-28.

137. This feature of public service work is emphasized in M. LIPSKY, *supra* note 71; J. WILSON, VARIETIES OF POLICE BEHAVIOR (1968). The critical factor of scarcity in public assistance work concerns advice and assistance.

decentralization, and professionalism valuable in medical triage are shared to a lesser but important degree in public assistance.[138]

If medical triage seems too exotic an analogy, consider the enforcement systems of private insurance companies, which handle high volumes of claims and seem likely to have been designed with some view to minimizing costs. As described by Laurence Ross,[139] they involve a high degree of informality and decentralization apparently because of the problems of close supervision, worker alienation, and claimant (customer) alienation.

Thus, the arguments for external differentiation have not been plausibly sustained.

## III. Class

If the preceding argument is correct, one cannot account for the course of welfare jurisprudence and welfare reform in recent years in terms of the general goals of efficiency, freedom, and fairness and the general conditions of modern society. One has to look to more concrete social and historical contingencies. The most interesting of these contingencies are variations on the theme of class.

Although explicit reference to class is considered vulgar in legal professional circles, a vague but important set of assumptions about class lies beneath (and sometimes even above[140]) the surface of most contemporary public law discourse. These assumptions tacitly mediate the simultaneous tendencies of public law discourse to deny and affirm the possibility of organization premised on shared values and trust. To put it crudely but not unfairly, organization premised on shared values is considered possible as long as the values are those of elite professionals; organization premised on trust is considered possible as long as those to be trusted are elite professionals.

Thus, one way to interpret recent welfare jurisprudence is as an expression of the efforts of professionals to define their place and relationships in the course of the recent expansion of the welfare state. Legal doctrine has played a role in the structuring of class relations within the welfare state that overlaps and parallels the role of technological doctrine in structuring relations in the private economy. For example, the role of

138. The susceptibility of the poor to crisis and emergency, arising in part from inability to make financial provision for the future, is often portrayed as the central characteristic of the "culture of poverty." *See* E. LIEBOW, TALLY'S CORNER: A STUDY OF NEGRO STREETCORNER MEN (1967).

139. L. ROSS, SETTLED OUT OF COURT 32-33, 45-66, 96-116 (1970). Ross describes the approach to claims determination of the adjusters that he observed as "principled contextualization of fairness." *Id.* at 52. He also suggests that the adjusters view their role as that of providing advice and assistance to claimants in accordance with relatively complex distributive judgments. *Id.* at 46-47, 52-54.

140. *See* Neuborne, *supra* note 116, at 1126.

the legal distinction between enactment and enforcement in rationalizing the boundary between professional policy and judicial officials on the one hand and ministerial officials on the other in the public sphere seems analogous to that of the technical distinction between conception and execution that rationalizes the boundary between elite managers and workers in the private sphere.[141]

The issue of class with which welfare jurisprudence has been most concerned is situating the large number of service roles created by the welfare expansion of the 1960's and 1970's.[142] This expansion involved roles that, at various points since the beginning of the welfare state, have seemed ambiguous both in their functional definition and their position in the social hierarchy. Many of them implicated occupations such as social work, nursing, and teaching, which have long claimed professional status but with mixed success. In these fields, the gap between aspiration and reality has at times inspired attempts at redefining the functional content and social status of occupational role. In the 1960's and 1970's, the expansion of welfare activity, the demand for institutional reform, and the creation of new contexts of practice temporarily unsettled the definitions of a variety of these service roles. Jurisprudence contributed to the resolution of this indeterminacy in favor of a proletarian definition of the welfare worker's role.

There are at least two promising approaches to interpreting this development; one emphasizes the constraints of social structure, the other the limited goals of the liberal welfare politics of the 1960's and 1970's. The two approaches are not really distinct. Social structure is simply congealed politics. Whether one explains events in terms of social structure or politics depends on whether one regards society as relatively open to purposive transformation (so that social structure appears as a transitory manifestation of collective action) or as relatively closed to such transformation (so that social structure appears as a fixed limit on collective action).[143] Thus, whether one regards the two approaches as mutually exclusive or as complementary depends on where one draws the line between social structure and politics.

141. *See* H. BRAVERMAN, LABOR AND MONOPOLY CAPITAL 85–138, 184–235 (1974).

142. On the expansion of white collar service and governmental work roles during this period, see Freeman, *The Evolution of the American Labor Market, 1948-80,* in THE AMERICAN ECONOMY IN TRANSITION 349, 362–66 (M. Feldstein ed. 1980); on the ambiguous status of some of these roles, see Scott, *supra* note 22.

On the parallel developments in the intermediate level roles in health care and education during the past two decades, see A. WISE, LEGISLATED LEARNING: THE BUREAUCRATIZATION OF THE AMERICAN CLASSROOM (1979); Kanter, *Work in a New America,* DAEDALUS, Winter 1978, at 47, 65. For an account of an earlier episode of formalization and bureaucratization in education, see D. TYACK, THE ONE BEST SYSTEM (1974).

143. I owe this conception of politics to Roberto Mangabeira Unger.

A. *Social Structure*

The approach based on social structure explains the triumph of the dominant vision by asserting that social structure precludes the downward extension of professionalism that would be required by the application of the opposed vision to welfare administration. This interpretation rests on the view of class implicit in contemporary public law discourse.

At the center of this view stands the professional class. The professional class is distinguished from the class above it (the upper class) by relatively lesser wealth, power, and status, and from the classes below it (the working class and the poor) by relatively greater wealth, power, and status. It is distinguished from all the other classes by a distinctive ethical orientation toward work. This orientation is expressed in the premise of universality in Hegel's notion of the "universal class."[144] It views work as expressing and implementing values that rise above the competing ends of antagonistic individuals and groups. It repudiates the ideal of work as instrumental to the satisfaction of private ends or as a means of imposing one's will on the world and asserts an ideal of work as an intrinsically satisfying form of participation in the life of the community. It is this transcendent, universalistic orientation to work that requires and makes possible autonomy and responsibility in the organization of professional work.

This vision of class plays an important, though only partially explicit role in two prominent streams of contemporary legal thought: the legal process and the rights-and-principles schools. The legal process school emphasizes professionalism as part of the solution to the question of trust.[145] It proposes to secure the goals of social order through fair procedures, and considers professional decisionmakers an essential part of such procedures. People are said to accept the decisions of such decisionmakers in disputed cases in part because they have confidence that their professional status is a guarantee of fairness. The rights-and-principles school looks to the professional class as part of the solution to the problem of value. It proposes to make legal norms determinate by interpreting them in the context of the discursive practices of a particular community. Although the rights-and-principles writers are notoriously vague about the boundaries of the community they are talking about, these boundaries

144. G. HEGEL, *supra* note 93, at 188–93. For varying contemporary perspectives on the notion of a professional class, see E. BANFIELD, THE UNHEAVENLY CITY 48–54 (1970); H. GANS, THE URBAN VILLAGERS 229–62 (1962); A. GOULDNER, THE FUTURE OF INTELLECTUALS AND THE RISE OF THE NEW CLASS (1981); THE NEW CLASS? (B. Bruce-Briggs ed. 1980); Ehrenreich & Ehrenreich, *The Professional-Managerial Class*, in BETWEEN LABOR AND CAPITAL 15–45 (P. Walker ed. 1979).

145. *See* Wellington, *Common Law Rules and Constitutional Double Standards: Some Notes on Adjudication*, 83 YALE L.J. 221, 248–49 (1973); H. Hart & A. Sacks, *supra* note 116, at 117–78; Chayes, *supra* note 116, at 1307–08; Neuborne, *supra* note 116, at 1126.

Welfare System

seem to be located within the confines of the professional class.[146]

There is, however, a second premise in this view of the professional class, the premise of exclusivity. This premise holds that the distinctive experience of transcendence and universality involved in professional work is necessarily limited to a small minority, that the rest of society is necessarily left to work roles in which the immediate experience is the pursuit of self-interest or group interest (however much the role occupants may convince themselves that *in the long run* such pursuit serves universal ends). The argument from social structure asserts that the possibilities for the expansion of professionalism are subject to severe limits.

There are two types of explanation of these limits. One sees them as structures of hierarchical privilege protected by patterns of defense on the part of the privileged and of acquiescence on the part of the unprivileged so entrenched as to be immune to political challenge.[147] The other type of explanation sees the limits as functional adaptations to general constraints on social organization that could be altered only at the cost of leaving the society as a whole worse off. There are many variations on the functionalist explanation, some of which can be sampled in the recent literature lamenting the expansion of the federal judiciary.[148] There is, for example, the explanation of *cost*, which asserts that further professionalization would require too many resources to adequately educate workers and structure their work setting in a manner consistent with professional norms.[149] There is the explanation of *aptitude and character*, which asserts that professionalism depends on qualities of intelligence and fair-mindedness that are in short supply.[150] One version of this argument assumes that aptitude and character are innate and that everyone who has enough of them has already been recruited into the professional class. Another version assumes that at least character depends on childhood socialization and that lower class socialization handicaps people for professionalism by inculcating moral parochialism and an instrumental attitude toward work.[151] There is the argument from *size*, which asserts that the

146. *E.g.*, Fiss, *Objectivity and Interpretation*, 34 STAN. L. REV. 739, 746–47 (1982). The rights-and-principles writers show little interest in the beliefs of anyone other than legal professionals. Those who have investigated such beliefs have found important differences and discontinuities between the perspectives of those inside and those outside the professional culture. *See* F. PARKIN, CLASS INEQUALITY AND POLITICAL ORDER 79–102 (1971); Casper, *Having Their Day in Court: Defendant Evaluations of the Fairness of Their Treatment*, 12 LAW & SOC'Y REV. 237 (1978); McCloskey, *Consensus and Ideology in American Politics*, 58 AM. POL. SCI. REV. 361 (1964); Sarat, *Studying American Legal Culture: An Assessment of Survey Evidence*, 11 LAW & SOC'Y REV. 427, 435–41, 464–69, 471–77 (1977).

147. *Cf.* Ehrenreich & Ehrenreich, *surpa* note 144, at 5.

148. *See* H. FRIENDLY, *supra* note 117; McCree, *supra* note 117.

149. *See* Scalia, *The ALJ Fiasco—A Reprise*, 47 U. CHI. L. REV. 57 (1979).

150. *See* McCree, *supra* note 117, at 780, 782–783.

151. *See* E. BANFIELD, *supra* note 144, at 48–54; H. GANS, *supra* note 144.

collegiality and peer relations required by professionalism can be achieved only within a small group.[152] And there is the argument from *differential status and reward*, which asserts that professionalism is dependent on hierarchical status that would be diluted to the point of inefficacy by expansion: without differential status either the professional's motivation to perform would be diminished or she would lose the ability to inspire in others confidence in the validity of her decision.[153]

None of these arguments has ever been established or even systematically articulated, and none seems obviously correct on reflection. The privilege explanation usually turns out to be simply a *description* of the social structure coupled with an expression of vague skepticism about the possibility of changing it. The functional explanations tend to be more ambitious but not necessarily more plausible. The explanation of aptitude and character suffers from an inability to define the relevant aptitude or character and to measure its availability. This explanation is also challenged by evidence that people's moral and technical capacities vary significantly with the circumstances of their work-setting and are generally enhanced by conditions of responsibility and autonomy.[154] As for cost, it may be that the added cost of educating and equipping professional workers could be offset by reductions in the costs of supervision or by savings through the more flexible and efficient deployment of resources that professionalism might make possible. Moreover, to the extent that there is a scarcity of educational resources, it is partly a function of the fact that many occupational groups—the legal profession is one I am sure of—are vastly overeducated relative to the demands of their jobs; to the extent that the professionalization of the lower tier public work force could be accomplished by redistributing resources from the overeducated groups, there would be no net cost. The explanation of size encounters the difficulty that the American welfare state is already fragmented into programs and organizational structures of widely varying sizes and degrees of specializa-

152. *See* Schwartz, *The Reorganization of the Legal Profession*, 58 TEX. L. REV. 1269, 1278–79 (1980).

153. H. FRIENDLY, *supra* note 117, at 28–30.

154. *See* C. SABEL, WORK AND POLITICS: THE DIVISION OF LABOR IN INDUSTRY (1982); *see also* Scott, *supra* note 22 (effects of education on attitudes toward work among welfare workers).

As Paul Bator puts it:

> Competence and sensitivity are themselves not static phenomena. Conscientiousness, dedication, idealism, openness, enthusiasm, willingness to listen and learn . . . are at least to some extent evoked by a sense of responsibility, by the realization that one has been entrusted with a great and important task. I can think of nothing more subversive to the . . . inner sense of responsibility than the notion that, to the greatest possible extent, all the important shots will be called by someone else because we don't believe in his or her competence and sensitivity.

Bator, *The State Courts and Federal Constitutional Litigation*, 22 WM. & MARY L. REV. 605, 624–25 (1981). Bator is arguing here that state judges are qualified to determine federal constitutional claims, but the point is applicable to the role of the welfare worker as well.

tion; there is simply no reason to believe that whatever limits collegiality and peer relations impose on size could not be accommodated from among this broad variety of organizational structures. The explanation of differential status and reward appears to be contradicted by examples of lower status workers who seem to perform responsibly under conditions of autonomy[155] and by indications that the high status of judges does not prevent people adversely affected by their decisions from feeling dissatisfied with them.[156]

But the basic problem with the argument from social structure is not the implausibility of the premise of exclusivity, but its incompatibility with the premise of universality. This problem is reflected in the basic ambiguities of the jurisprudence of the legal process and rights-and-principles schools: In the legal process school, are the decisions of the professional decisionmakers effective because they are substantively correct or because people acquiesce in them regardless of their substantive validity? To assert that they are always or usually correct would be inconsistent with the fact, acknowledged by the legal process writers, of widespread disagreement within the society and the professional class.[157] But if the assertion is that they are effective merely because people acquiesce in them, then the legal process school seems to have betrayed the goals of efficiency, freedom, and fairness to the sanctification of mere stability and constituted power.[158] In the rights-and-principles literature, are the values articulated by the professional class merely the contingent norms of this particular group, or are they universal (in at least the sense that they cut across divisions in the society)?[159] If the answer is that the rights-and-principles literature has merely described the values of a particular class, then it has no plausible response to the question of value. But if the answer is that the values are universal, then the writers have to account for the fact that the values can be discovered only in the discourse of the professional class. The common problem of both approaches is the difficulty of reconciling the premise that direct experience of and responsibility to legal norms is possible only for a privileged minority with the premise that legal norms are universal in any meaningful sense.[160]

155. L. ROSS, *supra* note 139, at 24–135 (insurance adjusters).

156. Casper, *supra* note 146, at 240–49.

157. *See* Bator, *Finality in the Criminal Law and Federal Habeas Corpus for State Prisoners*, 76 HARV. L. REV. 441, 446-51 (1963).

158. *See* Gunther, *The Subtle Vices of the "Passive Virtues,"* 64 COLUM. L. REV. 1, 1–13 (1964).

159. *Compare* Soper, *Legal Theory and the Obligation of a Judge: The Hart/Dworkin Dispute*, 75 MICH. L. REV. 473 (1977) (Dworkin's rights and principles are descriptive accounts of practices of particular community) *with* Fried, *The Laws of Change: The Cunning of Reason in Moral and Legal History*, 9 J. LEGAL STUD. 335 (1980) (Dworkin's rights and principles are universal).

160. *See* K. Marx, *Critique of Hegel's Doctrine of the State*, in EARLY WRITINGS 100–16 (R. Livingstone & G. Benton trans. 1975) (arguing that Hegel's idea of universal class is self-

A recent response to this problem combines themes from the legal process and rights-and-principles schools in a theory of adjudication that emphasizes dialogue and participation.[161] As in the legal process school, fairness is conceived in terms of procedure, but procedure is conceived here as the arena of an ongoing substantive discourse of the type described by the rights-and-principles writers. By emphasizing the professional decisionmaker's duty to listen to the arguments advanced by the litigant and to explain her decision in a manner responsive to these arguments, this view suggests that the professional can mediate between the universalistic moral culture that is her special province and the concerns of ordinary citizens. For the citizen, the judicial proceeding is an initiation into the universalistic moral culture; for the professional, the citizen's participation is a safeguard against excessive differentiation of the universalistic culture from the concerns of civil society.

I think this view rests on a naive understanding of how people experience judicial proceedings.[162] But for present purposes, it is sufficient to emphasize how little the view promises, even within the framework of its own assumptions. The initiation it promises is merely a momentary ad hoc response to disputes that have found their way into the privileged forums of the professional decisionmakers. But few people ever enter these forums, and the factors that determine when and whether they do are to a large extent arbitrary in terms of the values of the universalistic moral culture. The setting in which most people, especially most poor people, confront the state is the bureaucratic setting of the lower tier public work force.

The argument from social structure against the downward expansion of the opposed vision thus has a depressing implication: At least for the poor, the experience of dignified, responsible, just treatment at the hands of the state must be a rare and random event. Except in those few and unpredictable moments when claims are precipitated into the privileged forums of the opposed vision, the experience of such people in their everyday dealings with the state must continue to be alienation and bewilderment.

### B. *Politics*

The political approach interprets the dominant vision as ideology. By ideology I mean discourse that tends to portray as functions of fixed social structure what are in fact contingent political choices. As I use the term, it

contradictory).

161. Fiss, *supra* note 116; Mashaw, *Administrative Due Process: The Quest for a Dignitary Theory*, 61 B.U. L. REV. 885 (1981).

162. *See* Simon, *The Ideology of Advocacy: Procedural Justice and Professional Ethics*, 1978 WIS. L. REV. 29, 94–99; Sarat, *supra* note 146, at 441, 466–67.

does not imply anything about the motivations of the people who engage in such discourse. Ideology is not necessarily propagated in bad faith; it is a kind of failed social theory. Nor do I mean to suggest that such discourse expresses the choices of a single class or group. Political choices typically reflect compromises or alliances among groups, and one use of ideology is to codify such compromises and alliances. The political interpretation of the dominant vision starts with the hypothesis that the liberal welfare jurisprudence of the 1960's and 1970's expresses such compromises and alliances. It proceeds by speculating about whether the groups involved—especially the liberal professional reformers and the lower-tier public work force—might have understood their interests and options in a way that made the reforms prescribed by the dominant vision seem a plausible political choice.

The political posture of the professional class toward the welfare state is framed by a tension or ambiguity in its relation to the upper class. On the one hand, the most important and lucrative market for professional services is the upper class. Yet, the upper class is a threat to the attainment of the ideal of universality and transcendence. It will generally be in the interest of the upper class to demand a degree of loyalty and subordination inconsistent with the professional ideal. And the more the profession as a whole is seen to be in the service of the upper class, the less plausible become the pretensions to serve universal interests. There are many strategies of accommodation to this situation (some involving exploitation of the upper class, some involving concessions to the other classes), but during some periods these strategies fail to prevent unease among large numbers of professionals and even rebellion by a few of them. Richard Hofstadter has identified the Progressive Era as a period in which professional aspirations fueled reformist politics;[163] the recent period of welfare legalism is another.

There is an important congruence between the expansion of the welfare state and the aspirations of the professional class. Since at least the New Deal, the national state has sought to mediate and to neutralize class antagonisms by integrating all classes into a national political process committed to universal norms. The professional class has a dual affinity for this effort: first, as an activity that respects its aspirations to universality, and second, as an alternative source of employment to the dominant class. The role envisioned for the state by the New Deal was precisely the role that Brandeis had earlier prescribed for the professionals[164]—broker of class compromise—and the New Deal activities created a strong demand

163. R. HOFSTADTER, THE AGE OF REFORM 131-73 (1955).
164. L. BRANDEIS, BUSINESS—A PROFESSION (1926).

for professional services. This affinity makes the professional class a potential ally of the lower classes when they make demands for the recognition and institutionalization of their interests in ways that expand the national state. The debates about the welfare system I have been discussing got underway during a period of such an alliance.

The liberal professional reformers of the 1960's sought both to expand the welfare system and to make it more responsive to the poor. They exercised their influence through the federal judiciary and the upper levels of the federal executive. From this perspective, the expanding corps of lower level service roles of somewhat ambiguous status presented them with a political choice analogous to one faced by some of the reforming monarchs of modern Europe.[165] The choice is between professionalizing and proletarianizing strategies of transformation of the state. In the professionalizing strategy, the reformer creates an organizational structure designed to foster autonomous, responsible activity by people socialized in the reformer's own perspective; in the proletarianizing strategy, the reformer creates an organizational structure designed to subject subordinates to her direct control. The appeal of the professionalizing strategy is that it promises to overcome some of the deficiencies of Weberian bureaucracy as an instrument of control and, by extending the reformer's own mode of life and work, to create valuable allies for her. The disadvantages are, first, that if the strategy fails to inculcate the reformer's perspective, organizational autonomy may be used in ways that will frustrate her ends; and, second, that the expansion of professional status dilutes the exclusivity of the positions and perhaps the privileges of the reformer and her present allies. Thus, one explanation for the embrace of the proletarian strategy by the liberal reformers of the 1960's is that downward professionalization might have seemed to pose unacceptable risks to their own positions.[166]

165. *See* R. WORTMAN, THE DEVELOPMENT OF A RUSSIAN LEGAL CONSCIOUSNESS (1976).

166. For the social workers the choice of reforming strategies involved distinctive considerations. On the one hand, the social work profession had long claimed public assistance as its province and had prescribed the integration of counseling and financial assistance. This position was premised on the notion that the personal problems of the poor were a function of their material condition. This premise had in turn inspired the view, traditional with an important segment of the profession, that the distinctive concerns of the profession were linked to the goals of redistributive social change. *See* Chambers, *An Historical Perspective on Political Action vs. Individual Treatment*, in PERSPECTIVES ON SOCIAL WELFARE 89-106 (P. Weinberger ed. 1969); Towle, *supra* note 15. On the other hand, financial eligibility tasks were the aspect of social work regarded as least prestigious and least integrated into the profession's academic paradigm, which, since the 1920's, has been drawn from psychology. Thus, for the social workers, the political compromise represented by the proletarianization strategy had a special significance. The profession retreated from its general redistributive political goals, ceded its influence over public assistance, and gave up the project of expanding downward. In return, it strengthened its claims to elite status by disencumbering itself of the tasks that were least prestigious and most difficult to rationalize in terms of its academic paradigm and by limiting its claims to a smaller, more clearly bounded segment of the public work force. *Cf.* Wyers, *Whatever*

Welfare System

A related explanation looks at the problem from the perspective of the lower-tier public work force. The roles this group occupies are not entirely the creatures of elite professionals; the workers themselves have participated in designing them. The choice between professionalizing and proletarianizing strategies of elite reform correspond to a choice between strategies of worker politics.

For the workers, the professionalizing strategy would have involved pursuit, not only of material reward and personal comfort, but of a part in interpreting the purposes and structure of the programs they administered. It would have involved attempts to interpret the public purposes of the programs in ways that linked workers' interests with the interests of the beneficiaries. It would also have involved appeals to these purposes against formality and organizational hierarchy. The most notable illustration of such a strategy in the recent history of the American welfare system is the one through which the Social Security ALJs (formerly "hearing examiners") have transformed themselves since World War II. The ALJs have long been a class-conscious group, politically active in support of reforms to increase their organizational autonomy and the status, reward, and educational requirements of their job. Their activity has been particularly vigorous in recent years—including a series of lawsuits against the Social Security Administration in opposition to its efforts to formalize eligibility criteria, to prescribe job performance in detail, to impose productivity standards, and to use reversal rates and quality control data for personnel purposes. In the course of these efforts, the ALJs have appealed to the notions of legality and organization of the opposed vision in a way that links their own interests with those of beneficiaries. They argue that autonomy and professional status are necessary for them to perform their duty to enforce the rights of claimants. Understanding this duty to require a complex, particularized judgment, they assert that its performance is compromised by hierarchical supervision, which is inevitably less sensitive to the needs of the particular case and undermines devotion to the goal of justice to the individual client.[167]

*Happened to the Income Maintenance Line Worker?*, 25 SOC. WORK 259 (1980) (ambivalent account of separation suggesting tradeoff between profession's broader political goals and security of professional status).

167. *See* Scalia, *supra* note 149, at 66; Macy, *The APA and the Hearing Examiner: Products of a Viable Political Society*, 27 FED. B.J. 351, 352–94 (1967); SUBCOMM. ON OVERSIGHT OF GOVERNMENT MANAGEMENT, *supra* note 110; SUBCOMM. ON SOCIAL SECURITY, H. COMM. ON WAYS & MEANS, SOCIAL SECURITY ADMINISTRATIVE LAW JUDGES: SURVEY AND ISSUE PAPER 1-3, 76-84, 111-17 (Comm. Print 1979).

The style of worker politics that links interests of the worker in autonomy and participation with the interests of the beneficiaries of their work has been legitimated by the courts in cases involving professional litigants. These decisions infer rights in the professionals from laws designed to protect the beneficiaries of their work. *See* Nash v. Califano, 613 F.2d 10 (2d Cir. 1980) (inferring right of "decisional independence" allowing ALJs to challenge administrative supervisory and productivity

The competing option of worker politics, the proletarian strategy, involved retreating from goals other than material reward and personal comfort. It involved a compromise with hierarchy in which formality was embraced as a shield against the demands of superiors. In this compromise, the workers relinquished their claims to participate in interpreting the goals of the program in return for a guarantee of some autonomy in pursuing private and material goals. Instead of developing the kinds of work protest exemplified by the ALJs based on appeals to program purposes, they fell back on conventional forms of protest such as strikes and slowdowns that disrupted the programs in ways that hurt beneficiaries. In effect, they exchanged the possibility of solidarity with claimants for the option of holding the interests of claimants hostage to their private demands.

To the workers, the professional strategy held the promise of a nobler and more satisfying life at work and of political solidarity with a wider segment of the society. But it was also a riskier strategy. It was a strategy that, if implemented broadly, would have made much greater redistributive demands on the society. And it was a strategy that would have depended on alliances with professionals and poor people from whom many of the new service workers were divided by ethnicity, education, and status, and whose reliability they might well have suspected.[168]

From the point of view of the liberal reformers' goal to make the system more responsive to the poor, the proletarian strategy had severe drawbacks. The dominant vision obscured the difficulties of translating influence over the upper levels of the system into control of a lower-tier work force alienated from the purposes of those at the top. Moreover, the liberal strategy depended on liberals retaining influence over the upper levels. When in fact liberal influence waned and control passed to conservatives relatively indifferent to beneficiary interests and more intent on curbing expenditures, the proletarian strategy was easily co-opted for quite different purposes. (To be sure, the proletarian strategy has some of the same disadvantages as a means of controlling expenditures that it has as a safe-

controls); *cf.* Griswold v. Connecticut, 381 U.S. 479, 481 (1965) (inferring right of medical professionals to challenge restrictions on practice from patients' privacy rights).

168. Thus, while the interpretation based on social structure sees admininistrative reform as in part a response to the economistic orientation of the work force, the political interpretation sees the economistic orientation of the work force as in part a response to administrative reform. The difference lies in the extent to which one sees the way people view their interests in work as given on the one hand or as a matter of politics on the other. My political interpretation of worker politics was inspired by conversations with workers in Massachusetts during 1979–1981. It does not purport to be anything more than a speculative hypothesis.

For an account of a strike involving an unsuccessful attempt by welfare workers to ally themselves with recipients and professionals, see Weber, *Paradise Lost: Or Whatever Happened to the Chicago Social Workers?*, in COLLECTIVE BARGAINING IN GOVERNMENT 163–77 (J. Loewenberg & M. Moskow eds. 1972).

guard of beneficiary interests, but the political liabilities of the alternative professionalizing strategy would have seemed even greater to the conservatives than to the liberals.) As the conservatives implemented the strategy in a way that reallocated enforcement resources away from beneficiary interests, its adverse consequences to recipients were exacerbated.

The course of administrative reform paralleled in some respects the larger political process by which broad segments of the working class came to see their interests as in conflict with those of the beneficiaries of welfare expansion, and by defecting from the progressive constituency of the Democratic Party, brought the expansion to a halt.[169] Much of the expansion of the 1960's took the form of institutional structures designed to link the federal government with the urban poor while bypassing state and local governments with strong working class representation.[170] For the most part, the expansion was financed through fiscal policies that a broad segment of the working class came to see as burdening them unfairly.[171] In one respect, the failure of administrative reform mirrors the failure of the broader program of welfare expansion: in each case, the ambitions of the liberal reformers were thwarted by the tendency of their program to alienate the working class.

If one adopts this political explanation of recent welfare jurisprudence, then the future prospects of the opposed vision would seem to depend on political factors, in particular, on the possibilities of reestablishing the New Deal alliance of professionals, workers, and the poor. From this perspective, an interesting feature of the opposed vision is its capacity to link the interests of the public work force in dignified, satisfying working conditions with the interests of the poor in dignified, responsible treatment by the welfare state.

### C. *The Ambiguity of Professional Culture*

There is a further objection to the opposed vision as an ideal of public administration. This objection focuses, not on the premise of exclusivity, but on the premise of universality. It denies that the public culture of the professional class has been or could be anything but an expression of the contingent views or interests of the professionals themselves or their allies or patrons. Although this objection rests on a powerful critique of professionalism, it remains to be seen whether it can be maintained against a

169. *See* F. PIVEN & R. CLOWARD, REGULATING THE POOR 348-410 (1971); D. MOYNIHAN, MAXIMUM FEASIBLE MISUNDERSTANDING (1969).

170. *See* Musgrave, *Theories of Fiscal Crisis: Notes on Fiscal Sociology*, in 1983 BROOKINGS PAPERS ON ECON. ACTIVITY 361, 383-88.

171. *See* Burnham, *The 1980 Earthquake: Realignment, Reaction, or What?*, in THE HIDDEN ELECTION 98-140 (T. Ferguson & J. Rogers eds. 1981).

version of professionalism that dispenses with the premise of exclusivity.

Most contemporary critiques of professional culture present an ambiguity. They both attack the culture and rely on it. This is particularly so of critiques that explicitly adopt the professions' norms in order to demonstrate how their members have betrayed them.[172] Even critics who attack the structure of professional doctrine often do so in order to transform rather than repudiate it.[173] And the more uncompromising critics who deny any normative status to professional doctrine have yet to show that they are capable of a plausible programmatic discourse that escapes reliance on the practices they reject.

There is a parallel ambiguity in critical accounts of professional practice and organization. On the one hand, the professions, even in their compromised state, provide evidence of the possibility of universalistic and altruistic commitment in public life and of autonomy and responsibility in work. On the other hand, they seem to institutionalize and rationalize illegitimate privilege and domination.

The case for the opposed vision suggests that the implausibility of the professional project lies less in its aspirations to universality than in the premise of exclusivity. This suggestion depends on at least two conditions. First, the tendency in the legal professional culture to criticize and transform hierarchical social relations in the name of the ideals of efficiency, freedom, and fairness would have to be developed even in the face of severe social strains; the countervailing tendency to qualify and sublimate these ideals in the name of social stability would have to be muted.[174] The less the culture feels bound to defer to the constraints of social hierarchy, the more plausible become its claims to be more than an apology for that hierarchy. Second, downward professionalization would have to mean, not simply exposure or indoctrination of new recruits in the currently prevailing doctrines of the professions, but the downward extension of the social circumstances associated with the limited but significant amount of trust that is currently accorded professionals: education, reward, status, collective work experience, peer culture, and work roles incorporating autonomy and responsibility. Expanding the boundaries of the professional class in this way would affect the development of professional doctrine. There is no guarantee that such development would vindicate the aspiration to universality. The hope that it would is grounded in the notion that the larger the range and number of people who participate directly in the professional culture (and the less differentiated the culture becomes from

172. *E.g.*, J. AUERBACH, UNEQUAL JUSTICE: LAWYERS AND SOCIAL CHANGE IN MODERN AMERICA (1976).
173. *See* Unger, *The Critical Legal Studies Movement*, 96 HARV. L. REV. 561, 576-83 (1983).
174. *Id.*

Welfare System

its surroundings), the stronger become its claims to universality.

The basic jurisprudential questions raised by the critique of the dominant vision turn on this possibility. The answer to the questions of value and trust and the response to the deficiencies of the Weberian vision of legality and organization—the problems of communication, supervision, alienation—all turn on some variation of the principle of social order through participation in a common culture.[175] This response to the deficiencies of Weberian formality and bureaucracy has been well known to American legal and social thought throughout this century. But lawyers have tended to mistake this theoretical insight for a practical achievement. They have alternated between the mistaken view that their own normative culture is shared throughout the society and the vain hope that the limitations of a culture common only to their own class could be cured through the readmission of formality and bureaucracy.

In fact, the solution of the common culture has never been anything more than a political prospect. The downward professionalization of public administration is a reform inspired by this prospect.

## Conclusion

The opposed vision of welfare administration could be implemented in many ways at varying levels of ambitiousness. For example, one modest reform would involve the abolition of the AFDC Quality Control system and its replacement with an expanded system of quasi-adjudicatory review. Review for all purposes would be superintended by an expanded corps of hearings officials.[176] Two changes in current practice could be made to remedy the problems that arise from the current hearing system's dependence on recipient initiation. First, in addition to cases initiated by recipients, review of a representative sample of cases could be administratively triggered.[177] Centrally triggered cases would be reviewed by an auditor and by either an ombudsman-type official charged with protecting the claimant's interests or a representative of the claimant's choosing. If the reviewers disagreed with each other or the worker who made the initial decision, the disagreement could be resolved by decision at a hearing in which all participate. Second, review could also be triggered by eligibility workers who disagreed with their supervisors about any eligibility de-

175. *See* Fuller, *Human Interaction and the Law*, in THE RULE OF LAW (R. Wolff ed. 1971).

176. The proposal contemplates that the hearing officers have a degree of organizational autonomy and professionalism comparable to the Social Security ALJs or the hearing officials in the more professionalized state appeals systems, such as that of the Massachusetts Welfare Department. Substantial reform would be required in many state systems to attain this condition.

177. For a discussion of one method of triggering cases for review, see J. MASHAW, C. GOETZ, F. GOODMAN, W. SCHWARTZ, P. VERKUIL & M. CARROW, *supra* note 123.

cision. There could be selective publication of hearing decisions and the workers would be taught to regard adjudicatory decisions as precedent to be followed in similar cases.

From the perspective of the opposed vision, this proposal has several virtues. It shifts a major part of the supervisory process to forums in which the contingencies of the particular case can be explored, in which both claimants and workers can participate and confront the decisionmaker, and in which the decisionmakers understand their roles as involving responsibility to both claimants and to the public. It involves a modest expansion in the part of the system that most closely approximates the ideal of the opposed vision (an expansion that would be accomplished by a shift of resources from the present quality control system).[178] Most importantly, it narrows (if only slightly) the gulf between regular eligibility work and the privileged process of review. By increasing the worker's participation in the review process and by prescribing that the worker attempt to apply the doctrine developed in that process to initial decisions, it encourages the worker to view the review process, with its commitment to complex judgment and respect for the claimant, as an integral extension of routine eligibility work. The more modest ambition of the reform is to increase the control of review procedures structured in accordance with the opposed vision; the less modest ambition is to change, however marginally, the way the eligibility workers view their own work and interests

178. An important issue that can only be mentioned briefly here concerns the extent to which the opposed vision depends on adversary representation. If the efficacy of the decisionmaker's role in the opposed vision requires adversary representation, then the applicability of this role to the task of deciding welfare claims in a non-adversary context would seem questionable. I think the opposed vision depends on adversary representation only to a limited extent.

Those who assert that adversary representation is essential presume that there is a high danger that the decisionmaker will have preconceptions or interests adverse to the claimant. *See* J. HANDLER, *supra* note 24, at 3-25. The argument above suggests that this danger is not inevitable, that it is a function of the way decisionmakers are recruited and socialized and the way their roles are structured. In particular, the argument suggests that the danger could be reduced most effectively through downward professionalization. On the other hand, if my argument is wrong, it is not at all clear that adversary representation can provide a more satisfactory response to the danger. The partisans of adversary representation have never been able to show that it overcomes bias, rather than simply introducing new biases or confusion; their argument rests on faith that opposing biases neutralize each other through some mechanism they cannot explain. *See* Damaska, *Presentation of Evidence and Factfinding Precision*, 120 U. PA. L. REV. 1083, 1091-95 (1975); Simon, *supra* note 162, at 75-83. Moreover, adversary representation displaces the problem of trust and bias onto the role of the representative; given skepticism toward the professional solution, this role may seem as problematical as that of the impartial decisionmaker. *See* Skolnick, *Social Control in the Adversary System*, 11 J. CONFLICT RESOLUTION 52 (1967).

My illustrative reform proposes to extend adversary representation to cases other than those appealed by claimants, not in deference to the assertion that the opposed vision requires adversary representation, but in recognition of how very limited a step toward the opposed vision such a reform would be. One of the advantages of adversary representation in the current system is that it is the principal form of decisionmaking in which the system tolerates complex judgment, decentralization, and professionalism. A more ambitious and thoroughgoing reform of the initial decisionmaking role would reduce the importance of the expansion of adversary representation.

by encouraging them to see themselves as autonomous, responsible participants in the implementation of a public program designed to alleviate individual need.

More thoroughgoing reforms would require more adventurous decentralization and redistribution of wealth, power, and status. Whether one views such reforms as serious options depends on whether one adopts the perspective of social structure or the perspective of politics on the current limitations of the system, and, from the latter perspective, the course of future political struggle over the system.

This kind of speculation about the possibilities for the progressive transformation of public administration or the welfare system may seem hopelessly utopian in a time when conventional perceptions about the range of political possibility seem steadily narrowing. But to write off such possibilities is to abandon hope for the vindication of our most ambitious and most plausible notions of the ideal of law.

# [17]

# Discretion in Social Welfare: The Uneasy Position in the Rule of Law

**Joel F. Handler†**

Prior to the routinization and bureaucratization of public welfare, the system could be loosely described as discretionary, professional, and decentralized. In general, eligibility was not clear-cut; budgets were individually determined. But even in those days, there were rules. Professionalization was the ideal, but most workers were in fact not professionals. And there were efforts at centralization at both the federal and state levels. Certainly as compared to the present, however, the public assistance programs had far more play.

What was that system like? Then, as now, there was great variety, but some generalizations can be made. Wisconsin was a benign, liberal system. Basic grants were relatively generous, there was an elaborate system of special grants to meet both emergency and rehabilitative goals, and there was a considerable degree of professionalism. In practice, however, the system was quite routinized. The special needs program was not utilized in any significant amount; it depended, for the most part, on client initiative and clients lacked information or were hesitant to ask. The caseworkers, a shifting sea of people who used their public assistance jobs as way stations, were not particularly interested in spending more agency resources or engaging in more paperwork. At that time, home visits were mandatory, but, for the overwhelming majority of recipients, the visit was pleasant and attitudes toward the caseworker were positive. For the most part, these were friendly, non-threatening social calls. But in the rare situation in which caseworkers did have control over something that the clients wanted, then negative feelings arose—feelings of dependency and coercion.[1]

The next example comes from Professor Mashaw's empirical work in Virginia, but is a story that has been found many times over in many parts of the country. These are the depressing tales of refusals to take

† Vilas Research Professor of Law, University of Wisconsin.

1. J. HANDLER & E. HOLLINGSWORTH, THE "DESERVING POOR": A STUDY OF WELFARE ADMINISTRATION 119-28 (1971) (Wisconsin case study). Susan Sheehan's story of a Puerto Rican family on welfare illustrates most of these points. The mother enjoyed the caseworkers' visits. The workers (there were many changes) were pleasant, young, college-educated women, who did not know very much, but were nice to chat with. However, when the mother needed something—in her case, permission to move—her relationship with the workers became dominating, hostile, and ugly. S. SHEEHAN, A WELFARE MOTHER 19-24, 60-66 (1976).

applications, harrassment of applicants and recipients, imposition of crude moralisms, midnight raids, threats to take away children. Protective rules were flouted with impunity. This is the story of racism, sexism, and traditional, long-standing hostility toward the "undeserving" poor.[2]

The third example involves the "welfare mess." Again, our time period is before the conservative reaction to welfare. In the large city departments, the offices simply became overwhelmed with numbers. Administration became chaotic, arbitrary, random. The concept of individual treatment broke down; many recipients experienced routinization, while many others got lost in the bedlam of the offices. Almost none had the professional recipient-caseworker relationship contemplated in the program.[3]

## I.

These stories are familiar, but what are the underlying reasons and what implications do they have for the problems that we are now discussing? One could, of course, find many causes contributing to the manner in which large public programs developed, but I would like to stress three: volume, values, and the distribution of wealth and power. Volume need not detain us very long. It is a brutal fact of the welfare state. In the 1930's, we thought that welfare (public assistance) would wither away. Now, we have become reconciled to the fact that vast numbers of people in our society, as presently organized, will need financial and other assistance. This is especially true for the client group on which we focus: female-headed households. Volume is the cardinal enemy of discretion, professional judgment, individualization; heavy caseloads force routinization. All programs, if we are to be at all realistic, must deal with the problem of workload.

The second cause is far more important: Values and attitudes toward the poor are varied, long-standing, and greatly affect how the poor are treated. Society has always distinguished between the deserving and undeserving poor, those whose poverty is blameless and those who are blameworthy. In a prior age, the blind, the halt, and the lame were in the former category; those who could work but failed were in the latter. Today, the aged and the disabled have joined the former, but the non-

2. *See, e.g.*, Mashaw, *Welfare Reform and Local Administration of Aid to Families with Dependent Children in Virginia*, 57 VA. L. REV. 818 (1971); Reich, *Midnight Welfare Searches and the Social Security Act*, 72 YALE L.J. 1347 (1963). An interesting contemporary example concerns the enforcement of criminal cohabitation statutes. The man-in-the-house rules were declared invalid by the Supreme Court in King v. Smith, 392 U.S. 309 (1968), and Lewis v. Martin, 397 U.S. 552 (1970), but the cohabitation statutes are enforced by local prosecutors. The choices offered in the plea bargain are to marry, to move out, or to get off welfare. Fineman, *Law and Changing Patterns of Behavior: Sanctions on Non-Marital Cohabitation*, 1981 WIS. L. REV. 275, 289-97.

3. Lipsky, *Bureaucratic Disentitlement in Social Welfare*, 58 SOC. SCI. REV., Mar. 1984, at 3.

aged—the childless adults, and the female-headed households—are still the undeserving. It is not only the failure of work that draws the community's hostility; fueling the furies are race, sex, and various forms of deviant behavior and life style.[4]

Attitudes toward the poor are reflected in the organization and structure of programs. For pensioners, the Social Security system is federal, rule-bound, relatively evenhanded in its administration, and with little reported hassle. Similarly, now that the aged poor have passed the line from undeserving to deserving, their progam—Supplemental Security Income—which in the 1920's bristled with moralistic conditions, is also now federalized, relatively condition-free, and evenhanded. But programs for the undeserving are very different. They are state and local, discretionary, decentralized, and subject to a great many moralistic and punitive practices. In addition to the Aid to Families with Dependent Children (AFDC) program discussed by Professor Simon, I am referring to General Assistance, and state and local emergency and special needs programs. The one exception to this pattern is the food stamps program, which has its own special history.

In sum, the organizational and structural arrangements of the public assistance programs are not accidental. Instead, they are profoundly affected by views on how to regulate deviant behavior in this country—the undeserving poor have always been considered deviant.[5]

The final cause of the ills of public assistance programs is the distribution of wealth and power. One can never forget that the people we are talking about are extremely dependent. They are ill-prepared to effectively participate in public programs, and, in particular, to understand the procedural systems designed to secure benefits and rights for them. The bureaucracy has control over the information, the resources, the staying power, the power of retaliation; workers, even if well-meaning, are pressed for time, short of money, and, in all honesty, feel that they know what is best for the clients. Discretion, in its lawful, positive sense (as distinguished from Professor Mashaw's examples from Virginia), implies, at the minimum, a discussion, a dialogue, a bargain of some sorts, a minimal sharing of power. But how are the poor, the really dependent poor, to participate in these decisions? And if they cannot cope when the administration of the program is benign and supporting, imagine their situation

4. *See* J. HANDLER, REFORMING THE POOR: WELFARE POLICY, FEDERALISM, AND MORALITY 138-41 (1972); J. PATTERSON, AMERICA'S STRUGGLE AGAINST POVERTY 1900-1980, at 99-126 (1981); Rosenheim, *Vagrancy Concepts in Welfare Law*, in LAW OF THE POOR 187 (J. tenBroek ed. 1966).

5. *See* J. HANDLER & E. HOLLINGSWORTH, *supra* note 1, at 33-37; J. HANDLER, *supra* note 4, at 138; J. HANDLER & M. SOSIN, LAST RESORTS: EMERGENCY ASSISTANCE AND SPECIAL NEEDS PROGRAMS IN PUBLIC WELFARE (1983).

when it is hostile, abusive, and vindictive.

The old system of public assistance was predicated on individualism, professionalism, and decentralization, but the caseload and working conditions forced routinization at best, and chaos and arbitrariness more often. In this situation, hostile attitudes toward the undeserving poor, combined with extreme dependency, led to widespread abuses.

## II.

It was against this depressing background that liberals attempted to reform welfare. The liberals sought to attack the three problems of volume, values, and distribution. To deal with the problem of volume, they pressed for the routinization of the welfare grant—called the consolidated or flat grant—based on the concept of horizontal equity.[6] Advocates of horizontal equity recognized that concepts of equality of treatment ultimately depended on arbitrary inclusions and exclusions, but their central animating principle was that in light of the great arbitrariness and chaos of the welfare mess, more equality could be achieved through rough measures than through individualized treatment. But in doing so, they failed to pay enough attention to the need for emergency assistance to help those who could not get by on the flat grant.[7]

The second issue, the corrosive hostility toward the underserving poor, was addressed through a profound change in our legal culture, where relationships with government were reconceived from privileges to rights. Instead of discretionary decisions, officials could work out their own and the community's hostilities, citizens would be protected by substantive and procedural rules; they would be rights-bearing citizens, not supplicants. It was a re-conception of the poor; they were not deviant, they were not in need of rehabilitation. They needed income, not social services.[8]

The third issue, the distribution question, was to be handled by providing a full array of procedural protections to vindicate substantive rights, and legal and other advocacy services.[9]

The liberal program did not work out; maybe it was doomed from the start. Instead, the conservative approach carried the day. The flat grant did become nationwide, but grant levels (particularly in AFDC) were

6. Actually, the trend toward the consolidated grant had been established in the prior decade because of the workload pressure.

7. The development of the consolidated grant, its ideology, and its limitations, are discussed in J. HANDLER & M. SOSIN, *supra* note 5, at 23-28.

8. Handler, *Controlling Official Behavior in Welfare Administration*, in LAW OF THE POOR, *supra* note 4, at 155, 157-58; Reich, *The New Property*, 73 YALE L.J. 733, 734-39 (1964).

9. J. HANDLER, E. HOLLINGSWORTH & E. ERLANGER, LAWYERS AND THE PURSUIT OF LEGAL RIGHTS 185-89 (1978); Cahn & Cahn, *The War on Poverty: A Civilian Perspective*, 73 YALE L.J. 1317, 1344-52 (1964).

The Yale Law Journal Vol. 92: 1270, 1983

kept low, and only pitiful amounts of money went into special needs and emergency assistance programs. The result has been the rising demand on private charity—the food lines, the shelters. Legal services and other advocacy resources, never sufficient for the task, have been seriously curtailed. Negative attitudes toward the undeserving poor have been fueled; the current conservative policy is to further segregate and categorize, to increase the severity of the work test and of other conditions for receiving public assistance for this class. Then, in further efforts to reduce costs, the administrative practices that Professor Simon has described have been introduced. I agree with his description, but would add two additional comments: first, the utter chaos that one witnesses in the public assistance offices—the crowds, the waiting, the shouting, the maze of cubicles, the forms, the fear and resignation of the applicants, and the anger and frustration of the workers; second, that by forcing public assistance recipients to supplement their welfare grants by resorting to General Assistance and private charity—where available—the recipients are now confronting the most discretionary, moralistic public and private programs, in which there are virtually no legal protections.

## III.

These are the realities of the administration of public assistance for the undeserving. What happened? What went wrong with the liberal program? Was it a failure of implementation or a failure in concept as well? One side of the story is familiar—the conservative takeover and the distortion of liberal ideals. But was this outcome inevitable?

As E.P. Thompson reminds us, any system of law in a society of great maldistributions of wealth and power will be suspect.[10] We have many prominent examples. Our streets are filled with confused and pitiful wanderers who are not considered dangerous to themselves and others, and teenagers who, for whatever reason, no longer find home tolerable. Was it wrong or misconceived to insist that these people no longer remain locked in dungeons or red-brick institutions even though the liberals could not carry through and provide for community services?[11] The answer is not clear.

Similar questions could be raised about the history of welfare reform. Faced with the arbitrariness, the abuses, and the randomness of the welfare system, was it wrong to press for horizontal equity, entitlements, legal services—in short, the rule of law? Was it wrong to think of the poor

10. E.P. THOMPSON, WHIGS AND HUNTERS: THE ORIGIN OF THE BLACK ACT 258-69 (1975).

11. The story of the mentally ill is well known. For the deinstitutionalization of juvenile status offenders, see NEITHER ANGELS NOR THIEVES: STUDIES IN DEINSTITUTIONALIZATION OF STATUS OFFENDERS (J. Handler & J. Zatz eds. 1982).

as rights-bearing citizens entitled to the same procedural regularities as other citizens?

Events turned out badly in AFDC, mental health, for status offenders. One could name many other programs as well. But why? The liberals would blame the conservatives. Professor Simon apparently feels that the liberal program (the "dominant vision") is conceptually flawed; if not responsible for the transformation of public welfare, it helped pave the way. Most of the horror stories that he recounts, however, are the results of the zeal of the Reagan Administration. One can hardly blame the liberals for the current excesses.

The social reforms in public assistance were intimately connected to the broader changes in our legal culture starting with the civil rights movement of the mid-1950's and early 1960's. The ideology of that movement stretches all the way back to the foundations of liberalism. The liberal vision viewed man as autonomous and in an adversarial, conflictual relationship with the state. Under the rising market economy of the seventeenth and eighteenth centuries, man pursued his individual interests free from governmental restraints.[12] The role of law was to protect the individual from the sovereign, to provide order and security in a competitive society. Neutral principles of law applied by an independent judiciary would curb the discretionary authority of the rulers; they, too, would be subject to the rule of law. Absolute monarchy ceased to the extent that law became absolute. In Nonet and Selznick's terms, law became autonomous.[13] Through the use of autonomous law, rights would be enforced by reducing the discretionary powers of government. Government would be subject to law.

There is still a great deal to be said in favor of the liberal vision. Think of the Social Security retirement system. Despite its size, as far as I know, it is a relatively well-run, smoothly operating program. Would we want that system to be based on standards, decentralization, and profession rather than on rules, centralization, and routinization? Voter registration in the South used to be based on "organic social norms"; one of the great, successful social reform efforts in recent decades has been the transformation of that system from discretion to rules.[14] We witnessed a similar struggle in school desegregation. Other examples could be given. Professor Simon thinks that most of social order depends on the law not being enforced. Are we describing the same elephant? It seems to me that large

12. C. MACPHERSON, THE POLITICAL THEORY OF POSSESSIVE INDIVIDUALISM: HOBBES TO LOCKE 209-10 (1962).

13. P. NONET & P. SELZNICK, LAW AND SOCIETY IN TRANSITION: TOWARD RESPONSIVE LAW 53-54 (1978).

14. The reform effort in voting is described in J. HANDLER, SOCIAL MOVEMENTS AND THE LEGAL SYSTEM: A THEORY OF LAW REFORM AND SOCIAL CHANGE 103-53 (1978).

areas of society are subject to relatively clear rules (both public and private); there is a vast amount of law abidingness and regularity.

The point, I think, is that some areas lend themselves to legal and bureaucratic routinization, while other do not. They do not because of the changed role of government. Liberal legalism has failed to take account of this change, and this, at least on a conceptual level, has contributed to the trends that Professor Simon has described. Let me explain.

The modern welfare state has changed the relationship of the citizen to the state. Instead of the old liberal vision of the individual asserting his independence from the state, we now see interdependence. We see relationships that are both continuous and discretionary—education, health, mental health, parts of welfare, social services, and so on.

The result of this change is that large numbers of citizens, of necessity, have to deal with the discretionary powers of officials on a more or less continuous basis, but, because of the maldistribution of wealth and power, they lack the capacity to deal with government in these situations. The result is familiar. Discretion becomes professionally or bureaucratically dominating. There is a loss of both substantive and procedural rights.

The liberal legalism vision of the relationship of the citizen to the state is individualistic, conflictual, adversarial. It seeks to achieve the values of individualism—autonomy, dignity, responsibility—through the assertion of rights vindicated in courts of law. This is the ideology of the legal rights revolution. But in areas where the social relationship between the citizen and the state is discretionary and continuous, the legal rights approach has not succeeded. It has failed conceptually and empirically.

The conceptual failure lies in that the situation calls for continuity and consensus whereas liberal legalism emphasizes a discontinuous, adversarial conflict. The empirical failure lies in the distribution of wealth and power. The bureaucracy has the information, the resources, the staying power, and because of the continuing relationship, the power of retaliation. Legal services and laws are not sufficient to overcome this imbalance. The empirical results of the operation of due process procedures in social welfare confirm these results. In many systems, including AFDC, procedural rights are routinely subverted by the bureaucracy. The harsh, negative values and attitudes toward the poor, the minorities, the weak, the deviant still work their way. The burdens of asserting the rule of law, especially in the discretionary, continuous relationship, are just too great for the vast majority of the poor.[15]

15. There is a large empirical literature documenting this point. *See, e.g.*, D. BAUM, THE WELFARE FAMILY AND MASS ADMINISTRATIVE JUSTICE 1-13 (1974); J. HANDLER, PROTECTING THE SOCIAL SERVICE CLIENT 47-69 (1979); Kirp, Buss & Kuriloff, *Legal Reforms of Special Education: Empirical Studies and Procedural Proposals*, 62 CALIF. L. REV. 40, 117-23 (1974).

Comment on Simon

Liberal legalism expresses our deepest ideals of individualism, freedom, and social ordering. In many areas, both historically and today, it has served us well, and in my opinion, will continue its vital, humanistic role. The inadequacy of liberal legalism is that it has tried to either stamp out discretion or control it through the adversarial assertion of legal rights, and this appproach is inappropriate for certain areas.[16]

Professor Simon would have us abandon liberal legalism altogether, in favor of standards, decentralization, and profession. But because he has not addressed the fundamental problems of volume, values, and distribution, his proposals are unsatisfactory. We are dealing with massive numbers of people and claims. While one should not reject proposals out of hand during the present period of economic stringency, we will never be in a world of unlimited resources, especially administrative resources for public welfare. It is always going to be a world of relative scarcity. At the minimum, then, one must pick and choose. There are large areas of public welfare that do lend themselves to routinization, where rules are efficacious, not perfect but reasonably satisfactory for most cases. In those areas, rules are preferable to a discretionary system of standards and decentralization.

A central, preliminary question is to determine which areas lend themselves to routinization and which areas require discretion. What are the criteria for deciding appropriateness? The next line of inquiry is to structure procedures for both routinization and discretion that will further the basic values of a liberal society.

While the liberal legal tradition founders over discretion, Professor Simon goes too far the other way. Without addressing the problems of volume, values, and the distribution of wealth and power, the direction he proposes (which has been tried in many situations) poses great dangers. He asserts that his system—the original understanding of the New Deal—was never tried; in fact, it was tried. It was the system prior to the legal rights revolution. In some areas of the country, it worked moderately well, but it also led to the widespread, serious abuses that became so familiar. Standards, professionalism, and decentralization foundered on the corrosion of volume, values, and power.

16. There is a question of whether some aspects of the legal rights changes in our culture could be characterized as "autonomous law" or "responsive law." Nonet and Selznick define responsive law as emphasizing purposiveness and participation, which is the thrust of much of public interest law. P. NONET & P. SELZNICK, *supra* note 13, at 73-78; *see* B. WEISBROD, J. HANDLER & N. KOMESAR, PUBLIC INTEREST LAW: AN ECONOMIC AND INSTITUTIONAL ANALYSIS 457-59 (1978). There was also a purposive and participatory aspect to welfare reform, but, by and large, I think that the dominant movement was toward the development of legally enforceable rights through the application of formal due process procedures. This movement was closer to autonomous than responsive law. *See* Teubner, *Substantive and Reflexive Elements in Modern Law*, 17 LAW & SOC'Y REV. 239 (1983).

Volume will, of necessity, produce routinization of practices. In a discretionary system, such practices will be unwritten. Thus, there will be even greater problems of indeterminacy and disparities in access to information. Standards and professionalism exacerbate the problems caused by society's values and attitudes towards the poor. First, there is at least some law abidingness in our society and rules influence some behavior in some situations. This restraint is lessened in a regime of standards (let alone organic social norms).

Second, the professions do not have an enviable record in fulfilling values of individualism.[17] For example, the queen of the professions, medicine, is paternalistic in the extreme. It is solely the physician who makes the judgment as to what is in the best interests of the patient. The focus is strictly on outcomes, not on the decisionmaking process. Now it is true that there is a movement in medical ethics to change this approach, to move toward a balance between professional and patient autonomy and responsibility, to try to achieve genuine informed consent, but the movement's philosophy has not been accepted by the medical profession.

The training and orientation of professionals emphasizes their scientific expertise, that they have superior knowledge and judgment. And they are under time constraints as well. Professionals, whether in organizations or not, are busy, they are instrumental, and feel that ultimately they will be making the decision anyway.

In addition, the unequal distribution of power encourages professional domination. The poor and the near poor are at a considerable disadvantage in dealing with professionals. They often have feelings of insecurity, fears of imposing themselves, of taking up valuable time, of feeling stupid. Many legal services lawyers and physicians, as well as other professionals, who are fully committed to dialogue and patient autonomy complain of the frustrations in trying to get clients to take responsibility for their decisions. The inexorable social relation is that of *dependency*, and this fact casts serious doubt on the prospects of approaching the values of individualism in a regime of standards, decentralization, and profession. The only hope offered is that the professionals (officials) will change their ways. That is a thin reed; something more must be provided.

How, then, should we think about the issue of discretion in social welfare programs? People in roughly equal positions have no problems with discretion; they bargain, and for both parties to the bargain there is auton-

17. For medicine, see Katz, *Informed Consent—A Fairy Tale?: Law's Vision*, 39 U. PITT. L. REV. 137, 168-69 (1977). For mental health, see Rapapport, *In Praise of Paradox: A Social Policy of Empowerment over Prevention*, AM. J. COMMUNITY PSYCHOLOGY 1, 15-21 (1981). For social work, see R. LUBOVE, THE PROFESSIONAL ALTRUIST 118-24 (1965); J. GALPER, THE POLITICS OF SOCIAL SERVICES 31-36 (1975). For law, see Spiegel, *Lawyering and Client Decisionmaking: Informed Consent and the Legal Profession*, 128 U. PA. L. REV. 41 (1979).

omy, dignity, and responsibility. But the kind of rough equality that is necessary for this kind of relationship will not be achieved through the Legal Services Corporation or any other program of client resources in the likely future. As a realistic matter, the issue of discretion has to be faced in a world of dependency. This means paying more attention to structures and incentives to encourage and support the changes in attitudes that are necessary to make discretionary decisions compatible with liberal values.

First, let me make some suggestions in what I call mixed areas, where there has to be both routinization and discretion. The example I have in mind is public assistance. There, large areas, of necessity, have to be routinized. Volume alone dictates this result, but there also are affirmative reasons. There is considerable evidence that many people are comfortable with an adequate basic grant. (I emphasize adequate, because this research was done in a different time, and certainly these results would no longer be applicable when grants continue to decline in real terms.) Such people prefer to live their lives with a minimum of contact with government and take pride in their ability to manage, pretty much as they did before assistance. Now I do not want to exaggerate this point. There may be a sense of false pride, feelings of stigma, lack of information, and real suffering. Certainly, there is a problem of lack of expressed dissatisfaction based on lack of awareness of opportunities.[18] It is also true, however, that there are people who do want to get along on their own terms.

But this, of course, is not the whole problem. Although considerable areas of public assistance can be handled in a routinized way, there are also large areas where discretionary determinations have to be made. This is especially true for emergencies and special needs. Public assistance recipients run out of money because of unforeseen events (for example, diabetes), or because of mismanagement (a problem not confined to the poor, as all of us well know). A system of public assistance has to provide for individual, discretionary decisions to handle these emergencies and special needs.

Today, in an era of cutbacks and harshness toward the most vulnerable of our society, the bottom line public assistance programs are a disaster. The basic grants have been flattened and reduced dramatically in real terms; this is especially true of AFDC (although the effect has been mitigated somewhat by food stamps). But no attention has been paid to the emergency assistance and special needs programs. The programs that exist

18. For example, there appears to be a persistent problem in the take-up rate of the Supplemental Security Income program. Some who do not apply are close to the eligibility line, and the small amount of benefit might not be worth the cost, but this group by no means accounts for the discrepancy between potential eligibility and actual enrollment. Part of the explanation is that there are difficult problems of communication with the elderly poor. *See* J. HANDLER & M. SOSIN, *supra* note 5, at 237-42.

are extremely small, limited to a few items that do not involve "moral hazard," and most public assistance recipients have to rely on whatever General Assistance might have to offer, or on private charity. And, as already noted, the full force of society's negative attitudes toward the undeserving poor is manifest in this part of public and private assistance.[19]

A major failure of the liberal reformers was not to recognize the importance of maintaining a discretionary system for emergencies and special needs along with a system of entitlements. The failure is not confined to the United States. At the end of World War II, when the British installed the Beveridge reforms, the strong emphasis was on a system of entitlements with a basic, minimum floor. The vision of the government was that the poor were like everyone else, except that they lacked sufficient income resources. The concepts of discretion, professional assistance, and decentralization lost favor because they carried connotations that the poor were somewhat deviant and needed rehabilitation. But special needs and emergencies arise in real life, regardless of the vision of political leaders, and over time, so many recipients also received some form of discretionary assistance that on three separate occasions the entire system had to be overhauled. Despite this experience, the British still resist the idea that a bottom line public assistance program has to be both routinized and discretionary. They still insist that a large, massive program can only be fair if it is completely routinized.[20]

The first step toward creating a desirable mixed system is to recognize the importance of discretion, think about it constructively instead of as a necessary evil, and then design structures and incentives to make sure that it works properly and is capable of being monitored. I cannot go into details here, but will suggest that it may be that separate organizational structures, even private structures, would be desirable, that many items for special needs and emergencies can be prescribed by rules, and that in general professional assistance may not be necessary or desirable.[21] Nonetheless, there still will remain the trouble spots. In particular, people will run out of money and need additional funds for items that were supposed to be covered by the basic grant—for example, rent, utilities, food, clothing. This happens all the time, but, of course, will occur far more frequently during times like the present. The English call this "double payments" and they raise the most difficult problems. Administrators fear the runaway quality of these demands and the disincentives to budget. The

19. *See id.* at 241.
20. For a description of the British experience, see *id.* at 215-35.
21. *See* J. Handler, "Proportional" vs. "Creative" Justice—Discretionary Benefits in Income-Maintenance Programs: The British Supplementary Benefits Scheme (Inst. for Research on Poverty, Univ. of Wisconsin, Discussion Paper No. 603-80, 1980).

public and other recipients think it unfair that they have to get along on their grants when others are rewarded for either negligence or fraud. Nevertheless, the problem persists, and needs have to be met.

It would be primarily in this area that special units should be created, equipped with a high degree of professional training, operating under standards. The units would have to be decentralized so that they could operate flexibly and efficiently. In addition to helping these people, the demands made on these offices (as well as the other emergencies and special needs) should be viewed as a window on the operation of the basic program and other social and economic conditions facing the poor. This is where shortages in housing, rises in fuel prices and other necessities will appear. It will also indicate malfunctions in administration of the basic program. It will identify families that need professional help.[22]

There is another area where discretion is also needed. In thinking about the inadequacies of the routinized welfare system, we tend to focus on the recipient who comes for help, but we know that there are others who need help and do not ask. The problem is probably most acute with the elderly on public assistance. In England, for example, the elderly poor can have extra heating grants for the asking, but many do not ask and suffer. There are many reasons for the failure to ask, but to get them to ask is not simply a matter of providing information. Studies have shown that requests will only be made after intensive social work with a fairly high per capita administrative cost.

One of the curious ironies about emergency assistance and special needs programs is that the intense opposition to them seems to be out of proportion to their costs. In the United States, such programs are small and haphazard, so costs are not very relevant, but in England, where extensive programs did develop, they never accounted for more than about five to six percent of the total public assistance payments budget.[23] Although roundly criticized as being administratively intensive, the administrative costs of these programs were comparable to those of their routinized counterparts. Nevertheless, discretionary programs are severely attacked from both the right and the liberal professional reformers. The right's attack is predictable. The liberal reformers insist that discretion is inconsistent with the ideal of rights-bearing citizens and that a large-scale public assistance

22. The fair hearing system can also be used as a window on the operation of the program, but again, one has to pay attention to structures and incentives. In Wisconsin, state district directors used to use fair hearing requests to help spot weaknesses in county administration. Handler, *Justice for the Welfare Recipient: Fair Hearings in AFDC—The Wisconsin Experience*, 43 SOC. SERV. REV. 12, 28-32 (1969). For a later use of negotiators, which contrary to state expectations increased the number of hearing requests, see Project, *Procedural Due Process and the Welfare Recipient: A Statistical Study of AFDC Fair Hearings in Wisconsin*, 1978 WIS. L. REV. 145.

23. J. HANDLER & M. SOSIN, *supra* note 5, at 220-25.

program cannot be both fair and discretionary.

The truth, of course, is that regardless of the liberal program, necessity requires a discretionary element. The question is whether this need will be openly acknowledged and programs restructured according to decent, humane values or, as in the United States, the public assistance recipients will be thrown to the mercies of General Assistance and private charity. But to bring the discretionary system out of the closet certainly does not imply that the routinization of public assistance has to be scrapped and the whole system reconverted into standards, decentralization, and profession.

## IV.

I come now to the final point, that is, how to structure a discretionary decisionmaking process that reaches intelligent substantive decisions and, at the same time, enhances the autonomy, dignity, and responsibility of the participants.

I start with a concrete example in an area where I am currently working—special education. Special education decisions are discretionary and continuous. They are discretionary in the sense that we really do not know the causes for why children do not do well at school, or what to do for these children.[24] Thus, the facts are indeterminate. The statute—the Education for All Handicapped Children Act[25]—is also indeterminate; it merely guarantees the right to an "appropriate" education.[26] The decision is continuous in that the relationship lasts during the school life of the child.

Growing out of the changes in our legal culture previously described, the substantive right to an appropriate education is coupled with extensive procedural safeguards. An informed consent form has to be signed by the parent or guardian before *every* formal decision is taken by the school—the identification and selection of the child for testing, the evaluation conference and decision, the placement, the re-evaluation. If the parent objects, he is entitled to two administrative hearings—one at the school district level and one at the state level, and there is judicial review.[27]

Nationwide, the procedural system, for the most part, is a failure. The school system has the information, the professional expertise, and is sad-

24. See *Placement in Public Education: Historical Developments and Current Procedures*, in PLACING CHILDREN IN SPECIAL EDUCATION: A STRATEGY FOR EQUITY 23 (K. Heller, W. Holtzman & S. Messick eds. 1982).

25. 20 U.S.C. §§ 1400-1420, 1453 (1982).

26. *Id.* § 1400.

27. See Bickel, *Classifying Mentally Retarded Students: A Review of Placement Practices in Special Education*, in PLACING CHILDREN IN SPECIAL EDUCATION, *supra* note 24, at 182, 209-13.

dled with the resource constraints. Historically, the educational establishment was never keen about special education; it views its mission as the education of those students that will further its organizational goals; the Act was thrust upon it. Most parents, especially the ones that we are concerned about (the lower social classes, minorities) face tremendous odds in trying to cope with the school system. For many, having a handicapped child is a matter of shame and denial; they are only too glad if the school bus will take their child away for the day. For others, there is lack of understanding, fear of antagonizing the school people, fear of appearing stupid, or taking up valuable professional time. They do not understand the scientific jargon. The result is that many parents have contact with the schools but no real communication, they passively accept the school's decisions, they sign consent forms in blank, and the schools regard the Act's procedures as giving rise to unnecessary paperwork and bother—a situation totally predictable given the problems of volume, values, and the distribution of wealth and power. When the distribution is altered, the system is altered. Middle class and rich parents (or poor people with vigorous advocates) can and do use the system successfully when high stakes are involved—for example, forcing the school to provide an expensive private placement—but such situations are rare.[28]

The school district in Madison, Wisconsin, operates differently.[29] The prevailing view there is that the system can succeed in helping a handicapped child only if the parent fully understands the nature of the problem. The Madison school people point out that the child spends only five or six hours each day in the school. For the Madison school people, informed consent is not an obstacle to be overcome, but is a positive organization goal. They implement this program by a series of informal conferences prior to the institution of the formal educational steps; these conferences take place at each stage of the process. Every decision is viewed as experimental and subject to evaluation and re-negotiation. Neither the parents nor the school people feel that they are in a zero-sum game. This immediately reduces the level of conflict and allows for negotiation and compromise. The attitude toward experimentation, combined with a healthy professional skepticism as to the state of the art, leads the school to be flexible as to a range of alternatives. If the parents really want plan *A*, the school will go along even though the school would prefer plan *B*, as long as plan *A* is reasonable and the parties understand that all

28. *Id.* at 224-25.

29. The description of the Madison program is based on approximately twenty interviews I conducted with parents of handicapped children, parent advocates, the head of a citizens advocacy group specializing in special education, the director and assistant director of the program, teachers, social workers, and school psychologists. Additional interviews are being scheduled. This case study is part of larger work that I am engaged in, which explores alternative procedures for discretionary decisions.

decisions will be re-evaluated. In those cases, the school regards the parents' cooperation as worth more than the additional benefits of plan *B*. Parents, on the other hand, also feel that particular decisions can be renegotiated, and can therefore afford to be flexible as well.

Well and good, but, given the distribution question, how can the parents participate in this process? Aren't they still subject to co-optation, and if this is true, aren't they in an even worse position than under the formal system? The school recognizes this problem and through oral and written communication, strongly encourages the parents to contact voluntary organizations that will supply parent advocates. The parent advocates themselves are usually parents of handicapped children and are knowledgeable volunteers. In addition, the state department of instruction also provides training sessions and workshops for parents of handicapped children.

The parent advocates attend the conferences and act on behalf of the parents. Why does the school district encourage this? In their words, the parent advocates do not have to be "polite." "They will ask questions that the parents are afraid to ask." And—this is the important point—it is out of this conflict that better communication and understanding will be achieved.

The Madison system, of course, is not perfect and there are many unanswered questions and problems, but at this point, I want to draw some generalizations to show two things: first, how this procedure differs from and is superior to the liberal legal model, and second, that to achieve individual values in this kind of procedure, one must go beyond standards, decentralization, and profession.[30]

The Madison procedure is consensual rather than conflictual. The goal is to reach a cooperative solution rather than to determine winners and losers. In a relationship that is both discretionary and continuous, this makes far more sense than adversarial advocacy, which is discontinuous, cross-sectional, and pulls the parties apart. As Stewart Macaulay has pointed out in his seminal work on the use of contract law in business relations: When businessmen want to continue to deal with each other, they bargain, they do not go to law. If the continuing relationship is worth preserving, they do not sue.[31] With handicapped children, the relationship

30. The Madison system, of course, does not replace the Act's procedures, but only three formal appeals have been filed since 1974. The research, however, is only preliminary. I still lack information on very crucial matters—for example, the number of conferences, the percentage of parents who in fact participate, caseloads, resources, and so forth. But the fact that there is a high degree of consensus among a variety of sources gives me some confidence that the description in the text is reasonably accurate. It is certainly accurate in theory.

31. Macaulay, *Non-Contractual Relations in Business: A Preliminary Study*, 28 AM. SOC. REV. 55, 60-62 (1963).

continues. The question is whether it is alienating and dominating or is consensual and cooperative.

The Madison procedure is continuous rather than discontinuous. And again, this makes more sense. The procedure should last as long as the substantive relationship. This does not mean that there has to be one continuous conference, but it does mean frequent meetings, communication, and an experimental, flexible approach rather than finality.

The distributional issue is lessened if two conditions are fulfilled. If the parent advocate and the other resources are supplied (help and support from voluntary organizations and the state workshops) *and* if the school is interested in genuine informed consent, then the parent is in a better position to participate. But both conditions have to be fulfilled. If the school treats informed consent as an obstacle rather than as an organizational goal, then client resources will not be sufficient to overcome the advantages of the bureaucracy. The school has to want the parents to understand and agree.

How, though, is individualism to be preserved in this communitarian, consensual decisionmaking procedure? Here lies the special role of conflict—the use of the parent advocate. In adversarial relations, conflict and advocates are integral parts of the procedure. In cooperative or consensual systems, conflict is suppressed; it is negative, and, for this reason, there is considerable concern about the loss of autonomy and responsibility.[32] The Madison system takes a unique approach to conflict. Conflict is necessary to gain consensus, to aid in communication and understanding. Conflict is a positive good, not something to be avoided. Conflict, in the form of the parent advocate, preserves individualism. It allows the parent to exercise autonomy, dignity, and responsibility. It is communicative conflict, not adversarial conflict.

The core of liberalism is that each individual is to be considered an end, never a means. Adversarial advocacy cannot meet this ideal; there is always a winner and a loser. Communal decisionmaking threatens the individualism of the participants, who may become means to the group decision. The Madison system, by treating genuine informed consent as an important organizational goal, overcomes the means-ends distinction; the school and the parents have to be both means and ends simultaneously. Conflict, structured into the consensual decisionmaking, is the mechanism by which the individualism of the parent is preserved.

32. *See* Mashaw, *Administrative Due Process: The Quest for a Dignitary Theory*, 61 B.U. L. REV. 885, 922-25 (1981).

In adversarial advocacy, it is assumed that individualism is preserved. Profesor Simon questions this assumption in a powerful critique. *See* Simon, *The Ideology of Advocacy: Procedural Justice and Professional Ethics*, 1978 WIS. L. REV. 29.

The Yale Law Journal Vol. 92: 1270, 1983

To sum up, for many parts of the welfare system, as well as for other social programs, the ideals of the legal rights approach, I believe, are valid, necessary, and productive of much social good. But, as long as we have problems of volume, there will be routinization; it might as well be in the open and dealt with constructively.

For significant aspects of social welfare programs, discretion will be necessary, but more needs to be done than trying to refurbish the old system of standards, decentralization, and profession. The Madison school district experience suggests a model. We have to abandon the traditional view that discretion is incompatible with a liberal society, that individualism can be preserved only through adversarial advocacy. The suggestion is that autonomy, dignity, and responsibility can be enhanced in consensual decisionmaking through the positive use of conflict.

There are other really knotty problems. A great deal more thought has to be given to the problems of informed consent in dependent relationships—what are its elements, what are its limits, how does one evaluate it in real life? Client resources (parent advocates, voluntary organizations, information, training) do not seem to raise great conceptual issues, and there is a great deal of experience from the past two decades to draw upon. The problem of organizational behavior, however, is far more elusive. How does one make the lower levels of the bureaucracy view informed consent in positive terms? This is not merely a question of attitudes; careful attention has to be paid to structures and incentives, to facilitate and reward flexibility and experimentation. As far as I can tell, this is still largely an unchartered area, but the problem has been recognized, promising real-life examples have been identified, and analysis has taken some preliminary steps.[33] How did the Madison school district system get that way? Under what conditions can it be replicated in other school districts, in other social welfare programs where discretion is an important aspect of citizen-state relations?

33. *See, e.g.*, Elmore, *Backward Mapping: Implementation Research and Policy Decisions*, 94 POL. SCI. Q. 601 (1979); Elmore, *Organizational Models of Social Program Implementation*, 26 PUB. POL'Y 185 (1978); Sabatier & Mazmanian, *The Implementation of Public Policy: A Framework for Analysis*, 8 POL'Y STUD. J. 538 (1980).

# [18]

# WELFARE "RIGHTS", LAW AND DISCRETION

RICHARD M. TITMUSS

THE administrative merging in Britain in 1966 of the non-means-tested and the means-tested income maintenance programmes has made more explicit some of the fundamental issues of precedence or innovation, precision or flexibility, rule or discretion, equity or adequacy in regard to social security. They were all there and in conflict before the Social Security Act of 1966, which established the Supplementary Benefits Commission and placed it inside the Department of Social Security. Administrative discretionary powers and responsibilities for adjudicating on a comprehensive scale were, for example, built into the national insurance, industrial injuries and war pensions " as of right " contingent schemes, just as they were in the work of the National Assistance Board. The consequences of integration have made these issues more apparent. The social policy choices that continually have to be made in income maintenance programmes between these conflicting and often overlapping principles are now clearer. The act of integration brought more choices to the political surface. It is the purpose of this paper to discuss the nature of some of these choices, and particularly the choice between legal rule and administrative discretion.[1] It will thus draw on American experience in the field of public assistance in considering the Supplementary Benefits Commission's attempts to follow a different route to individualised justice.

## Dicey and Discretion

If all decisions involving social security justice to individuals were lined up on a scale with those governed by precise eligibility rules at the extreme left, and those involving complete individualized discretion at the extreme right, and those based on various mixtures of rules, principles, standards and discretion somewhere in the

* The author is Professor of Social Administration at the London School of Economics and Political Science and Deputy Chairman of the Supplementary Benefits Commission. This is an expanded version of a talk given at the Department of Health and Social Security Summer School, Cambridge, July 1970.

[1] The distinction between " rights " schemes and means-tested schemes is also discussed in Richard M. Titmuss, " Equity, Adequacy and Innovation in Social Security ", *International Social Security Review*, 1970, Vol. XXIII, No. 2.

middle, where on the scale might be the most serious and the most frequent injustice?

It would be hard to find anyone today in Britain or North America who would publicly support in the whole field of income maintenance the principle of complete individualised discretion. To do so would involve the destruction of millions of acquired and inherited rights to social security contributory programmes. For many it would signal a reversion to a mass "poor law age". Powerful objections to individualised discretion would also come from others who we may describe as the new "Diceyists", a movement that has emerged in recent years in unexpected and strange disguises in Britain and the United States.

Dicey, we may recall, was obsessed by fears of administrative discretion subject to control by administrative tribunals.[2] Discretionary power by government officials and administrative tribunals composed of lay people would both be subject to and tainted by political influence; more administrative discretion would mean more "socialistic ideas"; more administrative justice would sap the foundations of precedence and judicial case-law "which has been for generations a leading feature of the English constitution". In his concern for the freedom of the individual citizen, Dicey was basically opposed to the growth of public government. Less government spelt more individual freedom, dignity and self-determination. Less precedence based on case-law implied more social policy innovation and more benefits for the "undeserving". Less "judicial impartiality" meant more citizen (non-legal) participation in decision-making processes.[3] In sum, he was echoing William Pitt, "Where law ends tyranny begins".

Modern "Diceyism" is now to be found, on the political right, in the philosophy expounded by Professor Friedman of Chicago and many other economists, sociologists and politicians in the United States and Britain who advocate negative income taxation and Speenhamland wage supplementation systems as the answer to the problem of "minority poverty", and as a means of radically reducing the role of government in the direct provision of social services.

The extraordinary popularity in recent years of negative (or reverse) income taxation and other presumptive mechanical means

[2] For a recent summary of Dicey's formulation of the rule of law, see K. Bell, *Tribunals in the Social Services*, 1969.

[3] A. V. Dicey, *Law of the Constitution*, 1885, and *Law and Opinion in England*, 2nd ed., 1914. See also other references in Professor W. A. Robson's classic appraisal of Dicey's views, *Justice and Administrative Law*, 1951.

of distributing some income to some poor people is in part accounted for by a growing distrust of the exercise of administrative power in governmental systems of income maintenance, and in part as an ideological movement to transform policies into rules. Such proposals, while being advanced in the cause of less government intervention in the lives of upper and middle income groups, will also mean, it is argued, less bureaucratic control over the lives of poor people. More freedom for the poor, still needed by society as price stabilisers, will follow automatically from giving more freedom to the rich.

These mechanical means of distributing some income to " poverty groups " are also seen by critics of public social services as one way of reducing lay participation in dispute and complaint procedures. The " amateurish, inquisitorial and moralising " participation of ordinary citizens in the work of thousands of administrative tribunals in Britain would be abolished. In so far as disputes arose in negative income taxation and similar schemes they would be handled by the courts and by lawyers.

To account fully for the widespread popularity of such schemes since the " re-discovery of poverty " in the late 1950s would involve a lengthy digression. One further important reason should, however, be mentioned. For many supporters their appeal lies in the belief that they would concentrate income redistribution on " those whose needs are greatest ". And they would do so with a minimum of government; a minimum of discretionary power exercised by officials, and a minimum of participation by lay people and " social controllers " (such as social workers).

President Nixon's Family Assistance Plan (1970 version) embodies and expresses these values and beliefs.[4] It attempts to create a differential between the working rate (low wages) and the welfare rate (public assistance). Its " new social wonder drug " is the work incentive.[5] Thus, its core proposal is wage supplementation for the " working poor "—a new version of Speenhamland. It is aimed to apply—and the words used are similar to those in the Act of 1795— " . . . to labourers in the lower paid employments, and only to them ".[6]

[4] H.R. 16311, the Family Assistance Act of 1970 (revised), U.S. 91st Cong., 2d Sess., 1970.

[5] So described in an analysis by R. Pruger, " Reciprocity and the Poor ", Ph.D. thesis, University of California, Berkeley, 1970.

[6] Karl de Schweinitz writing on the 1795 Act in *England's Road to Social Security*, 1937, p. 240, and E. G. Levi, " Mr. Nixon's Speenhamland ", *Social Work*, January 1970, p. 7.

RICHARD M. TITMUSS

In proposing to supplement the wages of the "working poor" with dependent children it will thus discriminate against those on welfare who cannot work or who cannot get full-time work who will be taxed at a higher rate on any part-time earnings.

Critics of the plan have also argued that it will operate as an incentive to family break-up (the earnings of wives will be counted in "family income"); that by contrast with universal programmes, *e.g.*, family allowances, it will act as a divisive "dependency-creating programme"; that it will confuse and frustrate an already heavily means-tested population; and that the recoupment of F.A.P. payments from a deserting husband's eventual social security pension will increase the number of "disappearing men" in North America. Lastly, and to quote Professor Burns,

> "Programmes that deal only with 'the poor' run the danger, not only of being poor programmes, but also of polarising society into two groups, the poor and non-poor, the one receiving benefits and the other footing the bill. There is growing evidence of a rising resentment on the part of those just above the poverty line that everything is being done for the poor while they are neglected. A programme that perpetuates this polarisation is inefficient."[7]

It could also bring about a sharper polarisation in American society between black and white because a large proportion of the "working poor" are black people.

Some of these criticisms may also be applicable, with appropriate qualifications for differences in scale, content and objectives, to the British Government's Family Income Supplements plan and associated means-testing programme.

However that may be, what is relevant to the themes of this paper is the assumption in the Nixon plan that it will reduce the area of administrative discretion. In terms of eligibility, assessment and administration it looks simpler when contrasted with the complexities of American public assistance. Hence its popularity on the political left as well as on the political right. It is seen as an impersonal plan with precise eligibility rules. The interfering, moralising, judgmental caseworker (portrayed by many supporters of the "Welfare Rights" movement) will have no place in its administration. Instead of the home visit and personal contact with a caseworker there will be substituted the postal application, the computer and the postal payment. The new Diceyists of welfare reform on the left and the "economic man" Diceyists on the right both

[7] E. M. Burns, "Welfare Reform and Income Security Policies", National Conference on Social Welfare paper, June 1970.

acclaim the plan on this score though they may differ on the value of the cash benefits to be provided, the scope of the plan itself and the labour control mechanisms involved.

## Law and Opinion

It is a paradoxical alliance. For the Chicago School to say, in effect, "where law ends tyranny begins" is ideologically consistent. The presumed automatism of the rules of F.A.P. and N.I.T. will—like the rules of monetary supply reform—assist the workings of "the market". Organised, militant "consumerism" and "tax avoidance to the limit" will be encouraged as cash is substituted for services and the market for bureaucracy and government.

All this is logical enough though it begs some fundamental questions. To understand, however, the support of welfare rights reformers we need to see it as part of the more general protest and liberation movement.[8]

It is a phenomenon which has been gathering force in recent years in most countries of Western society. In Britain it is symbolised and expressed in the growth of organised groups and associations of many different kinds: poverty groups, organisations for widows, the disabled, old-age pensioners, single women, liberated women, gay people, parents of handicapped children, minority religious and ethnic groups, student action groups, anti-drug addict groups, tenants' groups, squatters, neighbourhood, territorial and amenity groups, and many others. Some are claiming equal or preferential treatment in the form of cash, goods or services. Some are demanding rights of participation in what is called "the decision-making process". Others more explicitly are claiming representation on committees and executive bodies of institutions which influence or affect their welfare—from secondary schools to industrial organisations. New forms of democracy are breaking out all over the place, and particularly in some politically unexpected quarters. More people are demanding rights to a greater say in what happens to them. It is an international phenomenon linked, some would argue, to a "libertarian explosion",[9] and not peculiar to Britain or to the Supplementary Benefits Commission.

This is the social and political context within which we should discuss the growth of demand for income-maintenance rights, judicialised appeal systems and equality of access to material facts

[8] See, for example, J. R. Gusfield, *Protest, Reform and Revolt*, New York, 1970.

[9] See, for example, G. Ionescu (ed.), "Anarchism Today", *Government and Opposition*, Vol. 5, No. 4, L.S.E., 1970.

RICHARD M. TITMUSS

contained in files or office procedural books (from confidential student files to so-called " secret " Code As). To be the keeper of secrets these days, it seems, is both a mark of stigma and a definition of old age. Only youth has no secrets.

These populist movements for social rights and participation are as difficult to define in terms of ends as democracy itself. Like democracy it is easier to say what the social rights movement is against than to say what it is for. It is against power, the arbitrary non-accountable exercise of power, against imposed stigma, against charity as opposed to rights, against the use of discretion, against discrimination on grounds of age, sex, class, colour and religion, and against moral judgments being made about claimants by social workers as well as administrators.

These, it is argued, are some of the tyrannies of the so-called bureaucrat of the public welfare system. One answer, according to leaders of the movement particularly in the United States, is increasingly to call in the lawyer and base welfare decisions on a massive body of precedent and case-law. Thus, the conclusion follows, personalised discretion in giving or withholding cash grants would be abolished. Hence the attractions to some of Nixon's Family Assistance Plan.

There are a number of basic assumptions in these arguments which may be said to relate to the functions of the Supplementary Benefits Commission in Britain and to Welfare (Public Assistance) Departments in the United States. They are all founded on the theory that case-law or lawyer's law (as in some parts of National Insurance) contains no element of discretion whereas administrative discretion contains no element of law. In other words, law is as different from discretion as day is to night.

Therefore it is assumed that justice will be advanced if case-law is substituted for administrative decision; if all appeal systems are judicialised and claimants are represented by lawyers; if all discretionary cash additions are abolished; if access to the courts is made available to all claimants, and if the adversary system replaces the inquisitorial lay tribunal.

Underlying these assumptions there are many others, insufficiently defined and inadequately discussed by welfare rights reformers: that lawyers are morally infallible and do not unprofessionally " stir up strife and litigation " [10]; that they are as interested

[10] For a discussion of the ethics of the legal profession, see P. Nonet, *Administrative Justice*, New York, 1969.

—or more interested—in poor people as in rich people; that there are enough of them everywhere to replace all administrative tribunals and to handle all disputes and complaints in the health and social services fields[11]; that citizen participation in the work of tribunals should be abolished; that the law is as speedy, cheap, effective and creative as administrative tribunals and governmental rule-making procedures; that case-law when built up in the world of public assistance will be administratively manageable and intelligible to both parties on the counter late on a Friday afternoon; and that massive case-law accumulations will be as flexibly responsive to changes in the values prevailing in society as discretionary rule-making procedures by, for example, the Supplementary Benefits Commission.

We cannot examine all these assumptions here. But the belief that lawyer's law contains no element of discretion is completely false. Law and discretion are not separated by a sharp line but by overlapping zones. Exercising discretion may be a part of finding facts and applying law, and finding facts may be a part of exercising discretion. As Roscoe Pound has said: "in no legal system, however minute and detailed its body of rules, is justice administered wholly by rule and without recourse to the will of the judge . . .".[12] In the history of the administration of criminal justice in England, discretion has been more important than rule. Other criticisms of the quaint belief in the mechanistic objectivity of lawyer's law and the impartiality of judges are contained in the works cited below.[13]

To these we would add one further comment. It is insufficiently recognised today that rule-making procedure is one of the greatest

11 The immensity of this problem in the context of a national shortage of lawyers is indicated by some statistics for tribunals under the general supervision of the Council on Tribunals. In 1969 over 150,000 cases were handled by more than 21,000 appointed members the great majority of whom were lay people (*Annual Report for 1969–70*, H.M.S.O., 1970).

12 R. Pound, *Jurisprudence*, 1959, p. 355.

13 *Justice Out of Reach*, a Consumer Council Study, marshals a formidable indictment of lawyers for their neglect, indifference, delays and charges in the matter of small claims by consumers. It concludes that the admission of lawyers to a proposed small claims court should not be allowed if justice is to be obtained by consumers (H.M.S.O., 1970). The harmful and undesirable effects of legal representation before administrative tribunals are discussed in *Administrative Justice*, H. J. Elcock, Longmans, 1969. See also *Complaints Against Lawyers*, which assembles the evidence of some 4,000–5,000 complaints per year by dissatisfied consumers (A Report by *Justice*, Knight & Co., 1970); *Legal Aid as a Social Service* which criticises lawyers for their failure to service poor people and poor areas (Cobden Trust, 1970); *Tribunals in the Social Services*, 1969, and "Administrative Tribunals Since Franks", *Social and Economic Administration*, Vol. 4, No. 3, 1970, by K. Bell; *In Search of Justice*, B. Abel-Smith and R. B. Stevens, Allen Lane, 1968; R. B. Stevens, "The Role of a Final Appeal Court in a Democracy: The House of Lords", *Modern Law Review*, September 1965; P. Nonet, *Administrative Justice*, 1969.

RICHARD M. TITMUSS

inventions of modern government. In this belief we are supported by a perceptive American lawyer, Professor K. C. Davis, who, after surveying the American legal system, concluded: " . . . the creation of new law through either statutory enactment or administrative rule-making is much more desirable than creation of new law through either judicial decision or administrative adjudication." [14]

## The American Experience

All these assumptions—intimately related to the issue of Welfare "Rights"—merit more discussion than they have so far received in Britain. Meanwhile, we can ask: What evidence is there on which to test these assumptions? Do public assistance claimants as a whole —and not just one lone claimant—benefit in terms of the claims they make when systems are judicialised? Are the rights of poor people "grossly restricted" if they are not represented by lawyers? [15] Does the "anarchy created" by the absence of case-law in the work of the Supplementary Benefits Commission penalise claimants? [16] Should the assistance system be judicialised on the American pattern following the precedent of the Industrial Relations Bill based, as it is, on American legal experience? [17] Does court action represent a better or more effective "quality control" over administrative behaviour than rule-making procedures operated by administrative systems?

While we can—and, indeed, should—discuss more fully these questions and assumptions, hard evidence and unassailable facts are not easy to come by. While there is a vast literature on case-law and endless volumes of digests of decisions in the field of national insurance, there are few thorough studies of administrative rule-making and the exercise of discretion. The Franks Committee *Report on Administrative Tribunals* in 1957, for instance, and the Lord Chancellor's Advisory Committee which considered and rejected in 1968 the possibility of extending the legal aid scheme to cover the cost of legal representation before Supplementary Benefit Appeal Tribunals, these were not founded on any searching

[14] K. C. Davis, *Discretionary Justice*, Louisiana State University Press, 1969, p. 65.

[15] Alleged by the Child Poverty Action Group in *Poverty*, Pamphlet One, 1969, p. 3, but contradicted by *Justice out of Reach : A Case for Small Claims Courts*, A Consumer Council Study, H.M.S.O., 1970.

[16] Alleged by Tony Lynes in *The Fifth Social Service* (Fabian Essays, 1970). *New Society* has consistently taken the line that the "Poor Law" will not be abolished in Britain until "the present anarchic situation in which each appeal is considered without regard for decisions made in earlier cases" is ended (see, for example, issues of April 30 and September 10, 1970).

[17] *The Economist*, October 10, 1970.

statistical studies. This is not to say they were wrong; it is merely to point out that the conclusions of these committees were largely matters of opinion.

In the absence of any studies in depth in Britain we summarise here the findings of some American research in the public assistance field. It is moreover appropriate to do so, first, because of the widespread view that this country should adopt the American case-law approach which would encourage claimants "to extort the last penny from the system"[18] and, secondly, because the Welfare "Rights" movement originated in the States and was indirectly supported by the Federal Government's Office of Economic Opportunity (the War on Poverty programme). The Director of that Office, Mr. Sargant Shriver, said in 1965 at the Annual Convention of the American Bar Association:

> "There is a growing awareness across the country that the poor have, in fact, been deprived of their rights. . . . With this awareness, there is a new appreciation of the contributions the law and lawyers can make to get poor people out of poverty."[19]

One of the more searching studies of "Welfare Rights" undertaken in the States was carried out in California by Professor Scott Briar.[20] He investigated 1,088 fair hearing (welfare appeal) cases for 1965–66. All the case files were read, analysed, coded and compared statistically for relationships among them. He also observed hearings and interviewed welfare officials (variously described as caseworkers or social workers).

The legal criteria for the hearing process appear in the Federal public assistance statutes, the Californian statutes in the Welfare Code, and the policy interpretations and rules to be found in the Federal Handbook of Public Assistance Administration. The requirements of the hearing process include provisions for an informal demand for a hearing, notice of the right to a hearing, and specified time limits. Recipients have the right to examine evidence, to call witnesses and to employ lawyers or be represented by lawyers. There is also a provision for the publication of decisions in the form of an indexed digest. Hearings may further be reviewed by the courts. Testimony offered by clients may be criminally prejudicial.

Professor Briar remarks, in his report, on the "incredibly complex series of statutes, rules, regulations and guidelines under

[18] T. Lynes, *op. cit.*, p. 122.

[19] *First Annual Report of the Program of the Office of Economic Opportunity to the American Bar Association*, August 1966, p. 1.

[20] Draft copy of the Report, dated July 11, 1968, provided by the author. To be published under the title *Welfare from Below*.

which public assistance is administered ". Another student of this system, Mr. Michael Evans, an ex-public welfare worker, has said: " The volumes of case reports are fast exceeding any law library's capacity to house them." [21]

Some of Professor Briar's findings can be summarised thus:

1. Two-thirds of the appeal cases involved clients who would have lost public assistance altogether had they not appealed.

> " These claimants, who feel they have nothing to lose, do not perceive the hearing process as a ' right '. Most are afraid to appeal if they are getting any money or services through public assistance. They prefer to live with an inequity rather than challenge a system they consider a ' charity '."

One reason why appeals are not made is that in the American system the claimant generally has to deal with the same caseworker who has the duty of providing or determining access to social services as well as cash—a relationship reminiscent of the role of the old Poor Law relieving officer in Britain. Clients in the States have to " live " with their caseworkers after a hearing.

2. Clients who were represented at hearings did better than clients who were not. Lawyers were not markedly more successful than lay representatives.

3. The Californian digest of all decisions (required by law) was (a) incomplete, (b) had no page numbers, and (c) was not indexed. Thus, it was only helpful to those who had the time, energy and money to undertake a case-by-case search through tens of thousands of cases.[22]

4. A large proportion of clients did not know that the police and representatives of other prosecuting agencies were present at the public hearings.

5. As the hearings became more " legal " (*i.e.*, as the presence of lawyers at the hearings increased) the content became more esoteric and mystical to claimants. A similar finding has been reported by Professor Nonet in an American case study of workmen's compensation. The aims of health and rehabilitation programmes were increasingly frustrated by case-law, legal mystification and a litigious courthouse atmosphere.[23]

[21] M. Evans, *The Courts as Social Change Agents*, National Association of Social Workers, Washington, 1969, p. 24.

[22] A study in Cleveland concluded that the State Welfare Manual of case-law was incomprehensible to clients and social workers alike. " Even experienced lawyers were puzzled." (Herman D. Stein, *The Crisis in Welfare in Cleveland*, Report of the Mayor's Commission, 1969.) See also *Judicial Control of the Administrative Process*, Ditchley Paper No. 22, Ditchley Foundation (especially pp. 18, 19 and 31), 1969.

[23] P. Nonet, *op. cit.*, pp. 155–157.

WELFARE "RIGHTS", LAW AND DISCRETION

Professor Briar concluded:

"Designed to insure against bureaucratic intransigence and programmed to encourage dignity and self-help to assistance recipients, the system instead serves frequently to reinforce the claimant's weaknesses. Confusion reigns and the client stands helpless while his complaint is processed through a system whose adversary nature is frequently invisible."

To improve the system, the lawyer had little to contribute.

In a series of studies in Wisconsin, Professor Handler and his colleagues at the Institute for Research on Poverty have demonstrated the extent to which the public assistance system in the United States is fundamentally an adversary system.[24] The essence of an adversary system is challenge. Those clothed with discretionary authority must be continually challenged—and challenged with legal hostility. Hence it is logical that the fair hearing process is set within the administrative context and is presumed to operate as a "quality control" over administrative behaviour.[25] In Britain, by contrast, the appeal tribunals are not considered part of the administration. The Franks Committee Report said (para. 130):

". . . we cannot accept the view that tribunals are part and parcel of the ordinary machinery of administration. We consider that they are properly to be thought of as independent organs of adjudication."

Professor Handler also found that in a system designed to create challenge the percentage of appeals heard to recipients was only 1·1 per cent. (average 1959–65). This, the author said, was "disappointingly low".

In Wisconsin, lawyers appeared in about 12 per cent. of appeal hearings. They seem to have had no effect on the success rate which was approximately the same as for those not represented. Professor Handler has clearly become sceptical of lawyers. In pointing out that there is little direct American evidence on the total and long-term effects (the harm-cost equation) on relationships (and on society) of legalised hostility in the welfare system he does, however, cite evidence from studies of the administration of juvenile justice. The introduction of lawyers in juvenile justice is viewed, he says, as a hostile act (as it is in the commercial world) and

". . . there is evidence now that lawyers function poorly in the administration of juvenile justice. As public defenders for juveniles, they deal with cases

24 See, in particular, J. F. Handler, "Justice for the Welfare Recipient: Fair Hearings in AFDC—The Wisconsin Experience", *Social Service Review*, Vol. 43, No. 1, March 1969.

25 Appellate bodies consist of persons employed by Welfare Departments.

routinely and perfunctorily, they plead the 'bad' cases to bargain the 'good ones', and they are cynical and jaded towards their clients." [26]

## The Pathology of Legalism

At this point we venture on a broad generalisation. The adversary public assistance system seems to produce (at one extreme) a small proportion of hostile, near-desperate appellants and (at the other extreme) a very high proportion of clients characterised by Briar, Handler and others as "submissive", "inert" and "coerced" who themselves believe (in about half the cases studied on "attitudes to welfare") that many recipients "cheat" the welfare departments.

In this belief they were, it has been reported, simply reflecting society's attitude towards welfare recipients.[27] The stigma of receiving "unearned benefits"—a stigma which American society apparently needs—has led to what Nonet has termed "moral captivity"—an acceptance and incorporation by recipients of the terms and consequences of society's definition of a recipient as a person occupying a degraded role.[28] Hence, some welfare rights organisations encourage recipients to lie and "cheat" the system: for example, by starting small fires in order to claim for fire-damaged goods.

Attitudes, behaviour and relationships which take these forms are the product of many economic, cultural and institutional factors. Certain primary ones may, however, be singled out. First, public assistance in the United States is almost entirely discretionary and it is still possible to deny eligibility on grounds of "non-cooperation". Secondly, in the spirit of less eligibility the great majority of welfare payments are significantly below "official" poverty levels. Thirdly, the widespread assumption that claimants need "rehabilitation"—hence the association of social work with money payments. Fourthly, the dominance of the work ethic as the "final solution" involving arbitrary tests of "work-worthiness" for women as well as men (as, for example, in Nixon's Family Assistance Plan which shifts the exercise of such discretionary power from welfare departments to labour departments so as to "strengthen the will to work"). Fifthly, the extent to which the administration of assistance is rooted in adversariness and a pathology of "legalism".

By "legalism" we mean an insistence on legal rules based on

[26] Cited from A. Platt *et al.*, *Indiana Law Journal*, 43, Spring 1968, p. 619.

[27] N. G. Streshinsky, "Welfare Rights Organizations and the Public Welfare System", Ph.D. thesis, University of California, Berkeley, 1970. This study also summarises the results of other surveys of welfare attitudes.

[28] P. Nonet, *op. cit.*, p. 91.

precedent and responsive only very slowly to rapidly changing human needs and circumstances. The increasing application of "legalism" to the public assistance system combined with rising demands for "welfare rights" has led, all over the United States, to a massive fragmentation of entitlement. Itemised legal entitlements, in the assessment of needs and resources, now embrace hundreds of visible articles and objects—practically everything that bedrooms, living-rooms, kitchens and lavatories may contain; most normal articles of clothing, day, night, summer and winter, for individuals of both sexes, all ages and nearly all shapes and sizes. For example: in New York City in 1968 (with one million people on public assistance) a man had a "right" to possess one pair of winter trousers at $7.50 (regular sizes); the household had a right to possess in the kitchen one can-opener at 35 cents and, in the lavatory, one toilet tissue holder at 75 cents "*but only if your landlord does not have to give you one*". And so on and so on through hundreds of itemised entitlements from scrub brushes to panties.[29]

Similarly and logically, the Welfare Department has legal rights. It has a right to compel clients to sell things they do not need; it has a right to take over houses (owner occupied) and to sell houses on the market, if clients are on assistance for more than one year. "Legalism" (to quote Nonet) "tends to weaken the authority of the law in the eyes of those whose needs and aspirations are frustrated; legal institutions come to seem ineffective and arbitrary, and tend to lose their claim to reasoned obedience."[30] The consequences for the American public assistance system have been far-reaching: more concealed discretionary power not less (for example, in the assessment of itemised needs); more frustration, bewilderment and apathy among claiments as fair hearings become more esoteric; more inequitable treatment with the growth of itemised entitlements; more administrative inefficiencies and fewer "quality controls"; and more hostility and fear on both sides of the counter not less.

## Precision versus Flexibility

Against this background of American experience we may now consider the Supplementary Benefits Scheme in Britain and set down some general principles relevant to the Commission's attempts since 1966 to find a balance between precision and flexibility, rule and

29 L. Marks, *Your Right to Welfare*, Citizen's Committee for Children of New York, Inc., 1968.

30 P. Nonet, *op. cit.*, p. 265.

RICHARD M. TITMUSS

discretion, in following an alternative route to individualised justice. In what follows I express my own views as a member of the Commission.

1. *People should be helped to know their rights.* It must be common ground, and accepted as a fundamental principle, that everyone as citizens should know their rights. As Professor Raphael has stressed, social rights are essentially rights of access and recipience; not rights of action.[31] It must follow that the Commission can never afford to relax its efforts to make people aware of their rights to claim and their rights to appeal. In four years, the Commission have made substantial progress in this direction, developing new leaflets and booklets and, in particular, producing the *Supplementary Benefits Handbook*—a comprehensive guide to the scheme and to the ways in which the Commission's discretion is exercised. At the outset the *Handbook* was seen to be important because helping people to know their rights is a responsibility not merely for the central department concerned but for society as a whole, and particularly for those organisations, agencies and groups who are involved in a variety of ways in meeting needs for services in kind or in cash or pressing for needs to be met—social and welfare workers, doctors, teachers, citizens advice bureaux and so forth.

2. *The need to reduce or eliminate unnecessary discretionary power*: (a) *The need for some discretion.* The Ministry of Social Security Act lays down a minimum standard in financial terms, with discretion given to the Commission to vary these where circumstances warrant it and a right of appeal if the claimant is dissatisfied with the Commission's decision. This has the advantage of flexibility and of preserving the dignity of the individual recipient of supplementary benefit by allowing him some choice in how his income is expended. Of course it can be criticised as giving too much power to officials in the exercise of discretion and of leaving the claimant in the dark as to his precise entitlement, but both of these disadvantages can be countered through the appeals system and by action under the previous head. A definition of entitlement in precise material and itemised terms would deprive the recipient of choice, and by prohibiting flexibility would mean that whatever the level of provision it would become maximum which no official *or* tribunal could exceed. A legalised itemised prescription of minimum entitlement would become a rigid ceiling against which cases

[31] D. D. Raphael (ed.), *Political Theory and the Rights of Man*, 1967.

crying out by any human standards for extra help—demanding individualised justice—would press in vain. Nor would such a system eliminate arbitrary decisions—" Your dustbin does not need renewing and your tooth brush is not worn out yet."

In fact—and what is insufficiently recognised—the scheme does provide fully legalised basic rights, but it also provides for additional grants which allow flexible responses to human needs and to an immense variety of complex individual circumstances.

Just where the line should be drawn between legalised basic rights and discretionary additions is a problem which a fully legalised system based on case-law and precedent cannot even begin to consider. It is, however, a constant challenge to any system like the Supplementary Benefits Scheme which continues to recognise the need for individualised justice.

3. *The need to reduce or eliminate unnecessary discretionary power:* (b) *The proper scope of discretion as the indispensable tool for the individualisation of justice.* As Professor Davis has warned in another context, " Let us not over emphasise either the need for discretion or its dangers; let us emphasise both the need for discretion and its dangers." [32] No one wants discretion unless it serves a positive purpose, for two important reasons. First, it is an expensive way of administration; the Commission would prefer to spend money on basic entitlements rather than on administrative overheads. Secondly, more discretion means more resources by way of public education, information, advice and appeal machinery, to provide adequate safeguards against the misuse of discretion—officials, like claimants, are people.

The central concept for progress under this head is the definition of contingencies which can be met, without discretion, either by flat-rate benefits, or benefits varying with precise conditions such as the number of children or a fixed relationship with previous earnings or both. The obvious example is contributory insurance programmes making provision against loss of income because of the interruption or cessation of earnings. But it is not confined to contributory schemes (both those which have contribution conditions for benefit and those which, like the Industrial Injuries Scheme, have not) but extends to non-contributory schemes like Family Allowances and War Pensions. The latter scheme, incidentally, has the same provision by way of basic rights and discretionary additives as the Supplementary Benefits Scheme (and some of its benefits

[32] K. C. Davis, *op. cit.*, p. 25.

are means-tested). The balance between the two was the subject of lively controversy in the 1940s but now after thirty years' experience seems to be generally accepted as about right.

Whether a contingency can be defined in these ways is a matter for judgment on a balance of relevant considerations at any given time. Regrettably, these considerations—whether (to take one example) a benefit proposed for a particular contingency could in fact be operated in ways seen to be fair, which is closely linked with whether the contingency can be defined to this end—have received far more intensive study by government departments and their related advisory bodies (the National Insurance Advisory Committee, the Industrial Injuries Advisory Council and the Central Advisory Committee on War Pensions) than in academic circles. One of the advantages of discretionary powers is that, when for the time being it is considered impracticable to define the contingency for a non-discretionary benefit, experience can be gained in the relevant field upon which an operational definition may be formulated. An example of this process was the experience of administering discretionary additions to national assistance; this made it possible for a policy decision to be taken to introduce the long-term addition as a basic benefit in the Supplementary Benefits Scheme.

4. *The need to develop sounder and more sensitive quality controls in the administrative process.* The development of techniques of quality control is essential under any scheme containing elements of discretion. These include supervision of subordinates by superiors, the intervention of checks by one officer of another, audit and inspection controls, random sample checking, administrative surveys, the analysis of statistical data, research and so forth. The Commission have expanded the development of these techniques in a variety of ways, including utilisation studies, statistical assessments of performance and the setting up of a Policy Inspectorate reporting directly to them, and are particularly anxious to respond positively to any constructive criticism of performance from outside organisations and individuals. It is sometimes assumed—particularly in the United States—that a fully judicialised system ensures better quality control but, given the desire to operate as efficiently and humanely as possible, there are at least two important and highly relevant considerations which point the other way.

First, an official who just has to apply a rigid code of case-law is not in a position of really having to justify his decision—particularly on appeal. If challenged he has in effect simply to say he did his best to apply the code; the matter is then for disputation by lawyers. But an official exercising discretion can never forget he may have to make a reasoned case for his decision to a superior and before a tribunal which has the same discretionary power as he had. Accountability to others is linked to accountability to one's own ideal of a civil servant; this, as Sir William Armstrong has said, can be a greater check than many technical checks and balances.[33]

Secondly, the aim of achieving a better quality of work in assessment is basically a matter of the quantum of resources which can be directed to the end product of adequate numbers of trained and competent staff. Given that, under either system, society will make the best allocation of resources it can against their competing demands (such as health and education services) the administrative overheads of a judicialised system will be substantially heavier. The partisan attitudes inseparable from the concept of contending parties —as distinct from the concept of a *service*—must inevitably cause heavy investment in the staff and procedures required for legalised hostility, with at least a danger that the ablest staff will be trained, and will spend their time, as advocates rather than in raising standards of local and regional office performance and in developing co-operation with those agencies responsible for services in kind.

5. *The need for a continual process of clarification and classification in administrative rule-making.* This is vitally important when staff have to exercise discretion and need the best possible guidance. It is also an integral part of the need to inform the public of the way discretion is exercised. In a society of changing values, the substitution of clarity for vagueness is a never ending process.

It is a need which clearly does not arise in the same way in schemes based on precedent and where there is presumed to be no discretion. Such schemes, of course, require the modernisation of the long itemised lists of " rights "; the risk here, however, is that responses to changing human wants may be inordinately slow because of their legal imprisonment in precedence and the cumbrous processes of gladiatorial combat. Schemes based on a mixture of basic rights and discretionary powers can lead to more innovation and creativity in the broader context of social needs.

[33] *Public Administration*, Summer 1970, p. 130.

RICHARD M. TITMUSS

6. *The need for more and better training, retraining, education and staff development programmes.* This is of crucial importance to either type of system but again the shift of resources and priorities to cover legal processes and partisan procedures inherent in a fully judicialised system gives a decisive advantage to a mixed basic rights and discretionary system. The problem—that officials like claimants are people who reflect the limitations of their particular cultural environment—is well illustrated by Mr. Michael Hill's illuminating and balanced essay "The Exercise of Discretion in the National Assistance Board".[34] It is one which the Commission have attempted to tackle in various ways, for example, by revising training programmes at all staff levels following the recommendations they received from their social work consultant, Miss Olive Stevenson; by giving more prominence to the "social services" and "human relations" content in training programmes; and by developing integrated programmes of technical training, role-playing, behaviour and attitude assessment with the use of such aids as closed-circuit television. Fundamentally, however, all the crucial issues of training and quality control are, quite simply, a matter of resources. In this area of the Commission's responsibilities as in others—as well as the personal social services—our society is failing to invest enough resources in manpower, staff development and training programmes.

7. *The need for adequate time and adequate facilities.* The need for more and better trained manpower cannot be separated from the need to provide adequate facilities and conditions for staff in local offices. In the *Supplementary Benefits Handbook* it is written:

> "[The Commission] believe that claimants have a 'right' to courtesy and understanding relations, and that Commission's staff too, have a 'right' to expect understanding from the public in the difficult tasks and pressures of work that often confront them. These are rights that cannot be laid down or ensured by law or regulation."

But they are, it must be said, extremely difficult to accord to both claimants and staff in Dickensian conditions of overcrowding, discomfort, psychological stress and overwork which, if they prevailed in the universities, would bring all (or most of) the staff and students out on the streets. While, since 1966, commendable efforts have been made to improve premises and conditions, the fact remains

[34] M. J. Hill, *Public Administration*, 1969, Vol. 47.

that there are still offices which are a disgrace in the 1970s. Administratively and financially, few objectives are as difficult to attain, without massive public support, as compensating in full for the long years of public assistance neglect. It is in essence a matter of society itself accepting—and understanding—the choices and the priorities involved.

8. *The need to reduce the scope and coverage of means-tested supplementary benefits.* Under this last heading we return to the question of choice: the choices that continually have to be made between precedence and innovation, precision and flexibility, rule and discretion, equity and adequacy. Much of the discussion in this paper has been devoted to the issues of proportional (equitable) justice and creative (individualised) justice.

As I see it, the British income maintenance system needs both. It needs an element of flexible, individualised justice for two fundamental reasons. First, because as far as we can see ahead and on the basis of all we know about human weaknesses and diversities a society without some element of means-testing and discretion is an unattainable ideal. It is stupid and dangerous to pretend that such an element need not exist; that all will be resolved by the automatism of negative income tax, the money market, consumerism and the lawyer. Secondly, we need this element of individualised justice in order to allow a universal rights scheme, based on principles of equity, to be as precise and inflexible as possible. These characteristics of precision, inflexibility and universality depend for their sustenance and strength on the existence of some element of flexible, individualised justice. But they do not need stigma.

The essential problem is to find the right balance. Britain has not yet done so. The situation today is one of *deteriorating unbalance.* Because, in recent years, the definition of "subsistence" or "poverty" has in relative terms been substantially raised, and for many other reasons besides, the Commission has attracted more and more clients, more and more duties, and more and more victims of the "diswelfares" and moral confusions of modern society. With no immediate prospect of being relieved, it is in danger of being overwhelmed. Already it has too many claimants, too many callers, too many clients, too large a case-load. For the consequence of this its staff is unjustly criticised. The more this happens the harder will it become to avoid "the stigmatising process" demanded—if American experience is any guide—by a materialistic market

RICHARD M. TITMUSS

economy. I believe—because I do not wish to see poorer people stigmatised as poor people—that it is possible to develop a system of flexible, individualised justice based on considerations of dignity and self-respect. But not with millions of clients and inadequate resources in manpower. Nor will it assist to call in the lawyer—even if, by the year 2000, he was marginally interested.[35]

35 The author wishes to acknowledge with gratitude the valuable comments and criticisms he received in revising this paper from Professor W. A. Robson, Professor Scott Briar, Mrs. Kathleen Bell, and officials of the Supplementary Benefits Commission.

# [19]

# WELFARE, RIGHTS AND DISCRETION

ROBERT E. GOODIN*

Theorists in a variety of disciplines have, for quite some time now, been saying that a—perhaps the—defining feature of the welfare state is its commitment to providing a certain range of goods and services to its citizens 'as of right'.[1] From T. H. Marshall's classic lectures on 'Citizenship and Social Class' forward, we have grown accustomed to tracing the history of the welfare state in terms of the expanding 'rights of citizenship'.[2] From the welfare rights movement of the 1960s onward, we have grown accustomed to thinking of welfare rights as the clear alternatives to more odious forms of official discretion.[3] And so on.

Many have probably always felt some lingering unease when employing such formulations. Many—especially those touched by modern analytic philosophy—probably have long suspected that the concept of 'rights' was not exactly what was needed in such contexts. But although perhaps not quite right, it was a fair approximation and would serve perfectly adequately for the purposes at hand. So, swallowing hard, they have tended to make do with the concept of 'welfare rights', promising to come back to the conceptual issues some day and sort them out properly. It is that kind of long-overdue promissory note that I shall here be attempting to honour.

Straightaway I should say that I shall be raising none of the once-standard philosophical objections to the very notion of a 'welfare right' as such. Early critics of the UN Declaration of Human Rights, for example, used to protest that the notion of positive rights is a nonsense, insisting that we can properly talk only of negative rights against interference from others.[4] But that claim has now been effectively withdrawn; it is now well-established that certain rights of both a negative ('security') and a positive ('subsistence') kind are not only compatible with but are actually presupposed by all rights claims.[5]

*Senior Lecturer in Government, University of Essex. An earlier version of this article was read to the Social Administration Association's annual conference in York, July 1985. I am grateful for helpful comments, then and later, from Michael Adler, P. S. Atiyah, David Bull, Paul Spicker, Jeremy Waldron and a reader for this *Journal*.

1 A standard definition would be that 'the welfare state necessarily entails compulsory, collective provision for certain basic needs as a matter of right': R. E. Goodin, 79 *American Political Science Rev* 784 (1985). See more generally R. E. Goodin, *Protecting the Vulnerable* (Univ of Chicago Press 1985) chaps 6 & 7.

2 *Class, Citizenship and Social Development* (Univ of Chicago Press 1964) 71–134 and 13 *Sociological Rev* 261 (1965).

3 R. M. Titmuss, 42 *Political Q* 113 (1971). J. Jowell, *Public L* 178 (1973).

4 D. D. Raphael, ed., *Political Theory and the Rights of Man* (Indiana Univ Press 1967).

5 J. Waldron, ed., *Theories of Rights* (Oxford Univ Press 1984) 11. H. Shue, *Basic Rights* (Princeton Univ Press 1980).



 

My worry with welfare rights is less fundamental and more pragmatic. I am concerned, not with any incoherence in the concept itself, but rather with the question of whether such rights are what people really need in order to secure their welfare interests. Threats to those interests arise from nature on the one side and petty officials on the other. It is the latter sort of threat—arising from abuse of official discretion—that provides the principal focus for this paper.

My conclusions are largely discouraging. Some kinds of discretion are ineliminable, and some problems with discretion are apparently insurmountable. After having mapped the dimensions of the concept (Section I) and shown why some forms of discretion are logically ineliminable from any system of rules (Section II), I proceed to survey four major moral objections to discretionary powers (Section III). These problems all seem to be inherent in discretion, in the sense that there is no way to curtail the problems without curtailing the discretions themselves (Section IV). But in three out of the four cases, rules designed to overcome these problems with discretion could—and probably would—reproduce the very same problems themselves (Section V). Thus, of the many things wrong with discretion, there seems to be only one—its tendency to manipulation and exploitation—that a regime of strict rules could hope to remedy. Even then, that is best accomplished through rules different in form from the standard 'welfare rights', and focusing instead on notions of officials' duties and responsibilities (Section VI). As for those problems with discretion that rules cannot hope to remedy, the best strategy would probably be to try to circumvent them through more generous funding of the social services (Section VII).

## I. DEFINING 'DISCRETION'

'Discretion' admits of two types of characterization, one positive and one negative. On the positive characterization, an official can be said to have discretion if and only if he is empowered to pursue some social goal(s) in the context of individual cases in such a way as he judges to be best calculated, in the circumstances, to promote those goals.[6]

The negative characterization of discretion is well-represented by Dworkin's remark that 'discretion' is 'like the hole in the doughnut', which does not exist except as an area left open by a surrounding belt of restriction'.[7] On that negative analysis, 'discretion' is a residual notion, defined in terms of its opposite: viz, official outcomes (typically, officials' decisions) being strictly determined by rules, and rules alone. The sheer absence of rules is not enough to qualify the situation as 'discretionary', however. There is, for example, no rule governing the colour I as a homeowner paint my bathroom; yet it seems distinctly odd to prattle on about my 'discretion' in the matter. Where freedom is taken for granted, the situation seems ill-described in terms of discretion at all. Only when there is some

6 I am indebted to Jeremy Waldron, personal correspondence, for this formulation.

7 R. M. Dworkin, *Taking Rights Seriously* (Butterworth 1977) 31.

prima-facie expectation that the decision will be subject to constraints of a particular, rule-like form is the absence of such constraints a matter for comment. And, more to the present point, only then is it describable as an occasion for the exercise of 'discretion' at all. Were I a public housing tenant, subject to various other rules about repainting, then I might be said to have discretion if those rules left open the question of bathroom colours in a way that as a homeowner (not ordinarily subject to any such rules) I am not. Thus, discretion refers to an area of conduct which is generally governed by rules but where the dictates of the rules are indeterminate. In short, discretion refers, negatively, to a lacuna in a system of rules.

These two characterizations, one positive and the other negative, perhaps give a different flavour to discussions of discretion. Formally, however, I take them to be extensionally equivalent. Since my focus here is upon ways of limiting discretion rather than of extending it, the negative characterization—emphasizing the role of rules in restricting discretion—will prove the more useful.

Various different *types* of discretion can be identified by reference to rules of the general form:

*Rule R:* If some individual *I*, who satisfies certain background conditions *B*, displays characteristics *K* in circumstances *C*, then an individual *O*, who occupies official position *P*, should do thing *T* to or for that individual *I*.

In the context of social welfare policy, *I* will typically be a claimant, *O* a caseworker (and *P* the position of 'caseworker'). *K* will refer to the claimant's personal characteristics (e.g., old age, blindness), and *C* to various other impersonal features of the claimant's circumstances (e.g., homelessness, joblessness). *B* will refer to background conditions required for the claimant even to have legal standing to file a claim (e.g., citizenship, residency, paid-up National Insurance contributions). The treatment *T* will characteristically refer to the providing or the withholding of some particular benefits or services stipulated in social security legislation.

With this general characterization of a rule in hand, we can now distinguish several varieties of discretion.

*(1) Strong discretion.* To say that an official *O* enjoys 'strong discretion' in respect to some treatment *T* is to say that: (a) there is some rule *R* allowing the official *O* to provide treatment *T* to or for individuals; but (b) the rule imposes no constraints on what treatment the official gives to any particular individual *I* (i.e., the rule contains no reference to factors *B*, *K* or *C*).

Strong discretion is sometimes defined, more simply but less precisely, as the *absence* of any rule *R*.[8] Although this may be a useful shorthand, it is strictly

8 Dworkin's comment that, in cases of strong discretion, the official 'is simply not bound by standards set by the authority in question' admits of such a reading, although that is probably not the one he intended; Dworkin, *supra* n 7, 32.

speaking incorrect. Discretionary power is power exercised *under* some rule. Those exercising it have broad latitude under that rule in deciding how to exercise that power. But unless the power derives from some rule in the first place, it would not constitute a case of discretionary power at all. Hence the necessity of clause 1(a) in the above definition.

The opposite of strong discretion is, obviously, weak discretion. This can be defined as follows:

*(2) Weak discretion.* An official *O* can be said to enjoy 'weak discretion' if: (a) there is some rule *R* directing official *O* to provide treatment *T* to or for individuals *I* under certain conditions *B, K* and *C*; but (b) that rule leaves the official with some latitude in deciding either *who* (i.e., which *I*) is to benefit or *what* (i.e., which *T*) beneficiaries are to receive.[9]

Official rules are sometimes explicitly permissive in these respects. Rules sometimes say, for example, that anyone displaying certain attributes *may* be given certain benefits (e.g., job training), without requiring that everyone displaying those attributes *must* be given such benefits. Or sometimes rules say that anyone meeting certain descriptions should receive treatment within some specified range (e.g., for convicted thieves, one to five years' imprisonment), while leaving the choice of the precise treatment within that range to the official's discretion.

This suggests another pair of contrasts:

*(3) Formal discretion.* If options as regards beneficiaries (*I*) or treatments (*T*) are explicitly written into rule *R*, officials *O* will be said to have 'formal discretion'.

*(4) Informal discretion.* Officials *O* will be said to enjoy 'informal discretion' if they enjoy options as regards beneficiaries (*I*) or treatments (*T*) that are merely implicit in the statement of rule *R*.

Typically, informal discretion derives from vagueness in the formulation of the rule-statement. Vagueness in specifying who is to receive benefits (i.e., in specifying *C*) or under what circumstances they are to be received (i.e., in specifying *K* or *B*) might leave officials with substantial effective discretion in applying a rule. Formulae like 'exceptional needs' or 'exceptional circumstances', built into the UK Supplementary Benefits scheme by the Social Security Act of 1966, were very permissive indeed. So too might vagueness in specifying treatment (*T*) leave officials with considerable latitude. Familiar fudges of this sort trade on notions of 'suitable' or 'appropriate' treatment, 'treatment in the best interests of the child', and so on.[10]

These two distinctions cut across one another, yielding four composite categories. Officials can enjoy *weak formal* discretion, where their options are explicit in the rule; or they can enjoy *weak informal* discretion where they are not.

9 T. D. Campbell, in N. Timms and D. Watson, eds, *Philosophy in Social Work* (Routledge and Kegan Paul 1978) 50–77.

10 E. Freund, 30 *Yale LJ* 437 (1921) and J. Handler, *Protecting the Social Service Client* (Academic Press 1979) 8–9.

They can enjoy ***strong formal*** discretion, where the rule granting them power pointedly refrains from setting conditions for the exercise of that power. They can also enjoy ***strong informal*** discretion. This is perhaps a less obvious category, but it is nonetheless real and nonetheless important. It is often unclear whether rule *R* (or any rule *R*) applies, either because it is unclear whether official *O* satisfies all the conditions laid down by the job description *P* or else because it is unclear whether claimant *I* satisfies background conditions *B*. By virtue of these ambiguities, the official would then be said to enjoy strong informal discretion in applying rule *R*.

There is yet another set of distinctions that cuts across all those others:

*(5) Provisional discretion.* An official *O* is said to have 'provisional' discretionary power if: (a) rule *R* gives that official some discretion, either strong or weak, formal or informal, in deciding what treatment *T* to provide to or for individual *I*; and (b) official *O*'s decision in that regard is subject to review, and possible overturning, by some other official *OO*.

Clause 5(b) makes the lower-level official's discretion 'provisional' in the sense of being 'temporary', i.e., pending higher-level review.[11]

*(6) Ultimate discretion.* An official *O* is said to have 'ultimate' discretionary power if: (a) rule *R* gives that official *O* some discretion, either strong or weak, formal or informal, in deciding what treatment *T* to provide to individual *I*; and (b) official *O*'s decision in that regard is not subject to review or possible overturning by any other official *OO*.

Obviously, strong and weak discretionary powers can come in either of these two forms, provisional or ultimate. Similarly, provisional or ultimate discretionary powers can be either formal or informal, i.e., either explicit or implicit in the statement of the rules. The case of formal, explicit grants of either form of discretion is utterly straightforward. The fact that such powers are sometimes granted informally and implicitly is equally undeniable.[12] But it is a phenomenon that is slightly more complicated to analyze. Essentially the informal, implicit granting of ultimate discretionary power amounts to a failure of the rules to empower any other official *OO* to review the judgments of official *O*; then, by implication if not by formal edict, official *O*'s discretion in the matter is ultimate. The informal granting of provisional discretionary powers amounts to the explicit granting of rights of review to some other official *OO*, conjoined with an implicit pledge on the part of the official *OO* that such power will not in fact be used to override official *O*'s decisions.

11 Dworkin, *supra* n 7, 32, runs together 'weak' and 'provisional' discretion.

12 A striking case in point is early Victorian emigration officers. The discharge of their duties was characterized by 'the absence of a real superintendence. No person or department within the colonial office was directly and specifically responsible for the officers. Hay acknowledged and filed their correspondence; but otherwise, unless a scandal arose or an expenditure was proposed, they were left entirely to their own devices'; O. MacDonagh, *A Pattern of Government Growth, 1800–1860* (MacGibbon & Kee 1961) 108.

For the sake of brevity, I shall in the balance of this paper refer to the situation in which an official has formal, strong, ultimate discretion as being a situation in which he has 'complete' discretion in the matter.

## II. INELIMINABLE DISCRETIONS

It is widely agreed that a certain amount of discretion will inevitably prove necessary. Those concerned with social assistance typically give examples such as the need to leave officials with discretionary powers to make extraordinary payments to people in truly exceptional circumstances, such as fire or flood.[13]

Now, it may well be a bad idea—for all sorts of reasons—to curtail such discretion, either by prohibiting such payments altogether or by codifying them in the ordinary rules of social service departments. But all of those reasons, whatever they are, are of a practical character. The 'necessity' in view there is pragmatic rather than logical necessity. Eliminating such discretions may be inadvisable, but it is not logically impossible.

That weaker sense of inevitability does not here concern me. I shall instead be discussing two ways in which discretion is inevitable in the stronger sense. These are discretions that are inevitable, in the sense that they are logically necessary to the operation of a system of rules at all. Such discretions are truly ineliminable: they cannot be eliminated except by eliminating the system of rules itself.[14]

The first such aspect of discretion concerns the fundamental choice of which rules to adopt in the first place. Such discretion is ineliminable, in that it cannot be removed from the system altogether. Of course, it can be removed from any particular official or level of officials. Indeed, such discretion can be moved all around the system: it can be shifted from lower-level officials to higher ones, or onto judges, or onto Parliament, or whatever. There may be meta-rules telling us when to apply particular first-order rules; there may be meta-meta-rules telling us when to apply particular meta-rules; and so forth. But at some point the regress must stop.

In a straightforward analogy to Gödel's theorem,[15] a system of social rules simply *must* appeal to something outside itself at some point or another. To what it appeals is an open question. For John Austin it is a 'general habit of obedience' to Sovereign; for H. L. A. Hart it is some combination of 'serious social pressure' externally applied and a 'critical reflective attitude' internalized by those subject to the rules.[16] But wherever and however you stop the regress, it is clear that there

13 Supplementary Benefits Commission (SBC), *Annual Report 1976* cmnd 6910 (HMSO 1977) para 7.54. D. Donnison, 41 *New Society* 534 (1977). Department of Health and Social Security (DHSS), *Social Assistance* (DHSS 1978) para 9.47. J. Handler and M. Sosin, *Last Resorts* (Academic Press 1983).

14 And since 'no rules' is itself a rule, they cannot be eliminated in that way, either.

15 E. Nagel and J. R. Newman, *Gödel's Proof* (Routledge and Kegan Paul 1959).

16 H. L. A. Hart, *Concept of Law* (Clarendon Press 1961).

must be something standing outside and underlying the system of rules. Insofar as it does, then someone, somewhere must enjoy discretionary power in adopting one set of rules rather than another. The question is not whether someone somewhere in the system will have discretion of this sort, but merely who.[17]

A second respect in which discretion is ineliminable is in the act of bringing particular cases under the ambit of general rules. Acts imply agency; and rules, whatever might be said about them, cannot plausibly qualify as agents in their own right. As Hart wryly remarks, 'Particular fact-situations do not await us already marked off from each other, and labelled as instances of the general rule, the application of which is in question; nor can the rule itself step forward to claim its own instances.'[18] Here, too, there is necessarily scope for independent judgment.[19]

Even where fairly precise decision criteria are laid down (as in the British Social Security Act of 1980, for example) the criteria still admit of substantial scope for interpretation in their application. A rule that says 'Pay an old age pension of £60 per week to anyone over 65 years of age' would seem to admit of relatively little discretion in its application to any particular case. The presentation of a birth certificate would usually settle the question of the applicability of this rule to the case of any particular claimant. But even in such relatively clear-cut cases, there is always still some scope for independent judgment: officials must exercise discretion, for example, in deciding whether or not they believe the document to be genuine.[20]

Again, although the exercise of this second sort of discretion is inevitable, the question of *who* is to exercise it remains open. At least in the first instance, it will typically be exercised by the line staff, who are the ones that initially confront clients and render a decision on their pleas by bringing their cases under the ambit of various general rules. Caseworkers' discretion in classifying claimants may, of course, be merely provisional and subject to higher-level review. When such review is undertaken, discretion passes from the caseworkers to their superiors. And if superiors' decisions are themselves subject to appeal and review by still higher-level officials, the discretion migrates still further up the hierarchy. Here again, however, the buck must stop *somewhere.* This form of discretion, like the last, must be exercised in an ultimate way by someone somewhere in the system. The only question is, *by whom*?

17 R. M. Dworkin, 60 *J of Philosophy* 624, 628 (1963). H. van Gunsteren, *Quest for Control* (Wiley 1976) chap 4. Notice that questions about the derivation of rules are different from questions about the enforcement of rules. Problems of infinite regress in the latter realm can be solved by 'self-referring laws', as shown by H. L. A. Hart, *Essays in Jurisprudence and Philosophy* (Clarendon Press 1983) 170–78; but this solution cannot be plausibly employed in the former realm as well.

18 Hart, *supra* n 16, 123.

19 Some prefer to call this 'judgment' rather than 'discretion' at all. See Titmuss, *supra* n 3, 119; SBC, *supra* n 13, para 1.39; Donnison, *supra* n 13, 534.

20 R. M. Titmuss, 23 *International Social Security Rev* 259, 264 (1970).

Saying that it is 'just' a question of who exercises these discretions is not to say that we are indifferent as between the various possibilities. On the contrary, we seem to have strong views on these matters. We would much prefer rule-making discretions to be exercised by legislators, and ultimate rule-applying ones by judges; and we worry much less than we might (and perhaps should) about leaving such discretions to those agents.[21] Part of the reason may have to do with their greater capacities to make substantively correct decisions: legislators can take a broader view than can a caseworker who is immersed in the details of some particular case, and judges can reach a more considered opinion on a particular case than can a harried caseworker who is preoccupied with the details of many complicated claims all at once. Another important part of the reason may have to do with their greater accountability: legislators and judges, even, are more powerfully and directly accountable to the Sovereign (construed as the electorate or the Crown) than lowly caseworkers. But whatever reasons we may have for thinking that some allocations of these ineliminable discretions are superior to others, they cannot change the fact that those discretions are indeed ineliminable.

## III. PROBLEMS WITH DISCRETION

Here I shall trace four distinct strands to the opposition to discretionary powers. For these purposes, I shall focus upon the limiting case of 'complete' (strong, formal, ultimate) discretion. The objections which I here canvass pertain to discretion quite generally, as the breadth of my examples will show. But I shall also try to show through the use of actual examples or 'stylized facts' that these general problems are of particular relevance to the social services.

### *(1) Manipulation and Exploitation*

The classic objection to one person having discretionary control over the disposition of resources which another needs is that that person thereby acquires *power* over the other. Such a person can lay down all sorts of demands and back them up with threats to withhold the needed resources from the other unless that person complies with those demands. If the threatener really does have complete discretion in the disposition of those resources, there would seem to be nothing to prevent the making or carrying out of those threats. And if the other person really does need the resources in question, there would seem to be little that that person could do but to comply with the demands.[22]

Possibly the most dramatic example of such manipulation *via* discretionary powers comes in connection with the penal sanction in eighteenth-century England. The gentry enjoyed substantial discretionary powers, firstly, in deciding whether or not to prosecute, since the vast majority of prosecutions were then private prosecutions. Secondly, there was considerable scope for judges to exercise

21 P. S. Atiyah, *From Principles to Pragmatism* (Oxford Univ Press 1978).

22 Goodin, *Protecting the Vulnerable, supra* n 1, chap 7.

discretionary power in recommending 'mercy' for convicted criminals. (Fully half of those convicted of hanging offences in this period were not, in fact, hanged.) Parasitic upon that discretion was the further discretionary power of local gentlemen and peers either to lobby or not to lobby for a pardon for the convicted criminal. From all that discretionary control over the criminal sanction, the gentry derived substantial power to control the population at large in a variety of ways not formally covered by the law. Since poor people could never know when or in what ways they might need to appeal to the gentry's mercy, and since that mercy was wholly discretionary, they dared not do anything to offend them. 'Discretion allowed a prosecutor to terrorize the petty thief and then command his gratitude.... In the countryside the power of gentlemen and peers to punish or forgive worked in the same way to maintain the fabric of obedience, gratitude and deference.'[23]

That is a particularly dramatic example of discretion serving as a source of illicit power. It is widely remarked, however, that social welfare programmes serve the same social-control functions, and that they do so in much the same ways. 'The law of social welfare grew up on the theory that welfare is a "gratuity" furnished by the state, and thus may be made subject to whatever conditions the state sees fit to impose.'[24] Legislatures, exercising their undoubted discretionary powers, sometimes impose social-control riders on welfare legislation. Some of the conditions they lay down bear some obvious, direct relationship to the purposes of the programmes. Others do not. Notable among these is the requirement in the US Economic Opportunity Act of 1964 that participants in Lyndon Johnson's Great Society must swear allegiance to the United States Constitution.[25]

Administrators of welfare programmes, too, often exercise their discretionary powers 'to impose standards of morality [on welfare recipients] not imposed on the rest of the community'.[26] Some of the more striking examples of abusing discretion to control client conduct grow out of the discretionary powers of administrators of public housing projects to evict or to deny admission to those who are, in some ill-defined way, 'undesirable tenants'.[27]

The truth of these criticisms is so undeniable that the point is now officially conceded. In its review of the UK Supplementary Benefits scheme, the Department of Health and Social Security acknowledges that the discretionary elements formerly contained therein were 'an element of the scheme ... open to exploitation and pressure'.[28]

23 D. Hay, *Albion's Fatal Tree* (Allen Lane 1975) 49.

24 C. A. Reich, 74 *Yale LJ* 1245 (1965). See similarly: A. D. Smith 63 *Harvard LR* 266 (1949); C. A. Reich, 72 *Yale LJ* 1347 (1963) and 73 *Yale LJ* 733 (1964); and Handler, *supra* n 10, 3–8. There is surprisingly strong adherence to this view even among claimants, judging from S. Briar, 54 *California LR* 370 (1966).

25 C. A. Reich, 74 *Yale LJ* 1245, 1250 (1965).

26 C. A. Reich, 72 *Yale LJ* 1347, 1359 (1963). See similarly Reich, *supra* n 25, 1247 and Campbell, *supra* n 9, 66–7.

27 K. C. Davis, *Discretionary Justice* (Louisiana State Univ Press 1969) 78.

28 DHSS, *supra* n 13, para 9.10; see similarly D. Donnison, 5 *J of Social Policy* 337, 348 (1976).

Note that the objection is not to the laying down of conditions *per se*. There is nothing that is always and ever wrong, either conclusively or even just presumptively, with laying down conditions that others must meet before you do something good (or refrain from doing something bad) to or for them. My greengrocer offers me beans on condition I pay for them; whether he provides me with beans is entirely within his discretion, and no one would regard it as an unacceptable exercise of that discretionary power for him to make delivery of the beans conditional upon receipt of my money. Likewise, no one would regard it as an unacceptable exercise of discretionary powers for a judge or parole board to release prisoners on condition that they not make contact with known felons. Nor, presumably, would most of us regard it as an unacceptable exercise of discretionary power for the leglislature to make employment benefits conditional upon the recipient trying to find work.

The central issue is what conditions are acceptable, and what ones are not. Existing philosophical literature on the permissibility of threats and offers more generally does not provide as much leverage on this question as might be supposed. The standard conclusion there is, basically, that it would be wrong to threaten to do what it would be wrong to do.[29] But that cannot be the whole problem here. Surely at least *some* instances of discretionary power are wholly justified; and what it means to say that they are wholly justified is that it would *not* be wrong for the bearer of this discretionary power to withhold the benefits or to impose the burden. How, then, could it be wrong to do conditionally what it is not wrong to do unconditionally?

The problem must lie in the *nature* of the condition imposed. The real objection, I suggest, is to taking advantage of the situation in which your discretion gives you power over others to realize benefits (or to pursue projects, more generally) in some other sphere altogether. The inappropriate taking advantage of a situation in this way constitutes 'exploitation'.[30] Admittedly, 'inappropriateness' is a slippery notion, and formalistic analyses (dealing in terms of 'structural similarities' between treatment and justificatory circumstance) will clearly not suffice to explicate it completely. In the end, we will have to fall back on only slightly less slippery notions of the 'official purpose' and 'underlying principles' of the programme to guide us. The weakness of that approach is that it never yields a clear-cut, conclusive answer as to whether any instance of the conditional exercise of discretionary power counts as exploitative.[31] But the strength of that approach lies in drawing out most dramatically precisely what is

29 V. Haksar, 4 *Political Theory* 65 (1976).

30 R. E. Goodin, 'Exploiting a Situation and Exploiting a Person', Paper Presented to ECPR Joint Sessions, Barcelona, 1985.

31 Indeed, the reason the law was left vague, and administrators therefore enjoy the discretion they do, was often precisely that legislators could not agree on any single purpose or goal: they adopted vague formulae to patch over cracks in the enacting coalition. T. Prosser, in M. Adler and S. Asquith, eds, *Discretion and Welfare* (Heinemann 1981) 148–70.

at issue between those who deride discretion in any particular instance as exploitative and those who do not: viz, what precisely the goals, purposes and underlying principles of the programme in question actually are, or should be.

This analysis of the exploitation of discretionary powers bears close relation to the notion of 'abuse of process' found in tort law.[32] A standard example from that domain would be this: If I have injured you, then you may prosecute me for it. But you may not threaten to prosecute me, merely with a view to obtaining money from me to induce you to drop the threat. To do so would be to abuse the legal process—to use the law allowing prosecution of those who have caused injuries in a way that is wholly inappropriate, contrary to its intentions and true purposes.[33] So, too, does the setting of certain sorts of preconditions that must be met before you will exercise your discretionary powers to another's advantage constitute an exploitative abuse of the purposes for which the discretion was granted in the first place.[34]

### *(2) Arbitrariness*

A second objection to discretionary powers is couched in terms of arbitrariness. Insofar as someone enjoys complete (strong, formal, ultimate) discretionary control over some matter, then it follows from the definitions offered in Section I that that person is not obliged to have, much less to give, any reasons whatsoever for deciding one way rather than another. That is to say, someone with complete discretion is at liberty to act 'arbitrarily' not only in the weak sense of 'acting without reasons that are known to and can be relied on in advance by those affected by his actions', but also in the strong sense of 'acting without reasons' altogether. That follows simply from the definition of 'complete discretion'. (Whether or not anyone ever actually enjoys such complete discretion is, perhaps, another matter.)

Whereas with rule-governed decisions one is obliged to demonstrate that one has made the right decision, with completely discretionary decisions one need merely demonstrate that one was within one's rights in making the decision as one has done.[35] There will typically be review bodies charged with the task of determining whether or not officials have kept within their powers. Such reviews designed to preclude officials from acting outside their proper spheres do not, in and of themselves, necessarily diminish the discretionary powers of officials to act within their proper spheres. In practice, however, this power of review tends to be used in such a way as to render officials' discretion substantially less complete

32 W. Prosser, *Handbook of the Law of Torts*, 4th ed (West 1971) 856–8.

33 G. Williams, *Criminal LR* 79 (1954).

34 Courts similarly construe the notion of 'abuse of discretion': 'discretion must be exercised in the manner intended by the empowering Act', and will be held *ultra vires* if it is not; H. W. R. Wade, *Administrative Law*, 5th ed (Clarendon Press 1982) 353, 355, 361. Invalidating administrative acts in this way, however, constitutes solving the problems with discretion by eliminating discretion, as Section IV will argue.

35 J. L. Mashaw, *Bureaucratic Justice* (Yale Univ Press 1983) 9–10.

than it might at first appear to be. From Coke's day forward, English courts have imposed substantive tests as well as formal ones in determining whether officials have acted within their proper powers. Discretionary power, it is said, is granted to officials in order for them to make 'reasonable' decisions; unreasonable decisions thus exceed their powers, and are to be held *ultra vires*.[36] That is merely to say that the official's discretion is not 'complete' (because it is not 'ultimate'). The problems with discretion (here, arbitrariness) are solved merely by reducing discretion.

Insofar as some matter truly is within the *complete* discretion of some official, there is very little for others (be they that official's national superiors, or other agencies or branches of government) to consider on appeal. In such cases, appeals panels will have to confine themselves to a very narrow range of questions. They may ask whether the case was indeed one over which the official in question truly enjoyed discretionary power, and whether the decisions rendered actually fell within the limits of that official's discretion. They may even go so far as to enquire whether there was at least *some* reason for front-line officials to decide the case as they did.[37] But insofar as complete discretionary power is truly lodged with those lower-level officials themselves, a 'higher-level' appeals tribunal cannot properly substitute its judgment for theirs.[38]

Avoiding appeals is sometimes precisely the intention underlying the grant of discretion. One early and particularly dramatic case in point comes in Oliver MacDonagh's study of early Victorian policies concerning the powers of emigration officers at UK ports to set and enforce standards governing the stowage of iron cargoes on passenger ships. When one such officer came under threat of suit for abusing that authority, the powers-that-be responded by giving such officers absolute and complete discretionary powers in such matters, explicitly with a view to preventing any further such second-guessing of officers' judgments.[39]

Opposition to the arbitrariness of discretionary powers has a long and glorious

36 Wade, *supra* n 34, 353 and chaps 2 and 12, passim. Ruling on a complaint against arbitrary administration of public housing programmes, a US Court of Appeals has similarly held that, 'The government as a landlord is still the government. It must not act arbitrarily, for, unlike private landlords, it is subject to the requirements of due process of law. Arbitrary action is not due process'; Davis, *supra* n 27, 80.

37 Wade, *supra* n 34, 289–90. Handler, *supra* n 10, 51.

38 Wade, *supra* n 34, 34–6; see similarly G. Marshall, *Constitutional Conventions* (Oxford Univ Press 1984) 82 on the powers of the UK Parliamentary Commissioner (the Ombudsman). Insofar as appeals tribunals *do* substitute their judgment for that of lower-level officials (in effect, rehearing the case), then the ultimate discretionary power rests with the appeals tribunal and the lower-level official only enjoys 'provisional' discretion; that was the case with UK Supplementary Benefits Appeal Tribunals prior to the 1980 reforms, for example (DHSS, *supra* n 13, para 3.6). Jeremy Waldron is right to point out, in personal correspondence, that there is often a good reason for insulating the grant of discretion from appellate review: viz, if discretion is given to officials so that decisions can reflect the full facts of particular circumstances, then it would be counterproductive to allow a superior body which is less well-acquainted with the particular circumstances to substitute its judgment for theirs.

39 O. MacDonagh, 2 *Victorian Studies* 29 (1958).

history. It figures centrally in Dicey's plea for a 'rule of law, not men'. On his analysis, the 'rule of law . . . means . . . the absolute supremacy or predominance of regular law as opposed to the influence of arbitrary power, and excludes the existence of arbitrariness, of prerogative, or even of wide discretionary authority on the part of the government'.[40]

That case against *complete* discretion has been made so often and so persuasively over so many years that there are relatively few offenders left. Nowadays the argument is principally levelled against parole boards, which insistently (and, in the US, in defiance of the clear provisions of the Administrative Procedure Act) refuse to give reasons for their decisions on the parole petitions which come before them.[41]

Until surprisingly recently, however, the failure to give reasons for action (at least to give them as a matter of course) characterized the administration of social welfare policies as well. Supplementary Benefit claimants in the UK were not routinely given an explanation of how the officer in charge of their case arrived at the figure representing how much they would receive in benefits; they had to ask for an A124 if they wanted such an explanation.[42] And the same was, until recently, true even on appeal. Since the decision of the Appeal Tribunal was to be final, it was long held that 'there was "absolutely no reason at all" why reasons should be given if there was no further right of appeal'.[43] Later it was decided that appellants should be supplied with written reasons for the Tribunal's decision, but only upon specific request; such requests were received from only two percent of appellants.[44] Now, at last, written statements of Tribunals' reasons are compulsory. But it is still the case that claimants are unclear in their own minds 'about the extent to which they are eligible for discretionary payments, and are critical of what appear to be arbitrary and discriminatory benefits which some receive but others do not'.[45]

### *(3) Uncertainty and Insecurity*

From arbitrariness flows uncertainty, unpredictability and insecurity. Insofar as some matter is completely discretionary, and depends wholly upon some official's

40 A. V. Dicey, *The Law of the Constitution*, 7th ed (Macmillan 1908) 198. Administrative lawyers now seem satisfied that discretions can coexist with the rule of law. The review mechanisms they trust to guarantee the absence of arbitrariness, however, do so only by reducing discretionary powers, thus confirming the thesis of Section IV below. See Wade, *supra* n 34, 22–6 and chap 12; and Davis, *supra* n 27, 27–44.

41 Davis, *supra* n 27, 126–33.

42 E. Briggs and A. M. Rees, *Supplementary Benefits and the Consumer* (Bedford Square Press/NCVO 1980).

43 Testimony of Sir Harold Fieldhouse, secretary of the National Assistance Board, to the Franks Committee; quoted in A. Bradley, in M. Adler and A. Bradley, eds, *Justice, Discretion and Poverty* (London: Professional Books 1975) 33–54, 40.

44 M. Herman, *Administrative Justice and Supplementary Benefits* (Bell 1972) 56.

45 DHSS, *supra* n 13, para 9.5.

own arbitrary will, those who are subject to the decision will have no good way of predicting what the outcome will be.[46] At most, they might try to make some inferences based on the official's past practices. But since there was never any compelling reason for the official to behave in one way rather than another in the past (or at least since no reason was enunciated in the past), there is no particularly good reason to expect similar decisions in the future, even from the same official. Still less is there any reason to expect that other officials will fit the pattern of the first.

All those points are familiar from the arguments of legal philosophers of the Realist School. To those arguments must be added another, this one owing to rule-utilitarians. Many worthwhile projects can be realized only insofar as we can confidently predict what others will do, and frame our own action-plans accordingly. Hence, discretion-mad act-utilitarians, choosing to do exactly the right thing in each and every circumstance, may by reason of the unpredictability of their behaviour end up doing more (indirect) harm than (direct) good.[47]

Throughout history, this unpredictability objection has been central to arguments against discretionary powers. Coke picturesquely contrasts 'the golden and straight metwand' of law with 'the uncertain and crooked cord of discretion'.[48] Hayek inveighs against social planning on account of its 'progressive introduction of . . . vague formulas into legislation . . . and of the increasing arbitrariness and uncertainty of, and the consequent disrespect for, the law. . . .'[49] Merchants and manufacturers whose activities are subject to state regulation constantly complain that, when those regulations are enforced by officials with broad discretionary powers, uncertainty and unpredictability is thereby engendered.[50] Even those who would have little sympathy with the cause of business in general nonetheless see an important connection between procedural due process and fixed, predictable rules.[51]

The poor are, and rationally should be, particularly sensitive to any such uncertainties. The poorer one is, the more urgent one's need to be able to budget in advance. Even subsistence farmers in Southeast Asia clearly prefer a lower average payoff with less variation from year to year to a higher average payoff with more variation, as is evidenced by their continuing to plant traditional strains of rice in preference to the new strains of 'wonder rice'.[52] In Tawney's analogy,

46 F. A. Hayek, *The Road to Serfdom* (Routledge 1944) 72. O. S. Franks, *Report of the Committee on Administrative Tribunals and Enquiries* cmnd 218 (HMSO 1957) 6.

47 D. H. Hodgson, *Consequences of Utilitarianism* (Clarendon Press 1967). F. E. Kydland and E. C. Prescott, 85 *J of Political Economy* 473 (1977). Atiyah, *supra* n 21, 20–3.

48 Coke, 4 Inst 41, quoted in Wade, *supra* n 34, 22. See similarly Hart, *supra* n 16, chap 7; and Atiyah, *supra* n 21, 32.

49 Hayek, *supra* n 46, 78.

50 MacDonagh, *supra* n 39.

51 L. Fuller, *The Morality of the Law* (Yale Univ Press 1964). T. R. Kearns, in J. R. Pennock and J. W. Chapman, eds, *Nomos XVIII: Due Process* (New York Univ Press 1977) 229–56.

52 J. C. Scott, *The Moral Economy of the Peasant* (Yale Univ Press 1976).

the poor are like people up to their necks in water. Any slight wave will drown them.

Many see the modern welfare state as an instrument for providing the poor of our own societies with a certain level of 'security' akin to that offered by traditional modes of rice cultivation in peasant societies. That is certainly what Charles Reich thinks the 'new property' is—or could and should be.[53]

On this account, what is wrong with the charity-based approach to welfare is that charitable contributions are discretionary, and being discretionary they are (from the point of view of the recipient) utterly unreliable. There is no particular reason for any particular individual to be favoured by such benefices in the first place. Neither is there any particular reason to expect that such benefices will continue, once they have started. Such is the way of discretion.

Parallel complaints are, not surprisingly, lodged against discretionary elements in modern social welfare programmes. 'Discretion means uncertainty', some bluntly say.[54] Various examples lend credence to that claim. In the US, for example, public housing authorities have broad discretionary powers to evict 'undesirable' tenants, and they exercise that power by instituting a regime of 'month-to-month leases [that] maintain tenants in a state of insecurity' constantly.[55]

Again, however, the broad point is by now pretty well accepted. Even the Department of Health and Social Security, in its review of Supplementary Benefits, describes as the prime failing of the discretionary components of that scheme the fact that 'they make it more difficult for claimants to understand the extent of their entitlement to benefit'; and the DHSS report elsewhere says, 'It is essential that the detailed rules and practices of the scheme should be set out publicly in a sufficiently authoritative form for them to be followed consistently by both the officials administering them and the appeal tribunals'.[56]

### *(4) Privacy and Intrusiveness*

A fourth broad class of objections to discretionary powers is couched in terms of privacy and intrusiveness. The ethos of discretionary judgment is that they are able to be made on the basis of the 'full facts' of the particular case: such decisions are to be made with reference to 'the case in the round', rather than some selective aspects of it artificially isolated by some narrow rules; and so on. Now, if this advantage is to accrue, officials guided by discretion must necessarily base their decisions on more information about individual claimants than would officials guided by rules alone. Such an argument may not justify officials in gathering any

53 C. A. Reich, 73 *Yale LJ* 733 (1964) and *supra* n 25, 1255–6.

54 Briggs and Rees, *supra* n 42, 4. See similarly Jowell, *supra* n 3, 189–90 and Campbell, *supra* n 9, 64–5.

55 Reich, *supra* n 25, 1250.

56 DHSS, *supra* n 13, paras 9.10 and 3.13. See similarly Supplementary Benefits Commission (SBC), *Annual Report 1975* cmnd 6615 (HMSO 1976) para 2.17 and Donnison, *supra* n 28, 348.

and all information that they might like about claimants; it only justifies their gathering information arguably relevant to the decision at hand. But it remains inevitable nevertheless that in order to get the positive benefits we desire from discretion (treatment better fitting the particular case), there must necessarily be a more intrusive administrative apparatus prying more deeply into the private affairs of claimants.

Charges of 'snooping' are levelled with some regularity—and often with considerable justification—against officials enjoying discretionary power in the administration of social welfare programmes. One interwar example from Britain concerns the investigations of officials responsible for payment of unemployment benefits only to those 'available for work' but unable to find it. The Divisional Controller for the South-East reportedly advised investigators, 'It has proved more fruitful to call, ostensibly in error, at a neighbour's house instead of the correct address and to allow the line of inquiry to develop in accordance with the reception given by the neighbour. . . .'[57]

Similarly, in our own day, Supplementary Benefits officers administering discretionary clothing allowances under provision for payment for 'exceptional needs' often ask claimants to present their old shoes or overcoats to demonstrate that they are indeed in need of replacement. Supplementary Benefits officers sometimes impose a scheme of 'voluntary' savings for claimants who have demonstrated themselves incapable of handling their own money by making regular deductions from their entitlements.[58] The discretionary means chosen to enforce cohabitation ('man under the bed') provisions in welfare laws involved, in the US at least, 'midnight searches' of the most intrusive kinds.[59] While those particular practices have now ended, similar ones continue. Still we find in the US that 'merchants may be asked for information' about applicants for public welfare, 'financial data is checked, the whereabouts of relations is sought, . . .' and so on.[60] There is simply no settled judgment as to how much personal information administrators should, or legally could, collect about applicants for public relief.[61]

## IV. ARE THE PROBLEMS INHERENT IN DISCRETION?

Next I shall pose essentially the 'reformist' question. Is there any way to overcome the problems with discretion, described above, that does not entail depriving officials of discretion? I shall argue that the answer is 'no'. The problems are inherent in the practice of discretion, and can be overcome (if at all) only by removing discretion from officials.

57 Quoted in A. Deacon, *In Search of the Scrounger* (Bell 1976), 59–60.
58 SBC, *supra* n 13, para 1.43.
59 Reich, *supra* n 26, 1347.
60 Reich, *supra* n 25, 1247–8.
61 Handler, *supra* n 10, 110–116.

The clearest example of such an inherent problem is 'arbitrariness'. Insofar as an official has complete discretion, then to that extent the official is not *bound* by anything (rules, reasons, or what have you) to decide one way rather than another. The official may, and usually will, have various reasons for deciding a case as he did; the official might volunteer (or might even be legally obliged to enunciate) the reasons. But the point about completely discretionary decisions is that, being completely discretionary, those reasons were not (and are not, in the future) binding. The official was (and is) free to act on those reasons. Equally, the official was (and is) free to act on any of several others.[62] Completely discretionary judgments are, to that extent, always and necessarily 'arbitrary' decisions in that sense.

It may well be true that few decisions are ever completely discretionary, of course. Discretions are often hedged with guidelines, standards, principles, parameters, and so on. Court-imposed standards of 'reasonableness', already referred to, are one important example; and Kenneth Culp Davis's various proposals for further 'structuring discretion' would all further hedge discretion in this way.[63] Likewise, discretions are often hedged with review and appeals procedures; and Davis's various proposals for further 'checking discretion' would also further hedge discretion in this way.[64] But insofar as guidelines, etc. are binding rather than being merely advisory, or insofar as higher tribunals substitute their judgment for the official's own on the particulars of the case, then to that extent the official is thereby deprived of discretion. Our objection to the arbitrariness of that official's discretionary power may have been overcome, but only by removing discretionary power from that official.[65]

Much the same is true—and for much the same reasons—of the 'insecurity' objection. Insofar as completely discretionary decisions are necessarily arbitrary, they are to that extent necessarily unpredictable. Those who must rely upon them for needed resources suffer a certain amount of insecurity in consequence.

Again, there are various ways to ameliorate this insecurity. Probably the best proposal is for everyone to be guaranteed a certain baseline—a 'security level'—with deviations from that being permitted only in the upward direction.

62 There may be some reasons which he cannot act upon—his discretion may be narrowed in that way, while remaining complete over the narrower range of reasons for which he may still act or refrain from acting. But proscribing some reasons as bad ones is not the same as prescribing others as mandatory ones.

63 Davis, *supra* n 27, chap 4. Notice, however, that insofar as officials who have formally been granted discretion by the legislature exercise that discretion by blindly following some rule, courts will strike their decisions down as 'unreasonable'; Wade, *supra* n 34, 330.

64 Davis, *supra* n 27, chap 5.

65 The same is true of 'due process' constraints on discretion. Insofar as that is a purely procedural test, demanding merely proper procedures (fair hearing, adequate notice, etc), then there is no guarantee that the decision was reached for the 'right' reasons, or indeed for any non-arbitrary reasons. Insofar as 'due process' contains some substantive test (such as that the decision be 'reasonable'), then to that extent it limits the arbitrariness of discretionary judgments—but only by limiting the discretionariness of discretionary judgments.

Much of the social security system is now like that. Everyone is guaranteed a basic pension or grant, and deviations from that (e.g., Supplementary Benefits) only make people better off than they would have been at that baseline.[66] Notice, however, that this guarantee of a 'security level' works only by depriving officials of some of their discretionary powers. Specifically, it deprives them of discretion to vary the payment below the baseline: they enjoy only unidirectional discretion, to raise but not to lower the award. Thus, the 'insecurity' objection too can be solved only by depriving officials of some (although not necessarily all) discretion.

Broadly the same is true of the objection that discretion opens the way to exploitation. This, too, seems to be an inherent feature of any system of discretionary powers. There is of course one easy way to eliminate the risk of exploitation. The root of the problem, as shown above, is that the official might lay down illicit conditions upon the exercise of his discretion; and if that is the problem, the remedy is simply to prohibit the laying down of such conditions. That (or, more precisely, its converse) is what we already do through laws prohibiting the bribery or corruption of public officials. Once again, however, this amounts to overcoming the problems with discretion by curtailing discretion itself. Officials can be prevented from exploiting the power their discretion gives over claimants only by curtailing their power to exercise that discretion conditionally.[67]

With the 'intrusiveness' objection, the story is only slightly different. I must concede that I find nothing in the notion of 'discretion' itself that makes this an inherent consequence of its exercise. It is perfectly possible for officials to exercise discretionary power without knowing anything at all about the people and their problems. Under such circumstances, of course, the arbitrariness objection would begin to bite all that much harder. But, more to the point, discretion would defeat its own purpose. The whole rationale for giving officials discretionary power rather than obliging them to follow slavishly some rule is to allow (indeed, to require) them to tailor their treatment of individuals to the peculiar circumstances of those particular individuals. If they are to do this, it seems that a good deal of 'intrusiveness' *is* a necessary concomitant.

How much intrusiveness is strictly necessary may, of course, be debatable. It may well be that caseworkers characteristically collect far more information than they really need. But I am inclined to suppose that this matter admits of no more general a resolution than the other. How much information it is necessary to

66 Marshall, *supra* n 2, 111–3. R. E. Goodin, 52 *Social Research* 99 (1985).

67 Some may deny this, saying that although officials' power to exercise discretion conditionally is restricted, the *scope* of discretionary powers (i.e., the *range of options* they may exercise unconditionally) remains as broad as ever. But surely the proper way to define the extent of an official's discretion is in terms of the *number* of options rather than merely the range of options available to him. Someone who can choose to give a claimant £1 or £5 or £10 or £20 surely has more discretion than someone who can choose to give a claimant either £1 or £20 but nothing in between, even though the 'range' of options (defined in terms of endpoints) is the same in both cases.

collect should, I suspect, best be left to the caseworker's discretion for the selfsame reason as we left the broader decision of how to handle the case to the caseworker's discretion in the first place. In this way, I think we can reasonably say that 'intrusiveness'—or at least the risk thereof—is inherent in the *rationale* for discretion, if not in the notion of 'discretion' itself.

## V. ARE RULES THE ANSWER?

Logically, the opposite of enjoying discretion is being bound by a rule. So, logically, the natural response to finding that certain problems are inherent in discretion is to impose rules in the place of those discretions. The assumption that that will automatically solve the problem of discretion, however, entails an unwarranted presumption that every problem necessarily has a solution. Saying that the problems identified above are inherent in discretion means that those problems can be resolved, if at all, only by curtailing that discretion through rules. But it is perfectly possible that those problems cannot be solved in that way, either.

The problems discussed above may be inherent, not merely in discretion, but also in the purpose which those discretions were supposed to serve. If so, then any system (rules, or anything else) that also serves those purposes will also necessarily display those same faults. Here I shall argue that this is true of three out of the four objections to discretion canvassed above. Specifically, I shall show that, for those three problems: (1) the objectionable features which are inevitable in discretionary powers are nonetheless possible in a system of rules; and (2) the same considerations that drove us toward discretion in the first place would drive us to use rules in such a way as to reproduce the same problems there as well. Only the 'manipulation/exploitation' objection escapes that trap.

Consider first the 'arbitrariness' objection. The problem there was that officials with complete discretion did not have to give any reasons for their actions. With rules, *almost* the same is true. Admittedly, officials do, after a fashion, have to offer a 'reason' for their decisions: they have to point to some rule or another. But rules typically serve as shields, permitting 'unreasoned legalistic official behaviour with no apparent rational relation between fidelity to the rule and [the] original ends' for which the rule was promulgated.[68]

A rule is not a reason. There may or may not be any logic behind the rule—either in general, or in its application to this particular case or to cases of this kind. But even if there were some compelling logic underlying the rule, a rule-following official would not be obliged to communicate that underlying logic to claimants when rendering a rule-based decision on their cases. Insofar as he is officially obliged to 'give reasons' for his decisions, the giving of reasons need consist in no more than citing the rules.

68 Jowell, *supra* n 3, 193. See also Titmuss, *supra* n 3, 128–9.

There are, moreover, powerful pragmatic reasons for officials not going beyond the mere 'citing of rules' to explain the underlying logic and principles of the rules to claimants. If officials were to do so, then claimants whose petitions fell outside the strict letter of the law would begin arguing with officials, trying to show that their cases really did come within the spirit of the rule nonetheless. Insofar as the officials are bound by a strict set of rules (as would seem to be required to curtail arbitrary discretion), however, officials would have no scope for deciding cases according to the spirit rather than the letter of the law. Since they do not, explaining rules' underlying logic to claimants would be powerfully counterproductive.[69]

The same sort of conclusion holds, for different reasons, as regards the 'insecurity' objection. The problem there is that claimants never know what they are going to receive when officials have complete discretion over their grants. But the unpredictability of discretionary official decisions derives, at least in part, from the variety of considerations which should legitimately be taken into account in deciding the proper award. Insofar as the rules that replace discretion attempt to capture the same range of considerations, their operation may (at least from the clients' point of view) be as unpredictable as the discretionary caseworker's.[70]

We can, of course, reduce the unpredictability of the verdicts rendered by rule-abiding officials by restricting the range of considerations that the rules direct them to take into account. But if those considerations were ones that really needed to be taken into account in rendering the 'right' decision, then predictability of this sort is gained at the cost of rendering objectively 'worse' decisions.[71]

69 Indeed, there may be an underlying logic, principle or reason that would dictate the *opposite* conclusion to that which follows from a strict application of the rule to the present case; yet it is the latter direction in which non-discretionary, rule-bound officials must move. This fact is what gives rise to complaints of penalizing 'technical violators' (Jowell, *supra* n 3, 192), and to complaints of 'regulatory unreasonableness' (E. Bardach and R. A Kagan, *Going by the Book* (Temple University Press 1982)).

70 When pre-1980 Supplementary Benefit claimants were supplied with a Form A124 detailing the basis of the officer's decision, 22 per cent reported not understanding the calculations, 16 per cent the language, and 19 per cent the whole thing; Briggs and Rees, *supra* n 42, chap 6. The 1980 reform of Supplementary Benefits moved away 'from a scheme with relatively loose legislative framework and many discretionary provisions . . . to one governed by regulations covering all aspects of entitlement'; G. Beltram, *Testing the Safety Net* (Bedford Square Press/NCVO 1984) 3. But 'by November 1981 there were not only 13 sets of incredibly complex supplementary benefits regulations plus seven sets of amendments, but also a very extensive internal code of instructions for benefit officers'; P. Foster, *Access to Welfare* (London: Macmillan 1983) 125. Not surprisingly, Beltram, 4, reports that caseworkers administering the reformed scheme say that claimants still do not 'understand how the scheme works'. As the SBC, *supra* n 56, para 2.20 had anticipated, complexity proves as baffling to claimants whether codified in formal rules or embodied in informal practices.

71 Hart, *supra* n 16, 126 says, 'We may fasten on certain features present in the plain case and insist that these are both necessary and sufficient to bring anything which has them within the scope of the rule, whatever. . . . To do this is to secure a measure of certainty or predictability at the cost of blindly prejudging what is to be done in a range of future cases, about whose composition we

*(continued on page 252)*

Much the same tradeoff reappears with respect to the 'intrusiveness' objection. Officials following rules might be just as intrusive as officials following their own discretion. It all depends on what sorts of factors (e.g., 'cohabitation') the rules direct (or allow) them to take into account, and what sorts of powers (e.g., midnight searches) the rules give them to acquire those facts. We can of course reduce the intrusiveness of rule-governed officials by restricting the range of things the rule instructs (or allows) officials to do or to consider. And in the particular case just mentioned—of midnight searches for men under the bed—I suppose we are probably all inclined to opt for that solution. But more generally, a certain amount of intrusiveness is inherent in tailoring the treatment to the claimant's peculiar circumstances; and rules can eliminate that intrusiveness only by forsaking that goal

Thus, I am left with the conclusion that the problem to which stricter rules governing official behaviour is the solution is *not* the problem of arbitrariness or insecurity or intrusiveness. There is nothing in the nature of rules to guarantee that they will necessarily, automatically solve those problems; and there is much in the background circumstances to suggest that, whenever we are tempted by discretionary solutions, the same things that tempt us in them are likely to make any rules we adopt as bad as discretionary powers in all three ways. With respect to the third problem (intrusiveness) in particular, rules are in exactly the same position as discretionary powers: the evil in view is a necessary concomitant to a valued end, and the same considerations that led discretion-based regimes to countenance intrusiveness would exert the same sort of pressure on rule-based regimes as well.

Ultimately, the only problem with discretion to which rules are the solution is the problem of 'manipulation/exploitation'. If an official's treatment of some particular individual is strictly dictated by some rule, then that official cannot (legally, at least) threaten or offer to vary the treatment depending on the claimant's conforming to some other illicit conditions the official might care to lay down.[72] Of course, rules may be more or less precise; and insofar as they allow officials some leeway for choices in how to treat claimants, then to that extent the officials can still attempt to exploit that position of power over claimants. But that is just to say that rules may still allow officials some (weak) discretion. If we fear exploitation of such discretion, then the solution is merely to eliminate it: i.e., to write rules that dictate officials' decisions strictly, tightly and unambiguously in each case, insofar as possible.

## VI. WHICH KIND OF RULE?

A regime of rights is one alternative to a regime of discretionary powers. Contrary to what is sometimes implied, especially by writers in social administration, however,

*(continued from page 251)*

are ignorant. We shall thus indeed succeed in settling in advance, but also in the dark, issues which can only reasonably be settled when they arise and are identified'. A. D'Amato, 71 *California LR* 1 (1983) shows how relatively precise rules become increasingly uncertain over the course of time and applications for just such reasons.

72 A. D. Smith, *The Right to Life* (Univ of North Carolina Press 1955) and *supra* n 24. Goodin, *Protecting the Vulnerable*, *supra* n 1, chap 7.

that is not the only alternative. Here I shall first set out, in fairly formal fashion, the three distinct rule-based alternatives to a regime of discretionary powers. Then I shall discuss the appropriateness of each alternative remedy for the problems with discretion discussed above.

### *Alternative Types of Rule*

All alternatives to discretionary powers are, generically, strategies for using a formal set of *legally-binding rules* to exercise *control* over *lower-level agents* of state authority. That far, all the strategies here to be discussed are alike. They are all essentially variations on that one same theme.

The distinctive feature of *rights* is that they constitute *control from below*. Specifically, rights allow citizens to exercise control over agents of authority by stipulating certain things that those agents must do to or for the rights-holders, or certain things that those agents must not do to rights-holders. Rights thus constitute one clear way of diminishing the discretionary power of state officials, by giving those subject to their authority a certain measure of legal control over them.

Broadly speaking, the alternative to rights-based controls on official discretion is a system of controls based on notions of officials' *obligations*. This strategy, in its various forms, constitutes *control from above*.[73] A regime of official obligations provides a mechanism for higher officials to control lower ones, and (assuming no slippage) ultimately for the highest—in a democracy, the sovereign electorate—to control the lowest minion. That is the other logically possible way of limiting the discretion of intermediate state officials.

This second, obligations-based strategy, admits of two basic variants. Obligations can come in the form of either duties or responsibilities. *Duties* stipulate particular *actions* which state agents must take or refrain from taking. *Responsibilities*, in contrast, stipulate particular *outcomes* which state officials must produce or avoid producing. In the former case, lower-level officials are answerable to higher-level ones for what they did or did not do. So long as they did what they were duty-bound to do, they will be deemed to have discharged their duties, no matter what happened in consequence. In the latter case, the lower-level officials are answerable to higher-level ones for what happened. So long as the right consequences have been produced (and no duties violated in the process), the officials' responsibilities will be deemed to have been discharged, regardless of how in particular those results were brought about.[74]

### *Problems with Rights*

Let us first consider the choice between 'rights' and other forms of rule-based controls on official discretion. There are, of course, various rival theories of

73 Handler, *supra* n 10, 101–2, similarly distinguishes top-down approaches to the control of official behaviour from the bottom-up approach of the welfare-rights movement.

74 R. E. Goodin, 36 *Philosophical Q* 50 (1986).

rights.[75] This is hardly the place to enter into that controversy. For present purposes, it is enough to note that the only theory of rights which makes them importantly different from other forms of rule (obligation, duty, responsibility) in constraining official behaviour construes rights as 'powers'.

The chief rival to the Power Theory of rights is the Benefit (or interest) Theory. On that account, to be a right-holder is merely to be the direct, intended beneficiary of another's duty-bound performance. But if that is all there is to rights-based controls on official behaviour, then rights-based controls just reduce without residue to duty-based controls. Talk of rights might serve some rhetorical function in persuading legislators to impose certain duties on officials. Once imposed, however, it is the duty that does all the work in constraining official behaviour. Rights serve no further purpose.

The Power Theory envisages a larger and more distinctive role for rights in constraining official behaviour. On that account, rights are 'protected choices': to have a right is to have a legally-protected power to choose between demanding or waiving your right to the other person's duty-bound performance. That makes rights and duties correlative, once again: if what it means to have a right is to have the legal power to manipulate another's duty in the ways just described, then it is logically impossible to have a right without someone else's having such a duty in the first place. But whereas on the Benefit Theory rights-based controls on official behaviour are just duty-based controls and no more, on the Power Theory rights-based controls are duty-based controls plus something more. What 'more' is the right-holder's power of choice in claiming or waiving his entitlement.

Thus, even at their most distinctive, rights-based controls on official behaviour are just duty-based controls plus something more. I submit that the strength of rights-based control strategies in solving that one problem which rules in general can solve at all (i.e., manipulation/exploitation) derives from what rights-based and duty-based control strategies share in common. The weakness of the rights-based control strategy derives from what is peculiar to it alone.

The strength of the strategy is this. Where welfare recipients have a right to welfare payments, officials have a correlative duty to supply them. (At least they have such a duty if the claimants do in fact apply for such benefits.) That being so, officials cannot exploit claimants by threatening to withhold benefits unless certain preconditions are met. The crucial thing in that argument, however, is the official's duty—not the claimant's right.

The weakness of the rights-based strategy is that, insofar as it is a distinctive control strategy at all, it depends upon rights-holders actually claiming or demanding their rights. In a purely rights-based system, the rights-holders alone have legal standing to complain if officials fail to do their

75 Waldron, *supra* n 5, 9–12.

correlative duties. It seems to be sheer folly, however, to make their getting their due contingent upon their demanding it, since we know so well that (for one reason or another) a substantial number of them will in fact not do so.[76]

The central plank in this argument is, obviously, an empirical one. Yet, empirically, it is pretty well incontestible. Even businesses subject to state regulation are reluctant to press their 'rights' against administrators guilty of abusing them: 'the costs or risks involved are too high', more often than not.[77] The poor are more reluctant still to press a claim. This is true even of straightforward legal claims against private individuals for, e.g., compensation in cases of automobile accidents.[78] And it is all the more true of other, more complicated claims.[79]

The poor are particularly unlikely to press any legal claims to welfare rights, especially. Just consider all the steps involved in the process, and all that might prevent a poor claimant from proceeding at each step.

> In order for this system to function, . . . the potential claimant has to be aware of the fact that he has a legal right that has been violated; he has to be aware that a remedy is available; he has to have the resources with which to pursue the remedy; and he has to make a calculation that the expected benefits of pursuing the remedy outweigh the possible costs. Only if all of these conditions are fulfilled will the adversary [i.e., the rights-based] system work. If any of them is not fulfilled, there will not be a complaining client and the alleged deprivation of a legal right will not be challenged.[80]

Empirical evidence, however, suggests that each of those conditions is likely not to be fulfilled. Many poor people are simply unaware of their legal rights and of the remedies available in case of breach; and many more, although informed of 'fair hearings' provisions and such like when first applying for aid, found the

76 Given all these problems with the rights-based strategy, it might pay to reflect on how we ever got the idea of enforcing social welfare claims in that way. Historically, the answer is tied up with arguments for 'social insurance', which was to be insurance in just the same sense as private insurance. The political point of this analogy was that insurance schemes cannot be means-tested: anyone who paid insurance premiums is entitled to benefits whenever any of the insured-against contingencies actually occurs. See W. H. Beveridge, *Social Insurance and Allied Services* cmd 6404 (HMSO 1942) para 402 and Marshall, *supra* n 2, 265. The reason the problems sketched in the text were not immediately apparent is that most previous experience with insurance (be it private, or even the earlier forms of social insurance) had been of a rather different kind, in two respects. A different social strata had participated in traditional insurance schemes, and to some extent continued to predominate in early forms of social insurance (old age pensions, national insurance) as well. And they did so under much clearer terms of what precisely constituted a relevant 'contribution' to the insurance scheme (i.e., National Insurance contributions), and to what precisely that contribution entitled one. When the Social Security Act of 1966 vested an analogous welfare right in every Briton, both those latter points were powerfully ambiguous.

77 J. F. Handler, 54 *California LR* 479 (1966).

78 J. E. Carlin, J. Howard and S. C. Messinger, 1 *L & Society Rev* 9, 69–84 (1966).

79 SBC, *supra* n 13, para 7.43–7.48.

80 Handler, *supra* n 10, 48.

information simply not relevant at the time and forgot all about it.[81] Resources—of time, psychic energy and expert advice—are all desperately short among the poor. Furthermore, even if they could muster such resources, it is far from clear that it would be wise for the poor to invest them in pursuing a welfare-rights claim that might alienate an agency with which they have to have a continuing relationship, and upon whose continued decisions they will be forced to rely. Empirical evidence on the behaviour of welfare claimants suggests that each of these steps individually constitutes a serious obstacle to claiming.[82] Cumulatively, the obstacles will typically prove insurmountable. In light of them, it is pure folly to trust clients' pursuing their own claims to exercise comprehensive, effective control over officials.

A system of obligations-based controls on official discretion, in contrast, does not depend upon social-welfare clients themselves to exercise the controls.[83] Obligations-based systems can give all sorts of different people legal standing to intervene to demand that officials do in fact discharge their obligations.[84] There are good reasons (mostly to do with self-respect and dignity) for counting would-be beneficiaries among these potential plaintiffs.[85] But there is no good reason to make them the *only* potential plaintiffs, as purely rights-based control strategies would

81 N. Bond, in E. Butterworth and R. Holman, eds, *Social Welfare in Modern Britain* (Fontana 1975) 134–40. Handler, *supra* n 10, 48–9.

82 Handler, *supra* n 10, 48–51. See also Briar, *supra* n 24; Handler, *supra* n 77; J. F. Handler and E. J. Hollingsworth, 118 *Univ of Pennsylvania LR* 1167 (1970); S. A. Scheingold, *The Politics of Rights* (Yale Univ Press 1974).

83 Similar reasoning underlies sec 38 of the UK Powers of Criminal Courts Act of 1973, allowing criminal courts to issue a 'criminal compensation order' for convicted defendants to pay compensation to their victims: in that way, 'the victim will not be deprived of compensation simply because he lacks the courage or determination to pursue a civil remedy'; G. Williams and B. A. Hepple, *Foundations of the Law of Tort*, 2nd ed (Butterworth, 1984) 6.

84 Petitioners would be seeking not their rights-based entitlements but rather a writ of mandamus to compel officials to do their duties or, in dramatic cases, criminal prosecution for breach of duty; Williams and Hepple, *supra* n 83, 8, 62–3; Wade, *supra* n 34, chap 19. Under such rules, various people other than the direct, intended beneficiaries *can* be accorded standing. That is not to imply that they necessarily *will* be. A revised and more generous notion of standing is also required. According to the Poor Law conception of standing, which persisted into the 1940s, paupers themselves lacked standing to complain, having forfeited their rights of citizenship quite generally upon applying for relief; Marshall, *supra* n 2, 262–3. Yet according to the prevailing notion of standing, no one else had standing to take public officials to court to demand performance of their duties toward the poor, either: only those with a 'legally protected interest' in the administrative action in question were traditionally thought to have standing; and the public at large had no such 'interest', narrowly construed. From the 1960s onward, however, notions of standing have been broadening to allow a wide variety of people to challenge a wide variety of administrative actions. This has now happened in both British and American law. On the former, see Wade, *supra* n 34, 572–9, 640–3. On the latter, see L. L. Jaffe, 74, 75 *Harvard LR* 1265, 255 (1961); K. C. Davis, 37 *Univ of Chicago LR* 450 (1970); L. A. Albert, 83 *Yale LJ* 425 (1974); R. B. Stewart, 88 *Harvard LR* 1669 (1975).

85 J. Feinberg, *Rights, Justice and the Bounds of Liberty* (Princeton University Press 1980) chap 7.

do.[86] There would be more and more effective test cases brought the more people who, under obligations-based strategies, would be allowed to bring them.

*The Relative Merits of Duties and Responsibilities*

Next let us consider the choice between duties and responsibilities, the two obligations-based strategies for controlling official behaviour. The difference between them, as described above, is between act-oriented and results-oriented modes of control. Sometimes we might have some independent moral concern with the way people are treated (e.g., wanting them to be treated courteously by welfare workers), regardless of the end-results of the administrative process. Deontological moral theories make a fetish of such concerns. However, more often—and especially with regard to welfare policy—we seem principally concerned with consequences. If so, then we should choose between these two control strategies depending simply upon their relative efficacy in producing the outcomes we desire.

Both duty-based and responsibility-based strategies are, at root, strategies for superiors exercising control over subordinates. In the duty-based approach, what superiors are trying to control is behaviour of subordinates. For this sort of control to be effective, superiors need to be able to monitor and control effectively the activities of subordinates—and, through them, of subordinates' subordinates, and so on down the chain of command. Often this is impossible, by the nature of the task. Michael Lipsky's 'street-level bureaucrats', for example, must by the nature of their jobs (teaching, policing, etc.) do their work well away from their supervisors' prying eyes.[87] The more slippage there is in any step in this monitoring and control process, the less effective the duty-based strategy of control will be.

In the responsibility-based strategy, what superiors are trying to control is outputs. For this sort of control to be effective, superiors need to be able to monitor and to control effectively the outputs of their subordinates.[88] This might appear, at first blush, to be the easier of the two approaches, but appearances may well be deceptive. Arguably, it is precisely the inability to monitor outputs that forces governments to provide certain services directly themselves, rather than contracting out to private suppliers.[89] And the difficulties with meaningful

86 In practice, of course, the co-operation of claimants is often pragmatically required—e.g., in testifying against officials who abuse their powers and violate their obligations. Hence, some of the same problems are bound to reappear under an obligations-based system; but not all of them will.

87 M. Lipsky, *Street-level Bureaucracy* (Russell Sage Foundation 1980).

88 For arguments in favour of such results-based controls, see: C. L. Schultze, *The Public Use of Private Interest* (Brookings Institution 1977); B. A. Ackerman and W. T. Hassler, *Clean Coal/Dirty Air* (Yale Univ Press 1981); R. E. Goodin, *Political Theory and Public Policy* (Univ of Chicago Press 1982) chap 4.

89 P. Blau, *The Dynamics of Bureaucracy*, rev ed (Univ of Chicago Press 1963) chaps 3 and 11. Lipsky, *supra* n 87, 48–53. D. M. Gibson, R. E. Goodin and J. LeGrand, 13 *Policy & Politics* 109 (1985).

statistical reporting of the *real* outputs—the ones that matter— are particularly acute in social welfare policy.[90] Thus, the relative effectiveness of these two control mechanisms comes down to a question of whether officials' superiors are better able to monitor and control the officials' activities or their outputs. This is an empirical question, the answer to which is likely to vary from case to case.

Our particular concern, in the present context, is not with the relative effectiveness of these two control strategies *tout court*, but rather with their relative effectiveness at remedying abuses of discretion (and, more particularly still, the exploitation and manipulation of that discretion). At first glance, it might seem that responsibility-based controls must always prove inferior in that particular respect. After all, they leave officials with substantial residual discretionary power in deciding how best to accomplish the prescribed results.[91]

Certainly it is true that responsibilities entail formal discretionary powers of a particular kind. Where responsibilities prove to be more effective control strategies than duties, however, the implication must necessarily be that in those circumstances a regime of strict duties would, in effect, leave subordinates with even broader (albeit informal) discretionary power. (Remember, the reason responsibilities prove superior to duties is that superiors are relatively powerless to monitor or control the behaviour of subordinates.) Hence, the question of effective control of subordinates *tout court* and the question of how best to prevent abuses of discretionary powers by subordinates is one and the same question. Where responsibility-based regimes prove superior on the former criterion, they prove superior on the latter one as well.

## VII. INTERIM CONCLUSIONS, AND A PARTIAL 'SOLUTION'

The arguments offered above lead to a pair of pretty depressing conclusions. First, as shown in Section II, discretionary powers are to a certain extent *ineliminable*. Worse still, some of the more worrisome aspects of discretionary powers seem to be among these.

By their very nature, rules must be interpreted by officials in the process of applying them to particular cases. In the course of interpreting the rules, however, those officials often subtly redefine them. 'Bureaucratic disentitlement' is a popular way to cope with cutbacks in agency funding.[92] But this process must be seen for what it is: the administrative arrogation of what is properly a legislative function. There have been several compelling studies illustrating this practice among street-level professionals.[93] More worrying still, there is a substantial body

90 Handler, *supra* n 77, 181–3.

91 Feinberg, *supra* n 85, 137. Goodin, *supra* n 74.

92 M. Lipsky, 58 *Social Service R* 3 (1984).

93 Lipsky, *supra* n 87 and 92. D. A. Stone, *The Disabled State* (London: Macmillan 1984).

of evidence that the very lowest-level functionaries, such as clerks and receptionists, are among its most common practitioners.[94]

Second, the problems we find with the exercise of discretionary powers are to a large extent *insurmountable*. Of the many problems posed by officials possessing discretions, a regime of rights is the proper solution to none, and a regime of rules more generally to only one. It is important to see what rules can do: they can prevent the manipulation and exploitation of those dependent upon state services by officials responsible for the administration of those services. It is equally important to see what they cannot do. They cannot (necessarily, or without substantial costs in other respects) prevent intrusiveness, arbitrariness or insecurity. For much the same reasons that discretionary decisions *must* display those attributes, rule-based decisions *can*, and *probably will*. That, too, is an important finding.

Those latter problems associated with discretion are, in some deep sense, insoluble. Insofar as they trouble us, therefore, the proper way to handle them is not to try resolving them at all. Rather, we should try *circumventing* them. That is to say, we should seek ways to avoid the circumstances that push both discretion-based and rule-based systems in these undesirable directions.

The problems described above all seem to arise, most fundamentally, from the effort to make sure that assistance is granted to everyone who needs/deserves assistance, and *only* to those who need/deserve it. That is why, even within a rule-based system, we are required to take account of a vast array of personal circumstances, thus rendering decisions unpredictable, and leaving claimants feeling insecure. That is why, even with a rule-based system, we must collect vast amounts of personal information, with all the intrusiveness that that inevitably entails. That, too, is why even with a rule-based system officials dare not (for fear of inviting still more formally invalid claims) enunciate any principles they might perceive underlying the rules—thus giving rise to arbitrariness, or at least the appearance thereof, from the claimant's point of view. All these things stem from the attempt to make sure that *only* the needy/deserving receive the benefits.[95]

Imagine, in contrast, a world in which officials were guided only by the first half of that twin obsession: suppose officials are anxious to ensure that everyone who needs/deserves benefits gets them, but that they are utterly unconcerned to ensure that only they receive them. By adopting a rule of systematically erring on the side of generosity in this way, officials could obviate the need for any of the mechanisms that give rise to the objections of arbitrariness, insecurity or intrusiveness as described above. Of course, it is still perfectly possible that those disagreeable attributes might be displayed (quite needlessly) in a discretion-based

94 Blau, *supra* n 89, chaps 2 and 5. Lipsky, *supra* n 87, 198. D. Mechanic, 7 *Administrative Science Q* 341 (1962). D. H. Zimmerman, in J. D. Douglas, ed, *Understanding Everyday Life* (Routledge & Kegan Paul 1971) 221–38. A. S. Hall, *The Point of Entry* (Allen & Unwin 1974). Foster, *supra* n 70.

95 See similarly Donnison, *supra* n 13, 535 and M. J. Hill, 47 *Public Administration* 75 (1969).

system: those possibilities, as I have shown in Section IV, are inherent in any such system. But working with a rule-based system, we could guarantee that the rules governing official behaviour (operating under a meta-rule of generosity) would display none of those disagreeable attributes.

A rule of generosity would have one further advantage. In Section II it was argued that someone, somewhere always has to have some discretionary power in any system of rules. That is inherent in the nature of rules themselves. But it is important, morally, that the *right people*—or at least the *people in the right positions*—be the ones to exercise such discretions. There are various considerations to be taken into account in deciding what is the right place to settle discretionary power. On the one hand, the greater capacity of lower-level officials to produce an answer that takes full account of the particular circumstances of the particular case argues for vesting discretion at a lower level; on the other hand, the greater accountability of higher-level officials to the Sovereign (the Monarch, Parliament, electorate, etc.) argues for vesting discretion at a higher level.

An underfunded discretionary authority, however, brings us the worst of both worlds. Overworked caseworkers or their immediate superiors are forced to adopt rules of their own devising to batch-process claimants.[96] We thereby lose whatever advantage we might have expected from vesting discretion lower down. But at the same time, we put into operation a system of rules promulgated by those not in authority to make rules. If we were going to have cases being decided by rules rather than individualized discretion, we should have had the rules enacted in the proper way by the proper authorities rather than being made up by beleagured street-level bureaucrats as they went along.[97] More generous funding would solve these problems, too, allowing street-level bureaucrats to exercise discretion as it was meant to be exercised.[98]

In certain respects, my 'rule of generosity' is merely an artful dodge around problems of discretion. It certainly does not meet the problems head-on. But I

96 Lipsky, *supra* n 87. Donnison, *supra* n 13, 535 similarly bemoans as 'clumsy local improvisations' the sorts of rules the Supplementary Benefits system was forced to adopt in light of rising caseloads conjoined with severe staffing restraints. Ironically, this seems to be just the sort of thing Davis, *supra* n 27, chaps 2 and 3 is advocating as 'administrative rule-making'.

97 That is to say if, we are to have something like the A-Code guiding the behaviour of National Assistance and, later, Supplementary Benefits officers, it should be regularized by approval of Parliament—as has now been done by the Social Security Act of 1980—rather than being merely an in-house invention. Beltram, *supra* n 70, 23. Alternatively, if we leave discretionary power in the agencies, we should make those agencies more directly politically accountable—e.g., by popular election of agency officials as one American suggests (Stewart, *supra* n 84, 1791–3).

98 P. S. Atiyah, in personal correspondence, has similarly suggested that some of the reasons we are relatively comfortable with judges exercising discretions have to do with the time and money lavished on judicial proceedings, thereby increasing the odds of a 'correct' determination. There is no reason to believe most welfare claims require anything like so much attention; but, on a small scale, more generous funding might help make us more comfortable with those exercises of discretion, too.

am inclined to think that it is none the worse for that. If the dodge really is a *successful* dodge—if it really does get around the problems—then that is, for all intents and purposes, just as good as solving the problems.

Some will no doubt find more principled objections, couched in terms of the 'inequity' and 'injustice' done to the truly needy/deserving by giving benefits to the unneedy/undeserving as well.[99] Sometimes it is true that 'supply-side solutions' are unsuccessful evasions of distributional problems; and sometimes it is true that people are made worse off by another person's being made better off.[100] However, the benefits provided by the social services do not seem to display any of the more specific characteristics that are required for any of that to be true.

The only real objection to my 'rule of generosity' is the economic one. Systematically erring on the side of generosity would indeed cost the Treasury, and perhaps cost it dearly. If my other arguments are correct, however, doing otherwise has its costs, too. It might be harder to put a price-tag on moral affronts, like arbitrariness, insecurity and intrusiveness. But the mere fact that we cannot count them quite so readily does not make them any less of a cost.[101]

99 Cf. Handler and Sosin, *supra* n 13, 6–7.

100 R. E. Goodin, 18 *Politics* 57 (1983). F. Hirsch, *Social Limits to Growth* (Harvard Univ Press 1976). A. Sen, 35 *Oxford Economic Papers* 153 (1983).

101 Elsewhere I have shown that on straightforward welfare-economic calculations we should be *more* inclined (not *less*) to err on the side of kindness in deciding social welfare entitlements in bad times, when claim levels are legitimately high. See R. E. Goodin, 18 *Policy Sciences* 141 (1985). That is merely to say we should be more willing to commit more social resources to welfare programmes when need for them is high. Of course, resources may be genuinely scarce, and not all claims may be able to be met: then we would be in a genuinely 'tragic' situation, where distributions might have to be governed by very different principles.

# [20]

JOURNAL OF LAW AND SOCIETY
VOLUME 14, NUMBER 4, WINTER 1987
0263-323X $3.00

# Welfare Benefits, Administrative Discretion, and the Politics of the 'New Urban Left'

IAN LOVELAND*

## INTRODUCTION

Empirical studies of welfare service decision-making have frequently drawn the conclusion that there exists a significant gap between the apparent objectives of the 'law' as articulated in legislation or by judges and the concrete social relations produced by the activities of government employees seeking to put such ideas into practice. Investigations into the allocation[1] and management[2] of council housing, into the administration of supplementary benefit[3] (formerly national assistance[4]), and into the behaviour of the quasi-judicial supplementary benefit appeal tribunals,[5] have identified widespread ignorance and/or evasion of legal obligations by the administrators involved, particularly when exercising discretionary powers. The arguments for and against the retention of lawfully-exercised discretionary powers within welfare services have been thoroughly and frequently rehearsed,[6] and need not be repeated here.

Of more concern to this paper are the various analyses advanced to explain administrators' wilful or uninformed transgression of the lawful limits of such discretion. Blame has been laid on inadequate employee training,[7] on insufficient staffing levels,[8] on administrators' desire to make their on-going tasks less burdensome,[9] on employees' attribution of greater legitimacy to their own moral prejudices (particularly regarding racism[10] and the notion of a deserving and undeserving poor[11]) than to legislative or judicial prescription. Blame has also been laid on claimants' inability to gain access to sources of legal competence,[12] and on lack of political will on the part of law-makers to pursue their ideas to material completion[13] – some commentators have suggested that such political faint-heartedness is quite deliberate, with

**Centre for Socio-Legal Studies and Nuffield College, Oxford University, Oxford OX1 1NF, England.*

This paper won the Journal of Law and Society Student Essay Prize in Socio-Legal Studies 1986-87. The editorial board wishes to thank the judges, Dr. R. B. Ferguson, Tony Bunyan, and in particular Dr. P. Carlen for undertaking the onerous task of assessment.

proposals to judicialise[14] welfare service decision-making being designed to produce only "symbolic reassurance".[15]

While much impact analysis[16] of legal reform has centred on Department of Health and Social Security (D.H.S.S.) decision-making, similarly diffusive processes have been observed in the making and implementation of local government policy. Honestly-held policy statements made in committee are subjected to obstruction and dilution as they filter down through the organisational structure before emerging into society as effective determinants of claimant/council relations.[17]

Central government, in seeking to reform the procedural conduct or substantive content[18] of the supplementary benefit system, may do so fairly unproblematically through legislation.[19] However, council autonomy regarding its own welfare policy is constrained within a legal framework set by the centre,[20] and although the widespread use of discretionary powers affords councils room for manoeuvre within that framework, its boundaries can rarely be adjusted without central approval. While local authorities have frequently resorted to the courts in their attempts to overcome central government constraints on their autonomy – with occasional successes[21] – central/local dispute as to the correct parameters within which to confine that autonomy has periodically led local councillors to step beyond legal confines.[22] Poplar[23] and Clay Cross[24] are oft-cited examples of this, as is the current controversy over the rate-capping of 'new urban left'[25] Labour authorities by the Thatcher government.[26] This paper focuses, however, on the rather more modest attempts by one new urban left authority to manipulate the provisions of the housing benefit scheme, with the intention of producing concrete social relations between the citizen and the state which are entirely inconsistent with the Thatcher government's political philosophy.

## A BRIEF NOTE ABOUT THE HOUSING BENEFIT SCHEME

The housing benefit scheme was introduced in 1982-83[27] and transferred to local housing authorities' sole responsibility for the administration of rent and rate subsidies to occupants of rented and owner-occupied accommodation. The scheme embraces both supplementary benefit claimants (who receive 'certificated' housing benefit) and other low-income groups (who receive 'standard' housing benefit). Implementation of the scheme, which is a blend of centrally-defined rules and discretionary powers which remain to be interpreted by the administering authority, has been widely criticised as slow, prone to error, and inconsistent.[28] Dissatisfaction with housing benefit administration led the then Secretary of State for the Environment to commission a review of the scheme's operation. The review team reported in 1985.[29] The team identified many areas of concern involving both rule-bound and discretionary elements of the scheme. They put forward a lengthy list of recommendations for reform.

## NORTH LONDON BOROUGH COUNCIL

North London Borough Council (a pseudonym is used for reasons of confidentiality) has been fixed with the 'loony left' label by senior members of the Conservative party, and has additionally been subjected to rather more sober criticism by the Audit Commission concerning management of its finances.[30] In recent years the council's history has been one of trenchant resistance to government welfare policies, which have involved the complete loss of rate support grant, recurrent disputes over rate-capping, and the threat of disqualification and bankruptcy to many members of the Labour group.

Although containing some of London's most exclusive residential areas and an expanding 'yuppie' population, North London Borough Council also contends with a large and poorly-maintained public housing sector and a multiplicity of private rented sector dwellings, many involving multiple occupation and most let under contracts which pay scant attention to any legislation regulating the landlord/tenant (licensee) relationship.

The Labour group's housing benefit policy has been basically two-pronged. The council has campaigned relentlessly against central government's repeated erosion of the substantive benefits paid to claimants, while its administration of the scheme has been underpinned by the twin objectives (i) to maximise the number of claimants receiving benefit; and (ii) to be as substantially generous to those claimants as current regulations will allow. While such policy objectives might be dismissed merely as abstract expressions of political will, a shortage of 'political will' is often advanced as an explicator of the failure of the welfare state to live up to legislation's good intentions. It has been suggested that radical social democracy will be effective only if its principles are pursued at every stage of both the legislative and administrative process.[31] One of the aims of this paper, therefore, is to trace the fate of the new urban left political will as it descends from the council chamber to senior and then junior officers, before finally emerging in the outside world as the 'benefit' which claimants actually receive. Consequently, the first step must be to explore the authority's councillor/officer relationships.

## COUNCILLOR/OFFICER RELATIONSHIPS – PRESCRIPTIVE INFLUENCES

Hill's influential critique of public administration has identified two basic models of politician/officer relations.[32] The first model of 'administrative politics' locates power primarily with senior officers, who both devise and oversee implementation of policy, simultaneously seeking to legitimise their power base by co-opting elected representatives into the policy-making process, while carefully ensuring that co-optees absorb officers' values and objectives.[33] Hill's second model of 'ideological politics' envisages a member/officer partnership, with both sides deeply involved in policy design and implementation, and with staff recruitment geared towards selection of administrators sympathetic to the ruling group's political ideals. Recently, following increased political polarisation within local government – in particular the emergence of the new urban left and the new radical right – the 'ideological politics' model has assumed growing prominence.[34]

North London Borough Council's housing benefit office is a sub-division of the finance department (see Figure 1). The office employs some ninety people and occupies an entire floor of the council's main building. Each team deals with a geographically-defined area of the borough. Teams have between ten and fifteen members according to the size of each area's claimant population. Five of the six team managers were officers in North London Borough Council's rate rebate/allowance department before the introduction of housing benefit; they have considerable experience of benefits administration, of the political orientation of the ruling Labour group, and of the chief officer's managerial style. The only exception, team manager 1, joined the office three years ago at interviewer grade. Decision-making is undertaken almost entirely within the division and very rarely involves the Director of Finance. Effective overall control rests with the Chief Housing Benefits Officer (hereafter referred to as the chief officer), who has spent over ten years with the council both as a benefits administrator and as a trade union official for the National Association of Local Government Officers (N.A.L.G.O.).

The chief officer's personal politics and those of the team managers are entirely congruent with the ruling group's and have been carried whole-heartedly into the design and supervision of the administrative process. During the survey the chief officer explained that she felt her job required her to be:

> ... tremendously aware of the political pulses of the borough. The politicians shouldn't be paying me the salary I'm on and have to hold my hand, telling me at every inch along the way "this is what you should do". You should be able to anticipate their wishes.

An example of this anticipatory variant of 'ideological politics' was displayed by the chief officer's response to the plight of the trade union members of the Society of Graphic and Allied Trades (S.O.G.A.T. '82) and the National Graphical Association (N.G.A.) who were involved in industrial action with Rupert Murdoch. Although the strikers were ineligible for supplementary benefit (and thence certificated housing benefit) they were eligible for standard housing benefit if their incomes were low enough. Applications from strikers were encouraged by the council's welfare rights service, but even after receiving standard housing benefit many strikers were left with incomes below the supplementary benefit level. The chief officer, however, anticipated that the Labour group would support the printworkers' cause and decided to apply regulation 25 of S.I. 1985 No. 677 to the strikers' claims. Regulation 25 provides that in standard cases an authority may grant an applicant an additional amount of benefit if it considers the person's circumstances "exceptional", and the chief officer used this power to increase the strikers' housing benefit payments to a level that raised their total income to the supplementary benefit threshold. The ruling group had made the

FIGURE 1 *The formal structure of North London Borough Council's housing benefit office*

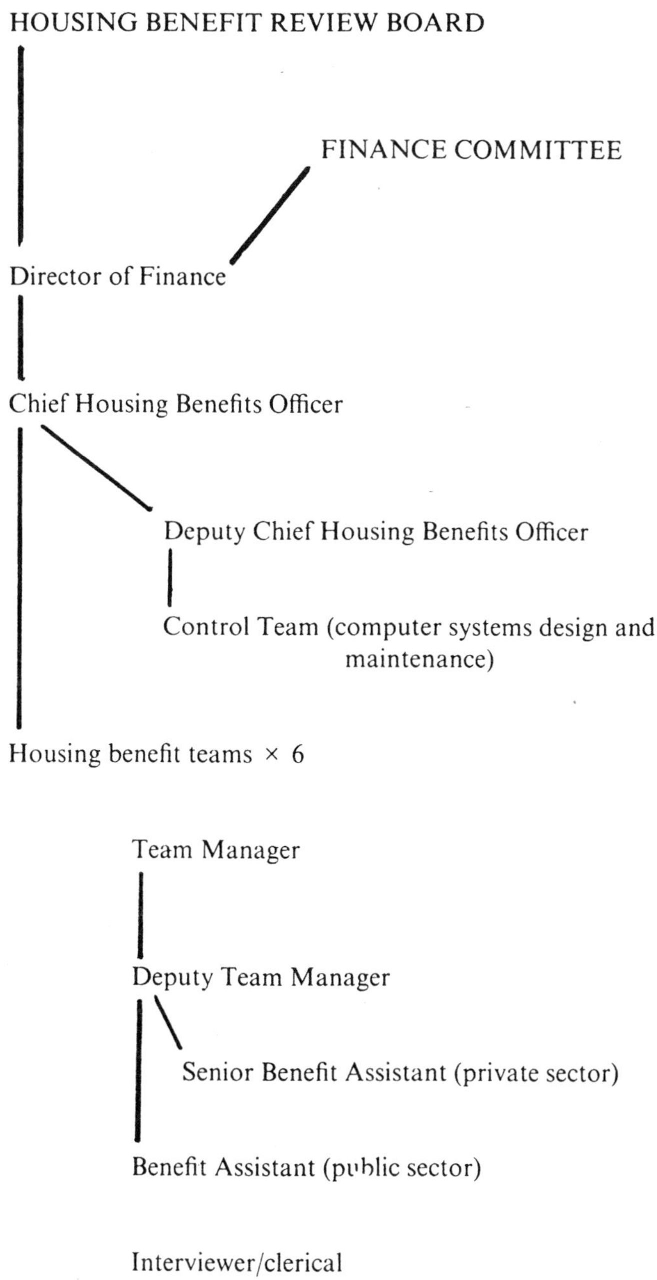

initiative possible, in so far as it had voted a budget for the chief officer to use for regulation 25 cases,[35] but this particular initiative was entirely the chief officer's creation; as far as she knew, the councillors were not even aware that the action had been taken. She felt that this use was an accurate anticipation of the council's political will.

## THE TAKE-UP OF HOUSING BENEFIT

The extremely low take-up rate of the rent/rate rebate scheme which preceded housing benefit had been much criticised,[36] and government proposals introducing the housing benefit scheme had laid considerable stress on the claim that the new system would reach those most needing assistance more effectively.[37] However, such stress was not reflected in subsequent legislation. Central government placed no specific obligation upon authorities to maximise take-up. Rather, s.31(1) of the Social Security and Housing Benefit Act 1982 provides that councils shall:

> . . . take such steps as may appear to them appropriate for the purpose of securing that the provisions of the scheme come to the notice of any persons who may be entitled to a rebate or allowance under the scheme.

Clues regarding the Thatcher government's perception of "appropriate steps" are perhaps found in the Minister of State for Social Security's recent denunication of Labour-controlled councils which have increased the government's welfare benefits bill by vigorously encouraging their citizens to claim their legal entitlements.[38] North London Borough Council's chief officer, however, gave such sentiments short shrift:

> How can you ignore, when you look very quickly at someone's application, that they could be entitled to F.I.S., one-parent benefit, attendance allowance, all that sort of thing – even their tax code being wrong.
>
> How can you, if you've got any heart at all, just ignore it, when all it needs is an application form or a letter sent . . . or something said at interview? It wouldn't be right.

This personal conviction has been mirrored in the office's exhaustive efforts to publicise the scheme through constant leafleting of libraries, leisure centres, and through advice agencies (and always in ethnic minority languages as well as in English); advertisements and articles in the local press and in the council's own magazine; explanatory visits to local voluntary organisations; and a computer system that automatically identifies applicants' eligibility for other state benefits. Such activities are indicative of office attempts to give substance to the new urban left's political will.

The political will has been mediated through the chief officer to a generally appreciative audience of senior and junior employees. One interviewer/clerical grade worker who had been a recent 'defector' from a local D.H.S.S. office recalled that his first impression of North London Borough Council's office was to think "My God, they're really trying to help the public here". In contrast, he suggested that the D.H.S.S. managerialist ethos was to "try to fob people off from benefits to save a bit of money; you start believing it yourself after a while".

Accounts of service delivery in D.H.S.S. offices frequently focus on the slow, inexpert attention of employees, the grimey surroundings, and the cage-like interviewing facilities.[39] The inhospitable environment which interacts with claimants' sometimes urgent – if not desperate – need, is presumed to engender in claimant and administrator alike a hostile 'counter culture', punctuated alternately by aggression and despair.[40] The chief officer visited several D.H.S.S. offices before the housing benefit scheme was introduced, and used what she found there as a guide to how *not* to run a welfare service. North London Borough Council's reception area is light and airy, furnished with comfortable seating, assorted plants, a water dispenser, and toilet facilities. Perhaps more importantly, the office ensures that no claimant waits more than ten minutes to be interviewed even if, as is quite frequently the case, this requires that employees up to team manager level drop whatever they are doing to conduct an interview. Consequently, Blau's notion of "poverty shock"[41] has no place in North London Borough Council's office – officers need not expend time and energy devising techniques to survive the 'nine to five'.

In part, North London Borough Council's high quality service delivery has been designed to enhance administrative efficiency but, as team manager 1 suggested, it also derives from a rather more deep-rooted political value judgement about the social status of welfare claimants:

> . . . the managers see their role as providing the best possible service . . . because after all that's what people deserve. Why should they be treated like rubbish just because they're on housing benefit? They're getting what they're entitled to!

The best possible service", however, is not provided by substantive political generosity alone. North London Borough Council's officers are withering in their criticism of the administrative chaos faced by nearby Lambeth's housing benefit office, recently threatened with an application for judicial review by its own welfare rights service. For North London Borough Council's administrators, good intentions are of little value to claimants unless accompanied by good administration. Thus, much thought, time, and effort has been given to the design of administrative systems, to the purchase of computer technology, and to the recruitment and training of employees. Employee enthusiasm is also fostered by frequent and rapid promotion opportunities within the department; team manager 1 had moved from interviewer grade to his current post in just three years. Delegation of decision-making powers from the chief officer to team managers and then within teams is also the norm, affording all but the interviewer/clerical grade staff significant decision-making power.[42] Generally, individual cases only reach the chief officer if councillors become involved with the decision-making process, discussed further below.

Therefore, the notion of welfare bureaucracies as "gatekeepers"[43] would seem quite inappropriate for North London Borough Council's housing benefit office. A more apposite analogy might perhaps be that of 'pathfinder', actively marking the route along which claimants can maximise their welfare entitlements. And although the chief officer recognised during her discussions for the survey that there are several "awkward" employees in the office, she said that she regarded them as unfortunate individual aberrations rather than as a systemic obstacle to realisation of the political will.

Thus far, however, this paper has sought the council's political will only at the abstract level of statement of intent. In seeking the influences which act on discretionary decison-making it is necessary to examine actual decisions made over specific issues, and I now turn to this task.

## COHABITATION – IDEOLOGY, POLICY, AND PRACTICE

The imagery of the nuclear family as the ideal unit of social organisation[44] in advanced capitalist societies, though somewhat inaccurate as a guide to household composition,[45] powerfully affects both the design and implementation of welfare provision.[46] In particular, the notion that women and children should be dependent on the male wage-earning head of household finds legislative expression in requirements that a woman's supplementary benefit entitlement must be constructed with reference to her 'husband's' financial circumstances. Not only do such requirements generally produce a family benefit of lesser substance than two single persons would receive, but they also limit or remove entirely a woman's financial autonomy from the man, given that the family's benefit is paid to him.[47] Moreover, although the emphasis on the family as the 'natural' provider of welfare support has increased under the Thatcher administration,[48] maximising family self-sufficiency has been a central tenet of all post-war governments' welfare policies in both Britain and the United States of America.[49]

The principle generally applies both to married couples and cohabitees. The zealous attempts of welfare officials in the United States of America to uncover suspected cases of cohabitation among women claimants, which culminated in forcible night-time entry into claimants' homes, has been of considerable importance in provoking the new property thesis there.[50] In Britain, where one might note that citizens have no constitutional 'right' to privacy, the activities of D.H.S.S. 'snooper squads' have been less spectacular, but nonetheless represent a significant and continuing governmental intrusion into people's domestic circumstances.[51]

A feature of the new urban left's political posture, however, is a marked antipathy to the subordinate economic position of women. Many councils have taken steps to redress this imbalance through equal opportunity employment policies, expansion of child care facilities, and the establishment of women's committees.[52] A corollary of this stance is the presumption that citizens' sexual and emotional relationships are not a fit subject of enquiry for government welfare institutions.

The housing benefit scheme drafted by central government requires under regulation 11(2) that cohabitees be assessed as a family unit rather than as individuals. The scheme's application can seriously affect benefit levels, particularly where the claimants have widely disparate incomes. Local authorities have no discretion to assess cohabitees individually – if they are satisfied a couple are cohabiting any claims must be dealt with jointly.

However, cohabitation must first be established. While discretion is not granted regarding councils' responses to such established circumstances, the substance and conduct of the evidentiary process through which such facts are found is subject to local authority discretion. Thus, discretion is displaced essentially one step further back in the decision-making process;[53] the point being, of course, that 'facts' do not have independent existence, but are the creation of social actions.

Simply put, the Labour group has no wish to pry into claimants' sexual relationships and, since there is no obvious legislative duty on the council to ask claimants if they cohabit, the office's application form does not raise the issue. Nor do officers assume cohabitation exists simply because claimants of opposite sexes are sharing accommodation, be it a flat or even a room. The political will does not permit officers to ask legally unnecessary questions when honest answers might reduce claimants' benefit entitlements. For example, officers accept that claimants meet the 'exceptional circumstances' criterion required under regulation 28(2)(b) to permit back-dating of standard housing benefit simply by claiming to have been ill – claimants are not required to produce medical corroboration. In team manager 1's words:

> Frankly, the council would go up the wall if we did something like that. They wouldn't allow it! It wouldn't be part of [North London Borough Council] policy.

However, while the evidence from the survey showed that the chief officer and her team managers had supported this non-intrusive approach enthusiastically, it was clear that they were not prepared to disregard cohabitation if it should come to their attention. They explained that where the scheme afforded officers discretion they would use it to bend rules to give effect to the political will – but they would not (knowingly) break rules.[54] As team manager 1 put it:

> Our first duty is to implement the legislation. We always work on the legislation – we never go outside it. But the legislation is filled with potholes and discretions, and in those areas it's up to [us] as to how they are implemented. Now . . . there is a political dimension. . . .

This acceptance by officers of the sanctity of legal boundaries contrasted clearly with the stance taken by some councillors against central government over the rate-capping issue. Some members considered their political preferences to be sufficient justification to pursue action which either clearly was – or might subsequently be proven to be – unlawful.[55] From their comments it was clear that while officers might dislike the regulatory constraints on their political autonomy, nonetheless they reluctantly accepted those constraints as legitimate determinants of administrative activity. As we shall see below, this divergence of officer/member opinion has occasionally led to tension in their normally harmonious relationship.

## CURATIVE ASPECTS OF THE OFFICER/MEMBER RELATIONSHIP

The regulations require councils to inform claimants that all office decisions are subject to a two-stage appeal process under regulation 50. Stage one is an initial review by officers under regulation 51; thereafter claimants may request a hearing before the authority's housing benefit review board under regulation 52. This apparently quasi-judicial body is formally independent of the council under regulation 52(3), although its members are the authority's councillors and the authority determines its precise composition and procedures under Schedule 5. Little is known about review board operations, few cases have been recorded, and many councils apparently have yet to hold a single hearing.[56] Concern has also been voiced regarding the boards' likely competence and impartiality.[57]

Early studies have suggested that many councils accord little importance to the potential role of review boards.[58] In North London Borough Council, however, a joint officer/member working party was set up to determine how best to maximise claimants' procedural and substantive entitlements. The substantive political alignment adopted by the review board's potential members is, perhaps, of most interest to this study. In the chief officer's opinion the councillors' emphasis was:

> ... very much on fairness for the claimant.... I was the enemy there if you like. They made it quite clear to me ... that if things were fairly even and they had to make a decision one way or another they'd swing towards the claimant. They wouldn't be seen to be on the side of the officer, no matter what.

While the councillors have clearly institutionalised a pro-claimant bias into review board operations (in complete contrast to the anti-claimant bias recorded by many observers of supplementary benefit appeal tribunals[59]) the imagery of radically political councillors championing claimants' rights against conservative bureaucrats is inapplicable to the dynamics of the office's decision-making processes – officers have enthusiastically sought to give new urban left politics as much concrete effect as the regulations will allow; mistakes have not been made in the application of the scheme's rule-bound elements, and discretionary powers have been interpreted to the claimants' maximum advantage. Consequently, as the chief officer expected when the scheme was introduced, the council's political will has been realised during the initial stage of the administrative process. The chief officer suggested that a review board case could result from only three causes: political meanness, administrative incompetence, or quite unsustainable claimant demands. She explained that while the office considered itself neither 'mean' nor 'incompetent', it had been under the third head (with specific reference to the cohabitation rule) that the generally pervasive congruence between the councillors' political will and the officers' behavioural rationality had broken down.

1. *Modifying the Political Will – the Administrative Process and the Influence of "Intuitive Rationality"*[60]

The emphasis that officers place on constraining their behaviour within their interpretation of the regulations has affected both the application of discretionary powers to established facts and the discovery of those facts themselves. Thus, just as the office would not ignore regulatory provisions, neither would it turn a blind eye to obvious circumstances, even if such circumstances might reduce a claimant's entitlements.

Claimants N.L./C.H.B.1 and N.L./C.H.B.2 in my survey shared a two-bedroom flat; one of the claimants was a former employee of the council's social services department, and through the office grapevine it was widely known that she cohabited with the other claimant. However, the claimants applied individually, one for certificated benefit, the other for standard benefit on fifty per cent of the flat's rent and rates. To team manager 1 this was "a blatant case of fraud" – he suspected that the claimant had sought legal advice as to how to manipulate the scheme. Consequently, he visited the claimants' home, where he found "the second bedroom piled high with junk and only one double bed in the place".

Team manager 1 informed the chief officer of his suspicion, but although she agreed with his analysis, she was reluctant to refuse the claim; she felt that the claimants would appeal to the review board and was quite certain that the councillors would disapprove vehemently of the team manager's 'snooping', irrespective of his motives or the evidence uncovered; in her opinion not only would the review board consider such evidence inadmissible,[61] but the very fact that it had been gathered would offend against the political will. However, since one claimant was a certificated case, the chief officer passed her suspicions onto the D.H.S.S. in the hope that she could present to the review board the evidence thereby uncovered as a 'fact' which the office had no choice but to accept. But, when a D.H.S.S. investigator visited the flat he found two fully furnished bedrooms, each with a bed, bookcase, television, and radio; as far as the D.H.S.S. were concerned the claimants lived separately.

The visit was followed immediately by a letter to the office from a Citizens Advice Bureau on the claimants' behalf, suggesting that an appeal to the review board would be made if the claims were not assessed individually. The chief officer explained that she invariably considered the office's position before the review boards to be completely untenable if she was advancing an argument less generous to the claimant than that supported by the D.H.S.S. – consequently the claim was granted. As team manager 3 remarked, the review board would not decide "according to the spirit of the legislation; they would go on how to get the best deal for the claimant. As I cynically said years ago . . . 'anything for a vote'."

Team manager 1 was extremely annoyed by this outcome, partly because the unwitting intervention of the D.H.S.S. had frustrated his attempt to prevent a "blatant fraud", but also because he believed that the Citizens Advice Bureau had actively connived with the claimants in dishonestly manipulating the scheme. This annoyance was in part based on a fear that news of the case would rapidly spread throughout the borough's many para-legal agencies, triggering a flood of such illegitimate claims. His major irritation, however, was at the balance of political forces within the housing benefit decision-making process which meant that such claimants would always be assured of success merely by raising the 'threat' of a review board hearing.

Whereas officers would attribute a rush of such claims to deviant claimants, the chief officer explained that she considered that the councillors would regard a plethora of review board cases as an indication that their political will was not being done, and "it would only take months for enough evidence to build up against an individual to require a change, and the change they'd have is a new manager, I'm sure. And quite rightly so." Officers at all levels of the hierarchy are, therefore, acutely aware that their promotion prospects and job security are to a large extent dependent on furthering achievement of the political will. Councillors, after all, are "our bosses . . . they're the ones who hire us and fire us", and it was clear from the survey that their displeasure would not be lightly incurred.

## THE CONSTRUCTION OF DEVIANCE IN A SOCIAL DEMOCRATIC ENVIRONMENT

However, the disjunction between the officers' and members' respective political alignments in North London Borough Council appeared to be only a rarely occurring phenomenon. It was clear from that survey that the disjunction had arisen primarily because, while councillors have construed the distribution of housing benefit entirely in terms of claimants' status – that is, that claimants by their very status must be afforded maximum protection against the Thatcher government's welfare policy – officers have regarded this status essentially as a starting point from which to construct a response to particular claimants. Since it is officers who are involved in the maintenance of an administrative system, their general mobilisation of bias in the claimants' favour may be undermined or overturned by events uncovered during their attempts professionally to discharge the sometimes dissonant task of effecting lawful realisation of the political will.

Thus, although traditional distinctions concerning the 'deserving' and 'undeserving' poor did not feature in the survey of North London Borough Council's decision-making processes – wherein radical social democracy has virtually hegemonic influence, or is 'common sense' in Gramscian terminology[62] – the officers have, nonetheless, occasionally identified claimants whom they considered undeserving of the full benefit of the council's new urban left political will. This claimant deviance has arisen from one or both of two sources.

First, as in the case discussed above, deviance might be behaviourally based, stemming from manipulative or fraudulent claimant activity which officers have stumbled across during the routine course of claim processing. Officers would not actively look for such behaviour, indeed they would assume claimants to be invariably honest, but evidence of deviant behaviour has occasionally been glaringly obvious. Moreover, following years of experience in administering welfare benefits, officers suggested that they had built up patterns of claimant behaviour – an "intuitive rationality"[63] – which has sensitised them to the possible presence of deviant activity in circumstances which might look quite innocuous to observers lacking such inside knowledge.

While officers surveyed accepted as a general premise that welfare claimants did not receive enough help from the state, manipulative claimants were felt to be taking unfair advantage of North London Borough Council's political stance and, in team manager 3's opinion, "the country will never be able to afford to give them more with all these abuses going on". Whether this assertion indicates the vestiges of a gift-based[64] perception of welfare benefits within new urban left ideology – or rather a deviation from that ideology – is a matter for speculation.

However, councillors who lack such intuitive rationality retain their purely abstract status-based perception of claimants' deservingness of full access to the political will. According to the survey, behaviourally-induced deviance has been constructed only by the officers and was reported to be a non-issue for review board members. Consequently, officers have been able to maintain their notion of a correct determination of a behaviourally deviant claimant's case if the claimant has not appealed to the review board. However, since the office's fundamental adherence to the political will has meant that claimants have always been notified of their procedural rights of appeal, and since the council has funded a plethora of para-legal agencies capable of providing legal competence,[65] appeals have been frequently forthcoming. And, by appealing, behaviourally deviant claimants have ensured – albeit unwittingly – that their claims have been met.

However, officers also discussed their perception of a status-based form of deviance which has led to the creation, in effect, of a sub-group of claimants one might label 'the undeserving rich'. Team manager 1, echoing his colleagues' views, considered the housing benefit scheme "ungenerous", and said that he had found that being as substantively generous to claimants as the regulations allow had become an automatic response. However:

> There are some cases where I feel, it has to be said . . . the scheme is far too generous. We have someone who has investments of £150,000 who . . . qualified for a rate rebate, incredibly, because all the money was invested in very low-yield shares, which were very growth-orientated, in Japan.

Team manager 1 was equally incredulous on receiving an application for rate rebate from a claimant who owned two houses in London, had £20,000 in a Jersey bank account, and had returned from the Gulf to go back to university while living off his savings. "Frankly, I feel that I don't want to give him rebate. I don't think he deserves it when there are all those pensioners who can hardly make ends meet who need the money much more."

Regulation 16(4) of S.I. No. 677 provides that:

> In so far as a person's income does not consist of earnings from a gainful occupation, its weekly amount shall be calculated or estimated on such basis as appears to the appropriate authority to be reasonable in the circumstances of the particular case.

Although this affords officers some discretion in assessing claimants' income, both the above claimants had provided accurate evidence of their limited interest-based incomes, and the regulations do not permit authorities to take claimants' capital resources into account. Thus, team manager 1 had felt compelled to base assessment on the claimants' limited incomes. Although the claimants' affluence essentially had made them political undesirables within the office, officers would not countenance breaking rules in attempts to effect their own preferred solutions. Nor would officers expect review board support for rule breaking. One does see here, however, the apparent paradox of an officer who, while supportive of the council's political orientation, could draw on his experience of the administrative process and welcome the Thatcher government's proposals to introduce a capital cut-off for housing benefit eligibility[66] – a proposal against which the councillors have vigorously campaigned.

However, it was clear from the survey that in cases involving the 'undeserving rich' where officers have discretion to produce 'ungenerous' decisions they would do so and, moreover, would expect the review board to support them if the claimant should appeal. Officers explained that they presumed that affluent claimants would forfeit the review board's usual 'generous as possible' mobilisation of bias, thereby affording the office at least the prospect of a 'fair trial' before the board.

An example of this genre was claimant N.L./U.D.R.3, a young woman student living alone in a three-bedroom flat which she owned, but on which the mortgage payments were met directly by her father. Team manager 3 construed the mortgage payments as income within the meaning of regulation 16(4). However, the claimant's father (who was also a solicitor) wrote to the office maintaining that since the mortgage payments did not pass under his daughter's control they were not income. Team manager 3 thought this argument outrageous:

> . . . it seems stupid to me that . . . because the money doesn't come into [her] hands one can't count it as income. To me it's grossly unfair . . . because if you don't count that as income what do you count?

With the chief officer's support. team manager 3 determined to resist the claim, and approached the D.H.S.S. central office, hoping to buttress her argument with an 'expert' opinion. To her dismay the D.H.S.S. supported the claimant's contention, which left the team manager with two unpalatable choices: either to go before the review board as someone 'less generous than the D.H.S.S.', or to grant a 'grossly unfair' claim. The first option was considered untenable, even with respect to one of the undeserving rich, until the team manager came across *R. v. Oxford City Council, ex parte Jack*,[67] which is one of the very few housing benefit cases yet to have reached the courts. This case reinforced the team manager's contention and encouraged her to present the D.H.S.S. opinion to the review board as simply wrong in law. Pending appeal by the claimant, team manager 3 based the benefit on an income which included the mortgage payments – whether the chief officer would in fact resist any such appeal was unclear. By the end of the fieldwork period the claimant had yet to put the question.

## THE WELFARE STATE AND THE RULE OF LAW: A NEW URBAN LEFT RATIONALE

Maintenance of 'the rule of law' has latterly assumed a high profile in the Conservative government's political rhetoric.[68] In particular, members of the Thatcher administration have recently suggested that the principles of democratic government which the rule of law is presumed to guarantee are under threat from striking miners,[69] 'loony left' councils,[70] and S.O.G.A.T./N.G.A. pickets at Wapping, among others. As Fine has observed, however, despite the supposed intellectual and philosophical links between the *realpolitik* of the new right and nineteenth-century *laissez-faire* individualism,[71] the current government's perception of the rule of law is entirely at odds with the meaning accorded to the concept by classical liberalism which, as restated by Hayek, provides "that government in all its actions is bound by rules fixed and announced beforehand".[72]

The classical liberal definition is essentially a procedural mechanism, premised upon a (fictional[73]) constitutional separation of powers between the executive and judiciary and designed to maintain substantively minimal government interference with individual liberty and private property rights.[74] The Thatcher government, in contrast, advances a definition which requires that citizens exhibit "unconditional obedience to the state".[75]

The liberal ideal, perhaps somewhat ironically, has long been used by social democratic political parties and interest groups as a procedural route to achieve a more substantively interventionist role for state institutions.[76] Indeed, we currently face the apparent paradox that while central government castigates new urban left Labour councils for transgressing the rule of law (according to the Thatcherite model) those same authorities have been making frequent resort to the courts to establish that central government is consistently breaching the classical liberal variant of the concept. While much litigation has centred on increasing attempts by the Secretary of State for the Environment to curtail local government's financial autonomy,[77] social democratic councils and interest groups have also sought to use the procedural mechanisms of the rule of law to resist central government's cutbacks in welfare provisions (the Cotton case being the most obvious example[78]).

What conclusions, then, might one draw from this brief study of new urban left administrative decision-making? One is that the vast body of case law containing judicial prescription regarding the procedural and substantive constraints on bureaucratic behaviour are virtually invisible within the housing benefit office. That decision-making does appear closely to approximate to Jones's "adjudicative ideal"[79] is a consequence not of the penetrative impact of judicial review, but of the council's political philosophy and, more importantly, of the fundamental congruence between the personal politics and morality of councillors and administrators.

The survey of North London Borough Council's housing benefit office has provided a clear example of Hill's "ideological typology". Equally, there is no suggestion of either loose coupling or de-coupling[80] between the formal structure of the decision-making process and the effective distribution of power. From the survey it was clear that councillors functioned overtly in their dual formal roles of delineators of policy and judges of administrative behaviour. It cannot credibly be argued that the twin roles of elected politicians as policy-makers and quasi-judiciary provide merely 'symbolic reassurance', or act solely as legitimating devices to the council's claimants.

The inference is, perhaps, that realisation of Reich's new property thesis within welfare state bureaucracies is dependent on far more than the mere promulgation of procedural legal reform. The fact that disciples of Reich's seminal analysis are so often disappointed by the limited material impact of efforts to judicialise administrative decision-making is the result, perhaps, of a somewhat myopic reading of his work. Nascent within the new property articles, it may be suggested, were the seeds of what amounted to advocacy of a cultural revolution, a pleading for a totally radicalised perception of citizen/state relations. This proposed cultural transformation was only fully articulated in a later, avowedly non-legalistic book[81] in which Reich – albeit not explicitly – slipped into a basically Gramscian critique, premising his analysis of prevailing power and wealth distribution on the relative strength of competing multi-facted modes of 'consciousness', and basing hope for reform on the emergence and consolidation of the new 'consciousness'.

The effective attachment of the adjudicative ideal to welfare services is, as Reich has made clear, dependent upon public and judicial opinion which would accord welfare benefits the political status of property rights, whose protection against arbitrary state interference is the basis of the liberal rule of law concept.[82] And, despite the Thatcher government's protestations,[83] the rule of law is breached only by governments and not by their citizens. In essence, the new property thesis seeks to take hold of the liberal rule of law ideal and apply it, through the medium of administrative law,[84] to achieve social democratic ends.

However, despite the disjunction between the market liberalism of the Thatcher government and the social democracy of previous post-war governments,[85] the idea of welfare benefits as an inalienable right held by citizens against the state and protected by the rigours of legal due process has never effectively fastened itself upon post-war British public opinion. Popular perception of welfare benefits continues to construe them broadly as gifts[86] and, as Reich took pains to emphasise, legal protection cannot be extended effectively to gifts.[87] Indeed, the (temporary) successes of the welfare rights movement in the United States of America may have been largely attributable to its proponents' ability to attack administrative practices in terms of infringements of citizens' traditional constitutional rights rather than as a realignment of political and economic power with its own substantive integrity, given that the constitution has a certain sanctity in the 'common sense' of the people of the United States of America.

The welfare rights movement in Britain[88] has had no such traditional bastion to support its innovative political demands; the presentation of welfare as a legal right continues to challenge the dominant political and moral order.[89] However, the element of political pluralism within British society does offer local government some scope to create a cultural environment where the concept of welfare benefits as a right is entirely accepted. The process observed in North London Borough Council is one in which a political and bureaucratic organisation has used the autonomy afforded it by central government to engineer an 'administrative culture' dedicated to the maintenance of rights and, effectively, to upholding the rule of law.

What I have sought to convey is that the maintenance of the rule of law in the welfare state presents a cultural rather than simply legal challenge. It is dependent on a number of factors: the substantive personal and corporate politics and morality of politicians and officers, the bureaucratic efficiency of employees, staffing levels, investment in new technology, and the provision of legal expertise to claimants. Perhaps ironically, threats to the maintenance of the rule of law in North London Borough Council's office have emanated from central government's continuing efforts to curtail the council's financial autonomy, thus raising the spectre of reduced staffing levels and the disqualification of members. There is, of course, a significant divergence between the perceptions of central government and the new urban left as to the substance of state interventionism which the rule of law exists to control. That both groupings seek to legitimise their politics through a demonstration of allegiance to the same procedural ideal is, perhaps, the most accurate indicator of its complexity.

## NOTES AND REFERENCES

1 See E. Birney, *Housing on Trial* (1967) chap. 3; J. Rex and R. Moore, *Race, Community and Conflict* (1967); D. Hughes and S. Jones, "Bias in the Allocation and Transfer of Local Authority Housing: A Study of the Reports of the Commissioner for Local Administration in England" (1979) *J. Social Welfare Law* p. 273.

2 S. Merret, *State Housing in Britain* (1979); A. Murie, *Housing Inequality and Deprivation* (1983); D. Donnison and C. Ungerson, *Housing Policy* (1982).

3 M. Hill, *The Sociology of Public Administration* (1972), and *The State, Administration and the Individual* (1976); N. Lewis, "Discretionary Justice and the Supplementary Benefits System" in *Justice, Discretion and Poverty* (1976; eds. M. Adler and A. Bradley).

4 M. Hill, "The Exercise of Discretion in the National Assistance Board" (1969) XLVII *Public Administration* p. 75.

5 R. Lister, *Justice for the Claimant* (1974); J. Fulbrook, *The Appellant and his Case* (1975); K. Bell, *Tribunals in the Social Services* (1969), and *Research Study on Supplementary Benefit Appeal Tribunals* (1975); H. Street, *Justice in the Welfare State* (1968); N. Lewis, "Supplementary Benefit Appeal Tribunals" (1973) *Public Law* p. 257.

6 For an overview see R. Titmuss, "Welfare Rights, Law and Discretion" (1971) *Political Q.* p. 42. See also the argument between Donnison and Jordan in D. Donnison, "Against Discretion" *New Society*, 15 September 1977; B. Jordan, "Against Donnison" *New Society*, 13 October 1977; D. Donnison, "Dear Bill Jordan" *New Society*, 21 September 1978. More recently, see R. Goodin, "Welfare, Rights and Discretion" (1986) 6 *Oxford J. Legal Studies* p. 232.

7 Hill, *supra*, n. 3.

8 P. Moore, "Counter-culture in a social security office" *New Society*, 10 July 1980.

9 Birney, *op. cit.*, n. 1, chap. 5.

10 Lewis, *supra*, n. 5; Rex and Moore, *op. cit.*, n. 1; Birney, *op. cit.*, n. 1.

11 Lister, *op. cit.*, n. 5; Fulbrook, *op. cit.*, n. 5. See also the collection of articles in M. Adler and A. Bradley, *op. cit.*, n. 3. On the place of the deserving/undeserving distinction within popular culture, see P. Golding and S. Middleton, *Images of Welfare* (1982); P. Moore, "Scroungermania again at the D.H.S.S." *New Society*, 22 January 1981; A. Deacon, "The Scrounging Controversy: Public Atttitudes towards the Unemployed in Contemporary Britain" (1978) 12 *Social and Economic Administration* p. 120.

12 See R. Lawrence, "Solicitors and Tribunals" (1980) *J. Social Welfare Law* p. 13; D. Williams, "Social Welfare Consumers and their Complaints" (1979) *J. Social Welfare Law* p. 257. For a more generalised review of the spatial distribution of legal services see K. Economides *et al.*, "Law and Geography" (1986) 13 *J. Law and Society* p. 161.

13 T. Prosser, "Poverty, Ideology and Legality: Supplementary Benefit Appeal Tribunals and their Predecessors" (1977) *Brit. J. Law and Society* p. 40.

14 For an explanation of the 'adjudicative ideal' see H. Jones, "The Rule of Law and the Welfare State" (1958) *Columbia Law Rev.* p. 143.

15 J. Jowell, "The Legal Control of Administrative Discretion" (1973) *Public Law* p. 178.

16 A term coined by political scientists in the United States of America for empirical and theoretical investigations into the material influence of judicial decisions on, among other things, administrative processes, public opinion, legislatures, and other judges. For an early example, see T. Becker and M. Feeleym, *The Impact of Supreme Court Decisions* (2nd ed. 1973).

17 See J. Gyford, *Local Politics in Britain* (1976).

18 This dual nature of discretion is something lawyers are often accused of overlooking while concentrating solely on procedural issues. See, for example, M. Adler and A. Asquith (eds.), *Discretion and Welfare* (1982).

19 Although the government's recent setbacks over amendments to board and lodgings regulations are demonstrative of some limits on government behaviour (see below, n. 79). On the limited utility of the welfare rights movement's procedural victories to which the governmental response was to introduce amending legislation, see T. Prosser, *Test Cases for the Poor* (1983).

20 In the housing context, see Merret, *op. cit.*, n. 2; Donnison and Ungerson, *op. cit.*, n. 2, p. 21. More generally, see M. Loughlin, "Administrative Law, Local Government and the Courts" in *Half a Century of Municipal Decline* (1985; eds. M. Loughlin *et al.*).

21 [footnote missing]

22 For a variety of assessments of the current scope for local autonomy from central control see the essays in M. Loughlin, *op. cit.*, n. 20; M. Boddy and C. Fudge (eds.), *Local Socialism* (1984).

23 N. Branson, *Poplarism* (1979).

24 D. Skinner and J. Langdon, *The Story of Clay Cross* (1975).

25 On the emergence and consolidation of this new political grouping see Gyford, *op. cit.*, n. 17, and "The Politicisation of Local Government" in M. Loughlin, *op. cit.*, n. 20, and *The Politics of Local Socialism* (1985); Boddy and Fudge, *op. cit.*, n. 22.

26 See M. Loughlin, *Local Government in the Modern State* (1985) chap. 2; M. Boddy, "Local Councils and the Financial Squeeze" in Boddy and Fudge, *op. cit.*, n. 22.

27 Social Security and Housing Benefits Act 1982. The Act is merely an enabling instrument; current details of the scheme are contained in the Housing Benefit Regulations 1985, S.I. 1985 No. 677 to which all citations in the text refer.

28 See A. Erskine, *The Housing Benefit Bungle* (1983); N. Fielding, "The Housing Benefit Fiasco" *ROOF*, November 1983 p. 19; P. Kemp, *The Cost of Chaos* (1984).

29 *Housing Benefit Review* (1985; Cmnd. 9520).

30 Precise details are not given in order to preserve the anonymity of the field. Extracts from interviews with personnel are also anonymous for the same reason. Information about the survey can be obtained from the author.

31 Titmuss, *supra*, n. 6.

32 Hill, *op. cit.*, n.3.

33 For a refutation of the popular myth that councillors create policy while officers merely implement it, see Gyford, *op. cit.*, n. 17.

34 J. Gyford, *op. cit.*, n. 25; Boddy and Fudge, *op. cit.*, n. 22.

35 Regulation 25 expenditure is not eligible for D.H.S.S. subsidy, whereas subsidy is available for 100% of certificated benefit and 90% of standard benefit.

36 Donnison and Ungerson, *op. cit.*, n. 2.

37 See the Department of Environment, *Assistance with Housing Costs* (1981; Cmnd. ??).

38 *The Guardian*, 26 February 1986. See also the report in *New Society*, 23 January 1987, which revealed the existence of a 'deal' between senior officials in the Strathclyde social services department and local D.H.S.S. offices to reduce the D.H.S.S. workload by deliberately failing to inform claimants of their procedural rights to challenge D.H.S.S. decisions.

39 Moore, *supra*, n. 8.

40 *Id.*

41 P. Blau, "Orientation towards Clients in a Public Welfare Agency" (1960) *Administrative Science Q.* p. 5.

42 The office provides an exception to Braverman's notion of the progressive proletarianisation of white collar work in *Labour and Monopoly Capital* (1974), suggesting perhaps that proletarianisation is a process owing as much to the political and organisational context within which work is conducted as to the intrinsic nature of the work itself.

43 Hill, *op. cit.*, n. 3.

44 See the collection of articles in M. Freeman (ed.), *The State, the Law and the Family* (1984); J. Gardiner, "Women, Recession and the Tories" in *The Politics of Thatcherism* (1983; eds. S. Hall and M. Jacques).

45 See J. Nixon, *Fatherless Families on Family Income Supplement* (1979).

46 See I. Gough, *The Political Economy of the Welfare State* (1979).

47 J. Pahl, "The Allocation of Money within the Household" in Freeman, *op. cit.*, n. 44.

48 Gardiner, *op. cit.*, n. 44.

49 See E. Wilson, *Women and the Welfare State* (1977); R. Titmuss, *Essays on the Welfare State* (1958) especially chaps. 5 and 6. With respect to public sector housing, see Donnison and Ungerson, *op. cit.*, n. 2; Merret, *op. cit.*, n. 2. In the context of the United Stated of America, see L. Komisar, *Down and Out in the U.S.A.* (1974).

50 C. Reich, "The New Property" (1964) *Yale Law J.* and "Individual Rights and Social Welfare – The Emerging Legal Issues" (1965) *Yale Law J.*

51 Hill, *op. cit.*, n. 3; Goodin, *op. cit.*, n. 6.

52 S. Goss, "Women's Initiatives in Local Government" in Boddy and Fudge, *op. cit.*, n. 22.

53 For further examples of this use of 'displaced discretion' as a means to sidestep seemingly

binding rules see R. Baldwin and K. Hawkins, "Discretionary Justice: Davis Reconsidered" (1984) *Public Law* p. 570.

54 The chief officer's S.O.G.A.T. initiative was undertaken without reference to the council's solicitors; that the measure might be substantively *ultra vires* was not a factor that entered into her decision-making equation.

55 *Supra*, n. 30.

56 J. Luba, "Decisions of Housing Benefit Review Boards 1" *Legal Action Group Bulletin* August 1985, p. 117.

57 M. Partington and H. Bolderson, *Housing Benefit Review Procedures: A Preliminary Analysis* (1984); Q. Oliver, "The Final Appeal" *ROOF*, March/April 1984, p. 15.

58 *Id.*

59 *Supra*, n. 5.

60 J. Mashaw, *Bureaucratic Justice* (1983).

61 On the admissibility of evidence in Supplementary Benefit Appeal Tribunals see C. Yates, "Supplementary Benefit Appeals and the Rules of Evidence" (1980) *J. Social Welfare Law* p. 273.

62 R. Simon, "Gramsci's Concept of Hegemony" *Marxism Today*, March 1977, p. 17; L. Migliaro and P. Misuraca, "The Theory of Modern Bureaucracy" in *Approaches to Gramsci* (1982; ed. A. Showstack-Sassoon); C. Buci-Glucksman, *Gramsci and the State* (1980).

63 *Supra*, n. 6.

64 Reich, *op. cit.*, n. 50.

65 The phraseology being Nonet's (P. Nonet, *Administrative Justice* (1969)).

66 Which is expected, general elections results permitting, in 1988.

67 17 H.L.R. 419.

68 See Bob Fine, *Democracy and the Rule of Law* (1984).

69 For the reverse view see the collection of essays in Bob Fine and Robert Millar (eds.), *Policing the Miners' Strike* (1985).

70 That such posturing by Conservative politicians is designed primarily as fodder for the popular press, at whose hands it is magnified into an inaccurate but effective form of electioneering by scaremongering, is an argument advanced by J. Jenkins, "Madness and Delusion: The Green Sheep in Colonel Gaddaffi Drive" *New Statesman*, 9 January 1978.

71 Hall and Jacques, *op. cit.*, n. 44.

72 F. Hayek, *The Road to Serfdom* (1944) chap. 6. See also F. Hayek, *The Constitution of Liberty* (1960), and "Will the Democratic Ideal Prevail?" in *The Coming Confrontation* (1978; ed. A. Seldon).

73 See L. Lustgarten, *The Governance of Police* (1986) chap. 1.

74 Hayek, *op. cit.*, n. 72 (1944) and (1960).

75 Fine, *op. cit.*, n. 68, p. 8.

76 Jones, *op. cit.*, n. 14 (1958); Reich, *op. cit.*, n. 50 (1964) and (1965).

77 For the political parties' perspective on the latest round in the continuing controversy between Nicholas Ridley and the new urban left, this time concerning rate support grant payments for non-existent roads, see *The Times*, 6 March 1987.

78 See S. Stewart *et al.*, "The Right Approach to Social Security: The Case of the Board and Lodgings Regulations" (1986) 13 *J. Law and Society* p. 371. For the latest development see *R. v. D.H.S.S. ex parte the London Borough of Camden*, *The Times*, 6 March 1987.

79 *Supra*, n. 14.

80 See W. Starbuck, "Congealing Oil: Inventing Ideology to Justify Acting Ideologies Out" (1982) *J. Management Studies* p. 19.

81 C. Reich, *The Greening of America* (1970).

82 Hayek, *op. cit.*, n. 71 (1944). See also M. Loughlin, "Procedural Fairness: A Study of Crisis in Administrative Law Theory" (1978) *University of Toronto Law J.* p. 215.

83 Fine, *op. cit.*, n.68.

84 Jones, *op. cit.*, n. 14.

85 Hall and Jacques, *op. cit.*, n. 44.

86 See Taylor-Gooby, *Public Opinion, Ideology and State Welfare* (1985).

[87] Reich, *op. cit.*, n. 50.

[88] D. Bull, "The Anti-Discretion Movement in Britain: Fact or Phantom?" (1980) *J. Social Welfare Law* p. 65.

[89] See Enoch Powell's assertion in *Still to Decide* (1972) p. 12 that "the translation of a want or need into a right is one of the most widespread and dangerous of modern heresies."

# Part V
# Gender and Welfare

# [21]

*Jnl Soc. Pol.*, 7, 3, 257–84 

# Who Cares for the Family?*

HILARY LAND†

## ABSTRACT

Although Britain has never had a set of policies explicitly labelled 'family policies', most if not all social policies are implicitly family policies because they are based on certain assumptions about the nature of relationships between the sexes and the generations. By careful examination of the detail of the legislation and administrative rules, together with the way in which services are allocated and used, it is possible to expose these assumptions and show that they are not only consistent between policies but very persistent over time. This paper first examines the assumptions concerning the division of unpaid labour within the family whereby women care for the young, the sick and the old and for able-bodied adult men (their husbands). The examples are selected from a variety of income maintenance systems and services for children, the old and the disabled. Particular attention is focused on the extent to which it is recognized that women are at the same time workers in the labour market *and* unpaid domestic workers in the home. The second part of the paper analyses the impact on their participation and opportunities in the labour market of the ideology which accords to women the primary responsibilities for caring for other members of their family. The perpetuation of such an ideology favours the interests of men and frequently the interests of the economically powerful, but it is not assumed that these interests always coincide.

---

'The family must be regarded as the bulwark of a stable society', said the Archbishop of Canterbury in the opening speech in a major debate on the family which took place in the House of Lords in the summer of 1976.[1] There is no doubt that the family is a powerful force for maintaining the

* A paper given at the annual conference of the Social Administration Association at the University of Bristol in July 1977. For help in developing my ideas for this paper I am indebted to colleagues in my department and to Miki David, Paddy Hillyard and Roy Parker in particular, and also to Diana Barker, Christine Delphy, Leonora Davidoff, Jalna Hamner and Jenny Shaw and to those who attend the Women's Research and Resource Centre seminars.

† University of Bristol.

[1] *House of Lords Debates*, Vol. 371, col. 1,260.

*status quo*. In particular it is an important mechanism for the transmission of existing inequalities. On the other hand the family manages, or is expected to manage, the tension between order and change and in this sense may facilitate rather than inhibit change. Paradoxically therefore the family both transmits culture *and* provides a counter-culture. Hence both the causes of and the solutions to various social ills are looked for within the family. It is not surprising that a government spokesman in the same debate declared 'The government believe implicitly in the family and recognise that the family needs all the support that society can give it...'[2] In other words governments do care about the family but the form which their concern takes is an important and delicate issue because the family is portrayed as a sanctuary – warm, welcoming and intimate, unlike the cold, ruthless, competitive society outside. Unless this haven, which is thought to be a frail institution, remains private and free from state intrusion then it will not be able to counteract the increasingly alienating effects of social and economic change.

The extent of state intervention in the family has therefore been obscured in order to maintain the illusion that the family is a private domain. Those pressing for new or different social policies and those managing existing services have presented these policies as defending the 'normal' or 'natural' pattern of dependencies and responsibilities already existing within the family. In addition benefits and services are provided to individuals defined to be without families, or at least 'normal' families. Thus, by narrowing the definition of 'normal' family, it has been possible to develop a wide range of services for children, and to a lesser extent for adults, without appearing to impose particular patterns of responsibilities within the family. At the same time those family obligations which are held to be important are emphasized.

Social policies are *implicit* family policies therefore because most, if not all, of them are based on certain assumptions about the pattern of 'normal' relationships between the sexes and the generations within the family. If these assumptions can be shown to be consistent between a variety of policies and also to persist over long periods of time then we need to know how and why these particular patterns are sustained and perpetuated. This means exposing the ideological dimensions of a range of social policies as they affect the family and abandoning the view that the state does not interfere in the family, which anyway is somehow separate from other major social, political and economic institutions. It also means recognizing that individual family members may have quite different and even opposing interests. Resources and responsibilities are not shared equally within the

[2] *Ibid*. col. 1,361.

family. Just as the concept of 'the national interest' makes obscure crucial conflicts of interest within the nation, thus favouring the superordinate in society, the demand to preserve and protect 'the family' is to the advantage of its more powerful and privileged members, and some of those who voice such a demand may represent deeply conservative forces.

This paper will first examine the assumptions underlying a variety of social policies which concern the division of unpaid labour within the family whereby women care for the young, the sick and the old and, most important, for able-bodied adult men (their husbands). While acknowledging that the time and work involved are not the only dimensions of caring and that particularly in the context of a loving relationship there are other aspects which are positive and rewarding, it is important for us to recognize that, if we ascribe to women the primary responsibility for providing domestic services for other members of the family, their daily lives are structured in a way which profoundly affects their opportunities in the wider society in general and the labour market in particular. Moreover, the fact that this work is unpaid means that women do not acquire any direct financial independence by doing it. The second part of the paper therefore will indicate how the division of unpaid labour within the family is an important determinant of women's opportunities in the labour market.

In order to appreciate the full extent of the work of caring within the family it is important not to restrict an examination of the family to the child-bearing stage of the life cycle. Social policies are most likely to be discussed explicitly in terms of their impact on family relationships and responsibilities in the context of demographic objectives, because it is legitimate for governments to be concerned with the size and structure of the population. The focus is then on the nuclear family and the obligation that parents have for their dependent children. However, the child-bearing and rearing stage of the family life cycle lasts a shorter time than formerly because fertility within marriage starts later and ends earlier. Today men and women can expect to live another forty years after the birth of their last child so active parenthood does not occupy all or even most of a man's or a woman's married lifetime.[3] The work of caring does not come to an end when children have attained adulthood. Adults have relationships with and obligations towards their middle-aged and elderly parents. For example, on the basis of a study of home helps in 1967, Audrey Hunt concluded that 'Between the ages of 35 and 64 roughly half the housewives can expect at some time or another to give some help to elderly or infirm persons.'[4]

[3] D. Eversley, 'Demographic Change and the Demand for Housing', in M. Buxton and E. Craven, *The Uncertain Future*, Centre for Studies in Social Policy, London, 1976, p. 32.

[4] A. Hunt, *The Home Help Service in England and Wales*, Government Social Survey, HMSO, London, 1970, p. 424.

260 *Hilary Land*

Her study showed that one in five housewives (that is, the person other than a domestic servant who is responsible for most of the domestic duties) aged between thirty-five and forty-nine years of age had a disabled person or someone aged over sixty-five in the household and that among those aged between fifty and sixty-four one in four had an elderly or infirm person present. (Not all those aged sixty-five or over were necessarily infirm, but in time many would become so. Peter Townsend's studies of the elderly suggested that nearly half of them had difficulty doing heavy housework.)

Significantly, the formula used by *The General Household Survey*, which is one of the largest ongoing government surveys, defines the family in such a way that it is impossible to discover how many elderly people live with their children, either married or single: 'In general families cannot span more than two generations; that is grandparents and grandchildren cannot belong to the same family.'[5]

A further reason for looking beyond the child-rearing stage is that it is essential to distinguish the needs and obligations which are presumed to arise from marriage from those which are presumed to arise from parenthood. When we are looking at families with young children it is too easy to equate marriage and parenthood. Marriage is after all a social contract regulated by church and state. With it goes a set of financial obligations for the man – in particular he must participate in the labour market in order to support his children and his wife. Women acquire a set of domestic duties which include caring for their children, their elderly or sick relatives and of course their husbands. One important consequence of the difference between the meaning of marriage for men and its meaning for women is that there is a conflict between a woman's responsibilities towards other members of her family and her activities in the labour market, whereas for most men there is not. As Alfred Marshall wrote at the turn of the century, when commenting on recent increases in women's wages, 'This is a great gain in so far as it tends to develop their faculties but an injury in so far as it tempts them to neglect their duty of building up a true home and of investing their effort in the Personal Capital of their children's character and abilities.'[6]

This paper will attempt to show that the priorities which women must accord to their paid work in the labour market. their unpaid work in the home and their leisure are as much a product of being wives as of being mothers. A number of social policies will be examined and the underlying assumptions about the nature of the obligations between different members

[5] Office of Population Censuses and Surveys (OPCS), *The General Household Survey, 1973*, HMSO, London, 1976, p. 135.

[6] A. Marshall, *Elements of Economics of Industry*, third edition, Macmillan, London, 1901, p. 342.

of the family disentangled. The examples will be selected from the income maintenance system and services for children, the old and the disabled. Other social policies could be analysed in the same way, but space allows only a few policies to be examined. Examples will be drawn from past as well as present policies, to demonstrate the persistence of the underlying assumptions. Attention will be focused particularly on the extent to which it is recognized that women are at the same time workers in the labour market *and* unpaid domestic workers in the home.

## INCOME MAINTENANCE SYSTEMS AND RESPONSIBILITIES FOR CARING

The majority of married women have paid employment for most of their married lives. The economic activity rates for childless married women under forty years of age are the same as those for single women, and increasingly women with children have paid employment.[7] In half of all married couples under retirement age both husband and wife are earners. On average a wife's earnings represent 25 per cent of the family income.[8] For some families the wife's financial contribution is a very important means of keeping a family out of poverty. For example the Department of the Environment's second Inner Area study in Lambeth showed that among married couples with children under fifteen years of age in which the mother had full-time paid employment all had an income at least 20 per cent above supplementary benefit level. However, in those families in which the mother had part-time employment 6 per cent had an income below 20 per cent of supplementary benefit level, and where the mother did not have paid employment at all nearly one in four fell below this level.[9]

A wife's earnings then are an important means of maintaining a family's standard of living. It seems at first a little surprising therefore that among unemployed men the overall proportion with wives in paid employment is low. Among men dependent on supplementary benefit the proportion is even lower – one-third of the childless and only 1 per cent of those with children.[10] Part of the explanation lies in the fact that the social security system is based on the concept of one male breadwinner upon whom the rest of the family relies or *should* rely for financial support. The importance of the wife's financial contribution to the family is therefore ignored.

[7] OPCS, 1971 *Census*, HMSO, London, 1971 – household composition tables: 10 per cent sample, Table 50.

[8] L. Hamill, *Wives as Sole and Joint Breadwinners*, unpublished paper given to the Social Science Research Council Social Security Workshop, 1977.

[9] Quoted from the Department of the Environment's second Inner Area study in P. Willmott, 'The Role of the Family', in Buxton and Craven, *op. cit.* p. 53.

[10] Supplementary Benefits Commission (SBC), *Annual Report* 1976, Cmnd 6910, HMSO, London, 1977, p. 46.

Currently only £4 a week of a wife's earnings are disregarded. If she earns more than this then the extra dependency benefit is lost and in addition, for those on supplementary benefit, the benefit is reduced pound for pound. There is therefore a substantial incentive for a woman to give up paid work once her husband becomes unemployed, unless she has high enough earnings to maintain the whole family. Similarly there is evidence that the wives of men who become chronically sick are more likely to give up than to take up employment.[11] In other words the social security system ignores the fact that most families are dependent on two earners (and for many working-class families this has always been so);[12] it actively discourages role reversal and it encourages women to give priority to their responsibilities in the home. As a result the division of labour within the home remains unchanged even when the man is out of the labour market and dependent on state benefits. At the same time the experience of unemployment for the man is less intolerable than it might otherwise be. George Orwell, writing forty years ago about the lives of the unemployed, drew attention to the same phenomenon:

> . . .so long as a man is married unemployment makes comparatively little alteration to his way of life. His home is impoverished but it is still a home, and it is noticeable everywhere that the anomalous position created by unemployment – the man being out of work while the woman's work continues as before – has not altered the relative status of the sexes. In working class homes it is the man who is the master and not, as in a middle class home, the woman or baby. Practically never, for instance, in a working class home, will you see the man doing a stroke of the housework. Unemployment has not changed this convention which on the face of it seems a little unfair. The man is idle from morning to night but the woman is as busy as ever – more so indeed, because she has to manage with less money. Yet so far as my experience goes the women do not protest. I believe that they, as well as the men, feel that a man would lose his manhood if, merely because he was out of work, he developed into a 'Mary Ann'.[13]

The interpretation of 'incapacity to work' in the national insurance scheme provides further examples of the assumptions made about a woman's primary responsibilities. The national insurance scheme created in 1911 was based on a large number of friendly societies and industrial associations which had developed during the previous century. Although some of them extended membership to women, the number of married women who joined was quite small because few could afford the premiums and in any case benefit was rarely paid during illness arising from pregnancy or childbirth.

[11] See J. Martin and D. Morgan, *Prolonged Sickness and the Return to Work*, OPCS, HMSO, London, 1975.

[12] See H. Land, 'The Myth of the Male Breadwinner', *New Society*, 29:2 (1975), 71–3.

[13] G. Orwell, *The Road to Wigan Pier*, Penguin Books, Harmondsworth, 1937, p. 72.

However, the new national insurance scheme had a much broader membership and included 700,000 married women, insured in their own right, many of whom had not been eligible for benefit before. Difficult questions about the circumstances in which sickness benefit should be paid were therefore raised on a much larger scale than hitherto. These issues could not be ignored because in the first years of the scheme many more women than had been expected to do so claimed sickness benefit, and in 1913 a committee was set up to find out why these 'excessive claims' had been made.[14]

The committee gave careful consideration to the meaning of 'incapacity to work'. Did it mean inability to follow one's usual occupation? For short periods of sickness when there was a good chance of returning to the same job, this was a reasonable interpretation, at least as far as men were concerned. For women it was different. As one witness explained, 'A man is working or he is ill. A woman is perhaps not working because some of the family are ill, or perhaps she is cleaning the house.'[15] Provided they were capable of doing the housework they were not deemed to be ill and therefore women found doing housework when the sick visitor called had their benefit withdrawn in spite of the fact that they were not fit enough to return to the mill or factory. What was recognized by only a few witnesses was how hard it was for a woman *not* to do any domestic work, however ill she felt. For example Marion Phillips, representing The Women's Labour League, told the committee:

> It is a very difficult problem to deal with mothers who are so used to waiting on the rest of the family that they do it unconsciously. . .the working woman who has been so used to serving other people that even when she is ill she will go on doing it and it is recognized in her family as a natural thing.[16]

Men caught working on their allotment or garden were likewise disqualified, but, as Sidney Webb said to the committee, 'Gardens are not quite as common as teacups.'[17]

It was feared by many of the witnesses and indeed by the majority of the committee that the availability of sickness benefit had encouraged women to take time off from their paid employment. The secretary of an approved society with a membership of about 24,500, a third of whom were married, explained:

> With sickness benefit and husband's wages, she has sufficient to keep the family going, because she is saving the money she would have had to pay for having the

[14] Departmental Committee on Sickness Benefit Claims under the Insurance Act, appointed in September 1913.

[15] Sickness Benefit Claims Committee, *Report and Minutes of Evidence*, Cd 7688, Vol. 1, HMSO, London, 1914, p. 4.

[16] *Ibid.* Vol. 3, p. 311.

[17] *Ibid.* Vol. 2, p. 435.

children looked after. . .and then there is washing and baking. She would have that to pay for. I consider that seven shillings and sixpence at home and being able to look after the children and to do the washing and baking herself would be equal to what she got by going out to work and having to pay for all these things.[18]

(This is evidence that, even when a woman does not actually do the household work herself, she is responsible for arranging *and* paying for it to be done.)

The committee (bar Mary Macarthur) found it easier to accept that the unexpectedly high number of claims for sickness benefits from women was due to an ignorance about insurance principles and a greater tendency to malinger than that it was because the health of many working women was very bad and because for the first time they could afford to take time off from work when they were ill. The committee therefore recommended that societies should convince women of the necessity to abstain from housework while they were receiving sickness benefit and should generally educate them about the principles of insurance.

Those who administer the national insurance sickness benefit scheme today still assume that if a woman is capable of housework then she is not in fact ill. The instructions issued by the Department of Health and Social Security (DHSS) to doctors concerning medical evidence for social security purposes ask them to consider the question of fitness for alternative work after a lengthy period of illness. As far as women are concerned this means assessing their capacity to perform household duties. The instructions state:

If a woman has for some considerable time (perhaps 6 months or so) been advised to refrain from her normal paid employment but is nevertheless doing an amount of housework in her own home for which she could reasonably expect to be paid if it were done for an employer, there will generally be no grounds for continuing to issue statements of advice to refrain from work.[19]

Similarly DHSS visiting officers fill in a form which has a separate section for a woman ascertaining whether 'she is able to look after her family (if any) and do her own housework and laundry'. At the time of writing there were no such questions for men, either living alone or married. In other words in the last resort *all* women were expected to do housework in order to maintain themselves, or be maintained by a man. Men were not expected to do so until August 1977, when this assumption was challenged and a national insurance commissioner ruled that, where a man's capacity for work was at issue, 'If the evidence showed that he undertook household chores, as many men now do, or worked in the garden, that evidence would be admissible on the question whether he is capable of remunerative work.'

[18] *Ibid.* Vol. 1, p. 2.

[19] *Medical Evidence for Social Security Purposes*, DHSS, London, 1976, p. 3.

As a result the instructions issued to doctors and DHSS visiting officers are going to be amended to apply to *all* claimants.[20]

Recently two non-contributory benefits have been introduced which are also based firmly on the assumption that upon marriage (or indeed cohabitation) women undertake to care for the men with whom they are living, for the children and for sick or elderly relatives – the non-contributory invalidity pension for married women and the invalid care allowance. Men and single women are eligible for the former on the basis of an inadequate national insurance contribution record and incapacity for paid work. Their eligibility for benefit is not affected by their ability to cook, clean or do their washing. However, a married woman will only qualify if she is too disabled to perform normal household duties. The invalid care allowance of £10.50 is paid to men and women who give up paid employment (which means earning less than £9 a week) in order to care for a sick or elderly relative. So this allowance does not help many of those who combine paid employment with the care of the sick or elderly. (In 1965 one in twelve of all women in paid employment also had the care of an elderly or infirm person.[21] We do not know how many men were in this position.) However, a married woman or a woman cohabiting with a man is not eligible at all. Even when the EEC directive on equal treatment for men and women in the social security system is signed it will not be possible to challenge the discriminatory nature of these two new benefits because the commission's view is that the directive will not include housewives and therefore will not affect these benefits.[22]

Before leaving examples from the social security system I should point out that these assumptions do not always work to the disadvantage of women. In 1966 the Supplementary Benefits Commission inherited a policy from the National Assistance Board of paying an exceptional circumstance allowance to cover Class Three national insurance contributions (thus maintaining the claimants' rights to a pension) in the following circumstances:

> If a *female* claimant has left employment in order to look after elderly or sick parents or other close relatives, or if a daughter has given up work to look after a younger brother or sister, the amount of the non-employed persons national insurance contributions should be treated as a reckonable expense. . .If any one else asks for help to pay contributions *he* should be told that it cannot be given.[23]

In future all recipients of the invalid care allowance will be credited with national insurance contributions, as will those who are out of the labour

[20] Personal communication from Stanley Orme, Minister of Social Security, to Jo Tunnard, 26 October 1977.
[21] A. Hunt, *A Survey of Women's Employment*, OPCS, HMSO, London, 1968, p. 176.
[22] *House of Commons Debates*, Vol. 941, col. 453.
[23] SBC, *Policy Guidelines*, para. A3,011 (my italics).

market because of home responsibilities. The latter will include married women who are at home looking after children of any age up to sixteen.

The British income tax system recognizes a variety of family responsibilities by means of a series of allowances which the taxpayer is allowed to offset against his (or less often her) taxable income. Among these allowances is one for housekeepers, and the reasons given for their introduction show similar assumptions about who does the work in the home. The housekeeper's allowance was first introduced in 1918. Initially it was only for widowers with dependent children but a year later it was extended to widowers without children. The Board of Inland Revenue in its evidence to the Royal Commission on the Taxation of Profits and Income of 1951–5 explained that 'The reason for this extension appears to have been the largely sentimental one that when a man's wife dies he cannot be expected to give up his home and therefore he must have someone to look after him . . .(the widow). . .is already accustomed to look after the home herself.'[24]

Widows with children were, however, included in 1920; four years later the allowance was extended to childless widows. This seemed surprising in retrospect because, as the Inland Revenue Staff Federation told the same royal commission, 'It is not the death of the spouse but the lack of a *wife* who can keep house which may necessitate a housekeeper.'[25] Until the Second World War the tax system only recognized housekeepers who were female relatives and resident in the taxpayer's home. Evidence that they were being paid was not necessary. In other words women do the housework and look after a man and his children in return for their maintenance.

During the Second World War the definition of 'housekeeper' for tax purposes was broadened to include non-relatives, and any taxpayer with children employing a resident female housekeeper could claim it. However, a married man could only claim if his wife was permanently incapacitated, and a female taxpayer could only use the allowance if she was disabled or chronically sick, or supporting herself by full-time employment. In 1960 an additional allowance was introduced for taxpayers with children in the above categories. They did not have to have a resident housekeeper. However, married women with permanently incapacitated husbands were not eligible for either allowance because, a government spokesman explained, 'Though the work of looking after an invalid husband may be a serious tie to the wife, it does not prevent her from undertaking the normal responsibilities of looking after the children.'[26] It is clear that, even if married women are in full-time paid employment because their husbands cannot

[24] Royal Commission on the Taxation of Profits and Income 1951–5, *Evidence*, Vol. 4, HMSO, London, 1953, p. 55.

[25] *Ibid*. Vol. 3, p. 18.

[26] *House of Commons Debates*, Vol. 621, col. 1,558.

earn, they are still expected to carry out their 'normal responsibilities' in the home. Only women with children but without husbands to care for get additional tax relief. (In other words the key determinant is a woman's marital status rather than whether or not she is a mother.) In contrast men are not expected to combine paid employment with domestic work and are therefore helped with the cost of providing a substitute for a sick wife as well as an absent one. The substitute must be another woman.

### FAMILY RESPONSIBILITIES AND COMMUNITY CARE FOR THE SICK AND THE OLD

The examples of the different treatment of men and women in the British systems of income maintenance described above result as much from assumptions actually contained in the legislation as from administrative practices. The next set of examples will examine policies relating to the provision of services for the elderly, the sick and the young which do not discriminate between men and women in the legislation but which are still differentially allocated and utilized. I shall also look briefly at who staffs the services and at the assumptions made about the work done by male employees on the one hand and female employees on the other.

The vast majority of the elderly, including the majority of the bedfast and the house-bound, live in their own homes or with their children: only a small proportion (fewer than 2 per cent in 1975) are in residential institutions provided by voluntary organizations or local authorities. The characteristics of old people living in institutions are significantly different from those of old people who remain in private households. Ethel Shanas, on the basis of her study of old people in three countries conducted in the sixties, concluded:

> There would appear to be a marked inverse correlation between the numbers of close relatives and the likelihood of institutionalisation in old age. When incapacity is also taken into account this correlation becomes more marked, but two variables also seem to be important – the sex of the close relative and *their* incapacity. More people in institutions than outside who have children have sons only. . .[27]

Altogether she found that in Britain three times as many old people lived with married daughters as those living with married sons. Even when they were living separately, daughters were the most likely relatives to be relied upon for help with housework and personal care. Old people with sons but no daughters were more likely to be close to a daughter-in-law, especially if the daughter-in-law in question had no surviving parents. She also found

[27] E. Shanas, P. Townsend, D. Wedderburn, H. Friis, P. Milnøj and J. Stewhouwer, *The Old in Three Industrial Societies*, Routledge and Kegan Paul, London, 1968, p. 112.

that it was more common for men to be looked after in their own homes by their wives than the reverse. Thus admission to an institution depended a great deal on the existence of a daughter or daughter-in-law or a wife and not only on the degree of infirmity of the old person.

The provision of domiciliary services to old people is also allocated in a way which reflects assumptions about the availability of help from female relatives in general and daughters in particular. Audrey Hunt's study of the home help service in 1967 revealed that old people living alone and at a distance from children were more likely to receive a home help than those living with their families. Since the more severely handicapped old people are, the more likely they are to be living with their children, home helps do not necessarily go to the most infirm old people. Fewer than one in ten of the elderly recipients of a home help had children living in the same household. Three-fifths had children living elsewhere, but these were more likely to be sons than daughters.[28] A similar pattern was found among chronically sick recipients of the home help service. Her study also showed that women living alone had to be more infirm before receiving a home help than men living alone. She reported:

> There are indications that men are more likely to receive home helps simply because they are elderly and living alone: for example 89 per cent of men were able to go out compared with 68 per cent of women; 29 per cent of men compared with 8 per cent of women had no difficulty with personal tasks involving mobility.[29]

It is clear then that men are not expected to look after themselves as much as women are and that they are accordingly given more help from publicly provided support services. Neither is it assumed that they will be able to look after elderly or infirm relatives: their primary commitment must be to the labour market and when they have retired from it they are not expected to acquire domestic skills. This of course makes it difficult for a man to care himself for a sick or elderly member of his family should he wish to, but because he is probably earning substantially more than a woman at least he is more likely to be able to afford to buy help. Moreover, as is shown above, if he is married, his wife's duties include the care of his relatives unless she has overriding commitments to her own family. In contrast women must put their domestic responsibilities first, and little account is taken of the financial necessity for many of them to remain in paid employment. Even less consideration is given to women who would simply prefer to continue with their paid work outside the home and shoulder some, but not all, of the responsibility for caring.

The division of labour within the family in determining who uses the

[28] *Ibid.* p. 178.

[29] *Ibid.* p. 61.

social services was just as important years ago when the only alternative to family care and maintenance was either the Poor Law or charity. The Royal Commission on the Poor Laws noted that in 1906 there were many more old men than old women in workhouse wards. This was not because men were more infirm or liable to illness: the surplus was found almost entirely in the wards of the workhouses *not* appropriated to the sick or infirm. Conversely there were twice as many old women as old men receiving outdoor relief. Alderman Mcdougall, a leading member of the Manchester Board of Guardians offered the royal commission the following explanation:

> The large majority of those who endure biting poverty without seeking relief from the Guardians are women. Men do not so frequently attain to old age under disadvantageous circumstances as women do. Old men go more readily into the workhouse than old women. Women struggle longer and with greater determination with the difficulties of poverty and the incapacities of old age. Families in poor circumstances find it less possible to provide food and shelter for an old man who is a relative than for an old woman. He is more in the way, he expects not only a larger portion of the food, but to share in the better portions. He does not fit into the household of a working family as an old woman does and is not so useful in domestic matters. His welcome is colder and he desires to get out of the way and goes to the workhouse. A decent old woman will cling to a home where she may be regarded as a drudge rather than as the grandmother or the aunt, and she will exist on the plainer portions of the meals and wedge in both day and night without encroaching much on the means of the family.[30]

He was drawing attention to the differential allocation of resources within the family as well as the division of domestic duties and suggesting that both are factors in determining how and where men and women are looked after in their old age.

Although there is much talk of 'shared care', in fact the social services on the whole only provide domiciliary or residential services to the sick and the old either when they have no relatives or when their relatives cannot cope. Legitimate reasons for not caring differ between men and women, as do acceptable reasons for being out of the labour market. It would seem that it is feared that if the social services actually provided supportive services of a high standard and made them widely available then women's incentive to carry out their primary duties in the home would be diminished in the same way in which state income maintenance, whether in the form of wage subsidies or unemployment benefit, is alleged to diminish male work incentives in the labour market. The myth that families no longer care for their kin as much as they used to do is as long-standing and as prevalent as the belief that the unemployed are mainly work-shy scroungers. (It is not

[30] *Report of the Royal Commission on the Poor Laws and Relief of Distress*, Cd 4499, Vol. 3, HMSO, London, 1909, p. 259, quoted by R. Moroney in *The Family and the State*, Longman, London, 1976. He makes no comment on the differences between men and women.

possible in the space of one article fully to explore the function of these myths, but it is a topic worthy of further analysis.)

### THE INTERRELATIONSHIP BETWEEN MOTHERS' AND FATHERS' EMPLOYMENT AND DAY CARE PROVISIONS FOR CHILDREN

The provision of services which either share or replace the care which parents give their young children is based on similar assumptions. Although in the past hundred years the state has gradually taken from parents responsibilities for *educating* their children, it is not yet considered legitimate in Britain for the state to provide pre-school child *care* services either free or on anything approaching a universal basis. Since the Second World War local authority day nurseries have declined in number while nursery education places have doubled, and there are plans to provide sufficient places for all children from three to five years old whose parents wish them to attend. However, these nursery school places will only be provided for the majority on a part-time basis. The extension of nursery education is therefore not considered in the context of enabling mothers to take paid work outside the home but rather as a way of supplementing their skills and expertise. In other words education for the under-fives is increasingly seen as the province of professionals. The result is, as Bridget Plowden has pointed out, 'The confidence of parents in themselves as parents, in this rapidly changing society, where the urgent need is for confidence and security, has been lessened. It is "they" in nurseries and schools who know best, from the earliest months and years of a child's life. . .'[31]

In contrast the work of caring is still firmly seen as the responsibility of the mother. Day care facilities do exist, but in 1975 two-thirds of legal day care (that is, day nurseries and registered child-minders) was provided by voluntary or private organizations. Even when numbers attending play groups are included, in 1974 only about a third of all children under five in England and Wales were known to be receiving some form of organized day care outside their families. This is half the number whose parents would like to use day care services. Access to a local authority day nursery is difficult, if not impossible, for the child from a 'normal' two-parent family. Even one-parent families may be refused a place, and some authorities will only accept children who are believed to be in danger of being battered and who are therefore on their 'at risk' register. Most mothers who do have paid work – and in 1974 it was estimated that one in three mothers of children under five were economically active (the majority part time) – have to

[31] B. Plowden, 'Low Cost Day Care Facilities and the Part Which is Being and Can be Played by Voluntary Organisations', in *Low Cost Day Provision for the Under Fives*, DHSS, London, 1976, p. 17.

rely on relatives (often grandmothers), neighbours or their own husbands. However, fathers of young children help mainly when the mother works part time: they rarely give sufficient help to enable the mother to take full-time employment.[32]

The justification for not providing more day care services, particularly nurseries, which are costly to run, is often based on a concern not to harm the emotional development of young children as well as on economic considerations. However, the evidence that the experience of day care outside the family is damaging to a child is not convincing. As Jack Tizard argued recently:

> Those such as Pringle (1974) who think that day care outside the home must be inevitably detrimental to the child's development (though it may be the lesser of the two evils) base their views essentially on two premises: first that the young children cannot accommodate to two environmental schemes rather than one (and this carries further implications that the home environment of a young child is in an undefined sense constant), secondly, that because of the child's attachment to his mother he can only function normally in her presence. Neither premise is true.
>
> The view that young children require constant mothering by the child's own mother or by a single mother substitute is of more than academic interest. *It provides the ideological (as opposed to the economic) basis both for the discouragement of daycare services,* and for the current enthusiasm for the expansion of child-minding services rather than nursery services for those young children who simply cannot stay at home all day with their mother.[33]

Moreover, because the issue of day care for pre-school children is discussed predominantly in relation to mothers' employment, the use of such an ideological justification for restricting day care facilities serves to confirm the view that women's attachment to the labour market is, and should be, of secondary importance only. As the Plowden committee, investigating the primary school system, stated in 1967, 'The extent to which mothers of young children should be encouraged by the provision of full-time nursery places to go out to work raises a question of principle.'[34] What is the principle? It is not that the needs of children must always take priority, although those who believe that day care outside the family is harmful to the child often present it as if this were so. For example the Plowden committee acknowledges that some mothers for 'exceptionally good reasons'

[32] P. Moss, 'The Current Situation', in N. Fonda and P. Moss (eds), *Mothers in Employment*, Institute of Education, London, 1976, p. 24.

[33] J. Tizard, 'Effects of Day Care on Young Children', in Fonda and Moss, *op. cit.* p. 67 (my italics).

[34] *Children and Their Primary Schools* (Plowden Report), Central Advisory Council for Education, Vol. 1, HMSO, London, 1965, p. 127.

might need full-time nursery places for their children although on the basis of its evidence the committee felt it generally undesirable, except to prevent a greater evil, to separate mother and child for a whole day.[35] These exceptionally good reasons included the necessity for the mother to make a financial contribution to the family income and the needs of the government's economic policy to employ women, as well as the importance of providing a child with an alternative to an inadequate home and poor parenting. However, the committee also stated that full-time day care was undesirable 'even for children who might tolerate separation *without* harm'. In other words it seems to be saying that a mother's place is in the home unless *economic* priorities require otherwise. However, this is not the full story.

During the Second World War, the economy required women, including women with young children, to participate fully in the labour market. The attitude towards day care services changed dramatically, and day nurseries were provided on a more extensive basis than ever before or since. Commenting on this change in government policy, Ferguson and Fitzgerald later wrote:

> Without this emphasis on child care would any government have embarked on a campaign – such a successful campaign – to encourage married women to work? Nurseries were partly an expression of the *right* of mothers willing to contribute to the war effort, to this sort of service. . .The nursery. . .was a contribution toward the feeling of *mutual responsibility* between government and the family.[36]

There were other policies too which helped women to combine paid work with their domestic responsibilities, for example the rapid development of the school meals service, factory canteen meals and civic restaurants. Government nutrition and food experts even went so far as to state publicly that the production of individual meals by individual housewives was wasteful both in economic and nutritional terms.[37]

As soon as the war was over, however, the propaganda switched to emphasizing the importance of 'the home' once again. The feeling of 'mutual responsibility' for child care dwindled rapidly and women were no longer considered to have the right to paid work. As a group of Oxford economists wrote in 1947, 'Custom also will fix a reasonably clear line of demarcation between those who may be regarded as employable and those

35 *Ibid.*

36 S. Ferguson and K. Fitzgerald, *Studies in the Social Services*, HMSO, London, 1954, p. 211 (my italics).

37 Royal Institute of Great Britain, *The Nation's Larder*, George Bell and Sons, London, 1940, p. 95. This was a series of lectures given at the Royal Institute in the summer of 1940. Contributors included Lord Woolton, Minister of Food, John Boyd-Orr and Professor Mottram.

(especially married women with children) who may be considered for practical purposes outside the field of paid employment.'[38]

This can partly be explained by the government's concern in the post-war period about its ability to maintain full employment, meaning a job for nearly every man – and so women were expected to make way for men returning from the armed forces. In the event many married women did continue to participate in the labour market, but it should be remembered that the fifties were a time when the government made bigger efforts to recruit immigrant labour from the Commonwealth than to recruit married women, even those with qualifications. The other factor at work here may be men's concern not only that their wives are at home to look after their children but that they are available to provide domestic services for them.[39] Is it not more than a coincidence that the period in Britain when the state made the biggest deliberate attempts to relieve women of some of their responsibilities for caring for their children was a time when many men were absent from their homes? (It was estimated that by 1944 two-and-a-half million men in the armed forces were separated from their wives.) There is therefore a complex interaction between economic priorities and the wish of men to preserve the benefits which accrue to them from the traditional division of labour within the home.

Further evidence that it is easier to maintain this division of labour if women have the responsibility for looking after children *at home* can be seen from the Hungarian experience of the child care grant which was introduced in 1967. It is available for mothers who stay at home to care for their children until the age of three. The grants are generous and by 1973 78 per cent of mothers entitled to claim the grant were doing so.[40] However, there are some unfavourable consequences for women. There has been a growing reluctance of employers to take a young married woman for a qualified or responsible job (employers are obliged to keep the woman's job open for her or to offer her a similar one). In addition Zsuza Ferge writes that research 'revealed that a significant proportion of mothers on grant claimed that their husbands did less housework than before the grant was consented. . .though the amount of work obviously increased. *Thus the increased opportunity for the wife to fulfil the mother's function turns into an obligation to play the housewife role in full.*'[41]

In Hungary therefore it is acknowledged that the grant cannot altogether replace the nurseries and the emphasis is shifting from discussion of a

[38] P. Worswick, 'The Stability and Flexibility of Full Employment', in T. Balogh (ed.), *Economics of Full Employment*, Basil Blackwell, Oxford, 1947, p. 60.

[39] I am indebted to Diana Barker for first pointing this out to me.

[40] Z. Ferge, 'The Relation between Paid and Unpaid Working Women', *Labor and Society*, April 1976, p. 46.

[41] *Ibid.* p. 47 (my italics).

*mother's* wage to that of a *parent's* wage which would enable fathers to take a bigger share in the responsibility for children. (A father can already claim the grant if his wife is ill or absent.) This means that the responsibilities of child care are beginning to be discussed in relation to men's as well as women's employment patterns.

This has yet to happen in Britain. Much research has been done on the impact of the mother's employment on the development of children, but the effect of the nature of the father's occupation on family life has been largely neglected.[42] Those who are concerned about the effects of mothers' paid employment outside the home on the development of children would do well to examine the families of men whose jobs require them to work 'unsocial hours' or to be frequently absent from home or to be geographically mobile. An extreme example is the life of the families of men in the army.

In 1974 half of all men in the army were married and between them they had approximately 157,000 children. Roughly a third of the children were under five years, a third were of primary school age and the remainder were of secondary school age or over. The amount of mobility and separation experienced by these families was considerable. For example nearly a third of the families of soldiers and junior officers had moved at least four times in the previous five years. As a result two-thirds of secondary school children in the families of the senior ranks had been to at least six schools and nearly one in six had been to nine or more different schools. On average for all families except those of senior officers the husband had been absent for a total of three to four months out of the previous twelve. One in four soldiers and one in five junior officers had been separated from their wives for at least six out of the previous twelve months. This separation did not take place in a single block of time: there could be many distinct periods of separation of varying duration ranging from a four months' unaccompanied tour in Northern Ireland to two or three weeks' training. Altogether over a third had experienced six, seven or eight periods of separation in the previous two years and a further two-fifths had had nine or more periods of separation.

This combination of mobility and separation called 'turbulence' could occur at crucial times particularly for the young married soldier. In the first year of marriage a junior rank soldier had experienced an average of twenty weeks' separation from his wife and between one-quarter and a third had been absent during their wife's confinement.[43] Not surprisingly the wives,

[42] There have been a few recent studies. See for example G. Cohen, *Absentee Husbands in Spiralist Families*, mimeograph, Civil Service College, London, 1975.

[43] *Army Welfare Inquiry Committee Report*, Appendix C, HMSO, London, 1976.

particularly of the young soldiers, experienced considerable loneliness and stress. Because the demands of army service gave them little opportunity to settle into a stable civilian community they were divorced from much of the resources and support to which civilians have access. Nevertheless their problems are only just beginning to be acknowledged by the army (not, however, to the extent of its agreeing to establish a family welfare service, as recommended by a recent committee of inquiry). It is assumed that, as long as the men are well provided for, the welfare of their families is assured.

It is to be hoped that this is an extreme example of the disruptive effects that a father's occupation can have on family life. Meanwhile most research studies measure a father's occupation in terms of the status or the economic resources which it brings to the family rather than in terms of how the nature of the job structures the daily lives of other members of the family and affects the emotional and intellectual development of the children. Conversely studies of mothers' employment tend to underplay the resulting financial contribution made to the family income and to emphasize the impact on children of their mothers' outside interests and absence from the home.

## RESIDENTIAL CHILD CARE AND THE DIVISION OF RESPONSIBILITIES BETWEEN STAFF

Stability for the children of families which are very mobile can be achieved at least in part by the provision of boarding schools. The army recognizes this and in 1975 it spent £9.3 million on allowances to enable its personnel to send their children to boarding schools. The majority (75 per cent) of those who make use of the allowance are officers, which is not surprising, as working-class families have not traditionally used boarding education. In any case most of the schools are in the private sector because residential care in the form of boarding schools has low priority and the state directly finances only a few of them. Therefore the only residential care outside their families which the majority of working-class children are ever likely to experience will not be of their parents' choosing but will result from decisions taken by social services departments and the courts. In 1975 nearly two-fifths of the 99,000 children in the care of local authorities were in community homes.[44] Of the remainder a third were boarded out and nearly a fifth were being supervised in their own families. On the whole then the state does not provide residential care for 'normal' children, and since the end of the Second World War there has been a shift towards foster care and keeping children with their own families. Foster care, like child-minding,

[44] Central Statistical Office, *Social Trends*, no. 6, HMSO, London, 1976, p. 80.

is a closer replica of the relationship in the nuclear family and is therefore cheaper than institutional care.

Although the experience of residential care is different in many respects from that of living with parents or parent-substitutes, children will still learn about the division of domestic labour between the sexes. Lady Williams wrote in 1967 in her report on residential staffing carried out on behalf of the National Council of Social Services:

> Children need the influence of both men and women in their lives. For a girl of school age the presence of men as a normal part of the social pattern is essential to develop the understanding of the parts played by men and women in the world; and there are many play activities in which the man's contribution can be outstanding. Hiking, exploring, camping, hill-climbing, a host of do-it-yourself jobs can help children to learn to act independently and to expand their mental and spiritual horizons.[45]

More recently, in 1976, an equal pay tribunal refused an appeal by a house-mother in a children's home on the following grounds:

> A housemother is engaged to look after the younger boys and carry out domestic duties. A housefather is engaged to lead the growing boy to a better approach to life and help him in his problems. The roles are largely those of a mother and father in ordinary life: they are both important, but they are different. . .for these reasons we find that the applicant is not engaged on like work with a man – full of admiration as we are for the work which she is doing.[46]

The characteristics of residential staff in themselves are also indicative of assumptions about who does the work of caring and on what terms. Lady Williams found that in ordinary children's homes 80 per cent of the resident care staff were women and in particular two-thirds were *single* women. In old people's homes 62 per cent were single women. In contrast only a small proportion of residential staff were single men.[47]

This study of residential institutions was based on 1963 figures, and, as a significant proportion of the staff were then over fifty years of age, they reflected past processes whereby single women, unless they had capital of their own, had even less direct access to the housing market than they have today. The majority of women could only keep or acquire a roof over their heads by taking on an obligation to care for someone – elderly parents if they stayed in the parental home or their own husbands and children if they married, and, if they did not marry, someone else's relatives. As well as accommodation they received maintenance but rarely little more. Indeed their lives were often very restricted. As Lady Williams commented of resi-

[45] G. Williams, *Residential Staffing*, Allen and Unwin, London, 1967, p. 149.

[46] Quoted in J. Coussins, *The Equality Report*, National Council for Civil Liberties, London, 1977, p. 47.

[47] Williams, *op. cit.*

dential staff, 'There are large numbers who resign themselves to long hours of work, poor accommodation and exclusion from the normal social life of the neighbourhood.'[48] The situation has changed a little now because far fewer women remain single; there are more employment opportunities for them, and the increase in the number of married men and women among residential staff has raised standards of remuneration and conditions of employment. Nevertheless single people in general still have limited access to the housing markets. Marriage improves the chances of getting housed for both men and women. In return men assume the obligation to take paid work in order to maintain their families and women take on the obligation to care.

## THE IMPACT OF DOMESTIC WORK ON MEN'S AND WOMEN'S PARTICIPATION IN THE LABOUR MARKET

The above analysis of a few social policies shows that they are indeed based on consistent assumptions about the division of unpaid labour in the home and the respective priorities which men and women should accord to participating in the labour market. That these assumptions do not always have to be made explicit in the legislation or administrative rules suggests that we are looking at the outcome of a powerful set of ideologies concerning the family and that state social policies are one of the means by which these ideologies are sustained. The question now to be answered is who benefits from the maintenance of this pattern of dependencies and responsibilities within the family? In order to explore the economic benefits I shall examine the impact of women's domestic responsibilities on their opportunities and activities in the labour market. It would, however, be wrong to assume that the ideologies are solely a product of a capitalist economic system. The subordination of women is a phenomenon which predates the rise of capitalism in this country, and, although we need to know far more about how and why their subordination has been maintained although transformed as capitalism developed, we should also consider ways in which patriarchal values have interacted and even conflicted with economic priorities.

The amount of time taken up by women's domestic duties is one of the most important constraints on their daily lives. Hannah Mitchell, a working-class suffragette, described this graphically in her autobiography:

> The tyranny of meals is the worst snag in the housewife's lot. Her life is bounded in the north by breakfast, south by dinner, east by tea and in the west by supper, and the most sympathetic man can never understand that

[48] *Ibid.*

meals do not come up through the tablecloth but have to be planned, bought and cooked.[49]

But meals are only one of the many regular domestic tasks for which women are responsible. The physical care of young children requires attention at frequent intervals. Indeed the attendance allowance paid to those who are so ill that someone is needed to be present with them for a substantial part of the day or night (or both) is not available for children under the age of two years on the grounds that they all need constant attention. School-aged children do not require an adult's presence in the home to the same extent as a younger brother or sister but their mother's daily routine will have to become geared to the school day, which is shorter than a normal working day. In any case schools are not open for all fifty-two weeks of the year. The care of a sick or elderly person will demand differing amounts of attention spaced at varying intervals depending on the degree of their infirmity and their capacity for self-care. The domestic routine of all married women is likely to be affected to some extent by their husbands' working hours. In other words a woman's daily activities have to be timed to fit the needs of other members of the family. It is true that a man's paid employment fixes his hours too, but – with the reduction in the length of the working day which has taken place over the past hundred years – to a lesser extent, as William Beveridge noted thirty years ago – 'The housewife's job with a large family is frankly impossible and will remain so, unless some of what has now to be done separately in every home – washing all clothes, cooking every meal, being in charge of every child every moment when it is not in school – can be done communally outside the home.'[50] He therefore advocated amongst other services day and night nurseries and he went on to say, 'Nothing short of a revolution in housing would give to the working housewife the equivalent to the two hours of additional leisure a day on five days a week that has come to the wage earner in the past 70 years. . .'[51] In these proposals Beveridge was trying to remedy what he called 'the defective appreciation of the housewife as an unpaid worker'. Unfortunately his assumptions about the economic dependency of married women led him to disregard the importance of their financial contribution to the family. He therefore helped to perpetuate a social security system which failed to meet the needs of many women.

It is often argued that the amount of time a woman need spend on her household tasks has been considerably reduced and that therefore she has more leisure or greater opportunities to take paid employment. There are two reasons put forward – technology has rendered domestic chores less

[49] H. Mitchell, *The Hard Way Up*, Virago, London, 1977, p. 113.
[50] W. Beveridge, *Voluntary Action*, Allen and Unwin, London, 1947, p. 264.
[51] *Ibid.* p. 275.

labour intensive,[52] and husbands help in the home far more than used to be the case. On closer examination, however, this argument is not as soundly based as it first appears to be.

It is true that the development of a variety of household appliances has removed some of the drudgery from many domestic tasks, but this does not necessarily mean that women have to spend less time on their domestic responsibilities. First, not all households have labour-saving appliances. *The General Household Survey* shows that nearly three-quarters of households with economically active heads of households have a washing machine, although among the unskilled and semi-skilled the proportion is less than two-thirds.[53] Audrey Hunt found that among elderly recipients of a home help half had a vacuum cleaner, a fifth had a washing machine and nearly a quarter had no hot water supply.[54] Their housework could still be very hard work. The families most likely to have all the labour-saving devices are those which would have had domestic servants fifty years ago – instead of supervising people they now operate machines. Secondly, time-budget studies show that the total time women spend on their domestic tasks has declined very little in the last half-century. Full-time housewives living in urban areas still spend an average fifty-three hours a week.[55] What has changed is the way in which their time is distributed among the various tasks. The proportion of time spent on child care has increased and the time spent on cooking and cleaning has decreased. Data from the United States show that the more educated a mother is the more time she spends on child care.[56]

There is evidence that husbands help in the home more than they used to but the data need careful interpretation. Peter Willmott's and Michael Young's study, *The Symmetrical Family*, was based on couples aged between thirty and fifty, so their sample underrepresented those with very young children as well as those with sick or elderly dependants. We have already seen that the care of the sick, the young and the old falls disproportionately on women in the family. Willmott and Young also excluded some activities which require *regular* time and attention. For example they state that 'Such things not recorded as work might actually be so for housewives. A meal for example, is not counted as work although some mothers would think that feeding young children was.'[57] More comprehensive time-budget

[52] See for example Department of Employment, *Gazette*, January 1974, p. 9.
[53] OPCS, *The General Household Survey*, 1974, HMSO, London, 1977, p. 84.
[54] Hunt, *The Home Help Service in England and Wales*, p. 191.
[55] A. Leibowitz, 'Women's Work in the Home', in C. Lloyd (ed.), *Sex Discrimination and the Division of Labour*, Columbia University Press, New York, 1975, p. 223.
[56] *Ibid.* p. 230.
[57] P. Willmott and M. Young, *The Symmetrical Family*, Routledge and Kegan Paul, London, 1973, p. 112.

studies show, with remarkable consistency between countries, that women spend substantially more time on housework than men.[58]

Moreover a careful analysis of the tasks which men do in the home suggests that they do not substitute for their wife's time very much. Thus a study conducted in 1967 in the United States showed that in couples in which men helped with the physical care of the children the wife spent even *more* time herself on this task. If they helped with the preparation of meals the amount of the wife's time saved was only half that spent by the husband. In any case women spent ten times as much time as their husbands on meal preparation and the physical care of children.[59] Men helped more in activities relating to the children's social and educational development – activities which women also preferred but of which they did proportionately less. All these figures are averages, and, while some men do more, many do less. Audrey Hunt's study of women's employment in 1965 found that nearly a third of men gave their wives no help in the home. Altogether she found that a fifth of wives in paid employment had no help at all from other members of the household and had no paid help either.[60]

Women then are much more likely than men to be responsible for the routine domestic tasks in the home. It is therefore not surprising to find that 84 per cent of the four-and-a-quarter million part-time employees in 1975 were women, most of them married. In 1965 Audrey Hunt found that two-fifths of those working part time said that this was a consequence of having children to look after. One in six gave their responsibility for caring for their husbands as a reason.[61] The hours worked by those with children were often geared to the school day – a third of those working part time only did so during school hours and a further 7 per cent worked only evenings, early mornings or nights. 13 per cent gave up paid work during school holidays. Women with very young children were more likely to do paid work in their own homes – 16 per cent of working women with children under two years old did home work compared with 8 per cent of those with school-aged children.[62] Altogether a fifth of women working part time did so because they had the responsibility of an elderly or infirm person who was not necessarily living in the same household. Women responsible for an old person who was bedfast were the least likely to have paid employment at all.[63] So, although in some respects the national data on women's employment are incomplete and out of date, it is clear that a woman's

[58] E. Boulding, 'Familial Constraints on Women's Work Roles', in M. Blaxall and B. Reagan, *Women and the Workplace*, University of Chicago Press, Chicago, 1976, p. 112.

[59] Leibowitz, *op. cit.* p. 239.

[60] Hunt, *A Survey of Women's Employment*, Vol. 2, p. 205.

[61] *Ibid.* p. 52.

[62] *Ibid.* p. 164.

[63] *Ibid.* p. 180.

availability for work is considerably constrained by her domestic circumstances.

From the employers' point of view this can be an advantage. Part-time employees have fewer rights than full-time employees (the *Employment Protection Act* has only recently been extended to those working sixteen or more hours a week). They therefore form a more flexible part of the labour force. Audrey Hunt's study of management attitudes towards women workers showed that one of the main advantages of part-time workers was that 'You can have them when you need them.'[64] They were also useful for jobs which did not require a full-time worker. In addition to greater flexibility they may also be cheaper. Married women with low earnings (less than £15 a week in 1977) will be counted as 'non-employable' and therefore no national insurance contribution need be paid. They are also less likely to have rights to sick pay or pensions from their employers. Promotion prospects are very limited – in only 17 per cent of the establishments included in Audrey Hunt's study did part-time workers have opportunities for promotion. Employers were sympathetic to women who needed time off to care for sick children and a fifth had a formal policy on the matter. However, less than 3 per cent granted *paid* leave for this reason.[65] In the face of this evidence it would be wrong to conclude that opportunities for part-time employment have grown out of a concern to enable women to combine paid employment with their domestic responsibilities.[66]

## CONCLUSIONS

What needs to be understood is the complex interaction between the factors which structure the supply of particular sorts of jobs and those which determine the supply of certain types of labour. It is clear that many women and the minority of men with sole responsibility for the *care* of dependent children or adults[67] exchange some flexibility in working hours for considerably lower pay and prospects except when demand for their labour is *exceptionally* high, as it was during the Second World War.

There are other factors relating to a woman's primary commitment to her family which put her at a disadvantage in the labour market. First, she must find employment near home and, secondly, she is less likely than her husband to move in order to enhance her employment opportunities.

64 A. Hunt, *Management Attitudes and Practices Towards Women at Work*, OPCS, HMSO, London, 1975, p. 14.

65 *Ibid.*

66 Department of Employment, *op. cit.* p. 9.

67 See for example P. Wilding and V. George, *Motherless Families*, Routledge and Kegan Paul, London, 1970.

Research in the United States has shown that, whereas a quarter of unemployed women mentioned their husband's job as a reason for not wanting to leave the area in which they were currently living, only 3 per cent of unemployed men gave their wife's job as a reason for wanting to stay. Looking at the employment prospects of those who had moved, the study concluded, 'For male workers inter-State mobility had the effect of decreasing the unemployment rate. However geographic mobility, especially long distance, decidedly worsens the unemployment situation for women, indicating that such migration was governed by factors other than personal economic opportunity.'[68]

In Britain *The General Household Survey* showed that in 1974 60 per cent of women who were out of the labour market gave domestic circumstances or pregnancy as a reason for leaving their last job.[69] When women do return after a break in employment they are often treated as new entrants and paid accordingly. Marriage and motherhood effectively 'deskill' women. Moreover in times of economic recession if one has left employment it becomes increasingly difficult to re-enter it. Unfortunately the official unemployment statistics in this country grossly underestimate the number of unemployed women because the figures are based on the number registering for work. Married women are less inclined to register because the majority are neither entitled to unemployment benefit, having 'opted out' of the national insurance scheme, nor able to claim supplementary benefit. As this 'option' is gradually withdrawn women's unemployment will become more visible. In the United States, where unemployment statistics are collected on an entirely different basis, the data show not only that women have higher rates of unemployment than men but that the unemployment situation of women has worsened over time.[70] It is not known whether this is the situation in Britain because the concept of the male bread-winner which is still deeply embedded in our social security system conveniently obscures the true dimensions of female unemployment, which in any case is regarded as a less important problem.

The perpetuation of an ideology which accords to women the primary responsibility for caring for other members of their family but at the same time takes for granted and therefore undervalues the time, work and skill which this involves ensures that there is always a supply of workers who are prepared to offer their labour on terms which are very favourable to employers. For this reason there have been periods when, in certain sectors of the economy at least, women have been used to undercut male wage

[68] B. Neimi, 'Geographic Immobility and Labour Force Mobility: A Study of Female Unemployment', in Lloyd, *op. cit.* p. 76.

[69] OPCS, *The General Household Survey*, 1973, p. 119.

[70] Neimi, *op. cit.* p. 86.

rates or to drive some men out of the labour market altogether. Male trade unionists have understandably resisted such attempts on the part of employers, and one strategy they adopted was to restrict the sphere of women's employment. The Trades Union Congress told the Royal Commission on Equal Pay in 1944 that 'The trade unions have been compelled not only to uphold *but to promote*, a clear demarcation between men's and women's work – where such demarcation was possible – in order to protect the men's and thus indirectly women's rate of pay.'[71]

Thus the largely sex-segregated labour market observed in this country and many others is the result of the activities of organized labour as well as of changes in the technical means of production and the overall demand for labour. It should be noted that by behaving in this way men are acting in their own interests not only as workers but also as husbands and fathers who wish to retain as much as possible of the woman's labour in the home. Paradoxically the more men emphasize the importance of their own employment and their own wages, which must be higher than women's because unlike women they have families to support, the more they are bolstering up an ideology which says that men have a *duty* to take paid employment. However, there never has been a time in Britain when all, or even most, men have been able to earn wages high enough to support a family unaided. Consequently the reality for many women is that they have always had to combine paid employment with their domestic tasks. Most men do not have this obligation, and that is one of the advantages that marriage has for men. Moreover it is an advantage which is not exclusive to capitalist economies. Lenin, nearly fifty years ago, in a letter to Clara Zetkin, wrote that 'Very few husbands, not even the proletarians think of how much they could lighten the burden and worries of their wives or relieve them entirely, if they lent a hand in their "women's work". But no, that would go against the "privilege and dignity" of the husband. He demands to have his rest and comfort.'[72]

The particular assumptions about the division of responsibilities between the sexes and the generations in the family which have been described in this paper therefore have an important impact both on the interests of the economically powerful and on those of individual men. These interests are not always entirely coincident. The state *does* intervene in the family, and it is not a question of whether or not to have family policies but of how explicit the values on which they are based are to be made. The fact that certain values favouring the interests of men rather than women have been

[71] *Report of the Royal Commission on Equal Pay*, Cmd 6937, HMSO, London, 1944, p. 191 (my italics).

[72] Quoted in H. Scott, *Women and Socialism: Experiences from Eastern Europe*, Allison and Busby, London, 1976, p. 199.

embodied in a variety of social policies over a long period of time, both formally in the legislation and by the way in which they are allocated or used, indicates that social policies are a very important means by which these values, and hence major inequalities between the sexes, are maintained.

# [22]

# FEMINISM AND SOCIAL POLICY

Mary McIntosh

This article is based on a paper given by the author at the Critical Social Policy Conference, 'Crisis in the Welfare State' in November 1980.

## Abstract

**Feminists have a specific critique of state services and social security because of the way women are made individually dependent on men and yoked with the state in meeting needs. There are two key guidelines for planning any socialist welfare policy in capitalist society: (1) advances are possible, because popular demands are not merely antithetical to capitalist interests, but (2) advances that would destroy the capital-labour relation cannot be achieved under capitalism. In this context the feminist campaign for 'disaggregation' is a promising one. Feminist campaigns involve work within and in alliance with many existing organisations and men should recognise that feminist demands are central to any socialist strategy on social policy.**

During the 1970s, feminists developed a critique of the welfare system that was both sophisticated and damning. It began in a fragmentary way in the early seventies with specific protests about issues like the 'cohabitation rule' and the 'tax credit' proposals. There was a growing awareness that women figure prominently among the clients of social workers, the inmates of geriatric and psychiatric hospitals, the claimants of supplementary benefits — despite the fact that married and cohabiting women are not eligible for many benefits. There was resentment about the degrading way that women are treated when they need state benefits and state services.

The first responses were articulated most clearly by libertarian feminists, who could express vividly what women know of the conditions under which welfare is granted. They know the queues and the forms, the deference, the anger, the degradation, the sense of invisibility and the loss of autonomy. They see the mean, withholding face of the state and can readily take up the negative cry of 'smash the state!' But the cohabitation campaign also raised deeper issues. It was not just that the 'SS' were 'sex snoopers' who prevented women claimants from drawing their benefit if they were suspected of living with a man. They also tried to force women into prostitutional dependence on the men they slept with. This raised the whole question of women's dependence on men and the fact that women were second class citizens. The Women's Family Allowance Campaign against the Tory Government's 1972 tax-credit proposals focussed on the same problems. The family allowance, paid directly to a mother was preferable to the same, or even a greater, amount paid in tax credits through a father's pay packet. The model of the couple as a financial unit bore little relation to reality as many women experienced it. In the end, after we had defeated this aspect of the tax-credit scheme, the trade unions' reluctance to accept the loss of the child tax allowance that accompanied the improved child benefit only verified what we already knew: that money in a husband's pay packet was not equivalent to a direct payment to his wife.

In the context of the women's liberation movement, the developing awareness of women's relation to the welfare state was crystallised at the national conference in 1974. Elizabeth Wilson's pamphlet *Women and the Welfare State* (1974) was launched there and a new demand, for 'legal and financial independence', was adopted. The new demand, the fifth to be adopted by the movement, recognised clearly the relevance of the state in solving the problem of women's dependence upon men. The other demands (concerned with equal opportunities in jobs and training, equal pay, nurseries, abortion and contraception) all had a bearing on women's independence in their different ways. But this one, as the paper calling for it to be adopted expressed it, 'highlights the links between the state and the family, and the way in which the state systematically bolsters the dependent-woman family' (Gieve et al., 1974). It saw the relevance of state policy not merely to those categories of women who receive or are denied state benefits of various kinds — not merely to mothers and non-mothers, wives and non-wives, earners and non-earners — but to women as a whole category. For it saw how state policies play a part in constructing that category and in constructing the idea of the family in which it exists. All women suffer from the stereotype of the woman as properly dependent upon a man. But all women also suffer in quite practical terms from the fact that there are few viable alternatives to such dependence. (For an argument against this view, see Bennett et al., 1980.)

Since then, this critique of state policy has been detailed and sustained. Academic articles have been published (especially by Hilary Land, 1976, 1977), and so have pamphlets (for instance, Streather and Weir, 1974; Lister and Wilson, 1976). Many a parliamentary select committee and inter-departmental working party has been told of our views by various women's groups. Wider campaigns, like the rousing but in the end rather abortive one on wives' treatment under income tax, have been mounted. What is disappointing is how little this critique has really affected thinking among other radicals about social policy. Goodwill towards feminism expresses itself in manning the creche, going on the abortion demo and avoiding sexist styles of behaviour. But how many critics of the DHSS review of Supplementary Benefit a year or so ago — apart from women — argued against the aggregation of the income and resources of husband and wife? Yet separate treatment has been our demand ever since the first feminist critiques of the Beveridge Report in the early 1940s (see, for instance, Abbott and Bompas, 1943; Pierce, 1979).

At the same time as this awareness of how the state constructs dependent women, there was a growing awareness of women as state employees. Both the state bureaucracies and the institutions of health, education and welfare employ enormous numbers of women in their lower ranks; often their clients are women; and often they are engaged in classically 'feminine' types of work both in terms of the contents of their tasks and in terms of the social functions they fulfill. In fact, insofar as previously domestic functions like healthcare, childcare and personal services have become socialised, the social tasks are frequently performed by women just as the private ones were. In struggles to improve social services and nurseries, and in struggles to unionise women workers and advance their position, feminist issues and the question of what women in different situations have in common were fought out time and again. 'The patter of tiny contradictions' was how Val Charlton (1973) described a childcare centre started by some women's liberation groups in London.

All of these critical approaches to social policy were the feminist version of the radical and marxist critiques of the 1960s and 1970s. The burden of these was that the welfare state is nothing of the kind: that it is not redistributive as between the social classes, but makes the working class pay for its own social casualties, that it does not even eliminate poverty at the bottom end of the scale, that it is not the harbinger of socialist provision according to need — neither in its style nor in its effects — and that it is an instrument of bourgeois control, forcing people to work and imposing standards of morality, decency and household management. To this, feminists add that the welfare state is especially oppressive to women, in that it harnesses them into the team that pulls the whole welfare charabanc along.

What was new, though, was that there was a clear recognition at the same time that women need state provision. Faced with a choice between a chancy dependence on a man on the one hand and dependence on the state or exploitation in waged work on the other, feminists opt for the state and the wage.

Personal dependence carries with it a whole baggage of psychological dependence. Lack of autonomy, deference, the need to manipulate personal relations, all tend to stunt women's potential and make us insecure and unadventurous. Indeed the characteristics of femininity which Juliet Mitchell (1974) has explained in terms of the experience of infancy — passivity, masochism and narcissism — could equally be explained by the adult experience of dependence and the practical need to seek support. This explanation would in fact fit better the reality, which is one of public passivity, based on self-repression and often masking an underlying attitude of cynicism and rebellion, similar to that of Franz Fanon's colonised people.

With all their problems, then, the state and the employer can be fought collectively and unlike modern marriage they are not intrinsically patriarchal. And whenever feminists have formulated the demand for the socialisation of housework and of personal care, it has been state provision rather than private commercial provision that they have had in mind.

Feminists in this country have never been for very long attracted to purely anti-statist positions. Such utopian individualism (or even small-scale collectivism) is a possible dream for men who can envisage a world of self-supporting able-bodied people. But women are usually concerned with how the other three-quarters live. They have argued for new forms of interdependence based in the community and not in the family, and these necessarily involve the state at one level or another.

There have been some interesting debates in the women's movement about the development and provision of feminist services. The question has been: should we provide these ourselves or should we demand state provision and then fight about the form that provision should take? Nurseries, playgroups, healthcare, advice on contraception and abortion, refuges for battered women, rape crisis centres, legal and welfare rights advice — all clearly fall within the ambit of things that we expect to be provided by state agencies. Yet these are either not available or, when they are, are inadequate and unfeminist in their approach. Setting up services like this is a way both of meeting women's needs and also of developing public awareness of the effects of women's oppression, and providing a base for feminist analysis and agitation around the issue (Flaskas and Hounslow, 1980). In Australia and in the United States there has been a great proliferation of feminist health and welfare services and the results have sometimes been disappointing in that the energies of the women involved have been used up in providing a good service so that the more forward-looking political tasks have been neglected. In this country, with the notable exception of the network of Women's Aid refuges for battered women, the tendency has been to set up very few feminist agencies but to concentrate on campaigning for state provision. The more developed social and health services in this country have made this a more promising direction to work in. It also seems to me to be the right approach, since it can lead to more long-term and more universal provision than any voluntary efforts are likely to do. The character of such campaigns is also different and in some ways more outgoing politically. Instead of the independent and sometimes rather inward-looking group work involved in establishing and running a feminist service, there is the need to make alliances and work in the existing political arena. The struggle to develop the present services in a feminist direction involves work in the uions and professional bodies of the service workers as well as organising among clients and users.

Making claims on the state thus involves fruitful political work and agitation at many levels and is far from being confined to the politics of Westminster. So in this respect, as in some others, women have been at the forefront of the rethinking of the rather facile radical libertarianism of the 1960s and early 1970s. (The other things that feminists questioned were the general assumption that decriminalisation, decarceration and de-institutionalisation were unambiguously progressive. Sometimes they have gone too far as in calling for exceptionally heavy punishments and the suspension of the usual rights of the accused in cases of rape and of violence against women, and in calling for increased state control over pornography. In some spheres we have not yet gone far enough: we should be mounting a much stronger criticism of present ideas of 'community care' and fighting for new forms of institutional care that avoid the problems earlier radicals have pointed to.)

Now, at the beginning of the 1980s, we have reached the point, feminists and socialists alike, that it is generally agreed that we cannot afford the luxury and purity of a simply critical stance. This, I take it, is why our journal is called *Critical Social Policy,* rather than *Critique of Social Policy.* We have to develop ideas and organisations that enable us to engage with social policy as it forms. And this will mean discussing what sort of welfare state we do want, not just sniping at the existing one and waiting for The Revolution to put everything right.

However, for marxists this cannot mean a fabian-style formulation of gradual ameliorative goals and means. It must mean taking a very clear class position and working within the labour movement and all organisations that can take up an anti-capitalist position. It means working out what gains can be made in any given situation and what threats most need defending against, not assuming that social policy makers are people of good will who will see reason when a clear and forceful case is put to them. I suggest that at the most general level there are two key points to remember.

i The first is that although the dominant factor affecting state policies will always be the long-term interests of the ruling class and although the central interests of the working class and the capitalist class are antagonistic, it is not necessarily the case that their interests will be opposed on every single issue of social policy. The most fundamental reason for this is that, despite the fact that the wage relation is an antagonistic one, workers' and capitalists' interests coincide in requiring the satisfaction of the workers' basic needs, whether through the wage or by other means. The capitalist requires the reproduction of labour power; the worker requires food and clothing. Of course, they will differ widely over what sort of needs should be met and under what conditions: over what constitutes 'adequate' reproduction of labour power; and this is where struggles over social policy come in. The history of the growth of the welfare state and the growth of collective consumption (Grevet, 1976; Castells, 1973) in general in capitalist societies is thus neither a history of cherries snatched from the greedy hands of capitalists by a militant working class, nor is it a history of a crafty capitalist plot to control and enfeeble the workers in the interests of guaranteeing the reproduction of labour power and of the relations of production. It is both. The gains and losses have to be figured partly in terms of some felicific calculus and partly in political terms: are we better placed for the next battle? Has morale improved?

ii The second key point is that we need to keep in mind the limits that are set on social policy by the capital-labour contradiction. In particular, we need to recognise that the wage system is fundamental to capitalist production and that the primary means of the reproduction of labour power will be the wage. Social security provisions and collective consumption will be designed in such a way as to minimise their interference with the labour market and with the existence of a proletariat obliged to sell its labour power in order to survive.

This means that demands for a 'guaranteed minimum income' have no connexion with social policy in capitalist society. The 'guaranteed minimum income' is a demand adopted by the Claimants' Union as a radical solution to their degrading experiences at the hands of the social security officials. They see the problems of the means test, the search for a 'liable relative', and the obligation to sign on for employment as ways in which the working class are harassed and controlled. So they demand their abolition, the right of everyone to a guaranteed income regardless of whether or not they are willing to look for waged work. As a Claimants' Union representative argued in one of the workshops at the 'Crisis in the Welfare State' conference: 'People who don't have jobs need an income as much as those who do; it is hard work just staying alive in capitalist society.' The demand is thus very different from a demand for a minimum wage coupled with improved social security benefits at the same level. It is a demand that the need to sell one's labour power in order to survive should be abolished. So it is nothing less than a demand that socialism be introduced: but a demand ostensibly made of the capitalist state and a demand that socialism should enter through the back door, the relations of distribution; rather than the front door, the relations of production. It is thus, as its proponents are well aware, an unrealisable demand under capitalism, since it negates the wage relation which lies at the heart of capitalism. Any of their supporters who join the ranks because they think they might actually gain the demand have been sadly deceived. But the existence of such demands can have the depressing effect of making all real current struggles over policy look paltry and reformist by comparison.

Feminists have been very aware of this problem in relation to the demand for 'wages for housework', rejected by the women's liberation movement in this country in 1972, but still having a small, vocal following. Effectively this is a demand that women should have a guaranteed minimum income, since the idea that there should be any check on whether they actually do any housework is rejected. It is thus a demand that all women should be lifted out of the proletariat and put on a pension. It, too, can be dispiriting if it has the effect of making current struggles over matters like invalid care allowances or the infamous 'Housewife's Non-Contributory Disability Allowance' seem trivial and reformist.

Though dependence on the wage will continue to be the primary means of support for the working class, we have seen during the twentieth century a notable narrowing of the range of people who are expected to depend upon a wage. A wage-earner is no longer expected to provide the main support for old and disabled relatives, only for his wife and children (or, more rarely, her husband and children). The welfare state has defined whole categories of people out of the labour market — the old, the young, the disabled — enabling the capitalist work process to be intensified and many welfare benefits to be offered unconditionally and apparently benevolently.

But there cannot be an infinite extension of such benefits unless the working class is to be de-proletarianised altogether.

These two key points are proposed as basic considerations for the formulation of any socialist strategy for social policy in capitalist societies. But I shall illustrate their importance by looking at the problems of feminist strategy. Women have to consider whether they have gained or lost by the policies accepted by the working class in the past, and how they should relate to working-class political organisation for the future. And we have to consider what relation we want women to have to wage labour. Should we become more fully proletarianised or should we seek better conditions of dependence on husbands or on state benefits?

I shall turn now to these more specific questions of feminist strategy. In some ways, the central problem is the same one that has plagued feminism ever since the achievement of the vote left the movement without a central rallying cry. The problem is whether to press for equality with men, usually in terms of legal, political and citizenship rights, or to press for greater support and respect for women in their roles as housewives and mothers: a right to an independent income and a recognition of the importance of their contribution.

The second position was that of the 'new feminists' who emerged after the First World War. So Eleanor Rathbone argued in 1925 that the point had been reached where women could say:

> At least we have done with the boring business of measuring everything women want, or that is offered to them, by men's phraseology. We can demand what we want for women, not because it is what men have got, but because it is what women need to fulfill the potentialities of their own natures and to adjust themselves to the circumstances of their own lives (Rathbone, 1929, quoted in Lewis 1973).

The argument against the older equalitarianism took the form of a rejection of male definitions of women's work as inferior and a plea for a new dignity and new measures of protection. In some respects it was more progressive than equalitarianism: it sought to change the world, not merely to give women access to the better places in it. But in the end it was less radical because the changes it sought were too shallow. They were designed to ease the suffering where the shoe pinches rather than build a new shoe on a better last. For modern feminists it is easy to see why Rathbone's mountainous ideal of Family Endowment brought forth the rather ridiculous mouse of Child Benefit and why women's dependence is still a key issue today. As Hilary Land (1980) put it:

> Eleanor Rathbone laid much emphasis on the unequal economic relationship between husband and wife but had far less to say about the division of responsibilities for child care and housework.

A deeper analysis would have led her to see the two as inseparable within any wage-based economy. The problem as it was posed then is that of the impossibility either of the equalitarian ideal — which asks for equal treatment for unequal people — or of the 'new feminist' ideal — which asks for women to be treated as different but equal.

It is interesting to ask whether the difference between these two strategies has been transcended by the more recent feminism of the women's liberation movement. Certainly it is not the basis for the main divisions within the movement at present. And the modern movement is characterised much more by methods that have nothing to do with legal changes or state policies and so may appear to sidestep the problems of equalitarianism: cultural politics, the politics of lifestyle and changing household relationships, self-help and self-defence, support for victims of rape and violence, forming international links and (perhaps most distinctively) developing theoretical analyses of women's oppression.

Yet in many fields of work, the choice between those two strategies remains and continues to pose thorny problems. These tend to be the modern versions of the very issues of law and social policy that exercised our feminist grandmothers. The issue of protective legislation, restricting the hours and conditions of women's work in factories, is a conspicuous example. Feminists have been divided over it ever since it was first introduced during the nineteenth century. At that time equalitarianism was the dominant approach and such feminists as took an interest in the question opposed the legislation on the grounds that it infringed women's liberty and put them at a disadvantage in the labour market — a view which I think is justified by the historical evidence (Barrett and McIntosh, 1980; but for the opposite view, see Hutchins and Harrison, 1911; Humphries, 1977, 1981). Later the 'new feminists' attacked this stance and argued that women's functions of home-making and child-rearing could not be carried out properly if they were forced to work long hours and at night outside the home. This is not, of course, a defence that appeals to women's liberationists today.

However, the situation today is not at all comparable to that in the past. For one thing, we have formulated the goal of transforming the processes of home-making and child-rearing, so that if these are to be done privately we want men's factory hours to be limited as well. For another, while the CBI wants protective legislation ended, the TUC wants it continued and extended to cover men and to cover workers everywhere, not just in factory production. So when the Equal Opportunities Commission (1979) recently recommended abolishing the legislation it was siding with the bosses as well as taking an unhistorical perspective and thinking in terms of immediate equality of treatment (for the unequal) rather than of working to eliminate the underlying inequality.

However, it should be noted that the position that women's liberationists usually adopt on this issue depends upon trusting the TUC. If they are not genuine in their commitment to extend protection to men — or if they have no hope of carrying it through — our position becomes one that simply accepts the present role of women and seeks to protect us from some of its worst penalties. I shall come back later to the questions of political practice that this raises. I want first to say something about strategy in relation to one particular feminist campaign, that for 'disaggregation'. I focus on this campaign because it raises important problems and also because I happen to have been involved in it, rather than because I believe it to be any more or less important than other campaigns. It is obviously just one part of a wider struggle.

Socialist feminists in the women's liberation movement have transcended the old divide in the sense that they have questioned not only masculinity and femininity, not only man's place and woman's place, but also the very existence of social division and difference based on sex. We have firmly located the origin and support for this division in the family. This does not mean that we locate it in individual kin-based households, but in the institution of the family, with its ideology, its imperatives and its constraints, which spread far beyond households themselves and both cause and enable the organisation of everything else to be marked by gender division. Women's liberation depends upon the radical transformation of that family. However, although there is much disagreement about the relation of that family system to capitalism, most socialist feminists agree on two things: that the specific character of women's oppression at present is related to the articulation between the family system and the wage system; and that we should start working now towards the transformation of the family system and that it will not automatically arrive along with socialism. Indeed, I would add that the family system is changing and is under great strain at present (and not only because of the resurgence of feminism), so that it is incumbent on us to play a part in determining what form that change takes.

On the whole we choose to campaign for those things that we know will both help the immediate problems of many women and also help to open up possibilities for further and more far-reaching change. The demand for 'disaggregation' in social security, income tax, student grants and so on, is a good example. The aggregation of the married couple into a tax unit and into a means-testable unit — however it may be dressed up in unisex clothing — represents women's dependence on their husbands. This is a dependence that is unreliable and degrading when it does exist and which in any case is a less common pattern than is often supposed, since most women are breadwinners Hamill, (1978). In terms of social security, disaggregation would mean that a married women who could not get a job could claim supplementary benefit regardless of her husband's income. But it would also mean that a married man would get a single person's benefit with no allowance for the wife; she would have to claim herself and fulfill the usual conditions: unless she was responsible for caring for small children or an invalid or something like that, she would have to sign on for employment.

This is a demand that comes out of our own experience. Several of the group which formulated it had suffered indignities and deprivation at the hands of the social security. Even so, the chief argument for it is not that thousands of women will be better off. It is that all women will have rights to full social security and that all men will lose the right to state back-up for keeping their wives in dependence. We realise that some women, especially older ones who have not had recent experience of going out to work, will be disadvantaged. We realise that forcing women onto the labour-market as it exists for them now is painful. But we believe that married women's dependence is in part responsible for their dreadful position in the labour-market, and the movement is simultaneously fighting for better pay and conditions at work, including the part-time and low-paid jobs that many women are forced to take.

We realise, too, that many who are concerned about poverty will tell us that there are other groups worse off than married women, whose needs should be met first. I think that argument reveals one of the weaknesses of the approach to social policy that focusses on questions of income equality, in terms of the outcome of distributional and redistributional processes, and does not look at the structure of relations involved in producing those outcomes. Our concern is with moving towards a structural change; by unhitching marriage from the social security system we hope to contribute to loosening its ties to the welfare system in general and ultimately to the wage system itself. We do believe that many unemployed married women are in poverty; those who are may benefit from the change. So we think that disaggregation would meet important immediate needs for some women, but more importantly it would help undermine the existing unequal marriage system. (Incidently, I am not much swayed by the argument that disaggregation would remove one of the few advantages of forming households not based on the heterosexual pair-bond, and so provide another bonus for traditional marriage. For one thing, the argument considers individual types of household rather than the institutions as a whole. But more importantly, it assumes that marriage would be strengthened because more people would be motivated to enter it, or to stay in it, and I doubt whether this would be true for many people.)

In the present situation, the main point of arguing for disaggregation is to get an acceptance of the principle as widely as possible: to get to the point where the chief basis for resistance to it is cost and all the objections on principle have been rejected, both within the labour movement and in official circles. Some of the strongest arguments for it will, of course, be equalitarian ones, not because we want to conceal our real aims, but because equality is indeed an important dimension of the demand and one that people most readily latch on to. (In the social security field, arguments for equality will be undermined by some meretricious wording in the forthcoming legislation, which will use some euphemism like 'main breadwinner' to mask its sex discrimination.)

The day-to-day battles, unfortunately, are much more defensive ones against the cuts. But it is important to give these a feminist dimension, which often means one informed by the perspective of disaggregation, so that we recognise and attack cuts that force women further into dependence as well as those that take away their jobs or give them extra unpaid work. Disaggregation and protective legislation are only two examples. Similar strategic decisions have to be made in relation to almost every field. Should we press for a share of the matrimonial home and adequate maintenance for wives on the breakup of marriage? (Law Commission, 1980) Should we press for cohabitant women to be given rights equivalent to those of married women? (Anne Bottomley *et al.* 1981) These fields need to be linked and seen as part of the overall strategy for women's liberation, which of course goes far beyond the confines of social policy, even in its broadest sense.

The positions that I have argued for here are adopted in the light of the two key points of guidance for socialist social policy that I outlined earlier. They are based on the belief that there can be significant gains for women and for the working class (real gains for women are also gains for working-class unity) within capitalist society, since not every working-class gain is an immediate capitalist loss. And they are based on the belief that the wage system is fundamental to capitalist society, so that despite all the disadvantages of wage work, the way forward must be through furthering the process of proletarianisation of women and rescuing women from preproletarian dependence. The struggle to end capitalist wage labour cannot be helped by women opting out and can only be undertaken by a working class that is less divided by male domination than the present one.

I want to end with some remarks about problems of organisation in pursuing feminist goals in social policy. I shall not discuss questions of organisation for women's liberation in general, though what I shall say clearly reflects certain views on that.

Firstly, I think we have got to develop a feminist presence in all the places where changes in social policy are fought for. This means within the left political parties, within the labour movement, within all the campaigning and lobbying bodies, and as much as possible in the women's organisations. Building up such a presence is often an unattractive activity for contemporary women's liberationists. Once we have experienced the joys and terrors of swimming in structureless movements like the women's liberation movement (if we managed to keep our heads above water), whose favourite forums are the mass meeting in an overcrowded school hall with an inadequate PA system and the small intimate and supportive workgroup, we find it hard even to tread water in the structured world of jockeying for office, juggling agendas and bowing to the constraints of representative democracy. But we cannot by-pass those organisations; they exist, and each of them has carved out its own space of power. If we are not to be in constant opposition to them we must work within them as well as working in our own ways outside them. Sometimes this means challenging and transforming their styles of work and approach. Often, though, it means forming alliances where we have only a few points of agreement; and often it means compromises: avoiding taking a line that will lose us the support that we need for other more important battles. The question of protective legislation and the TUC, which I discussed earlier, is a case in point. Above all, it means getting in there and arguing our case in the context of on-going work.

The second remark I want to make is about men's relation to feminist social policy and to the women's liberation movement. I think it may be true to say that there is never an entirely acceptable stance for outsiders towards a movement of liberation. I have experienced this as a white person in relation to the black movement in the 1960s and as a Briton in relation to anti-imperialist movements. It is easy to be caught in the double bind of being told simultaneously that we should not interfere, not impose our ideas, not assume we can escape being oppressors by an act of will, leave the oppressed group to constitute its own autonomous movement. But it is easier still to use that double bind as an excuse for doing nothing to support the cause of liberation for carrying on with our own struggles quite unaffected by those of our neighbours. Many men have used that double bind as a way of getting off the hook in relation to women's liberation. They respect the autonomy of the women's movement, wish it well, and there the matter can rest.

But such an easy benovolence is not appropriate to the case. We aim to overthrow men's dominance and remove their privileges as a gender. Our cause cannot just be added on to the list of radical causes. We are not a newly discovered minority group like dyslexics or people whose homes are threatened by road-widening, because our oppression is built in to the very structure of production and reproduction. So anyone concerned with social policy must decide what stand to take on the issues we raise and must see the question of women as integral to any analysis of social policy. We have been talking and writing for many years now about the inadequacy of existing analyses. Yet those of us who are teachers still find that our well-meaning male colleagues invite us to give a lecture or two on 'women and welfare', 'women and crime', or whatever. This is done with a modest, 'I am only a man; I can't speak for women'. But I sometimes wonder what they think the other eighteen lectures in their course are about: men? neuters? a gender-free society? The welfare system as it stands (or totters) is utterly dependent upon a specific construction of gender. The Department of Health and Social Security is well aware of that and it is time that critics of social policy were as well.

# References

Elizabeth Abbot and Katherine Bompas, *The Woman Citizen and Social Security: A Criticism of the Proposals Made in the Beveridge Report as they affect Women*, London: Mrs. Bompas, 1943.

Sandra Allen, *et al.*, eds, *Conditions of Illusion*, Leeds: Feminist Books, 1974.

Michele Barrett and Mary McIntosh 'The Family Wage' *Capital and Class*, No. 11, 1980.

Fran Bennett, *et al.*, 'The Limitations of the Demand for Independence' *Politics and Power*, No. 1, 1980.

Anne Bottomley *et al.*, *The Cohabitation Handbook: A Woman's Guide to the Law*, Pluto Press, 1981.

Manuel Castells, 'Collective Consumption and Urban Contradictions in Advanced Capitalism' reprinted in Castells *City, Class and Power*, Macmillan 1978.

## FEMINISM AND SOCIAL POLICY

Valerie Charlton, 'The Patter of Tiny Contradictions' *Red Rag*, No. 5, reprinted in Sandra Allen *et al.* eds, *op.cit.* 1974.

Equal Opportunities Commission, *Health and Safety Legislation: Should we Distinguish between Men and Women?* HMSO, 1979.

Carmel Flaskas and Betty Hounslow, 'Government Intervention and Right-Wing Attacks on Feminist Services' *Scarlet Woman* (Australia) No. 11, 1980.

Katherine Gieve, *et al.*, 'The Independence Demand' in Sandra Allen *et al.*, eds, 1974.

Patrice Grevet, *Besoins Populaires et Financement Public*, Paris, Editions Sociales, 1976.

Lynn Hamill, 'Wives as Sole and Joint Breadwinners', paper presented to the Social Science Research Council, Social Security Research Workshop, 1978.

Jane Humphries, 'Class Struggle and the persistence of the working-class family' *Cambridge Journal of Economics*, Vol. 1, No. 3, pp 241-58, 1977.

Jane Humphries, 'Protective Legislation, the Capitalist State and Working-Class Men: 1842 Mines Regulation Act' *Feminist Review*, No. 7, 1981.

B.L. Hutchins and A. Harrison, *A History of Factory Legislation*, 2nd edition, P.S. King and Son, London, 1911.

Hilary Land, 'Women: Supporters or Supported?' in Diana Barker and Sheila Allen, *Sexual Divisions and Society: Process and Change*, London: Tavistock, 1976.

Hilary Land, 'Social Security and the Division of Unpaid work in the Home and Paid Employment in the Labour Market' in Department of Health and Social Security, *Social Security Research Seminar*, London: HMSO, pp 43-61. 1977.

Hilary Land, 'The Family Wage' *Feminist Review*, No. 6, 1980.

Law Commission, *Family Law: The Financial Consequences of Divorce: The Basic Policy: A Discussion Paper*. (Law Com. No. 103) London, HMSO, Cmnd. 8041, 1980.

Jane Lewis, 'Eleanor Rathbone and the New Feminism During the 1920s' Unpublished mimeograph, 1973.

Ruth Lister and Leo Wilson, *The Unequal Breadwinner*, London: National Council for Civil Liberties, 1976.

Juliet Mitchell, *Psychoanalysis and Feminism*, London: Allen Lane, 1974.

Sylvie Pierce, 'Ideologies of Female Independence in the Welfare State: Women's Response to the Beveridge Report' Paper given at British Sociological Association Annual Conference, 1979.

Eleanor F. Rathbone, *Milestones: Presidential Addresses at the Annual Council Meetings of NUSEC*, London, 1929.

Anne Bottomley *et al.*, *The Cohabitation Handbook: A Woman's Guide to the Law*, Pluto Press, 1981.

Jane Streather and Stuart Weir, *Social Insecurity: Single Mothers on Social Security*, Child Poverty Action Group, Poverty Pamphlet No. 16, 1974.

Elizabeth Wilson, *Women and the Welfare State*, Reg Rag Pamphlet No. 2, 1974.

# [23]

# Women and the Welfare State*

CAROLINE ANDREW *University of Ottawa*

As political scientists one of the things that interests us—or that falls within our domain—is the nature and shape of government intervention. This is not only one of the important areas of scientific investigation in Canada but also one of the important questions of public debate. Many of the assumptions of the postwar Canadian society and polity about the nature and shape of government intervention, such as the universality of social programmes or the importance of Keynesian spending, are being questioned. In other words we find ourselves in a crisis of the welfare state.

It is my contention that in order to analyze this crisis, and therefore in order to understand the welfare state itself, it is necessary to examine the question of gender, the relations between women and the welfare state. These relations are ambiguous, perhaps even contradictory, but they are vital. Without this analysis our understanding of the welfare state is incomplete, partial and I would even go as far as to say inadequate.

What I shall endeavour to demonstrate—very rapidly and very schematically—is a reinterpretation of the welfare state by insisting upon the role played by women in its development and ongoing functioning. At the broadest level, students of the welfare state agree that it refers to governments assuming responsibility for activities that were previously private, either in the sense of the private sector or the private realm. By the private sector I refer to those activities regulated by the market; and by the private realm or sphere, to those activities which are part neither of the market sphere nor of the state sector. These private activities were in some cases the responsibility of social institutions such as the churches, but in many cases were activities that went on within the family. Given the traditional gender-based division of labour in our society, family responsibilities were, generally speaking, women's responsibilities. It is then clear that the transfer of activities

* Presidential address to the Canadian Political Science Association, Guelph, June 1984. The author acknowledges with thanks the comments and suggestions of Duncan Cameron, Denyse Côté, François Houle, Jane Jenson and Jeanne Laux on a first draft of the address.

**Canadian Journal of Political Science / Revue canadienne de science politique, XVII:4 (December/ décembre 1984). Printed in Canada / Imprimé au Canada**

from the private to the social realm has had a dramatic impact on women. What is perhaps less clearly understood, and therefore what needs to be emphasized, is the active role women played in this development. Women were not simply passive recipients of social change; they were not merely objects but also subjects of history. This is becoming abundantly clear in the exciting literature being produced in all areas of feminist scholarship. What I want to do here is to suggest how the insights of this literature allow us to better make sense of the welfare state. I will do this by looking at the major roles women have played and continue to play in relation to the welfare state, in terms of their organizational activities, in terms of their role as workers in the welfare state and in terms of their role as clients of the welfare state.

Before getting into this description, it is important to look somewhat more closely at the definition of the welfare state in order to see why women have, until the present, formed such a small part of our examination of this phenomenon. We could perhaps simply reiterate that women have been largely invisible in whole areas of scholarship; but this is not really a satisfactory answer. How have scholars understood the dynamics of state intervention in the modern period? As I stated earlier, a common core—albeit very general—can be found in most interpretations of the welfare state. It is the taking over by government of responsibilities previously not part of the public sector. What largely characterizes these activities is that they relate to the reproduction of the labour force. Workers must be housed and cared for when sick; they must also be maintained between periods of employment; future workers must be educated. In modern societies these tasks have increasingly been taken on by the state. In Canada all these are increasingly public: nonmarket and nonprivate. The welfare state is, to quote Ian Gough, "the use of state power to modify the reproduction of labour power and maintain the non-working population in capitalist societies."[1] A similar definition is given by Alain Lipietz to describe the roots of "l'État-Providence, la gestion collective de la reproduction de la force de travail."[2]

In explaining this move from private to social responsibility, attention has been focussed largely on the needs of the productive system to have a stable and continuing labour force. Therefore, in terms of explaining the development of the welfare state, emphasis has been put on why production needs reproduction rather than on the activities whereby the reproduction of the labour force is assured. This is not, of course, to say that all explanations have been similar. Pluralist theorists have disagreed with marxists, and among marxists wide differences exist in the relative importance given to the needs of capital or to the

1 Ian Gough, *The Political Economy of the Welfare State* (London: Macmillan, 1979), 44-45.

2 Alain Lipietz, "Crise de l'État-providence," *Politique* 4 (1983), 56.

**Abstract.** The article presents a reinterpretation of the welfare state dealing with the role played by women in the development and on-going function of the welfare state. Three roles are emphasized: women's organizing and the role of women's organizations in pressuring for the measures making up the welfare state, women as workers in the welfare state and, finally, women as clients of the welfare state. Having described these roles, the current politics of the welfare state are examined in order to illustrate the importance of understanding the relations between gender and politics.

**Résumé.** L'article se veut une réinterprétation de l'État-providence qui insiste sur les rôles joués par les femmes dans le développement et le fonctionnement actuel de l'État-providence. Trois rôles sont soulignés: celui joué par les organisations de femmes qui ont fait un travail d'organisation et de mobilisation en faveur des mesures de l'État-providence, le rôle des femmes comme travailleuses de l'État-providence et celui des femmes comme clientes de l'État-providence. Après la description de ces rôles, certains enjeux politiques de l'État-providence actuel sont étudiés de façon à démontrer l'importance de l'analyse des relations entre les femmes et la politique.

demands of labour. But the broad concentration on economics and production has meant that gender has not been given a central importance in analyses of this process.

In addition to the broad macro-economic explanations, scholars have also tried to deal with certain specific historical patterns that have played a role in fashioning the welfare state in individual countries. Even here the emphasis has been on elements within the productive system. The more gender-based specificity of activities relating to reproduction is less often dealt with. As simply one example let me quote Claus Offe, from *Contradictions of the Welfare State:*

> Historically, the Welfare State has been the combined outcome of a variety of factors which change in composition from country to country. Social democratic reformism, Christian socialism, enlightened conservative political and economic elites, and large industrial unions were the most important forces which fought for and conceded more and more comprehensive compulsory insurance schemes, labour protection legislation, minimum wages, the expansion of health and education facilities and state-subsidized housing, as well as the recognition of unions as legitimate economic and political representatives of labour.[3]

I am not trying to say that these factors did not play major roles, but rather to point out that others did too and that, if reproduction of the labour force is a central focus of what defines the welfare state, the politics of the activities of reproducing the labour force ought also to be examined.

Where studies have focussed on the evolution from the private realm to the public one, more attention has been given to religion than to the family, so gender has once again not become a central focus.[4] The move from church to state activities has certainly been one of the main

3 Claus Offe, *Contradictions of the Welfare State* (London: Hutchinson, 1984), 148.

4 An interesting example is the article by Arnold J. Heidenheimer on "Secularization Patterns and the Westward Spread of the Welfare State" which appeared in the special number of *Comparative Social Research* 6 (1983) on the welfare state.

themes of accounts of the development of the welfare state within Quebec society. Léon Dion, in his study of the creation of the Quebec Ministry of Education, *Le bill 60 et la société québécoise*,[5] indicates that this legislation represented a fundamental shift in societal power, with the state assuming responsibility for areas previously organized by the Church. In *La longue marche des technocrates*, Jean-Jacques Simard makes much the same point: "Or, comme on n'accepte plus le rôle de l'Église en tant qu'arbitre des luttes sociales ni comme guide ultramontain du destin collectif, il faudra pour y parvenir faire appel à la seule institution 'nationale' qui puisse prétendre agir au nom de toute la collectivité: l'État provincial."[6]

Analyses of the welfare state have therefore given little consideration to women as primary participants in the private realm and their role as positive elements in the construction of the welfare state. In order to substantiate my argument that this should be done, I will turn to a description of the roles women have played vis-à-vis the welfare state in Canada.

While it is usual to think of the welfare state as referring to the period since the Second World War, its origins clearly go back well beyond this period. Allan Moscovitch begins his bibliography of the welfare state in 1840, linking the early development of capitalism in Canada with "the establishment of the legislative and institutional precursors of modern Welare State policy."[7] Others, such as Goran Therborn in his *Studies in Political Economy* article, highlight 1883 and the introduction of Bismarck's Health Insurance Act.[8] Guest, once again in the Canadian context, argues that the introduction of the Ontario workmen's compensation legislation in 1914 marks "the beginning of the modern era in social security."[9]

I wish to begin by focussing on the period of the reform era from 1880 to 1920 and its important links to the development of the modern welfare state. In many cases the concerns raised, and the forms of public and private assistance put in place, set the stage for the later development of the fully-formed welfare state. And it is my contention that women's organizing and women's organizations are crucial to the developments of this period. The very broad background to understanding the reform era is undoubtedly the intricate and complex

5 Léon Dion, *Le bill 60 et la société québécoise* (Montréal: HMH, 1967).

6 Jean-Jacques Simard, *La longue marche des technocrates* (Montréal: Éditions coopératives Albert St-Martin, 1979), 28.

7 Allan Moscovitch, *The Welfare State in Canada* (Waterloo: Wilfrid Laurier University Press, 1983), iii.

8 Goran Therborn, "Classes and States: Welfare State Developments, 1881-1981," *Studies in Political Economy* 14 (1984), 7-41.

9 Dennis Guest, *The Emergence of Social Security in Canada* (Vancouver: University of British Columbia Press, 1980), x.

interrelations of industrialization, urbanization and immigration as they worked themselves out in the Canadian context. Women's lives were dramatically affected by these processes and their experience, reactions and attempted solutions both reflected and acted upon the broad factors.

To describe briefly the impact of the movements of industrialization, urbanization and immigration on women is to run the risk, if not the certainty, of excessive simplification. But, having acknowledged this risk, I plunge ahead. Industrialization brought about the separation of work and home, and this became cemented into the physical form of the urban environment with the growth and development of our large modern cities. This separation of home from remunerated employment meant that women, at least those from the bourgeoisie, were removed from productive activities and increasingly associated with the home and the private sphere. As Aries has argued, this corresponds to the development of a new role and a new definition of the family as a unit organized around the education and protection of children, emotional fulfillment and consumption. The family takes on an increased importance as a vital unit of society and women's role within the family becomes increasingly the primary definition of women's role in the larger society.

This family-centred and family-bounded definition of women's activity corresponded perhaps to the reality of the bourgeoisie in the latter part of the nineteenth century, but certainly not to the lives of the working class women who were moving into industrial employment. But they, too, were influenced by the new view of the family and the increased social importance given to its role.

The family, with women as its centre, was seen as a vital social unit in terms of maintaining the cohesion of the society in a time of tremendous social change. Here industrialization and urbanization are joined by immigration as factors producing a society seen as potentially near chaos, or even worse, social revolution. The leaders of the society became preoccupied with the instability of this population—living in large cities; working in large factories and therefore in contact with other workers, but with little or no contact with their employers; in addition, comprised of a multitude of different nationalities and cultures who by the very nature of their recent arrival were unrooted in Canadian society. Living and working conditions were often appalling. Improving these conditions was a goal in itself and also a means of reinforcing social cohesion. The family was the natural focus for concerns related to the living conditions of this urban population. The centrality of women to the family meant that women would be central to these concerns. But more than that, women were important social actors in movements that arose to deal with these concerns.

Recent work in Canada is beginning to highlight the specific contribution of women to the reform era. Pioneering works in this area,

*The Neglected Majority*[10] and *A Not Unreasonable Claim: Women and Reform in Canada,*[11] cover studies of the Women's Christian Temperance Union (WCTU), the National Council of Women of Canada, the Fédération nationale Saint-Jean-Baptiste, the suffragette movement, and so on. Yolande Pinard's more recent study of the emerging women's movement in nineteenth-century Montreal also underlines the role of women in pushing for social reform: "Le mouvement des femmes qui apparaît à la fin du siècle dernier au Québec émerge principalement à Montréal, dans un contexte de crise urbaine. Le mouvement montréalais articule ses principaux objectifs autour de la réorganisation du travail philanthropique dans la métropole, de l'amélioration de la situation des travailleuses et de la promotion plus globale des droits des femmes."[12]

The interpretation that I wish to suggest here has been more fully articulated in a number of studies of the American experience,[13] notably Barbara Berg's *The Remembered Gate: Origins of American Feminism*, Nancy Cott's *The Bonds of Womanhood* and Keith Melder's *Beginnings of Sisterhood*. I feel that the Canadian evidence bears out a similar interpretation. Women, largely of the middle class, were extremely active in forming associations, many of which were formed to work towards the amelioration of the living conditions of other women. In pushing for and organizing services and programmes designed to improve the social conditions resulting from industrialization, urbanization and immigration, women played an important role in setting the stage for the development of the welfare state. In coming together, these women were motivated by, among other factors, a sense of the restrictions placed on them by the ideology of "separate spheres," a sense of sisterhood in relation to the conditions endured by working class women as well as an essentially class-determined sense of social concern for the unsettled and potentially chaotic conditions of urban existence.

These studies underline the dual impact of industrialization on the position of women. Middle class women were removed from the sphere of production, making them creatures of leisure. As Barbara Berg puts it, "the effects of urban and industrial growth combined with the tenets of the woman-belle ideal to produce an anomalous sector of society: the

10 Susan Mann Trofimenkoff and Alison Prentice (eds.), *The Neglected Majority* (Toronto: McClelland and Stewart, 1977).

11 Linda Kealey (ed.), *A Not Unreasonable Claim* (Toronto: The Women's Press, 1979).

12 Yolande Pinard, "Les débuts du mouvement des femmes à Montréal, 1893-1902," in Marie Lavigne and Yolande Pinard (eds.), *Travailleuses et féministes* (Montréal: Boréal Express, 1983), 177.

13 Barbara Berg, *The Remembered Gate: Origins of American Feminism* (New York: Oxford University Press, 1978); Nancy Cott, *The Bonds of Womanhood* (New Haven: Yale University Press, 1977), and Keith E. Melder, *Beginnings of Sisterhood* (New York: Schocken Books, 1977).

useless lady."[14] At the same time women of the working class were undergoing the brutal social conditions of industrialization: long hours in poor working conditions and inadequate housing in urban slums.

Women's groups proliferated, as places where women could both break out of the isolation of the home and also work for social change. To quote Berg once more, "woman's voluntary associations arose in combined response to personal needs and social demands in the growing cities."[15] Melder makes the same point. "By working and associating for some common purpose, whether sociability or social change, women could experience the accomplishment of group effort, in contrast to the isolation so many wives and mothers endured in individual households."[16]

These associations illustrated class loyalty both in their largely middle class composition and in their sense of noblesse oblige, but they also illustrated and developed gender loyalty. For Berg, feminism is a product of the cities:

> Women's sense of the oppression of her sex originated in American cities. It matured slowly as upper- and middle-class women began to assimilate the meaning of their intense involvement both with one another and with the destitute of their sex. Woman's recognition of the privations, responsibilities, and rights of her sex could only be gained through intimate association with women of every background.[17]

To return to the Canadian experience, we can see these same themes being played out. Women—largely from the bourgeoisie—came together and organized and pressed for reforms designed to improve the living and, to a lesser extent, the working conditions of other women. Mothers' Union—concerned with Child Care, Mothers' Pensions, Free Kindergarten Associations, Home and School Associations, reforms for juvenile delinquents and, of course, temperance campaigns—all can be seen, at least in part, as women's issues. They were women's issues because women were seen as particularly affected by the problem but also because women had been involved in the solutions. Furthermore, it was women that were pressing for change.

To illustrate the point we can look at specific cases. Wendy Mitchinson's study of the WCTU underlines its importance as "an example of the emergence of women from the domestic sphere to an active participation in society."[18] Joey Noble's study of the Women's Christian Association Mission and Relief Committee in Toronto also provides some evidence for my insistence on the active role taken by

14 Berg, *Feminism*, 96.

15 Ibid., 145.

16 Melder, *Sisterhood*, 47-49.

17 Berg, *Feminism*, 7.

18 Wendy Mitchinson, "The WCTU: 'For God, Home and Native Land': A Study in Nineteenth-Century Feminism," in Kealey, *Claim*, 154.

women. Although the author's analysis is in terms of the class relation between the visitors and the visited, it does provide evidence of the close relationships established between the women members of the voluntary association and the women being given charity. Noble indicates that it was women who were chiefly active: "During this period it was the lawyers, the merchants, the bankers—or more frequently, their dedicated wives—who were going door-to-door making personal contact with the impoverished."[19] Further, "the impulse to make personal contact could be a powerful one."[20]

The directions taken by these associations and the direction of their pressures were both towards the provision of certain social services by volunteer agencies and towards the state provision of these services. These groups created institutions and programmes of social reform but also, very often, they pressured for government activity. Carol Bacchi makes this clear in her analysis of the reform movement: "They saw the continued decline of familial authority and the general failure of their efforts to stop it. Increasingly, they turned to secondary institutions and agencies, to school, social work centres, and reformatories. And, increasingly, they asked the government to supervise these agencies and co-ordinate services."[21]

The same was true of the temperance groups. "Only the State, through legislation, could ensure a temperate society. To persuade the various levels of government to respond, the WCTU became actively involved in the public sphere."[22] These groups worked towards the improvement of conditions seen to be essential to life in the modern society, particularly conditions affecting women. In some cases this meant direct state intervention, in other cases indirect.

These organizational activities of women were inextricably linked to the role assigned to women in the family and to the vital social role attached to the family. Women were defined by the family and the family was defined by women's role. The need for social reform was argued in terms of the impact of unsatisfactory social conditions not on women but on the family. The universe of political discourse of the time defined women in terms of their family role. This concept of the universe of political discourse, developed by Jane Jenson in her analysis of the women's movement in France,[23] is very useful in our understanding of the goals being pursued by these women's groups. At any given point in

19 Joey Noble, "Class-ifying the Poor: Toronto Charities, 1850-1880," *Studies in Political Economy* 2 (1979), 114.

20 Ibid.

21 Carol Lee Bacchi, *Liberation Deferred?* (Toronto: University of Toronto Press, 1983), 103.

22 Mitchinson, "The WCTU," 155.

23 Jane Jenson, "Women on the Agenda: Mobilization for Change in France," paper delivered at the Conference of the Council for European Studies, Washington, DC, April-May 1982.

time the existing universe of political discourse provides a framework within which groups must work. This discourse can be and is modified but, at the same time, the existing universe influences the way in which issues will be defined and will develop.

Clearly the universe of political discourse of the time defined women in terms of the family. Both Michinson and Trofimenkoff insist on the mutual elements of reality and ideology in this association of women and the family. According to Michinson, "Women's reform organizations were one way in which Canadian women hoped to protect the family and assert themselves in an acceptable way."[24] For Trofimenkoff,

> The feminists thought so too. When they took on public tasks beyond the home, they did so to protect the home. They were merely enlarging their maternal sphere for the benefit of society. If their entrance into the public arena of education and social welfare was in fact a criticism of the extent of the industrial mess men had created or of the efficacy of religious institutions to cope with it or even of the shifting role that the ideology of separate spheres thrust upon them, few of them said so.[25]

Articulation of these questions in terms other than that of supporting the family would have been difficult. At the same time this definition of the issue influenced the thrust of the activities.

These organizational activities of women, setting up services and pushing for greater public support of these services, were not merely a phenomenon of the reform era of the late nineteenth century. This role has continued up to the present. Even now, the universe of political discourse is such that these organizational activities were often not articulated as being by women and for women. Yet many examples of citizen groups, such as low-income centre-city neighbourhoods, groups supporting daycare, and groups pushing for improved health services, have been predominantly female and concerned to provide and improve services to predominantly female populations. Denise Ventelou underlines this point in a recent analysis of a successful struggle led by a largely female citizen group in centre-city Montreal: "Ce sont essentiellement des femmes, à tous les niveaux, qui l'ont menée, et ce sont surtout des femmes qui se sont mobilisées. L'approche et les moyens d'action ont été colorés de cette réalité. En particulier les liens entre lutte politique et vie privée n'ont pas été laissée de côté. . . ."[26]

In general, these activities have been undertaken by women in the name of the preservation and the strengthening of the family. They have also been undertaken by women because of their belief that there are

24 Mitchinson, "The WCTU," 153.

25 Trofimenkoff, *The Dream of Nation* (Toronto: Gage, 1983), 199.

26 Denise Ventelou, "Le point de départ: une lutte," in Gisèle Ampleman et al., *Pratiques de conscientisation* (Montréal: Nouvelle Optique, 1983), 39.

peculiarly female talents that should be given a greater weight in the public realm. In Canada social feminism has been extremely important. And, to refer to Naomi Black's analysis:

> Social feminists believe that women have produced a set of values and practical skills that are excluded, along with women, from the larger society that is organized and run by men. The female virtues are nurturant, cooperative and peaceful. The female skills are productive of orderliness, plenty and security. An authoritative public role for women is therefore necessary to improve the defective social system.[27]

These organizational activities of women have played an important role over the past century in directly providing, and in pressuring for increases in, the services that now make up the welfare state. But as the welfare state develops fully, and the state increasingly takes over control of, and more often responsibility for, these services it is the state that increasingly decides the form of its own intervention. This leads us to the second of our roles, that which women play in the welfare state as workers for the state.

Our definition of the welfare state, linking it to the reproduction of the labour force, suggests that a number of central welfare state activities relate to the caring professions that were, in many cases, carried on by women. "In the modern welfare state, caregiving functions of the family and informal social networks have gradually been taken over by public welfare or social service institutions. These tasks, however, are still predominantly performed by women, even though financial compensation is paid for this work."[28]

However, what we find in the modern welfare state is that although women are very present as workers of the state, they are not in the most powerful positions. They are the executants and not the deciders. As Alison Prentice says for women teachers in the nineteenth century:

> The entry of large numbers of women into public school teaching was thus accepted because their position in the schools was generally a subordinate one. Their move into public teaching facilitated—and was facilitated by—the emergence of the public school systems, in which hierarchical professional patterns were feasible.[29]

The link between professionalization and women's subordinate role is an important one. The areas of employment of the welfare state have all been characterized by a strong move to professionalization. This development has been accompanied by a trend towards the

27 Naomi Black, "Virginia Woolf: The Life of Natural Happiness," in Dale Spender (ed.), *Feminist Theorists* (New York: Pantheon Books, 1983), 300.

28 Elina Haavio-Mannila, "Caregiving in the Welfare State," *Acta Sociologica* 26 (1983), 61.

29 Alison Prentice, "The Feminization of Teaching," in Trofimenkoff and Prentice, *Majority*, 65.

masculinization of some of these professions, as in the case of school teachers in the recent past.[30] Social work is another example where professionalization, statization and masculinization have followed parallel lines of development. Social work was first dominated by women, but the concern for professionalization brought with it the increased importance of formal education and, with this, an increased presence of men. By the mid-1970s a report on the status of women for the Canadian Association of Schools of Social Work would signal "a picture of discrimination . . . for women in the social work profession."[31]

The subordinate position of women workers within the state bureaucracy can be simply illustrated. For instance, considering government departments closely linked to welfare state activities, 46.5 per cent of the total work force of Quebec's Ministère des affaires sociales in 1983 were female, but only 9 per cent of the "cadres."[32] Ontario is similar; in 1983 the Ministry of Community and Social Services had 62 per cent women employees.[33] But once we look at nonclerical positions, the figure drops—the largest nonclerical category has 37 per cent women. And so it continues to the top of the ministry—neither the deputy minister nor any of the three assistant deputy ministers were female. Overall figures reveal the same pattern. In a review of 1980-1981 the City of Toronto listed 20 department heads, 19 of them men.[34] In Quebec in 1983, 4 per cent of "les cadres supérieurs" were women.[35] In Ontario, the top category of the service had, in 1983, 51 women out of a total of 574, or about 8 per cent.[36]

As for the federal government, Carolle Simard's study *L'administration contre les femmes*, demonstrates clearly that the civil service reproduces the segregated nature of the job market in general.

> C'est sur la division par groupes occupationnels que repose cette structure profonde et dualiste, puisqu'il y a des groupes pour les hommes et d'autres pour les femmes. Parmi ces derniers groupes, plus d'un (en fait presque tous) ne sont que les prolongements de certains rôles sociaux que l'on continue d'attribuer

30 Pat Armstrong and Hugh Armstrong, *The Double Ghetto* (Toronto: McClelland and Stewart, 1978), 38.

31 Joan Turner, "There Comes a Time," in Joan Turner and Lois Emery (eds.), *Perspectives on Women in the 1980's* (Winnipeg: University of Manitoba Press, 1983), 8.

32 Gouvernement du Québec, *Présence des femmes et des hommes dans la fonction publique du Québec* (Québec: Ministère de la fonction publique, 1983).

33 Women Crown Employees Office, *Report 1982/83* (Toronto: Ontario Women's Directorate, 1983).

34 City of Toronto, *Equal Opportunity Review 1980-81* (Toronto: City of Toronto, 1982), xvii.

35 The category "cadres supérieurs" contained, in 1983, 2,700 individuals, including 125 women.

36 The executive compensation plan group was therefore only 8 per cent female. See Women Crown Employees Office, *Report 1982/83*, 42.

uniquement aux femmes. Cette division sexuelle se retrouve par ailleurs dans la répartition des femmes au sein des ministères et dans la structure hiérarchique.[37]

Although our analysis is in terms of women as workers in the state bureaucracy and not as decision-makers, it is worth making the point briefly that this subordinate role for women is also true at the political level. Certainly the studies done by Jill Vickers and Janine Brodie have indicated the very limited role women play. "Since women's emancipation their integration into Canadian legislative assemblies has been slow and tenuous";[38] "women's political opportunities are severely restricted by Canadian political parties."[39] Strong impetus for change to the gender-based division of power within the state bureaucracy is unlikely to come from the male-dominated political leadership. But similarly, as Varda Burstyn argues, it is unlikely to come from within the bureaucracy. In addition to the sexual division of labour which limits women's participation, women are penalized by the informal norms of promotion. "Women who are aggressive, verbal and decisive are judged negatively and rejected for breaking gender rules, yet upper echelon positions demand aggressive, decisive and literate qualities in their members."[40] Or, as Dorothy E. Smith says in "Women, Class and Family," "the ruling apparatus of managerial practices, state, textual discourse, professional organization and so on is gender organized and still dominated by men."[41]

Women play a very major role as workers in the welfare state but their power is limited. They provide many of the front-line direct services but they do not determine the form of these services. They care for the clients of the welfare state but they have little influence on the direction of the welfare state.

And, coming to my third role, women also influence the welfare state by being its clients. In a large number of the programmes making up the welfare state, women are the principal clients. Two groups of women are particularly significant as clients of the welfare state: the elderly and single mothers. The poorest group in our society is elderly women.[42] Owing to the considerably lower income of working women, the lower labour force participation of women, and their higher life expectancy, many women find themselves extremely poor and therefore extremely

37 Carolle Simard, *L'administration contre les femmes* (Montréal: Boréal Express, 1983), 14.

38 Jill McCalla Vickers and M. Janine Brodie, "Canada," in Joni Lovenduski and Jill Hills (eds.), *The Politics of the Second Electorate* (London: Routledge and Kegan Paul, 1981), 70.

39 Ibid., 66.

40 Varda Burstyn, "Masculine Dominance and the State," in Ralph Miliband and John Saville (eds.), *The Socialist Register 1983* (London: The Merlin Press, 1983), 76.

41 Dorothy E. Smith, "Women, Class and Family," ibid., 40.

42 National Council of Welfare, *Sixty-Five and Older* (Ottawa: Government of Canada, 1984), 64.

dependent in their old age. They depend on the state provision of income and social services.

Women raising children alone represent one of the most rapidly growing groups in our society and, once again, a group that uses extensively the services of the welfare state. For example, nearly one-half of the Family Benefit Assistance recipients in Ontario are mother-led households.[43] The same phenomenon can be seen in the area of public housing—more and more, public housing is women's housing.[44] Daycare subsidies are another area of welfare state services that are used, to a high degree, by women raising children on their own.

Although women make up the significant clientele groups of these programmes it can be argued that, in many respects, these programmes do not respond to the real needs and to the real situation of their clients. The reality of family organization has changed greatly within the last half century, but often these programmes are designed as though the whole of society were organized neatly in nuclear families. Pension plans assume that women will be provided for by men, whereas the reality is that "the vast majority of women are obliged at some point in their lives to take charge of their own economic needs."[45] Welfare programmes still make it difficult for women to work at the same time as they receive benefits. Further, the law defines moral standards for receipt of assistance: "one has to be living as a single woman in order to get family benefits, irrespective of whether the woman actually gets any money from a man."[46] Public housing regulations have, up until the very recent past, continued to act as though the nuclear family were the only acceptable living arrangement, despite the ever growing number of women in public housing clearly not conforming to this pattern. It was, for instance, very difficult to convince housing authorities to allow two women and their children to share one unit.

As Elizabeth Wilson argues in her book, *Women and the Welfare State*: "The welfare state is not just a set of services, it is also a set of ideas about society, about the family, and—not least important—about women, who have a centrally important role within the family, as its linch pin."[47] This underlines the fundamental ambiguity of the welfare state in relation to its women clients. The services of the welfare state

43 *And the Poor Get Poorer* (Toronto: Social Planning Council of Metropolitan Toronto and the Ontario Social Development Council, 1983), 58.

44 Beth Moore-Milroy, *Woman and Housing* (Ottawa: Social Planning Council, Housing Committee, 1984). See also Janet McClain and Cassie Doyle, *Women and Housing: Changing Needs and the Failure of Policy* (Toronto: James Lorimer, 1984).

45 National Council on Welfare, *Women and Poverty* (Ottawa: National Council on Welfare, 1979), 25.

46 Margrit Eichler, "Women, Families and the State," in Turner and Emery, *Perspectives on Women*, 122.

47 Elizabeth Wilson, *Women and the Welfare State* (London: Tavistock Publications, 1977), 9.

are useful, but at the same time these programmes impose stereotypes of behaviour. The state gives, but it also controls. Or, as Nicole Laurin-Frenette states in her analysis of "Féminisme et anarchisme":

> C'est l'État qui initie, implante, oriente, réglemente, encadre, directement ou indirectement, les politiques, programmes et services d'éducation, d'acceuil, de santé, de garde, de récréation, de réhabilitation et autres, qui sont destinés aux femmes et à leurs enfants.... Nombre de ces services et de ces ressources sont nécessaires aux femmes: dans bien des cas, elles ont lutté pour les obtenir. Il n'en demeure pas moins qu'ils permettent une régulation plus centralisée et plus efficace des agents, dans et par l'État.[48]

The clients of the welfare state are aware of these contradictions; they deal with them as part of their daily lives. A British study on the crisis of the welfare state, *In and Against the State*, reports the reflections of a welfare mother:

> After all, social welfare has enabled her to bring up her family without depending on a man or his earnings.... And it is the welfare state that has made this small degree of independence possible for the first time. But to Maureen even these advantages do not seem to quite outweigh the power that the state has over you—especially the power to remove your children from your care.[49]

Dorothy O'Connell has also vividly portrayed in her book, *Chiclet Gomez*, the management of officialdom that becomes necessary for women to survive as public housing tenants: "If Edna was wearing the Dumb Look, it meant her visitors were official. Could be a public health nurse, social worker, or Housing Authority minion."[50] The welfare state provides assistance to women but at the cost of dependency.

It is these ambiguities of the welfare state—particularly in its relations with women—that make the present period so interesting. What are the current politics of the welfare state? And to what extent can the political manifestations of the welfare state be understood in terms of gender? I wish to discuss briefly two types of politics of the welfare state. The first can best be described as "clientelism"; the second includes both the neo-conservative and budget-cutting attack on the welfare state, and the organized reactions to cutbacks.

The very pervasiveness of the welfare state means that enormous numbers of people in our society are its clients, and are brought together to react to and attempt to influence government decisions and policies affecting them. Public housing tenants, welfare recipients, daycare users—these groups become significant political actors. These groups are, as we have seen, increasingly likely to be made up of women:

48 Nicole Laurin-Frenette, "Féminisme et anarchisme," in Yolande Cohen (ed.), *Femmes et politique* (Montréal: Le Jour éditeur, 1981), 178.

49 London Edinburgh Weekend Return Group, *In and Against the State* (London: Pluto Press, 1980), 15-16.

50 Dorothy O'Connell, *Chiclet Gomez* (Ottawa: Deneau & Greenberg), 116.

therefore gender is and will increasingly be important to the politics of clientelism.

These politics reflect all the ambiguities of the relations between welfare state clients and the state that we outlined previously—the importance of the services provided and the degree of financial independence achieved, together with the costs in terms of control, the reinforcing of stereotypes and a loss of autonomy. Should the future be greater autonomy in relation to the state, or closer links to it? Both positions are argued by those involved in the politics of clientelism. My example of authors arguing for greater autonomy comes from women involved in providing transition homes for battered women. Their argument is that a totally women-controlled programme could give a different model of providing services—a specifically female model. A state-controlled programme could never do this.

> Plus les femmes prennent conscience de l'originalité de leurs démarches et des acquis des groupes de services et de lutte contre la violence, plus se dégage un modèle qui leur est propre.... Face à l'autonomie, l'ensemble des maisons est traversé par un double courant oscillant entre l'allégeance au gouvernement et l'opposition à ses politiques.... Sommes-nous déjà à l'étape de l'histoire des refuges où il faut parler de redonner aux femmes leurs maisons?[51]

The argument for autonomist political activity for women is also made by Claire Duguay and Micheline de Sève in their article, "Tant d'amarres à larguer." They insist on the creativity demonstrated by feminist political practices.

> Nous nous attacherons à montrer d'autre part, comment les groupes autonomes de femmes, parce qu'autonomes précisément, ont rencontré moins d'obstacles pour défendre leurs revendications.... Nous avançons l'hypothèse que les groupes autonomes de femmes en particulier sont en voie d'implanter par leurs actions, leurs productions littéraires ou artistiques, leur humour, leur folie(?) une nouvelle culture politique qui traduit en termes socialement significatifs la richesse de l'expérience des femmes jusqu'ici confinée à la sphère de la vie privée.[52]

But not all authors argue that greater autonomy from the state serves the interests of women. Quite the opposite in fact is true in the case of those who feel that "the state is turning out to be the main recourse of women."[53] Frances Fox Piven bases her case for a favourable view of the welfare state in relation to women on the argument that women are in a weaker position, and have less power in the private sector and increasingly so even in the private realm.

51 Micheline Beaudry, *Les maisons des femmes battues au Québec* (Montréal: Éditions Saint-Martin, 1984), 23.

52 Claire Duguay and Micheline de Sève, "Tant d'amarres à larguer: une analyse des pratiques du mouvement des femmes," *Politique* 5 (1984), 52.

53 Frances Fox Piven, "Women and the State: Ideology, Power and the Welfare State," *Socialist Review* 74 (1984), 14.

Women are losing their old rights and their limited forms of power in the family. In the market place their position is weak; they are not likely to gain forms of mass power in production, and prospects for advancement through market processes are dim. As a consequence, women have turned to the state and specially to the expanding programs of the welfare state.[54]

The state becomes, in this argument, the area of greatest benefit to, but also of greatest potential influence by, women.[55] Instead of rejecting the state, clients of the welfare state should increase their links to it.

These differing interpretations reflect the contradictory nature of the relations between clients and the welfare state. These contradictions become even greater in periods, such as the present, of political attacks on the welfare state, of the politics of budget-cutting and reactions to budget-cutting.

Allan Moscovitch has outlined a number of the forms that the erosion of state social welfare has taken in Canada, indicating their impact on women:

The closing of institutions for the psychiatrically disabled, an otherwise often progressive activity, without appropriate provision for the necessary community based facilities may put the burden of care onto the family, most often on women. Similarly restrictions on the expansion of child care facilities creates a situation in which either care is provided at home largely by women, or it is purchased privately from other women.... A further aspect of the restructuring of welfare has been the attempts by both state and capital to encourage the substitution of the services and assistance of charitable institutions, provided by volunteers, for state social welfare. This approach reflects not only a denigration of human service but also a pronounced anti-feminism.[56]

Gender is an important variable in these political struggles. The programme cuts affect women both because of the importance of women within the clientele groups served by the programmes, and because of the importance of women as front-line workers for the state and therefore as those whose jobs are most likely to be eliminated by the cutbacks. As an article on the cutbacks in British Columbia states, "women immediately recognized the crushing impact these measures would have on them as workers and on social services for women and children."[57] Gender becomes even more important to the politics of these issues because of the potential for alliances—between clients and workers but also between clients, workers and women of the general

54 Ibid.

55 One could also argue that recent efforts to recruit women to senior bureaucratic positions support this position. See the 1983 annual report of the federal *Public Service Commission* for figures showing the increase in the recruitment of women in the senior ranks.

56 Allan Moscovitch, "The Welfare State since 1975," paper presented to the annual conference of l'Association d'économie politique, Montreal, October 1983, 21-22.

57 Cynthia Flood, "Women Against the Budget," *Canadian Dimension* 18 (1984), 13.

population who are motivated by gender solidarity. The "bonds of sisterhood" relevant to the organizational activities of middle class women of the nineteenth century are a factor today and certainly explain, for instance, some of the current "gender gap" and the lower female support for neo-conservative policies. Again the British Columbia example provides a description of this kind of broadly based political alliance.

> An extraordinary range of individual women and representatives of women's groups converged on the women against the Budget meeting-room to form an umbrella organization. Public sector unionists, teachers, lesbian rights activists, long-time general-issue feminists, church women, artists, writers, left-wingers of gaudily-varied stripes, daycare activists, rape crisis workers, students, librarians, old women, young women—all came to argue and act.[58]

Attempts to link public sector workers, welfare state clients and feminist activists can also be seen in welfare state workers' efforts to develop consciously feminist work strategies, as in this example from *Breaking the Silence*, a newsletter on feminism in social welfare: "This type of negotiation of the system, to enable people to bend rules and develop strategies in the interest of women clients, is something that a feminist social worker must learn."[59]

Gender, therefore, is an important part of the politics of the welfare state—today and in the future. It will likely become an increasingly explicit part of these politics given the changes occuring in the universe of political discourse. Changes are occuring, but they are happening slowly. It is at this point that I come to my exhortation. Political scientists are one of the groups in our society that can influence the development of the universe of political discourse. We are, of course, not the only group. Political discourse, however, is changed not only by political practitioners but also by theorists and observers of politics. Our teaching and our writing does have an impact on the way in which Canadian society defines that which is political. Analyzing and articulating the relations between gender and politics is one of the vital tasks that confronts Canadian society as a whole and certainly us as Canadian political scientists. I hope that we will accept this challenge.

58 Ibid.
59 Pamela Connolly, "Issues Facing a Feminist Counsellor in a Traditional Setting," *Breaking the Silence* 2 (1983), 14.

# [24]

# The Gender Basis of American Social Policy

VIRGINIA SAPIRO

During the last quarter of the nineteenth century, women—thousands of them—became increasingly organized and active in the attempt to promote the general welfare, especially by helping the most vulnerable members of society. As individual leaders and as group participants they were instrumental in organizing and nationalizing movements for public health (mental and physical), poor relief, penal and other institutional reform, education for the previously uneducated, and child welfare. As the nineteenth century waned and the twentieth dawned, women were prominent among proponents of a principle which was hitherto nearly alien to American ideology but which has now, a century later, come to be an accepted part of our political views: the government and, they increasingly argued, the national government, have a responsibility to promote the general welfare actively by providing initiative and support where necessary. The degree and types of support remain, perhaps more now than then, matters of profound political contention, but in the late twentieth century even the most conservative ideologues tend to agree that government must provide a "safety net" for its people.

The late nineteenth and early twentieth centuries was also a time during which thousands of women, many of them the same as those involved in the general welfare movements, were agitating to promote women's welfare specifically.[1] The

[1] On women's movements of this period see Barbara Berg, *The Remembered Gate: Origins of American Feminism: Women and the City, 1800–60* (New York: Oxford University Press, 1978); Ellen DuBois, *Feminism and Suffrage: The Emergence of An Independent Women's Movement in America, 1848–69* (Ithaca, N.Y.: Cornell University Press, 1978); Eleanor Flexner, *Century of*

VIRGINIA SAPIRO is professor of political science and women's studies at the University of Wisconsin, Madison. She has published books and articles on gender including *Women in American Society* and *The Political Integration of Women.*

suffrage movement, aimed at providing women with what we now regard as the basic right of citizenship and the basic means of leverage within a democratic political system, is only the best known facet of the women's movement of that era. As many historians have demonstrated, a large proportion of nineteenth-century feminists came to their concerns for women through their charitable and political efforts aimed at the needy.[2] Moreover, many nineteenth-century feminists conceived of their woman-directed activities as means to improve the lot not just of women but of women's families and communities.[3]

The development of American social welfare policy was heavily influenced by women, who often saw themselves acting on behalf of women. These women—many of them feminists—were instrumental in the development of the American social welfare state, such as it is: the efforts in the 1840s of Dorothea Dix to get Congress to provide money and land for the construction of mental institutions (the bill passed but President Franklin Pierce's veto was sustained); the establishment of the U.S. Sanitary Commission; Josephine Shaw Lowell's New York Charity Organization Society and its counterparts; the settlement movement; Josephine Kelley's National Consumers League; many Progressive leaders; the instigators of the Children's Bureau; and the authors and primary promoters of the 1921 Infancy and Maternity (Sheppard-Towner) Bill.

The history of movements for women's welfare and for the general welfare are virtually inseparable. But we can go further and argue that it is not possible to understand the underlying principles, structure, and effects of our social welfare system and policies without understanding their relationship to gender roles and gender ideology. Three examples suggest how important understanding this relationship is: widows' or mothers' pensions, protective labor legislation, and the Sheppard-Towner Act of 1921.

In 1911, Missouri became the first state to provide for cash assistance to widows with dependent children. By 1935, the date of the nationalization of this policy through Title IV (Aid to Dependent Children) of the Social Security Act, all states except South Carolina and Georgia had acted similarly. As Walter Trattner argues, "Widow's pension laws marked a definite turning point in the welfare policies of many states. In theory at least, they removed the stigma of charity for a large number of welfare recipients. They also broke down the nineteenth-century tradition against public home relief."[4] Before the advent of widows' pensions, public pensions were limited to military personnel or civil servants, people whose willingness to work for limited public salaries would be re-

---

*Struggle: The Women's Rights Movement in the United States* (Cambridge, Mass.: Harvard University Press, 1975); and Stanley Lemons, *The Woman Citizen: Social Feminism in the 1920's* (Urbana: University of Illinois Press, 1972).

[2] For example, Berg, *Remembered Gate*; and DuBois, *Feminism and Suffrage.*

[3] For example, Linda Gordon, *Woman's Body, Woman's Right: A Social History of Birth Control in America* (New York: Viking Press, 1977).

[4] Walter I. Trattner, *From Poor Law to Welfare State: A History of Social Welfare in America* (New York: Free Press, 1974), 190.

warded with security.[5] Widows' pensions were different in that they provided for needy private persons. The Social Security Act, through Aid to Dependent Children (ADC), did the same at the federal level.

Protective labor legislation offers another example of the role that gender differentiation played in promoting social welfare ideas within the United States. At the turn of the century, efforts to provide for public regulation of working conditions advocated by both trade unions and groups such as the National Consumers' League were turned back consistently on the grounds that they would conflict with the right of employers and employees to make contracts freely and unimpeded by forces outside the market. The major turning point in employment and workplace policy came in 1908 when the Supreme Court, in *Muller v. Oregon*, upheld the right of a state to limit the working hours of women.[6] Although protective labor legislation has been highly contentious among feminists from the first for reasons that will be discussed below, the "thin edge of the wedge" for regulation of the workplace was provided by policies based on a particular construction of gender ideology.

A third example of the importance of gender in the expansion of American social policy is the Sheppard-Towner Bill, enacted in 1921 and in force until Herbert Hoover assured its demise in 1929. Sheppard-Towner provided for the first time for matching federal grants-in-aid to states for the purpose of promoting child and maternal health services. This was the first time the federal government provided grants for state welfare programs other than education,[7] and it provided the precedent for later efforts. The program was widely attacked as the first incursion of "bolshevism" into the United States and was the subject of the first major—but certainly not the last—campaign against "state medicine."[8] Anxiety over socialism was one of the major reasons for the demise of the pure laissez faire system of labor contract in the marketplace. Sheppard-Towner put government, notably the federal government, in the business of providing the public with social services other than protective services and education.

These cases mark turning points in American political ideology. The notion that "that government governs best that governs least" was transformed, at least to the degree that the standard of what constitutes "least" was questioned. To the belief that people should be self-reliant, which meant providing for themselves and their families, was added the idea that it was good for private individuals to engage in charitable acts (although it was not good for individuals to expect to depend upon these acts), and also that government had some responsibility to provide. Government was now to promote the general welfare not just by assuring civil order, but by providing for that welfare directly.

Of crucial importance here, women were the apparent beneficiaries of these

[5] James Leiby, *A History of Social Welfare and Social Work in the United States* (New York: Columbia University Press, 1978), 212.

[6] *Muller v. Oregon*, 208 U.S. 412, (1908).

[7] Trattner, *From Poor Law to Welfare State*, 187.

[8] Lemons, *Woman Citizen*.

policies. When these policies were first set in place, there was no intention on the part of most policy makers to set any precedents for other parallel reforms or, certainly, for more widespread changes in the structure or theoretical basis of political economy. Indeed, there was considerable opposition to these changes, specifically because they might turn out to be turning points and precedents, as some interest groups such as the labor and the Progressive movements hoped they might be. Why were women so central to these changes? What does this "coincidence" tell us about the development of gender ideology, political ideology, and social policy in the United States?

Unfortunately, the standard treatments of social policy offer little assistance in answering these questons because the relationships among gender, feminism, and the development of social welfare policy has generally been neglected outside of feminist scholarship. Marxists and non-Marxists alike have identified the development of the welfare state as a part of the political process of the development of capitalist industrialism; to the non-Marxist especially it is a part of the political transformation of societies into mass democracies. Within the standard view of the history of welfare states, as Peter Flora and Arnold J. Heidenheimer write, "one may interpret the welfare state as an answer to increasing demands for socioeconomic equality or as the institutionalization of social rights relative to the development of civil and political rights."[9] Just so; but academic analyses tend to focus on demands and rights specifically relevant to class conflicts within society, thus obscuring the roles of women and gender. This, interestingly, is the case as much for non-Marxists as for Marxists. A woman's economic interests are generally assumed to follow from a husband when the woman is married, and especially a homemaker, and to be defined adequately by standard class definitions in cases where women are employed. The problem is that standard views of economic interest and organization are defined primarily through male history and experience, and feminist activists have often been aware of these differences.[10]

Analysis of the theory and practice of social policy has rarely taken full account of the relevance of gender, and often implicitly accepts without examination certain paternalistic and patriarchal assumptions about the nature of gender that are also embedded in the policies themselves. As a result, there is little understanding of how social policy affects women in particular and, more generally, how women's welfare is linked to general welfare.

The remainder of this article examines the relationship between women's welfare and the general welfare within the framework of American social policy, especially as it treats economic dependency. Women have been defined primarily

[9] Peter Flora and Arnold J. Heidenheimer, "The Historical Core and Changing Boundaries of the Welfare State," in Flora and Heidenheimer, eds., *The Development of Welfare States in Europe and America* (New Brunswick, N.J.: Transaction Books, 1981), 22.

[10] For further discussion see Christine Delphy, *Closer to Home: A Materialist Analysis of Women's Oppression* (Amherst: University of Massachusetts Press, 1984); and Lydia Sargent, ed., *Women and Revolution: A Discussion of the Unhappy Marriage of Marxism and Feminism* (Boston: South End Press, 1981).

as dependents, *because* others depend upon their dependency. American social policy, it shall be argued, not only assumes, but helps to maintain this state of affairs. Further, many social policies that most affect women are not, in fact, aimed primarily *at* them but rather, in many senses, *through* them. Finally, analysis of the relationship between women and social policy does not teach us "only" about women and social policy, but about our construction and understanding of social policy and the general welfare more broadly.

## American Social Policy: The Standard Version

Social policy is, as Albert Weale has written, "a deliberate attempt by governments to promote individual and social welfare in certain specific dimensions using any suitable policy instruments."[11] This definition is useful because it underscores the point that social policy is not a matter simply of social services or even more narrowly (and perhaps more commonly believed) social services for the poor. Social policy, in other words, is not always what it seems to be to the untrained eye. Some of the most important social services are not aimed at the poor (for example, public universities), and many of the social policies that might do the most to promote individual and social welfare are not services (for example, occupational safety and health regulations or benefits policies and nondiscrimination policies). Indeed it has been argued repeatedly that it is not easy and not always worthwhile to draw definite boundaries among social policy and fiscal or civil rights policies.[12]

For the first century and more of American history, social policy basically rested on the belief that the welfare of the society and its component parts could best be assured by allowing—encouraging—individuals to pursue their own interests freely. This notion was as much a moral as an economic belief. What came to be known as the "protestant work ethic" supported moral and policy distinctions made among the "just" desserts earned by the diligent well-off and the shiftless poor and the unfortunate "deserving" poor. As Robert Goodin has pointed out, the emphasis on self-reliance was, at its heart, a concern about the moral character of individuals.[13] Conservatives continue to maintain, despite empirical evidence to the contrary,[14] that provision of welfare benefits makes individuals psychologically dependent and removes their motivation to pursue their interests in the marketplace and, therefore, short circuits the entire system. In other words, provision of welfare changes the character of individuals so as to make them bad and unproductive members of society.

[11] Albert Weale, *Political Theory and Social Policy* (London: Macmillan, 1983), 5.

[12] Weale, *Political Theory and Social Policy*; Richard M. Titmuss, "The Social Division of Welfare: Some Reflections on the Search for Equity," in Titmuss, ed., *Essays on the Welfare State* (London: Allen and Unwin, 1958), 34–55.

[13] Robert E. Goodin, "Self-Reliance versus The Welfare State," *Journal of Social Policy* 14 (January 1985): 25–47.

[14] Ibid.

In practical terms, therefore, the nation was to be composed of diligent hardworking individuals who competed in the marketplace (or, for the agrarian ideal of self-sufficiency, worked their land) to make something of themselves and to provide for themselves. With the growth of industrialism and the ascendency of a middle class, the principle of individualistic competition in a free market to assure self-sufficiency became a moral, social, political, and economic ideal. The implications of this set of beliefs for social welfare have been well summarized by Ramesh Mishra: "Paternalism—of the state but also of the employer—is frowned upon."

> Not the bonds of status but those of contract between "free" men typifies the basic model of social relationship outside the family. Translating these generalities into patterns of welfare, we might say that the middle-class society is likely to develop a "residual" system of welfare. In the early states of industrialization neither state nor enterprise welfare is favored. Instead, friendly societies, voluntary organizations, charities, and market responses to the various problems and needs are encouraged.[15]

This is precisely what happened during the second half of the nineteenth century in the United States. There was an impressive growth of charity and social action (a growth especially among women) as the more negative by-products of industrialism became more obvious, but this "social action was largely a voluntary do-it-yourself arrangement among individuals with a common interest."[16]

Should individuals be in need of assistance or cooperation, such arrangements were to be made on a voluntary basis. There were clear hierarchies of responsibility or, as Michael Walzer puts it, spheres of justice.[17] The core in which assistance could be freely sought and in which others had the most responsibility to provide was the immediate family followed by more distant relatives. At the next stage were neighbors and others in the local community. As the public domain began to share in provision, the state was seen as more obliged than the federal govenment. Above all, aid and cooperation were to come from the private world rather than from government. As James Leiby notes, only in the twentieth century was "social welfare" rather than "charity and correction" widely used to label assistance. "Social welfare," he argues, connotes "a recognition of human interdependence. . . , a sense of mutual responsibilities and goals among [society's] classes and parts, and of the need for common policies to realize them."[18]

The earliest social policies fall into two general categories. The first, into which we might put social insurance (originally called "workingman's insurance") and pensions, were aimed at helping or providing some added security to those who were working to help themselves and their society. The second was assistance aimed at those who seemed most inevitably dependent: paupers

[15] Ramesh Mishra, *Society and Social Policy: Theories and Practice of Welfare* (London: Macmillan, 1981), 41.

[16] Leiby, *A History of Social Welfare*, 33.

[17] Michael Walzer, *Spheres of Justice* (New York: Basic Books, 1983).

[18] Leiby, *A History of Social Welfare*, 2. For a parallel discussion of charity versus justice, see Robert E. Goodin, *Protecting the Vulnerable* (Chicago: University of Chicago Press, 1985), chap. 2.

without relatives to help, children and especially orphans, and "defectives" such as the insane and criminally inclined. Later a third type of social policy developed, but did not really flower until the post-World War II era: social regulation or government intervention in the rules and procedures of the market. Above all, American social policy was developed with a continuing distaste for paternalism and an emphasis on allowing individuals, and by later policies helping individuals, compete as individuals in an open market in order to achieve self-sufficiency and self-reliance.

The previous paragraphs offer little more than a standard, albeit boiled down, rendition of American social policy thinking and practice. Turning our attention to the place of women in this story we find that this rendition is seriously flawed. It is written in apparently generic gender-neutral terms and, therefore, masks an extremely gender-based story.

## The Revised Version: Beyond Gender Neutrality

In order to see the fault in analysis of social policy and in social policy itself, let us look again at the main themes: dependence and self-reliance, individualism and paternalism. In fact, if we consider the subjects of policy not in the apparently gender-neutral terms (such as individual, worker, family) usually used, but in the explicit terms of male and female, we find that the dominant ideology underlying social-policy thinking and action has never stressed individualism pure and simple. It has never been uniformly opposed to either dependency or paternalism, and it has never supported a universal value of self-reliance, especially in economic terms. Instead, it has supported individualism, independence, and self-reliance for some people (primarily men) and dependence and reliance on paternalism for others (primarily women). This is largely because individuals have been viewed in terms of functional roles depending upon gender. Men are regarded as breadwinners for themselves and their families, and women are regarded as wives and mothers who are and should be economically dependent upon those breadwinners.

In order to understand the relationship of women to social policy, it is necessary to consider policy directly regarding the ability of women to provide for themselves. As we have seen, the primary purpose of most American social policy is supposed to be to allow "individuals" to provide for themselves, to reward those who have done so, and to provide a back-up for those who have not been able to do so because of circumstances beyond their own control. If, however, this really was "the" American approach to social policy, it should apply in a gender-neutral way. In fact, this view did not apply to women; indeed, throughout most of American history it has been contradictory to the predominant prescription for women.

Until the enactment of the Married Women's Property Acts in the 1840s, women could not own property including that which they inherited or earned through their own labor, and they could not make contacts without their husband's consent. In other words, women were barred by law from engaging in the activities that were supposed to be the primary principle of political economy and the civil right most fiercely protected by American law up to the twentieth century—the right to contract freely to pursue one's economic interest. The reason was the common law principle of *femme couverte*. Women's economic and political identities and interests were incorporated into (not with) those of their husbands. Women's only voluntary contract was the marriage contract, by which they were thought to be giving blanket tacit consent to most future decisions made by their husbands.[19]

Even when free women gained the right to own and manage property and to make contracts, they did not gain the right to provide for themselves. If employers wanted to bar women as a class from employment, their right to do so was protected by the principle of governmental noninterference in private contracts. Moreover, as women began to seek training and jobs outside the women's sphere of employment (domestic labor and sewing) states stepped in to help bar women's further progress.

The first Supreme Court case concerning women's economic rights was *Bradwell v. Illinois*, which in 1874 upheld a state's right to prohibit women's admission to the bar.[20] Although the main reason offered by the Court was the principle of state's rights, the concurring opinion expressed the paternalistic view that has been repeated in law and political argument numerous times. "Man is, or should be, woman's protector and defender," and, therefore, must protect her from the world of work and individualistic competition. Further, "the harmony, not to say identity, of interests and views which belong, or should belong, to the family institution is repugnant to the idea of a woman adopting a distinct and independent career from that of her husband." Most telling of all, the prohibition covered not just married but all women, because women are defined by their actual or potential statuses as wives and mothers. "The paramount destiny and mission of women are to fulfill the noble and benign offices of wife and mother. This is the law of the Creator. And the rules of society must be adapted to the general constitution of things and cannot be based upon exceptional cases." Whereas the Protestant work ethic as applied to income-producing work was a moral and economic principle for men, economic dependency was a moral, God-given principle for women.

Government became increasingly involved in restricting women's ability to provide for themselves and their families and even, in denying women their own rights of citizenship separate from those of their husbands.[21] Public institutions of higher education, including the land grant colleges, were generally sex segregated and, therefore, kept women from the programs that might lead them

[19] Carole Pateman, "Women and Consent," *Political Theory* 8 (May 1980): 149–68; and Virginia Sapiro, "Women, Citizenship, and Nationality: Immigration and Naturalization Policies in the United States," *Politics and Society* 13 (1984).

[20] *Bradwell v. Illinois*, 83 U.S. 130, (1874).

[21] Sapiro, "Women, Citizenship, and Nationality."

to professional careers. Women were barred from certain job classifications and in some jobs such as teaching, they were refused employment if they were married or certainly, if they were pregnant. Female employees were fired if they got married or if they became pregnant. Government discriminated against women in pay. Even the National Industrial Recovery Act (NIRA) signed by Franklin Delano Roosevelt in 1933 provided for sex differences in pay despite intensive lobbying by women's groups and assurances by Eleanor Roosevelt and Labor Secretary Frances Perkins. Moreover, women's jobs were especially likely to be excluded from minimum wage regulations, and the Public Works Administration and Federal Emergency Relief Administration tended to emphasize projects that involved male jobs.[22]

Not until nearly a century after *Bradwell*, in Title VII of the 1964 Civil Rights Act, did the federal government take a stand against sex discrimination in hiring; only in 1971 did the Supreme Court, in *Phillips v. Martin Marietta*, argue that employers may not discriminate against women, in this case women with children.[23] Following a case in which the Supreme Court upheld the right of an employer to discriminate against pregnant women in occupational benefits,[24] Congress passed the 1978 Pregnancy Discrimination Act, which incorporated into Title VII the principle of nondiscrimination against pregnant women.

Because social policy tends to be analyzed as a class issue, we tend to look to labor movements and unions as some of the primary instigators of progressive social policy insofar as their role is to pursue the interests of workers. Although women have benefited from labor organization in gender specific ways (for example, gender differentials in pay are lower among unionized than nonunionized workers), the early history of the labor movement shows considerable support for paternalistic and exclusionary treatment of women in the job market.[25] Although women constituted about 30 percent of printers by 1831 and 16 percent of newspaper compositors by 1850, for example, print unions would not accept women to full membership until 1873.[26] Other unions continued to bar women. Samuel Gompers, among other union activitsts, was opposed to women workers on the grounds that they took wages from men and destroyed the family. In 1898 he urged the government to prohibit women from federal employment.

[22] Lois Scharf, " 'The Forgotten Woman': Working Women, the New Deal, and Women's Organizations," in Lois Scharf and Joan M. Jensen, eds., *Decades of Discontent: The Women's Movement, 1920–40* (Westport, Conn.: Greenwood Press, 1983), 243–60. On women in the New Deal see also Susan D. Becker, *The Origins of the Equal Rights Amendment: American Feminism Between the Wars* (Westport, Conn: Greenwood Press, 1981); and Susan Ware, *Beyond Suffrage: Women in the New Deal* (Cambridge, Mass.: Harvard University Press, 1981).

[23] *Phillips v. Martin Marietta*, 400 U.S. 542, (1971).

[24] *General Electric v. Gilbert*, 429 U.S. 125, (1976).

[25] Bettina Berch, *The Endless Day: The Political Economy of Women and Work* (New York: Harcourt, Brace, Jovanovich, 1982).

[26] Maron Marzolf, *Up From the Footnote: A History of Women Journalists* (New York: Hastings House, 1977); and DuBois, *Feminism and Suffrage*.

The perspective of labor unions leads us back to specific consideration of social policy. The labor movement and its leaders such as Gompers were among the most committed supporters of protective labor legislation for women. Their reasons varied. Certainly some of the motivation was the desire to assist those in a relatively weak position in the labor market. As suggested earlier, unions saw woman-directed policies as the "thin edge of the wedge" of more widespread protections for all workers. But another major motivation in the U.S. as in other countries was to use legislation directed at women to protect male jobs and wages. Protective labor legislation for women could directly and indirectly keep women out of competition for "male" jobs and make them less desirable to employers. Indeed, "protection" has generally been applied less strenuously to "female" than to "male" jobs. Hours and weightlifting limits, for example, were never applied to domestic labor, paid or unpaid. Protective labor legislation made women more expensive to hire than they had been. As femininst observers have often remarked, this type of policy has served at least as much to keep women out of higher paying jobs as it has to improve their working conditions. This has been true of later types of protective legislation as well.[27]

Another early proposal of the labor and other movements concerned with workers was not just the provision of a *living* wage, but of a family wage; that is, a wage that would give the (male) breadwinner the ability to support his family without needing to depend on a wage-earning wife. Again, the thinking did not simply concern the economic situation of a family, but the character of those in the family. Women, it was thought, should not have to seek employment because their jobs were to care for the other members of the family. Men should not have to compete with women for jobs; after all, men need to support their families. Most important, "manhood" was defined in part by the ability of a man to support his family. Men were—and still to some degree are—taught to feel emasculated when they depend on women's wages. The goodness or badness of dependency depends on who is depending on whom. Husbands' economic dependence upon wives is bad. Wives' economic dependence upon husbands is good, in part because it is often thought to allow men to be more independent.[28]

Most social policy aimed at women has been designed explicitly to benefit them in their capacity as wives and mothers and more particularly, to benefit those who depend upon them for nurturance and domestic service: husbands, children, and elderly relatives. The widows' pensions and Sheppard-Towner Act mentioned above are early examples. In an important sense, women have not been the main targets of these policies but rather, they were the main conduit of these policies, which were aimed at providing for children. The original con-

[27] On occupational safety and health, for example, see Wendy Chavkin, ed., *Double Exposure: Women's Health Hazards on the Job and at Home* (New York: Monthly Review Press, 1984).

[28] For an economic history that treats the changing psychology of gender divisions of labor, see Julie A. Matthaei, *An Economic History of Women in America: Women's Work, The Sexual Division of Labor, and The Development of Capitalism* (New York: Schocken, 1982).

struction of ADC provided for support of the children in one-parent families. Only later was support extended to the caregiver.[29]

Social policy aimed at women has been designed to benefit them in their capacity as wives and mothers only in a limited sense. Its intention has been to enable them to *care* for their families and not, by and large, to *provide* for them in the sense that is expected of a breadwinner. Often, as in the case of ADC (and its later incarnation as AFDC (Aid to Families with Dependent Children)), it has been aimed at relieving mothers of the "need to work." Women were expected to remain economically dependent because of domestic responsibilities assigned to them. In contrast, the "man in the house" provisions, which allowed administrators to withhold funds if any evidence was found to indicate a man (related or not) was living in, or even a frequent visitor to the house, underscores the degree to which men were still regarded as responsible for economic support.

Only in the late 1960s and especially the 1970s were any serious efforts made to enable women to be economic providers for themselves and their families. Title VII of the Civil Rights Act was given some force in 1971 when the Equal Employment Opportunities Commission (EEOC) gained power to litigate. The growth of affirmative action programs signaled governmental support for improving the employment prospects of women, even if no employers were actually punished for failing to achieve hiring goals. The Work Incentive (WIN) Program established at the end of the 1960s began to suggest that even for women, "work goes with welfare." At first, however, men were given priority in WIN funding, followed by women on a first-come-first-served basis.[30] In 1971, AFDC regulation required for the first time that female recipients of AFDC funds with children over six years old should seek employment.[31] Even the relatively meager efforts to provide women with the means and incentive to seek employment have remained controversial and, during the Reagan administration, have been attacked and reduced.[32]

Even if there is more widespread support for the breakdown of familial gender roles in the marketplace, support for traditional gender roles within the home remain firm even, in a sense, with regard to families in which there is no adult male. Programs of employment incentives and supports for women have not included provision of child care services, which remain the responsibility of mothers. A bill passed through Congress that would have provided federal funds for day care centers was vetoed by Richard Nixon on the grounds that such services would break up "the family." Despite the pro-nationalist claims of recent administrations, the United States remains one of the few Organization for Eco-

[29] Dorothy C. Miller, "AFDC: Mapping a Strategy for Tomorrow," *Social Service Review* 57 (December 1983): 599–613.

[30] Sar A. Levitan, Martin Rein, and David Marwick, *Work and Welfare Go Together* (Baltimore: Johns Hopkins Press, 1972), 77.

[31] Deborah K. Zinn and Rosemary C. Sarri, "Turning Back The Clock on Welfare," *Signs* 10 (Winter 1984): 355–70.

[32] Ibid.

nomic Cooperation and Development (OECD) nations that lacks a maternity leave policy. It lags in other supports for pregnant women and families with children as well.

It is important to note that although women and children are supposed to depend upon a male breadwinner for financial support, public policy has not been vigorous in enforcing this goal. Marital law still assumes that husbands are responsible for financial support, but court cases continue to conclude that if a woman is actually residing with her husband that is proof enough that he is supporting her adequately regardless of what he provides or what he is capable of providing. This is an unwarranted assumption either that husbands provide adequate allowances to their wives or that married couples pool their resources in such a way as to allow each individual to draw on them freely. One of the major causes of poverty among women and children in recent decades has been the refusal of divorced husbands to comply with court orders for support payments. Only when the Reagan administration realized that considerable sums of AFDC money could be saved was a serious policy of enforcement initiated, but it was originally designed to encompass only women who were eligible for AFDC funding. The implication was that support of women by their husbands is a private matter of no concern to government unless or until women became public charges because of lack of spousal support. If for much of our history, women's welfare was supposedly safeguarded by a husband, we are led to the deduction that for most of our history, women's welfare has been of little concern to government, except insofar as it served instrumental purposes in providing care and services for others.

Women's primary relationship to the structure of the general welfare is to provide essential services that might otherwise cost money either to the private or public sector.[33] As many feminist observers have pointed out, when it is said that families have the primary responsibility to care for themselves, what one really means is that women have the primary responsibility to care for others in the family.[34] Given the continuing gender division of labor in the family, it is not the family as a unit but rather women in families who care for children, the elderly, and other dependents, including breadwinners who are dependent upon these services for their own day-to-day maintenance. Of course, given gender divisions of labor in the marketplace, when people are employed to replace what has previously been women's domestic labor, these services continue to be rendered by women. A major and generally hidden question in social policy, therefore, is whether women should be required to provide for the general welfare in a way that often necessitates that they remain economically dependent and ultimately perhaps in need of social welfare provisions themselves. Or can women and others provide for the general welfare in a way that allows women to provide for themselves as well?

[33] See, for example, Gerdt Sundström, "The Elderly, Women's Work, and Social Security Costs," *Acta Sociologica* 25 (1982): 21–38.

[34] Michele Barrett and Mary McIntosh, *The Antisocial Family* (London: Verso, 1982).

Women's contribution to the general welfare goes beyond the provision of services that need to be done. Even in the minority of cases in which women do not contribute wages to a household, they help determine the worth of the wages that are contributed by others. Again, because of the continuing gender division of domestic labor, women's efforts in shopping, cooking, and other household tasks affect the value of each dollar brought in. Although public pronouncements have often acknowledged the importance of women's contribution to the home, there has been little effort to give women a return. Only in this decade, for example, have courts begun to recognize women's investment in domestic labor as an economic contribution to be considered in dividing household assets following divorce. Homemakers do not receive their own social security benefits but rather are supposed to benefit through their husbands' contributions. In fact, only 54 percent of women receiving social security benefits make their claims on the basis of their own work records; the other 46 percent claim as wives.[35] In the case of divorced women, however, only those who qualify under very stringent conditions find that their years of contributing to their husband's maintenance and worth results in payment.

It is women's provision of care and the expectation that they should do so that does the most to make women dependent. Those who are most economically vulnerable are the women who do the most to fulfill a paternalistic and patriarchal gender ideology: they devote themselves full time to caring for their families. Any human capital investment they made in earlier years through education, training, or employment becomes devalued with each year they are homemakers,[36] and they lack the further benefits afforded by continuing job experience. They foresake both the independent security of employment and employment-related benefits including pensions, and they foresake a considerable amount of ability to provide for themselves should the need arise. Women's economic activities, however, cannot be regarded as choices in the full sense of the word. Our social policies assume that women are the primary care givers, which means there is little assistance to be offered to women who are, in addition, breadwinners. Our social welfare system depends on women either being dependent or taking on what has become to be known as the "double burden." Even when women attempt to seek employment, they continue to face job discrimination based on this gender ideology. Although it is illegal for employers to take marital or maternal status into account, they continue to devalue women as employees because of the assumption that women's primary focus of attention is the home.

Reality contradicts the persistent view that women are not providers. The majority of women are now in the labor force, including the majority of women

[35] Barbara J. Nelson, "Women's Poverty and Women's Citizenship: Some Political Consequences of Economic Marginality," *Signs* 10 (Winter 1984): 223.

[36] Marnie Mueller, "Applying Human Capital Theory to Women's Changing Work Patterns," *Journal of Social Issues* 38 (Spring 1982): 89–96.

with children as young as two.[37] They now spend relatively few years out of the labor force. Women make important financial contributions to their households. Many people have noted that women who do not have a husband to help support themselves and their families are particularly likely to suffer from poverty. In 1983, more than one quarter of all divorced and separated women were on welfare. Thirty-seven percent of single mothers with one child were poor, as were 85 percent of single mothers with four children. But married men are also poorer if they do not have a wife who makes financial contributions to the home. Among married white couples, 9 percent of the families in which the husband was the only earner were poor compared with 3 percent in which both spouses worked. The difference is even more stark among black families, where we find 24 percent were poor if only the husband was a wage earner compared with 4 percent if both were.

## Beyond Gender-Biased Social Policy

Women constitute a majority of the beneficiaries of most major social welfare programs in existence today—with the exception of unemployment insurance. Among adults receiving AFDC, the largest single item in what is regarded as the welfare budget, over 80 percent of the beneficiaries are women. As Barbara Nelson reports, women constitute 70 percent of the housing beneficiaries, 65 percent of Medicare users, 62 percent of beneficiaries of social security (Old Age, Survivors and Disability Insurance or OASDI), 57 percent of food stamp recipients, and 56 percent of Medicaid users.[38] It is no wonder. These programs are intended primarily for the poor and aged, and women are a majority of both. Indeed, they are an increasing proportion of the poor (now roughly two thirds), a phenomenon known as the "feminization of poverty."

American social policies, including those targeted particularly at helping the economically vulnerable, are not simply part of the solution, they are part of the problem. They have helped women primarily in their capacity as wives or, especially, as mothers, and not because any positive value has been placed on removing women from a dependent state. As Barbara Nelson observes, "The poorer a woman, the greater the likelihood that she makes a claim for benefits on the basis of her position as a wife or mother."[39] One of the reasons is that women's poverty is increased substantially by their economic dependence brought on by the dependence for care that others place in them. Here it must be reemphasized that those who depend on women's care include not just children and elderly relatives, but able-bodied working husbands. Moreover, whereas the more obviously vulnerable such as children and elderly relatives depend on women's care and caring, husbands have also depended psychologically

[37] Elizabeth Waldman, "Labor Force Statistics from a Family Perspective," *Monthly Labor Review* 106 (December 1983): 16–20.

[38] Nelson, "Women's Poverty and Women's Citizenship," 209–231.

[39] Ibid, 223.

on women's dependency itself, a point made as long as a century ago by John Stuart Mill in his "Subjection of Women."[40] Although this point might suggest that gender divisions of labor make women and men mutually and, therefore, acceptably dependent upon each other, the dependency of men on women's dependency and the particular vulnerabilities of women created by others' dependence on them means we cannot properly say that the women and men in this relationship are truly interdependent, a term that would suggest more symmetry of power.[41]

Because of gender role assumptions, the family presumption in caring—that those outside the family, and especially government, have only a residual role to play—is really a presumption that women should have the primary role in caring or offering personal services and only a secondary role in financial provision. Conversely, this outlook defines men's primary role as provision and their secondary role as caring. Contrary to the standard rendition of social policy, we do not assume a single line of responsibility for caring that runs from family to other private individuals and organizations to government. Predominant beliefs and attitudes encompass a dual hierarchy of responsibility, one for provision and one for caring. For provision the line extends from the male "head of the family" outward, in ideological terms skipping over the female adult on the grounds that it is less demoralizing for a man to be supported by outside males (or agencies) than to be supported by a woman. For caring, the line extends from the wife and mother outward, in ideological terms skipping over the male adult on the grounds that men are not competent at caring or that their primary role is provision. Here lies another interesting assumption: a man cannot provide *and* care, a combination of efforts faced by most married women today. The reality contradicts the belief; women do indeed provide. There has been somewhat less change in familial patterns of caring men; their assumption of the caring role has not increased as dramatically as has women's assumption of the provision role.

In order for our policies to cease supporting the dependency of women, it is necessary for society to cease depending on women as women; that is, it is necessary that we do not define women in terms of what have up to now been considered women's unique roles and propensities toward caring. This also requires that we no longer depend on men as men or, in other words, on the man's exclusive roles as provider.

The pressing policy question that arises from this discussion is: If we abandon the gender division of responsibility in the family, who will provide and, especially, who will care? Do we place the primary responsibility on governmental

[40] John Stuart Mill, "The Subjection of Women," in Alice Rossi, ed., *Essays in Sex Equality* (Chicago: University of Chicago Press, 1970), 123–242. For a psychoanalytically based attempt to explain this relationship, see Nancy Chodorow, *The Reproduction of Mothering: Psychoanalysis and the Sociology of Gender* (Berkeley: University of California Press, 1978).

[41] For more discussion of intrafamilial vulnerability and dependence see Goodin, *Protecting the Vulnerable*, chap. 4; and Patricia Tulloch, "Gender and Dependency," in Dorothy Broom, ed., *Unfinished Business: Social Justice for Women in Australia* (Sydney, Australia: Allen and Unwin, 1984).

institutions? This is certainly the view taken by conservative critics of feminist arguments, who see women's apparent abandonment of exclusive domestic roles as both the cause of the need for social services and as a force that will weaken men's incentives to be providers. It has also been the suggestion of some early Marxist theorists, who called for the "socialization" of domestic labor, and of the influential Progressive, Charlotte Perkins Gilman, who at the turn of the century offered a slightly different picture of taking domestic labor out of the home and out of the realm of women's familial responsibility.[42]

It would be a sad commentary on the human state if our acceptance of responsibility to help others is based only on a structure of gender inequality and power hierarchies. As Robert Goodin has argued, our fundamental moral responsibilities spring from the situation of being able to help those who are vulnerable and dependent, and especially those who are vulnerable to us.[43] We have these responsibilities regardless of gender. One cannot shirk moral responsibilities on the basis of a functionalism of gender.

Goodin's theory of responsibility and vulnerability is important, because it provides a way of analyzing and assessing our hierarchies of responsibility for others. It is in the intimacy of the family that we are most likely to find both vulnerability and ability to help that is linked to specific individuals, especially with respect to the kind of necessary caring that has been defined as women's responsibility. Responsibility does move outward to family, friends, community, and others most likely to be aware of the situation and have individual and mutual ties to those who need help. By emphasizing the notion of those who are next most responsible, Goodin draws the line of caring to the community as a whole and its administrative voice, government, which, he argues, has responsibility under three circumstances: "when no one has been assigned primary responsibility," when "those with primary responsibilities . . . prove unable to discharge them," and when "the persons with primary responsibilities prove unwilling to discharge them."[44]

This construction of the residual responsibility of government does not leave us where we started, with government providing only the barest of safety nets for those who have already fallen. We know, for example, that parents are unable to work at full time jobs with inflexible schedules (as most have) and take care of dependent children at the same time. If we, as a community know this to be a pattern in a significant proportion of economically active members of our society, we could argue that we as a community, through government, have a responsibility to help. Alternative means of assistance include workplace policies that mandate more flexible job schedules; parental leave policies that allow parents leave time without making them and their families more vulnerable through loss of pay, benefits, or career opportunities; and direct or indirect provision of child care servies. Goodin argues that the purpose of social policy is

[42] Charlotte Perkins Gilman, *Women and Economics* (New York: Harper and Row, 1966).

[43] Goodin, *Protecting the Vulnerable.*

[44] Ibid, 151–52.

to protect the vulnerable and dependent. Protecting the vulnerable implies protecting those at particular risk, not just those who are already in trouble. It follows that social policy, in seeking to protect the vulnerable and dependent, should not at the same time create vulnerability and dependency. Our minimalist social policies up to this point have done just that.

Women have suffered, in a sense, from the tendency to make relatively rigid distinctions between *social* policies and *rights* policies. There is not a space here to repeat in full the arguments that claim that the distinctions are not great and that some social policies, including the provision of certain services, constitute rights.[45] Let us, rather, briefly consider one example that has served as a theme throughout this discussion. For most of our history, Americans have accepted the idea that women should be dependent upon their husbands and that they should not, if possible, provide for themselves through gainful employment. Following from this idea, men have been accorded higher priority in training and jobs, even when there were more qualified women available. In public debate today, policies aimed at securing education and jobs for women are labelled rights policies. If we also thought of them in terms of social policy, we would be more likely to define the goals of these policies as providing for the general welfare—that is, of providing the means whereby a significant portion of the society could become more economically secure and less dependent and vulnerable. We would then not only allow women to become self-reliant, we would encourage it.[46]

This is a call for collective as well as individual responsibility and it is a criticism of crass individualism, even if that individualism is softened with an overlay of voluntaristic altruism. Advocacy of collective responsibility does not, as some critics would argue, mean the demise of the individual as an agent in society. To the contrary, it is entirely consistent with Albert Weale's argument that "there is one overriding imperative to which government action ought to be subject to its authority. This principle of autonomy asserts that all persons are entitled to respect as deliberative and purposive agents capable of formulating their own projects, and that as part of this respect there is a governmental obligation to bring into being or preserve the conditions in which this autonomy can be realized."[47]

This is precisely what has been missing in social policy as it concerns women: the preservation of conditions of autonomy. In a sense this is true for men as well, because their roles also have been dictated by prescriptions that are made on the basis of sex. But for women the prescription is dependency including dependency of identity itself.[48] Social policy has assumed that women are not au-

[45] See, for example, T.H. Marshall, "Citizenship and Social Class," in Marshall, *Sociology At The Crossroads and Other Essays* (London: Heinemann, 1963); and Mishra, *Society and Social Policy.*

[46] For a parallel discussion of policies of toleration versus liberation, see Virginia Sapiro, *The Political Integration of Women: Roles, Socialization, and Politics* (Urbana: University of Illinois Press, 1983), chap. 8.

[47] Weale, *Political Theory and Social Policy*, 42.

[48] For the classic development of this theme, see Simone de Beauvoir, *The Second Sex* (New York: Knopf, 1953).

tonomous individuals and moral agents, but that they live contingent lives. With specific regard to their economic lives, their ability to provide for themselves and others is supposed to be contingent upon whether others around them need their caring services. Choice as a moral agent is missing. Women are defined as individuals who place themselves second. The irony is that this "altruism" often keeps them from helping not only themselves, but others they would wish and feel obligated to help.

We are in great need of constructing more humane social policy for the future and also of reinterpreting what has gone before. Historically, for vast numbers of men the individualistic ideology of self-reliance has not worked. For women it never existed.*

* I would like to thank Graham Wilson and Bob Goodin for their helpful comments and criticisms.

# [25]

*Acta Sociologica* 1987 (30), 3/4:255–270

# The Scandinavian Welfare States – Towards Sexual Equality or a New Kind of Male Domination?

*Birte Siim*
Institute of Social Development and Planning, Aalborg University

This paper studies the debate about the Scandinavian welfare states from a feminist perspective, focusing on the differences between a feminist perspective and the dominant liberal and critical Marxist understanding of the welfare state. In particular it focuses on the argument that the Scandinavian welfare states are the most advanced in relation to women and discusses both the potentialities and dangers in the Scandinavian welfare states in relation to women. Feminists have pointed out that the concept of gender has been disregarded from a theoretical and methodological point of view in both liberal and Marxist analyses of the welfare state. The fundamental concepts have been either the individual or the class, and the determining forces of the development of the welfare state have been found in the political sphere or in the economy or in the interrelation between the two spheres. The paper points to the need to integrate gender relations in the theoretical model for an analysis of the welfare state and emphasizes the need to explore the relationship between the family and the state (and the family and the economy) in the different welfare states. The paper emphasizes that the qualitative differences in the organization of care work are important for understanding the institutional differences between the welfare states, and especially the Scandinavian welfare states, where motherhood and care work has today become a part of social citizenship. The author argues that even though women have in important ways become empowered in the Scandinavian welfare states as mothers, workers and citizens, they have at the same time become subsumed under a new kind of male domination in the public sphere. A further exploration of this new kind of male domination must transcend the theoretical framework of both Marxism and liberalism and must begin to rethink such central concepts as citizenship, power and interests.

During the last 25 years we have witnessed dramatic changes in both socioeconomic structures and in the position of women in society. Industrialization, urbanization and development of the modern welfare state have radically changed people's daily lives and their perceptions about themselves. During the 1960s and 1970s women have gradually become integrated as workers on the labour market and at the same time the family has changed and the state has taken over some of the responsibilities for care of the elderly, the sick, children and the disabled. As a result the meaning and practice of motherhood, housework and care work has changed. The new women's movement has been both an integrated part of and an independent response to these changes. Women have fought for the right to abortion, for equal pay and for abolishment of the sexual division of labour and male dominance.

During the 1970s and 1980s we have witnessed an institutionalization of an official equality policy through legislation and through the establishment of such new institutions as the Equality Council. It is paradoxical that at a time when women's political activity as citizens has increased greatly both within the formal and the informal political system there is a tendency towards a growing rate of unemployment and an economic marginalization of especially older and unskilled women and of young women. The position of women in the modern welfare state has been researched, but there have been few attempts to study the potentialities and dangers for women in the Scandinavian welfare states.[1]

During the last 20 years there is no doubt that women have obtained more power and influence in the public sphere as workers, mothers and citizens. But the fact that sex is no longer a legitimate base of male domination does not necessarily mean that male domination no longer exists. On the contrary, it can be argued that in the modern welfare states women have become subjected to a new kind of male domination in the public sphere (Hernes 1982, 1983, Borchorst & Siim 1984, 1985).

Liberal analyses have often focused on the positive aspects of the Scandinavian welfare states towards women as individuals, while Marxist analyses have focused on the double oppression of women as workers and mothers within the capitalist state. In contrast, I argue that the Scandinavian welfare states have had contradictory effects on women's lives: On the one hand the specific character of the social state[2] with an institutionalization of motherhood and care work as a part of social citizenship and the specific character of women's integration on the labour market, where women have become part of the permanent labour force with relative high wages, has been favourable to women. On the other hand women have primarily been objects in the development of the modern welfare states and have not been able to determine their interests as social and political agents, and the development of the corporate state structure with a high degree of centralization has been detrimental to women's collective interests. There seems to be a double relationship between women and the Scandinavian welfare states: On the one hand, in different ways the state has helped produce and reproduce the sexual division of labour and male domination. But on the other hand the state has also in certain areas helped to change the sexual division of labour and male dominance and has attempted to create a greater equality between men and women, especially on the labour market and within the educational system (Borchorst & Siim 1984).

In the following I look firstly at different neo-Marxist attempts to explain the development of the Scandinavian welfare states, and then I discuss a recent attempt to analyse the position of women in the Scandinavian welfare states from within the neo-Marxist framework. Secondly, I present the feminist critique of the liberal and Marxist understanding of the Scandinavian welfare states. And then I look at future development of the welfare state from a feminist perspective and discuss women's role in changing the social and political institutions of the welfare state. Finally, I discuss some of the theoretical challenges to both Marxists and feminists from the Scandinavian experiences.

## 1. The neo-Marxist understanding of the Scandinavian welfare states

Neo-Marxist analyses of the Scandinavian welfare states have focused primarily on structural class conflicts and on the need to increase the power of the working class through political and economic struggle. In this perspective the Scandinavian welfare states are built on a 'class compromise', i.e. an alliance between the interests of the capitalist class and the interests of the working class that is an expression of the relative strength of the working class vis-à-vis the capitalist forces. Gender relations have usually been absent from the theoretical model or gender has been subsumed under the dominant category of class and gender conflicts have been understood as a part of the struggle between organized capital and labour.

In the following I focus specifically on Gøsta Esping-Andersen's model for an analysis of the Scandinavian welfare states, using it to illustrate some of the strengths and weaknesses of the neo-Marxist approach (Esping-Andersen 1980, 1981 and 1984). Then I analyse how the 'women question' has been integrated into the neo-Marxist model by looking at the work of Mary Ruggie, who understands the position of women as a reflection of the position of the working class within society (Ruggie 1984). Finally, I present a recent interpretation of the Danish welfare state by Niels Ole Finnemann, who has focused on the contradictions and continuity in the Danish political culture by looking at the development of ideas of the Social Democratic party (1985). Finnemann deals with gender relations within the context of the changes of the paternalistic spirit of the Social Democratic party and is aware of gender conflicts. His analysis therefore raises important questions about women's values and interests in relation to the Social Democratic party and the working class, and represents an interesting attempt to incorporate a feminist perspective in a Marxist analysis of the Scandinavian welfare state.

### *The Scandinavian welfare states as a model of social citizenship*

Gøsta Esping-Andersen has interpreted the Scandinavian welfare states as a prototype of Marshall's ideas about a social citizenship. In this model the welfare of citizens is not only related to social reproduction of individuals and households, social and welfare policy is defined in a broad sense linked to the economic policies. In the Scandinavian welfare states social policy is built on an institutionalized reallocation of welfare which is contrasted to a model of social policy built on the residual welfare model and a model built on the social insurance model, where recipients receive only what they have paid for (Esping-Andersen 1984).

In his theoretical model for comparing the development of the Danish and Swedish welfare states Esping-Andersen combines three variables: class structure, class politics (or class formation) and state politics (1980). Class structure influences class politics which in turn influences state policies, but there is a dialectical relationship between class politics and state policies in the sense that specific state policies influence the way class politics develop. In Esping-Andersen's work politics matter in the sense that the state is semi-autonomous vis-à-vis the economy, which means that specific state policies must be explained in a historical context. The leading hypothesis in the book *Social Class, Social Democracy and State Policy* is the claim that 'unless social democratic parties break with the "consensus" politics and move in the direction of reforms which aim at controlling capital, they will tend to decompose' (Esping-Andersen 1980:13). This means on the one hand that it is possible for the state to act as an independent variable in relation to a specific class structure, and further that it is the relationship between the state and the market economy that matters, whereas the relationship between the state and the family (or civil society) is not an integrated part of the model.

Esping-Andersen has used his model in an illuminating historical analysis of the differences between the Danish and the Swedish welfare states using three case studies – the pension reforms, economic democracy and housing reforms – to illustrate the differences between state policies in the two countries. On this basis he concludes that the Danish, but not the Swedish, social democrats were in a process of realignment to the detriment of the social democrats. There are many strong points in his approach compared with other interpretations of the Scandinavian welfare state, especially the emphasis on the differences in state policies and on the role of social and political agents in the development of the welfare state. People are not reduced to objects of the dominant economic structures. On the contrary, the aim of the analysis is to study in what way the working class has influenced state policies, and how different types of state intervention affect people.

There are, however, also some weaknesses in his approach which result in a somewhat one-dimensional analysis of the welfare state, and specifically of the differences between Denmark and Sweden. Contrary to the intentions, I find that the model is reductionist, because it focuses primarily on state intervention and state control of the economy, and the major categories of state policies are reduced to commodity and production policies. This means that the model leaves out the interrelation between the state and the family and consequently does not explain the different organization of social care and human reproduction. This is surprising, because the specific character of social citizenship in the Scandinavian welfare states has been the analytical starting point for his analyses (see esp. Esping-Andersen 1981 and 1984). It would be important to explore more precisely what it is that determines the different character of social citizenship, and to study how the concept can be used in an analysis of the different types of welfare states. Esping-Andersen has compared the decommodification in social welfare policy in relation to income maintenance programmes, but has not explored the differences in relation to collective services. Using case studies in relation to the collective organization of services would no doubt have brought the comparative analysis to a different conclusion. I find that there is a contradiction in his framework of analysis: On the one hand the specific character of social citizenship is used to define the different types of welfare state, while on the other the different organization of collective services in relation to care for children, the elderly, the sick and disabled is viewed as methodologically irrelevant and collective services are defined solely as unproductive activities and expenses.

The concept of social citizenship is in itself gender neutral, and so it is important to analyse to what extent and in what way it can be used in an analysis of gender conflicts and of differences in gender interests? I have argued elsewhere that analysing the different organization of social care is an important part of understanding the reproduction of the social organization of society (Siim 1987a). These differences in the organization of social care cannot be explained solely with reference to class structure, class formation or state policies. An important characteristic of the Scandinavian welfare states has been the development of a specific division of work between the family and the state integrating motherhood and social care as part of social citizenship. It is important to ask how this specific type of state intervention developed, what it means to people, and how this specific character of social citizenship has affected gender relations. Looking at the different organization of care for children, the elderly, the sick and disabled as a necessary part of the social division of labour and not as an unproductive activity may give a more positive picture of the Danish welfare state.[3] The differences in the organization of social care cannot be explained solely with reference to class relations. Historically there have been agents other than class agents which have played an important role in the development of the welfare state.[4] It is therefore necessary to develop a more complex theoretical model that (a) incorporates social structure (family structure), (b) acknowledges social actors other than class, (c) differentiates between different categories of state policies in relation to social care, and finally (d) integrates gender relations and gender conflicts into the model.

### *Women's position in the Scandinavian welfare states*

The neo-Marxist understanding of the welfare state has also been used to analyse the position of women. Mary Ruggie has compared the positions of women in Sweden and Britain in her book *The State and Working Women* (1984). She contrasts the neo-Marxist understanding of the state with the pluralist understanding where the state is seen as a neutral agent and with the feminist understanding where the state is seen as predominantly oppressive as capitalist or patriarchal or both. In her analysis she attempts to explain the differences in women's position in Sweden and England by looking at: (a) economic determinants, (b) women-specific factors, and (c) the role of the state. Ruggie acknowledges that each of the three factors plays a certain part in explaining the differences in women's position, but she argues that 'the state is critical, for it mediates the effect of the two factors in addition to having an independent impact of its own'. The state is therefore understood as both an independent and an intervening factor.

Ruggie's understanding of the state as an independent and intervening variable and her emphasis on the importance of state policies for the position of women could be an important starting point. She argues further that the key to the changes that have occurred in Swedish policies for working women is 'the close association between concern for women, the labour market, and economic productivity'. She tries to explain the position of women solely by reference to the position of the working class:

> It is my thesis that the differential role of the state vis-à-vis women workers in Britain and Sweden reflects the differential status of labor more generally (Ruggie 1984:298).

There is no doubt that women's position is in some way linked to the position of the working class in society, but she actually subsumes the situation of women completely under the position of the working class. This thesis is apparently deduced from the theoretical model which raises fundamental theoretical and empirical problems. One problem is that historically there does not seem to be any automatic relation between a specific state policy and a specific policy towards women workers. The state often has a general policy which for some reason does not apply to women, exactly as a result of 'women-specific factors', like the ideology and meaning of women and the family in the dominant political culture. Another problem with the approach is the tendency to see women primarily as workers, thereby subsuming women's position as mothers, and citizens, under their position as workers. This is a consequence of subsuming gender relations under class relations. Whether this is the case is not solely a theoretical question. It is also a historical-specific question which must be studied in relation to the different types of welfare state.

I have argued that in the Scandinavian welfare states it is not possible to understand women's position without studying the relationship between the women's position as mothers, workers and citizens. In countries like Britain the political culture and public policies are familist in the sense that women's position as workers has actually been subsumed under their position as mothers.[5] Ruggie has argued that the Swedish state has to a large extent represented women's interests, even though she acknowledges that women have allowed other parties speaking on their behalf to pursue their interests (1984:345). Feminist scholars have recently stressed that women have a common interest in being present in the social and political institutions of the modern state as women, even though they do not necessarily pursue the same political goals. The implication of this would be that women's interests cannot be interpreted and represented adequately by other parties such as the state, the Social Democratic party or the working class (Jonasdottir 1985, 1987).

*Paternalism in the political culture of the Scandinavian welfare states*

Niels Ole Finnemann has analysed the political culture of Denmark by focusing on the development of the ideas of the Social Democratic party (1985). He argues that there has been continuity in the ideas of the Social Democratic party about the meaning of fundamental concepts like the state and nature. The state was understood as the incarnation of reason and nature as a rational universe. In contrast, he finds that there has been a radical change in the conception of the private sphere since the Second World War. One main thesis in his analysis is that there has been both a 'male' and a 'female' perspective on the development of the welfare state, specifically in relation to the family and on democracy. Although the 'female' perspective was never influential he has attempted to trace it empirically through what is called the existing 'female voices' within the Social Democratic party.

Finnemann calls the Social Democratic spirit 'the spirit of brotherhood', which is defined as a specific form of community and solidarity. This spirit of brotherhood has been formulated and reformulated in different historical periods. He argues that the political culture of paternalism has changed radically since the development of the modern welfare state: On the one hand there has been *'a liberation from the personal-patriarchal aspects of brotherhood where there is no longer given any priority to the male sex with reference to sexual power. On the other hand there has been a subsumption of the subjective female values under the objective male values of rationality' (Finnemann 1985:340–341).*

According to Finnemann the female perspective is connected with the 'values of family life and a dream about a democratic harmony between the sexes in the family and in the public sphere and with an ambivalence towards wage work'. The dominant political culture of the Social Democratic party after the Second World War is called state reformism in contrast to the earlier form of proletarian and popular reformism. State reformism has strived towards a rational organization of both the public and the private sphere by building a new net of state institutions to take over part of the care for the elderly, the sick, the children and the disabled. The kind of rationality which became the governing principle of state reformism was at the same time the male principle of rationality connected to the values of the public sphere. Although the modern welfare state was built on a new understanding between the public and the private sphere, Finnemann argues that it was still created on a gender-dualist foundation based on a split between technical rationality on the one hand and subjectivity and human creativity on the other. 'In this perspective male domination then is both expressed by and an expression of the priority given to the values of objectivity and technical rationality over values of care, creativity and subjectivity' (Finnemann 1985:332).

Finnemann's analysis of the Social Democratic spirit represents a serious attempt towards a comprehensive historical analysis of the political culture of the Scandinavian welfare states. His approach focuses on the values and ideas of the dominant Social Democratic party, on the relationship between the public and the private sphere and attempts to incorporate a gender perspective. The approach is inspiring and leaves both Marxists and feminists with a number of questions to be pursued. One main question for feminists is, what exactly is a female perspective and what does the female perspective on the family and on democracy that is put forward represent? How is it possible to talk only about one female perspective? And to what extent could this perspective ever be developed as an alternative to the dominant male view given the differences in women's social and economic situation? What is the material basis of the female perspective and of the new form of male domination in the modern welfare state?

Finnemann has presented us with an impressive critique of the dominant male form of rationality which he places within the Social Democratic party. I find, however, that there is a tendency to idealize the female perspective and to place it outside history. Historically there has been a tension between the values and interests of women in different positions and in different classes which it is important to analyse and which calls into question the formulation of only one female perspective on the development.[6] It is therefore necessary to analyse in what way and to what extent it would have been possible to develop an alternative female perspective within a given historical period. There is a dualist tendency in Finnemann's approach that causes him to focus on the split between the dominant male rationality and the dominated female subjectivity. This may be connected with the methodological emphasis on the history of ideas and the consequent under-evaluation of the practical realization of these ideas in social institutions and state policies. It can be argued that the Social Democratic party has been characterized by contradictions within the values and ideas, which have also affected the principles of organization within the modern institutions of the welfare state. The dominant values of rationality and objectivity have been in conflict with other values, like the rationality of care and the values of equality and solidarity. Therefore the institutions of the family, the state and the economy are in different ways and to a different extent all influenced by these contradictions. There is no 'haven in a heartless world' (Widerberg 1985).

## 2. The feminist critique of the Scandinavian welfare states

The feminist critique of the Scandinavian welfare states has been a critique of both the dominant liberal and of the critical Marxist framework trying to transcend them both. The feminist critique of liberalism has focused on women's activities as citizens and on the relationship between the public and the private sphere, while the feminist critique of Marxism has focused on the structural relationship between the family and the state and on women's relations to the modern welfare state as mothers and workers.[7] Feminist scholars have analysed different aspects of the welfare state in relation to women: The immediate objectives and the content of public policies, the values and assumptions behind them and the interests that have guided them, and finally the consequences of different public policies for women. From this perspective the welfare state has not been gender neutral, rather the welfare state has through its public policies, political ideologies and organizational principles helped produce and reproduce a sexual division of labour and male domination.

In the following I look first at the feminist critique of liberalism and on the attempts to transcend it by focusing on women's participation as citizens in the formal and informal political system (Hernes 1982, 1985; Halsaa 1977; Togeby 1985). Secondly, I look at the feminist critique of Marxism and the attempts to transcend it by developing the concept of human reproduction and by rethinking the concept of patriarchy in connection with the analysis of women and the welfare state (Liljestrøm 1982; Edvuards 1986; Borchorst & Siim 1984, 1987). Finally, I discuss the future development of the Scandinavian welfare states focusing on women's role as citizens and political agents.

*The critique of the public–private split in liberal thinking*

Feminist scholars in political theory have developed a radical critique of the classical liberal thinkers and of the modern conception of democracy and citizenship (Eisenstein 1981; Pateman 1985a, 1985b; Hernes 1982). One of their main points is the contention that the conception of citizenship and democracy is based on a division between the ideas of individual freedom and equality in the public sphere and the values of dependency and inequality connected with the private sphere of the family. Feminists have documented that the universal categories of the individual and the citizen are not really universal, but are sex/gender specific, or masculine. The conclusion is that the public world of politics can only be understood in connection with the private world of the family, and in this perspective it becomes necessary to rethink fundamental categories of liberalism like the concept of the individual and the concept of citizenship (Pateman 1985a).

Political scientists like Helga Hernes have focused predominantly on women's position within the institutional structure of the state and in the formal and informal political system (Hernes 1982, 1983). Although women's representation in the formal political system has been growing in all the Scandinavian countries during the 70s and was by 1985 around 25%, which is the highest in the western world, this growing representation has not necessarily given women more power in relation to men. There is still an unequal power relationship between men and women, and women are still absent from the central arenas of decision-making, i.e. the powerful economic and political elites. It has been documented that women's representation in the corporate system of interest organizations, state administrators and experts is only around 10%, which is much lower than in the parliamentary system. Hernes' conclusion is that in the Scandinavian welfare states men have mainly been the participators and women the receivers in the political process:

> From this perspective one can describe the Scandinavian state form as a tutelary state for women since they have had a minimal role in the actual decision-making process concerning the distribution of power (Hernes 1983:7).

An increase in women's representation in the parliamentary system, then, does not necessarily mean an increase in the participation of women in the political process. Likewise, an increasing women's participation in the political system does not necessarily mean that women increase their real power in society in relation to men. Hernes has argued that in the Scandinavian welfare states women's relations to the state have become critical for women, because they have moved from the private dependency of their individual husbands to the public dependency of the state. This new dependency is connected with women's three different but interrelated roles as clients, employees and citizens. The conclusion of her analysis is therefore that although the development of the modern welfare state has given women important social and economic advantages, women have become subordinated to a new sexual power hierarchy within the political system. Men are still the agents and women the objects in the political system (Hernes 1983).

Other political scientists, like Lise Togeby and Drude Dahlerup, have analysed women's growing participation within the political parties, trade unions and within the new social movements. Although women and men today participate to the same extent in the new social movements, there is apparently still a gender profile in the kind of activities women and men engage in. This growing mobilization and participation of women in politics as citizens is an important feature of the modern welfare state which must be explored further. At the same time women are still underrepresented in the leadership of the political parties and within the leadership of the trade union movement. An increase in the participation of women in the political process apparently does not by itself give women more real power in relation to men within the political system or in society as a whole.

Hernes has documented women's low participation and lack of power in the formal political system, and Togeby and Dahlerup have documented women's growing participation in the informal political system and the growing participation at the basis level of the formal political system. The different conclusions point towards the need for more comprehensive analyses comparing women's different kinds of activities within the different parts of the political process. And it points towards the need for analyses that combine structural and more action-oriented approaches to politics. There is no doubting the importance of studying why women participate more in the social movements than in other political activities, and of studying why women are better represented in the parliamentary than in the corporate channel and of asking what difference it makes for women's position in society as mothers and workers. It is likewise important to study what the connection is between women's activities as citizens and the changes in women's socioeconomic position in society.

The feminist critique of liberalism has been the basis for a debate among feminists about the understanding of the public/private split, the meaning of politics and the perspective of the political struggle. Some have argued the need to abolish the distinction between the public and the private sphere altogether, while others have argued that it is important to maintain a difference between the different dimensions of human activities.[6] I tend to agree with Pateman, who has argued that the aim of the critical feminist theory of liberalism is not to make the political dimension of life disappear but to make it part of everyday life and to change the power relations in the private and public world in a way that makes women's participation in political life as social and political agents possible (Pateman 1985a).

### *The feminist critique of the patriarchal–capitalist state*

Marxist feminists have analysed women's relations to the welfare state by focusing on the structural contradictions between the labour market, the family and the state and between women's different position as workers and mothers. Some have emphasized the oppressive character of the capitalist state vis-à-vis women. Others have emphasized the new form of male domination in the public sphere and have tried to rethink the concept of patriarchy and use it in connection with the analysis of the modern welfare state (Einstein 1983; Liljestrøm 1982; Borchorst & Siim 1984). There have been several attempts to differentiate between a patriarchal family and social patriarchy, i.e. 'between the hierarchical sexual organization for reproduction of sex-gender as it exists in the family and the organization of sex-gender as it exists throughout society understood as a totality'. In this perspective patriarchy cannot be understood simply as 'the rule of the father' or as 'the power of men over women'. Instead the emphasis has been on the historical changes in patriarchy and on the transformation of patriarchy from the power of men in the families to the power of men through the state (Brown 1979; Boris & Bardaglio 1983). In this perspective the welfare state can be described as a form of 'social' or state patriarchy (Borchorst & Siim 1984).

In my own comparative work, and in the analysis of the Danish welfare state with Anette Borchorst, we have emphasized the contradictory character of women's integration in the public sphere and the interrelation between women's different positions as mothers, workers and citizens (Borchorst & Siim 1985; Siim 1987a). In Denmark the modern welfare state has been based on a new form of partnership between the state and the family – and to some extent between women and the state. Under the leadership of the Social Democratic party the state has formulated a conscious policy of socializing important parts of human reproduction such as care for children, the sick, the elderly and the disabled by building a network of public institutions. On this basis it can be argued that motherhood and care work in the Scandinavian countries have become part of social citizenship (Siim 1987a and 1987b).

The Scandinavian welfare states have been based on the most extensive usage of the universal rights of the individual vis-à-vis the state, but this right of the individual became a working-class ideal which was nowhere automatically extended to women. It is therefore necessary to examine separately to what extent and in what ways these rights have applied to women in the different Scandinavian countries. Furthermore, it becomes necessary to explore in what ways and to what extent activities from the private sphere of the family, like motherhood and care work, have become incorporated into the understanding of social citizenship. In this perspective the concept of social citizenship as originally formulated by Marshall has to be reformulated (Marshall 1984).

The Scandinavian development of the 'social state' or 'social citizenship', which has been most advanced in Denmark and Sweden, has been interpreted in completely different ways: One interpretation, like Ruggie and to some extent Dahlerup and Togeby, emphasizes the positive aspects of this development and sees the socioeconomic improvements in women's situation, women's increasing integration on the labour market and their growing participation in the political process as an illustration of the strength of the Scandinavian 'model' in relation to women. Others, like Helga Hernes, emphasize the continued reproduction of unequal power relations in the public sphere and on women's object status and lack of power in the corporate state structure and in the central political and economic institutions of the state. On this basis it can be argued that the Scandinavian welfare states are still dominated by a sexual division of labour and male domination although the patriarchal power hierarchy has taken on a qualitatively new form. Both interpretations cover important aspects of the contradictory character of the Scandinavian experience for women and must therefore be incorporated in a theoretical framework of analysis.

I have argued that specific organization of care work built on the partnership between the state and the family in relation to human reproduction can be seen as one precondition for empowering women as a group in relation to men both as workers and mothers and citizens by decreasing women's economic dependency of their individual husbands (Siim 1987b). This transformation of social citizenship has also influenced women's political activities as citizens, but there is no automatic connection between women's socioeconomic position and the sexual power relations in the public sphere. Women have become integrated into a new kind of sexual power hierarchy within the administrative and political system of the welfare state. In this perspective the development of the modern welfare state can be interpreted as a change from a family to a social patriarchy. The welfare state can be said to be patriarchal to the extent that women have been absent from the decision-making process and to the extent that public policies have been governed by male assumptions and male values and have predominantly served male interests.[7]

Women's experiences illuminate the two contradictory aspects of the Scandinavian welfare states – the oppressive and the supportive: On the one hand the welfare state has been supportive towards women and has helped to decrease women's personal dependency of individual men as mothers and workers. On the other hand the welfare state has also been oppressive towards women, has subsumed women under a new kind of centralized power hierarchy and has disregarded the collective interests of women or subsumed women's interests and values under the dominant state rationality. The political culture has also been ambivalent towards women: On the one hand it has stressed the general values of equality and solidarity and accepted motherhood and care work as part of social citizenship. On the other hand the conception of motherhood and care work has been governed by male assumptions and has served male interests. The general belief in equality has only recently included equality policies between men and women and then only to a very limited extent.

*The future development of the welfare state*

Evaluation of the future development of the Scandinavian welfare states, and specifically the future role of women in the welfare state, cannot be separated from the theoretical understanding of the nature of the state and of the historical interpretation of the determinant forces behind the development welfare state. Women's growing political mobilization and the increase in women's participation in politics during the 1970s and 1980s is one important aspect of the modern welfare state. Yet there is no agreement among feminists of what women's interests are or of how to define women's issues (Peterson 1984), and it is still an open question what impact women's political mobilization can have on the recent attempts to restructure the welfare state.[8]

What are women's interests today, and what do women want from the state? Historically, women have only to a limited extent been politically active in the formal political system, and there are many examples of how women have at times expressed different interests in relation to specific political issues. Women have disagreed about issues, like the right to abortion and the right to voluntary motherhood. On the other hand women have at times also expressed common interests and have built alliances around common goals, as e.g. the right to vote and the right to education and equal pay.

Women's socioeconomic position, sociopolitical profile and culture have changed dramatically during the last 20 years. Today there are strong socioeconomic and sociopolitical factors that both unite and divide women. In the Scandinavian countries there is a fundamental difference between the position of the young and well-educated women on the one side and the older and unskilled women on the other. Still an open question is the extent to which, and on what subjects, women will be able to unite and fight for common interests. It has been argued that women have a common interest in politicizing motherhood and care work, but they do not necessarily have the same solutions as to how these issues should be organized (Halsaa 1977; Stacey 1983). Eisenstein has argued that women today have a common interest as working mothers, but women also have a very different position on the labour market and can therefore also be expected to develop different solutions and strategies towards the labour market.

Political scientists have traced a gender gap and a specific gender profile in relation to politics. Women have a tendency to vote to the Left compared to men and women to a larger extent than men support the development of the 'social state' and are more positive than men towards a decrease in military spending and more positive than men towards the peace movement (Goul Andersen 1985; Peterson 1984). On the other hand women today disagree markedly in some countries around such feminist issues as abortion and equal rights and on moral issues connected with the family (Stacey 1983; Luker 1985). It is therefore necessary to explore further what the gender profiles in politics mean and in what way they can influence politics. It is no longer enough to define women's issues either as issues connected to human reproduction, especially motherhood and care work, or to women's position as working mothers.

There have been attempts to link differences in women's sociopolitical profiles to differences in women's socioeconomic and cultural position. It has been argued that there is an important difference between the old women's culture and the new women's culture in the sense that the old women's culture, centred predominantly around human reproduction in the family, has tended to pull women in a Conservative direction. In contrast, the new women's culture defined by women's double identification with the private and the public sphere has tended to pull women towards the Left (Goul Andersen 1985; Haalsaa 1985). From this perspective women could play an important role in the economic crisis in the present struggle to change the social and political institutions of the welfare state in a more democratic direction.

## 3. Theoretical challenges from the Scandinavian experiences

In order to grasp the complexities and contradictions of the Scandinavian welfare states and the contradictory experiences of women (and other social groups) it has become necessary to transcend both the liberal and the Marxist understanding of the welfare state and start to rethink central concepts like citizenship, power and interests. The Marxist perspective has emphasized the structural oppression of women on the labour market, within state institutions and in the family. From a structural perspective women have never obtained equality or equal power to men on the labour market, neither within state institutions nor in the family. This does not mean, however, that women have been powerless objects of the patriarchal-capitalist state. In a historical-dynamic perspective women have on the other hand also become empowered as workers, mothers and citizens and have increased their participation in the political process. The liberal perspective has emphasized women's activities as citizens and women's growing participation in the formal and informal political process. This growing participation of women as citizens is important, but must be combined with an understanding of women's structural oppression as mothers and workers and knowledge of the structural barriers on the labour market and in the political system to women's equality in the Scandinavian welfare states.

The changes in the nature of male domination with the advance of the modern welfare state appear to have shifted the locus of oppression from the private to the public sphere which has made the state a critical factor for women. In this perspective it becomes more important than ever that women strive collectively to be present as women within public institutions and organizations as one precondition for transforming the values, public policies and priorities and institutional structure of the welfare state. Even though there are today socioeconomic, cultural and political factors that both divide and unite women, women have a common interest in being present within the institutions in order to control the conditions for future choices and change them in a way that make them more responsive to women's needs and interests (Jonasdottir 1987).

The complex realities and contradictory experiences for women in the Scandinavian welfare states can be used as a basis for transcending the dualistic positions and for developing a more comprehensive framework of analysis: The welfare state has in some ways and in some areas given women more power and in this way it can be argued that the Scandinavian welfare states have given women an excellent foundation for collectively changing the social and political institutions and making them more democratic and more responsive to women's needs and interests. On the other hand there still exist strong structural barriers for any real empowering of women as social and political agents enabling them to determine their own interests. One of the most important barriers seems to be the high degree of centralization within the administrative and political system of the Scandinavian welfare states and a political culture that has subsumed women's needs and interests under the interests of economic class organizations, and which has only recently begun to recognize women's interests as separate and legitimate interests vis-à-vis the interests of the working class.

## Notes

1 The Unfinished Democracy was the first major research project focusing on women's position in the political system in the Nordic countries (Elina Haavia-Manila 1985). This study together with Helga Maria Hernes' work has contributed towards the debate about women's position in the Scandinavian welfare states (Hernes 1982, 1983). Feminist scholars outside the Scandinavian countries have been fascinated by the Scandinavian experiences, and they have usually been very positive towards the Scandinavian 'model' (see e.g. Teich Adams & Teich Winston 1980; Ruggie 1984).

2 The term the 'social' state is usually defined in relation to social policies in a broad Anglo-Saxon sense meaning 'education, health care, social security, housing and social services'.

3 I have argued that in relation to the organization of social care Denmark and Sweden are more advanced than Norway which actually resembles England more than the other two Scandinavian countries (Siim 1987b). Bent Rold Andersen (1984) has argued that Denmark is actually closer than the other Nordic countries to the Nordic principles of social policy in the sense that the rights of the individual are more universal.

4 In Denmark, social movement, like the Frøbel movement, has played a progressive role in relation to social care for children with demands for kindergartens. Several researchers have pointed to the historical importance of different kinds of women's reform movements for the advancement of social, educational and health policies (Zaretsky 1982; Sapiro 1986).

5 I have argued that the political culture of Britain is familist in the sense that (a) the family plays a primary role in the human reproduction and (b) state policies have predominantly reproduced a sexual division of work with a male breadwinner and a dependent wife (Siim 1987a).

6 Historically the class differences among women are very visible because women from different classes were organized separately. There has always been a tension between the fight for equality on the labour market and within the educational system and the identification with the values connected with the family, but this tension has had different expression at different times (Hirdman 1984).

7 This discussion is also part of the discussion about how to interpret the feminist slogan that 'the personal is political'. For an attempt to define politics see Halsaa 1977, ch. 2, Elshtain 1981 and Pateman 1985a.

8 This problem about how to decide more precisely when specific policies can be said to be patriarchal or not is important. Analytically it is important to differentiate between three different levels of analysis; one level where we study how the specific policies have come about and what their immediate objectives are. Another level which focuses on the assumptions and values behind them and the interests that have guided them, and finally

one level where we focus on their implementation and the consequences of these policies for women (Randell 1982; Siim 1987b).

9 I have focused on women's situation in the economic crisis in another paper arguing that the crisis has in different ways tended to politicize the family, the sexual division of labour and male dominance in the U.S., Britain and Denmark (Siim 1986).

## References

Adams, T. C. & Winston, T. K. 1980. *Mothers at Work. Public Policies in the U.S., Sweden and China.* Princeton: Princeton University Press.

Andersen, B. R. 1984. Kan vi bevare velfærdsstaten. I og II (Can We Preserve the Welfare State). Amtskommunernes & Kommunernes Forskningsinstitut.

Andersen, G. J. 1984. *Kvinder og politik* (Women and Politics). Århus: Politica.

Borchorst, A. & Siim, B. 1984. *Kvinder og velfærdsstaten. Mellem moderskab og lønarbejde i 100 år* (Women and the Welfare State Between Motherhood and Wagework in 100 Years). Aalborg: Aalborg University Press.

Borchorst, A. & Siim, B. 1985. Women and the Advanced Welfare State – a New Kind of Patriarchal Power? Forthcoming in Showstack-Sassoon (ed.), *From a Women's Point of View: New Perspectives on the Welfare State.* London: Hutchinson.

Boris, E. & Bardiglio, P. 1983. The Transformation of Patriarchy: The Historic Role of the State. *In* I. Diamond (ed.), *Families, Politics and Public Policies. A Dialogue on Women and the State.* New York: Longman.

Brown, C. 1979. Mothers, Fathers and Children. From Private to Public Patriarchy. *In* L. Sargent (ed.), *Women and Revolution.* New York: Monthly Review Press.

Dahlerup, D. 1984. *Is the New Women's Liberation Movement Dead? Social Movement Decline and Change: The Case of the Danish Feminist Movement 1970 till Today.* Paper for the Conference "Political Systems and the Women's Movement: A Comparative Analysis of Barriers and Openings". Sofia, Bulgaria, October 15–20.

Edvuards, M. 1986. Køn, stat och jæmstællhetspolitik (Gender, State and Equality Policies). *Kvinnovetenskaplig tiddskrift nr. 3.*

Eisenstein, Z. 1981. *The Radical Future of Liberal Feminism.* New York: Longman.

Eisenstein, Z. 1983. The State, the Patriarchal Family and Working Mothers. *In* I. Diamond (ed.), *Families, Politics and Public Policies. A Feminist Dialogue on Women and the State.* New York: Longman.

Eisenstein, Z. 1984. *Feminism and Sexual Equality. Crisis in Liberal Feminism.* New York: Monthly Review Press.

Elshtain, J. 1981. *Public Man – Private Woman. Woman in Social and Political Thought.* Oxford.

Elshtain, J. 1982. *The Family in Political Thought.* Harvester Press.

Esping-Andersen, G. 1980. *Social Class, Social Democracy and State Policy.* Copenhagen.

Esping-Andersen, G. 1981. *Politics Against Markets.* The Swedish Institute of Social Research.

Esping-Andersen, G. 1984. *The State as a System of Stratification: Capitalism, Liberalism and Socialism in the Organization of Welfare Programs.* First Draft of a Working Paper. Harvard.

Finnemann, N. O. 1985. *I Broderskabets Ånd. Den socialdemokratiske arbejderbevægelses idehistorie 1871–1977* (In the Spirit of Brotherhood). Gyldendal.

Haavio-Manila, E. et al. (eds.) 1985. *The Unfinished Democracy. Women in Nordic Politics.* Oxford: Pergamon Press.

Halsaa, B. 1977. *Kvinner og politisk deltagelse* (Women and Political Participation). Oslo: Pax Forlag A/S.

Halsaa, B. 1985. Kvinder og politik (Women and Politics). *Velfærdsstaten i krise II. Gløder nr. 9,* Aalborg.

Hernes, H. 1982. *Staten – kvinder ingen adgang* (The State – No Admittance for Women). Oslo: Universitetsforlaget.

Hernes, H. 1983. Women and the Advanced Welfare State – the Transition from Private to Public Dependence. Paper presented in Bellagio, Italy and later appeared in H. Holter (ed.), *Patriarchy in a Welfare State.* Oslo: Universitetsforlaget, 1984.

Hirdman, G. 1984. *Särart och Likket. Kvinnorörelsens Scylla och Carybdis* (Sexual Difference and Equality. The Scylla and Carybdis of the Women's Movement). Stockholm Universitet.

Jonasdottir, A. 1985. Kvinnors interessen och andre værden (Women's Interests and Other Values). *Kvinnovetenskaplig tidsskrift nr. 2.*

Jonasdottir, A. 1987. Women's Interests and Other Values" forthcoming in A. Jonasdottir & K. Jones (eds.), *The Political Interests of Gender, Developing Theory and Research with a Feminist Face.* London: Sage Pub.

Liljestrøm, R. 1982. Planning and Organizing Alternatives Stemming from the Sphere of Reproduction. *Acta Sociologica* 25 (suppl.).

Luker, K. 1984. *The Politics of Abortion.* University of California Press.

Marshall, A. 1984. Citizenship and Social Class. *In* D. Held & S. Hall (eds.), *State and Society in Contemporary Britain. A Critical Introduction.* Oxford: Polity Press in ass. with Blackwell.

McIntosh, M. 1984. The Family, Regulation and the Public Sphere. *In* D. Held & S. Hall (eds.), *State and Society in Contemporary Britain. A Critical Introduction.* Oxford: Polity Press in ass. with Blackwell.

Pateman, C. 1983. Feminism and Democracy. *In* D. Graham (ed.), *Democratic Theory and Practice.* Oxford: Polity Press.

Pateman, C. 1985a. *The Problem of Political Obligation. A Critique of Liberal Theory.* Oxford: Polity Press.

Pateman, C. 1985b. *Women and Democratic Citizenship.* The Jefferson Memorial Lectures, Berkeley.

Peterson, A. 1984. 'The Gender-Sex Dimension in Swedish Politics. *Acta Sociologica* 27:1.

Peterson, A. 1985. The New Women's Movement. Where have All the Women Gone? Women and the Peace Movement in Sweden. *Women's International Forum* 8(6).

Petersen, A. 1986. Power and Authority in the Feminist Theory and Practice. Forthcoming in A. Jonasdottir & K. Jones (eds.), *The Political Interests of Gender, Developing Theory and Research with a Feminist Face.* London: Sage Pub.

Randell, V. 1982. *Women and Politics.* London: Macmillan Press.

Ruggie, M. 1984. *The State and Working Women. A Comparative Study of Britain and Sweden.* Princeton: Princeton University Press.

Sapiro, V. 1986. The Gender Basis of American Social Policy. *Political Science Quarterly* 101(2).

Siim, B. 1986. Kvinder og Velfærdsstaten i et komparativt perspektiv (Women and the Welfare State in a Comparative Perspective). To appear in A. Saarinen, E. Hännen-Salmehn & M. Kernen (eds.), *Kvinnor och Makt. Kvinnoperspektiv på 'välfärdsstaten.* Nordisk Antologi. Institut for kvinnoforskning ved Åbo Akademi, 1987.

Siim, B. 1987a. Women and the Welfare State. Comparative Perspective on the Organization of Care Work in Denmark and Britain. Forthcoming in C. Ungerson (ed.), *Women and Community Care. Gender and Caring in the Modern Welfare State.* London: Wheatsheaf.

Siim, B. 1987b. Rethinking of the Welfare State from a Feminist Perspective. Forthcoming in A. Jonasdottir & K. Jones (eds.), *The Political Interests of Gender. Developing Theory and Research with a Feminist Face.* London: Sage Publications.

Stacey, J. 1983. The New Conservative Feminism. *Feminist Studies*, Fall.

Therborn, G. 1986. Classes and States: Welfare States Developments 1881–1981. Papers on Labour History. *Det nordiske i den nordiske arbetarroralsen.* P. Kettunen (ed.), Helsinki.

Togeby, L. 1985. *Politik – også en kvindesag* (Politics – also a Female Concern). Politica, 1984.

Togeby, L. 1985. Starka, aktiva och arga kvinnor (Strong, Active and Angry Women). *Kvinnovetenskaplig tidsskrift* nr. 2.

Widerberg, K. 1985. Ett kvinnoperspektiv på velfærdsstaten, marknaden och det civile samhälle (A Women's Perspective on the Welfare State, the Market and Civil Society). Velfærdsstatens krise II. *Gløder nr. 9*, Aalborg University.

Zaretsky, E. 1982. The Place of the Family in the Origin of the Welfare State. *In* B. Thorne & M. Yalom (eds.), *Rethinking of the Family.* New York.

# Name Index